MODERN PACING SIRE LINES

John Bradley

The Russell Meerdink Company, Ltd.
Neenah, Wisconsin USA

Copyright © 1999 John Bradley. All rights reserved.

All Rights Reserved. No part of this book may be reproduced or transmitted in any form or by any means, electronic or mechanical, including photography, recording or by any information storage or retrieval system, without permission in writing from the publisher.

Library of Congress Cataloging-in-Publication Data

Bradley, John, 1942-
    Modern pacing sire lines / John Bradley.
    Includes bibliographical references and index.
    ISBN   0-929346-56-4
    1. Standardbred horse--United States--Pedigrees. 2. Harness racehorses--United States--Pedigrees.
    3. Harness racehorses--United States--History.   I. Title.
SF293.S72B7 1998   98-36915
636.1'7522--dc21   CIP

Published by:

The Russell Meerdink Company, Ltd.
1555 South Park Avenue
Neenah, WI 54956 USA
(920) 725-0955 Worldwide

Printed in the United States of America

*To my parents, Jack and Eileen Bradley,
who encouraged me to follow my dream
of a harness racing career.*

About the Author

John Bradley is internationally recognized as a leading Standardbred pedigree authority. His inside knowledge of the Standardbred breed, the bloodlines, horses, races, and people is a result of over 32 years in the industry.

Bradley saw his first harness race in 1959 at Yonkers Raceway. A native of Queens, New York, Bradley began attending the Roosevelt and Yonkers races on a regular basis as a teenager and has seen all of the stars from the "golden age" of harness racing to the modern speedsters.

Bradley's first position in harness racing was Program Director and race charter at Brandywine and Rosecroft Raceways, a position he held for eight years. A former Journalism major at the University of Maryland, Bradley also became a free lance writer and has now been a member of the U.S. Harness Writers Association for over 30 years.

He developed a keen interest in pedigrees, which led to a 10-year position at Lana Lobell Farms as Vice President and Sales Manager of its Harness Breeders Sales Co., which conducted yearling and mixed sales at Liberty Bell Park and Lana Lobell Farm in New Jersey.

Since 1985, Bradley has owned and operated Bradley Standardbred Agency, a full-service bloodstock consulting firm located in Versailles, Kentucky. Presently, Bradley is the General Manager of the Tattersalls sale company, located at The Red Mile in Lexington, Kentucky, which holds one of the premiere yearling sales in North America.

Bradley has also been a successful market breeder with yearlings selling at the major sales and is a former member of the Board of Directors of Goshen's Historic Track and the Harness Horse Breeders of New York State. He is also a contributor to *Times: in harness* magazine as well as several European publications. Bradley's first book, *Modern Trotting Sire Lines*, was published in 1997.

John Bradley resides near Lexington, Kentucky with his wife, Joan Van Blarcom, and has two grown daughters.

If you would like to contact John Bradley, he may be reached at:

John Bradley
2610 Keene-Troy Road
Versailles, KY 40383
606-887-9184
606-881-5957 Fax
johnb10532@aol.com

Acknowledgements

There are many who deserve thanks for their assistance with this work. Publishers Russ, Jan and Todd Meerdink had many ideas for the content and layout of the book and provided guidance every step of the way. Carolyn Koehler was especially helpful in editing final copy.

Some statistics and pedigree information was provided by the USTA's Information and Research Dept. along with access to the USTA computer database. The Harness Racing Museum provided use of its wonderful library for research on the older stallions.

The magazines *Times: in harness*, *Horseman & Fair World* and *Hoof Beats* were invaluable sources of information as was the Tesio Power computer pedigree program by Syntax Software. And, many thanks to those farms and individuals who provided the necessary photographs.

Of course, this book would not have been possible without the help of many friends and associates during my harness racing career. Special thanks to Nick Parker who opened harness racing's door by hiring me to chart races and edit track programs while teaching me the ways of the business.

Many thanks to Alan Leavitt and Jim Harrison who provided much pedigree and breeding expertise during my decade at Lana Lobell Farm, to Hal Jones for his many insights on stallions, conformation and breeding and to Dr. John Egloff for his lessons on broodmare and stallion reproduction.

Thanks to Curt Greene who wrote the introductory portions of 15 chapters which enabled us to stay on production schedule when I was temporarily sidelined.

Sincere appreciation to Dr. John Cronin, Dr. William Walton and Lynne Maner who have guided me through a serious medical crisis and enabled me to complete this work.

Contents

Foreword	8
Introduction	9
From Hambletonian to the 21st Century	12
Pedigree Crosses of 1:51 Pacers	18
Abercrombie	34
Adios	42
Adios Vic	52
Albatross	58
Albert Albert	66
Artsplace	72
B.G.'s Bunny	80
Beach Towel	86
Big Towner	94
Bret Hanover	102
Bye Bye Byrd	112
Cam Fella	120
Cam's Card Shark	130
Cambest	136
Camluck	144
Dexter Nukes	150
Die Laughing	156
Direct Scooter	164
Dragon's Lair	172
Falcon Almahurst	180
Falcon Seelster	188
French Chef	196
Gene Abbe	202
Good Time	208
Jate Lobell	214
Jenna's Beach Boy	222
Laag	230
Life Sign	238
Magical Mike	246
Matt's Scooter	252

Meadow Skipper 260	*Race Time* 340
Most Happy Fella 268	*Run The Table* 346
Nero 276	*Shadow Wave* 354
Niatross 284	*Sonsam* 360
Nihilator 290	*Storm Damage* 366
No Nukes 298	*Strike Out* 372
On The Road Again 306	*Tar Heel* 378
Overtrick 316	*Tyler B* 384
Pacific Rocket 322	*Western Hanover* 390
Precious Bunny 328	*Index* 398
Presidential Ball 334	

Foreword

When the great racing historian John Hervey died in Chicago 50 years ago, it left a huge void in the sport of horse racing - and particularly harness racing - in North America. Hervey was the only journalist who could - and did - command an encyclopedic knowledge of both harness and Thoroughbred racing on this continent wide enough to write authoritative books on both sports.

Hervey's *The American Trotter*, published in 1947, traced the history of the harness sport and its great horses from the beginning to his death, and it has remained the definitive work on the subject for half a century. During that time, John Bradley was building the foundation of information and the depth of knowledge to enable him to undertake the gargantuan task of filling Hervey's shoes.

When his *Modern Trotting Sire Lines* appeared last year, it provided a fascinating insight into the 51 leading trotting sires of the modern era, and through their breeding, racing background and siring accomplishments provided a worthy follow-up and continuum to Hervey's monumental work.

Now comes the eagerly awaited sequel - *Modern Pacing Sire Lines* - and the world of the pacing horse, primarily centered in North America and Australasia, gets a fascinating view of the horses that have written its history since Hervey's classic work.

From Abercrombie to Western Hanover, we can relive the entrance, exploits and in many cases exits of those giants in harness who fashioned the pacing sport as it exists today. Through Bradley's deft writing we can relive and relish once again their days of glory on the track and their contributions since they left it. And through the pictures of each of the 50 horses profiled we get to see the stars themselves.

There is the story of Adios, who wrote his own illustrious chapter in harness racing history as a sulking race horse and super sire; of phenomenal Bret Hanover, winner of 62 of 68 career races, and his arch-rival Adios Vic, who ended Bret's undefeated skein after 35 consecutive victories and handed him 4 of the 6 losses of his career; of Albatross, leading sire of money-winners of any horse breed in the world with sons and daughters that have won more than $130 million.

There is currency, with the racing career and sensational siring start of Artsplace and all of the top stallions standing today.

This is not simply a book for breeders, although it is an invaluable reference for them.

It is a history book, and a well-written one.

For those too young to have shared the thrills of the explosive growth of the sport in the 1960s, the narrative is there in the career sketches of the horses of that glorious era.

For those deeply immersed in the sport today, there is a guideline to the future as far as breeding and sire lines and nicks are concerned.

For the casual fan, there is an insight into the horses that fashioned the sport as we know it, and that produced stars of today.

And for those who simply love horses or horse racing, there is wonderful reading that will deepen one's appreciation through these tales of greatness.

Since John Hervey's work is long out-of-print and difficult to find, Bradley provides a quick recap from the founding father Hambletonian to the 21st century, and for those interested in breeding better pacers he provides the pedigree crosses of all of the pacers with mile records of 1:51 or faster.

The time and effort and research and writing that went into this major addition to the literature of harness racing is overwhelming. It is a literary triumph for John Bradley. It is a gift of enormous value to all who enjoy harness racing.

Stanley F. Bergstein

Stanley F. Bergstein
Executive Vice President
Harness Tracks of America

Introduction

This book is my second detailed study of successful sires in the Standardbred breed. The first, *Modern Trotting Sire Lines*, focused on trotters; this work is about pacing sires. It's purpose is to help point you in the right direction when you make decisions about where and how to breed your stallions and mares. I hope it will serve as a valuable reference book for years to come. In addition, the information presented here can also help yearling and broodmare buyers.

Researching this book was a complex task since there are far more pacing sires than trotting sires and more male lines involved in producing successful racehorses and breeding stock. In addition, approximately three-quarters or all North American Standardbreds are bred to be pacers.

Modern Trotting Sire Lines focused primarily on the male lines of Star's Pride, Noble Victory and Speedster, which have proven the most dominant lines over the last half-century. This book will cover the same time period, from the 1950s onward. However, there have been more successful sire lines for the pacing gait with descendents of Adios, Meadow Skipper, Good Time, Gene Abbe, Bye Bye Byrd, Direct Scooter and Tar Heel to consider. Also, from those horses are sub-sets of sire lines through Bret Hanover, Abercrombie, Albatross, Cam Fella, French Chef, No Nukes and Tyler B.

As I did in my earlier book, I want to stress that this research is not based upon strict scientific guidelines and genetic formulas. What I have written is based upon over 38 years of close observation of racehorses, stallions and broodmares, and many years of researching and preparing pedigrees for sales catalogs, major farms and individual breeders. The one rule I have come to respect the most regarding breeding champion horses is this - "there are no rules."

Each stallion is an individual and has his own set of genes which work differently with each broodmare. However, patterns sometimes develop in which a particular sire seems to produce his best performers from mares from certain other sire lines, or combination of sires. This is not true of every sire, but there are noticeable trends. If one wishes to breed champions, it is essential to understand what has worked in the past and draw conclusions about what may work in the present and future.

For hundreds of years, breeders have tried to quantify certain physical and performance qualities of stallions and broodmares in an attempt to devise some formula which would produce champions. Many faddish theories come and go and a few carried on for generations. Some are valid, some are proven wrong quickly and others are resurrected from time to time by breeders in search of "nature's secret."

The Thoroughbred breed has received far more attention than the Standardbred in terms of devising formulas and averages which may or may not lead to better success at breeding. The Thoroughbred breeders have such things as "dosages," "Bruce Lowe family numbers" and other analysis techniques which are used by many breeders. There are also other factors which can be considered, things like the X-Factor heartscores and the measurement of air flow passages, all of which have their proponents and detractors. None of these tools can be written off and I'm sure there is some merit to each. However, my opinion is that none, by itself, or even in combination, can predict racing success, because in the end everything comes down to the flesh and blood horse, its soundness, heritage and inborn will to be a competitor. We need to remember that although we can now breed for type, certain conformation traits, speed and soundness, we can never be absolutely certain of what we will get when that newborn foal grows, is trained and begins racing. It is still a roll of the dice. The best a breeder can do is eliminate as many negative aspects as possible by adhering to the old adage, "breed the best to the best," and raise and feed the youngster properly, using experienced and successful trainers. Even then, the breeder will still need some luck.

Today, nutrition, training methods and race tracks are vastly better than they were a half-century ago. Breeders have played their part in this by constantly improving the looks and speed of the average Standardbred. There has been one casualty, however. Due to the economics of having rich purses for youngsters, the Standardbred pacer is being asked for more extreme speed at a very early age. We are seeing two-year-olds able to pace as fast as their older counterparts. Unfortunately, we are also seeing too many of these youngsters unable to hold that form and come back successfully at three without some soundness problems.

Some sires are able to produce extreme and precocious speed in their youngsters while others sire colts and fillies that may not be world champions at two, but who are sounder, get faster later and are able to race for several years. It is to be hoped that breeders will be able to sort this out and come up with a happy medium in which our fastest horses also stay sound. One sire noted for his soundness is Abercrombie, and his sons and daughters may help in this quest.

This book contains chapters about sires currently standing at stud and others which have helped form the breed over the last 50 years and who are still very influential in the second, third and fourth generations of current stars. Many of the older sires are now important as broodmare sires and should be recognized since their daughters are responsible for half of a foal's genes.

There are a number of new stallions profiled in this book - those who do not yet have youngsters of racing age. Some will become successful sires and some will not. But it is these sires who will lead the breed into the future and we should study how their pedigrees may have been important to their racing performance and how they may link up with the available broodmare pool to produce the stars of the future.

Sons of Abercrombie, Cam Fella and No Nukes seem to be those who will lead us to the new millenium. Mother Nature, though, has always been full of surprises in horse matters and who knows, maybe Matt's Scooter, or one of his sons, or a Big Towner son, will take the sport by storm and start the rebirth of an older sire line. This is all part of the challenge of the breeding business - and part of its charm and allure.

As I cautioned in the Introduction of the first book, always follow the rules of good horsemanship before following any theories or ideas. Do not breed conformation faults to conformation faults; or a bad dispostion to a bad dispostion. Always look to maximize the positive attributes whether they are size, conformation or speed. Above all, don't forget the quality of the broodmare. The sire does not do it all - at the genetic level, it's still a 50-50 proposition.

It is true that certain great sires, like Adios, Meadow Skipper and Direct Scooter, to name a few, have demonstrated the ability over the years to sire top horses from ordinary mares. But keep in mind that many stallions were bred to 100 or more mares every year and just by the law of averages some offspring should have turned out well. Other stallions, because of early success, were later able to attract the finest quality broodmares and then went on to even more success. The broodmare plays an extremely important role.

Some breeders use the term "prepotent" of certain stallions - meaning being greater in power or influence than their peers. Among the prepotent trotters are Volomite, Star's Pride, Super Bowl, Speedy Crown and Valley Victory. Pacing sires Adios, Albatross, Meadow Skipper, Most Happy Fella, Abercrombie and Cam Fella certainly fall into that same class.

Consider, also, that there are prepotent broodmares. Some mares have produced multiple 1:52 or 1:55 performers, five or more $100,000 winners, a dozen in 2:00 and so on. And these mares have done so with just a fraction of the number of foals for an average stallion; many have done it with foals by several different stallions. Remember too that the mare also has the chance to "move up" a stallion; so, you must also include this aspect of breeding. Playing the percentages, I would chose a foal by an average stallion from a great producing mare over a foal by a great sire from an average mare. Obviously, the best course of action would be to have a foal by a great stallion from a great mare, but we are not all so blessed.

Introduction

The records and statistics contained in this volume are current at least through the end of 1997 and I've included as many 1998 records as time allowed up to publication deadline. Time and earnings records have been obtained through computer access to the United States Trotting Association data through the first half of 1998. For pedigree chart and sire and dam crosses information, I have used the Tesio Power computer program, which provides six-generation printouts and color-coded inbreeding information. These tools were unavailable to pedigree researchers of earlier years and I don't think I would have undertaken this project had it not been for the computer age. I have great respect for my predecessors who spent hours with paper, pencil and dusty old books sketching out pedigree charts which are now available at the touch of a button.

However, even with computer technology, I don't know if we are really that much closer to being able to predict with any certainty the performance level of particular horses. I do think breeders are improving the product and with each generation of horses are on the road to understanding more. But the mystery is still there for all to investigate.

I hope the reader enjoys this book and can see that there are certain patterns at work within the Standardbred breed. These patterns are constantly changing, but they do serve as guideposts for some success.

John Bradley

The pacing sires reviewed in this book are those which have been active from 1950 to today, along with a few which will take us into the next century. My purpose is not to write a long, detailed history of the foundation of the Standardbred breed since that ground has already been covered in several previous books by other authors.

For those interested in a deeper research of the historic sires from Messenger to Hambletonian and his sons, I recommend several books. The first is The American Trotter by John Hervey which was published in 1947. This is a detailed and historic work and is the best of its kind. In 1968, the United States Trotting Association published *Care & Training of the Trotter and Pacer* which includes a wonderful chapter on Bloodlines and Breeding written by pedigree authority James C. Harrison. The information and insights are classic and takes the reader to the mid-1960s period. In 1970, The Complete Book of Harness Racing by Philip A. Pines, former Director of the Harness Racing Museum, was published and this provides an interesting and shorter review of the major old sires as well as the history of the sport. Now, the USTA has released the *New Care & Training of the Trotter and Pacer* which contains an opening chapter entitled Perspectives on Bloodlines & Breeding written by Curt Greene. This chapter updates and carries forward the bloodlines chapter written by Harrison in the original Care & Training book. All of these works should be in the library of, and read by, every serious student of Standardbred breeding. The Hervey and Pines books are hard-to-find, but the *New Care & Training* is available through the USTA.

However, I will give you a brief history of how we came from "there to here" during the last 200 years. A foal of 1780 in England, Messenger was a grey Thoroughbred stallion who was imported to America in 1788. He was a good runner in England and won eight of his 14 starts, including all of his stakes races. Messenger was well-bred and traced back to the Darley Arabian on his sire's side and to the Godolphin Arabian and Byerley Turk on his dam's side. Thus, his pedigree contained all three founders of the Thoroughbred breed. Messenger stood 15.3 hands which was a little above average for racehorses of his day.

Messenger continued as a sire of good Thoroughbred running horses in America. He also founded a separate and distinct breed of trotter which far surpassed all others in speed and quality. As his sons and daughters bred on, their progeny became widely known as superior performers and established Messenger as a truly historic stallion. The grey stallion also appears in the ancestry of such great American Thoroughbred legends as American Eclipse, Whirlaway, Equipoise, Man O'War, Sea Biscuit, Gallant Fox and Exterminator. Thus, Messenger is a foundation horse of both major racing breeds.

We now skip through a couple of generations and point out that Messenger's son Mambrino, a foal of 1806, was bred to the mare Amazonia to produce the stallion Abdallah I, in 1823, who later became the sire of Hambletonian who had a 3x4x4x4x5x6 cross to Messenger.

The story of Hambletonian, the "father" of the Standardbred breed, began at the farm of his breeder Jonas Seeley in Sugar Loaf, New York - just a few miles from Goshen. Seeley was a prosperous farmer who was in the cattle business and also bred some horses. In 1844, Seeley was in New York City to deliver some steers to the marketplace when he came upon a mare owned by a butcher named Charles Kent. He kept the mare in a stable behind his shop and Seeley recognized her as being a daughter of the mare, One Eye, which had belonged to his father. The mare was crippled from injuries received in a runaway accident and Seeley felt sentimental and purchased her from the butcher for $135. She had no official name and became known simply as the Charles Kent mare.

The sire of this mare was the Norfolk trotter Bellfounder and her dam, One Eye, was by Bishop's Hambletonian - a son of Messenger. Her second dam was a mare named Silvertail who was by also by Messenger, making One Eye intensely inbred. Both Silvertail, and her dam Black Jin, were renowned runners of their time and Silvertail's long-distance exploits were well-known.

Seeley bred the Charles Kent mare and her fourth foal, by the Messenger grandson Abdallah I, was born on May 5, 1849. William Rysdyk was a young farmhand from nearby Chester who worked for

Seeley and he immediately fell in love with the young colt. Rysdyk asked Seeley to put a price on the colt and his employer said he would take $150 for the mare and foal plus $10 for the Abdallah I stud fee. Rysdyk, who had no ready cash, offered $125 which Seeley accepted and agreed to give payment terms.

Rysdyk felt he could make his fortune with the colt he named Hambletonian and immediately started promoting him throughout Orange County. He was shown with success as a yearling at the Orange County Fair and came back again as a two-year-old and three-year-old to take top honors. He was making a name for himself without ever setting foot on a racetrack. In 1851, Rysdyk bred the two-year-old Hambletonian to four mares for free and the next year raised the stud fee to $25. At four, Hambletonian bred 101 mares at a stud fee of $35 which resulted in 78 foals. Rysdyk was making money and the Hambletonian offspring had not yet set foot on a racetrack.

Hambletonian and groom.

In those days, horses were not raced until they matured and Hambletonian was over ten-years-old when his first sons and daughters began their racing careers. Once they did, it became obvious Hambletonian was to be a sire without peer and his stud fee rose to $75 in 1863 and to $100 in 1864. That year, Hambletonian covered 217 mares and got 148 of them in foal. Rysdyk then raised the stud fee to $300 in 1865 and $500 in 1866. It remained at that level for several years. At age 19, in 1868, Hambletonian was exhausted and held back by Rysdyk for that breeding season. Beginning in 1869, Rysdyk limited Hambletonian's book to just 22 mares and it never again exceeded 30 mares.

Hambletonian stood his final year at stud in 1875 and died in his stall on March 27, 1876 at the age of 27, two years after the death of Rysdyk. Estimates are that Rysdyk received in excess of $200,000 in stud fees from Hambletonian as a result of his $135 investment in 1849. Hambletonian's remains are buried in a grave site next to the Rysdyk house and the location is marked by a tall, Missouri granite shaft.

All told, Hambletonian sired over 1,330 foals during his years at stud and over 99% of today's Standardbreds can be traced back to him. Today, four major sire lines come from Hambletonian through his sons Happy Medium, George Wilkes, Electioneer and Dictator. Many of Hambletonian's descendants were exported from America and established additional male lines in Europe, Australia and New Zealand. In North America, all breeding farms wanted sons and grandsons of Hambletonian as stallions and they stood at stud in all areas which had harness racing.

Photos and descriptions of Hambletonian show that he was not a handsome horse, but had an excellent disposition, a rich bay coat and glossy black stockings. He stood 15.1 hands at the withers and was two inches taller at the rump. He was described as moving "with cat-like grace and ease." Historian John Wallace described Hambletonian as "supple as a cat." Wallace added, "As he walked, he kept pushing those crooked hind legs away under him in a manner that gave him a motion peculiarly his own, suggesting immense possibilities of stride when opened out on a trot."

The four main sire lines from Hambletonian are through his sons George Wilkes (1856), Happy Medium (1863), Dictator (1863) and Electioneer (1868). They were all trotters, but today Electioneer is a root sire of the best pacers since he was the great-grandsire of The Abbe whose sons, Abbedale and Bert Abbe, are responsible for all the Adios, Meadow Skipper and Gene Abbe line sires. There is no Electioneer male line of trotters to have survived past the early 20th Century. The line of Dictator, who was a full brother to the world champion trotter Dexter, suffered a similar fate by not producing a trotter to carry on the male line. However, the Dictator line prospered for awhile with pacers through Billy Direct and Tar Heel, but later fell into obscurity when the major Tar Heel sons did not leave sons to carry on. The last of that line seems to be the pacer Steady Star.

We are interested here in the pacing sire lines, but I do want to point out that Hambletonian's son Happy Medium founded a line of great trotting sires. He is also responsible for the male line of pacing sires Matt's Scooter, Direct Scooter, Overtrick and Harold J., as they are all descendants of Volomite. The Direct Scooter branch of this pacing line is the only one with a reasonable chance to continue in North America.

Turning to the pacing male lines, the Electioneer and Happy Medium lines appear to be the only ones which will make it to the 21st Century with success. The George Wilkes line leads to two of the greatest Standardbreds ever, the pacer Dan Patch and the trotter Greyhound. Unfortunately, Dan Patch was not successful as a sire and Greyhound was a gelding.

Looking at the major sire lines descending from Hambletonian, we find that the Electioneer line has now divided into two distinct branches - one through Hal Dale and one through Gene Abbe. The Hal Dale male line has been incredibly successful and has dwarfed all other pacing sire lines in the second half of this century. The primary sons of Hal Dale are Adios, Dale Frost and Good Time.

As you will read later, Adios is one of the greatest, if not the greatest, pacing sire of all time and his descendants are still high achievers on the race track. His son Bret Hanover was a top sire and a great broodmare sire. Another son of Adios, Henry T. Adios, is the grandsire of Abercrombie who has had great success and appears to have a few sons who will carry on in his tradition, especially his son Artsplace.

Hal Dale's son Dale Frost is the sire of Meadow Skipper, another all-time great who took the breed to new heights during the latter quarter of this century. Until the recent emergence of Abercrombie and his sons as challengers, the Meadow Skipper line completely dominated the sport through his great siring sons Albatross and Most Happy Fella. It is through Most Happy Fella that two of today's great pacing lines have sprung - those from Cam Fella and No Nukes. Both have several successful sons at stud and the future of these branches of the Meadow Skipper sire line seems assured.

The other son of Hal Dale to achieve success is Good Time who gave us the good sires Race Time, Best Of All and Columbia George. Unfortunately for the sport, this line has now come to and end of it's commercial viability.

Gene Abbe heads the other branch of the Electioneer sire line and he single-handedly saved this line. His son Big Towner has been an outstanding success both as a sire and broodmare sire and Walton Hanover is a successful grandson of Gene Abbe. The line, however, seems to be in a bit of a precarious situation unless a son of Big Towner or Walton Hanover moves forward to the top levels of pacing sires.

Hambletonian's son Happy Medium established a successful pacing sire branch since it was his line which led to the absolutely wonderful sire Volomite who was dominant both as a pacing and trotting sire during his prime years. Volomite's influence in both the male and female lines of the Standardbred sport is incredible and he was certainly a horse for the ages. Volomite had four sons who carried his line forward for a few more decades - Poplar Byrd, King's Counsel, Worthy Boy and Sampson Hanover.

Poplar Byrd is the sire of the great Bye Bye Byrd who made an attempt at continuing the line through his top sons Armbro Nesbit, Keystone Ore and Bye And Large. Today, they are mostly noted as broodmare sires since none provided long-lasting, commercially successful sons. King's Counsel is the grandsire of Overtrick who was also a good broodmare sire, but who left no successful sons. Worthy Boy, also a noted sire of trotters, particularly Star's Pride, is the sire of

Harold J. who was a decent "blue collar" sire and the sire of the dam of the fastest pacer in the sport's history - Cambest. Finally, Sampson Hanover is the grandsire of the wonderful Direct Scooter who has been an outstanding sire and who appears to be the only one able to save the Volomite line through his sons Matt's Scooter and In The Pocket. However, this line, like that of Gene Abbe, is in a vary precarious position as we move to the new century.

The other mentioned son of Hambletonian, Dictator, is the direct ancestor of the great sire Tar Heel who was very successful from the 1950s through the 1970s and later became the sport's premier broodmare sire. Unfortunately, Tar Heel's sire Billy Direct died at a very young age when it looked as if he would go on to become a great sire. It was then up to Tar Heel to carry on this male line. Tar Heel had sons like Thorpe Hanover, Nansemond and Steady Beau who were successful for a time, but then their stars dimmed and were extinguished. The last hope for the Tar Heel line

Hal Dale

was the fast Steady Star who never provided a top son to carry on into the future. Thus, another male line came to a close.

In discussing the fate of these male lines, I am only referring to the situation in North America. Over the years, hundreds of stallions from all these male lines have been exported to Australia and New Zealand and there have been further successful extensions of some of these lines in those countries. They are also working with a different gene pool than breeders in North America and this may explain the success of certain lines there as opposed to those in North America. It is an interesting situation and one which will be followed into the next century.

Volomite

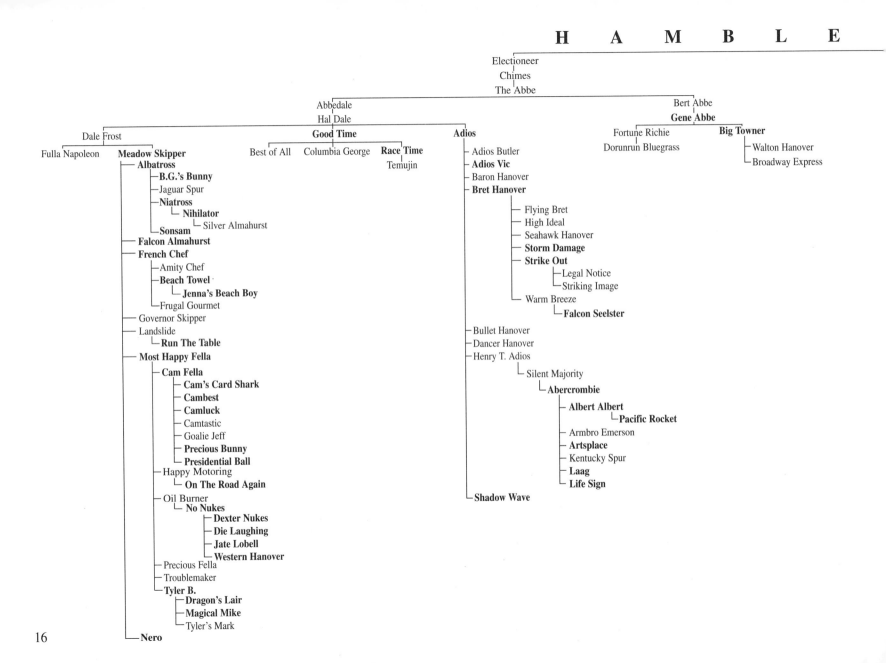

TONIAN

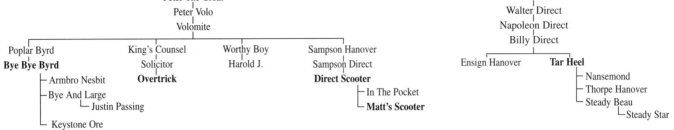

The best way to attempt a detailed study of pedigrees and bloodlines is to ascertain which horses have achieved a certain level of greatness or speed and focus on that group. Greatness and speed are not exactly the same since we all know horses that were extremely fast, but which did not exhibit the "class" or "heart" of truly outstanding champions.

However, my purpose here is to show which sire lines have been able to produce speed most consistently and it is speed which also leads to most of the pacing champions of recent years. Obviously, changes in track surfaces, sulkies, aggressive driving techniques and improvements in breeding, have all combined to allow the pacing Standardbred to achieve speeds inconceivable to most horsemen and fans just a few years ago. As this book is written, there are 74 pacers with records of 1:50 or faster with only six of them taking these records prior to 1990.

This book contains chapters 50 pacing sires, most of whom were also the outstanding racehorses of their own generations. Bear in mind that speed is a relative thing: a horse which could pace in 1:55 in the 1950s or 1960s is surely the equal of the sub-1:50 pacers of today. So although this particular chapter about the 1:51 pacers is skewed toward today's active stallions - which are those that breeders will look to for servicing their broodmares - many of these 1:51 performers are from daughters of the outstanding sires of one, two or three decades ago and their genes are also partly responsible for today's great speeds. For example, just because Meadow Skipper, Bret Hanover and Most Happy Fella don't have any 1:51 sire credits it does not mean each is any less of a sire than today's leaders Cam Fella, Abercrombie, Direct Scooter and Jate Lobell. They were still the best of their era and that is the main factor we should be concerned with - how a stallion compared to his own peers.

I chose the 1:51 time level for this chapter since it was four seconds lower than the 1:55 I used for Modern Trotting Sire Lines. This is about the difference between the best trotters and pacers. I could have easily chosen 1:50, but I opted for 1:51 since it provided for the study of more (262) horses which, by any standard, should serve as a reasonable number for a control group of the sport's fastest pacers.

It is very interesting that some stallions appear to have a genetic "speed limit" which makes their fastest performers capable of no more than a 1:51 time. Indeed, they may have many in the 1:51 area while other stallions may be capable of siring a 1:49 performer, but only one, with perhaps the next fastest being 1:52. This factor can be best illustrated by the chart at the end of this chapter which lists, separately, the sires of 1:50, 1:51, 1:52 and 1:55 performers.

For example, Cam Fella leads all three groups and clearly dominates the 1:50 level, with Dexter Nukes second and Abercrombie, Albatross, Direct Scooter and On The Road Again tied for third. At the 1:51 level only Abercrombie was able to keep pace with Cam Fella. No Nukes has never sired a 1:50 performer, but ranks tied for fifth in the 1:51 listing. At the 1:52 level, a major advance was made by Big Towner, who moves all the way up to seventh ranking. His fastest performer is in 1:49.4, but he has a large cluster between 1:51 and 1:52. The same holds true for Tyler B. Much of this can also be explained by the time period in which these stallions were at their peak. Tyler B. died early and Big Towner is now 24 years old and still doing very well. No Nukes is the clear leader of the 1:55 list while Albatross dominates the 2:00 list.

Looking at the broodmare sires, Albatross and Bret Hanover are at the top of each list. Meadow Skipper also ranked high on each list and Abercrombie and Most Happy Fella likewise at the 1:51, 1:52 and 1:55 levels. Those five, as broodmare sires, were also the best sires of their generations. This proves again that the best sires are always the best broodmare sires.

Of course, these rankings are always changing and we are now beginning to see the newly emerging top broodmare sires, like Niatross, Direct Scooter, Big Towner, No Nukes, B.G.'s Bunny and

Sonsam. It is also certain that Cam Fella will join this list, along with Nihilator and Tyler B. Cam Fella, in addition to everything else that makes him so great, is closely involved with the two fastest horses of all time he is the sire of Cambest and sire of the dam of Jenna's Beach Boy.

A study of the long list of 1:51 performers also reveals the crosses which work with the most frequency. Not surprisingly, the great sire and broodmare sire Albatross has the most prominent position within the leading crosses. In the top six crosses, he is the sire in one combination (with Bret Hanover) and the broodmare sire in four other leading combinations (with Cam Fella, No Nukes, Abercrombie and Big Towner). He also ranks high as a broodmare sire with Direct Scooter. It is most interesting that Albatross' daughters have worked extremely well to produce extreme speed with stallions from four different sire lines - Most Happy Fella (Cam Fella & No Nukes), Adios (Abercrombie), Gene Abbe (Big Towner) and Volomite (Direct Scooter).

The influence of Albatross on the Standardbred breed has been stunning and it may very well be his genes that have helped make other stallions successful. Don't forget, Albatross is the sire of the first sub-1:50 horse (Niatross in 1980) and he also has two other sub-1:50 performers. And this is by a stallion who was foaled in 1968 and who has been able to stay competitive with stallions three and four generations younger.

A study of the sires of the 1:50 sires reveals sire lines which seem to pass on the ability to sire the most extreme speed in the sport. Meadow Skipper and Most Happy Fella each have four sons who sired 1:50 performers, while Albatross, Tyler B. and Abercrombie each have three. Niatross and No Nukes have two each. All but Abercrombie are Meadow Skipper line stallions.

Looking at the sires of 1:50 broodmare sires, Meadow Skipper is the leader with six sons in that category, followed by Albatross and Bret Hanover with three each. Sires with two sons in this group are Adios, Bye Bye Byrd, Most Happy Fella, Dale Frost and Strike Out.

As you can see, Meadow Skipper has had a profound effect on the breed and is considered by many to be the most influential sire in pacing history. Others will argue Adios holds that position and a strong case can be made for either sire. Suffice it to say that both sires - one of which is a son, the other a grandson of Hal Dale, are legends.

I studied the various crosses shown by the six-generation pedigree charts for each of the 1:50 pacers to see if there were any trends or patterns throughout the group. As I found with the 1:55 trotters in Modern Trotting Sire Lines, success seems to come from a variety of breeding methods and from the crossing of many bloodlines in various ways. Outcrossing, linebreeding and inbreeding all had successful results with certain horses, but I was a bit surprised by the number of fast pacers which had no common ancestors in their first four generations. By today's standards, this is an outcross although technically there are hardly any true Standardbred outcrosses since we always see a number of common ancestors in the fifth and sixth generations.

Let's take a look at a few of the fastest horses, in order of their fastest time, and some aspects of their pedigrees. Cambest (Cam Fella-Oxford Mary Ann-Harold J.), the fastest of all, has his closest common cross as 4x4 to both Dale Frost and Adios, with Hal Dale appearing five times in the fifth generation - four through Cam Fella. Jenna's Beach Boy (Beach Towel-Five O'Clock Cindy-Cam Fella), with the fastest race mile ever, is 3x4x4 to Meadow Skipper with four other crosses to Adios and Dale Frost. Ultimate Falcon (Falcon Seelster-Caramel Sundae-Falcon Almahurst) is uniquely bred 3x3 to the full brothers Bret Hanover and Baron Hanover and 4x4 to Adios. He is a good example of a successful cross linking siblings. Staying Together (Panorama-Happily Involved-Armbro Alert) is also linebred 3x4 to Meadow Skipper. Armbro Alert is a full brother to the great mare Silk Stockings.

Matt's Scooter (Direct Scooter-Ellen's Glory-Meadow Skipper) is the fastest pacer with outcross breeding, since he has no common ancestors in the first four generations. His closest crosses go back to older foundation stallions; he is 4x5x5x6 to Volomite, 4x5x5 to Billy Direct, 5x4x5 to

Scotland and 4x5 to Hal Dale. Camluck (Cam Fella-Lucky Lady-Striking Image) is linebred 3x4 to Bret Hanover and is the fastest with a close cross to that great stallion.

The wonderful warhorse Riyadh (Jate Lobell-Malaysia-Bye And Large) also has no common ancestors close up and is 6x5x4 to Adios and his full sister Adieu. Albatross' fastest son, Ball And Chain (Albatross-Full Of Love-Bret Hanover), is 4x3 to Adios and 4x4 to Tar Heel - the golden cross of a generation ago. He also has an interesting 4x5 cross to the prolific half-sisters, The Old Maid and Lady Scotland.

The great Niatross (Albatross-Niagara Dream-Bye Bye Byrd) is another with no common ancestors in his first four generations. His closest cross is 4x5 to Hal Dale and 5x4 to the trotting sire Guy Abbey. In addition, he has a 4x4 cross to the full brother and sister Adios and Adieu and you can never have too much Adios blood. You will see this Adios/Adieu situation quite often since Adieu is the grandam of the top broodmare sire Bye Bye Byrd and there are many good horses with this combination of bloodlines.

Trump Casino (Falcon Seelster-Laker's Fortune-Fortune Teller) is another like Camluck with a 3x4 cross to Bret Hanover. In addition, he has five crosses to Adios and is 4x4 to the full brother and sister Adios Butler and Adios Governess. Tune Town (Big Towner-Paris Song-Colt Fortysix) has a dam inbred 3x2 to Tar Heel. The fast Red Bow Tie is bred 3x4 to Tar Heel and 5x6x5x5x6 to Adios. Artsplace (Abercrombie-Miss Elvira-Albatross) has a unique linebred cross and is 3x4 to the sire Duane Hanover, along with being 4x5 to Adios, Tar Heel and The Widower. He is also 5x4 to the three-quarter sisters Veda Hanover (grandam of Henry T. Adios) and Vibrant Hanover (grandam of Albatross).

Jaguar Spur (Albatross-J.D.'s Bret-Bret Hanover) has his closest cross as 4x3 to Adios and 4x4 to Tar Heel. T.K.'s Skipper (Governor Skipper-Shana Hanover-Armbro Nesbit) is 3x5x4 to Adios and has another cross in the fourth generation to Adios' sister Adieu.

The fastest of the three mares in the 1:50 list is Caesar's Jackpot (Walton Hanover-Tracy's Jackpot-Albatross) and she has no common ancestors in her first four generations. In fact, the closest is only a 5x5x5x4 cross to Adios and 5x5 to the half-sisters The Old Maid and Lady Scotland. Another outcross is Armbro Maestro (Dexter Nukes-Armbro Harmony-Legal Notice) who is 5x4 to both Meadow Skipper and Shadow Wave. Darth Raider (Laag-Barbara's Vic-Adios Vic) falls into this category with his 5x3 cross to Adios. He also has a couple of unusual crosses farther back - 4x5 to the full brothers Gay Song and Victory Song and 5x5 to the full brothers King's Counsel and Blackstone.

Stand Forever (Dragon's Lair-Niajet-Niatross) is 4x4 to both Meadow Skipper and Tar Heel. Tulane (Admiral's Galley-Burnish-Oil Burner) is 4x4x4 to Meadow Skipper and 4x4 to the half-sisters Baby Sitter and Laughing Girl. One of the closest bred among these fast pacers is Nihilator (Niatross-Margie's Melody-Bret Hanover) who is 3x3 to Meadow Skipper and 5x5x3 to Adios and his sister Adieu. Call For Rain (Storm Damage-Rain Proof-Meadow Skipper) has a similar 3x5x5 cross to Adios and Adieu, but no multiple Meadow Skipper cross. Triple Crown winner Western Dreamer (Western Hanover-Fits Of Fun-Panorama) is linebred 5x4x4 to Meadow Skipper.

Like Nihilator, Camtastic (Cam Fella-Lushkara-Albatross) is 3x3 to Meadow Skipper along with other crosses to Tar Heel and Adios. In The Pocket (Direct Scooter-Black Jade-Tar Heel) has Meadow Skipper only once in the third generation and his closest crosses are 4x3 to Billy Direct and 4x5x4x6 to Volomite. In addition, he sports a 4x5 cross to Scotland and his sister Rose Scott. He has some fairly old bloodlines for a 1998 stallion and is almost acting as an outcross stallion for many modern broodmares.

Cam Terrific (Cam Fella-The Booger Lady-Steady Star) is 4x4 to both Adios and Dale Frost and has double crosses to two significant broodmares back in his pedigree - 6x5 to Belle Mahone and 6x6 to Margaret Spangler. New Bucks (Nihilator-Candy Bucks-Sonsam) is what I call a "forward bred" horse in that he is 3x3 to a very modern sire, Albatross, and 3x4 to Bret Hanover. He is also 4x4x4 to Meadow Skipper.

At the other extreme is L.V. Whiskers (Armbro Aussie-Sarah Trick-Overtrick) with no common crosses in his first four generations. His closest crosses are 5x4 to King's Counsel and 6x4x5x5 to Billy Direct. He also has multiple crosses to strong mares - 6x5x6 to Margaret Spangler and 5x6 to Evensong. Sarah Trick, the dam of L.V. Whiskers, is very unique in that she has three separate crosses to very strong maternal lines. She is 4x5 to Margaret Spangler, 4x5 to Evensong, 6x6x6x6 to Nervolo Belle (dam of Peter Volo, Volga E. and The Great Miss Morris). I believe there are many instances in which great speed and class are derived from high class female blood.

Gee Gee Digger (Dignatarian-Gee Gee Gem-Counselor Bret) is inbred 3x3 to Bret Hanover and is also 5x4x4x4 to Adios and 4x5x5x5 to Tar Heel. One of two New Zealand-bred horses in the 1:50 list is Smart Son N. (Holmes Hanover-Smarty Pants-El Patron) who is 5x3 to Tar Heel and 5x5x4 to Adios. Holmes Hanover is a son of Albatross. For those unfamiliar with El Patron, I saw him as a youngster in the early 1970s and this son of Adios Butler had plenty of raw speed and always impressed me with his potential. Precious Bunny (Cam Fella-Bunny's Wish-B.G.'s Bunny) is linebred 3x4 to both Meadow Skipper and Bret Hanover.

Dorunrun Bluegrass (Fortune Richie-Delila Bluegrass-Sir Carlton) is a totally different animal than any other in the 1:50 list. He has no common crosses through his first five generations - almost unheard of among today's Standardbreds. The only modern horse in his pedigree is Meadow Skipper - one time in the third generation. In fact, his closest common ancestors are 5x6x6 to Volomite and 5x6 to Guy Abbey, which is ancient history in today's world. But he was a great racehorse and could be a solid outcross sire if he can pass on his speed and determination.

Jet Jockey (Abercrombie-Mississippi-Meadow Skipper) is 4x4 to Tar Heel and 4x5x5 to Adios and his sister Adieu. Silver Almahurst (Nihilator-Spiked Byrdie-Bye Bye Byrd) is interesting since he is inbred 4x2 to Bye Bye Byrd and has 4x4 crosses to Adios and Meadow Skipper. Catch A Flight (On The Road Again-Diana Lynn Lobell-Best Of All) is another linebred Meadow Skipper, being 4x4 to that stallion. Ash Blue Chip (On The Road Again-Breezie Skipper-Warm Breeze) is similarly bred with 4x3 to Meadow Skipper and additional crosses to Adios and Good Time, just like Catch A Flight and they are both by On The Road Again. Continuing with the linebred Meadow Skippers is Danger Of Fire (Flight Of Fire-Powder-Nero) who is 4x3 to that great stallion.

Misfit (Abercrombie-She's A Ten-Race Time) is one of those rare top pacers without any Meadow Skipper blood. His closest common crosses are 4x4 to Adios and 4x5 to Tar Heel - the old "golden cross".

Shadow Dance (Big Towner-Tango Almahurst-Falcon Almahurst) presents another interesting pedigree. He is 3x4 to Shadow Wave and 4x6 to old-timer The Abbe. In addition, he is 5x4 to the full sisters On Time and Olympia. On Time is the dam of the great racehorse and sire Good Time, and Olympia is the fourth dam of Big Towner.

The world champion race filly, Armbro Romance (Artsplace-Armbro Intimate-Cam Fella) is bred 3x4 to Albatross and 4x4x5 to Meadow Skipper.

Beach Towel (French Chef-Sunburn-Armbro Nesbit) has no common ancestors in four generations but has strength from several top lines - 4x6x6x5 to Hal Dale and 5x5x4 to Billy Direct. In addition, he is 5x5x4 to Adios and his sister Adieu. You will also note in Beach Towel's chapter how he nicks very well who have mares with plenty of Adios blood.

Cam's Card Shark (Cam Fella-Jef's Magic Trick-B.G.'s Bunny) is another classic linebred Meadow Skipper, being 3x4 to him and 3x4 to Bret Hanover. Bright As Day (Troublemaker-Sharper Image-Strike Out) is inbred 3x3 to Bret Hanover and linebred 4x4 to Good Time. Presidential Ball (Cam Fella-I Marilyn-Mountain Skipper) has plenty of

Hal Dale blood and is 4x4x3 to Dale Frost, 4x5 to Adios and 5x5x5x5x4x6 to Hal Dale.

Biba Fra (Tyler B.-Christine's Sister-Keystone Ore) has an unusual cross in that the closest common link is 3x3 to the half-brother and sister Meadow Skipper and Tarport Duchess. He is also 3x4 to Tar Heel, 4x4 to Good Time and 4x5x5x4 to Adios and Adieu. Another with a strong Tar Heel/Adios cross is Hometown Spirit (Slapstick-Ready Donut-Bret Hanover) who is linebred 3x4 to Tar Heel and 4x3 to Adios.

Keystone Endeavor (Storm Damage-Well Endowed-Albatross) has similar crosses, with 3x5x5 to Adios and 4x5x3 to Tar Heel, along with a 4x6 cross to the good broodmare Spinster. Without Reproach (Ideal Society-Above Board-Most Happy Fella) has multiple crosses to Adios, Tar Heel and Good Time, but his closest is the inbred 3x3 to Meadow Skipper. However, his dam is also inbred 3x3 to the full sisters Maxine's Dream (grandam of Most Happy Fella) and Dream Girl.

Nick's Fantasy (Tyler's Mark-Saraton-Trenton) is linebred 4x3x5 to Meadow Skipper and also has a 4x5 cross to world champion mare Adios Betty. Pacific Rocket (Albert Albert-Flat Foot Fluzy-Direct Scooter) is a good fit for many of today's mares since his closest crosses are 4x4 to Bret Hanover, 4x5 to Meadow Skipper and 4x5x5x4 to Adios. Village Jiffy is a 3x4 linebred to Meadow Skipper and 4x4 to Good Time.

Island Glow (Dragon's Lair-Three Mile Island-No Nukes) is another very "forward bred" horse with a 3x4 cross to Most Happy Fella and 3x3 to Race Time. He also has a very strong female cross with a 3x3 to three-quarter-sisters Tarport Cheer and Tarport Kathy - both very potent broodmares. Sands A Flyin (Beach Towel-Misty Bretta-Bret Hanover) is inbred 3x3 to Meadow Skipper and linebred 4x4 to Tar Heel. Dr. Lecter Lobell (On The Road Again-Bold Moment-Albatross) is linebred 4x3 to Meadow Skipper.

Others with linebred or inbred crosses to Albatross are Dream Away (Artsplace-Some Kinda Dream-Forrest Skipper) with a 3x4, B.J.'s Whirlwind (Precious Bunny-Tabloid-No Nukes) with a 4x3 and Armbro Pluto (Dexter Nukes-Leamlara-Niatross) who is inbred 3x3 to Albatross.

The lesson I have tried to point out through this exercise is that the 1:50 pacers can come from anywhere, through any sire line, and through any combination of sire lines. In fact, the 74 performers are sired by 43 different stallions and there are 46 different broodmare sires involved. Another aspect is the infusion of multiples of strong male and female blood through full, three-quarter or half-brothers and sisters. There are no sure formulas or recipes that guarantee breeding a 1:50 pacer; or, for that matter, a 2:00 pacer.

However, what we will learn is that certain patterns sometimes develop among sires and broodmare sires. While the 74 1:50 pacers may appear to come from anywhere, the picture becomes a bit more clear when we examine one sire at a time and see what works best for him. This is not an easy task, and it can become frustrating. But some crosses definitely do work better than others. Sometimes we need to look at the broodmare sires in the second or third generations of successful crosses in order to perceive a link. Other times, we may find fast horses resulting from a sire being bred to a certain maternal family.

Inbreeding, linebreeding and outcrossing all work in different ways with different stallions. The challenge is to find a pattern of success and that is what we are attempting to do in the stallion chapters.

The following is a listing of all the 1:51 pacers through late June of 1998, ranked by their time record. For ease of reading, the sires, dams and dam's sires have been placed in a column format, which will enable the reader to pick out certain sires which appear stronger at various levels. At the end are tables ranking the sires and broodmare sires in different categories.

1:51 Pacers

Horse	Time	Year	Sire	Dam	Dam's Sire
Cambest	p,T1:46.1	1993	Cam Fella	Oxford Mary Ann	Harold J.
Jenna's Beach Boy	p,4,1:47.3	1996	Beach Towel	Five O'Clock Cindy	Cam Fella
Ultimate Falcon	p,1:47.4z	1998	Falcon Seelster	Caramel Sundae	Falcon Almahurst
Matt's Scooter	p,3,T1:48.2	1988	Direct Scooter	Ellen's Glory	Meadow Skipper
Staying Together	p,4,1:48.2	1993	Panorama	Happily Involved	Armbro Alert
Pacific Fella	p,1:48.2z	1998	Cam Fella	One More Kiss	Big Towner
Camluck	p,T1:48.4	1992	Cam Fella	Lucky Lady	Striking Image
Riyadh	p,1:48.4	1996	Jate Lobell	Malaysia	Bye And Large
Ball And Chain	p,1:49	1996	Albatross	Full Of Love	Bret Hanover
Niatross	p,3,T1:49.1	1980	Albatross	Niagara Dream	Bye Bye Byrd
Trump Casino	p,4,1:49.1	1996	Falcon Seelster	Laker's Fortune	Fortune Teller
Northern Luck	p,3,1:49.1	1997	Camluck	Town Sweetheart	Big Towner
Tune Town	p,1:49.1	1997	Big Towner	Paris Song	Colt Fortysix
Palmetto Dear	p,1:49.1z	1998	Tyler's Mark	Yes Dear	Bret Hanover
Red Bow Tie	p,4,1:49.1	1998	Raging Glory	Cheers	Lauxmont Royce
Jaguar Spur	p,4,T1:49.2	1988	Albatross	J.D.'s Bret	Bret Hanover
T.K.'s Skipper	p,T1:49.2	1990	Governor Skipper	Shana Hanover	Armbro Nesbit
Caesar's Jackpot(m)	p,T1:49.2	1991	Walton Hanover	Tracy's Jackpot	Albatross
Artsplace	p,4,1:49.2	1992	Abercrombie	Miss Elvira	Albatross
Armbro Maestro	p,1:49.2	1996	Dexter Nukes	Armbro Harmony	Legal Notice
Darth Raider	p,1:49.2	1996	Laag	Barbara's Vic	Adios Vic
Stand Forever	p,4,1:49.2h	1996	Dragon's Lair	Niajet	Niatross
Tulane	p,4,1:49.2	1998	Admiral's Galley	Burnish	Oil Burner
Western Dreamer	p,4,1:49.2	1998	Western Hanover	Fits Of Fun	Panorama
Nihilator	p,3,1:49.3	1985	Niatross	Margie's Melody	Bret Hanover
Call For Rain	p,4,1:49.3	1988	Storm Damage	Rain Proof	Meadow Skipper
Camtastic	p,4,T1:49.3	1989	Cam Fella	Lushkara	Albatross
In The Pocket	p,3,T1:49.3	1990	Direct Scooter	Black Jade	Tar Heel
Cam Terrific	p,4,1:49.3	1995	Cam Fella	The Booger Lady	Steady Star
New Bucks	p,1:49.3	1995	Nihilator	Candy Bucks	Sonsam
L.V. Whiskers	p,1:49.3	1995	Armbro Aussie	Sarah Trick	Overtrick

Horse	Time	Year	Sire	Dam	Dam's Sire
Gee Gee Digger	p,3,1:49.3	1996	Dignatarian	Gee Gee Cam	Counselor Bret
Smart Son N.	p,1:49.3	1996	Holmes Hanover	Smarty Pants	El Patron
Hot Lead	p,4,1:49.3	1997	Jaguar Spur	J.M. Valinda	Bye Bye Byrd
Sports Town	p,4,1:49.3	1997	Die Laughing	Tyler Town	Tyler B.
Duke Of Abby	p,1:49.3	1998	Dexter Nukes	Mellowood Abby	Abercrombie
Oneinamillion N	p,1:49.3z	1998	Son Of Afella	Rippling River	Surmo Hanover
The Big Dog	p,4,1:49.3	1998	Dexter Nukes	Miss Donna Mayo	Silent Majority
Precious Bunny	p,3,1:49.4	1991	Cam Fella	Bunny's Wish	B.G.'s Bunny
Dorunrun Bluegrass	p,1:49.4	1992	Fortune Richie	Delila Bluegrass	Sir Carlton
Jet Jockey	p,1:49.4	1993	Abercrombie	Mississippi	Meadow Skipper
Silver Almahurst	p,4,1:49.4	1993	Nihilator	Spiked Byrdie	Bye Bye Byrd
Catch A Flight	p,4,1:49.4	1995	On The Road Again	Diana Lynn Lobell	Sonsam
Ash Blue Chip	p,1:49.4	1996	On The Road Again	Breezie Skipper	Warm Breeze
Danger Of Fire	p,1:49.4	1996	Flight Of Fire	Powder	Nero
Misfit	p,1:49.4	1996	Abercrombie	She's A Ten	Race Time
Shadow Dance	p,1:49.4	1996	Big Towner	Tango Almahurst	Falcon Almahurst
Stout	p,4,1:49.4	1997	Precious Bunny	Alison Sara	Keystone Ore
Village Jove	p,3,1:49.4	1997	Cam Fella	Village Jig	Direct Scooter
Armbro Romance (m)	p,3,1:49.4	1998	Artsplace	Armbro Intimate	Cam Fella
Mustang Hanover	p,1:49.4	1998	Colt Fortysix	Myrtle Direct	Sampson Direct
Beach Towel	p,3,1:50	1990	French Chef	Sunburn	Armbro Nesbit
Cam's Card Shark	p,3,1:50	1991	Cam Fella	Jef's Magic Trick	B.G.'s Bunny
Bright As Day	p,4,1:50	1993	Troublemaker	Sharper Image	Strike Out
Presidential Ball	p,3,1:50	1993	Cam Fella	I Marilyn	Mountain Skipper
Biba Fra	p,4,1:50	1993	Tyler B.	Christine's Sister	Keystone Ore
Hometown Spirit	p,1:50	1993	Slapstick	Ready Donut	Bret Hanover
Keystone Endeavor	p,4,1:50	1994	Storm Damage	Well Endowed	Albatross
Without Reproach	p,3,1:50	1994	Ideal Society	Above Board	Most Happy Fella
Nick's Fantasy	p,3,1:50	1995	Tyler's Mark	Saraton	Trenton
Pacific Rocket	p,4,1:50	1995	Albert Albert	Flat Foot Fluzy	Direct Scooter
Village Jiffy	p,1:50	1995	Cam Fella	Village Jig	Direct Scooter
Island Glow	p,1:50	1996	Dragon's Lair	Three Mile Island	No Nukes
Sands A Flyin	p,4,1:50	1996	Beach Towel	Misty Bretta	Bret Hanover

Pedigree Crosses of 1:51 Pacers

Horse	Time	Year	Sire	Dam	Dam's Sire
Armbro Operative	p,4,1:50	1997	Cam Fella	Cunning Bunny	B.G.'s Bunny
Dream Away	p,3,1:50	1997	Artsplace	Some Kinda Dream	Forrest Skipper
Dr. Lecter Lobell	p,1:50	1997	On The Road Again	Bold Moment	Albatross
Farlane Star	p,1:50	1997	Militant	Farlane Marg	Melvin's Strike
Mystical Maddy (m)	p,4,1:50	1997	Matt's Scooter	Mossy	Most Happy Fella
Strong Clan	p,1:50	1997	Direct Scooter	Village Jewel	Abercrombie
Armbro Pluto	p,4,1:50	1998	Dexter Nukes	Leamlara	Niatross
B J's Whirlwind	p,4,1:50	1998	Precious Bunny	Tabloid	No Nukes
Fearless Raider	p,1:50	1998	Keystone Raider	Freddi Fearless	B.G.'s Bunny
Midnight Stalker	p,1:50	1998	Cam Fella	Yarmila	Allwin Steady
Ramblin Storm	p,1:50.1	1988	Storm Damage	Elda Belle	Most Happy Fella
Kiev Hanover	p,3,1:50.1	1990	Albatross	Keystone Sandra	Bye Bye Byrd
Jake And Elwood	p,4,1:50.1	1991	Samadhi	Lil Pod's Fiddle	Gypsy Fiddle
Nuclear Siren	p,3,1:50.1	1991	No Nukes	Siren Almahurst	High Ideal
Lorryland Butler	p,1:50.1	1992	Skip By Night	Jud's Choice	B.G.'s Bunny
Odds Against	p,1:50.1	1992	Troublemaker	Cartier	Silent Majority
Holy Terror	p,4,1:50.1	1993	Troublemaker	Noble Feeling	Warm Breeze
Arrive At Five	p,4,1:50.1	1994	Nihilator	Lady Has Arrived	Safe Arrival
Silent Spring	p,1:50.1	1994	On the Road Again	Castleton Spring	Bret Hanover
No Laughs	p,1:50.1	1996	No Nukes	Laugher	Niatross
Splendid Splinter	p,4,1:50.1	1996	Beach Towel	Dime A Dip	Marauder
Sweetgeorgiabrown-m	p,4,1:50.1	1996	Jate Lobell	Armbro Georgia	Direct Scooter
Armbro Other	p,4,1:50.1	1997	Abercrombie	Thithter Thavage	Albatross
Final Cheers	p,4,1:50.1	1997	Champagne Lobell	Knight Caller	True Duane
Reactor Lobell	p,1:50.1	1997	Slapstick	Racy Heart	Race Time
Beach St Partners	p,1:50.1	1998	Beach Towel	Mow The Lawn	B.G.'s Bunny
Dauntless Bunny	p,4,1:50.1	1998	Precious Bunny	Everglade Angie	Abercrombie
Galleria (m)	p,3,1:50.1	1998	Artsplace	Emory Girl	Sherman Almahurst
Harden	p,1:50.1	1998	Precious Bunny	Keystone Flamingo	Keystone Ore
Here's A Quarter	p,1:50.1	1998	Big Towner	Rita Almahurst	Falcon Almahurst
Noble Ability	p,1:50.1	1998	Albatross	Myhalia Hanover	Tyler B
Barberry Spur	p,3,1:50.2	1986	Niatross	Etiquette	Bret Hanover
As Promised	p,4,1:50.2	1993	Abercrombie	Promised Princess	Niatross

Horse	Time	Year	Sire	Dam	Dam's Sire
Bilateral	p,4,1:50.2	1993	Laag	Kay Blue Chip	Most Happy Fella
Direct Command	p,4,1:50.2	1993	Direct Scooter	Brittany Lauxmont	Armbro Aussie
Exotic Earl	p,4,1:50.2	1993	Cam Fella	Armbro Exotic	Niatross
General Ring	p,1:50.2	1993	General Star	Star Ring	Dream Maker
Vine Street	p,3,1:50.2	1993	Storm Damage	Napa Valley	Most Happy Fella
Armbro Maneuver	p,3,1:50.2	1994	Direct Scooter	Cunning Bunny	B.G.'s Bunny
Magical Mike	p,3,1:50.2	1994	Tyler B.	Racing Date	Race Time
Cam's Catch	p,3,1:50.2	1995	Cam Fella	Lookin Fine	Albatross
Deadlock	p,1:50.2	1995	Nihilator	Karril Hanover	Albatross
Justabit Of Magic	p,1:50.2	1995	Chairmanoftheboard	Magic Touch	Set The Style
Lotta Soul	p,1:50.2	1995	No Nukes	Jazz Singer	Albatross
Make A Deal	p,4,1:50.2	1995	No Nukes	Leah Almahurst	Abercrombie
Mr. Panman	p,4,1:50.2	1995	Niatross	Palma Lobell	Nero
All Star Hanna	p,3,1:50.2	1996	Direct Scooter	Meadow Good Miss	Meadow Skipper
Arizona Jack	p,3,1:50.2	1996	Abercrombie	Concertina	French Chef
Bullvon's Dream	p,1:50.2	1996	Sonsam	Thelma's Dream	Most Happy Fella
Highly Promoted	p,1:50.2	1996	Praised Dignity	Vacation Bagel	Abercrombie
Road Happy	p,1:50.2	1996	On The Road Again	Happy Bottom	Abercrombie
Swingin Single	p,4,1:50.2	1996	Jate Lobell	Full Of Love	Bret Hanover
Free Spender	p,1:50.2	1997	Abercrombie	Dawn Michelle	Sonsam
Nicholas T.	p,4,1:50.2	1997	Falcon Seelster	Princess Pacific	Rashad
No Control N.	p,1:50.2	1997	Marked Man	Self Control	Tony Bucks
Road To The Top	p,1:50.2	1997	On The Road Again	So Precious	Most Happy Fella
Winning Goalie	p,1:50.2	1997	Goalie Jeff	Brenda Blue Chip	Overcall
Computer Scooter	p,4,1:50.2	1998	Matt's Scooter	Computer Chip	Bret Hanover
John Street North	p,1:50.2	1998	Precious Bunny	O J Almahurst	Abercrombie
Just Doodlin	p,1:50.2	1998	Royal Arms	K J Alert	Armbro Alert
Kendal Missile	p,1:50.2	1998	Camtastic	Miss Gold Skipper	Meadow Skipper
Little Steven	p,1:50.2	1998	Albert Albert	Lady Nelson	Landslide
Luren Lee	p,1:50.2z	1998	Lukan Hanover	Jerri Lee	Timely Adora
Magnetic Killean	p,1:50.2	1998	Run The Table	Magnetic Almahurst	Nihilator
Proud Albert	p,1:50.2	1998	Albert Albert	Tarport Clarabell	Most Happy Fella
Colt Fortysix	p,3,1:50.3	1984	Albatross	Hoopla	Tar Heel

Pedigree Crosses of 1:51 Pacers

Horse	Time	Year	Sire	Dam	Dam's Sire
Forrest Skipper	p,4,T1:50.3	1986	Scarlet Skipper	Camden Caroline	Tar Heel
Echelon	p,1:50.3	1991	Troublemaker	Cupid's Flight	Race Time
Prince Ebony	p,1:50.3	1991	Conquered	Fiji Islander	Most Happy Fella
Storm Compensation	p,1:50.3	1991	Storm Damage	Loren Messenger	Meadow Skipper
Life Sign	p,3,1:50.3	1993	Abercrombie	Three Diamonds	Albatross
Mystical Prince	p,3,1:50.3	1993	Jate Lobell	Mystical Mood	Trenton
Hi Ho Silverheel's	p,3,1:50.3	1994	Walton Hanover	Armbro Caprice	Abercrombie
Staff Officer	p,1:50.3	1994	Marauder	Sexy Dolly	Warm Breeze
Steady Freedom	p,3,1:50.3	1994	American Freedom	Steady Johnnie Sue	Steady Beau
Ellamony (m)	p,1:50.3	1995	Cam Fella	Ceremony	Race Time
Athena Blue Chip (m)	p,4,1:50.3	1996	Goalie Jeff	Athens Blue Chip	On The Road Again
Falcon Dakota	p,1:50.3	1996	Falcon Seelster	Picture Me Gone	Governor Skipper
Good News Scooter	p,1:50.3	1996	Matt's Scooter	Bit Of Good News	General Star
Lahar	p,1:50.3	1996	Abercrombie	Lismore	Albatross
Mustang Hanover	p,1:50.3	1996	Colt Fortysix	Myrtle Direct	Sampson Direct
Native Born	p,1:50.3	1996	Nihilator	Native Rita	Meadow Skipper
Private Ritual	p,4,1:50.3	1996	Kassa Branca	Romola Lobell	Precious Fella
Oye Vay	p,3,1:50.3	1996	Albatross	Armbro Glossy	Cam Fella
Cami Whitestocking (m)	p,4,1:50.3	1997	Camtastic	Allison Wonderland	Justin Passing
Spectacular Deal	p,1:50.3	1997	Topnotcher	Acquired Skill	Bret Hanover
Extreme Velocity	p,1:50.3	1997	Camtastic	Hasty Grand Slam	Nardins Grand Slam
Keystone Tad	p,1:50.3	1997	Cam Fella	Keystone Tulsa	Keystone Ore
The Wrath Of Pan	p,4,1:50.3	1997	Abercrombie	Infinite Wisdom	Seahawk Hanover
Kingdom Of The Sea	p,4,1:50.3z	1998	Jate Lobell	Kinway Heather	Ladatross
L Dee's Jonathan	p,1:50.3	1998	Die Laughing	L Dee's Leslie	Seahawk Hanover
Mattcheever	p,3,1:50.3	1998	Matt's Scooter	Breezy Road	On The Road Again
Mob Scene	p,1:50.3	1998	On The Road Again	Crowded	Albatross
Resurgent Dragon	p,3,1:50.3	1998	Dragon's Lair	Ghostly Returns	Laag
So Excited	p,4,1:50.3	1998	Laag	Excited	Troublemaker
Stampede Hanover	p,4,1:50.3	1998	Western Hanover	Sparkling Hanover	Abercrombie
Dare You To	p,1:50.4	1991	Abercrombie	Chickasaw Brave	Meadow Skipper
Fan Hanover (m)	p,4,T1:50.4	1982	Albatross	Farm Norah	Bret Hanover
Stoneridge Scooter	p,3,1:50.4	1991	Direct Scooter	J.N. Dynamic	Albatross
Marmaduke Hanover	p,3,1:50.4	1992	Walton Hanover	Manor Born	Bret Hanover

Horse	Time	Year	Sire	Dam	Dam's Sire
Western Hanover	p,3,1:50.4	1992	No Nukes	Wendymae Hanover	Albatross
Doctor Gerson	p,4,1:50.4	1993	Landslide	Damita Hanover	Best Of All
General Cochran	p,1:50.4	1993	Direct Scooter	Survival Kit	Most Happy Fella
Getting Personal	p,3,1:50.4	1993	Storm Damage	Fondle	Nero
All Da Time	p,1:50.4	1994	Keystone Ore	On Your Toes	Columbia George
Broadway Blue	p,4,1:50.4f	1994	No Nukes	Brunhilde Hanover	Albatross
Feree Hanover	p,4,1:50.4	1994	Big Towner	Farmstead's Future	Bret Hanover
Rayson Hanover	p,3,1:50.4	1994	Big Towner	Razzle Hanover	Albatross
Under Orders	p,4,1:50.4	1994	Silent Majority	Mc Toodles	Falcon Almahurst
Water Tower	p,3,1:50.4	1994	Abercrombie	Reservoir	Bret Hanover
Bad Self	p,1:50.4	1995	On The Road Again	Irma Blue Chip	Most Happy Fella
David's Pass	p,3,1:50.4	1995	Jate Lobell	Pass	Strike Out
J.C.'s Suprimo	p,4,1:50.4	1995	No Nukes	Town Tramp	Big Towner
Make Music	p,4,1:50.4	1995	Abercrombie	Evergreen Sandy	Most Happy Fella
Reality Check	p,4,1:50.4	1995	Laag	Hold True	Niatross
Richey Letsgo	p,1:50.4	1995	Abercrombie	Forever Sparkle	Storm Damage
Winning Goalie	p,4,1:50.4	1995	Goalie Jeff	Brenda Blue Chip	Overcall
Armbro Nest (m)	p,4,1:50.4	1996	Dragon's Lair	La Toya	Sonsam
Camtastic Dream	p,1:50.4	1996	Camtastic	Sonsam's Dream	Sonsam
Come Out Swinging	p,1:50.4	1996	Nihilator	Respectfully Yours	Big Towner
Orchard Street	p,4,1:50.4	1996	Goalie Jeff	Mulberry Street	On The Road Again
She's A Great Lady (m)	p,4,1:50.4	1996	Dexter Nukes	Miss Donna Mayo	Silent Majority
C.A. Connection	p,1:50.4	1997	Kassa Branca	Traci Miss	Peter Lobell
Gothic Dream	p,3,1:50.4	1997	Jate Lobell	Perfidia	Niatross
Jacsue Brooks	p,1:50.4	1997	Dennis Seelster	Sassy Becky	Nardin's Byrd
Longport	p,3,1:50.4	1997	Dragon's Lair	For Your Eyes Only	Jade Prince
Nuclear Design	p,1:50.4	1997	No Nukes	Nia Rita	Niatross
Ryan's Miracle	p,3,1:50.4	1997	Die Laughing	Watering Can	Meadow Skipper
Sharp Attack	p,4,1:50.4	1997	Direct Scooter	Betty Lobell	No Nukes
Stienam's Place (m)	p,3,1:50.4	1997	Artsplace	Stienam's Girl	Nihilator
Tune Town	p,1:50.4	1997	Big Towner	Paris Song	Colt Fortysix
At Point Blank	p,1:50.4	1998	Beach Towel	Bouvier	Big Towner
Armbro Oliver	p,1:50.4	1998	Cam Fella	Armbro Carmita	Abercrombie
Bad Bert	p,1:50.4	1998	Albert Albert	Sickem Cindy	Niatross

Pedigree Crosses of 1:51 Pacers

Horse	Time	Year	Sire	Dam	Dam's Sire
Color Striped	p,3,1:50.4	1998	Cam Fella	Keymona Rainbow	Keystone Ore
Dontgetinmyway	p,1:50.4	1998	Abercrombie	Seven O'Clock	Tyler B
Infellable	p,1:50.4	1998	Cam Fella	Albaquel	Albatross
Jet Laag	p,1:50.4z	1998	Laag	Truancy	Big Towner
Master Barney	p,1:50.4	1998	Armbro Emerson	Rake It In	Seedling Herbert
Master Miles	p,1:50.4z	1998	Praised Dignity	Silly Gamble	Bruce Gimble
Megamind	p,1:50.4	1998	Jate Lobell	Lady Genius	Tyler B
Stone Dragon	p,4,1:50.4	1998	Dragon's Lair	Keystone Native	Warm Breeze
Falcon Seelster	p,3,1:51h	1985	Warm Breeze	Fashion Trick	Overtrick
Run The Table	p,3,1:51	1987	Landslide	Hustler's Best	Best Of All
Shady Daisy (m)	p,3,1:51	1991	Falcon Seelster	Tika Belle	Skipper Walt
Carlsbad Cam	p,3,1:51	1992	Cam Fella	Perette Hanover	Albatross
Cam's Coal	p,3,1:51	1993	Cam Fella	Armbro Utrillo	Horton Hanover
Diablo Cedarn	p,4,1:51	1993	Armbro Aussie	Dancin' On Air	Sonsam
Direct Flight	p,4,1:51	1993	Direct Scooter	Oreo Byrd	Keystone Ore
Elegant Albert	p,3,1:51	1993	Albert Albert	D'Elegance	Escape Artist
Immortality (m)	p,3,1:51	1993	No Nukes	Jef's Eternity	Albatross
Incredible Aussie	p,4,1:51	1993	Armbro Aussie	Whimsical Lobell	Niatross
Ready To Rumble	p,3,1:51	1993	Laag	Miss Allison Plate	Nero
Survivor Gold	p,4,1:51	1993	Abercrombie	T.M.I.	Oil Burner
Apache Max	p,3,1:51	1994	Apache Circle	Maxine's Delight	Most Happy Fella
Call For Cash	p,3,1:51	1994	Matt's Scooter	Sable Hanover	Albatross
Expensive Scooter	p,3,1:51	1994	Direct Scooter	Expensive Lady	Tyler B.
Falcon's Future	p,3,1:51f	1994	Falcon Seelster	Margo Laporte	Oil Burner
Historic	p,3,1:51f	1994	Nihilator	Dateable	Race Time
Largo	p,1:51	1994	Cam Fella	Ombre Rose	B.G.'s Bunny
Lightening Speed	p,4,1:51	1994	Falcon Seelster	Visi D'Arte	Most Happy Fella
Lookout Man	p,3,1:51	1994	Jate Lobell	Ballycullun	Albatross
Too Much Trouble	p,1:51	1994	Troublemaker	Norahtross	Niatross
Forbidden Goal	p,4,1:51	1995	Goalie Jeff	Forbidden Love	Abercrombie
Hojo	p,1:51	1995	Del's Fella	G.P. Fancy	Laverne Hanover
No Standing Around	p,3,1:51	1995	Jate Lobell	Starfire Almahurst	Falcon Almahurst
Viking Commander	p,3,1:51	1995	Abercrombie	No Feathers	Albatross
Dixie Laag	p,3,1:51	1996	Laag	Dixie Clamp	Striking Image

Horse	Time	Year	Sire	Dam	Dam's Sire
Gabrielle (m)	p,4,1:51	1996	Dragon's Lair	Conquered Quest	Sonsam
Stout	p,3,1:51	1996	Precious Bunny	Alison Sara	Keystone Ore
Village Connection	p,4,1:51	1996	Cam Fella	Armbro Colleen	Abercrombie
Armbro Omar	p,4,1:51	1997	Abercrombie	May Wine	Most Happy Fella
Broadcast	p,4,1:51	1997	Abercrombie	Boobtube	Tyler B
Flow Control	p,4,1:51	1997	Precious Bunny	Sabra Almahurst	Bret Hanover
Hare Hare	p,1:51	1997	Precious Bunny	Joy Hanover	Big Towner
His Mattjesty	p,3,1:51	1997	Matt's Scooter	Lady Hathaway	No Nukes
J K Outlaw	p,3,1:51	1997	Artsplace	Mardi's Crown	Jamuga
Katorzheniki	p,4,1:51	1997	Kiev Hanover	Collector's Item	No Nukes
Kettle Bee	p,1:51	1997	Jate Lobell	Glamour Goes On	Abercrombie
Park Place	p,3,1:51	1997	Artsplace	Deneen's Delight	Most Happy Fella
Perfect Art	p,3,1:51	1997	Artsplace	Perfect Profile	Nihilator
Sakra Mania	p,4,1:51	1997	Laag	Rosellen Hanover	Tyler B
Thruway Hershey (m)	p,1:51	1997	On The Road Again	Easy Lovin	Sonsam
Village Jasper	p,3,1:51	1997	Jate Lobell	Village Jewel	Abercrombie
Albert T	p,4,1:51z	1998	Albert Albert	Charming T	Tyler B
Armbro Obliging	p,1:51	1998	Direct Scooter	Armbro Easy	Most Happy Fella
Artist Stena	p,3,1:51	1998	Artsplace	Loving Success	Jate Lobell
Cory's Big Guy	p,4,1:51	1998	Cam Fella	Florita Lobell	Albatross
Jules Jodoin (m)	p,1:51	1998	Laag	Myrtle Hanover	Armbro Nesbit
Launch Code	p,3,Q1:51	1998	No Nukes	Banshee Hanover	Albatross
Lead Me On	p,1:51	1998	Leading Edge	Foxy Windy	Jambooger
Little Bighorn	p,1:51	1998	Denali	War Chief's Sister	Conejo Chief
Rockapella	p,1:51	1998	Jaguar Spur	Impish Lobell	Temujin
Shania (m)	p,4,1:51	1998	Laag	Mission Of Truth	Albatross
Shotgun Scott	p,3,1:51	1998	Western Hanover	Barby's Makentrax	Barberry Spur
Swingin Glory	p,4,1:51	1998	Raging Glory	Swingin	Meadow Skipper
Take Down The Flag	p,3,1:51	1998	Western Hanover	Mable's Scooter	Sampson Direct

Leading Sires of 1:50 Performers

Sire	Count	Sire	Count
Cam Fella	12	Big Towner	2
Dexter Nukes	4	Dragon's Lair	2
Abercrombie	3	Falcon Seelster	2
Albatross	3	Nihilator	2
Direct Scooter	3	Precious Bunny	2
On The Road Again	3	Storm Damage	2
Artsplace	2	Tyler's Mark	2
Beach Towel	2		

Leading Sires of 1:51 Performers (2 or more)

Sire	Count	Sire	Count	Sire	Count
Cam Fella	24	Big Towner	6	Jaguar Spur	2
Abercrombie	19	Matt's Scooter	6	Kassa Branca	2
Direct Scooter	12	Storm Damage	6	Landslide	2
Jate Lobell	12	Beach Towel	5	Praised Dignity	2
Laag	10	Dexter Nukes	5	Raging Glory	2
No Nukes	10	Goalie Jeff	5	Tyler B	2
On The Road Again	9	Troublemaker	5	Tyler's Mark	2
Albatross	8	Camtastic	4		
Artsplace	8	Western Hanover	4		
Precious Bunny	8	Armbro Aussie	3		
Dragon's Lair	7	Die Laughing	3		
Falcon Seelster	7	Niatross	3		
Nihilator	7	Walton Hanover	3		
Albert Albert	6	Colt Fortysix	2		

Leading Sires of 1:52 Performers (5 or more)

Sire	Count	Sire	Count	Sire	Count
Cam Fella	51	Falcon Seelster	18	Western Hanover	10
Abercrombie	46	Tyler B	17	Denali	9
No Nukes	44	Dragon's Lair	16	Die Laughing	8
Direct Scooter	36	Nihilator	16	Goalie Jeff	8
On The Road Again	29	Storm Damage	14	Troublemaker	8
Jate Lobell	28	Beach Towel	13	Nobleland Sam	7
Big Towner	21	Walton Hanover	13	Armbro Aussie	6
Laag	21	Camtastic	12	Armbro Emerson	5
Albatross	20	Niatross	11	Jaguar Spur	5
Albert Albert	19	Precious Bunny	11	Nero	5
Matt's Scooter	19	Dexter Nukes	10	Run The Table	5
Artsplace	18	Tyler's Mark	10	Slapstick	5

Leading Sires of 1:55 Performers (40 or More)

Sire	Count	Sire	Count	Sire	Count	Sire	Count
No Nukes	332	Walton Hanover	123	Ideal Society	65	Western Hanover	50
Abercrombie	253	Matt's Scooter	111	Beach Towel	64	Vance Hanover	49
Albatross	236	Falcon Seelster	108	B.G.'s Bunny	62	Bret Hanover	48
Direct Scooter	228	Nihilator	107	Troublemaker	60	Die Laughing	44
Cam Fella	227	Albert Albert	98	Landslide	60	Incredible Finale	43
Big Towner	191	Sonsam	92	Camtastic	59	Denali	41
Jate Lobell	176	Falcon Almahurst	85	Meadow Skipper	58	Forrest Skipper	41
On The Road Again	161	Dragon's Lair	84	Most Happy Fella	58	Towner's Big Guy	41
Niatross	140	Nero	73	Armbro Emerson	56	Slapstick	40
Laag	139	Tyler's Mark	73	Nobleland Sam	54		
Tyler B	136	Artsplace	70	Goalie Jeff	51		
Storm Damage	135	Dexter Nukes	66	Kentucky Spur	51		

Leading Sires of 2:00 Performers (250 or More)

Sire	Count	Sire	Count	Sire	Count	Sire	Count
Albatross	1,163	Bret Hanover	546	Nihilator	368	Armbro Omaha	267
No Nukes	986	Tyler B	545	Landslide	347	Troublemaker	266
Direct Scooter	919	Nero	540	Precious Fella	343	High Ideal	258
Big Towner	889	Laag	492	Matt's Scooter	311	Ralph Hanover	255
Abercrombie	828	On The Road Again	462	Run The Table	304	Seahawk Hanover	251
Storm Damage	678	Meadow Skipper	454	Silent Majority	303	Keystone Ore	251
Niatross	637	Jate Lobell	440	Tyler's Mark	300	Dragon's Lair	250
B.G.'s Bunny	595	Walton Hanover	421	Warm Breeze	296		
Cam Fella	594	Ideal Society	406	Nobleland Sam	284		
Falcon Almahurst	556	Sonsam	386	Oil Burner	278		
Most Happy Fella	552	Falcon Seelster	381	Albert Albert	267		

Leading Sires of Dams of 1:50 Performers (2 or more)

Sire	Count	Sire	Count	Sire	Count	Sire	Count	Sire	Count
Bret Hanover	6	Direct Scooter	3	Big Towner	2	Most Happy Fella	2	Tyler's Mark	2
Albatross	5	Meadow Skipper	3	Cam Fella	2	Niatross	2		
B.G.'s Bunny	4	Abercrombie	2	Falcon Almahurst	2	No Nukes	2		
Bye Bye Byrd	3	Armbro Nesbit	2	Keystone Ore	2	Sonsam	2		

Leading Sires of Dams of 1:51 Performers (3 or more)

Sire	Count	Sire	Count	Sire	Count	Sire	Count	Sire	Count
Albatross	25	Meadow Skipper	10	Keystone Ore	7	Direct Scooter	4	Nihilator	3
Most Happy Fella	17	B.G.'s Bunny	8	Race Time	6	Nero	4	Oil Burner	3
Bret Hanover	16	Sonsam	8	Falcon Almahurst	5	Warm Breeze	4	On The Road Again	3
Abercrombie	14	Tyler B	8	No Nukes	5	Armbro Nesbit	3	Silent Majority	3
Niatross	11	Big Towner	7	Bye Bye Byrd	4	Cam Fella	3	Tar Heel	3

Leading Sires of Dams of 1:52 Performers (5 or more)

Sire	Count	Sire	Count	Sire	Count	Sire	Count	Sire	Count
Albatross	81	No Nukes	26	Keystone Ore	11	Precious Fella	8	Seahawk Hanover	6
Bret Hanover	48	Tyler B	22	Silent Majority	11	Storm Damage	8	Tar Heel	6
Meadow Skipper	40	Race Time	19	Bye Bye Byrd	10	Oil Burner	7	Overtrick	5
Most Happy Fella	37	B.G.'s Bunny	18	Direct Scooter	10	Strike Out	7	Temujin	5
Abercrombie	31	Nero	17	Cam Fella	9	Best Of All	6		
Niatross	27	Sonsam	16	Warm Breeze	9	Landslide	6		
Big Towner	26	Falcon Almahurst	12	Nihilator	8	Royce	6		

Leading Sires of Dams of 1:55 Performers (50 or more)

Sire	Count	Sire	Count	Sire	Count	Sire	Count	Sire	Count
Albatross	657	Nero	183	Falcon Almahurst	115	Adios Vic	75	Direct Scooter	58
Bret Hanover	409	Tyler B	180	Storm Damage	100	Keystone Ore	75	Nihilator	56
Meadow Skipper	357	Race Time	153	Bye Bye Byrd	93	High Ideal	70	Steady Star	55
Most Happy Fella	327	B.G.'s Bunny	147	Best Of All	88	Columbia George	68	Flying Bret	51
Niatross	210	No Nukes	138	Oil Burner	82	Strike Out	66	Overtrick	50
Abercrombie	199	Tar Heel	125	Precious Fella	82	Armbro Nesbit	63		
Big Towner	188	Sonsam	119	Silent Majority	82	Warm Breeze	59		

Leading Sires of Dams of 2:00 Performers (250 or more)

Sire	Count	Sire	Count	Sire	Count	Sire	Count	Sire	Count
Albatross	2,661	Best Of All	688	Storm Damage	544	Strike Out	434	Thorpe Hanover	334
Bret Hanover	2,069	Niatross	683	Steady Star	529	Good Time	429	Egyptian Dancer	323
Meadow Skipper	1,609	Adios Vic	675	B.G.'s Bunny	475	Silent Majority	429	Knight Dream	313
Most Happy Fella	1,593	Tyler B	654	No Nukes	462	Keystone Ore	420	Fulla Napoleon	296
Tar Heel	1,326	Abercrombie	650	Baron Hanover	447	Sonsam	406	Adios	296
Race Time	982	High Ideal	607	Precious Fella	446	Flying Bret	389	Direct Scooter	282
Nero	946	Columbia George	599	Shadow Wave	445	Nansemond	378	Harold J	282
Bye Bye Byrd	838	Overtrick	598	Airliner	443	Gene Abbe	351	Armbro Nesbit	276
Big Towner	761	Falcon Almahurst	571	Oil Burner	439	Warm Breeze	338	Adios Butler	260

Abercrombie

Abercrombie will most likely go down in Standardbred history as the stallion who saved the Adios male line from being totally overwhelmed by the Meadow Skipper line. In doing so, if the siring exploits of his son Artsplace are any indication, he may have even shifted the balance of power back to the Adios line.

Before we explore Abercrombie's career as a stallion, his greatness as a racehorse should be pointed out. He was voted Horse of the Year at three and became a world champion at four. Abercrombie possessed a flawless gait and a perfect temperament, characteristics which were passed on to many of his offspring - as well as a large dose of his racing courage.

Abercrombie was bred by the esteemed Walnut Hall Farm of Lexington, Kentucky, and purchased at the 1976 Tattersalls Yearling Sale for a bargain $9,500 by L. Keith Bulen who later sold half to Shirley Mitchell, both owners from Indiana. The colt was broken by Jerry Landess at the Indiana State Fairgrounds (Indianapolis) and trained by Cecil Peacock. Joe Essig, Ben Webster and Harold Barnes each drove him several times in his early races.

As a two-year-old, Abercrombie won seven of 20 starts and earned $49,379, his fastest win coming in a heat of the International Stallion S. in 1:56. He was also good on a half-mile track as attested by his 2:00 and 1:59 wins in the Ohio Standardbred S. at Delaware, Ohio. Although a good two-year-old, he was overshadowed by No No Yankee, who won divisional honors, and Say Hello. However, he showed he belonged with the best since his half-mile track clocking was the fastest of his age group and his mile record was second only to Say Hello.

It was in the second heat of the Ohio Standardbred S. that Abercrombie really came of age and showed his tenacity. He went off at odds of 17-1 and was still fifth, four lengths from the leader, at the top of the stretch. That's a lot of ground to make up at Delaware, but Abercrombie flew down the stretch and went on to win by almost three lengths. It was an extremely impressive performance. In terms of speed, Abercrombie's 1:56 in 1977 ranked him as the eighth fastest two-year-old in the sport's history at that time. Yes, Abercrombie had early speed.

The Delaware race was the first in which Abercrombie teamed up with trainer-driver Glen Garnsey who later went on achieve Hall of Fame honors. Garnsey drove Abercrombie in his final six starts as a two-year-old in which the colt had three wins, two seconds and a third; two of the losses were by only a half-length to Say Hello.

Garnsey was quoted after the 1977 season, "When I got Abercrombie he had been raced on the front end a lot and had a tendency to fall asleep, it's not that he doesn't have the ability to carry the speed or anything, but I just started racing the colt from behind and he improved. He won for me in 1:56 at Lexington, but he is a better half-mile track horse." Garnsey added, "He is a natural colt, good-gaited, doesn't wear anything but a pair of scalpers and a shadow roll and doesn't have a pimple on him."

At three, Abercrombie had made enough of an impression the prior fall to be ranked fourth in the Experimental Ratings. However, he would be facing the formidable group of No No Yankee, Say Hello, Falcon Almahurst and Flight Director, among others. Abercrombie was now in the Garnsey Stable and Glen Garnsey commented in a *Hoof Beats* interview, "I learned a lot about Abercrombie as I raced him that year. I tried not to use him too much. He was the kind who would lose interest if he got a big lead. He loved that head-to-head competition."

As a three-year-old, Abercrombie exceeded expectations compiling 22 wins from 33 starts, earning a single-season record of $703,260 and taking a mark of 1:54.3. For his efforts, Abercrombie earned Horse of the Year honors.

However, the colt began his season with a loss. After cutting the pace in a $2,000 overnight event at The Red Mile, he bounced back with wins in a Kentucky Sires S. and Scioto Challenge S. Abercrombie then shipped to The Meadowlands and won an elimination of the Oliver Wendell Holmes S. before finishing fifth in the Final after encountering traffic problems. Abercrombie then lost his next three starts including the Matron S. at Wolverine in which he had an eight-length lead in the stretch before illustrating the truth of Garnsey's remark that he would lose interest if he had a big lead. As

Abercrombie

Photo courtesy of Castleton Farms

Race Record Highlights

At 2
1st Ohio Standardbred S.
ITPHA S.
heat of International Stallion S.
2nd American National S.

At 3
1st Messenger S.
Adios S.
Prix d'Ete
Confederation Cup
Scioto Challenge S.
Reynolds Memorial
Queen City S.
James Dancer Memorial
Osborne P.
Geers S.

At 3 (continued)
T.W. Murphy Memorial
Hanover Colt S.
Mohawk Sophomore S.
Canadian Cup
Kentucky Sires S.
Cane Pace Elimination
Oliver Wendell Holmes Elimination

At 4
1st American-National Maturity
U.S. Pacing Championship
Hanover S.
two legs of Driscoll Series

Honors

Voted Horse of the Year at three

World Champion at four - fastest race mile ever

Set single-season money-winning record at three

Race Record

Year	Age	Starts	Wins	2nd	3rd	Earnings	Record
1977	2	20	7	3	3	$ 49,379	2,1:56
1978	3	33	22	6	0	703,260	3,1:54.3
1979	4	19	7	4	4	231,752	4,1:53
		72	36	13	7	$984,391	4,1:53

a result of this, he was caught at the wire again by Flight Director. It was then very evident that Abercrombie thrived on head-to-head competition.

At that point of the season, Abercrombie had won only three of his first eight starts and was considered a good, but not great, colt. Then things changed. He won five of his next six starts. Then, after dropping three in a row, including seconds in The Meadowlands Pace Elimination and Final, he finished his season with 14 wins in his final 16 starts to totally dominate the three-year-old ranks of pacing colts.

Among Abercrombie's major wins that year were the Messenger S., Adios S., Prix d'Ete, Confederation Cup, James Dancer Memorial and Cane Pace Elimination. In the Meadowlands Pace, Abercrombie took the lead past the quarter in his Elimination, but was passed again by Flight Director in the final strides to lose by a neck. In the Final, Garnsey raced the colt from behind, but just could not get up in time to catch the leading Falcon Almahurst. Abercrombie finished second.

Coming into the Little Brown Jug with an eight-race winning streak, Abercrombie was the heavy favorite. He was just not himself that day. His attitude was different and he seemed distracted by the large and boisterous crowd. In the first heat, Abercrombie was parked out first over for most of the mile - unable to go around the front-running Falcon Almahurst who won by a length. The second heat was a replay of the first. Falcon and Abercrombie waged a war for the lead with Abercrombie eventually tiring and finishing eighth. This was his last loss of the year.

Just nine days after the Jug, Abercrombie won in 1:54.3 at Lexington, his best time of the year, and began his season-ending six-race winning streak. He won four of those races by open lengths and then ended his season getting revenge over his great rival Flight Director in the Sophomore Championship and Labatts S. in Canada, closing fast through the stretch to win by a neck and by a half-length over Flight Director.

Following his great three-year-old season, Abercrombie was syndicated for $3,000,000 by Castleton Farm. Castleton purchased fifty percent, or 20 shares, of Abercrombie for $1,500,000 and sold the remaining 20 shares to major breeders to ensure that the horse received a good book of quality mares when he went to stud. Plans called for him to race again as a four-year-old and then be retired to stud.

Abercrombie's four-year-old season was good by most standards, but still a disappointment for Abercrombie's connections. He won seven of his 19 starts, was first, second or third in 15 of those races, and earned $231,752. However, a $3,000,000 stallion prospect, and Horse of the Year, had been expected to come back and dominate the competition. In Abercrombie's defense, both Glen Garnsey and assistant-trainer Steve Waller were quoted as saying there was something wrong in Abercrombie's hind end for much of that year that x-rays did not pick up. They said Abercrombie was pacing with his hind end leaning toward one side.

Whatever the problem, Abercrombie still won the American-National Maturity, the U.S. Pacing Championship at The Meadowlands, the Hanover S. and two legs of the Driscoll Series. The highlight of his 1979 season was his win in the U.S. Pacing Championship. Abercrombie got away dead last from post eight and was still eighth at the three-quarter pole which was reached in a fast 1:24.3. Garnsey then shook him loose and Abercrombie roared up like a runaway freight train, passing everything in his way. This burst of speed took him to the front in the middle of the track and he won by three-quarters of a length in a world record 1:53 - the fastest mile ever paced in a race. In his dramatic finish, Abercrombie had circled the field and paced a final quarter in :27.3.

That race was the highlight of his four-year-old season and another reminder that Abercrombie was a superstar and an excellent stallion prospect. Abercrombie ended his career with $984,391 in earnings, having won 36 of his 72 trips to the post. He retired as the sixth leading money-winning pacer of all time.

Glen Garnsey had some interesting published comments about Abercrombie. For example, "He's the ideal horse; the type of horse you'd like to pattern any horse after, but just couldn't." And after

Abercrombie's long three-year-old season, Garnsey commented, "He spent more time on the road last year than Bob Hope....and it seemed not to bother him. He is so steady." Garnsey estimated that Abercrombie shipped between seven and eight thousand miles during his three-year-old season. "That's one of Ab's strong points, he is an easy shipper. He's very easy on himself. He naps and sleeps. He'll just stretch out in his stall and sleep. People or photographers don't bother him. He's just nonchalant about everything he does. I think that's why he could race so many heats."

Garnsey added, "Nothing really affects him. I think you could drop a bomb and it wouldn't really shake him up. But when he sees a starting gate, he gets down to business. Actually, I am just a passenger. Sometimes he wants to leave and sometimes he doesn't. He lets you know when you get behind the gate. I let him do what he wants to do."

Sire Line

Abercrombie is from the first crop of Silent Majority who was another great racehorse. Silent Majority's sire is Henry T. Adios, also one of the greats on the track, who is a son of the great Adios. Thus, it is because Henry T. Adios and Silent Majority were able to sire their like that the sport has been blessed with a stallion such as Abercrombie and the continuation of this great pacing male line.

Silent Majority was a standout colt performer who raced at two and three. He was not staked to many Grand Circuit events and his freshman season saw him race mostly in Canada where he won 17 of 21 starts, including several Canadian Juvenile S. At three, he won 19 of 26 starts, was the leading money-winning three-year-old pacer, and was voted 1972 Canadian Horse of the Year. His major wins that year included the Messenger S., Battle of Brandywine, L.K. Shapiro P., Commodore P., American-National S. and Connaught Cup. Silent Majority won 36 of his 47 starts and his credentials were enough to put him in the Walnut Hall Farm stud barn.

From the non-record Tar Heel mare Hobby Horse Tar, Silent Majority is a half-brother to another decent stallion Landslide p,3,1:54 ($162,835) who also has an outstanding son at stud, the top Canadian sire Run The Table. Abercrombie is not Silent Majority's only star offspring. Some of his others include Meadowlands Pace winner Laughs p,3,1:52.1 ($1,383,172), Watering Hole p,3,1:54 ($303,183) and Breeders Crown-winning mare Samshu Bluegrass p,1:55 ($664,978) among a host of others.

Abercrombie's grandsire is Henry T. Adios. Then we go back to the inimitable Adios and to Hal Dale. As we can see, each male in this branch of the Adios line has sired at least one son who has moved the breed forward in giant steps. However, Abercrombie is special since he has done something his sire and grandsire could not do - sire multiple sons who are excellent sires and commercially viable. And, in Artsplace, Abercrombie may have sired a truly great son who will accelerate the forward movement of this powerful sire line.

Maternal Line

Abercrombie is the third foal of the Duane Hanover mare Bergdorf p,3,2:06f; 4,2:03.3 ($6,035). Walnut Hall Farm had purchased Bergdorf at the Old Glory Sale for $11,200 since they were looking for mares to breed to their new stallion Silent Majority. Walnut Hall had previously raised Bergdorf in partnership with Dr. Arthur Evans and sold her as a yearling. Her sire Duane Hanover p,4,1:58 ($280,288) was an excellent pacer in the mid to late 1950's and is a son of Knight Dream. We will see later that returning crosses to Knight Dream through mares bred to Abercrombie resulted in some of his top sons and daughters.

Bergdorf's first two foals were the Rivaltime daughters Bloomingdale p,3,2:02 ($51,478) and Bonwit p,3,2:02 ($12,469). Then came Abercrombie, her first colt. Bergdorf produced 12 foals, with six taking 2:00 records. In addition to Abercrombie, Bergdorf is the dam of stakes winner and sire Bruce Gimble p,3,1:54.4 ($203,655) (by Most Happy Fella), Federated p,3,1:57.3 (Niatross), Harrods p,3,1:58.1h (Silent Majority), Wannamaker p,2,1:58.4 (Niatross) and Altmans p,3,1:58.4 (Silent Majority). Obviously, none approached the quality of Abercrombie.

Despite producing five daughters, most of whom have had ample opportunity in the breeding ranks, only Bergdorf's daughter Cartier, a full sister to Silent Majority, has produced a top horse. Cartier is the dam of world champion, stakes and FFA winner Odds Against p,1:50.1 ($1,403,938) (by Troublemaker) and two others in 1:55.

Abercrombie's grandam is the mare Princess Best p,4,2:07f ($965) by The Widower p,3,T1:59½ (a son of Abbedale). She produced two in 2:00, but no major performers. His third dam is Princess Chief p,2:07h ($9,506) by Chief Abbedale p,2:00 (a son of Abbedale). Princess Chief produced 10 winners from 10 foals with none faster than 2:00, her best being her daughter Victoria Lind p,2:00.1 ($72,519) (by Peter Lind). Another daughter, Sally Lind p,4,2:04f (by Peter Lind) was also bred to Silent Majority and produced a top horse in Woodrow Wilson S. winner Carl's Bird p,2,1:55.3 ($1,180,292) (by Sundance Skipper). Thus, it appears this family seems to have an affinity for Silent Majority blood.

Another item to note is that Princess Best, Abercrombie's grandam, is inbred 2x3 to Abbedale. The maternal family here is known as Young Chicago Maid and is not one of the primary maternal families in the sport. In fact, it is still one of the lesser families by a wide margin. But it is not unusual for many top pacing and trotting stallions to come from such humble bloodlines.

Progeny of Note

This will give you an idea of Abercrombie's place in Standardbred stallion history: He is second only to Albatross in all-time money winnings by his offspring; he and Albatross are the only two pacing stallions ever to sire the winners of over $100,000,000; he ranks second to Albatross in career $100,000 winners, with nearly 300, and he is fifth on the all-time list of 2:00 sires with over 800 in that category.

When all is said and done, history should record Abercrombie as one of the greatest pacing sires ever. Certainly, Adios, Meadow Skipper and Albatross are at the top of the list, but Abercrombie has to rank with the best of the rest, such as Cam Fella, Most Happy Fella, No Nukes, Bret Hanover and Good Time.

From the outset, it was known that Abercrombie could not handle an extremely large book of mares due to the level of his fertility. However, he has been managed well by Castleton Farm. His book has been limited to less than 140 mares for the last decade and this is a figure with which he seems comfortable. I mention this only to point out the level of success he has achieved without books of mares in the 200 range which some popular stallions have enjoyed.

To date, Abercrombie has sired 11 winners of $1,000,000 or more with Artsplace being the leader ($3,085,083). Two of his $1,000,000 winners are the mares Anniecrombie p,1:52.3 ($1,414,477) and Leah Almahurst p,3,1:52.3 ($1,053,201) so it is evident Abercrombie can also sire his share of great daughters - although most breeders do not consider this one of Abercrombie's strengths. I suspect, though, his daughters will soon change a lot of minds in the breeding ranks.

In the speed category, Abercrombie has sired three sub-1:50 performers: Artsplace p,4,1:49.2 ($3,085,083), Jet Jockey p,1:49.4 ($390,430) and Misfit p,1:49.4 ($1,190,067). He also has 12 other sub-1:51 offspring.

The Abercrombies have won most of the sport's major events, including the Little Brown Jug, North America Cup, Woodrow Wilson S., Messenger S., Cane Pace, Prix d'Ete and numerous Breeders Crowns. Abercrombie has also sired a Horse of the Year and several divisional champions.

Of course, Abercrombie's number one son is Artsplace, one of the sport's all-time greats. Of Abercrombie's other sons, Life Sign's p,3,1:50.3 ($1,912,454) dramatic win in the Little Brown Jug has now become legend. (For more information on Artsplace and Life Sign, see their chapters.) Armbro Emerson p,3,1:52.3 ($1,414,477) won the Prix d'Ete and three and the Breeders Crown at four and has become a leading sire in Canada. Anniecrombie is Abercrombie's top daughter and has a world record, the Jugette and Breeders Crown among her list of credits. Leah Almahurst is another world champion Abercrombie daughter who won the Jugette and Breeders Crown.

World champion Kentucky Spur p,3,1:52 ($1,341,340) won the Breeders Crown at two along with the Messenger S. and Adios S. at three. Topnotcher p,4,1:52.3f ($1,340,840) won the Cane Pace and Canadian Pacing Derby. World champion Albert Albert p,3,1:52.1 ($1,237,070) won the Kentucky Pacing Derby and a heat of the Little

Brown Jug. He is now a successful stallion and has sired a $2,300,000 winner in Pacific Rocket p,4,1:50. Misfit p,1:49.4 is another fine example of how Abercrombie's offspring improve with age. Armbro Dallas p,3,1:52.3 ($1,401,201) was a major stakes winner at two and three. Dontgetinmyway p,1:50.4-'98 ($1,072,311) and Sportsmaster p,2,1:52.1 ($755,803) both won the Woodrow Wilson S. at two. Arizona Jack p,3,1:50.2 ($693,823) won the North America Cup.

This is just scratching the surface of outstanding Abercrombie sons and daughters. The list goes on and includes world champions such as Jet Jockey,1:49.4 ($390,430), world champion and top sire Laag p,3,1:51.2 ($642,995) and such daughters as Simply Ravishing p,3,1:54 ($547,035), Celebrity Girl p,3,1:52.1 ($535,726), On Her Way p,2,1:54.2 ($533,423) and Lisheen p,3,1:52.3 ($518,405).

Analysis

The great thing about Abercrombie has been his consistency in producing great racehorses. They may reach their peak a few months later than the young speed demons from other sires, but once they have attained it they keep it far longer. Some sires are noted for precocious two-year-olds, and Abercrombie has had his share of those, but he has added the important quality of soundness and endurance to most of his offspring. This quality is sadly lacking in the offspring of some other good sires whose sons and daughter peak early and then suffer the unsoundness which is their ultimate undoing. The Abercrombies just seem to go on and get better with age.

When Abercrombie went to stud, it was obvious that he would receive many broodmares from the Meadow Skipper line stallions. As a result, Abercrombie's eight richest performers are all from mares by Meadow Skipper line stallions - three by Albatross, three by Most Happy Fella and one each by Meadow Skipper and Windshield Wiper. In fact, 24 of Abercrombie's 25 richest performers - all winners of $500,000 or more - are from mares by Meadow Skipper line sires. Looking a little deeper, we find that mares with an Albatross/Bret Hanover cross have eight of Abercrombie's 38 richest sons and daughters and mares with a Meadow Skipper/Bret Hanover cross have four. These crosses account for almost one third of Abercrombie's 38 $500,000 winners. The only sire to break the Meadow Skipper line monopoly of the top 25 is the Race Time daughter She's A Ten by producing Misfit p,1:49.4 ($1,190,067) by Abercrombie.

Looking at another level of these statistics, we find that 15 of these 38 $500,000 winners have second dams by Bret Hanover. This is very interesting since Bret, like Abercrombie, is from the same Adios sire line. Thus, all the performers with Bret Hanover in that position are linebred 4x4 to Adios which turned out to be a very strong cross for Abercrombie. Another striking situation is that Abercrombie's richest son and richest daughter, Artsplace and Anniecrombie, each have second dams by Duane Hanover who is a son of Knight Dream. And Knight Dream shows prominently in the pedigrees of several of Abercrombie's other top horses.

For example, Life Sign is bred 4x4 to Adios and Knight Dream as is Albert Albert, Leah Almahurst, As Promised p,4,1:50.2 ($669,639), Lisheen, Curragh p,T1:51.4 ($509,740) and Lisryan p,1:52 ($507,621). Of Abercrombie's other million-dollar winners, Armbro Emerson is 4x3 to Tar Heel and 4x4 to Adios; Artsplace and Anniecrombie are 3x4 to Duane Hanover; Armbro Dallas is 4x4 to Adios; Kentucky Spur has no common ancestors in his first four generations since his dam is by the trotting sire Nevele Pride; Topnotcher is 4x4 to Adios and Tar Heel; Misfit is 4x4 to Adios and Dontgetinmyway is 4x4x5 to Tar Heel. There are several others with 4x4 crosses to Tar Heel, including Survivor Gold p,4,1:51 ($897,929), Sportsmaster p,2,1:52.1 ($755,803), Arizona Jack p,3,1:50.2 ($693,823), Jet Jockey p,1:49.4 and Armbro Other p,4,1:50.1.

As we have seen with many other pacing and trotting sires, some of their best offspring show interesting pedigree crosses to siblings - either to brothers, sisters or a brother and sister. Abercrombie is no exception and, in fact, some of his very best have these types of crosses. Anniecrombie's dam is bred 4x3 to Poplar Byrd and his full sister Poplar Ann; the very accomplished brothers Armbro Dallas and Armbro Cadet have a dam who is inbred 2x2 to the great half-brother and sister Meadow Skipper and Countess Adios; and Cimarron p,1:51.4 ($898,904) has a third dam who is inbred 2x2 to the half-sisters Honest Truth and Pleasant Surprise. In addition, Free Spender p,1:50.2 ($200,945) has a dam inbred 3x2 to Meadow Skipper.

Abercrombie has also become a great broodmare sire with 625 2:00 broodmare credits as of early 1998. His daughters have produced some top stars and seem to do best on a regular basis with Most Happy Fella line sires such as Precious Bunny, No Nukes, Cam Fella and Jate Lobell. They have also done very well when bred to Niatross and his great son Nihilator.

Daughters of Abercrombie have already produced three $1,000,000 winners, headed by Village Connection p,1:51h ($1,620,056) (by Cam Fella), Hi Ho Silverheel's p,3,1:50.3 ($1,074,671) (by Walton Hanover) and Village Jasper p,3,1:51 ($1,057,595) (by Jate Lobell). Jate Lobell has been an especially good consort for Abercrombie mares. In addition to millionaire Village Jasper, there are Bo Knows Jate p,1:51.2 ($921,603), Safely Kept p,2,1:52.4 ($866,999), Kettle Bee p,1:51 ($405,525) and Dodger Boy p,2,1:51.3 ($43,432) to name just a few. Precious Bunny also has stars from Abercrombie mares with John Street North p,1:50.2-'98 ($746,207), Paling Avenue p,3,1:52.2f ($644,762) and Dauntless Bunny p,4,1:50.1-'98 ($248,842). Niatross has sired the stars Ultra Jet p,1:51.1 ($756,571) and Miatross p,1:51.3 ($420,857) from Abercrombie mares.

A few other high money-winning credits for Abercrombie mares are Beach Ray p,3,1:53.1 ($742,149) (by Beach Towel), Duke Of Abby p,4,1:52.2 ($749,447) (by Dexter Nukes), Make A Deal p,4,1:50.2 ($610,249) (by No Nukes), Duke Duke p,3,1:52f ($553,048) (by Falcon Seelster) and Highly Promoted p,1:50.2 ($362,805) (by Praised Dignity). The fastest credit is Strong Clan p,1:50 ($663,377) (by Direct Scooter).

Abercrombie's own pedigree shows his closest common cross as the 4x4 to Nibble Hanover through his sire and his dam's sire. There does not appear to be anything especially interesting there except back in the six generation with the appearance twice of the mare Adioo who is the paternal grandam of Adioo Volo (the dam of Adios), and who also appears in the pedigree of the dam of Duane Hanover, Dorsh Hanover.

Abercrombie is now 23 years old but is still going strong and his offspring are still very competitive with those by stallions who are now a couple of generations ahead of him. He is one of today's greats and it appears that Artsplace will be able to successfully replace his sire as the prime representative of the Adios male line.

Leading Progeny by Abercrombie

Fastest
- Artsplace, h, p,4,1:49.2 $3,085,083
- Misfit, h, p,1:49.4 $1,190,067
- Jet Jockey, g, p,1:49.4 $390,430
- Armbro Other, g, p,4,1:50.1 $54,345
- As Promised, h, p,4,1:50.2 $669,639
- Arizona Jack, h, p,3,1:50.2 $693,823
- Free Spender, g, p,1:50.2 $200,945
- Life Sign, h, p,3,1:50.3 $1,912,454
- The Wrath of Pan, h, p,4,1:50.3 $524,425
- Lahar, h, p,1:50.3 $413,221

Richest
- Artsplace, h, p,4,1:49.2 $3,085,083
- Life Sign, h, p,3,1:50.3 $1,912,454
- Armbro Emerson, h, p,4,T1:51.4 $1,472,590
- Anniecrombie, m, p,1:52.3 $1,414,477
- Armbro Dallas, g, p,3,1:52.3 $1,401,201
- Kentucky Spur, h, p,3,1:52 $1,341,340
- Topnotcher, h, p,4,1:52.2f $1,340,850
- Albert Albert, h, p,3,1:52.1 $1,237,070
- Misfit, h, p,1:49.4 $1,190,067
- Dontgetinmyway, h, p,1:50.4 $1,072,331

Abercrombie, Bay Horse, 15.2 Hands, 1975
p, 2, 1:56; 3, 1:54.3; 4, 1:53 ($984,391)

Silent Majority, 1969 p, 3, 1:56.3 $362,369	Henry T. Adios, 1958 p, 6, 1:57 $706,833	Adios, 1940 p, T1:57½ $33,329	Hal Dale, 1926 p, 6, 2:02¼	**ABBEDALE**	**THE ABBE** Daisydale D.
				Margaret Hal	Argot Hal Margaret Polk
			Adioo Volo, 1930 p, 3, 2:05h	Adioo Guy	Guy Dillon **ADIOO**
				Sigrid Volo	**PETER VOLO** Polly Parrot
		Greer Hanover, 1948 p, 3, 2:06.2h $6,482	**NIBBLE HANOVER**, 1936 1:58¾ $25,599	Calumet Chuck	Truax Sumatra
				Justissima	Justice Brooke Claire Toddington
			Veda Hanover, 1943	**BILLY DIRECT**	**NAPOLEON DIRECT** Gay Forbes
				Vivian Hanover	Guy McKinney Guesswork
	Hobby Horse Tar, 1964	Tar Heel, 1948 p, 4, T1:57 $119,148	**BILLY DIRECT**, 1934 p, 4, T1:55 $12,040	**NAPOLEON DIRECT**	Walter Direct Lady Erectress
				Gay Forbes	Malcolm Forbes Gay Girl Chimes
			Leta Long, 1940 p, 4, 2:03¾ $9,321	Volomite	**PETER VOLO** Cita Frisco
				Rosette	Mr. McElwyn Rose Scott
		Wilellen, 1955 p, 3, 2:04.2h $16,994	Wilmington, 1938 p, 4, T1:59½ $7,988	Bert Abbe	**THE ABBE** Miss Ellah
				Miss Saginaw	Colonel Armstrong Miss Adioo
			Willola, 1941 2:11¼h	Willglow	San Francisco Worthy Spirit
				Romola	The Senator May Dodge
Bergdorf, 1967 p, 4, 2:03.3 $6,035	Duane Hanover, 1952 p, 4, 1:58 $280,288	Knight Dream 1945 p, 3, T1:59 $76,973	**NIBBLE HANOVER**, 1936 1:58¾ $25,599	Calumet Chuck	Truax Sumatra
				Justissima	Justice Brooke Claire Toddington
			Lydia Knight, 1929	Peter The Brewer	**PETER THE GREAT** Zombrewer
				Guy Rosa	**GUY AXWORTHY** Rosa Lake
		Dorsh Hanover, 1932 4, 2:15½h	Dillon Axworthy, 1910 3, 2:10¼	Axworthy	Axtell Marguerite
				Adioo Dillon	Sidney Dillon **ADIOO**
			Great Medium, 1921	**PETER THE GREAT**	Pilot Medium Santos
				Dorsch Medium	Red Medium Vicanora
	Princess Best, 1959 p, 4, 2:07f	The Widower, 1935 p, 3, T1:59½ $19,983	**ABBEDALE**, 1917 p, 2:01¼	**THE ABBE**	Chimes Nettie King
				Daisydale D.	Archdale Mrs. Trnolus
			Widow Grattan, 1923 p, T2:00	Grattan Royal	Grattan Mona
				I'm A Widow	Widower Peter Bessie Gilbert
		Princess Chief, 1945 p, 2:07h $9,506	Chief Abbedale, 1929 p, 2:00	**ABBEDALE**	**THE ABBE** Daisydale D.
				Marion Candler	**NAPOLEON DIRECT** Cherry Gentry
			The Gay Princess, 1932 4, 2:11h $1,391	Crispin	**GUY AXWORTHY** Jean Claire
				Princess Duffy	John A. McKerron Princess Pete

Adios

Adios is legendary in harness racing lore as a racehorse, as a stallion and for his connection with Hall of Famer Delvin Miller. Every now and then, a great sire comes along and shakes a breed of horses to its foundation. In the Standardbred sport that stallion was Adios.

Not since the Hambletonian era had the offspring of a single stallion dominated and shaped the sport of harness racing. There have been sires before and since who have stood well above their peers, but none have had more impact than Adios.

Yes, there are such greats as Peter Volo, Volomite, Hal Dale, Meadow Skipper, Albatross, Speedy Crown, Super Bowl, Cam Fella and Abercrombie, but history will record that Adios stood above them all. He single-handedly transformed the Standardbred pacing breed and his influence is still felt strongly more than three decades after his death. And now, through the efforts of Abercrombie and his sons, the Adios male line looks like it is about to regain the throne from the Meadow Skipper male line.

During his prime as a sire, there were many times when sons and daughters of Adios finished first, second and third in the sport's major stakes events. Sons of Adios were in great demand as stallion prospects and his daughters were highly prized by breeders. His influence continues strong today in North America, Australia and New Zealand. Adios was simply a stallion without peer, with a very interesting racing and ownership history.

Adios was such an historic stallion people sometimes forget his career as a racehorse in which he was one of the best of his era. He won 43 of his 87 heats and was first, second or third in 83 of those events. He showed tremendous speed as a two-year-old and passed that characteristic along to his offspring. At two, Adios set world records on half-mile tracks for one, two and three heats and just missed the mile track record by a couple of ticks. He was also the leading money-winning pacer in North America, regardless of age.

Adios also set world records at four, five and six, including both mile and half-mile tracks. So let's not forget the greatness of Adios as a racehorse. Although he earned only $33,329 during his five years on the track, Adios raced during the World War II years for paltry purses.

One of the greatest two-horse rivalries in harness racing history was that between Adios and King's Counsel. Both were foals of 1940 and began their racing careers in 1942. Adios and King's Counsel met in 67 separate heats, with King's Counsel having the slight advantage of 34 wins to 33 for Adios. This was a long-standing and hard-fought rivalry, the likes of which this sport has rarely seen.

Adios made his racetrack debut on July 21st, 1942, on the "kite" track at Old Orchard Beach in Maine. It was there that the great Adios-King's Counsel rivalry began. Adios won the first heat of a $5,000 event in 2:02½ with King's Counsel coming back to win the second heat in 2:01¼. King's Counsel's time was a world record, breaking the 2:02 set by His Majesty ten years earlier. King's Counsel then won the raceoff in 2:08. The two colts faced each other eight more times during their freshman season with Adios winning six of those races - mostly two heat affairs - and Adios ended the year with a 14 to seven heat advantage over King's Counsel. He was also the first two-year-old to pace a half-mile track faster than 2:05 and he did that three times with the fastest in 2:03¾ for the world record.

At three, Adios defeated King's Counsel in eight consecutive heats at the North Randall track in Ohio. King's Counsel rebounded by winning the next five races over Adios. During his three-year-old season, Adios was sold to E.J. Baker, the owner of Greyhound, for $20,000. At four, King's Counsel defeated Adios in five of seven meetings. But Adios set a world record for a two-heat race by four-year-olds when he paced in 1:58¼ twice to break the record for three-year-olds set by Directum. By the end of their four-year-old seasons, Adios and King's Counsel had each defeated the other 32 times! At six, King's Counsel defeated Adios in two of three starts and thus gained the lifetime advantage of 34 to 33.

Race Record Highlights

At 2
1st Fox S.
Geers S.
National S.
Ohio Horse Breeders Association S.
heat of N.T. Fox S.
2nd heat and Final of N.T. Fox S.
Defender S.
American S.

At 3
1st Matron S.
Geers S.
Championship Stallion S.
American S.

At 3 (continued)
Village Farm S.
heat of National S.
heat of Review Futurity
heat of Almahurst FFA P.

At 5
1st Star Pointer S.

Honors

At two, set world records on half-mile tracks for one, two and three heats

At two, the leading money-winning pacer regardless of age

At four, set world record for one and two heats for four-year-olds on a mile track and a world record on a half-mile track

At five, set world record for five-year-old pacers

At six, set world record for seven-eighths of a mile

Adios

Adios with Frank Ervin
Photo courtesy of the Harness Racing Museum

Race Record

Year	Age	Starts	Wins	2nd	3rd	Earnings	Record
1942	2	26	14	9	2	$ 16,188	p,2,2:02
1943	3	31	15	12	4	7,522	p,3,2:01¾
1944	4	21	7	9	3	2,678	p,4,1:58¼
1945	5	5	5	0	0	3,561	p,T1:57½
1946	6	4	2	0	1	3,380	
		87	43	30	10	$ 33,329	p,T1:57½

Adios

Racing opportunities were scarce for Adios at five in 1945. The great trainer and driver Frank Ervin, Adios' trainer at that time said, "In 1945, I couldn't get any races for Adios. I won only $2,500 with him all year. Seems nobody cared about free-for-allers, or no one dared race against Adios." Ervin shipped him to several tracks, but no one declared in against him. At DuQuoin, after no horses were entered against Adios, Ervin was offered $500 to break the track record. "Two minutes wasn't so damned easy to beat then, but I thought I'd better take a shot at it to get that $500. So, he went in 1:57½ that afternoon and I got the $500," said Ervin. The last half of that time-trial was paced in :57½. Adios won his final career start on May 16th, 1946, even after being handicapped by 130 feet.

Another aspect of the Adios legend, and one I started hearing at racetracks in the early 1960s, was that Adios and some of his sons were "sulkers" and would give up or not want to race. Of course, some were but the majority could not have been to have earned such fame and fortune.

However, there was one problem with Adios, which started when he was a two-year-old. He had a bad habit of stopping near the end of a mile. Several trainers tried to break him of that habit, but it was Frank Ervin who was successful. Since Adios would not give his best effort against King's Counsel after being pulled out of the pocket in the stretch, Ervin decided to race him on the front end and see what would happen. "I decided I wouldn't pull him anymore," Ervin was quoted in Marie Hill's book, Adios: The Big Daddy of Harness Racing, "I would let him go to the top and see how he raced there. To my surprise he went a great heat and beat King's Counsel very handily. From then on if I could get to the top with him I always raced him that way." Ervin added, "I also found out you could not whip him; if you did he would sulk and give up. I could threaten him with the whip and change the bit around with the lines and he would try his heart out for you."

Now that you have an idea of Adios the racehorse, I want to touch briefly on his early history. Adios was bred by Leo C. McNamara who stood his sire Hal Dale at his Two Gaits Farm in Carmel, Indiana. Adios was later sold as a yearling for $2,000 at the Indianapolis sale and purchased by the prominent owner Thomas Thomas, a Cleveland, Ohio, meat packer, who gave the colt to Rupe Parker to train.

Rupe Parker was the trainer of the four-year-old Adios but got sick during the racing season and asked his good friend Frank Ervin to take over the training until he got back in action. Unfortunately, Parker passed away a few days later and all his horses were left in Ervin's care.

Mr. Thomas wanted to sell Adios for $7,500 at the conclusion of his five-year-old season, but no one wanted to pay that price to race him or stand him at stud. At a sale in York, Pennsylvania, Ervin met some representatives of Harry Warner of the Warner Brothers Studio, who were looking for horses to race at the Santa Anita track in California for 1946. In January of 1946, the Warners, and their partner L.K. Shapiro, agreed to purchase Adios and the trotter Spengay, also trained by Ervin, for $27,500 for the pair. Ervin had priced Adios at $16,000 alone.

The new arrangement quickly ran into difficulties. Ervin and Warner did not get along and following a loss by Adios they had harsh words. Ervin told him to "take the horse and get him out of the barn." Adios pulled up lame after winning a race the following week. He was trained again the following two seasons, but never raced again.

In 1947, Adios was trained by Henry Thomas but did not get to the races and was retired to stud. Harry Warner planned to start a California breeding farm with Adios as his stallion and Adios was bred to a few mares in 1947 and 1948 while also training and failing to get back to the races. His first crop, which numbered just five, was foaled in California. The very first foal was a colt from the mare Josedale Dorcas and was born on February 26, 1948. He was a gelding named Que Tal who never took a record. However, that first crop did include the good performer Prince Adios p,4,1:58.

Adios was sent to the Tattersalls Mixed Sale in Lexington, Kentucky, in the fall of 1948 when the Warner brothers decided they did not want to be in the breeding business after all.

Now the Adios story begins to involve famed trainer, driver, breeder and harness racing's "Good Will Ambassador," Delvin Miller, who purchased the young stallion for $21,000 from the Harry Warner and L.K. Shapiro dispersal. Miller had always claimed he had only $20,000 available to purchase Adios. When someone else had the bid at $20,000, Miller raised one finger to the auctioneer, meaning to bid $20,100. However, auctioneer George Swinebroad took the bid to mean $21,000 and Adios was knocked down to Miller for that price.

The rest is history. Adios made Miller a rich man and provided his stable with champions for many years. Miller admired Adios as a racehorse and had also done his homework about him. In addition, he sought the advice of the great trainer "Doc" Parshall who had campaigned King's Counsel in the epic battles against Adios. Parshall told Miller he thought Adios would be the better sire of the two horses.

Miller took Adios to his Meadow Lands Farm in Pennsylvania and stood him at stud beginning with the 1949 breeding season. There were only 11 yearlings by Adios sold at public auction from his first three crops. When the offspring from the first two small crops by Adios began making waves, followed by the early crops from Miller's breeding, Adios became a hot commodity. It was the crop of 1951 which made breeders take notice. Adios had sired 2:00 performers from his first three crops, but it was the seven 2:00 pacers from the crop of 1951 which made Adios very legitimate in many eyes. That crop included such greats as Adios Harry p,4,1:55 ($345,433), Adios Boy p,2,T1:58.3 ($129,859) and Adios Betty p,2,T1:58.4.

In 1955, Hanover Shoe Farms' Lawrence Sheppard purchased Adios from Del Miller for $500,000. Later, Sheppard sold a one-third interest back to Miller and one-third to Max Hempt. Adios continued to stand at stud at Miller's farm with strong support from Hanover's great broodmare band.

Adios' stud fee began at $300 and was $15,000 at the time of his death on June 22nd, 1965 - the highest in Standardbred history at the time. Also at that time, Adios' sons and daughters had earned over $14,000,000 and went on to earn even more. That figure was higher than any Thoroughbred stallion in that era.

Del Miller, in addition to being a consummate horseman, was a good promotor. He had famous friends and acquaintances in sports, show business and politics and many availed themselves of "photo-ops" with Adios at Miller's farm. Adios became so well known, in and out of the Standardbred industry, that he even had bags of "fan mail" delivered at Miller's farm. So many top horses had the prefix Adios in their names that the public could not help but be aware of the stallion. For model horse collectors, the famous Breyer company manufactured an Adios model in the 1960s, and the aforementioned book about Adios, which was published in 1971 and still makes excellent reading, added further to his national reputation.

Yes, Adios was more than just a Standardbred stallion, he was an icon for harness racing and probably the most famous harness horse in the world during the golden era from the mid-fifties through the seventies.

Sire Line

What made Adios such a great sire? Unfortunately, the answer to this question is buried among the mysteries of nature. But, we do know that it does not hurt to have an outstanding sire and dam in a stallion's pedigree. Adios' sire was Hal Dale p,2:02¼ who, in addition to the Adios male line, also provided the male lines of Good Time and Dale Frost. Dale Frost happens to be the sire of the great Meadow Skipper who, along with his son Albatross, is the closest "impact sire" to Adios.

Leo McNamara had purchased Hal Dale at auction in 1936 for $2,000. Foaled in 1926, Hal Dale was raced free-legged as were his sire Abbedale p,2:01¼ and grandsire The Abbe p,2:04. Hal Dale raced only as a six-year-old in 1932. He won eight of his nine heats in races and was technically undefeated since in those days one race consisted of several heats. His only loss in a heat was as a result of a break.

Hal Dale never set foot out of Indiana. He was bred and foaled there, raced nowhere else, and stood at stud there. Hal Dale died at the age of 29 in 1955. Beyond Abbedale and The Abbe, Hal Dale's male line traces further back through Chimes and Electioneer to Hambletonian. Hal Dale's dam was the Argot Hal mare Margaret Hal and his second dam was a daughter of the great pacer of the 1890's who just missed becoming harness racing's first 2:00 performer - John R. Gentry p,T2:00½ in 1896.

Although Hal Dale was never a nationally known racehorse during his limited career, he had the ability to pass on speed and class and sired many sons who became successful at stud and carried on his male line. He was certainly blessed with prepotent genes.

Maternal Line

Adios' dam was a world champion and a speedy performer during her era. Adioo Volo p,3,2:05h, a foal of 1930, was a top filly who set a world record on a half-mile track at three. Her sire was Adioo Guy who left just a few foals in the United States before being exported "down under." Adioo Volo was a member of his final North American crop. She was the only foal of Sigrid Volo who was a daughter of the great sire Peter Volo. Adios' third dam, Polly Parrot, was a daughter of the noted racemare Lady Maud C. p,2:00½ who was a sister to the outstanding Hedgewood Boy p,2:01. They were one of the great brother-sister teams of all time and set a team-to-pole world record of 2:02¾ when hooked together in 1909. Due to a pasture injury, Lady Maud C. was bred at three to Jersey B.B. to produce Polly Parrot and it was later that she embarked on her storied racing career.

Adioo Volo was a very fast filly and won 11 of her 22 starts at three. She was bred at four, had a foal at five and was back at the races again at the age of six. However, she was entered in a claiming race and was claimed for $800 by Greyhound's owner E.J. Baker who raced her just a few times. Leo McNamara purchased Adioo Volo from Baker and bred her in 1937 to his new stallion Hal Dale. The result was the filly Adieu p,2:04½ who later became well-known as the grandam of the top racehorse and stallion Bye Bye Byrd p,T1:56.1 ($554,272). She then had another filly named Au Revoir before producing Adios in 1940.

One of the very interesting aspects in the pedigree of Adios is the appearance of incestuous inbreeding in Adioo Guy, the sire of Adioo Volo. He is bred 2x1 to the full sisters By Guy and Adioo. Take a look at Adios' six-generation pedigree chart and you will see that the dam of Adioo Guy is a full sister to the dam of his sire Guy Dillon.

Progeny of Note

Adios would have a place in Standardbred breeding history if he had done nothing other than sire Bret Hanover p,4,T1:53.3 ($922,616). That colt was the pinnacle of Adios' great career as a stallion, but he still would have been considered the all-time best even without a Bret Hanover. The mares bred to Adios during his California days, and during his first few years with Del Miller, were mostly just average. It was then up to Adios to show he could improve these mares by siring high-quality foals. He did just that!

Early world champions from his first small crops included Pleasant Surprise and Prince Adios. Then, in 1953, Adios set a record for 2:10 two-year-olds from a single crop with 16, including the world champions Adios Boy and Adios Betty - the first 2:00 two-year-old pacers ever. That same crop produced Adios Harry who went on to set a world record of 1:55 at four.

In 1956, Adios became the first stallion of any breed to sire the winners of over $1,000,000 in a single year. The first $100,000 yearling, Standardbred or Thoroughbred, was a son of Adios - Dancer Hanover, who brought $105,000 at auction.

The four-year-old Prince Adios became the first 2:00 performer for Adios in 1952 and it was he, campaigning in the United States and Canada, who first brought Adios national attention. Prince Adios won 16 of 26 starts at three and set a world record at four in a three-heat divided race. More importantly, he gave Adios some much needed publicity. Other early top performers for Adios included Shadow Wave p,3,1:56.3 in 1958 followed by the great two-time Horse of the Year Adios Butler p,4,T1:54.3 ($509,875) a year later. Adios Butler won 37 of 50 career starts and I still consider him among the fastest pacers I have ever seen. His blazing speed can be seen from his incredible clocking of :11.2 in the last eighth of a one and one-eighth mile race. This translates to a quarter rate of :22.4 which is thoroughbred speed.

Then came Bullet Hanover p,3,T1:55.3 ($132,578) and Dancer Hanover p,4,T1:56.4, followed by Henry T. Adios p,1:57 ($706,833) who is the grandsire of Abercrombie p,4,1:53 ($984,391), the horse now credited with extending the Adios male line. The 1962 crop of Adios is memorable since it included all-time great Bret Hanover p,4,T1:53.3, a winner in 62 of 68 starts, and his arch-rival Adios Vic p,3,1:56.3 ($455,896).

Daughters of Adios have done equally well. In addition to the aforementioned Adios Betty p,2,1:58.4, Adios is the sire of such female greats as Dottie's Pick p,4,T1:56.4 ($263,978), Countess Adios p,3,1:57.3 (t,T2:01.2) ($317,158) and Bonjour Hanover p,3,1:57 ($226,821) (a sister to Bret Hanover). Adios even sired a 2:00 trotter, the top filly Sara Black 3,2:00 who set a two-heat world record for trotting fillies. Just as Adios had become the sport's leading sire, when his daughters began producing racehorses, he quickly became the leading broodmare sire as well.

The Adios offspring mentioned here are just a small sample of the quality of his foals. His sons and daughters thoroughly dominated colt and filly stakes action in North America during the fifties and sixties. For example, during that time, the Messenger S. was the sport's richest race and Adios had the first, second and third place finishers in the 1959 and 1961 editions. In addition, many stakes fields showed Adios as the sire of half the entries.

Analysis

Bred before the era of artificial insemination, Adios' largest crop of foals was 51 in 1956. His total number of offspring from 19 years at stud was 597, 10 of which died as foals. Today's popular stallions can achieve those numbers in four or five years at stud. What Adios accomplished from this number of foals is simply amazing. To this day, he is still the standard by which modern sires can be measured. The big questions are - can a modern sire produce champions from average mares the way Adios did? And can any new stallion totally dominate the competition the way Adios did?

During his great career, Adios sired 79 2:00 performers - 78 pacers and one trotter. The earnings of his offspring totalled over $19,300,000 with 43 $100,000 winners. He nicked with a large number of mares, but there were several crosses which proved to be most prolific. Of course, you need to take into account the fact that Hanover Shoe Farm bred many top mares to him and also favored mares by certain sires. However, I must point out that the 79 2:00 performers were from mares by 32 different broodmare sires.

To provide perspective regarding Adios' domination of the racing scene, look at the winners of the Triple Crown races during the sport's glory years. Adios was the sire of eight Little Brown Jug winners during a 12-year period (including five consecutive winners). The Jug winners are Adios Harry, his full brother Noble Adios, Shadow Wave, Adios Butler, Bullet Hanover, Henry T. Adios, Lehigh Hanover and Bret Hanover. The Cane Futurity was won by Noble Adios, Raider Frost, Adios Butler, Countess Adios (against colts), Cold Front and Bret Hanover. The Messenger S. was won by Meadow Lands, Adios Butler, Countess Adios, Adios Don, Thor Hanover and Bret Hanover. In addition, the first two pacing Triple Crown winners were Adios' sons Adios Butler and Bret Hanover. Daughters of Adios have also produced the Jug winners Laverne Hanover (by Tar Heel), Nansemond (by Tar Heel) and Governor Skipper (by Meadow Skipper).

The most successful broodmare sire crosses for Adios came from mares by Volomite (15 2:00 credits) and Billy Direct (11 2:00 credits). Others with good numbers were Nibble Hanover (7), Chief Counsel (5) and King's

Counsel (4). Adios sired three 2:00 performers from Tar Heel mares. Since Tar Heel's first daughters were not born until 1954, Adios did not have access to many of them before he died. However, the reverse cross resulted in what was known as "the Golden Cross" - Tar Heel bred to Adios mares. Adios mares produced especially well with Tar Heel, his son Thorpe Hanover and Meadow Skipper.

Adios also gave us a number of sons who have impacted the Standardbred breed. Most notable among them are Bret Hanover, Henry T. Adios, Dancer Hanover, Adios Vic, Bullet Hanover, Shadow Wave and Airliner. The second greatest son of Adios, after Bret Hanover, was Adios Butler but he never really had a legitimate chance to succeed since he stood at a farm in Ohio without access to a good number of world-class mares. He did well for a period, but then his star dimmed.

Another son who was a good sire was Baron Hanover p,3,2:03.4f, the older full brother of Bret Hanover. Baron showed the ability to move mares up and sired 111 in 2:00 from very ordinary broodmares. In addition, his sons and daughters were the long-wearing type who were very well represented in the Invitational and Preferred classes at tracks all over the nation. It's unfortunate he never had access to the best mares. World champion Adios Harry had a similar situation in that he did not stand at a major farm when he retired. He was able to sire decent older performers, but was bred to just average mares and could not overcome that handicap.

In the 1997 edition of the Times: In Harness Almanac, which included 79 stallion pedigree advertisements featuring most of today's most popular sires in all parts of North America, there were only three stallions which did not have Adios blood in their pedigrees - Dorunrun Bluegrass, Direct Scooter, and his son In The Pocket. Many of the other stallions had multiple crosses to Adios through their sire and dam. Adios can reasonably be considered the modern day "Hambletonian" of pacing sires.

Looking at some of the crosses which worked best for Adios to produce his richest sons and daughters, there does not seem to be a major thread. Adios worked well with most any line. However, he had his best success with mares by Billy Direct, Volomite and Nibble Hanover. Adios' four greatest sons are Bret Hanover, Henry T. Adios, Adios Butler and Adios Vic. Bret Hanover is from a Tar Heel mare and Adios Butler from a Billy Direct mare - Tar Heel's sire. Henry T. Adios is from a Nibble Hanover mare while Adios Vic is from a Jimmy Creed mare. Another $400,000 winner is Cape Horn p,1:57.1 who is from a Billy Direct mare. King's Counsel, who was Adios' arch-rival on the racetrack, is the sire of the dam of one of Adios' most renowned daughters, Countess Adios.

In the speed department, it is much the same but with the addition of the fast Bullet Hanover who like many of the others was from a Billy Direct mare. The two world champion two-year-olds from Adios' 1951 crop, Adios Boy and Adios Betty, are from mares by Bonnycastle and Cardinal Prince respectively - hardly fashionable sires of their period.

Adios had 11 winners of $225,000 or more and there was only one with a common cross closer than a 4x4 relationship. That colt was Little Brown Jug winner Lehigh Hanover p,3,1:58.4h ($330,263) who is 3x4 to Dillon Axworthy. Of the others, Bret Hanover and his sister Bonjour Hanover are 4x5 to Peter Volo while Adios Butler, Countess Adios, Dottie's Pick and Adios Don p,3,1:58.4 ($236,154) are 4x4 to Peter Volo. Others with no common ancestors in the first four generations are Henry T. Adios, Adios Vic, Cold Front and Adios Harry.

With Adios on such a high pedestal, several major breeders tried inbreeding to Adios and produced foals with 2x3 an 3x3 crosses to him. Some of the results were excellent and Armstrong Bros. of Ontario, Canada, built a strong pacing broodmare band built upon several mares which were inbred to Adios. Their good pacing stallion Armbro Omaha was also bred 2x3 to Adios. The good Illinois sire

Shadow's Finale is another example of the 2x3 cross to Adios.

A few examples of outstanding broodmares with 2x3 crosses to Adios are the Bret Hanover mare Pleasure Seeker who is the dam of the fastest two-year-old pacer ever, regardless of sex, Miss Easy p,2,1:51.2; 3,1:51.1 ($1,777,656) and the Bret Hanover mare Ambiguity who is the dam of world champion Three Diamonds p,3,1:53.1 ($735,759) who in turn is the dam of Little Brown Jug winner Life Sign p,3,1:50.3 ($1,912,454). Life Sign is also a male-line descendant of Adios through his sire Abercrombie. Another Bret Hanover daughter with the 2x3 cross to Adios is Angel Hair who is the dam of Naughty But Nice p,3,1:54f ($1,062,197).

One other factor in the pedigrees of many of Adios top performers, as a sire and broodmare sire, is the presence of Knight Dream in their pedigrees. Ambiguity, Pleasure Seeker and Shadow's Finale all have Knight Dream blood and it must be remembered that Adios nicked very well with Nibble Hanover mares and he is Knight Dream's sire.

Today, the best way to get Adios blood close up in a pedigree is through daughters of Bret Hanover, Henry T. Adios and Adios Vic - although most will have some age at this point. But there are plenty of mares and stallions available with multiple crosses to Adios in their pedigrees. The blood of Adios changed harness racing forever and continues to be a major presence in modern great pacers in North America, Australia and New Zealand. He is truly a legend of the kind we may never see again.

Adios

Photo courtesy of the USTA

Leading Progeny by Adios

Fastest
- Bret Hanover, h, p,4,T1:53.3 $922,616
- Adios Butler, h, p,T1:54.3 $509,875
- Adios Harry, h, p,4,1:55 $345,433
- Bullet Hanover, h, p,3,T1:55.3 $132,578
- Adios Vic, h, p,3,1:56.3 $455,896
- Shadow Wave, h, p,3,1:56.3 $91,931
- Dottie's Pick, m, p,4,T1:56.4 $263,978
- Dancer Hanover, h, p,4,T1:56.4 $87,746
- Henry T Adios, h, p,1:57 $706,833
- Bonjour Hanover, m, p,3,1:57 $226,821

Richest
- Bret Hanover, h, p,4,T1:53.3 $922,616
- Henry T Adios, h, p,1:57 $706,833
- Adios Butler, h, p,4,:54.3 $509,875
- Adios Vic, h, p,3,1:56.3 $455,896
- Cold Front, h, p,1:57.1 $404,709
- Adios Harry, h, p,4,1:55 $345,433
- Lehigh Hanover, h, p,3,1:58.4h $330,263
- Countess Adios, m, p,3,1:57.3 $317,158
- Dottie's Pick, m, p,4,T1:56.4 $263,978
- Adios Don, h, p,3,1:58.4 $236,154

Adios, Bay Horse, 15 Hands, 1940
p, 2, 2:02; 3, 2:01¼; 4, 1:58¼; T1:57½ ($33,329)

Sire/Dam	2nd gen	3rd gen	4th gen	5th gen
Hal Dale, 1926 p, 6, 2:02¼	Abbedale, 1917 p, 2:01¼	The Abbe, 1903 p, 2:04	Chimes, 1884 3, 2:30¾	**ELECTIONEER** — **HAMBLETONIAN 10** / Green Mountain Maid
				Beautiful Bells — The Moor / Minnehaha
			Nettie King, 1887	Mambrino King — **MAMBRINO** / Belle Thornton
				Nettie Murphy — Hamblin Patchen
		Daisydale D., 1908 3, 2:15¼	Archdale, 1897	Expedition — **ELECTIONEER** / Lady Russell
				Aline — Allie West / Coquette
			Mrs. Tmolus, 1901	Pactolus — Patronage / Buda
				Flaxey
	Margaret Hal, 1914 p, 2:19½h	Argot Hal, 1903 p, T2:04¾	Brown Hal, 1879	**TOM HAL JNR** — Kittrel's Tom Hal / Julia Johnson
				Lizzie — John Nederland / Blackie
			Lady Wildflower, 1891	Duplex — Bay Tom Jnr
				Sally Ward — Bennett Chapman / Sweepstakes
		Margaret Polk, 1906	John R. Gentry, 1889 p, T2:00½	Ashland Wilkes — Red Wilkes / Daisy B
				Dame Wood — Wedgewood / Fancy
			Stella Hal, 1885	**TOM HAL JNR** — Kittrel's Tom Hal / Julia Johnson
				Dolly II — Pat Malone / Old Bald
Adioo Volo, 1930 p, 3, 2:05h	Adioo Guy, 1910 p, 2:00¾	Guy Dillon, 1902 T2:21¼	Sidney Dillon, 1892	Sidney — Santa Claus / Sweetness
				Venus — Captain Webster / Katie
			By Guy, 1894	**GUY WILKES** — **GEORGE WILKES** / Lady Bunker
				BY BY — **NUTWOOD** / Rapidan
		Adioo, 1895	**GUY WILKES**, 1878 2:15¼	**GEORGE WILKES** — **HAMBLETONIAN 10** / Dolly Spanker
				Lady Bunker — **MAMBRINO** / Lady Dunn
			BY BY, 1885	**NUTWOOD** — Belmont / Miss Russell
				Rapidan
	Sigrid Volo, 1921 p, T2:04	Peter Volo, 1911 4, 2:02	Peter The Great, 1895 4, 2:07¼	Pilot Medium — Happy Medium / Tackey
				Santos — Grand Sentinel / Shadow
			Nervolo Belle, 1906	Nervolo — Colbert / Nellie D
				Josephine Knight — Betterson / Mambrino Beauty
		Polly Parrot, 1904 p, 2:13¼h	Jersey B.B., 1900	Jersey Wilkes — **GEORGE WILKES** / Lady Patchen
				Blue Belle — Bartolomew Wilkes / Mamie Foster
			Lady Maud C., 1901 p, 2:00½	Chitwood — **NUTWOOD** / Maggie Wilkes
				Noretta — Norris / Maggie Yeaser

Adios Vic

Adios produced many fast horses, including world champions such as Bret Hanover, Bullet Hanover, and Adios Butler. Of those three, Adios Vic was most like Adios Butler. He could smoke! Whereas Bret Hanover was a big, massive horse who stood over 16 hands, and had a ground-devouring stride, Adios Vic and Adios Butler were smaller, more compact speed demons who were also good-gaited and extremely fast.

Adios Vic was a foal of 1962, as was his nemesis Bret Hanover, and both came from one of Adios' final few crops. Both were three in the summer of 1965 when their famous sire died at Delvin Miller's Meadow Lands Farm.

Adios Vic was bred and owned by Victor and Morris Zeinfeld of Illinois, and was trained and driven by California horseman Jim Dennis, one of the most accomplished horsemen of his era. At two, Adios Vic won six of 17 starts but earned only $24,945. But he showed flashes of dazzling speed, one victory coming in 1:59.3.

At three, he realized much of this exciting potential, winning 12 times in 32 starts, the most noteworthy of which was his legendary defeat of Bret Hanover in the opening heat of the 1965 Review Futurity at Springfield. This defeat was the first in 36 races for Bret Hanover, and established a career-long battle between the two vaunted sons of Adios. In fact, Bret Hanover lost only six races in his life, and four were to Adios Vic. Vic's three-year-old earnings were $123,195 and he returned at four to win another $152,617, winning the Washington Park Stake (over Bret Hanover), the Excelsior Stake and the Adios Butler Pace. At five, he won another $102,000, with major victories in the Good Time Pace and the National Championship Pace in New York. He also raced briefly at six, winning four of nine starts, closing out a career that saw him win $455,841. Adios Vic was syndicated for $500,000 by Lana Lobell Farm's Alan Leavitt and went to stud.

Adios Vic was a horse who no doubt would have prospered had he been allowed more racing opportunities on a mile track as a young horse. He had difficulty in the turns when he was young, but his spectacular brush of speed was clearly in evidence when he swept by Bret Hanover at both Springfield and Indianapolis. Adios Vic had much more raw speed than Bret, but lacked Bret's versatility over the smaller tracks. However, given cover over a mile track, his late kick was deadly. We are left to wonder what he could have accomplished had the early part of his career been developed over a track like the Meadowlands.

Sire Line

As we have seen, Adios Vic was a member of one of his sire's final five crops, and was born the same year as Bret Hanover, the legend to which his career would be linked. Adios is profiled in this book.

Maternal Line

Some observers believe that Adios Vic inherited his body type and speed from his female side. His dam is the Jimmy Creed mare Miss Creedabelle p,4,2:01.3, dam of ten winners including Majestic Lobell p,3,T1:55.4 ($125,273), and the dams of Norma Ruth Hanover p,2,T1:56.3 ($141,083), Trader Hanover p,1:57.1h ($301,141), Natrona Hanover p,2,T1:58.1 and Nate Hanover p,4,1:58.3.

Miss Creedabelle was also the dam of Rita Belle p,3,2:03.3, a Dancer Hanover three-quarter sister to Adios Vic who was the dam of the former world champion pacing filly Roses Are Red p,3,1:56.3h ($389,366). A full sister to Roses Are Red, the Meadow Skipper mare Native Rita p,4,2:00.4f, produced the millionaire Native Born p,1:50.3, a son of Nihilator, and the good Abercrombie horse Capital Spending p,4,1:51.4 ($110,836).

Adios Vic's Jimmy Creed dam is interesting only because Jimmy Creed is a son of Frisco Forbes, an all but forgotten sire who was a son of Frisco Dale, and grandson of Hal Dale. Since Adios Vic was by Adios, a son of Hal Dale, this meant that Adios Vic was linebred to Hal Dale in a pretty significant way in the male line of his sire and dam. This kind of breeding is all the rage in modern breeding circles, but was virtually untested in Adios Vic's day. It is possible that much

Race Record Highlights

At 2
- **1st** Batavia Colt S.
- **2nd** Arden Downs S.
  Ben Franklin P.
  Sportsmans Early Closer
- **3rd** heat of McMahon Memorial

At 3
- **1st** Dan Parish P.
  Horseman Futurity
  heat of Review Futurity
- **2nd** Spring Sophomore P.
  Cane Futurity Prep
  Commodore P.
  Grand Prix P.
  heat of Motor City P.
  heat of Review Futurity
  heat of Horseman Futurity
  American Pacing Classic
  Stepping Stone P.
- **3rd** Reynolds Memorial
  Arden Downs S.

At 4
- **1st** Washington Park S.
  Excelsior S.
  Adios Butler Pace
  Preview P.
  Golden West P.
- **2nd** California Elks P.
  Adios P.
  HTA P.
- **3rd** Californian P.
  National Championship P.
  HTA P.
  National Pacing Derby

At 5
- **1st** Good Time Pace
  International Championship Pace
  Hall of Fame P.
- **3rd** Spring Finale P.
  Washington Park P.

Honors
At three, set world record for three heats divided
At three, set world record for 1 1/16 miles

Adios Vic

Photo courtesy of The Horseman and Fair World

Race Record

Year	Age	Starts	Wins	2nd	3rd	Earnings	Record
1964	2	17	6	3	1	$ 24,945	p,2,1:59.3
1965	3	32	12	9	2	123,915	p,3,1:56.3
1966	4	28	8	4	4	152,617	
1967	5	11	6	0	2	102,000	
1968	6	9	4	2	1	52,250	
		97	36	18	10	$455,841	p,3,1:56.3

Adios Vic

of Adios Vic's speed came from the fact that he was linebred to Hal Dale through different branches of that vast family of sires. Later, we would come to understand that the melding of blood from the multiple and different branches of the Hal Dale line was a very effective way to produce good pacers (for example, Most Happy Fella, Albatross, Cam Fella, etc) Adios Vic's ability should have told us that this kind of breeding was very effective.

Progeny Of Note

With his renowned speed, and a pedigree that promised the delivery of future champions, Adios Vic was thought to have the material for a successful siring career. He began his stud duty at Lana Lobell Farms in Pennsylvania, and had good patronage from many of the sport's leading breeders, including the farm which stood him.

His first crop, however, produced no foals of note, and already Adios Vic was in trouble. The second crop, foals of 1971, showed some promise with pacers like the good colts Peter Lobell p,1:56 ($271,665), Armbro Ozark p,1:57.1f ($267,484), Armbro Ontario p,3,1:56.1 ($170,338), Right Tie p,1:57.3 ($289,462), Grateful Vikar p,1:59.3h ($263,705) and Armbro Ocelot p,1:58f ($258,084). In later crops, he produced the raceway star Newt Lobell p,1:55.1 ($982,828) and his richest performer J. D.'s Buck p,4,1:54.3 ($1,156,532). But after Peter Lobell, his only representative colt star was the attractive Adam Lobell p,3,1:57.3 ($403,588).

One of Adios Vic's problems was that like many sons of Adios, he failed to produce good fillies. His fastest female was the aged mare Gentle Miss p,1:56.2 ($251,329), and the only other high-profile female was the Chicago star Native Amber p,4,1:56.4 ($195,823).

Analysis

Aside from Bret Hanover, Adios Vic and Shadow Wave could easily be considered the next best siring sons of the great Adios. The other good racing sons of Adios - Adios Butler, Henry T. Adios, Adios Boy, Adios Harry, Bullet Hanover and Dancer Hanover - did not accomplish what Adios Vic did as a stallion. Adios Butler left nothing for the future on the male or female side, Henry T. Adios is primarily noted as the grandsire of Abercrombie and Dancer Hanover as the grandsire of Albatross.

Adios Vic sired the winners of nearly $30,000,000 during his North American career before being exported to Australia for stud duty. He had 137 2:00 performers, one $1,000,000 winner, four $500,000 winners, 20 $250,000 winners and 50 $150,000 winners. In addition, Adios Vic's sons and daughters were well-noted for their soundness and longevity on the racetrack.

Adios Vic did not begin his stud career until the age of seven. His first crop of foals arrived in 1970 and raced in 1972. Staying in the U.S. until the end of the 1979 season, Adios Vic had his largest crops, 144 and 153 foals, in 1976 and 1977.

The 2x5 cross to Hal Dale is very unusual and is the closest appearing in Adios Vic's pedigree. He is also 4x5 to Argot Hal and 5x5x4 to Grattan Royal since his dam is 4x4x3 to that stallion and his second dam is inbred 3x2 to Grattan Royal.

Like many decent sires, Adios Vic had plenty of stakes performers but could not hit the proverbial "home run" to make him a glamour sire. As the Meadow Skipper, Albatross and Most Happy Fella bandwagon started to roll, Adios Vic lost favor among breeders and his North American career was doomed. However, he has left a legacy of excellent money winners and daughters who went on to very productive broodmare careers as we will see. Adios Vic's primary siring son is Peter Lobell p,1:56 ($271,655) who stood in California for many years, dominated that state's program, and sired 144 2:00 performers. A few other Adios Vic sons were tried at stud with little success.

There is a very interesting aspect to Adios Vic's stallion career which must be noted. Armstrong Bros. farm bred a number of their good mares with Adios blood back to Adios Vic and achieved a 2x3 cross to Adios which was very successful. Elgin and Ted Armstrong believed so much in Adios that they had 40 Adios mares in their broodmare band at one point and later granddaughters and great-granddaughters which established the foundation of their prolific broodmare band. The Armstrong brothers also believed in inbreeding to such a great stallion as Adios. Thus, many of Adios' granddaughters found their way to Adios Vic to provide the offspring with the 2x3 inbreeding cross. Some of those 2x3 results are Armbro Ollie p,1:59.1f ($334,084), Armbro Rambler p,4,1:57 ($305,233), Armbro Ozark p,1:57.1f ($267,484), Armbro Rally p,2:00.2 ($239,468), Armbro Ontario p,3,1:56.1 ($170,338) and Armbro Rhythm p,1:57.2 ($139,336). Another with a 2x4 cross to Adios is Armbro Vienna p,1:55.4f ($382,517).

Armstrong was not the only breeder to try this close cross 2x3 to Adios and it also worked well for Cedarwood Chips p,1:56f ($532,560), Arion Lobell p,1:54.3f ($421,339) (Adios Vic's co-fastest performer), Adam Lobell p,3,1:57.3 ($403,588) and Alpha Lobell p,1:57 ($262,565) - the last three from the good producing Tar Heel mare Adiana Hanover.

But Adios Vic's co-fastest and richest performer is J. D.'s Buck p,4,1:54.3 ($1,156,532) who was from a mare by Harold J. His closest pedigree cross is 4x4 to Volomite since his dam is inbred 3x3 to Volomite. There is also an interesting connection regarding Harold J. He is the sire of the dam of the sport's fastest ever horse, Cambest, whose grandam is by Adios Vic. Here is the Harold J.-Adios Vic connection again. In addition, I must point out that Harold J.'s dam is Lady Scotland. I bring this to your attention because a great mare who enjoyed excellent success with Adios Vic was Prelude Lobell whose own dam is by Hodgen who is also a son of Lady Scotland. The melding of this blood is prolific and if you dig deep enough you can find some of these relationships which tend to reinforce the "nicking" theory.

Adios Vic's second richest son is the long-wearing Newt Lobell p,1:55.1 ($982,828) who took his record at 11 years of age. He is from a mare with an Overtrick/Tar Heel cross and is 3x4 to Hal Dale. Since Adios Vic's sire did so well with Tar Heel mares, and since they were in abundance when Adios Vic was in his prime, there were plenty bred to him and a few produced some of his best offspring.

The aforementioned Prelude Lobell was a Tar Heel mare and with Adios Vic produced Pegasus Lobell p,1:57 ($611,236), Patriot Lobell p,1:57.1 ($312,724), Peter Lobell p,1:56 ($271,655) and Perky Mindy p,3,1:59 who is the grandam of Caesar's Jackpot and another example of a classic successful "nicking" pattern for Adios Vic. Prelude Lobell has some power in her maternal family since she is linebred to two classic mares being 4x6 to Emily Ellen and 4x5 to Roya McKinney - both great foundation mares of the breed.

As a broodmare sire, Adios Vic has been very good. It is probably not often realized that he is the sire of the second dams of the fastest male and female in the history of the sport - Cambest p,T1:46.1 ($1,144,835) and Caesar's Jackpot p,T1:49.2 ($949,494). That is quite an accomplishment and it may, or may not, be a coincidence. He is also the sire of the grandams of such other successful performers as Tate Lobell p,1:51.2 ($175,004), Parson's Den p,4,1:51.4f-'98 ($269,476), Too Good p,3,1:52 ($356,373), Kelly Miles p,1:52.2f ($292,316), Lovin Yankee p,2,1:53 ($255,506), Timothy Lobell p,3,1:53.1 ($322,746), Yankee Co-ed p,3,1:53.4 ($671,110), Scoot Herb p,1:54.3 ($616,563) and Yankee Cashmere p,3,1:54.3f ($414,304) to name a few.

Switching from the granddaughters of Adios Vic to his daughters, we find that he is a top broodmare sire with 669 2:00 credits to date. Some of his fastest and richest broodmare credits are Darth Raider p,1:49.2 ($421,045) (by Laag), Lady Ashlee Ann p,3,1:51.3 ($95,481) (by Camtastic), Sun Damage p,1:52.1 ($175,668) (by Storm Damage), Dandy Promise p,4,1:52.1 ($324,323) (by Ahlberg), Forrest Eden p,4,1:52.4f (by Forrest Skipper), Choice Yankee p,2,1:52.4 ($732,442) (by Colt Fortysix), Miller's Aussie p,1:53f ($481,970) (by Armbro Aussie), Shipp's Fella p,4,1:53.1f ($478,191) (by Cam Fella), Joel's David p,4,1:53.1 ($430,694) (by Oil Burner), Armbro Vibrant p,3,T1:53.3 ($370,871) (by Armbro Nesbit), G.E.'s Karla p,1:53.3 ($406,969) (by G.E.'s Romanero), Soky's Atom p,3,T1:53.3 ($887,127) (by Albatross), Woodrow Wilson winner Grade One p,2,1:54.3 ($875,148), Armbro Dazzler p,2,1:55.4 ($577,915) (by Nero), Mostest Yankee p,1:56 ($484,248) (by Columbia George) and Areba Areba

Adios Vic

p,2,1:58 ($311,791) (by Nero). This is just scratching the surface, but you can see the types of horses involved here from Adios Vic's daughters.

Adios Vic mares work very well with Albatross and his sons and Most Happy Fella line stallions. Also very productive was the cross to Nero and his son G.E.'s Romanero - the latter an unsung stallion who produced three top horses from three different Adios Vic mares. Nero was especially prolific in producing great fillies like Areba Areba, Armbro Dazzler and Color And Light from Adios Vic mares.

Mares with the Nero/Adios Vic cross have done very well as producers. Yankeeland Farm of Maryland has plenty of mares with those crosses who have been producing prominent stakes performers from that nursery started years ago by the former New York Yankee baseball great Charlie Keller and now continued by his sons and grandsons.

Adios Vic's time may have passed, but you can still find his speed and strength in the pedigrees of many modern-day colts and fillies. He was definitely a sire in the Adios tradition.

Leading Progeny by Adios Vic

Fastest
- J.D.'s Buck, g, p,1:54.3 $1,156,532
- Arion Lobell, g, p,1:54.3f $421,339
- Newt Lobell, h, p,1:55.1 $982,838
- Smashing Vic, g, p,1:55.2 $174,028
- Searights, g, p,1:55.3 $301,122
- Chevy Chase A., g, p,1:55.3h $79,165
- Armbro Vienna, h, p,1:55.4f $382,517
- Cedarwood Chips, h, p,1:56f $532,560
- Peter Lobell, h, p,1:56 $271,655
- Pindari Way A., g, p,1:56f $181,604

Richest
- J.D.'s Buck, g, p,1:54.3 $1,156,532
- Newt Lobell, h, p,1:55.1 $982,838
- Pegasus Lobell, g, p,1:57 $611,236
- Cedarwood Chips, h, p,1:56f $532,560
- Arion Lobell, g, p,1:54.3f $421,339
- Native Leader, h, p,1:56.3f $411,424
- Adam Lobell, h, p,3,1:57.3 $403,588
- Armbro Vienna, h, p,1:55.4f $382,517
- K.C. Three, h, p,1:57f $354,897
- Armbro Ollie, h, p,1:59.1f $334,084

Adios Vic, Bay Horse, 1962
p,2,1:59.3; 3,1:56.3 $455,841

Sire/Dam	2nd gen	3rd gen	4th gen	5th gen
Adios, 1940 p, T1:57½ $33,329	**HAL DALE**, 1926 p, 6, 2:02¼ $595	Abbedale, 1917 p, 2:01¼	The Abbe, 1903 T, 2:10½	Chimes — Electioneer / Beautiful Bells
				Nettie King — Mambrino King / Nettie Murphy
			Daisydale D., 1908 p, 3, 2:15¼	Archdale — Expedition / Aline
				Mrs. Tmolus — Pactolus / Flaxey
		Margaret Hal, 1914 p, 2:19½h	**ARGOT HAL**, 1903 p, T2:04¾	Brown Hal — **TOM HAL JNR** / Lizzie
				Lady Wildflower — Duplex / Sally Ward
			Margaret Polk, 1906	John R. Gentry — Ashland Wilkes / Dame Wood
				Stella Hal — **TOM HAL JNR** / Dolly II
	Adioo Volo, 1930 p, 3, 2:05h	Adioo Guy, 1910 p, 2:00¾	Guy Dillon, 1902	Sidney Dillon — Sidney / Venus
				By Guy — **GUY WILKES** / **BY BY**
			Adioo, 1895	**GUY WILKES** — George Wilkes / Lady Bunker
				BY BY — Nutwood / Rapidan
		Sigrid Volo, 1921 p, T2:04	Peter Volo, 1911 T, 4, 2:02	**PETER THE GREAT** — Pilot Medium / **SANTOS**
				Nervolo Belle — Nervolo / Josephine Knight
			Polly Parrot, 1904 p, 2:13¼h	Jersey B.B. — Jersey Wilkes / Blue Belle
				Lady Maud C. — Chitwood / Noretta
Miss Creedabelle, 1952 p, 4, 2:01.3 $23,688	Jimmy Creed, 1942 p, T1:59.4 $108,919	Frisco Forbes, 1937 p, 3, 2:11h	Frisco Dale, 1934 p, 4, 2:00	**HAL DALE** — Abbedale / Margaret Hal
				Frances San Francisco — San Francisco / Dudie Egmont
			Elizabeth L, 1915 1, T2:29¼	J Malcolm Forbes — Bingen / **SANTOS**
				Nelle Worthy L — **AXWORTHY** / Miss Anna Jay
		Virginia Grattan, 1937	Silent Grattan, 1921 p, T2:09¾	**GRATTAN ROYAL** — Grattan / Mona
				Silent T — Silent Brook / Agave
			Myrtle McKlyo, 1926 p, 2:00¼	Peter Mcklyo — **PETER THE GREAT** / Klyo
				Red Chatham — Fuzzy Chatham / Macketta
	Belle Grattan, 1942 p, 4, 2:11h $3,853	Dexter Worthy, 1933 p, 2:03¼ $4,274	Full Worthy, 1923 2:02	Guy Axworthy — **AXWORTHY** / Lillian Wilkes
				Worthy Spirit — **AXWORTHY** / Great Spirit
			Daisy Grattan, 1921 p, 2:05½	**GRATTAN ROYAL** — Grattan / Mona
				Daisy At Law — Heir At Law / Daisy Rysdyk
		Iola Grattan, 1924 p, 2:09¾	**GRATTAN ROYAL**, 1908 p, 2:06¼	Grattan — Wilkes Boy / Annie Almont
				Mona — Robert McGregor / Jenny Bryan
			Iola Hal, 1907 p, 2:09¾	**ARGOT HAL** — Brown Hal / Lady Wildflower
				Bessie Louise — Mercury C / Barbette

Albatross

"He is, and was, simply the best horse I ever trained and drove." Those are the words of Hall Of Fame trainer-driver Stanley Dancer, describing Albatross. Few horses in the history of any breed have had such a notable racing life, followed by an even more profound and successful stallion career. Albatross was a foal of 1968, a member of Meadow Skipper's second crop, and was bred by John Wilcutts, Charlie Kenney, John Kenney, Elizabeth Peters and Mark Lydon. His dam, Voodoo Hanover, had been sold to Canadian owner Bert James when Albatross was a yearling as part of a package deal. The mare, Albatross and the mare's 1969 foal, a full sister to Albatross, were purchased by James for $11,000 from their breeders.

Albatross was offered for sale as a yearling at the 1969 Harrisburg sale, but was retained by James for a final bid of $7,000. Several subsequent attempts to sell the colt privately also fell short of James' price, and the decision was made, on the recommendation of Delvin Miller, to place him into training with Harry Harvey. The rest, as they say, is history.

Harvey developed Albatross into the leading two-year-old pacer in the country. He won 14 of his 17 starts, sweeping through all of the major two-year-old stakes of that era, including the Fox Stake, Roosevelt Futurity, Sheppard, Matron, Geers, American-National, Hanover-Hempt and Canadian Juvenile. Not surprisingly, he was voted Two-Year-Old Pacer of the Year. He won just over $183,000 as a freshman. His two-year-old mark was 1:57.4.

At three, following a sale reported at $1.25 million, and now racing for trainer Stanley Dancer, Albatross reasserted his dominance of his division, winning 25 of 28 races, earning nearly $560,000. He did not win the Triple Crown, dropping the Little Brown Jug to Nansemond, but he did capture the Messenger, Cane Pace, Adios, American Classic and Shapiro Stakes, the latter two races against the best older horses in North America. He was Harness Horse of the Year in 1971.

One of his most fascinating performances, and the one Dancer still recalls with wonder, was a double-heat triumph at The Red Mile near the end of his three-year-old season. In both heats, Albatross jumped offstride briefly at the start of each mile, spotting his foes several open lengths. However, he recovered to win both heats in then world record time of 1:54.4. These races, which came directly on the heels of his upset loss of the Little Brown Jug, truly showed Albatross' remarkable endowment. Dancer never time-trialed Albatross, but has said that he thought Albatross would have been capable of a 1:52 mile under the right conditions.

At four, after an eventful re-syndication, he won 20 of 26 races, earning $459,921 He completed a three year sweep of the American-National, and repeated his American Pacing Classic triumph as well. His 1:54.3f mark was taken at Sportsman's Park in Chicago when that track was still a five-eighth mile oval. To crown his season he was again voted Horse of the Year.

Albatross retired as the all-time record money-winning pacer, with career earnings of more than $1.2 million. He had 59 career wins in only 71 starts and was world champion at two, three and four.

However, Albatross' four-year-old season had begun in controversy. He lost his first three races, all to older horses early in the spring, and the syndicate which had purchased him as a three-year-old disagreed with the way Dancer was managing the horse. Ultimately, there was a quarrel about Albatross' immediate future. Some of the syndicate members wanted Albatross moved to another stable, but John Simpson, Sr., then president of Hanover Shoe Farms, stepped in with a compromise that mollified the disgruntled syndicate members. Albatross changed ownership once again but he stayed under Dancer's shedrow.

This was a most fortunate move for Hanover Shoe Farms. Albatross would close out his racing career in grand style, and then become the most successful stallion of any breed.

Albatross' hallmark, and his greatest contribution to the breed, was his gait. Dancer believes that Albatross could have raced free-legged,

Albatross

Photo by Monica Thors
Courtesy of The Horseman and Fair World

Race Record Highlights

At 2
- **1st** Fox S.
  Roosevelt Futurity
  L.B.Sheppard S.
  Matron S.
  Geers S.
  American-National S.
  Andy Kerr Memorial
  Hanover-Hempt S.
  Canadian Juvenile S.
- **2nd** Arden Downs S.
  Richelieu S.
- **3rd** Reading Futurity

At 3
- **1st** Messenger S.
  Cane Pace
  Adios S.
  American Classic
  L.K. Shapiro S.
  heat of Little Brown Jug

At 3 (continued)
- **2nd** heat and Final of Little Brown Jug

At 4
- **1st** American Classic
  Realization S.
  American-National S.
- **2nd** Clark Memorial
  Provincial Cup
  Suburban Downs Pacing Derby
  Oktoberfest P.

Honors

Voted Horse of the Year at three and four
Voted Two-Year-Old Pacer of the Year
At three, set all-age world record on mile track
At three, set all-age world record for two heats on mile track
At four, set all-age world record on five-eighth mile track and half mile track

Race Record

Year	Age	Starts	Wins	2nd	3rd	Earnings	Record
1970	2	17	14	2	1	$183,540	p,2,1:57.4
1971	3	28	25	2	1	558,009	p,3,1:54.4
1972	4	26	20	4	1	459,921	p,4,1:54.3f
		71	59	8	3	$1,201,470	p,4,1:54.3f

such was the pure quality of his motion. It was free-flowing, solid, and allowed Albatross to carry his speed through three demanding seasons. Some people described his gait as "the Meadow Skipper overdrive," but Albatross really made it his own trademark. He not only was great-gaited, but also a sound horse, and he passed those two remarkable qualities to his offspring, and to succeeding generations.

Albatross was a small horse, standing only 15.1 hands. This is unlike many of Meadow Skipper's most accomplished racing sons, who were bigger horses of more striking size and substance, most notably Most Happy Fella. Albatross was a long-barreled horse, however, and extremely well-balanced. Another of his distinguishing features was his unattractive head which seemed very disproportionate to the remainder of his conformation.

Sire Line

Albatross is a son of Meadow Skipper, the horse who transformed the modern-day pacer, and a grandson of Dale Frost, a son of Hal Dale. Thus Albatross represents a successful branch of the powerful Hal Dale sire line which dominates North American pacing.

Albatross was from the second crop of Meadow Skipper and provided one of the early indications that Meadow Skipper would be a sire of real quality. Dale Frost was an unlikely choice to be the sire of a horse as grand as Meadow Skipper, since the balance of his siring career did not produce a horse with even a hint of Meadow Skipper's renown. Meadow Skipper's own racing career also did not provide us with a glimpse of his siring punch. His development as a sire, and the ability to make a lasting impact, is the true mark of his contribution.

Maternal Line

Albatross' female lineage is most interesting. His dam, Voodoo Hanover, is by Dancer Hanover, a son of Adios, and his second dam is by Tar Heel, giving him an ample boost of the most popular blood of the generation that preceded him in the stud. This blending of the blood on top and bottom produces a 3 x 4 generation cross to Hal Dale. This mixing of the Adios and Tar Heel blood provided much of the siring power in the late 1950's and throughout the 1960's (as seen most notably with Bret Hanover) and it is no surprise to see the mingling of these two champions once again in Albatross' maternal pedigree. Dancer Hanover, Albatross' maternal grandsire, won 26 of his 48 lifetime starts, paced a half in :55.2, a quarter in :26 and an eighth in 12.2. Delvin Miller said, "I tell you, there were times he scared me to death he paced so fast."

Albatross hails from the noted Mamie maternal family, since his dam, Voodoo Hanover, is a 1964 foal by Dancer Hanover from Vibrant Hanover, a 1960 daughter of Tar Heel. The third dam is the Guy McKinney mare, Vivian Hanover, a foal of 1937, in the same branch of the family that produced the successful racehorses Henry T. Adios, the paternal grandsire of Abercrombie, and Little Brown Jug winner Dudley Hanover (Albatross' dam is a three-quarter sister to Dudley) although this branch of the family has fallen out of favor with most modern breeders. Other notable horses in the Mamie maternal family, albeit in different branches of the clan, that are still prized, are Valley Victory, Nihilator, Killbuck Mary and Gothic Dream.

Albatross was a very dominant racehorse, a product of the melding of the best blood available in his era. He was really the first great colt produced by Meadow Skipper, and is the only son of Meadow Skipper to outstrip his sire's own distinguished record. The fact he became an extraordinary sire (and later broodmare sire) of such enormous impact is testimony to his overall splendor.

Progeny of Note

Albatross' leading money winner is the two-time Horse of the Year and Triple Crown champion Niatross p,3,T1:49.1 ($2,019,213), who is remembered as being the first Standardbred to beat 1:50, in a memorable 1980 time trial at The Red Mile. The remaining five millionaires sired by Albatross include the Little Brown Jug winner Jaguar Spur p,4,T1:49.2 ($1,806,473); his fastest racing offspring, Ball And Chain p,1:49 ($1,435,390); the two-year-old star Praised

Dignity p,2,1:56.4f ($1,194,715); Woodrow Wilson winner Cullin Hanover p,1:53 ($1,118,774) and former world champion Tucson Hanover p,4,1:51.3 ($1,072,623).

Albatross has also produced a number of the breed's most memorable fillies, including his leading money-winning female, the Little Brown Jug winner and 1981 Horse of the Year, Fan Hanover p,4,T1:50.4 ($969,724). He also produced the sensational Jugette winners Cheery Hello p,3,1:52.3 ($869,619) and Turn The Tide p,3,1:53.2 ($860,993); the Breeders Crown champion Halcyon p,3,Q1:54.4 ($855,588) and the mercurial Three Diamonds p,3,1:53.1 ($735,759) (herself the dam of the Little Brown Jug winner Life Sign p,3,1:50.3 ($1,912,454).)

Other notable sons include Meadowlands Pace winners Sonsam p,3,1:53.2 ($820,104) and Conquered p,3,1:54.3 ($856,723); Kiev Hanover p,3,1:50.1 ($610,179); Breeders Crown winner Three Wizzards p,3,1:53.1 ($815,154) and Little Brown Jug winner Colt Fortysix p,3,1:50.3 ($232,538).

His broodmare credits, unparalleled in this, or any other breed, include the dams of such notable horses as world champion and Horse of the Year Artsplace; Little Brown Jug winner Life Sign; world champion Albert Albert; Breeders Crown winner Camtastic; Little Brown Jug and North America Cup winner Goalie Jeff; world champion Caesar's Jackpot; Meadowlands Pace winner and successful Canadian sire Dexter Nukes; Woodrow Wilson winner Die Laughing; and Cane and Messenger winner Western Hanover.

Albatross' sons have also made important contributions as broodmare sires themselves, although none appears to have the outright siring power of their own remarkable sire. B.G.'s Bunny, one of his earliest stars, is a broodmare sire of note, having produced the dams of such accomplished stars as Precious Bunny, Cam's Card Shark and Armbro Operative.

A remarkably virile horse throughout his stallion career, Albatross bred at least 100 mares for 18 consecutive seasons from 1976 through 1993. He has produced more than 2,500 foals, of which more than 2,000, or 80 per cent, have raced, earning an average of $64,000 per starter.

Analysis

Not only was Albatross one of the greatest racehorses of all time, but he is also among the most historically significant stallions in the sport. Albatross is the sire of the winners of over $129,000,000 - the highest ever among Standardbred or Thoroughbred sires. Albatross was the first to exceed the $100,000,000 plateau; the only others at that level are the trotting sire Speedy Crown and pacer Abercrombie.

To put Albatross in perspective as a stallion, he is the leading sire of 2:00 performers with over 1,150. He also leads in $100,000 winners, with over 360, and he was the leading money-winning sire from 1981 through 1984 and also in 1986. He has sired six $1,000,000 winners, 32 $500,000 winners, five Little Brown Jug winners and two Horses of the Year (Niatross twice and Fan Hanover). In addition, Albatross has always been the sire of great fillies and his $500,000 winners include 10 of that gender. Albatross' daughters are also some of the best broodmares in the sport and have produced over 2,300 2:00 performers, over 500 in 1:55 and the winners of over $230,000,000 to make Albatross the greatest broodmare sire in history by a wide margin.

In any ranking of harness racing's all time great racehorses, Albatross is easily among the top half-dozen and so, most likely, are his son Niatross and grandson Nihilator. There is inherent greatness in Albatross' genes which he was able to pass on to scores of sons and daughters.

It is true that Albatross did not produce a son anywhere near his equal as a sire, but he is an extremely hard act to follow and the same can be said about dozens of other great sires. Many Albatross sons have been given an ample opportunity at stud by being placed at major farms and having access to high-quality broodmares; but, although several have been reasonably successful as commercial stallions, none have really hit the "home run" and attained the heights of Albatross.

Albatross died in August of 1998 at the age of 30 so it is unlikely that one of his late in life sons will emerge as a great stallion. The main hope for a top siring son seems to rest with Ball And Chain p,1:49 ($1,435,390) who is Albatross' fastest son and third richest. He stands at stud at Hanover Shoe Farms in Pennsylvania.

Among Albatross' best siring sons are Niatross, Sonsam and B.G.'s Bunny. Niatross looked as if he was going to become a great sire from his first three crops but then tailed off quickly and dramatically. It was almost as if someone had replaced Niatross in the breeding shed with a lesser accomplished look-alike. In my mind, this is still one of the great mysteries of the sport. Sonsam appeared, for a time, to be on his way to becoming an outstanding sire, but fertility problems interfered and he soon lost favor among breeders. B.G.'s Bunny was a good, steady sire for years and his daughters have become excellent broodmares.

Other Albatross sons with some commercial success are Royce, Ideal Society, Coal Harbor and Jaguar Spur. Many Albatross sons have been exported to Australia and New Zealand and have become very successful, including Vance Hanover, Holmes Hanover and Soky's Atom. But as far as a son taking over from his great sire is concerned, the Albatross candle seems to be flickering in North America.

Looking at Albatross' top performers from a pedigree standpoint, it is interesting to note one of the greatest crosses ever - Albatross on a Bret Hanover mare. Nine of Albatross' 20 fastest performers are from Bret Hanover mares as are eight of his 19 richest sons and daughters. This list includes such outstanding horses as Ball And Chain, Jaguar Spur, Sonsam, Tucson Hanover and the fillies Fan Hanover, Three Diamonds and Forbidden Past. Bye Bye Byrd mares were also very productive with Albatross; they are responsible for two of his four fastest performers, Niatross and Kiev Hanover in addition to the great mare Jef's Eternity.

Mares by Tar Heel, whom Albatross eclipsed as the leading broodmare sire, are also prominent with Albatross; they have produced Praised Dignity p,2,1:56.4f ($1,194,715), Armbro Wolf p,3,1:54.1 ($869,987), Cheery Hello p,3,1:52.3 ($869,619) and the fast Colt Fortysix p,3,1:50.3 ($232,538), among others.

As with most successful sires, Albatross has worked well with broodmares from a variety of sire lines. The majority of Albatross' fastest and richest performers have multiple crosses to Adios, Tar Heel and Hal Dale which is to be expected given the availability of broodmares from those gene pools and Albatross' own pedigree which contained those three stallions in his third generation.

However, Albatross' greatest performer is Niatross and he has no common ancestors in his first four generations. The closest common cross in Niatross' pedigree is the 4x4 to the full brother and sister Adios and Adieu. Ball And Chain, the fastest son of Albatross, has crosses of 4x3 to Adios and 4x4 to Tar Heel and Hal Dale as does Albatross' other sub-1:50 performer Jaguar Spur p,4,T1:49.2 ($1,806,473), Fan Hanover p,4,T1:50.4 ($969,724), Forbidden Past p,4,T1:51.2 ($276,185), Three Diamonds p,3,1:53.1 ($735,759), Sonsam p,3,1:53.2 ($820,104) and Tucson Hanover p,4,1:51.3 ($1,072,623) are more examples of this dynamic cross - all are from Bret Hanover mares.

Among the top sons and daughters of Albatross, there were only a few with inbred crosses - Colt Fortysix, Cheery Hello p,3,1:52.3, Armbro Wolf p,3,1:54.1 and Praised Dignity p,2,1:56.4f who are 4x2 to Tar Heel, and Oye Vay p,3,1:50.3 ($969,493) who is 2x4 to Meadow Skipper. Armbro Wolf also has a 3x3 cross to the three-quarter sisters Veda Hanover and Vibrant Hanover (second dam of Albatross). Another with an interesting 3x3 cross to siblings is the top mare Turn The Tide p,3,1:53.2 ($860,993) who is 3x3 to the half-brothers Dancer Hanover and Thorpe Hanover.

Today, we look at Albatross as the premier broodmare sire. His daughters are still in demand and still producing many of the sport's greatest performers. Albatross dams have produced 13 $1,000,000 winners, second only to the 15 by Bret Hanover dams. Even if Albatross did not eventually leave a son who achieved greatness as a stallion, his daughters are doing their part. Some of today's leading sires with dams by Albatross are Artsplace p,4,1:49.2, Life Sign p,3,1:50.3, Western Hanover p,3,1:50.4, Die Laughing p,3,1:51.1f, Dexter Nukes p,3,1:51.3 and Albert Albert p,3,1:52.1.

As this is written, Albatross daughters have produced five in 1:50: Artsplace, Caesar's Jackpot p,T1:49.2 (the fastest filly ever), Camtastic p,4,T1:49.3, Dr. Lecter Lobell p,1:50 and Keystone Endeavor p,4,1:50; they are by five different sires: Abercrombie, Walton Hanover, Cam Fella, On The Road Again and Storm Damage. The Abercrombie/Albatross cross is especially prolific in the speed department; four of the 11 fastest credits for Albatross broodmares have been sired by Abercrombie: Artsplace, Armbro Other p,4,1:50.1, Life Sign and Lahar p,1:50.3.

Another sire who has had great success with Albatross mares is No Nukes whose progeny includes Lotta Soul p,1:50.2, Western Hanover, Broadway Blue p,4,1:50.4f, the great mare Immortality p,3,1:51, Die Laughing, Easy Goer p,3,1:51.1, Dexter Nukes, Silky Stallone p,3,1:51.3 and Nadia Lobell p,3,1:53.4f, to name a few. Cam Fella has had equal success from Albatross mares with Camtastic - Cam's Catch p,3,1:50.2, Carlsbad Cam p,3,1:51, Goalie Jeff p,3,1:51.2, Fake Left p,3,1:51.2 and many more. Matt's Scooter, Direct Scooter and Big Towner have also been extremely successful with Albatross mares.

Multiple crosses to Albatross seem to have some good success. Some examples of crosses which are 3x3, or a closer 3x2 and 2x3, include such standouts as New Bucks p,1:49.3, Deadlock p,1:50.2, Come Out Swinging p,1:50.4, Shore Patrol p,3,1:51.2 ($1,122,211), Cam's Jewel p,3,1:51.3 and Start The Fire p,1:52.1 ($541,876). In fact, the four fastest and three richest in this category are sired by Nihilator who sired some of his best performers when bred back to mares with Albatross (his grandsire) in their pedigree. Another sire with success is Albert Albert with Albatross mares even though his dam is by Albatross. The resulting foals from this cross are bred 3x2 to Albatross and include six sub-1:54 performers with $100,000 in earnings. So, don't be afraid to have multiple crosses of Albatross in a mare you are buying or in a yearling you are considering.

Albatross was truly a spectacular Standardbred from the standpoint of performance and siring ability. His own common pedigree crosses are 3x4 to Hal Dale, 4x4 to Billy Direct, 4x5 to Volomite and 5x5x5 to Guy Axworthy. Whatever magic took place with those genes, it enabled Albatross to take the sport to a new level of "extreme speed" never before witnessed, and his daughters have done the same in helping the newer stallions push the speed envelope even further. Albatross will forever be remembered and has certainly lived up to his nickname of "Super Bird" both on and off the track.

In fact, you may be able to find a copy of Donald Evans' book, <u>Super Bird - The Story of Albatross</u>, for additional information about the background and racing career of this great horse.

Albatross

Photo courtesy of The Horseman and Fair World

Leading Progeny by Albatross

Fastest
Ball and Chain, h, p,1:49 $1,435,390
Niatross, h, p,3,T1:49.1 $2,019,213
Jaguar Spur, h, p,4,T1:49.2 $1,806,473
Kicv Hanovcr, h, p,3,1:50.1 $610,179
Oye Vay, h, p,3,1:50.3 $969,493
Colt Fortysix, h, p,3,1:50.3 $232,538
Fan Hanover, m, p,4,T1:50.4 $969,724
Danny B., h, p,1:51.2 $292,055
Forbidden Past, m, p,4,T1:51.2 $276,185
Spectacle, g, p,1:51.2 $232,580

Richest
Niatross, h, p,3,T1:49.1 $2,019,213
Jaguar Spur, h, p,4,T1:49.2 $1,806,473
Ball and Chain, h, p,1:49 $1,435,390
Praised Dignity, h, p,2,1:56.4f $1,194,715
Cullin Hanover, h, p,1:53 $1,118,774
Tucson Hanover, h, p,4,1:51.3 $1,072,623
Fan Hanover, m, p,4,T1:50.4 $969,724
Oye Vay, h, p,3,1:50.3 $969,493
Soky's Atom, h, p,3,T1:53.3 $887,127
Armbro Wolf, h, p,3,1:54.1 $869,987

Albatross, Bay Horse, 15.1 Hands, 1968
p, 2, 1:57.4; 3, 1:54.4; 4, 1:54.3f ($1,201,470)

Meadow Skipper, 1960 p, 3, 1:55.1 $428,057	Dale Frost, 1951 p, 1:58 $204,117	**HAL DALE**, 1926 p, 6, 2:02¼	Abbedale, 1917 p, 2:01¼	**THE ABBE**	Chimes Nettie King
				Daisydale D.	Archdale Mrs. Tmolus
			Margaret Hal, 1914 p, 2:19½h	Argot Hal	Brown Hal Lady Wildflower
				Margaret Polk	John R. Gentry Stella Hal
		Galloway, 1939 p, 2:04½h $5,294	Raider, 1929 p, 1:59½	**PETER VOLO**	**PETER THE GREAT** Nervolo Belle
				Nelda Dillon	Dillon Axworthy Princess Nelda
			Bethel, 1926 p, 2:03	David Guy	**GUY AXWORTHY** Belle Zombro
				Annotation	Azoff Citation
	Countess Vivian, 1950 p, 3, 1:59 $43,262	King's Counsel, 1940 p, 6, 1:58 $44,930	**VOLOMITE**, 1926 3, 2:03¼ $32,649	**PETER VOLO**	**PETER THE GREAT** Nervolo Belle
				Cita Frisco	San Francisco Mendocita
			Margaret Spangler, 1918 p, 2:02¼	**GUY AXWORTHY**	Axworthy Lillian Wilkes
				Maggie Winder	Oratorio Clara Direct
		Filly Direct, 1941 p, 3, 2:06¾ $6,299	**BILLY DIRECT**, 1934 p, 4, T1:55 $12,040	Napoleon Direct	Walter Direct Lady Erectress
				Gay Forbes	Malcolm Forbes Gay Girl Chimes
			Calumet Edna, 1931 p, 2:08½h	Peter The Brewer	**PETER THE GREAT** Zombrewer
				Broncho Queen	Empire Direct The Broncho
Voodoo Hanover, 1964	Dancer Hanover, 1957 p, 4, T1:56.4 $87,746	Adios, 1940 p, T1:57½ $33,329	**HAL DALE**, 1926 p, 6, 2:02¼	Abbedale	**THE ABBE** Daisydale D.
				Margaret Hal	Argot Hal Margaret Polk
			Adioo Volo, 1930 p, 3, 2:05½	Adioo Guy	Guy Dillon Adioo
				Sigrid Volo	**PETER VOLO** Polly Parrot
		The Old Maid, 1945	Guy Abbey, 1925 3, 2:06¾	**GUY AXWORTHY**	Axworthy Lillian Wilkes
				Abbacy	**THE ABBE** Regal McKinney
			Spinster, 1930 4, T2:05	Spencer	Lee Tide Petrex
				Minnetonka	Belwin The Miss Stokes
	Vibrant Hanover, 1960	Tar Heel, 1948 p, 4, T1:57 $119,148	**BILLY DIRECT**, 1934 p, 4, T1:55 $12,040	Napoleon Direct	Walter Direct Lady Erectress
				Gay Forbes	Malcolm Forbes Gay Girl Chimes
			Leta Long, 1940 p, 4, 2:03¾ $9,321	**VOLOMITE**	**PETER VOLO** Cita Frisco
				Rosette	Mr. McElwyn Rose Scott
		Vivian Hanover, 1937	Guy McKinney, 1923 4, T1:58¾	**GUY AXWORTHY**	Axworthy Lillian Wilkes
				Queenly McKinney	McKinney Princess Royal
			Guesswork, 1916 p, 2:02¼	**PETER THE GREAT**	Pilot Medium Santos
				Elsie Leyburn	Expedition Skilful

Albert Albert

Albert Albert has been a very consistent horse both as a racehorse and as a stallion. He probably has not gotten as much respect as he deserves in both areas. On the track, Albert Albert was an excellent colt at two and then had to compete against Matt's Scooter, Camtastic and Runnymede Lobell - all of whom won over $1,000,000 at three.

As a stallion, Albert Albert, a son of Abercrombie, has an excellent percentage of starters, 1:55 and 2:00 performers and a $2,000,000 winner. He certainly is capable of siring fast, stakes-winning colts and fillies. And yet he's still somewhat overlooked in comparison to sires like Abercrombie, No Nukes, Artsplace, Jate Lobell, Big Towner, Matt's Scooter, Dexter Nukes, Beach Towel and so forth. Yet, Albert Albert ranked fifteenth among pacing sires in the money-winning list for the 1996 season and thirteenth for the 1997 season.

Purchased as a yearling for $42,000 at the 1986 Harrisburg Yearling Sale, Albert Albert was owned and raced by Proudfoot Farms of Michigan. Yonkers Raceway president Timothy Rooney, of New York, bred the colt.

Albert Albert was a world champion at two, winning 10 of his 18 starts and earning $591,999. He was second to Camtastic for divisional honors in 1987 since Camtastic won 13 of 14 starts and earned $7,000 more than Albert Albert. Trained and driven by Chris Boring, Albert Albert raced his first three starts at Michigan's Hazel Park and was second and third in baby races and then second in his first parimutuel race. The colt then won his next three starts at the same track - the fastest in 1:59.3 after coming from seventh at the half - before beginning his stakes schedule.

Albert Albert made his stakes debut on July 18th as a 15-1 longshot in the Hanover Colt S. at Freestate Raceway in Maryland. He finished a good third and was timed in 1:57.1. The following week he was third in the Potomac S. and then headed for The Meadowlands to race against the nation's best colts in the rich Woodrow Wilson S. Albert Albert was a 13-1 longshot in his Wilson Elimination, but even though leaving from the second tier in post 11, the colt had the lead at the half and carried it into the stretch before yielding to Camtastic in 1:55. The 1987 Woodrow Wilson S. had a purse of $1,422,500 and Albert Albert got a large piece of it, $170,700 to be exact, with his impressive third place finish at odds of 36-1. This was in spite of the fact that he had no luck in the race right from the draw for post positions. Albert Albert left from post 12 in the second tier, was seventh and three-wide looking for racing room at the three-quarters and around the final turn, and yet was still able to get up for third behind the winning Even Odds and Prince Royce, although he was four lengths behind the winner.

The colt had proven he belonged with the best and he began a seven-race winning streak which would only end in his last race of the season. Leaving The Meadowlands for Indianapolis, Albert Albert won his first heat of the Fox S. in 1:54.2 and the Final in 1:52.4, coming from well off the pace during the stretch drive and equalling Nihilator's world record for two-year-olds. A week later at the Louisville Downs half-mile track in Kentucky, Albert Albert put together another great two-heat performance in winning the Kentucky Pacing Derby with heats of 1:55.1 and 1:55.3 - both coming from off the pace again - and setting a world record for two-heats on a half-mile track. It was then on to Delaware, Ohio, for the Standardbred S., of which he won both heats. Albert Albert's final start of the year was in the International Stallion S. at Lexington in which he won the first heat in 1:53.3, but tired in the second and was out of the money. That defeat stopped his seven-race winning streak and ended his season.

For the three-year-old season, Robert Tucker's Stonegate Farm, of New Jersey, became a part-owner of Albert Albert with Proudfoot Farms. The colt was again trained and driven by Chris Boring. He won his first start of the year in a Kentucky Sires S. at Lexington in late May in 1:55. Then, in preparation for the rich North America Cup at Greenwood Raceway in Canada, Albert Albert raced in a three-year-old Open event, finishing third to Camtastic. A week later, the colt survived a parked out trip to finish second in the North America Cup Elimination. However, in the $1,043,000 Final, Albert Albert left from post six and suffered traffic problems throughout the race, never

Race Record Highlights

At 2
- **1st** Kentucky Pacing Derby Final and Elimination
  Fox S. Final and Elimination
  heat of International Stallion S.
  Ohio Standardbred S. Final
- **2nd** Woodrow Wilson Elimination
- **3rd** Woodrow Wilson Final
  Potomac S.

At 3
- **1st** Slutsky Memorial
  Oliver Wendell Holmes S.
  heat of Little Brown Jug
  heat of Horseman Futurity
  Adios S. Elimination
  Kentucky Sires S.
- **2nd** North America Cup Elimination
  Meadowlands Pace Elimination
  American-National S.
  Tattersalls S. Final
- **3rd** Jug Preview
  Bluegrass S.
  Tattersalls S. Elimination

Honors
Set world record for two-year-olds on half-mile track
Set two-heat world record for two-year-olds on half-mile track
Equalled world record for two-year-olds in a race on a mile track

Albert Albert

Photo by Monica Thors
Courtesy of The Horseman and Fair World

Race Record

Year	Age	Starts	Wins	2nd	3rd	Earnings	Record
1987	2	18	10	3	4	$ 591,599	p,2,1:52.4
1988	3	22	9	5	4	645,471	p,3,1:52.1
		40	19	8	8	$1,237,070	p,3,1:52.1

getting into the hunt and finishing seventh, but only two and one-half lengths from the winning Runnymede Lobell.

After another second at The Meadowlands, Albert Albert rebounded to win an Elimination and the $142,250 Final of the Oliver Wendell Holmes S. He then won an Adios S. Elimination at The Meadows, but was fifth in the Final to Camtastic. The colt came back again to win a heat of the Horseman Futurity at Indianapolis in 1:52.1, which was his lifetime record. In the Little Brown Jug, Albert Albert uncharacteristically went for the early lead in his Elimination which he gained at the quarter in :26.2 and held on for a 1:53.4 win. It was a gutsy performance. But the final heat of the Jug was another story. Boring wanted to take Albert Albert to the front again, but ultimate winner B.J. Scoot would have none of it and parked out Albert Albert first over in an unbelievable half in :53.4. After that brutal first half, Albert Albert eventually finished sixth.

In the Tattersalls Pace, Albert Albert again met up with Camtastic and finished third in the first heat. In the next heat, Albert Albert had a good trip and got to within a neck of his archrival at the wire; both were timed in 1:51.1. At Monticello Raceway two weeks later, Albert Albert scored a big victory in the $329,000 Slutsky Memorial, going wire-to-wire in 1:55.2 to defeat Matt's Scooter by a neck with Camtastic finishing only fifth. Driver Chris Boring said after the race, "I had the rail and wanted to take Albert Albert as far and as fast as we could go today." The owners had put up a $15,000 supplementary payment to get Albert Albert into this race and it paid off handsomely.

Albert Albert closed his racing days with a second place finish in the $384,500 American-National S. His career ended with 19 wins from his 40 starts and earnings of $1,237,070. In addition, he was a world champion and a very consistent performer, finishing first, second or third on 35 occasions against the best of his division for two years.

Sire Line

An important factor when Albert Albert went to stud at Stonegate Farm in 1989 was that he was the fastest son of Abercrombie as a two-year-old. Abercrombie had begun to make waves as a sire and breeders took note of Albert Albert's early speed, record and earnings.

Abercrombie is now regarded as the sport's premier active pacing sire and, as a result, the Adios male line is thriving again. And Albert Albert has plenty of Adios blood flowing through his veins. You can read more about Abercrombie in his own chapter; here it should be mentioned that Albert Albert is bred 4x5x4 to Adios through that great stallion's sons Henry T. Adios, Dancer Hanover and Bret Hanover.

Maternal Line

Albert Albert is another product of the very prolific Abercrombie/Albatross cross. Abercrombie's two best performers, Artsplace p,4,1:49.2 ($3,085,083) and Life Sign p,3,1:50.3 ($1,912,454) are also from Albatross mares. Albert Albert's dam, Lismore p,2,1:59.4f; 3,T1:57.2 ($150,309), was a good filly and a stakes winner at two and three. Lismore also has a lot more going for her from a pedigree standpoint since she is a full sister to world champion B.G.'s Bunny p,3,1:54 ($215,192) who has made a strong mark as a broodmare sire.

Lismore has been a world-class producer with 10 in 2:00 from her 13 foals of racing age to this point. But there's more - six of these performers are in 1:55 and five are sub-1:53. From an earnings standpoint, Lismore has produced seven $100,000 winners and four $500,000 winners. She has to be one of the greatest producing broodmares of any era.

Clicking especially well with Abercrombie, Lismore has given Albert Albert full brothers and sisters such as Curragh p,T1:51.4 ($509,740), Lahar p,1:50.3 ($413,221), Lisheen p,3,1:52.3 ($518,405) and Lisryan p,1:52 ($507,621). Several of Lismore's daughters are now producers and are the dams of such performers as Nude Beach p,3,1:52.2 and Redskin Rocky p,1:54.

Albert Albert's grandam is the Bret Hanover mare Bret's Romance p,3,2:04.3; 4,2:02f ($13,967) who has also been an outstanding broodmare with three in 1:55 and seven in 1:59. In addition to B.G.'s

Bunny, she is the dam of Refreshing Touch p,3,1:54.1 ($113,800) and Super Bradshaw p,4,1:54.3.

The name of the maternal family here is Betty Kellar, or Dora; but this branch, in modern times, has descended from the Bert Abbe mare Miss Reed, with the Bret's Romance branch being the strongest.

Progeny of Note

Through five full crops of racing age, Albert Albert has sired the winners of over $21,000,000, with two in 1:50, 86 in 1:55, 245 in 2:00 and 60 $100,000 winners. Not a bad performance for any sire.

Pacific Rocket p,2,1:53.3; 3,1:52.4; 4,1:50 ($2,333,401) is the best offspring by Albert Albert and a world-class performer on the track. He was one very tough competitor and never gave up. You can read more about Pacific Rocket in his own chapter since he is now at stud in Canada and very well received.

Albert Albert has also had his share of good fillies, headed by Ooh's N Aah's p,1:52 ($779,379), Petite Pan p,4,1:54.2h ($380,932), Roses For Emma p,1:52 ($420,511), One If By Pan p,3,1:53.3 ($449,955), Smarty Britches p,4,1:53.4 ($226,733), Slotting Allowance p,3,1:53, Grandpa's Ashley p,3,1:54.4 ($171,916), Fancy Boots p,4,1:53.1f ($125,416) and Fedorov p,3,1:53.3 ($119,042).

Some of Albert Albert's top colt performers, in addition to Pacific Rocket, are Pacific Sunshine p,1:51.3 ($387,229), Proud Albert p,1:50.2z-'98 ($146,396), Bad Bert p,1:50.4-'98 ($392,626), Little Steven p,1:49.4-'98 ($292,995), Ragtime Band p,3,1:53f ($303,560), Cafe Racer p,1:52.2 ($312,659), Brod p,4,1:51.4 ($306,916), Kazbek p,1:51.2 ($233,328), Stock Boy p,4,1:53.4f ($411,217), Big Elbert p,4,1:51.4 ($213,036), Pacific Missile p,1:51.3-'98 ($254,990), Raleigh Fingers p,4,1:51.2 ($276,114), Eicarl's Apache p,4,1:51.3 ($123,930), Some Albert p,1:51.2 ($191,329) and dozens of others.

Analysis

Albert Albert has worked well with a large variety of broodmare sires to produce his best offspring in terms of earnings and speed. Pacific Rocket, Albert Albert's fastest and richest offspring, and his full brother Pacific Missile are the only top performers from a Direct Scooter mare although with Albert Albert and Direct Scooter both standing at stud in New Jersey more might have been expected. But from his 40 fastest and 36 richest performers, the Direct Scooter daughter Flat Foot Fluzy is the only one, thus far, to produce top class Albert Albert offspring.

However, there is another broodmare sire who seems to be having outstanding success when his daughters produce foals by Albert Albert. That sire is the Meadow Skipper son Landslide, whose daughters have produced five of the 28 richest Albert Albert offspring and seven of the 33 fastest. Another factor is the presence of Race Time, or a close Race Time relative, in the pedigrees of these Landslide mares.

For example, Little Steven p,1:49.4-'98 ($292,995) is from a Landslide mare whose dam is by Storm Damage - a half-brother to Race Time. Slotting Allowance p,3,1:53 and Angeliou p,4,1:55.1h, both mares, are from Landslide mares who are full sisters and whose dam is by Race Time. Macadream p,1:52.3f is from a Landslide mare whose grandam is by Race Time. Fancy Boots p,4,1:53.1f is from a Landslide mare whose dam is by Steady Star and whose second dam is a full sister to Race Time. As you can see, there is a "nick" at work here with Landslide and Race Time and his relatives. This may be worth noting if you own a Landslide mare.

There are still other horses with close Race Time relative connections, but without the Landslide factor. Some Albert p,4,1:51.2 is from a Race Time mare and Eicarl's Apache p,4,1:51.3 is from a Steady Star mare whose second dam is a full sister to Race Time.

In terms of gender, only one of Albert Albert's 20 fastest horses are female. But his daughters shine in terms of earnings as three of his four richest performers, with over $350,000, are female. Another sire who seems to be "nicking" well with Albert Albert is Big Towner since his daughters have produced two of this stallion's six richest offspring.

Looking at the crosses at work in some of Albert Albert's best horses, we find that Pacific Rocket's closest common cross is 4x4 to Bret Hanover. The mare Ooh's 'N Aah's p,1:52 is 4x2 to Bret Hanover and 4x3 to Meadow Skipper. Petite Pan p,4,1:54.2h ($380,932) is also linebred to

Meadow Skipper. The next richest, Roses For Emma p,1:52, has no common crosses in her first four generations.

Albert Albert's fifth fastest record horse is Elegant Albert p,3,1:51, who is linebred 4x3 to Meadow Skipper and 4x4 to Bret Hanover.

Don't forget that Albert Albert has a dam who is a product of the great Albatross on a Bret Hanover mare cross which has produced so many champions over the years. As a result, you will see plenty of Albert Albert offspring with multiple crosses to those two great broodmare sires.

One very interesting cross is that in the pedigree of Pacific Sunshine p,1:51.3 and it may help explain the Albert Albert successes with Landslide mares. Albert Albert's grandsire is Silent Majority, who is by Henry T. Adios from the Tar Heel mare Hobby Horse Tar. Landslide is by Meadow Skipper from the same Hobby Horse Tar and the two stallions are half-brothers. Therefore, any foal by Albert Albert from a Landslide mare carries a 3x2 relationship to those half-brothers. This is a close cross, but one which the famous Italian breeder Federico Tesio used with great success with Thoroughbreds. I have also seen this type of breeding used very successfully with trotters. Pacific Sunshine, by the way, is also linebred 4x3 to Meadow Skipper.

I mentioned breeding back to the Albatross blood which already appears in Albert Albert's pedigree through his dam. One example is the closely inbred 3x2 cross to Albatross for the full brothers Cafe Racer p,1:52.2 ($312,659) and Brod p,4,1:51.4 ($306,916), and their full sister Fedorov p,3,1:53.3, who are all from the Albatross mare Zanzara. Albert Albert is, obviously, a great cross for this mare.

Some other successful examples of the 3x3 cross to Albatross are Bad Bert p,1:50.4-'98 ($392,626), Stock Boy p,4,1:53.4f ($411,217), Some Albert, mentioned above, and the brother and sister Smarty Britches p,4,1:53.4 ($226,733) and Pacific Devil p,4,1:53.3 ($196,590).

In closing this chapter, I want to note that Albert Albert seems to be a very versatile sire with respect to working with mares of varied pedigrees and producing foals with outcrosses, linebreeding and inbreeding. Everything seems to work, although I have pointed out certain "nicks" which work better than others.

Albert Albert was moved from Stonegate Farm in New Jersey to Glengate Farm in Ontario, Canada, for the 1997 breeding season and received a high-quality book of broodmares. With his future foals being eligible for nomination to the rich Ontario Sires S. program, Albert Albert's first crop of foals in Canada should be well-received at the sales.

Leading Progeny by Albert Albert

Fastest
Little Steven, h, p,1:49.4-'98 $292,995
Pacific Rocket, h, p,4,1:50 $2,333,401
Proud Albert, h, p,1:50.2z-'98 $146,396
Bad Bert, h, p,1:50.4-'98 $392,626
Albert T, h, p,4,1:51z-'98 $45,002
Elegant Albert, h, p,3,1:51 $83,326
Raleigh Fingers, h, p,4,1:51.2 $235,334
Kazbek, g, p,1:51.2 $233,328
Some Albert, h, p,1:51.2 $161,521
Pacific Sunshine, g, p,1:51.3 $387,229

Richest
Pacific Rocket, h, p,4,1:50 $2,333,401
Ooh's 'N Aah's, m, p,1:52 $648,974
One If By Pan, m, p,3,1:53.3 $324,530
Roses for Emma, m, p,1:52 $420,511
Stock Boy, h, p,4,1:53.4f $357,572
Bad Bert, h, p,1:50.4-'98 $392,626
Pacific Sunshine, g, p,1:51.3 $387,229
Petite Pan, m, p,4,1:54.2h $380,932
El Said, h, p,1:52.2f-'98 $364,074
Cafe Racer, g, p,1:52.2 $312,659

Albert Albert, Brown Horse, 15.3 Hands, 1985
p, 2, 1:52.4; 3, 1:52.1 ($1,237,070)

Sire/Dam	2nd Gen	3rd Gen	4th Gen	5th Gen
Abercrombie, 1975 p, 4, 1:53 $984,391	Silent Majority, 1969 p, 3, 1:56.3 $362,369	Henry T. Adios, 1958 p, 6, 1:57 $706,833	**ADIOS**, 1940 p, T1:57½ $33,329	**HAL DALE** — **ABBEDALE** / Margaret Hal Adioo Volo — Adioo Guy / Sigrid Volo
			Greer Hanover, 1948 p, 3, 2:06.2h $6,482	**NIBBLE HANOVER** — Calumet Chuck / Justissima Veda Hanover — **BILLY DIRECT** / **VIVIAN HANOVER**
		Hobby Horse Tar, 1964	**TAR HEEL**, 1948 p, 4, T1:57 $119,148	**BILLY DIRECT** — Napoleon Direct / Gay Forbes Leta Long — **VOLOMITE** / Rosette
			Wilellen, 1955 p, 3, 2:04.2h $16,994	Wilmington — **BERT ABBE** / Miss Saginaw Willola — Willglow / Romola
	Bergdorf, 1967 p, 4, 2:03.3 $6,035	Duane Hanover, 1952 p, 4, 1:58 $280,288	**KNIGHT DREAM**, 1945 p, 3, T1:59 $76,973	**NIBBLE HANOVER** — Calumet Chuck / Justissima Lydia Knight — Peter The Brewer / Guy Rosa
			Dorsh Hanover, 1932 4, 2:15½h	Dillon Axworthy — Axworthy / Adioo Dillon Great Medium — Peter The Great / Dorsch Medium
		Princess Best, 1959 p, 4, 2:07f	The Widower, 1935 p, 3, T1:59½ $19,983	**ABBEDALE** — **THE ABBE** / Daisydale D. Widow Grattan — Grattan Royal / I'm A Widow
			Princess Chief, 1945 p, 2:07h $9,506	Chief Abbedale — **ABBEDALE** / Marion Candler The Gay Princess — Crispin / Princess Duffy
Lismore, 1976 p, 3, T1:57.2 $150,309	Albatross, 1968 p, 4, 1:54.3f $1,201,470	Meadow Skipper, 1960 p, 3, 1:55.1 $428,057	Dale Frost, 1951 p, 1:58 $204,117	**HAL DALE** — **ABBEDALE** / Margaret Hal Galloway — Raider / Bethel
			Countess Vivian, 1950 p, 3, 1:59 $43,262	King's Counsel — **VOLOMITE** / Margaret Spangler Filly Direct — **BILLY DIRECT** / Calumet Edna
		Voodoo Hanover, 1964	Dancer Hanover, 1957 p, 4, T1:56.4 $87,746	**ADIOS** — **HAL DALE** / Adioo Volo The Old Maid — Guy Abbey / Spinster
			Vibrant Hanover, 1960	**TAR HEEL** — **BILLY DIRECT** / Leta Long **VIVIAN HANOVER** — Guy McKinney / Guesswork
	Brets Romance, 1968 p, 4, 2:02f $13,967	Bret Hanover, 1962 p, 4, T1:53.3 $922,616	**ADIOS**, 1940 p, T1:57½ $33,329	**HAL DALE** — **ABBEDALE** / Margaret Hal Adioo Volo — Adioo Guy / Sigrid Volo
			Brenna Hanover, 1956 p, 3, T2:01 $21,946	**TAR HEEL** — **BILLY DIRECT** / Leta Long Beryl Hanover — **NIBBLE HANOVER** / Laura Hanover
		Knight's Embassy, 1951	**KNIGHT DREAM**, 1945 p, 3, T1:59 $76,973	**NIBBLE HANOVER** — Calumet Chuck / Justissima Lydia Knight — Peter The Brewer / Guy Rosa
			Miss Reed, 1942 p, 4, 2:13h $1,289	**BERT ABBE** — **THE ABBE** / Miss Ella H. Four D McKinney — Wallace McKinney / Misty Maiden

Artsplace

Mention the name Artsplace around folks in the harness racing business and you will get a positive reaction. Many will vividly recall his incredible 1:51.1 mile in the Breeders Crown when he was two, his undefeated season at four, or perhaps his slick-gaited pacing action. He was a memorable horse on the racetrack, and the early indication, from the results of his first three crops of foals to race, is that he may become just as memorable as a sire.

Artsplace was bred by and owned during his racing career by George Segal and Brian Monieson of Chicago, Illinois. The colt was named for an art gallery in Lexington, Kentucky. Segal, who was inducted into the harness racing Hall of Fame in 1997, and Monieson, have owned top horses over the years in partnership and Segal alone through his Brittany Farms, one of the industry leaders. But Artsplace is something very special.

As with most of the Segal-Monieson horses, Artsplace was trained by Hall of Famer Gene Riegle. He broke easily as a yearling. "He was a very nonchalant, easy colt to do anything with. Nothing ever bothered him", said Riegle. Driver John Campbell agrees, "He's not sulky or balky. He takes life very easily and he's very easy on himself. He'll do whatever you want him to do."

At two, Artsplace began his career with a win in a Scioto Downs baby race on June 12th, 1990, in 2:01 for driver Bruce Riegle, Gene's son. He was fifth at the half and then came home in :58.1 to score a half-length win. He then won another baby race at the same track two weeks later for Jeff Fout in 2:00.1. Artsplace was then sent to The Meadowlands and won a qualifier in 1:59.3 before entering his first stakes race a week later at Vernon Downs.

Artsplace won his next three races, including the Hanover-Hempt in 1:57.3, a Scioto Downs Late Closer in 1:58.4 and the Arden Downs S. in an eased up 1:55.3 by seven lengths. At this point, heading into the Fox S. at Indianapolis in late August, he was undefeated in five starts. His earnings were only $20,000, but the rich events loomed ahead and Artsplace was not being overused too early. He tasted defeat for the first time in the initial heat of the Fox S. in which he drew post 10 in the second tier. The colt was parked out all the way and was still only seventh and almost five lengths behind in the stretch. However, in a great performance, he found room and was able to finish second, only a three-quarters of a length behind Deal Direct, who set a world record 1:51.4 mile for two-year-old colts.

A week later in the Champlain S. at Mohawk, Deal Direct once again defeated Artsplace as he was parked out first over all the way from post seven and just lost by a half-length in his first drive for John Campbell, who became his regular chauffeur. Artsplace won the Nassagaweya S. a week later, going wire-to-wire in 1:55, and followed that with another win in the Metro S. Elimination in 1:54.3 after surviving a tough parked out trip and getting up in the last strides to win by a neck.

The rich $797,400 Metro S. Final on September 22nd became Artplace's biggest payday of the year. His luck changed and he drew the rail, as he would for three of his last six starts of the year. Campbell took no chances and gunned Artsplace right to the lead in a fast :26.4 first quarter. He was able to back it down to a :57 half and had plenty left to score a three-length win over Stand And Deliver and Three Wizzards. With the Presidential S., the Governor's Cup and the Breeders Crown all coming up in a five-week period from late October through late November, Riegle gave Artsplace some time off.

The colt did not return until a 1:55.3 qualifying race win on October 20th at Garden State Park. Artsplace then suffered two of his four seasonal losses to Die Laughing with a second place finish in the Presidential S. Elimination and a fourth in the Final. That Final, however, must have toughened him up. He left from post eight, was parked out first over all the way and lost by less than two lengths to Die Laughing.

Again drawing post eight in the Governor's Cup Elimination at Garden State Park, Campbell was still eighth with Artsplace at the half, but powered around the field through the last turn and stretch to win going away. The following week, in the $655,600 Governor's Cup Final, Artsplace was second choice to Die Laughing but turned in one of his best miles, coming from behind in the stretch to win by a half-length over his tough rival.

Artsplace

Photo by Monica Thors

Race Record Highlights

At 2
- **1st** Metro S. Final and Elimination
  Governor's Cup Final and Elimination
  Breeders Crown
  Nassagaweya S.
  Hanover-Hempt S.
  Arden Downs S.
  Scioto Downs Late Closer
- **2nd** Champlain S.
  heat of Fox S.
  Presidential S. Elimination

At 3
- **1st** American-National S.
  Terrapin S.
  James Dancer Memorial Final and Elimination
  Gaines Memorial Final and Elimination

At 3 (continued)
  Tompkins-Geers S.
  Meadowlands Pace Elimination
  Adios S. Elimination
  Kentucky Sires S.
- **2nd** Meadowlands Pace Final

At 4
- **1st** Breeders Crown
  Molson Series Final and two legs
  American-National S.
  Stewart Fraser Memorial
  Driscoll Series Final and leg
  Nicole Hudock Memorial
  Two legs of U.S. Pacing Championship
  Des Smith P.
  Senior Jug P.

Honors

Set world record for two-year-olds on five-eighth mile track
Set world record for two-year-olds over any size track
Voted Two-Year-Old Pacer of the Year
Voted Horse of the Year as a four-year-old
Equalled world record for three-year-olds on five-eighth mile track
Set world records for four-year-olds on mile and half-mile tracks
Set all-age world race record on mile track

Race Record

Year	Age	Starts	Wins	2nd	3rd	Earnings	Record
1990	2	15	11	3	0	$1,180,271	p,2,1:51.1f
1991	3	18	10	4	1	972,487	p,3,1:50.4f
1992	4	16	16	0	0	932,325	p,4,1:49.2
		49	37	7	1	$3,085,083	p,4,1:49.2

Artsplace

If there were ever any doubts about who was the best two-year-old in 1990, they were put to rest by Artsplace in the $605,870 Breeders Crown on a very windy night at Pompano Park. He turned in one of the most incredible performances in Standardbred history. Die Laughing was the 3-5 favorite with Artsplace second choice at 9-5. However, Artsplace drew post four with Die Laughing right outside in post five. Campbell was not taking any chances and rocketed out of the gate with Artsplace, parking out Die Laughing to the first quarter in an astounding :26.2. Tooter Scooter was second on the rail, leaving no hole for Die Laughing to tuck in. Artsplace flashed past the half in :53.2 with Die Laughing third on the outside and three lengths behind. Campbell stole a breather in the :29.3 third quarter when no one came on the outside and Die Laughing began to fall back. In the final turn and into the stretch it was all Artsplace as he opened up a huge eight-length lead. The Abercrombie colt paced home in :28.1 to win by eight lengths in an electrifying 1:51.1 over Pompano Park's five-eighth mile track.

This was the fastest mile ever by a two-year-old over any size track. It was faster than Deal Direct's colt record of 1:51.4 and Miss Easy's filly record of 1:51.2, which were both set over faster mile tracks. And, it was over two seconds faster than any two-year-old had ever gone on a five-eighth mile track. This was, indeed, a landmark performance and one that has still not been equalled as this is written over seven years later. Artsplace's mile was even faster than the 1:51.2 track record set a month before by the three-year-old Beach Towel in his Breeders Crown win.

Winning driver John Campbell said after the race, "When I saw the half-time flash (:53.3) I smiled because he felt like a million bucks." Campbell added, "This is no ordinary colt. I just turned him loose and away he went. He could have gone more."

The big win did several things for Artsplace. It made him a world champion, guaranteed the divisional championship and raised his earnings to $1,180,271 for the season - with over $1,000,000 coming from his final six starts of the year. The big win also helped trainer Gene Riegle win the 1990 Glen Garnsey Trainer of the Year award.

At three, many observers expected Artsplace to rewrite the harness racing record books. He easily won his first five starts of the year, including a Kentucky Sires S., $150,948 Terrapin S., Tompkins-Geers S., $345,200 American-National S. and a Meadowlands Pace Elimination in 1:50.4. However, while he was beginning to look invincible, two other three-year-old colts were also making a big impact in this tough division: Precious Bunny and Artsplace's old nemesis, Die Laughing.

Artsplace was the 2-5 favorite in the $1,000,000 Meadowlands Pace Final, with Precious Bunny second choice followed by Die Laughing. Artsplace and Campbell left from post four and Easy Goer took off the fastest from post seven to gain the lead at the :26.4 quarter. Start The Fire was second on the rail, and Artsplace was third on the outside with Precious Bunny following his cover. Artsplace got to the front and then Precious Bunny moved up to take over the lead at the half in :54.2. That colt hit the three-quarters in 1:21.4 and took a one and one-half length lead into the stretch with Storming Jessie second on the outside and Artsplace third. Precious Bunny prevailed that night, pacing home in :28 to win in 1:49.4 by two lengths over Artsplace and Stormin Jesse.

Two weeks later, Artsplace came back to win the Gaines Memorial Elimination and Final, followed by another victory in an Adios S. Elimination in which he defeated Precious Bunny by a neck. At this point, Artsplace had won eight of his nine starts and had avenged his defeat by Precious Bunny. In the Adios Final, though, Precious Bunny got to the lead first with Artsplace racing third at the half. He pulled out and challenged at the three-quarters, around the turn and into the stretch, but Precious Bunny went on to win in 1:50.4 with Artsplace fading to fourth.

The rich $603,500 Prix d'Ete was a week later at Blue Bonnets and since Precious Bunny was not in the race, Artsplace was the favorite. But the race did not go as expected. Driver Richie Silverman had Dic Laughing full of pace that day and he took the early lead from post four and was never headed. Artsplace and Campbell left from post six and were parked out second at the quarter and could never find a hole. Die Laughing kept Artsplace outside the entire mile and won in 1:51.3, with Artsplace losing ground in the stretch and finishing third.

Riegle gave the colt a week off and he came back fresher to win the James Dancer Memorial at Freehold. He was parked out all the way in the Elimination and then went wire-to-wire in the Final. The Messenger S. was next at Rosecroft but poor luck in post position draws continued to plague Artsplace as he drew post nine. He was parked out all the way again, getting as close as third at the three-quarters, but then finished ninth for the worst finish of his career. Die Laughing was the victor.

After a two-week vacation, Artsplace was second in a heat of the Tattersalls S. at The Red Mile and second again a week later over the same track in the Bluegrass S. A week after that, he had another game effort against Precious Bunny in the Cleveland Classic at Northfield. He drew post nine again, was parked out the final three-quarters, and still battled Precious Bunny down the stretch, missing by only a head and finishing second. The final race of the year for Artsplace was the $357,406 Breeders Crown at Pompano Park in which he finished fifth.

So, in a season which had started so brightly with a string of victories, Artsplace had only three seconds among his last five starts, while Precious Bunny had gone on to win 20 of his 25 starts and take Horse of the Year honors. But even though Artsplace had a disappointing year in terms of not meeting the high expectations, his $972,487 in earnings placed him third behind Precious Bunny and Die Laughing and he won 10 of his 18 starts. But his owners, trainer and driver knew he was a better colt than his results suggested, and that he had been plagued by some bad luck, bad posts and a lingering foot problem. Artsplace was to come back at four, winning total vindication and establishing himself as one of the sport's all-time greats.

At four, in his undefeated season, Artsplace was trained by top Canadian conditioner Bob McIntosh. Only two horses got within a length of Artsplace at the finish that year - Dorunrun Bluegrass, whom Artsplace got up in time to defeat by a neck and Camluck, who closed to within a half-length during a :26.4 final quarter at Delaware, Ohio. In 13 of his 16 wins, Artsplace was already in front by the half. In his 1:49.2 mile at The Meadowlands, Artsplace left from post seven and was fourth at the quarter. Then driver Catello Manzi took him three-wide at the half to sweep to the lead during a :27.4 third quarter. He came home in :27.2 to win by three lengths over Dorunrun Bluegrass and Cambest. Artsplace had paced the fastest race mile in the long history of the sport.

During this spectacular season, John Campbell drove Artsplace nine times, Bill O'Donnell three times, Bill Gale twice, Dave Magee once and Cat Manzi once, in his fastest mile. Artsplace paced final quarters in :26.4 on both half-mile and mile tracks and twice paced opening quarters in :27. He won on a half-mile track in 1:52.1 at Yonkers and five-eighth mile track in 1:51.3 at Greenwood.

Artsplace was honored as the 1992 Horse of the Year. His wins included the Breeders Crown, Molson Series Final, American-National S. and a host of other FFA and Invitational events. He had nothing left to prove and retired as the second leading money-winning pacer of all time with earnings over $3,000,000.

Sire Line
The ultimate representative of the Abercrombie line, Artsplace is poised to successfully carry on for his sire, and for the Adios male line in general. As is pointed out in the chapter about Abercrombie, his line and those from Cam Fella and No Nukes should be vying for pacing stallion honors for the foreseeable future.

Maternal Line
The dam of Artsplace is the Albatross mare, Miss Elvira. George Segal said, in a *Hoof Beats* article, "Miss Elvira was a great mare, but she had an injury, and we always talked about her producing a champion." Miss Elvira was purchased at the 1983 Kentucky Standardbred Select Yearling Sale by Segal and Monieson for $220,000. Trainer Gene Riegle felt she was an outstanding horse and worth the money. Segal added, "In addition to that, the family had produced a lot of speed, and we felt that this would be our chance for a very good racehorse and a very good broodmare. And I love Albatross."

Gene Riegle trained the high-priced filly. He commented, "Miss Elvira was a slightly bigger mare than Three Diamonds (a world champion and dam of Life Sign), and we thought maybe she had just as much class. Her personality was great, and we thought she was as good-gaited as Three Diamonds." But fate intervened and Miss Elvira broke a bone in one of her early starts and never raced again. She had won a baby race in 2:05.4 and an Early Closer in 2:00.1 in her only two starts, both at Scioto Downs, and earned $1,800.

To date, Miss Elvira has produced seven winners from eight foals of racing age, including four sub-1:55 performers. Artsplace is, obviously, her best and he has a full brother named Chill Factor with a record of 1:52.4 at three. By Cam Fella, Miss Elvira has produced Stand Together p,3,1:53 and, by Jate Lobell, Key Prospect p,3,1:54.2. However, none of the Artsplace brothers or sisters have earned more than $66,000. Thus far, Miss Elvira has produced seven colts and only one filly of racing age.

The grandam of Artsplace is the Columbia George mare Ladalia Hanover p,2,2:01.4f; 3,Q2:00.1, who won over $72,000 and set a track record at Mohawk for two-year-old fillies. At three, she made only four starts and ended her racing career. Ladalia Hanover has produced four sub-1:57 performers from her ten foals, including Instant Rebate p,3,1:54.2f ($412,405) (by Niatross) and Merger's Cousin p,4,1:54.2 ($285,634) (by Albatross). Her Albatross daughter Silky's Gal p,3,T1:56, a full sister to Artsplace's dam Miss Elvira, is the dam of the outstanding performer Silky Stallone p,3,1:51.3 ($785,823) (by No Nukes) and her Merger (son of Albatross) daughter Ladalia's Girl p,3,2:01.1f is the dam of Duncan MacLeod p,3,1:51.4 ($273,369) (by Cole Muffler). Ladalia's Girl has an interesting pedigree since she is bred 3x2 to her second dam, Lady Kacne, who is also the second dam of her sire.

Lady Kacne p,3,2:03.4f (by Duane Hanover) is the third dam of Artsplace. She had 18 foals and her top performers were Landy Hanover p,3,1:53.1 (by Albatross) and Lemoyne Hanover p,4,1:54.3f ($343,218) (by Tyler B). The big star among Lady Kacne's immediate relatives was Merger p,2,1:53.4; 3,1:53 ($444,668), who set a world record for two-year-olds in 1981 and then won the Little Brown Jug at three. However, he was not successful as a stallion.

Artsplace's maternal family is that of Miss Bertha Dillon, one of the all-time best and a great producing family for many decades.

Progeny of Note

As this book is written, Artsplace has had two full crops to the races and he is already considered the leading pacing sire in North America. During the 1997 racing season, Artsplace's sons and daughters earned $8,917,716 to place him at the top of the all-age list of Standardbred sires. And, keep in mind that this was accomplished from just two crops of racing age and 213 starters. Several other sires had many more crops racing and some had over 400 starters. This is an incredible accomplishment for a young sire. Artsplace's sire, Abercrombie, was second on this list with earnings of $7,648,318 and with 378 starters.

The first crop of Artsplace yearlings to sell was in 1995 and they averaged $37,182. The second crop averaged slightly less at $34,558. However, in the fall of 1997, Artsplace yearlings were the hot numbers at the various sales and averaged $56,965 with 11 selling for $100,000 or more. Artsplace was by far the leading pacing sire in terms of average with Cam Fella next at $31,329 and Abercrombie at $31,295. In the eyes of breeders, owners and trainers, the pacing stallion torch has clearly been passed to Artsplace.

The first crop of Artsplace, racing in 1996, featured great racing fillies. His daughter Michelle's Jackpot p,2,1:54.4f ($695,439) (B.G.'s Bunny dam) was voted Two-Year-Old Pacing Filly of the Year, won the $452,600 Three Diamonds Final and was second in the Breeders Crown Final. The three richest performers of Artsplace were fillies as were eight of his ten highest money winners. Several of the top fillies went on to glory as three-year-olds, including Divisional Champion Stienam's Place p,3,1:50.4 ($1,402,301) (Falcon Almahurst dam) who won the $665,400 Sweetheart P. Final at two and the Breeders Crown, Mistletoe Shalee S. and Jugette at three. In addition, she set a world record for three-year-old fillies.

Other top Artsplace fillies in 1997 were Art In The Park p,3,1:52 ($533,784) (No Nukes dam), Artistic Pleasure p,3,1:52.4 ($401,170) (Ralph Hanover dam), Natchitoches p,2,1:54 ($300,970) (Big Towner dam), Fanciful Hanover p,3,1:54.2h ($281,010) (Tyler B dam) and Cohiba Mary p,4,1:52.1 ($245,669) (Niatross dam). Another world champion Artsplace filly surfaced in the spring of 1998 in Galleria p,3,1:50.1-'98 ($132,887) (Sherman Almahurst dam) who set a world record for her age and gender. Yes, Artsplace is a great sire of fillies and, to date, 17 of his 26 leading money winners are female as are two of his three fastest performers. Not many stallions, if any, have figures like these for their daughters.

In the glamour division, that for three-year-old colts, Artsplace has also been dominant. Two of Artsplace's sons became millionaires in 1997 - Arturo p,3,1:51.2f ($1,298,491) (Pirate Skipper dam) and Dream Away p,3,1:50 ($1,058,861) (Forrest Skipper dam). Arturo won the $500,000 New Jersey Classic and Dream Away won the $1,000,000 Meadowlands Pace. Another son, Perfect Art p,3,1:51 ($576,983) (Nihilator dam), won the $500,000 Hoosier Cup at three and was second in the Woodrow Wilson at two. Arturo now stands at stud at Hanover Shoe Farm while Perfect Art has been sold to an Australian syndicate and may see stud duty in both hemispheres.

The 1997 two-year-old colts by Artsplace were a stellar group and headed by Breeders Crown winner Artiscape p,2,1:52.3 ($495,501) (On The Road Again dam). This colt is one of the best youngsters I have ever seen and has an incredible brush of speed along with much courage and grit - much like his world champion dam Delinquent Account p,1:51.4 ($1,038,997). The only problem with Artiscape is that he was not completely sound at two and, therefore, his three-year-old status will be in question. If he is sound, he has the ability to become a great colt. Another two-year-old star is Real Artist p,2,1:52 ($417,747) (Big Towner dam) who won the 1997 $765,750 Woodrow Wilson. He is quite a colt with a big future.

The list of Artsplace's stars goes on and on and I suspect it will continue to do so for many years to come. He is a very special kind of sire.

Analysis

In addition to his speed and tenacity, breeders hope Artsplace is able to pass on to his foals his great gait. Horsemen always seem to comment about the gait of a great horse, and Artsplace had plenty of admirers in that area. Bill O'Donnell, who was Nihilator's regular driver, was quoted in *Hoof Beats* (January, 1993) about Artsplace, "He's the greatest horse I've ever driven. His gait is so effortless. No sooner did he hit the ground than he was back up off the ground and going again. There's no wasted motion. He's so athletic." Trainer Bob McIntosh who had Artsplace at four said, "He has such great balance he almost could have raced without an overcheck, to tell the truth. He's just perfect-gaited, with great balance."

Regular driver John Campbell echoed the sentiments of O'Donnell and McIntosh when he commented in the same January, 1993 article, "He's the best pacer I've ever driven." Campbell continued, "He was just a professional racehorse - very easy to drive, very surefooted, You didn't have to worry about his gait or him making a break on you."

Looking at his pedigree, Artsplace is almost an outcross sire, by today's standards, in that his closest common crosses are 3x4 to Duane Hanover, 4x5 to Adios, Tar Heel, Knight Dream and The Widower and 5x5x6x5 to Hal Dale. Another interesting cross in his pedigree is the 5x4 to three-quarter sisters Veda Hanover (second dam of Henry T. Adios) and Vibrant Hanover (second dam of Albatross). As a result, he can be bred to a large number of broodmares who are daughters and granddaughters of today's popular stallions. Even breeding granddaughters of Albatross to Artsplace would result in a 3x3 cross to that stallion, who has been the most prolific broodmare sire of all time. There are some breeders who have professed a belief that the 3x3 cross to Albatross has not worked well, but I believe time will prove that inbreeding and linebreeding to Albatross is very effective and that there will be plenty of top horses with 3x3 crosses to Albatross through his granddaughters by B.G.'s Bunny, Niatross and Sonsam.

The managers of Artsplace's first season at stud were extremely selective in accepting mares to him and the results have paid off. As this is written, Artsplace has 28 $100,000 winners and I examined the dams of those performers. A total of 23 of the 28 in this category had dams with 2:00 records, including 9 in 1:55 and 3 sub-1:52 performers.

The dams of the three millionaires have records of 1:53.2, 1:56 and 1:53.1. In the speed category, the dams of the three fastest have records of 1:53.1, 1:52.4 and 1:53.2. So, there appears to be plenty of evidence that breeding top race mares to Artsplace pays great dividends. In addition, some top performers by Artsplace are from non-record mares and they are Park Place

Artsplace

p,3,1:51 ($576,971) (Most Happy Fella dam), Tallulah Belle p,3,1:54f ($204,468) (Nihilator dam) and Armbro Romance p,3,1:52-'98 ($107,280) (Cam Fella dam).

Mares bred to Artsplace were the cream of the crop from a performance and production standpoint and every breeder knows the resulting foals get 50% of their potential from the sire and 50% from the dam. It appears, at this early stage, that Artsplace is able to sire the best from the best.

He also sired good performers from daughters of sires not known as leading broodmare sires, such as Pirate Skipper, Ralph Hanover, Forrest Skipper, Jamuga, Sherman Almahurst, Coal Harbor and Distant Thunder. In each case, however, those dams had fast records. Nihilator daughters are prominent as the dams of two of Artsplace's five richest performers to date, and mares with No Nukes, Jate Lobell and B.G.'s Bunny blood are also faring well. Big Towner mares are also doing well with three of the 19 $200,000 winners and the second dam of another.

It also seems Artsplace likes the return of some of his own Albatross blood through the broodmares. Four of the five richest performers in the first crop of Artsplace have Albatross through their dams as well as through Artsplace. His divisional champion Michelle's Jackpot is 3x3 to Albatross, as is Peace Of Art p,3,1:52½-'98 ($368,831), Art's Palace p,4,1:52.1-'98, Maybe Today p,4,1:51.4z-'98 and Cohiba Mary p,4,1:52.1-'98 ($245,669). Those with 3x4 crosses to Albatross are Stienam's Place, Decor p,2,1:54 ($376,168), Perfect Art, Tallulah Belle, Dream Away p,3,1:50 ($1,058,861) and J.K. Outlaw p,3,1:51 ($233,715). I also suspect that mares with the No Nukes/Albatross will be good producers with Artsplace and their foals should show some extreme early speed.

The presence of Bret Hanover in the broodmare's pedigree is always a plus and there are a few good examples with Artsplace performers. Dream Away's second dam is inbred 3x2 to Bret Hanover, Michelle's Jackpot's dam is 3x3 to Bret Hanover and Tallulah Belle's dam is 3x2 to Bret Hanover. In addition, Artiscape's second dam is bred 3x3 to the full sisters Beryl Hanover and Odella Hanover - Beryl Hanover being the second dam of Bret Hanover. There are also a couple of instances in which good ones have a sibling cross to the great Meadow Skipper and his half sister the champion Countess Adios - Art In The Park is bred 4x5x4 to that pair and Art's Secret p,4,1:53.3-'98 ($169,698) is 4x4 to that duo. Another with a similar sibling cross is Maybe Today who is not only 3x3 to Albatross, but 4x4 to Meadow Skipper and his full sister With Thanks. That's a lot of concentration of great blood.

Early returns show Artsplace is doing well with daughters from a large assortment of sires, as well he should with his pedigree. Based on his early performance as a sire, Artsplace should continue to get the best mares and there is every reason to think he will be a very successful sire for years to come.

Leading Progeny by Artsplace

Fastest
Dream Away, h, p,3,1:50 $1,058,861
Galleria, m, p,3,1:50.1 $132,887
Stienam's Place, m, p,3,1:50.4 $1,402,301
Perfect Art, h, p,3,1:51 $976,983
Park Place, h, p,3,1:51 $576,971
J.K. Outlaw, h, p,3,1:51 $233,715
Southwest Art, h, p,3,1:51.1f $76,524
Arturo, h, p,3,1:51.2f $1,298,491
Maybe Today, h, p,4,1:51.4z $32,540
Art In The Park, m, p,3,1:52 $533,784

Richest
Stienam's Place, m, p,3,1:50.4 $1,402,301
Arturo, h, p,3,1:51.2f $1,298,491
Dream Away, h, p,3,1:50 $1,058,861
Michelle's Jackpot, m, p,2,1:54.4f $695,439
Perfect Art, h, p,3,1:51 $976,983
Park Place, h, p,3,1:51 $576,971
Art In The Park, m, p,3,1:52 $533,784
Artiscape, h, p,2,1:52.3 $495,501
Real Artist, h, p,2,1:52 $417,747
Artistic Pleasure, m, p,3,1:52.4 $401,170

Artsplace, Bay Horse, 1988
p, 2, 1:51.1f; 3, 1:50.4f; 4, 1:49.2 ($3,085,083)

Abercrombie, 1975 p, 4, 1:53 $984,391	Silent Majority, 1969 p, 3, 1:56.3 $362,369	Henry T. Adios, 1958 p, 6, 1:57 $706,833	**ADIOS**, 1940 p, T1:57½ $33,329	HAL DALE	ABBEDALE Margaret Hal
				Adioo Volo	Adioo Guy Sigrid Volo
			Greer Hanover, 1948 p, 3, 2:06.2h $6,482	**NIBBLE HANOVER**	Calumet Chuck Justissima
				Veda Hanover	**BILLY DIRECT** **VIVIAN HANOVER**
		Hobby Horse Tar, 1964	**TAR HEEL**, 1948 p, 4, T1:57 $119,148	**BILLY DIRECT**	Napoleon Direct Gay Forbes
				Leta Long	**VOLOMITE** Rosette
			Wilellen, 1955 p, 3, 2:04.2h $16,994	Wilmington	Bert Abbe Miss Saginaw
				Willola	Willglow Romola
	Bergdorf, 1967 p, 4, 2:03.3 $6,035	**DUANE HANOVER**, 1952 p, 4, 1:58 $280,288	Knight Dream, 1945 p, 3, T1:59 $76,973	**NIBBLE HANOVER**	Calumet Chuck Justissima
				Lydia Knight	Peter The Brewer Guy Rosa
			Dorsh Hanover, 1932 4, 2:15½h	Dillon Axworthy	Axworthy Adioo Dillon
				Great Medium	Peter The Great Dorsch Medium
		Princess Best, 1959 p, 4, 2:07f	**THE WIDOWER**, 1935 p, 3, T1:59½ $19,983	ABBEDALE	The Abbe Daisydale D.
				Widow Grattan	Grattan Royal I'm A Widow
			Princess Chief, 1945 p, 2:07h $9,506	Chief Abbedale	ABBEDALE Marion Candler
				The Gay Princess	Crispin Princess Duffy
Miss Elvira, 1982 p, 2, 2:00.1f $1,800	Albatross, 1968 p, 4, 1:54.3f $1,201,470	Meadow Skipper, 1960 p, 3, 1:55.1 $428,057	Dale Frost, 1951 p, 1:58 $204,117	HAL DALE	ABBEDALE Margaret Hal
				Galloway	Raider Bethel
			Countess Vivian, 1950 p, 3, 1:59 $43,262	King's Counsel	VOLOMITE Margaret Spangler
				Filly Direct	**BILLY DIRECT** Calumet Edna
		Voodoo Hanover, 1964	Dancer Hanover, 1957 p, 4, T1:56.4 $87,746	**ADIOS**	HAL DALE Adioo Volo
				The Old Maid	Guy Abbey Spinster
			Vibrant Hanover, 1960	**TAR HEEL**	**BILLY DIRECT** Leta Long
				VIVIAN HANOVER	Guy McKinney Guesswork
	Ladalia Hanover, 1975 p, 3, Q2:00.1 $72,802	Columbia George, 1967 p, 3, 1:56 $398,324	Good Time, 1946 p, 1:57.4 $318,792	HAL DALE	ABBEDALE Margaret Hal
				On Time	VOLOMITE Nedda Guy
			Mitzi Eden, 1958 p, 2, 2:05 $14,946	**THE WIDOWER**	ABBEDALE Widow Grattan
				Tallulah Hanover	**BILLY DIRECT** Natalie Hanover
		Lady Kacne, 1967 p, 3, 2:03.4f $686	**DUANE HANOVER**, 1952 p, 4, 1:58 $280,288	Knight Dream	**NIBBLE HANOVER** Lydia Knight
				Dorsh Hanover	Dillon Axworthy Great Medium
			Lady Lunken, 1961	Goose Bay	VOLOMITE Her Ladyship
				Reba Hanover	**BILLY DIRECT** Bertha Hanover

B.G.'s Bunny

B.G.'s Bunny was a part of Albatross' exciting first crop, and the first to offer a glimpse of the promise to come. His hallmark as a racehorse and sire was aggressive speed, and as we shall see later, there was a good reason for his powerful racing persona.

Through only 26 lifetime starts, B.G.'s Bunny displayed abilities out of proportion to his experience and race conditioning. At two, he made 16 starts for trainer George Berkner, and had nine wins and three seconds. Although none of these were in high-level stakes competition, he did win two Pennsylvania Sires Stakes, and a pair of Maryland Development Fund Stakes. He was also second in the Hanover-Hempt at Vernon Downs. At three, B.G.'s Bunny developed into a blazing, but all-too-brief star. He won an elimination of the Cane Pace, and set a world record for three-year-olds on a mile track, winning a Meadowlands Pace elimination in 1:54. This was the inaugural Meadowlands Pace in 1977, which was eventually won by Escort. B.G.'s Bunny had only ten starts at three, before a sesamoid injury forced him to the sidelines and into a breeding career at Apt-To-Acres.

"B.G.'s Bunny had the kind of raw speed that only a few horses are born with," trainer Berkner has said. "He was a big, handsome colt, very much a Bret Hanover type. He didn't look anything like Albatross. When we bought him as a yearling (for $15,000 at the Old Glory Sale) he had a boggy hock, and that hock bothered him throughout his career. He tried to compensate for the soreness, and he was never really a sound horse. He got grabby and aggressive when he was hurting. When he was sounder, he was a nice horse to drive. But the night he set the world record in the Meadowlands Pace elim I was just a passenger. That was his last start."

B.G.'s Bunny was Albatross' first world champion, and the first to indicate that the cross of a Bret Hanover mare to Albatross would be the so-called "golden cross" of the generation. His dam was the Bret Hanover mare Bret's Romance.

B.G.'s Bunny was bred by Tim Rooney of the famed Rooney sports family empire, and raced for Bob Greenberg, a wealthy New Jersey land developer.

Sire Line

B.G.'s Bunny is a son of Albatross and grandson of Meadow Skipper, and was first thought to be his sire's best chance to continue this emerging sire line. He bred big foal crops in his early years at stud. In 1980, for example, he produced more than 200 foals, and his first two crops each won lifetime earnings of more than $7 million. His contributions, however, quickly diminished after a few seasons, and he was subsequently sold to Australia. His last 50 American foals hit the ground in the spring of 1993.

Maternal Line

As noted above, B.G.'s Bunny was from a Bret Hanover mare, Bret's Romance, a daughter of the Knight Dream mare Knight's Embassy. He was her second foal and first colt. The immediate family has become one of modern day pacing's strongest clans. Bret's Romance is a full sister to Bret's Knight p,2,T1:59 ($137,149) and to the grandam of Bond Street p,4,T1:52 ($541,297). Bret's Romance also produced the exceptional Niatross mare Refreshing Touch p,3,1:54.1 ($113,800), and that mare is already the dam of the fast mare Coast p,3,1:52.1 ($247,917).

Another of Bret's Romance's foals was the Albatross mare, Lismore p,3,T1:57.2, a full sister to B.G.'s Bunny, who has become one of the sport's modern broodmare stars. She has produced a number of quality progeny, all to the cover of supersire Abercrombie, including the world champion and respected sire Albert Albert p,3,1:52.1 ($1,237,070), Lahar p,4,1:50.3 ($347,685), Lisheen p,3,1:52.1 ($518,405), Lisryan p,1:52 ($450,541) and Curragh p,T1:51.4 ($509,740).

Race Record Highlights

At 2

1st two Maryland Development Fund S.
two Pennsylvania Sires S.

2nd Hanover-Hempt S.
Silver Spoon P.

At 3

1st Cane Pace Elimination
Meadowlands Pace Elimination

2nd Battle of Brandywine

Honors

Set world record for three-year-old pacers on mile track

Photo courtesy of The Horseman and Fair World

B.G.'s Bunny

Race Record

Year	Age	Starts	Wins	2nd	3rd	Earnings	Record
1976	2	16	9	3	0	$ 64,002	p,2,1:59.1
1977	3	10	3	2	2	151,190	p,3,1:54
		26	12	5	2	$215,192	p,3,1:54

B.G.'s Bunny

B.G.'s Bunny is like many of Albatross' most successful sons in that he carries a large quantity of Hal Dale blood. Albatross is by Meadow Skipper, a grandson of Hal Dale, and out of a mare by Dancer Hanover, also a grandson of Hal Dale. B.G.'s Bunny's dam, Bret's Romance, carries yet another cross to Hal Dale in that she is by Bret Hanover, also a grandson of Hal Dale, a pattern repeated over and over in modern pacing. An important footnote here is that the mating of Albatross mares with daughters of Bret Hanover combines the blood of Dale Frost with a double dose of Adios, since both Bret Hanover and Dancer Hanover are sons of Adios. It is also interesting to note that Lismore, sister to B.G.'s Bunny and thus bred exactly the same way, produced so outstandingly when she was bred to Abercrombie, who provided still another touch of the Hal Dale blood since Abercrombie traces directly to Hal Dale through yet another son of Adios, Henry T. Adios.

Progeny of Note

B.G.'s Bunny's biggest money winner came from his very first crop, the fast but troubled Woodrow Wilson winner, McKinzie Almahurst p,3,1:54.4 ($1,532,870). Subsequent crops included the fast Butler B G p,3,1:53.4f ($878,709), Awesome Almahurst p,1:52.4 ($578,238), Allwin Steady p,3,1:53 ($414,989) and the aggressive filly Armbro Bramble p,3,1:56 ($351,514) (dam of the seemingly iron-clad Cammie's Lady p,4,1:52.1, a lifetime winner of nearly $750,000.)

B.G.'s Bunny had at least 100 foals in seven of his first eight crops, so he did not lack opportunity. What he lacked as a sire was the same as what he lacked as a racehorse. His foals were never sound horses and as a result, the earnings of his late 1980's offspring dwindled under the onrush of his contemporaries, most notably Cam Fella. B.G.'s Bunny was buried in that landslide, but he was not alone.

In all, he was a remarkably gifted horse whose own enormous potential surfaced through his daughters, who have become prized broodmares, producing a slate of champions such as Precious Bunny, Cam's Card Shark, Armbro Operative, et al. Although Cam Fella was B.G.'s Bunny's siring nemesis, the daughters of B.G.'s Bunny seemed to click perfectly with Cam Fella, a horse with a definitive Hal Dale presence as well.

"Many of his foals were like him," trainer Berkner said. "He passed on both his best and worst characteristics. His offspring were very fast, and generally very unsound horses. Speed is a both a blessing and a curse sometimes, and it was never truer than in B.G.'s Bunny's case. The speed, though, helped his broodmares produce all out of proportion to their own ability."

B.G.'s Bunny produced more than 1,600 foals in 15 seasons in North America between 1979 and 1993, and a remarkably high number of those foals, 1,399 to be exact, were starters. That percentage of 83.5 per cent is good in anybody's league. However, those starters earned an average of only $35,000 each, a statistic that spelled doom for B.G.'s Bunny's continuing influence.

Analysis

B.G.'s Bunny never made an impact as a sire of sires and his best son appears to be Allwin Steady p,3,1:53 ($414,989) who has sired some nice performers but is not a major commercial stallion. Woodrow Wilson winner McKinzie Almahurst p,3,1:54.4 ($1,532,870) was also tried for a time but was not successful. Another fast son is Butler B G who was exported and is now a sire in New Zealand. However, B.G.'s Bunny has become an outstanding broodmare sire.

The closest common crosses in B.G.'s Bunny's pedigree are classic and outstanding stallions - 4x3 to Adios, 4x4 to Tar Heel, 4x5x4 to Hal Dale and 5x5x5 to Billy Direct.

B.G.'s Bunny sired over 1,600 foals during his U.S. stallion career and was a prolific sire during his early years at stud. His first five crops each had 149 or more foals, including an incredible 209 foaled in 1980. His progeny have earned over $50,000,000 at the races with 595 taking 2:00 records and 23 winning $250,000. Standing in New Jersey, B.G.'s Bunny had the benefit of many of his sons and daughters racing at The Meadowlands and taking fast records. His stud fee rose quickly to $15,000 for several years before he began losing favor among breeders.

I have always felt The Meadowlands skewed the ability of certain stallions since mile track racing was new in the east and many horses were taking fast and impressive records. Breeders seemed obsessed with speed at that time, rather than asking the question, "who did he beat?" and sires like B.G.'s Bunny and Oil Burner reaped the rewards of fast records by their offspring. As a result, I feel those particular stallions were thought to have a lot more ability than was the case.

On the other side of the coin, being New Jersey-based helped B.G.'s Bunny's daughters since there were so many of them in the east and they were bred to such New Jersey stallions as Cam Fella and Direct Scooter with whom they had great success as producers.

As a sire of racehorses, B.G.'s Bunny's fastest credits are two below the 1:53 level. Dome Patrol p,3,1:52.2 ($204,157) is his fastest and he is from the Computer mare Tandy. Dome Patrol, like several of B.G.'s Bunny's fastest performers, is inbred 3x3 to Meadow Skipper. Dome Patrol's dam, Tandy, has two interesting crosses in her pedigree - 4x3 to Bullet Hanover and his three-quarter sister Overbid and 4x3 to the full brother and sister Torpid and Torris. Awesome Almahurst p,1:52.4 ($578,238) is B.G.'s Bunny's next fastest son and he is also 3x3 to Meadow Skipper. In addition, Awesome Almahurst also has a common cross to siblings; he is 4x4x4 to the half-sisters Countess Vivian (dam of Meadow Skipper) and Filly Byrd.

In other chapters, and in my <u>Modern Trotting Sire Lines</u>, I have noted the incidence of common crosses to siblings in the pedigrees of many great horses. This situation seems to have worked very well for B.G.'s Bunny. In addition to the two horses mentioned above, world champion Stabilizer p,1:54.4 ($525,771) is bred 5x4x4x4 to Adios and his sister Adieu, as well as 4x4 to the full brother and sister Knight Dream and Marjorie Armstrong.

Another example is the B.G.'s Bunny daughter Bunny's Wish p,2,1:58.2 ($288,962) who is bred 5x4x4x5 to Adios and Adieu. She happens to be the dam of Precious Bunny p,3,1:49.4 ($2,281,142).

B.G.'s Bunny nicked well with daughters of Race Time, Best Of All and Columbia George - all sons of Good Time. Daughters of Most Happy Fella and his sons have also done well. B.G.'s Bunny also had success with mares whose dams were by trotting sires. For example, Allwin Steady has a second dam by Florican, Markim's Pride p,3,1:53.2 ($516,974) has a second dam by Speedy Scot, Que B. p,3,1:55.3 ($426,102) has a second dam by Hoot Mon as does the good mare Styx And Scones p,4,1:56.4 ($271,380).

B.G.'s Bunny did not need daughters of super sires to produce good horses. The broodmare sires of B.G.'s Bunny's four fastest performers are by Computer, Nero, Steady Beau and Nero. And McKinzie Almahurst, his richest son, is from a mare by Golden Money Maker.

As a broodmare sire, B.G.'s Bunny is well-respected and has had much success. To date, his daughters have produced over 640 in 2:00 and they include many top-notch performers. B.G.'s Bunny daughters are responsible for several young sires and sire prospects now in commercial service. Precious Bunny is at the top of the list along with new sires Cam's Card Shark p,3,1:50 ($2,498,204) and his brother Cam's Magic Trick p,3,1:52.4f ($469,899), Armbro Operative p,4,1:50 ($1,012,712) and Electric Yankee p,3,1:51.3f ($506,752) - all very accomplished racehorses. Another stallion, trying to make a mark in Ohio, is Tooter Scooter p,3,1:51.1 ($567,400).

B.G.'s Bunny mares have already produced three in 1:50, as above, along with such fast performers as Lorryland Butler p,1:50.1, Armbro Maneuver p,3,1:50.2, Largo p,1:51, Beach St. Partners p,3,1:51.1 and Cammie's Lady p,1:51.2 among others. All three in the 1:50 list are sired by Cam Fella as well as Largo and Cammie's Lady. This has been a prolific cross as has Direct Scooter with B.G.'s Bunny mares with such performers as Armbro Maneuver, Tooter Scooter, W R H p,2,1:54.1h and O K Bye p,3,1:54.2.

B.G.'s Bunny broodmares seem to like doubling up on certain crosses in their own pedigree. For example, the fast Lorryland Butler is sired by Skip

B.G.'s Bunny

By Night who is a Meadow Skipper/Knight Dream cross. Jud's Choice, the dam of Lorryland Butler, also has the Meadow Skipper line and Knight Dream line cross. Tooter Scooter is by a Sampson Hanover line stallion (Direct Scooter) and his second dam is by Sampson Hanover.

The best examples of this factor are shown by the three fastest, and only 1:50, credits for B.G.'s Bunny's daughters. B.G.'s Bunny has a Meadow Skipper line and Bret Hanover cross in his own pedigree and the sire of all 1:50 credits for his daughters is Cam Fella - also with the Meadow Skipper line and Bret Hanover cross.

There are still plenty of B.G.'s Bunny mares available in North America who are 10 years of age or under. Many are well-bred, have fast records, and would be nice additions to any broodmare band - especially with all the sons of Cam Fella now at stud.

Leading Progeny by B.G.'s Bunny

Fastest

Dome Patrol, h, p,3,1:52.2 $204,157
Awesome Almahurst, h, p,3,1:52.4 $578,238
Allwin Steady, h, p,3,1:53 $414,989
Lindsey's Bunny, g, p,3,1:53 $129,026
True Genius, h, p,1:53.1 $71,415
Markim's Pride, h, p,3,1:53.2 $516,974
Joey T., h, p,1:53.2 $265,423
Another Fishy, m, p,4,1:53.2 $158,579
Country Beau, h, p,1:53.3 $176,351
Sweet Surrey, m, p,4,1:53.3 $170,940

Richest

McKinzie Almahurst, h, p,3,1:54.4 $1,532,870
Butler B G, h, p,3,1:53.4f $878,709
Awesome Almahurst, h, p,3,1:52.4 $578,238
Stabilizer, g, p,1:54.4 $525,771
Markim's Pride, h, p,3,1:53.2 $516,974
Power Bunny, h, p,1:55 $438,443
Que B, h, p,3,1:55.3 $426,102
Allwin Steady, h, p,3,1:53 $414,989
Youra Jinx, h, p,3,1:54.1 $359,802
Armbro Bramble, m, p,3,1:56 $351,514

B.G.'s Bunny, Bay Horse, 1974
p, 2, 1:59.1; 3, 1:54 ($215,192)

Albatross, 1968 p, 4, 1:54.3f $1,201,470	Meadow Skipper, 1960 p, 3, 1:55.1 $428,057	Dale Frost, 1951 p, 1:58 $204,117	**HAL DALE**, 1926 p, 6, 2:02¼	Abbedale	**THE ABBE** Daisydale D.
				Margaret Hal	Argot Hal Margaret Polk
			Galloway, 1939 p, 2:04½h $5,294	Raider	**PETER VOLO** Nelda Dillon
				Bethel	David Guy Annotation
		Countess Vivian, 1950 p, 3, 1:59 $43,262	King's Counsel, 1940 p, 6, 1:58 $44,930	**VOLOMITE**	**PETER VOLO** Cita Frisco
				Margaret Spangler	**GUY AXWORTHY** Maggie Winder
			Filly Direct, 1941 p, 3, 2:06¾h $6,299	**BILLY DIRECT**	Napoleon Direct Gay Forbes
				Calumet Edna	**PETER THE BREWER** Broncho Queen
	Voodoo Hanover, 1964	Dancer Hanover, 1957 p, 4, T1:56.4 $87,746	**ADIOS**, 1940 p, T1:57½ $33,329	**HAL DALE**	Abbedale Margaret Hal
				Adioo Volo	Adioo Guy Sigrid Volo
			The Old Maid, 1945	Guy Abbey	**GUY AXWORTHY** Abbacy
				Spinster	Spencer Minnetonka
		Vibrant Hanover, 1960	**TAR HEEL**, 1948 p, 4, T1:57 $119,148	**BILLY DIRECT**	Napoleon Direct Gay Forbes
				Leta Long	**VOLOMITE** Rosette
			Vivian Hanover, 1937	Guy McKinney	**GUY AXWORTHY** Queenly McKinney
				Guesswork	**PETER THE GREAT** Elsie Leyburn
Brets Romance, 1968 p, 4, 2:02f $13,967	Bret Hanover, 1962 p, 4, T1:53.3 $922,616	**ADIOS**, 1940 p, T1:57½ $33,329	**HAL DALE**, 1926 p, 6, 2:02¼	Abbedale	**THE ABBE** Daisydale D.
				Margaret Hal	Argot Hal Margaret Polk
			Adioo Volo, 1930 p, 3, 2:05h	Adioo Guy	Guy Dillon Adioo
				Sigrid Volo	**PETER VOLO** Polly Parrot
		Brenna Hanover, 1956 p, 3, T2:01 $21,946	**TAR HEEL**, 1948 p, 4, T1:57 $119,148	**BILLY DIRECT**	Napoleon Direct Gay Forbes
				Leta Long	**VOLOMITE** Rosette
			Beryl Hanover, 1947 p, 2, T2:02 $29,076	**NIBBLE HANOVER**	Calumet Chuck Justissima
				Laura Hanover	The Laurel Hall Miss Bertha Worthy
	Knight's Embassy, 1951	Knight Dream, 1945 p, 3, T1:59 $76,973	**NIBBLE HANOVER**, 1936 1:58¾ $25,599	Calumet Chuck	Truax Sumatra
				Justissima	Justice Brooke Claire Toddington
			Lydia Knight, 1929 p, 4, 2:03	**PETER THE BREWER**	**PETER THE GREAT** Zombrewer
				Guy Rosa	**GUY AXWORTHY** Rosa Lake
		Miss Reed, 1942 p, 4, 2:13h $1,289	Bert Abbe, 1922 p, T1:59¼	**THE ABBE**	Chimes Nettie King
				Miss Ella H.	Mack H Nelly Patch
			Four D McKinney, 1927	Wallace McKinney	McKinney Leonor
				Misty Maiden	Pilot Burns Lottie Strathmore

Beach Towel

Horse of the Year, World Champion and Earnings Champion were titles bestowed upon Beach Towel during his racing career. What could he do for an encore in retirement? The answer is simple - sire multiple world champion Jenna's Beach Boy and a host of other speed demons.

One of the top racehorses of the modern era, Beach Towel was a dominant figure at two and three, winning 29 of 36 races and earning over $2,500,000.

Beach Towel was bred by Norman Woolworth's and Mrs. Alice Johnston's Stoner Creek Stud of Kentucky and sold at the 1988 Tattersalls Yearling Sale for $22,000 to the Uptown Stable, which was headed by young Seth Rosenfeld of New York City. Like Beach Towel, Rosenfeld has achieved harness racing success at an early age and on his own. Also like Beach Towel, he has a rich pedigree, being the nephew of Lana Lobell Farm founder Alan Leavitt who is now President of Walnut Hall Limited in Lexington, Kentucky.

Then only 22 years of age, but well-versed in harness racing and bloodlines, Rosenfeld was impressed with the yearling Beach Towel and entrusted the colt to Canadian-born trainers Ray Remmen and Larry Remmen, who have long been among the top trainers at The Meadowlands and who had success for several years with other Rosenfeld family horses.

Driven by Hall of Famer Ray Remmen, Beach Towel made his racing debut at The Meadowlands on May 20th, 1989 and won a baby race in 1:59.1 by a nose. He then won three more of these events, the fastest in 1:57.4, before entering his first parimutuel race - the Hopeful S. Elimination which he won in 2:00.2 at Buffalo Raceway. The first disappointment for Beach Towel's owners came in the $200,000 Hopeful S. Final when the colt made a break while heading for the lead in the first turn and was then hopelessly distanced. He came back a week later to win a division of the Potomac S. at Freestate Raceway in 1:56.4.

Beach Towel was then out of action from July 8th until August 30th when he won a qualifier at Brandywine and another qualifier two weeks later at Garden State Park. It was not until October 12th that Beach Towel returned to the parimutuel wars, recording a fast 1:54.1 win in an overnight event for two-year-olds at Garden State Park. He then won a Presidential S. Elimination at Rosecroft in 1:54 and followed this with an ultra-impressive victory in the $335,325 Presidential S. Final in 1:53.3. The Governor's Cup Elimination was next at Garden State Park and Beach Towel won his division in 1:53.3. Bet down to 1-2 favorite in the $681,100 Governor's Cup Final, Beach Towel was parked out first over to the quarter in :27.2. Then he assumed the lead and held it until the final stride before losing by a nose to In The Pocket in 1:54.2. The defeat was only the colt's second of the year and he came back two weeks later to end his season with a victory in the Matron S. at Pompano Park.

It was an excellent freshman season for Beach Towel; he won $478,497 from his 11 wins in 13 starts. However, he finished second in the balloting for divisional honors to Breeders Crown winner Till We Meet Again.

Coming back stronger at three, Beach Towel qualified in April at Pompano Park and The Meadowlands and made his first start in an Open event at Rosecroft on April 28th. Ray Remmen served notice that his colt was ready. Beach Towel was parked out first over to the half in :56.4, then took the lead and powered home in 1:52.4 in an impressive opening performance. Rosecroft was also the scene of Beach Towel's next two races, the John Miller Memorial Elimination and $315,000 Final. He won both, in 1:53 and 1:52.3. The colt won two more stakes at Rosecroft, the Hanover Colt S. in 1:54.1 and the $316,135 Terrapin S. in identical time.

Beach Towel had won his first five starts of the year and looked like a champion. It was then off to Canada for the rich North America Cup at Greenwood. Beach Towel won his elimination by five lengths in

Race Record Highlights

At 2

1st Presidential S. Final and Elimination
Matron S.
Potomac S.
Governor's Cup Elimination

At 3

1st Meadowlands Pace Final and Elimination
Little Brown Jug
Prix d'Ete Final and Elimination
Tattersalls S. Final and Elimination
Breeders Crown
Adios S.
American-National S.
Miller Memorial Final and Elimination
Terrapin S.
Hanover Colt S.
heat of Hayes Memorial

Honors

At three, voted Horse of the Year

At three, set world records for fastest first heat and fastest second heat on mile track

At three, set world record for fastest second heat and two-heat race on five-eighth mile track

Set record for single-season earnings

Beach Towel

Photo by Tony Leonard
Courtesy of The Horseman and Fair World

Race Record

Year	Age	Starts	Wins	2nd	3rd	Earnings	Record
1989	2	13	11	1	0	$ 478,497	p,2,1:53.3f
1990	3	23	18	4	0	2,091,860	p,3,1:50
		36	29	5	0	$2,570,357	p,3,1:50

Beach Towel

1:53 and after drawing the rail was made the heavy favorite for the $1,000,000 North America Cup Final. In this big race, Beach Towel left quickly but then made a break just before the first quarter and lost all chance. "I really don't have any explanation of why he broke stride," said a disappointed Ray Remmen. "He just overpaced himself and I don't think it had anything to do with the tight turns because he had no problem with them last week. It was just unfortunate timing for us."

Just a week later, Beach Towel pushed his lifetime earnings over the $1,000,000 mark with a dominating win in the $347,000 American-National S. at Sportsman's Park in 1:52.4. He was now primed for a try at another major race - the $1,153,500 Meadowlands Pace. Beach Towel drew the rail in his Elimination and raced conservatively in fourth to the half, made a challenge for the lead on the final turn and won by three-quarters of a length in 1:52.3. In the Meadowlands Pace Final, Beach Towel was not as fortunate in the post position draw, getting saddled with the outside post ten. The colt never saw the rail as Remmen left him in the outside flow following cover and he was still fourth at the three-quarter marker. On the front end, Till We Meet again and Apache's Fame were engaging in a suicidal speed duel which worked to the advantage of the trailers as the field turned into the long Meadowlands stretch.

Beach Towel then kicked into another gear and moved from fourth to the lead coming off the final turn as the leaders tired. Jake And Elwood went three wide for John Campbell and challenged Beach Towel in the stretch. The other colt put his nose ahead of Beach Towel's at one point but Beach Towel came back on the inside and was able to get his nose back in front of Jake And Elwood at the wire in 1:52.2. After the big win, Ray Remmen said, "Beach Towel fought back. I knew he'd never give it up. He fought back real, real hard." With the million-dollar Meadowlands Pace victory added to his previous wins in the Hambletonian (Shiaway St. Pat) and Woodrow Wilson S. (Grade One), Remmen became only the second driver, along with Bill O'Donnell, to win those three events.

Remmen gave Beach Towel a couple of weeks off and then qualified him at The Meadowlands in 1:53.4 with a final quarter in :26.1. The Adios S. was next on the colt's schedule. In the Elimination he was surprised again by In The Pocket as that colt came up in the stretch to defeat Beach Towel by a half-length in a world record 1:50.4 over The Meadows five-eighth mile track. Beach Towel turned the tables in the $295,905 Adios Final, scoring over In The Pocket by two lengths in 1:51.4. The Prix d'Ete was next at Blue Bonnets in Montreal, Canada; Beach Towel won his heat in 1:53.1 and the $265,400 Final in identical time.

It was then on to DuQuoin with Beach Towel going after the 1:49.3 world race record held jointly by Nihilator and Call For Rain. The setting was the first heat of the Hayes Memorial. Beach Towel exploded from the gate to pass the first quarter in :26.2 and the half in :53.4. He then paced another :26.2 quarter to hit the three-quarter mark in an unheard of 1:20.1. But the effort took its toll and Beach Towel tired in the stretch, passing under the timer in 1:50 flat - the third fastest race mile of all time and a fitting record for a great colt.

The Messenger S. was next at Rosecroft and Beach Towel suffered a surprising defeat in his Elimination, Kiev Hanover passing him in the stretch to win in 1:53.1. Remmen tried come-from-behind tactics in the Messenger Final, but even though Beach Towel paced home in :27.3 he was second to Jack And Elwood with Kiev Hanover taking third.

The Little Brown Jug was a different and happier story for Beach Towel and his connections. A field of 22 horses, perhaps encouraged by Beach Towel's defeat in the Messenger S., entered the Jug, necessitating three Elimination divisions. In The Pocket and Kiev Hanover won their Eliminations and then Beach Towel easily dispatched his field with a 1:54 four and three-quarter-length win. In the $253,049

Little Brown Jug Final, Beach Towel dominated the race, winning by one and one-half lengths in 1:53.3 over In The Pocket with Kiev Hanover third. Seth Rosenfeld told those assembled at the famed Delaware, Ohio, oval, "When you grow up in harness racing, you grow up wanting to win the Little Brown Jug."

Beach Towel then went on to win the Tattersalls S. at Lexington with a 1:51.3 Elimination and 1:51.1 in the Final; but he was second a week later in the Bluegrass S. to Kiev Hanover's 1:50.1 mile. The final race of Beach Towel's great career came almost a month later when he easily won the $366,933 Breeders Crown at Pompano Park in 1:51.2 by three lengths over In The Pocket. Beach Towel had closed out his three-year-old season with 18 wins in 23 starts and earnings of $2,091,860 to set a single-season earnings record for a Standardbred. He had also set world records for the fastest first heat on a mile track and the fastest two-heats on a five-eighth mile track. For his efforts, Beach Towel was rewarded with Horse of the Year honors for 1990.

Despite several lucrative offers to buy Beach Towel, Seth Rosenfeld and his Uptown Stable believed strongly in Beach Towel's future as a stallion and decided to maintain a large interest in his ownership. They sold a part-interest to Walnridge Farm of Cream Ridge, New Jersey, which has been Beach Towel's home as a stallion since 1991.

Sire Line

Breeders were a little skeptical about Beach Towel when he first went to stud since he is a son of French Chef p,2,1:54 ($371,445) whose two other millionaire sons, Amity Chef p,3,1:51.1 ($1,372,683) and Frugal Gourmet p,3,1:51.3 ($1,349,560) were not successful sires. French Chef has unusual breeding in that, although he is a son of the great Meadow Skipper, his dam is a mare who took a pacing record although she is by the top trotting sire Nevele Pride and from a great trotting maternal family.

French Chef was a great horse as a two-year-old, winning 21 of 23 starts and setting world records on every size track. He was not as good at three and was retired to Stoner Creek Stud, where his great sire once stood. French Chef was a decent sire, but never achieved a lofty status and was later exported.

Maternal Line

Beach Towel's maternal family is known as the Lida family. The particular branch of the family that includes Beach Towel has been by far the most active and successful. In more modern terms, this branch should be known as the family of Shy Ann and has been responsible for Adios Betty, the first 2:00 two-year-old filly, and her many descendants.

Beach Towel's dam is the Armbro Nesbit mare Sunburn p,2,1:58.3 ($52,096) who was a good stakes winner at two. Armbro Nesbit was a top son of Bye Bye Byrd and it should be noted that French Chef's other two great sons, Amity Chef and Frugal Gourmet, were both from daughters of Bye Bye Byrd. So, all three of French Chef's top sons have dams with Bye Bye Byrd blood up close.

Of course, Beach Towel is Sunburn's best foal, but she has also been the producer of 11 in 2:00 from 14 foals to date, including four sub-1:54 performers. Three of her four fastest performers have been by French Chef (Beach Towel p,3,1:50, Sun Lamp p,4,1:53.4f, Sun Prince p,3,1:53.4) and the other by Abercrombie (Lotion p,4,1:52.4f). Each of Sunburn's three daughters with foals of racing age have been 1:55 producers, but not of major stars as yet.

Sunburn's dam is the Tar Heel mare Sunbelle Hanover, who is a full sister to the dam of Royce p,4,1:53.4 ($437,177). The next dam is the Adios mare Suave Hanover p,3,2:03.3, who is a full sister to the aforementioned champion filly Adios Betty.

Progeny of Note

Beach Towel sired one of the sport's great horses, Jenna's Beach Boy p,2,1:51.4; 3,1:48.4; 4,1:47.3 ($1,972,172) in his first crop and breeders immediately took even more notice of him as a stallion. Jenna's Beach Boy was voted Two-Year-Old Pacer of the Year and equalled the world record for his division. You can read more about Jenna's Beach Boy in his chapter.

There were other stars in Beach Towel's first crop racing in 1994, which included five 1:55 two-year-olds, 27 in 2:00 and four $100,000 winners. Surf Party p,3,1:52.1 ($325,163), Sands A Flyin p,4,1:50 ($481,436), Beach The Clock p,3,Q1:54.1h ($219,518) and Only Pan p,2,1:53.2 ($78,992) scored good stakes wins. Beach Towel came back with another good crop of two-year-olds in the next year, including the Breeders Crown winning filly Paige Nicole Q. p,3,1:52 ($712,801), Beach Ray p,1:52.4f-'98 ($797,393) and Power Beach p,2,1:54.4 ($88,560). In 1996, Beach Towel had 31 2:00 two-year-olds, but not a major star and the same for 1997.

In addition to winning a Breeders Crown at two, Beach Towel's daughter Paige Nicole Q. won the Jugette at three. Beach Ray came back at three to win the $200,000 Provincial Cup and Beach Of Faith won the Western Canada Pacing Derby. Raycer Thad p,3,1:52.1 ($241,867) won the $310,500 Berry's Creek Final in 1997. Beach Towel has had good representation in the major stakes and has had nine offspring with earnings over $250,000.

Beach Towel is also no stranger to siring extreme speed. As this chapter is written, he has two 1:50 performers in Jenna's Beach Boy p,4,1:47.3 and Sands A Flyin p,4,1:50, with several others knocking at the door. Splendid Splinter p,4,1:50.1 ($265,278), Towel Me p,1:51.1 ($111,256), Beach St. Partners p,3,1:51.1 ($115,174), Timbo Timbo p,3,1:51.1 ($161,463), Barracuda Beach p,4,1:51.3 ($116,493) and Beach Of Faith p,4,1:51.3 ($310,852) have also shown flashes of extreme speed.

Analysis

As a result of Beach Towel's great first crop, he was bred to a large book of high quality mares in 1995, who had foals in 1996. Those foals will race in 1998 and have the potential to be Beach Towel's best crop. However, he will need to achieve high performance levels to keep breeders and yearling buyers interested in his foals. Unfortunately, the breeding business can be fickle and the question "what has he done lately?" is commonly heard when discussion turns to a stallion.

For Beach Towel to have continuing success at the highest levels, he will need to sire more colts and fillies like Jenna's Beach Boy and Paige Nicole Q., which is asking quite a bit from any stallion. There has also been some questions about Beach Towel fillies, but three of his top 13 earners are female, as are two of his 13 fastest performers. However, looking at the larger picture, 27 of his 30 fastest performers are male, as are 21 of his 25 richest. So although Beach Towel can sire top fillies, he has proven to be better with colts. Ironically, in the 1996 yearling sales Beach Towel fillies brought four of the six highest prices.

In my opinion, it is too early to make a judgment on the ultimate success or failure of Beach Towel. Yes, he needs to do more than just be the sire of Jenna's Beach Boy. But this could happen, given the numbers and quality of broodmares bred to him. During his first six years at stud, Beach Towel has been bred to between 131 and 185 mares each year and we have only yet seen the results of four racing crops. So I'm keeping an open mind and hoping for the best since his bloodlines offer a bit of an outcross for many of today's mares. Since his sire is from a Nevele Pride mare, and the sires close in the pedigree on his maternal side are Armbro Nesbit and Tar Heel, Beach Towel does not have the most common pedigree structure for a pacing stallion and is open to mares by most of today's best broodmare sires.

One major factor in Beach Towel's best performers is that he seems to have the ability to "move up" broodmares. By that I mean many mares which have produced at least three or more foals by other sires have had their best and fastest by Beach Towel. In some cases, the Beach Towel's were faster by several seconds. Of course, some of this may be due to the fact that Beach Towel is a New Jersey sire and many of his foals have the opportunity to race over New Jersey's two mile tracks - the Meadowlands and Garden State Park. Still, it is a factor worth noting.

Beach Towel has also worked well with a large variety of mares with good and poor performance records and pedigrees. There does not seem to be a particular "nick" which he needs to sire a good horse, although his best colt and filly, Jenna's Beach Boy and Paige Nicole Q., are both from mares by Cam Fella. As with many other sires, the more Albatross blood in the mare the better. Looking at the pedigrees of Beach Towel's 25 richest offspring, 12 have crosses to Albatross through their broodmare sires and dams and several had multiple crosses. Mares with Albatross blood have the ability to help most stallions.

Beach Towel appears to be working well with mares by sires from many different sire lines like Meadow Skipper, Adios, Bret Hanover, Gene Abbe and Direct Scooter. His top performers have come from all these lines. In addition, he has solid performers from daughters of such unheralded broodmare sires like Computer, Marauder, Striking Image, Sundance Skipper, Springfield and Steady Star.

Since Beach Towel stands at stud in New Jersey, he has been bred to a number of mares with B.G.'s Bunny and Direct Scooter blood - both of which are New Jersey sires - and he had done very well with them. B.G.'s Bunny mares appear as the dam and second dam of two of Beach Towel's five fastest performers. Also, Bret Hanover blood seems to be a very positive factor since six of Beach Towel's 31 $100,000 winners have his blood in their pedigrees. Another Adios line sire, Abercrombie, has daughters who are doing very well with Beach Towel as shown by Beach Ray p,1:52.4f-'98 ($797,393), Nude Beach p,3,1:52.2 ($172,973) and Angie Girl p,4,1:55.3 ($118,964). One of Abercrombie's daughters is also the second dam of At Point Blank p,4,1:51.4-'98 ($360,652).

I checked the six-generation pedigrees of Beach Towel's highest money winners to see if there was a particular pedigree pattern at work with his top horses. Since Beach Towel is a grandson of Meadow Skipper, that sire would show up in the third generation of any son or daughter of Beach Towel. In his own pedigree, Beach Towel has no common ancestors in the first four generations. This study showed that six of the seven richest Beach Towel sons and daughters were inbred 3x3 or linebred 3x4 to Meadow Skipper, but had no other common crosses closer than 4x4 to any other stallion. That makes sense considering Armbro Nesbit, Nevele Pride and Tar Heel would be the only sires which could achieve those crosses in Beach Towel's pedigree. In addition, four of Beach Towels five fastest performers were also 3x3 or 3x4 to Meadow Skipper.

We've already seen that Beach Towel is capable of siring world-class performers. The only question which needs to be answered is how many more can he sire in the future. And that should be answered in the next year or two which will decide whether Beach Towel will be judged a great sire or only a good sire.

Beach Towel

Photo courtesy of The Horseman and Fair World

Leading Progeny by Beach Towel

Fastest
- Jenna's Beach Boy, h, p,4,1:47.3 $1,972,172
- Sands A Flyin, h, p,4,1:50 $481,436
- Splendid Splinter, h, p,4,1:50.1 $265,278
- Timbo-Timbo, h, p,3,1:51.1 $161,463
- Beach St Partners, h, p,3,1:51.1 $115,174
- Towel Me, h, p,1:51.1 $111,156
- Vay is Mere, h, p,4,1:51.2z $84,825
- Beach Of Faith, h, p,4,1:51.3 $310,852
- Barracuda Beach, g, p,4,1:51.3 $116,493
- At Point Blank, h, p,4,1:51.4 $360,652

Richest
- Jenna's Beach Boy, h, p,4,1:47.3 $1,972,172
- Beach Ray, g, p,1:52.4f $797,393
- Paige Nicole Q, m, p,3,1:52 $712,801
- Sands A Flyin, h, p,4,1:50 $481,436
- At Point Blank, h, p,4,1:51.4 $360,652
- Surf Party, h, p,3,1:52.1 $325,163
- Beach Of Faith, h, p,4,1:51.3 $310,852
- Splendid Splinter, h, p,4,1:50.1 $265,278
- World Trade Center, g, p,1:52.4f $263,105
- Raycer Thad, h, p,3,1:52.1 $241,867

Beach Towel, Bay Horse, 16.1 Hands, 1987
p, 2, 1:53.3f; 3, 1:50 ($2,570,357)

Sire/Dam	2nd Gen	3rd Gen	4th Gen	5th Gen	6th Gen
French Chef, 1978 p, 2, 1:54 $371,445	Meadow Skipper, 1960 p, 3, 1:55.1 $428,057	Dale Frost, 1951 p, 1:58 $204,117	**HAL DALE**, 1926 p, 6, 2:02¼	Abbedale	The Abbe / Daisydale D.
				Margaret Hal	Argot Hal / Margaret Polk
			Galloway, 1939 p, 2:04½h $5,294	Raider	**PETER VOLO** / Nelda Dillon
				Bethel	David Guy / Annotation
		Countess Vivian, 1950 p, 3, 1:59 $43,262	King's Counsel, 1940 p, 6, 1:58 $44,930	**VOLOMITE**	**PETER VOLO** / Cita Frisco
				Margaret Spangler	Guy Axworthy / Maggie Winder
			Filly Direct, 1941 p, 3, 2:06¾h $6,299	**BILLY DIRECT**	Napoleon Direct / Gay Forbes
				Calumet Edna	Peter The Brewer / Broncho Queen
	La Pomme Souffle, 1972 p, 2, 2:02 $1,475	Nevele Pride, 1965 4, T1:54.4 $873,350	Star's Pride, 1947 5, 1:57.1 $140,969	Worthy Boy	**VOLOMITE** / Warwell Worthy
				Stardrift	**MR. McELWYN** / Dillcisco
			Thankful, 1952 4, T2:03.2 $31,104	**HOOT MON**	Scotland / Missey
				Magnolia Hanover	Dean Hanover / Melba Hanover
		Pompanette, 1965 3, 2:05h $39,004	Florican, 1947 5, 1:57.2 $152,222	Spud Hanover	Guy McKinney / Evelyn The Great
				Florimel	Spencer / Carolyn
			Spinster Hanover, 1952 4, T2:00.4 $17,496	Bill Gallon	**SANDY FLASH** / Calumet Aristocrat
				The Old Maid	Guy Abbey / Spinster
Sunburn, 1977 p, 2, 1:58.3 $52,216	Armbro Nesbit, 1970 p, 3, 1:56 $625,964	Bye Bye Byrd, 1955 p, 5, T1:56.1 $554,272	Poplar Byrd, 1944 p, T1:59.3 $69,300	**VOLOMITE**	**PETER VOLO** / Cita Frisco
				Ann Vonian	Grattan At Law / Margaret Vonian
			Evalina Hanover, 1946 p, 1:59.2 $12,420	**BILLY DIRECT**	Napoleon Direct / Gay Forbes
				Adieu	**HAL DALE** / **ADIOO VOLO**
		Armbro Impel, 1965	Capetown, 1954 p, 4, 1:58.3 $26,448	**HOOT MON**	Scotland / Missey
				Margo Mite	**VOLOMITE** / Margaret Castleton
			Dottie's Pick, 1952 p, 4, T1:56.4 $263,978	**ADIOS**	**HAL DALE** / **ADIOO VOLO**
				Pick Up	Follow Up / Mimzy
	Sunbelle Hanover, 1966	Tar Heel, 1948 p, 4, T1:57 $119,148	**BILLY DIRECT**, 1934 p, 4, T1:55 $12,040	Napoleon Direct	Walter Direct / Lady Erectress
				Gay Forbes	Malcolm Forbes / Gay Girl Chimes
			Leta Long, 1940 p, 4, 2:03¾ $9,321	**VOLOMITE**	**PETER VOLO** / Cita Frisco
				Rosette	**MR. McELWYN** / Rose Scott
		Suave Hanover, 1959 p, 3, 2:03.3 $5,696	**ADIOS**, 1940 p, T1:57½ $33,329	**HAL DALE**	Abbedale / Margaret Hal
				ADIOO VOLO	Adioo Guy / Sigrid Volo
			Shy Ann, 1943	Cardinal Prince	Peter Potempkin / Lillian L
				Bid Hanover	**SANDY FLASH** / Betty Blythe

Big Towner

There have not been too many colts more aptly named than Big Towner. For two years, he used New York's "big town" tracks of Yonkers and Roosevelt as his playground and won more often than he lost. Big Towner could have also been named "Big Timer" because he came up big on the racetrack and later in the breeding shed.

Big Towner has single-handedly kept the Gene Abbe male line at the top levels of the sport by siring four $1,000,000 winners and a number of world champion colts and fillies. His daughters are now making a major impact as broodmares and this will keep Big Towner in the limelight for several more generations.

All of this from a colt who sold for less than $6,000 as a yearling. Bred by Florence Startsman and Paul Gardner of Ohio, Big Towner was sold for $5,700 at the 1975 Ohio Tattersalls Sale to The Big Stable of Maryland.

As a racehorse, Big Towner was a precocious colt right from the start, as was seen when he made his two-year-old debut at Maryland's Rosecroft Raceway (then a half-mile track) on May 7th, 1976. In a $300 baby race, Big Towner drew post four and made a break right before the start. But in a preview of what was to come, the colt got back on stride, made up the lost ground and raced second all the way until the stretch when he took command and pulled away to a twelve-length win in 2:09.3.

Big Towner followed that opening performance with two more baby race wins in 2:07.4 and 2:08.1 before racing in two conditioned races for youngsters which he won handily in 2:05.4 and 2:07. He was then undefeated in his first five starts, with a combined victory margin of 31 lengths - all of this by June 10th. But the colt's owners only wanted to race him lightly at two and his season ended after a second place finish in the Reading Futurity on June 21st in which Big Towner was timed in 2:03.4h.

Trained by Lee Broglio, Big Towner came back for the big time at three, ready to take on the best. Driven primarily by Lucien Fontaine and John Chapman, Big Towner opened his season with three wins at Roosevelt and Yonkers, the fastest in 2:01. In a courageous effort in his first stakes race, Big Towner was parked out every step of the way in the Miller Memorial at Rosecroft but lost by only a neck to Nat Lobell in 1:59.1. With that effort, he established himself as a tough, game and fast colt who would be a factor in the major stakes the rest of the season.

Big Towner rebounded with a 1:58.3 win at Yonkers in a three-year-old Invitational, defeating the world champions Governor Skipper and Super Clint. Following a second place finish a week later, Big Towner again showed his speed and tenacity, this time in a New York Sires S. race at Yonkers in which he left from post nine in the second tier. Interfered with in the first turn, Big Towner was a distant eighth at the first quarter and still seventh on the outside at the half. Driver Lucien Fontaine was able to follow cover and moved up to fourth on the outside at the three-quarters and then set Big Towner loose around the turn and into the short Yonkers stretch. The colt responded and got up to win by a neck in 2:00.4.

The Cane Pace was a week later at Yonkers. Big Towner won his elimination on the front end in 1:58.2 by a neck over Governor Skipper and Nat Lobell. In the Cane Final, however, Big Towner was the victim of a horrible trip in which he tried for the lead at the half, was parked out and then shuffled back to fifth, before finishing third behind Jade Prince and Nat Lobell.

Big Towner saw the winners circle again at Roosevelt with a 1:59.2 win in a New York Sires S. and then saw a mile track for the first time when he went to The Meadowlands to compete in the Meadowlands Pace. In his elimination, Big Towner was parked out from post seven and never saw the rail as he challenged first over all the way before tiring in the stretch and finishing fifth. In the final, he had the lead parked out at the quarter, but was then a victim of the infamous "Meadowlands Shuffle" and wound up a disappointing and distant ninth.

Race Record Highlights

At 2

2nd Reading Futurity

At 3

1st Monticello Classic
Cane Futurity Elimination
New York State Fair S.
three New York Sires S.
2nd Miller Memorial
3rd Cane Futurity Final

At 4

1st U.S. Pacing Championship
six New York Sires S.

Big Towner

Photo by Monica Thors
Courtesy of The Horseman and Fair World

Race Record

Year	Age	Starts	Wins	2nd	3rd	Earnings	Record
1976	2	6	5	1	0	$ 3,972	p,2,2:05.4h
1977	3	22	12	3	3	295,012	p,3,1:56.1
1978	4	20	14	1	0	248,142	p,4,1:54.4
		48	31	5	3	$547,126	p,4,1:54.4

Big Towner

Better times were ahead. Big Towner won his Monticello Classic Elimination a week later in 1:59.3 and the $228,780 Monticello Classic Final proved a real showcase for his talents, as well as providing his owners with their biggest payday. Driven by John Chapman, Big Towner was the favorite in the race and left from post five. Chapman, apparently knowing he had the best horse, sat patiently on the outside in third and fourth position in order to stay out of any potential trouble. At the head of the stretch, Big Towner was fifth on the outside but only a length and a half from the leaders. Chapman tapped the colt and he took off around the field, getting up to nip the great filly Mistletoe Shalee by a neck at the wire in 1:58.3 to take the big prize.

Following a week's vacation, Big Towner made two breaks in his next start at Saratoga and finished a distant sixth. He then won a New York Sires S. at Syracuse in 1:56.1 followed by another at Batavia in 1:59.1. Following his scheduled stakes events, Big Towner went up against the Open Class pacers at Yonkers, which were a very strong group in those days. In four starts against the older horses, Big Towner defeated Silk Stockings in one and was third to Silk Stockings and Skipper Dexter in two other Open races at the conclusion of his season.

For the year, Big Towner won 12 of 22 starts, earned $295,012 and was the fourth highest money-winning three-year-old pacer of 1977. More important, he showed he could be very competitive with the nation's top older pacers, which was a good sign for the next year.

At the beginning of Big Towner's four-year-old season trainer Lee Broglio said, "I knew what kind of horse I had. I knew he had tremendous speed. Big Towner is better than his record - he didn't have too many opportunities over a big track last season - and definitely a fast horse."

At four, Big Towner lived up to expectations, winning 14 of 20 starts, including the U.S. Pacing Championship at Roosevelt, six New York Sires S. and seven Open-Handicap events at Yonkers and Roosevelt. Big Towner was a terror on half-mile tracks but he did not fare so well at The Meadowlands, where he was never better than fifth in his three starts at the New Jersey mile track. However, he was the FFA king of the New York tracks and made quite a name for himself, being the favorite in most of his starts. Big Towner was so good at the end of his career that he won his last nine races over six different New York tracks, including a 1:54.4 effort at Syracuse which was to be his lifetime record. An indication of Big Towner's determination is shown by the fact that he won 14 of 16 times he had the lead at the three-quarter pole.

Big Towner was impressive enough to be chosen as a stallion for Hanover Shoe Farm in Pennsylvania and syndicated among top breeders.

Sire Line

Big Towner is one of the very few non-Hal Dale line stallions to make it to the late 20th century while still achieving a high level of success. It was Gene Abbe, the sire of Big Towner (featured in his own chapter in this book), who had the success, against all odds, that made it possible for Big Towner to carry on this male line for a few more generations.

Gene Abbe was a good sire and an especially good broodmare sire - a trait which Big Towner should be able to duplicate given the great success of his daughters on the racetrack and the fact that most of them are very well bred. Big Towner has not yet sired a major stallion son who would be able to take this male line into future generations. This is a shame for the breed since this line has acted as a fine outcross for all the Adios and Meadow Skipper line stallions.

However, there is still time for a son to rise up and make himself known and popular among breeders. The Big Towner son Walton Hanover was popular for several years at Hanover Shoe Farms and had some decent success. He was an excellent percentage sire and could also get some top horses - but just not enough for the commercial marketplace. Another Big Towner son, Broadway Express, has had good success in the Illinois racing program but has not made a national impact. Apache Circle looked hot for a while after he sired the million-dollar winner Apache's Fame, but his flame also dimmed. Towner's Big Guy and Threefold are both adequate siring sons of Big Towner, but neither has made a firm impact among breeders.

There is one son of Big Towner who is doing a great job given the limited opportunities available to him. This horse is Raging Glory p,3,1:55.1, owned by veteran breeder Dana Irving, from the good Tar Heel daughter Farmer's Hostess. Raging Glory is standing in Florida, not a bastion of breeding strength or a high-visibility racing program. He has sired only 60 horses of racing age, but has one in 1:50, five in 1:55 and 27 in 2:00. His top star is the very fine stakes-winning pacer Red Bow Tie p,3,1:50 ($518,276). Unfortunately, Raging Glory turned 13 years old in 1998 and will probably never have the access to large groups of quality mares which he may have deserved.

Big Towner is not the only son of Gene Abbe who appears to have possessed the genetic make-up to become a top sire. Fortune Richie p,3,2:00.1f, an unheralded racehorse from the late 1970s, stood at stud for many years at a small farm in Kentucky and sent out a steady stream of good homebred performers which included the great Dorunrun Bluegrass p,1:49.4 ($1,880,235), now a sire at Blue Chip Farms in New York.

Yes, this Gene Abbe sire line has long been able to produce some "home run" type performers, but not as regularly as the Adios and Meadow Skipper lines. Interestingly, Gene Abbe is a son of Bert Abbe whose grandam is a daughter of the great and legendary Dan Patch. Perhaps a little of old Dan Patch surfaces every once in a while! Another interesting point is that the founding father of the breed, Hambletonian (a foal of 1849) is only six generations removed from Big Towner since Gene Abbe was a geriatric 30 years old when Big Towner was born. It is extremely rare for a sire to produce his most outstanding son at that advanced age.

To put the six-generation distance between Hambletonian and Big Towner in perspective, keep in mind that Jate Lobell and Western Hanover are 11 generations from Hambletonian, Artsplace is ten and Albatross is eight. Now, do you agree that Big Towner is a horse way ahead of his time?

Maternal Line

Big Towner is from the Shadow Wave mare Tiny Wave. Shadow Wave was a great broodmare sire and several of his daughters have produced sons that went on to become good sires. In addition to Big Towner, some other noteworthy stallions from Shadow Wave mares are Oil Burner, Falcon Almahurst and Happy Motoring.

When Big Towner went to stud, he did not bring with him a "blue-blooded" maternal pedigree. His grandam is Tiny Gold p,2:01.2 ($16,291) by Guinea Gold, and his third dam is Cynthiana 2:10.4h by Protector. His fourth dam is the non-record Volomite mare Olympia who has one in 2:00 and not much else.

But if you keep digging you can find a possible explanation for Big Towner's success both as a racehorse and a stallion. Olympia is a Volomite full sister to On Time p,3,2:03$\frac{1}{2}$, who happens to be the dam of the two-time Horse of the Year and great stallion Good Time p,1:57.4 ($318,792).

Big Towner was the first foal from Tiny Wave and by far the best of her later 13 foals. Tiny Wave produced seven in 2:00, but her fastest are only at 1:58 and, aside from Gleeful George's earnings of $122,496, none of her other foals earned more than $28,000. Tiny Wave has also had seven daughters who are producers, but only one has even produced a $100,000 winner - that being the Most Happy Fella mare Happy Tid Bit who is the dam of Lives On Laughter p,4,1:53.2f ($115,936), Heat Relief p,3,1:58h ($160,341) and Daylon Falcon p,3,1:53.1. Her two fastest are sired by Falcon Seelster who is also working well with Big Towner mares.

Progeny of Note

From his 16 crops of foals of racing age, Big Towner has been a spectacular success at stud with the winners of over $89,000,000 to his

Big Towner

credit along with two in 1:50, 200 in 1:55 and 885 in 2:00. Big Towner led the North American sires money-winning list in 1989 and was runner-up in 1988. In many other years he has been among the leaders and he continues to hold his own. On the all-time pacing sire leaders list, Big Towner ranks only behind Albatross, Abercrombie, Most Happy Fella and No Nukes. He also ranks fourth on the list of career $100,000 winners and in the production of 2:00 performers. Yes, he has quietly become one of the all-time great sires.

Although Big Towner took a race record of "only" 1:54.4, it must be remembered that he raced primarily on half-mile tracks. He had a world of speed and it was used judiciously in his races, many of which he had won by the three-quarter pole. Suffice to say that Big Towner was capable of far more speed than his record indicates and this is proven by his ability to sire sub-1:50 speed and for his daughters to produce the same.

A noted sire of great fillies, two of Big Towner's four millionaire offspring are female - Town Pro p,3,1:51.4 ($1,229,582) and Sweet Reflection p,3,1:53.1 ($1,004,639). His richest sons are Broadway Express p,4,1:56.1h ($1,141,726) and Sandman Hanover p,3,1:53.2f ($1,089,005). Five of Big Towner's 11 richest performers are fillies and he also has 26 $500,000 winners, eight of which are female.

In the speed department, Big Towner's fastest performers are Tune Town p,1:49.1 ($617,000) and Shadow Dance p,1:49.4 ($689,473) and he has a total of 21 sub-1:52 performers, six of which are fillies. Big Towner's fastest daughters are Trini Hanover p,3,T1:51.2 ($84,670), Towner's Image p,3,1:51.2 ($714,300), Hardie Hanover p,3,1:51.3 ($718,437), Kindly Hanover p,3,1:51.3 ($331,525) and the aforementioned Town Pro.

Big Towner has sired several divisional champions, including Walton Hanover p,3,1:53.2 ($802,741), Central Park West p,2,1:53.3f ($534,863), Town Pro (twice), Hardie Hanover and Sweet Reflection, the latter four fillies also being Breeders Crown winners.

Analysis

Considered an outcross stallion by today's standards, the only Hal Dale influences in Big Towner's pedigree are the appearance of Adios in his third generation (as the paternal grandsire of his dam) and the Hal Dale son Frisco Dale in the fourth generation. This places Adios in the fourth generation of any Big Towner offspring and another generation back in the offspring of Big Towner's daughters. Thus, Big Towner has access to broodmares from virtually every sire line except that of his own sire Gene Abbe. And he did well with many different sire lines.

The closest common crosses in Big Towner's own pedigree are 3x6x6 to The Abbe and 4x5 to Hal Dale.

Big Towner is not a large horse, standing just 15.2, but his sons and daughters race big and seem to have plenty of heart, stamina and soundness. Not only do Big Towners make themselves known in the two-year-old events, they are also racing all over North America as aged performers in FFA and Open events at ages eight, nine, ten and beyond.

Taking a look at Big Towner's 30 fastest sons and daughters, we see that eight are from Albatross mares, three from Tar Heel mares and two each from mares by Bret Hanover, Most Happy Fella, Meadow Skipper and No Nukes. In addition, three of Big Towner's fastest eight are from Albatross mares along with 12 of the 30 (40%) being from mares by Albatross and several of his sons. This is definitely a cross which works for extreme speed.

Turning to Big Towner's richest performers, there are 34 which have won $400,000 or more. Again, Albatross mares lead with nine followed by Meadow Skipper mares with four, Tar Heel and Most Happy Fella with three and Best Of All with two.

Big Towner is also capable of siring fast and rich performers from mares sired by less than mainstream stallions. Among the dams of

Big Towner's top performers are daughters of sires such as Bengazi Hanover, Captain Courageous, Hustling Time, Colt Fortysix, Maynard Hanover and Slapstick. He has also had success with several different sire lines - not just that of Meadow Skipper. Big Towner has clicked well with mares from Adios and Tar Heel sire lines.

I checked the pedigree crosses of 23 of Big Towner's $500,000 winners and was quite surprised at what I found. Knowing that Adios would be the most likely sire to be duplicated in performers sired by Big Towner, I was expecting to see several of the 4x3 and 4x4 crosses to Adios. What I did not expect was the frequency of top Big Towner performers with absolutely no Meadow Skipper blood. I had assumed that most mares going to Big Towner would have at least some Meadow Skipper blood since they were plentiful and Big Towner was the logical outcross sire for those mares. Obviously, many breeders were attempting to produce foals without Meadow Skipper blood and the results turned out to be quite startling.

Two of Big Towner's three richest performers, Broadway Express and Sandman Hanover have no Meadow Skipper blood and no common pedigree crosses within their first four generations. In addition, seven of Big Towner's 17 $600,000 winners have no Meadow Skipper blood flowing through their veins. Those other performers are Lustra's Big Guy p,1:52.4 ($977,914) and his full brother Towner's Big Guy p,3,1:52.1f ($616,841), Walton Hanover p,3,1:53.2 ($802,741), Towner's Image p,3,1:51.2 ($714,300) and Apache Circle p,2,1:55.2 ($660,248).

There is almost no such thing as inbreeding to Big Towner. Eleven of his 19 richest performers have no common ancestors in the first four generations. Interestingly, the closest cross is the 3x4 to Shadow Wave carried by Shadow Dance, who is one of Big Towner's two sub-1:50 performers, and Here's A Quarter p,1:50.1-'98 ($265,521). The other sub-1:50 horse, Tune Town, is linebred 4x3 to Tar Heel through his dam who is inbred 3x2 to Tar Heel. It's probably worth noting that Big Towner's three fastest offspring had the three closest common pedigree crosses.

Another noticeable fact is the very frequent presence of the stallion Good Time somewhere in the pedigrees of the dams of many of Big Towner's top performers. You may want to keep this in mind when choosing mares to breed to Big Towner sons. As you will read in other chapters, I am a strong proponent of the doubling of good female blood and the Good Time influence may be an illustration of the effectiveness of it. As mentioned earlier in this chapter, Big Towner's fourth dam, Olympia, is a full sister to On Time who is the dam of Good Time. Thus, there are several top Big Towner performers who are bred 5x4 to the full sisters Olympia and On Time. They are Sandman Hanover, Walton Hanover, Towner's Image, Apache Circle, Shadow Dance and Bree's Brief. In addition, there are several others bred 5x5 to that same cross.

As a broodmare sire, Big Towner has made great strides and his daughter's offspring ranked behind only those of Albatross and Abercrombie in the 1997 all-age money-winning list. For two- and three-year-olds, Big Towner ranked number one. Given the racing quality of his daughters, and that his own Gene Abbe/Shadow Wave cross reflects two of the all-time great broodmare sires, Big Towner's success should not be surprising.

The fastest horse of 1997, Northern Luck p,3,1:49.1 ($907,974), is by Camluck from the Big Towner mare Town Sweetheart p,3,1:57.3f who also has two other success stories - the Abercrombie son V P Finance p,1:51.4f-'98 ($532,453) and the good Presidential Ball 1997 two-year-old Bear Dance p,2,1:53 ($312,163). Big Towner mares are doing very well with Most Happy Fella line sires with such performers as Pacific Fella p,1:48.2-'98 ($641,341) (Cam Fella), J C's Suprimo p,4,1:50.4 ($487,797) (No Nukes), Hare Hare p,4,1:51 ($638,364) (Precious Bunny), Bingo Hanover p,4,1:51.1 ($334,547) (On The Road Again), Bahama Bunny p,3,1:52 ($464,661) and Tyler Town 3,1:54.1 ($783,093). The last mentioned mare is the dam of Sports Town p,4,1:49.2 ($631,555) (by Die Laughing).

Falcon Seelster has also clicked with Big Towner with Music Director p,1:51.1 ($796,593) and Southsider p,1:51.3 ($169,107). Other sires with

Big Towner

multiple fast performers from Big Towner mares are Nihilator, Laag, Artsplace and Abercrombie, to name a few. Big Towner's richest credit is Covert Action p,1:52.4 ($1,183,594), the long-wearing son of General Star. The cross of Artsplace with Big Towner mares should be fine if Woodrow Wilson winner Real Artist p,2,1:52 ($417,747) is any example. As you would expect with Big Towner's pedigree, his daughters fit many different sire lines and seem to be doing well with all of them. He would not have achieved such a high ranking as a broodmare sire had there been only certain niches. The same held true with Big Towner's sire Gene Abbe. Big Towner mares are the way of the future and there are plenty of them in production: he has sired 878 registered daughters from his 18 crops of foals.

Big Towner came along at the right time for the Standardbred breed and he, along with Direct Scooter, has offered an outcross choice for breeders who feel there is just too much Meadow Skipper blood. Big Towner has proven himself many times over and will be a factor in pedigrees for generations to come.

Leading Progeny by Big Towner

Fastest
- Tune Town, h, p,1:49.1 $663,500
- Shadow Dance, g, p,1:49.4 $691,073
- Here's A Quarter, h, p,1:50.1 $298,952
- Rayson Hanover, h, p,3,1:50.4 $659,342
- Feree Hanover, g, p,4,1:50.4 $139,551
- Keystone Raider, h, p,4,1:51.1 $946,914
- Threefold, h, p,3,1:51.1 $634,004
- Surburbanite, h, p,4,1:51.1 $457,224
- Townation, h, p,1:51.1 $345,402
- Towner's Image, m, p,3,1:51.2 $714,300

Richest
- Town Pro, m, p,3,1:51.4 $1,229,582
- Broadway Express, h, p,4,1:56.1h $1,141,726
- Sandman Hanover, h, p,3,1:53.2f $1,089,005
- Sweet Reflection, m, p,3,1:53.1 $1,004,639
- Lustra's Big Guy, g, p,1:52.4 $977,914
- Keystone Raider, h, p,4,1:51.1 $946,914
- Walton Hanover, h, p,3,1:53.2 $802,741
- Shipp's Scorch, h, p,3,1:54.1 $755,065
- Uptown Swell, m, p,3,1:54.2 $728,135
- Hardie Hanover, m, p,3,1:51.3 $718,437

Big Towner, Brown Horse, 15.2 Hands, 1974
p, 2, 2:05.4h; 3, 1:56.1; 4, 1:54.4 ($547,126)

Gene Abbe, 1944 p, T2:00.3 $51,239	Bert Abbe, 1922 p, T1:59¼	THE ABBE, 1903 p, 2:04	Chimes, 1884 3, 2:30¾	Electioneer	Hambletonian 10 Green Mountain Maid
				Beautiful Bells	The Moor Minnehaha
			Nettie King, 1887 4, 2:20¼	Mambrino King	Mambrino Patchen Belle Thornton
				Nettie Murphy	Hamblin Patchen
		Miss Ella H., 1913 p, 2:12¼	Mack H., 1909 2:29¼h	John A. McKerron	Nutwood Wilkes Ingar
				Wainscot	ONWARD Hecla
			Nelly Patch, 1903	Dan Patch	Joe Patchen Zelica
				Dun Daisy	
	Rose Marie, 1927 p, 2:05h	Martinos, 1913 4, 2:12¼h	Cochato, 1903 3, 2:11½	Todd	Bingen Fanella
				Castanea	Pistachio Lindora Wilkes
			Queen Audubon, 1905	Audubon Boy	J J Audubon Flaxy
				Miss Nutonia	Nutwood Iona
		Lady Permilia, 1912 p, 2:12¼h	Coastman, 1888 p, 2, 2:08¼	Bourbon Wilkes	George Wilkes Favorite
				Albatross	Coaster Calypso
			Virginia Alta, 1907	Anderson Wilkes	ONWARD Magnet
				True Lady	
Tiny Wave, 1970	Shadow Wave, 1955 p, 3, 1:56.3 $91,931	Adios, 1940 p, T1:57½ $33,329	HAL DALE, 1926 p, 6, 2:02¼ $595	ABBEDALE	THE ABBE Daisydale D.
				Margaret Hal	Argot Hal Margaret Polk
			Adioo Volo, 1930 p, 3, 2:05h	Adioo Guy	Guy Dillon Adioo
				Sigrid Volo	PETER VOLO Polly Parrot
		Shadow Grattan, 1943 p, 4, 2:07.1h $2,555	Silent Grattan, 1921 p, T2:09¾	GRATTAN ROYAL	Grattan Mona
				Silent T	Silent Brook Agave
			Peacedale, 1936 p, 2, 2:17h $45	ABBEDALE	THE ABBE Daisydale D.
				Miss Dorothy Dillon	Dillon Axworthy Zulu Belle
	Tiny Gold, 1956 p, 4, 2:01.2 $16,291	Guinea Gold, 1945 p, 9, 1:59 $118,155	Frisco Dale, 1934 p, 4, 2:00	HAL DALE	ABBEDALE Margaret Hal
				Frances San Francisco	San Francisco Dudie Egmont
			Goldie Grattan, 1934	Grattan At Law	GRATTAN ROYAL Daisy At Law
				Thais Direct	Walter Direct Wild Fire
		Cynthiana, 1951 2:10.4h $1,809	Protector, 1928 3, 1:59¼ $34,319	PETER VOLO	Peter The Great Nervolo Belle
				Margaret Arion	GUY AXWORTHY Margaret Parrish
			Olympia, 1943	Volomite	PETER VOLO Cita Frisco
				Nedda Guy	GUY AXWORTHY Nedda

Bret Hanover

A genuine Standardbred hero of the second half of the Twentieth Century, Bret Hanover has his place in history alongside of Dan Patch, Greyhound, Niatross, Albatross and Cam Fella. In fact, Bret Hanover was constantly compared to Dan Patch as he toured North America winning races, setting records, "bowing" to the crowds, and being responsible for record attendance at many tracks.

Bret was an "icon" for the harness racing industry during the 1964, 1965 and 1966 seasons, gaining fans and major publicity for the sport. Bret's racing ability drew most of the attention, but the efforts of his trainer-driver Frank Ervin had much to do with Bret's popularity. Ervin, 60 years old when Bret began his racing career, was the consummate showman and in his charge was a great horse "actor." Bret would "bow" in the winner's circle and the fans loved it. He was also well-known for his love of peppermints, but only of a certain kind - Brach's Starlight Mints. Once the media reported this, Bret's admirers made sure he was never without a plentiful supply of them.

The late Donald Evans wrote a wonderful book, entitled <u>Big Bum - The Story of Bret Hanover</u>, about the exploits of Bret and Frank Ervin. Although it is now hard to find, it should be sought out and read by harness racing fans and participants. It harkens back to the "golden era" of the sport which featured great horses, great competition and record crowds that appreciated a true champion. Evans' book chronicles Bret's career in almost race-by-race detail and what follows here is no more than an overview of that career. It's almost enough just to report that Bret Hanover won 62 of 68 starts and was voted Horse of the Year all three years he raced. He was a one of a kind legend and a true ambassador for harness racing.

Today, Bret is remembered not only as a great racehorse, but also as a great sire and broodmare sire. The only thing that kept him from being as dominant in the breeding shed as he was on the racetrack was the presence of Meadow Skipper and, later, Albatross, both of whom went on to become even greater stallions. However, Bret Hanover was extremely successful as a stallion and his blood is a major influence in the pedigrees of today's top performers.

Bret Hanover was an eye-catching colt right from the start and was the most impressive yearling in the Hanover Shoe Farm group selling in 1963. Bret was sold for $50,000 and was the highest priced yearling sold that year. The purchaser was Richard Downing of Shaker Heights, Ohio, and Bret's trainer was to be Frank Ervin, one of the sport's all-time greats who raced Bret's sire, Adios.

Downing had told Ervin he wanted to buy a Tar Heel colt at Harrisburg and Ervin agreed to check over all the Tar Heels. However, that was before he saw Bret Hanover being led at Hanover Shoe Farms. Ervin said, "Bret had the hobbles on and was a really good-gaited colt. The pony was running hard to keep up with Bret. I asked Marvin Childs about him and he said that Bret couldn't do a thing without the hobbles but he had been such a good-natured colt that they put the hobbles on him." Ervin added, "He was gaited just like Adios, had his hip movement and everything, but a lot bigger horse than Adios. He really put me in mind of Adios with his conformation and gait." Ervin was impressed and returned to the farm twice more to see the colt. At the Harrisburg sale Downing asked to see the colt with Ervin. They both agreed he was the colt they wanted to buy - and the rest is history.

Ervin was often asked to compare Bret Hanover to his sire Adios since Ervin trained and raced them both and Adios was also a champion. He said, "This colt is much finer than Tar Heel (the sire of Bret's dam) but he isn't as fine as Adios - especially over the rump. He looks a little like Adios around his head, but Adios had a finer head and a better ear than Bret. Sitting behind Bret, his motion and gait remind me of Adios. He was a fast gaited and good gaited horse and Bret is like a larger edition of him.

"Bret Hanover is a different dispositioned horse than Adios. I found that Adios was good in front but he was a sulky so-and-so when racing from behind. This big colt (Bret) has a good disposition and is kind and mannerly. But Adios was different. He was apt to stop just short of the wire. Without any warning he'd come to a sliding stop and he lost races that way. If you hit him and hurt him he wouldn't try. But I learned that I could threaten him and he would try for me. If he pinned

Bret Hanover

Photo by J. Noye
Courtesy of Castleton Farm

Race Record Highlights

At 2
1st Fox S.
Reynolds Memorial
Battle of Saratoga
Goshen Cup
Little Pat S.
Roosevelt Futurity
Ohio Standardbred Futurity
Meadow Lands Farm S.
Star Pointer S.

At 3
1st Little Brown Jug
Cane Futurity
Messenger S.
Arden Downs S.
Battle of Saratoga
American-National S.
Review Futurity
Scioto Challenge S.

At 3 (continued)
2nd heat of Review Futurity
heat and raceoff of Horseman Futurity

At 4
1st Realization S.
American-National Maturity
Empire P.
Autumn Classic P.
Governor's Cup
Revenge P.
HTA Final
2nd Pace of the Century
Preview Pace
3rd American Pacing Classic

Honors
Retired as fastest and richest Standardbred of all time
Voted Horse of the Year at two, three and four
Triple Crown winner
World Champion at three and four
World Champion for one and two heats on half-mile track
Set record for earnings by two-year-old
Set record for earnings by three-year-old

Race Record

Year	Age	Starts	Wins	2nd	3rd	Earnings	Record
1964	2	24	24	0	0	$173,298	p,2,1:57.2
1965	3	24	21	3	0	340,975	p,3,1:55
1966	4	20	17	2	1	408,343	p,4,T1:53.3
		68	62	5	1	$922,616	p,4,T1:53.3

Bret Hanover

his ears back, I would get my lines in one hand like I was getting ready to hit him, then I'd yell at him and he'd keep going."

Later, the mature Bret Hanover was tall, powerful and well-proportioned. Describing his demeanor, Ervin said "He's just a big ham."

Not only was Bret Hanover noticed and admired as a yearling, but his early training efforts also set him apart from other colts. This was noticed by Ervin's assistant Don Miller, who was based in Lexington, where Bret arrived after the Harrisburg sale. Bret was easy to break and after just a week, Miller told his wife "We've got a freak out there or he's the best natured colt I ever saw."

On the racetrack, Bret continued to live up to his early billing as a top prospect. At two, he went undefeated in all 24 starts and became the first two-year-old to win Horse of the Year honors. His earnings of $173,298 in 1964 were also the most ever by a youngster.

Bret Hanover was ready early and won the first race of his career on May 6th, 1964, in 2:07 at the Red Mile in Lexington with Frank Ervin in the sulky. That was a pretty early start by today's standards, as were Bret's 24 races at two. By the first week of June, Bret had four victories under his belt at the Red Mile, two with Ervin in the sulky and two for Dick Buxton. His fastest time was 2:04.2. It was then off to the stakes races in which Ervin's assistant Don Miller drove Bret to three consecutive wins - one at Buffalo and a two-heat affair in the Battle of Saratoga. The second of these, on July 1st, was timed in an unheard of 2:00.4 over that half-mile track.

Ervin was not in the sulky behind Bret Hanover from May 27th at the Red Mile until July 6th at Goshen due to injuries suffered during a freak incident at the Red Mile. Ervin had been warming Bret up before the races and as he rounded the final turn there was a Shriner's Band on the track near the grandstand. Ervin slowed Bret down and was just jogging the rest of the way when the band suddenly went into a turn maneuver and began playing loudly. Bret was spooked, backed up into the rail and then reared up. Ervin was dumped from the sulky and Bret fell over onto him. Bret escaped with minor scrapes and won his race later that night. However, his trainer was not as lucky. Ervin was diagnosed with two broken ribs, a pinched colon and a tear in his kidney which sidelined him for the next ten weeks except for Bret's two starts at Goshen. Ervin later admitted he came back too soon and then had to take additional time off. That's how assistant trainer Don Miller came to be in the sulky for Bret's 1:57.2 mile at Vernon Downs.

Now a star with an opening record of seven straight victories, Bret Hanover made his way to Goshen, New York and won both heats, with Frank Ervin in the sulky, in front of a large crowd which included this writer. I had gotten out of the Army just two weeks before and was privileged to see Bret Hanover this early in his career. Obviously, he made a lasting impression. A week after Goshen, Bret paced in 1:57.2 at Vernon Downs, which was to be his two-year-old record, although he also paced in 1:58 and 1:58.4 at Indianapolis. His main competition that year came from Adios Vic, Gee Lee Hanover, Tuxedo Hanover and Rivaltime, the last-named a colt who was partially owned by the great basketball star Wilt Chamberlain.

Bret Hanover ended his freshman season undefeated in 24 starts, 18 of them with Ervin in the sulky. In addition, he was harness racing's new hero and fans and horsemen alike could hardly wait for him to come back at three and show his full potential.

At three, everything Bret did enhanced his legendary status. He won his first 11 races which sent his career opening winning streak to 35 starts. Winning streaks were nothing new to Frank Ervin since he had previous streaks of 22 wins with Expresson and Yankee Hanover and 20 with Sampson Hanover.

The first loss Bret Hanover ever suffered came at Springfield, Illinois, on August 18th from the flashing hooves of the dynamic closer Adios Vic who had an incredible brush of speed in the stretch. Adios Vic had been second twice to Bret on half-mile tracks and third on a half-mile track and five-eighth mile track. However, Adios Vic was a terror on mile tracks and was able to defeat Bret three times that year over mile tracks. But the lifetime advantage went to Bret Hanover over Adios Vic by a score of 19 to 4.

Following the Springfield defeat in the first heat of the Review Futurity, Bret gained revenge in the second. In the first heat, Bret had dawdled to the three-quarters in 1:33 in a three-horse field with Adios Vic right behind. Jim Dennis pulled Adios Vic in the stretch and the battle was on with Vic outkicking Bret in a :27 final quarter to win by one and one-half lengths. There was joy in the Adios Vic camp and justifiable disappointment among the Bret Hanover group. However, Bret won the second heat by starting his stretch drive earlier and coming home in :27.1, holding off Adios Vic's closing rush.

Bret Hanover then won again at Sportsman's Park and DuQuoin, without having to face Adios Vic. His next engagement was on September 7th at Indianapolis in the Horseman Futurity. This race was to go down in history as a landmark event for a number of reasons. Adios Vic was in the field and everyone was eager for the rematch of the two great sons of Adios. In the first heat, Bret was on the front end and set fast fractions, passing the three-quarters in 1:27.1 and still in high gear. Ervin really let him ramble with a :27.4 final quarter and they passed under the wire in 1:55 flat - the fastest ever for a three-year-old and equalling the fastest ever mile in a race (set in 1955 by four-year-old Adios Harry - another son of Adios).

Since a horse still had to win two dashes to win the purse and the trophy, the field returned for the second heat. Ervin and Bret set slower fractions in this heat, passing the three-quarters in 1:29.4, which gave Adios Vic some reserve for his patented stretch drive. Jim Dennis and Adios Vic took dead aim at Bret and timed their drive just right to win by a neck in 1:56.3 with a final quarter in :26.4. Thus, the stage was set for a raceoff between the two colts.

Ervin decided to try a different strategy and took a good hold of Bret right after the start, allowing Dennis and Adios Vic to take the early lead in the two-horse race. Dennis took advantage of the opportunity by practically walking to the half in 1:08 before letting Adios Vic show his speed. The third quarter was paced in :30 with Bret still right behind Vic. But Dennis let his comet loose and brushed the final quarter in :26.2 to hold off Bret by a length in 2:04.2. Thus, the champ was not invincible, but only a horse with one of the greatest brushes of sheer speed ever seen could beat him.

These were the final losses of the year for Bret Hanover and he ended his season with a six-race winning streak to wind up his three-year-old year with 21 wins from 24 starts and another Horse of the Year trophy to go along with his 1:55 world record. Included in Bret's last half-dozen wins was the Little Brown Jug, in which he set six world records, and the Messenger S. Bret had earlier won the Cane Pace and now, along with all his other laurels, he became harness racing's second pacing Triple Crown Champion.

At four, Bret and Ervin had to face North America's best older pacers during a great season which saw him win 17 of 20 starts, set more world records, and earn another Horse of the Year trophy. Knowing that this was to be Bret's farewell tour of the nation's racetracks, harness racing fans, as well as the merely curious, came out in record numbers to witness this great horse.

One of the epic match-ups of great horses occurred when Bret Hanover met Stanley Dancer's great pacer, 10-year-old Cardigan Bay, at Roosevelt Raceway in the "Pace of the Century" in Bret's third start of the year. Cardigan Bay got the best of Bret that night, but there was a rematch a few weeks later called the "Revenge Pace" which Bret won easily over Rex Pick with Cardigan Bay third. Both races had tons of publicity and drew 37,000 fans for each event.

Bret's four-year-old season featured increased purses from tracks where he raced, appearance fees in some cases, and, usually, track record crowds. More important, in August of that year the story broke that Castleton Farm, of Lexington, Kentucky, had agreed to purchase a fifty percent interest in Bret Hanover for $1,000,000 - placing his value at $2,000,000. No horse of any breed had ever been worth as much as Bret Hanover.

A major highlight of Bret's season took place at Vernon Downs in early September. Ervin had agreed to a time-trial for his champion in hopes of breaking Adios Butler's 1:54.3 world record for pacers which was set at Lexington's Red Mile in 1960. That evening at Vernon conditions were not the best for a time-trial, being moist and foggy with a 15 mph breeze against the horses in the stretch. But this was Bret Hanover and nothing would hold him back.

Pacing with his big stride, with a lone prompter right behind, Bret passed the first quarter in :26.4 and reached the half in :55 - the fastest ever recorded. Bret went on to the three-quarters in 1:23.4 and passed under the finish line in 1:54 flat to erase Adios Butler from the record books. In doing so, Bret became the third consecutive son of Adios to hold the world record for pacers - preceded by Adios Harry and Adios Butler. Five weeks later, after a few more wins, Bret Hanover lowered that record again with a Red Mile time-trial in 1:53.3 with fractions of :27.4, :55.2, 1:24 and 1:53.3.

Bret later won the Autumn Classic Pace at Blue Bonnets in Montreal, Canada, and then headed out to California for the final two races of his career. At that point, Bret Hanover had won 62 of 66 lifetime starts - but the Canadian victory was to be his last. A delay at New York's Kennedy Airport during the trip from Canada to California caused Bret to be laid up in a temporary stall for an eight-hour period. He had also gotten cold and wet from a freezing rain during the loading process and Ervin felt this had compromised his health by the time Bret arrived in California.

Bret was to compete in the Preview Pace at Hollywood Park and then end his racing career in the $50,000 American Pacing Classic there a week later. The Preview Pace was over a one-mile distance and drew a stellar field of pacers, including Adios Vic, Cardigan Bay, Adios Marches and Glad Rags. While warming up for the Preview Pace, Bret "seemed dull and disinterested," Ervin later said. "He was not himself, not Bret Hanover at all that day; he simply had no wallop, no wallop whatsoever," Ervin was quoted by Don Evans.

Adios Vic, Bret's major career nemesis, benefited from a slow half in 1:02 by Bret. Then Jim Dennis had Adios Vic flying through the stretch as usual, going by Bret easily to win by two and one-half lengths in 1:59.2.

In an effort to thwart Adios Vic's closing drive in Bret Hanover's final race, the American Pacing Classic, Ervin planned to set a very fast pace on the lead to neutralize Adios Vic's rush. However, this event was over one and one-eighth miles - a distance Bret had never gone before in any race.

Over 23,000 fans turned out for Bret Hanover's final racetrack appearance and they were witness to an exciting drama. The same field that raced in the Preview Pace had returned with the addition of Easy Prom, Paper Boy and a budding three-year-old star named True Duane who was handled by Chris Boring. Bret Hanover was all fired up that day and Ervin had little control of his charge. Bret seemed to sense he was in some sort of time-trial and rammed the wing of the starting gate. Once loose, Bret stormed to the front and paced to the quarter in :27, the half in :56 and passed the three-quarter pole in 1:25.1. Ervin seemed to be just a passenger and Bret stormed forward, passing the mile marker in a blistering 1:54.3. Had the race ended at that point, Bret would have paced the fastest race mile in the history of the sport; no Standardbred had ever raced a sub-1:55 mile.

However, there was another eighth of a mile remaining. Ervin was later quoted, "He was like a crazy horse, an animal possessed. He was on the bit so hard I was powerless to check him. At the end of the mile I thought we might still win the thing; though my hold on him was beginning to tell. It had taken too much out of him and he was beginning to weaken. And then I saw True Duane coming."

Chris Boring had benefited from Bret Hanover's runaway antics and sat in the three-hole for the entire mile. Cardigan Bay had been right behind Bret with Adios Vic further behind True Duane. As the leaders turned for home, Boring took True Duane off the rail to go up and challenge Bret Hanover for the lead. The youngster quickly went around two of the greatest pacers ever to grab the lead and go on to victory. The mile and one-eighth time of 2:09.1 was a world record by a full two seconds. Cardigan Bay then put his nose in front of Bret's at the wire to take second with Bret Hanover finishing third for the only time in his career.

Sire Line

The male line of Bret Hanover is one of the finest of all time and he is the premier example of greatness in this line. Bret's sire is Adios, who still may go down in history as the greatest standardbred stallion ever. Bret's grandsire is Hal Dale who, in addition to Adios, is the sire of the great racehorse and stallion Good Time and the grandsire of

Meadow Skipper who many consider on a par with Adios as far as being the greatest influence on today's pacing breed.

Now, thirty years after Bret Hanover entered the stallion ranks, only to be eclipsed by Meadow Skipper and his son Albatross, the Adios line has come back in full force through Adios' great-grandson Abercrombie and his son Artsplace who seems to be taking pacers to a new level. Things have come full circle and there is now more parity among the Adios line sires and the Meadow Skipper line sires.

One would have thought the sons and grandsons of Bret Hanover, Adios's greatest son, would have been the ones to return the Adios male line to greatness. Bret did his best with sons like Storm Damage, Strike Out, Warm Breeze and High Ideal, and grandsons like Falcon Seelster. But the line reached the heights of success again through a different Adios son, Henry T. Adios, who was also a great racehorse. Abercrombie is a grandson of Henry T. Adios.

Many of the sires mentioned here are profiled in their own chapters, where you can see the twists and turns taken to get us where we are today with the Adios line.

Maternal Line

Bret Hanover's dam is the Tar Heel mare Brenna Hanover p,2,T2:02.2; 3,T2:01 ($21,946) who won the Flora Temple S., Breeders Filly S. and a heat of the Hoosier Futurity at two. She was a decent stakes filly and very well bred. Brenna Hanover produced seven living foals; Baron Hanover, Bret Hanover and Bonjour Hanover were her first three, all by Adios.

Baron Hanover p,3,2:03.4f ($1,974) never had much of a racing career but later went on to become an outstanding stallion in Ohio. He was noted for fast and long-wearing sons and his daughters became good broodmares. Like his sire Adios, Baron Hanover had the ability to "move up" poor-to-average bred broodmares. Frank Ervin was very familiar with Baron Hanover since he had seen him train as a colt the spring of the year Bret Hanover was sold as a yearling. Baron Hanover had talent and was an impressive training colt at Ben White Raceway training center in Florida. Leg problems ensured that he never reached his full potential, but Ervin knew the colt was meant to be a good one.

The Adios-Brenna Hanover cross produced more than Bret Hanover. His full sister Bonjour Hanover, a year younger, became the pacing filly version of Bret. She was an extremely dominant filly who set several world records and was the leading filly money winner at two and three. Hall of Fame trainer-driver Stanley Dancer, who trained and drove Bonjour Hanover, was quoted in a 1976 *Hub Rail* magazine article, "I think Bonjour Hanover was the greatest pacing filly I ever had. She was a full sister to Bret Hanover and she beat all the great fillies of her time week in and week out. At one time, she even held the track record of 1:57 at DuQuoin for all age and all sex. That was when she was a three-year-old in 1966."

Bonjour Hanover was, in fact, one of the sport's great filly pacers. She won 15 of 19 starts at two and 20 of 24 at three for a two-year total of 35 wins from 43 starts. At four, however, it was a different story. Bonjour won only three of her 20 starts against Invitational company and was retired to the broodmare ranks. Unfortunately for her owner Armstrong Bros., and for the Standardbred sport, she and her first foal died during a difficult birthing process.

Brenna Hanover's other foals included Betty Hanover p,3,T1:57.2 ($83,695) (by Dancer Hanover), Beau Dexter p,3,T1:59.1 ($9,606) (by Dancer Hanover) and Beautiful Hanover p,3,2:01.2 ($18,545) (by Adios). Another was the $105,000 yearling Bart Hanover p,2,2:06.2f ($502), a full brother to Bret Hanover, who was a terrible failure. Again, this proves the vagaries of genetics involving full brothers and sisters.

Bret Hanover's grandam is the stakes-winning world champion Beryl Hanover p,2,T2:02 ($29,149) by Nibble Hanover. The next three dams back in Bret's family tree are Laura Hanover 2,T2:15¼ (by The Laurel Hall), Miss Bertha Worthy 2,T2:21 (by Lee Worthy) and a Hanover Shoe Farm foundation mare Miss Bertha Dillon 4,2:02½ (by Dillon Axworthy). Yes, Bret Hanover had very high-class blood coursing through his veins.

Progeny of Note

Although Bret Hanover was ultimately overshadowed by Meadow Skipper and Albatross as a sire of racehorses, he certainly held his own during his most active period. Had there never been a Meadow Skipper, we would probably be singing the praises of Bret Hanover as an all-time great sire who followed in the footsteps of his own sire Adios. However, although history cannot be changed, don't think for a moment that Bret Hanover was not an excellent sire.

Bret Hanover sired two consecutive Little Brown Jug winners in 1972 and 1973 with Strike Out p,3,1:56.3h ($454,064) and Melvin's Woe p,3,1:57 ($157,902). Bret also sired his share of Divisional Champions, including two-year-old colt pacers Alert Bret and Strike Out and three-year-old colt pacers Strike Out, Melvin's Woe and Seahawk Hanover p,3,1:55.2 ($675,122). Bret's son Even Odds p,2,1:53.4 ($976,683) won the $1,422,500 Woodrow Wilson Pace in 1987. In other Triple Crown events, three Bret Hanover colts won the Messenger S.: Valiant Bret p,4,1:59.1h ($253,796) (1973), Bret's Champ p,3,T1:55.4 ($270,575) (1975) and Seahawk Hanover (1981) and the Cane Pace was won by Hilarious Way p,3,1:55.2 ($273,509) (1972).

Bret's greatest son as a racehorse could be Storm Damage p,3,1:53.2f ($659,296) who won 18 of his 36 starts at two and three, but had the misfortune of racing in the same crop as Niatross and Tyler B. In any other crop, Storm Damage could have been the top colt. He was tied with Niatross as the fastest two-year-old of 1979 with his 1:55.4 mile. At three, he won the Adios S. and was second to Niatross in the Meadowlands Pace Final and the Little Brown Jug. Along the way, Storm Damage set a world record of 1:53.2 on a five-eighth mile track. Storm Damage went on to become a good sire and you can read about him in his chapter.

A case can also be made for Strike Out being Bret Hanover's best son. This chestnut colt won 29 of his 44 starts, earning $454,064. Strike Out was voted Two-Year-Old Pacer of the Year and Three-Year-Old Pacer of the Year. He also set a half-mile track world record winning the Little Brown Jug, and he also won the Adios S. and Prix d'Ete. (See his chapter in this book.)

Another Bret Hanover star was Warm Breeze who, at three, equalled the 1:54.4 world record of Albatross for three-year-olds on a mile track. He came back the next year at four to pace in 1:53.1 at Golden Bear Raceway in California to become the fastest racing harness horse in history. Warm Breeze then went on to a long and successful stud career at Hanover Shoe Farms and Hempt Farms, although he never reached star status. Ironically, Warm Breeze is the Bret Hanover son who may be the link that extends the Bret male line through Falcon Seelster.

As a broodmare sire, Bret Hanover has Little Brown Jug credits with the great filly Fan Hanover p,4,T1:50.4 ($969,724), Nihilator p,3,1:49.3 ($3,225,653), Barberry Spur p,3,1:50.2 ($1,634,017) and Jaguar Spur p,4,T1:49.2 ($1,806,473) - the last-named with three consecutive wins in 1985, 1986 and 1987. In the Horse of the Year category, Bret is the sire of the dams of Nihilator (1985), Cam Fella (1982 and 1983) and Fan Hanover (1981). In the very important category of million-dollar winners, Bret Hanover is the leading broodmare sire with 15 grandsons and granddaughters having won $1,000,000 or more. Albatross is second to Bret with 13 credits, followed by Meadow Skipper and Most Happy Fella with eight and Bye Bye Byrd, Race Time and Tar Heel with seven each. When it comes to producing money winners, Bret Hanover's daughters are tops.

Analysis

Bret Hanover's own pedigree is interesting in that he is basically an outcross with the closest common pedigree cross being 4x5 to the historic stallion Peter Volo and 5x6x5 to Peter The Great. While he was a product of the most prolific bloodline cross of his era, Adios on a Tar Heel mare, Bret offered nice outcross possibilities to mares without Adios or Tar Heel blood. Of course, during the course of his long stallion career, he was also bred to plenty of mares carrying those bloodlines.

While Bret Hanover sired a significant number of sons who eventually went to stud, there were only a few who actually became commercial successes. Several were hot for a few years and would then cool off. The most important of his stallion sons would be Storm Damage, Warm Breeze, Strike Out, Seahawk Hanover, High Ideal and Flying Bret. Strike Out was able to sire speed and class, but due to limited fertility he never had the numbers needed for success. Two of

Strike Out's sons, Legal Notice and Striking Image, also had only limited success. Today, the main conduit for the continuation of the Bret Hanover male line would seem to be the Warm Breeze son Falcon Seelster who, although he has run hot and cold during his stud career, has the ability to sire high-class performers. Falcon Seelster was exported to New Zealand for a couple of years as a stallion and then returned to the U.S. for the 1998 breeding season.

Like many sires, Bret Hanover seemed to like the return of his own best blood through mares bred to him. Obviously, his "best blood" is Adios and he did well when bred to mares with some Adios blood. Bret's two richest performers, Even Odds and Farmstead's Fame p 4,1:55f ($764,598) are both linebred 2x5 to Adios. However, some of his other most notable performers are bred as follows: Seahawk Hanover 3x4 to Hal Dale; Storm Damage p,3,1:53.2f ($659,296) 5x6x4 to Peter Volo; Strike Out 4x3 to Billy Direct and Warm Breeze p,4,1:53.1 ($254,168) 3x3 to Hal Dale and 4x4 to Volomite. Some other blood that Bret did very well with was that of Nibble Hanover and his son Knight Dream. Bret's second dam is by Nibble Hanover.

Looking at Bret Hanover's highest money winners, four of his top six are from Albatross mares: Even Odds, Farmstead's Fame, Count N Sheep p,1:55.3h ($477,035) and Ultra Bright p4,1:54.4f ($472,598). Also in the top half dozen are Seahawk Hanover (from a Meadow Skipper mare) and Storm Damage (from a Worthy Boy mare). The larger picture shows that Bret Hanover sired 24 $300,000 winners with 15 being from Meadow Skipper mares and six from Albatross (son of Meadow Skipper) mares. These were crosses which really clicked for Bret Hanover.

Bret sired 47 1:55 performers during his career, and 38 of which were from mares by Meadow Skipper and his sons. Here is the breakdown - Meadow Skipper 22, Albatross 11, Race Time 4, Most Happy Fella 3, Good Time and Worthy Boy 2, and one each for daughters of General Star, French Chef and Precious Fella.

Although Bret Hanover never led the money-winning sires list, he was second in this category to Meadow Skipper during the 1975 and 1976 seasons and was in the top half-dozen sires for a number of years. In terms of his career statistics, Bret Hanover is tenth on the all-time money-winning sire list with the winners of over $64,000,000; seventh in the siring of $100,000 winners with 191, and tenth on list of the sires of 2:00 performers with 545 credits. Another Bret Hanover asset is that most of his foals made the races - 1,389 of his 1,724 foals, just over eighty percent were starters. Yes, Bret could hold his own with the greats of the breed.

For years, Bret Hanover was known as the consummate broodmare sire - a position now held by Albatross. And many of those successful Albatross mares are from Bret Hanover daughters. It was a match made in heaven and worked both ways - Bret on Albatross mares and Albatross on Bret Hanover mares. Bret was the leading money-winning broodmare sire for 1984 and 1985 and constantly among the leaders from the time his daughters began producing. In fact, he was still second to Albatross in this category for the 1995 and 1996 seasons, which shows his staying power. Bret also had stern competition in this category from Tar Heel early, and later from Meadow Skipper, Most Happy Fella and Albatross. Bret Hanover ranks as the second all-time leading 2:00 broodmare sire with 2,019 credits as this is written. He is behind only Albatross and ahead of Meadow Skipper, Most Happy Fella and Tar Heel.

The return of Adios blood worked especially well for mares by Bret Hanover. They have produced dozens of all-time great performers and many are inbred or linebred to Adios. To date, Bret Hanover has five 1:50 broodmare sire credits and all are linked to Adios. Ball and Chain p,1:49 ($1,435,390) and Jaguar Spur p,4,T1:49.2 ($1,806,473), both sired by Albatross, are 4x3 to Adios; Nihilator p,3,1:49.3 ($3,225,653) is 3x3 to Meadow Skipper and 5x3 to Adios; Sands A Flyin p,4,1:50 ($481,436) is 3x3 to Meadow Skipper and 5x3 to Adios; Hometown Spirit p,1:50 ($131,448) is 4x3 to Adios. In addition, there are two others knocking at the 1:50 door with even more intense Adios blood - Silent Spring p,1:50.1 ($981,177) is 5x5x3 to Adios and his full sister Adieu and Barberry Spur p,3,1:50.2 ($1,634,017) is 3x3 to Meadow Skipper and 5x5x3 to Adios and Adieu. It seems that when it comes to Adios blood, you can never get enough.

Five of harness racing's all-time best mares are from Bret Hanover dams and they have interesting crosses. Fan Hanover (Albatross) is 4x3 to Adios; Town Pro p,3,1:51.4 ($1,229,582) (Big Towner) is 4x3 to Adios; Three

Bret Hanover

Diamonds p,3,1:53.1 ($735,759) (Albatross) is 4x3x4 to Adios; Miss Easy p,3,1:51.1 ($1,777,656) (Amity Chef) is 5x4x3x4 to Adios and Adieu. Other good ones are Time Well Spent p,3,1:53.3 ($1,089,933) (Governor Skipper) who is inbred 3x3 to Adios and Naughty But Nice p,3,1:54f ($1,062,197) (Meadow Skipper) 3x4 to Adios. In addition, the latter's dam, Angel Hair, is inbred 2x3 to Adios.

Another great one from a Bret Hanover mare, Delinquent Account p,1:51.4 ($1,038,997) (On The Road Again), is 5x3x5 to Adios and 4x3 to Meadow Skipper. But wait -- she has an even more interesting aspect to her pedigree. Al Dente, the Bret Hanover dam of Delinquent Account, is inbred 2x4 to Adios and has an additional 3x3 cross to the Nibble Hanover full sisters Beryl Hanover and Odella Hanover. Beryl Hanover just happens to be the second dam of Bret Hanover! There is lightning in this blood and the additional return of the blood of two good full sisters does not hurt.

I must also point out here that Delinquent Account's 1997 two-year-old Artiscape p,2,1:52.3 ($495,501) (by Artsplace), is one of the most precocious and impressive youngsters I have ever seen in my long years in the sport. If Artiscape stays sound at three, he could be a true wonder horse. I'm sure Artsplace also has a lot to do with this colt's ability since that stallion is now clearly at the top of the pacing sire ladder.

A great pacing mare from a Bret Hanover daughter, without a second cross to Adios, is Armbro Feather p,1:51.3 ($1,454,927) whose closest cross is 4x3 to Knight Dream. But again, I've already mentioned this cross worked very well for Bret Hanover.

Sonsam p,3,1:53.2 ($820,104), a truly great racehorse and a major sire for a time, is from a Bret Hanover dam and is linebred 3x4 to Adios. However, another sire from a Bret Hanover dam does not have a double cross to Adios. This is Cam Fella p,4,1:53.1 ($2,041,367), the toughest racehorse ever, and also one of the best sires in history. Cam Fella's pedigree cross is an inbred 3x3 to Dale Frost and 4x4x4x4 to Hal Dale - the sire of Adios.

As you can see, Bret Hanover blood shows up in so many of the best horses in the history of the sport and that is no fluke. His blood and genes are part of these horses and it is clear that he has been able to be pass on much of his greatness to future generations.

Years ago, Frank Ervin referred endearingly to Bret Hanover as "just a big bum" which later became part of the title of the book about the great horse. Today, the memory and legacy of Bret Hanover is anything but that of a "Big Bum." Anyone who views the lifesize statue of Bret Hanover at Castleton Farm, or visits his gravesite at Kentucky Horse Park, can see the esteem in which this modern-day wonder horse is held. It was the same during his lifetime. Bret Hanover attracted visitors to his stall and paddock at Castleton Farm for many years before his death at the age of 30 in November of 1992. And many of those visitors remembered to bring Brach's Starlight Mints for "the Peppermint Kid," as he was fondly known.

Leading Progeny by Bret Hanover

Fastest
- Save Fuel, h, p,1:51.1 $325,377
- Bret's Avenger, h, p,4,1:51.3 $417,554
- Alert Move, h, p,1:51.4 $271,079
- Dangarvon, h, p,4,1:52 $273,227
- Ogden Lobell, h, p,1:52.1 $382,941
- Harada, h, p,1:52.2 $202,896
- Tropic March, h, p,1:52.4 $344,073
- Saute, g, p,4,1:53 $407,100
- Blitzen Almahurst, h, p,1:53f $205,490
- Warm Breeze, h, p,4,1:53.1 $254,168

Richest
- Even Odds, h, p,2,1:53.4 $976,683
- Farmstead's Fame, h, p,4,1:55f $764,598
- Seahawk Hanover, h, p,3,1:55.2 $675,122
- Storm Damage, h, p,3,1:53.2f $659,296
- Count N Sheep, h, p,1:55.3h $477,035
- Ultra Bright, g, p,4,1:54.4f $472,598
- Strike Out, h, p,3,1:56.3h $454,064
- Bret's Avenger, h, p,4,1:51.3 $417,554
- Saute, g, p,4,1:53 $407,100
- Raffi, h, p,4,1:53.3 $390,215

Bret Hanover, *Bay Horse, 15.3 Hands, 1962*
p, 2, 1:57.2; 3, 1:55; 4, T1:53.3 ($922,616)

Adios, 1940 p, T1:57½ $33,329	Hal Dale, 1926 p, 6, 2:02¼	Abbedale, 1917 p, 2:01¼	The Abbe, 1903 p, 2:04	Chimes	Electioneer / Beautiful Bells
				Nettie King	Mambrino King / Nettie Murphy
			Daisydale D., 1908 3, 2:15¼	Archdale	Expedition / Aline
				Mrs. Tmolus	Pactolus / Flaxey
		Margaret Hal, 1914 p, 2:19½h	Argot Hal, 1903 p, T2:04¾	Brown Hal	**TOM HAL JNR** / Lizzie
				Lady Wildflower	Duplex / Sally Ward
			Margaret Polk, 1906	John R. Gentry	Ashland Wilkes / Dame Wood
				Stella Hal	**TOM HAL JNR** / Dolly II
	Adioo Volo, 1930 p, 3, 2:05h	Adioo Guy, 1910 p, 2:00¾	Guy Dillon, 1902 T2:21¼	Sidney Dillon	Sidney / Venus
				By Guy	**GUY WILKES** / **BY BY**
			Adioo, 1895	**GUY WILKES**	George Wilkes / Lady Bunker
				BY BY	Nutwood / Rapidan
		Sigrid Volo, 1921 p, T2:04	**PETER VOLO**, 1911 4, 2:02	**PETER THE GREAT**	Pilot Medium / Santos
				Nervolo Belle	Nervolo / Josephine Knight
			Polly Parrot, 1904 p, 2:13¼h	Jersey B B	Jersey Wilkes / Blue Belle
				Lady Maud C	Chitwood / Noretta
Brenna Hanover, 1956 p, 3, T2:01 $21,946	Tar Heel, 1948 p, 4, T1:57 $119,148	Billy Direct, 1934 p, 4, T1:55 $12,040	Napoleon Direct, 1909 p, 1:59¾	Walter Direct	Direct Hal / Ella Brown
				Lady Erectress	Tom Kendle / Nelly Zarro
			Gay Forbes, 1916 p, 2:07¾	Malcolm Forbes	Bingen / Nancy Hanks
				Gay Girl Chimes	Berkshire Chimes / Miss Gay Girl
		Leta Long, 1940 p, 4, 2:03¾ $9,321	Volomite, 1926 3, 2:03¼ $32,649	**PETER VOLO**	**PETER THE GREAT** / Nervolo Belle
				Cita Frisco	San Francisco / Mendocita
			Rosette, 1933 2, 2:06 $4,222	Mr. McElwyn	**GUY AXWORTHY** / Widow Maggie
				Rose Scott	Peter Scott / Roya McKinney
	Beryl Hanover, 1947 p, 2, T2:02 $29,076	Nibble Hanover, 1936 1:58¾ $25,599	Calumet Chuck, 1929 2, 2:04	Truax	**GUY AXWORTHY** / Hollyrood Nimble
				Sumatra	Belwin / Sienna
			Justissima, 1915 6, 2:06¼h	Justice Brooke	Barongale / Expectation
				Claire Toddington	Toddington / Fruity Worthy
		Laura Hanover, 1931 2, T2:15¼	The Laurel Hall, 1918	**PETER THE GREAT**	Pilot Medium / Santos
				Baby Bertha	Silk Cord / Bertha Derby
			Miss Bertha Worthy, 1925 2, T2:21	Lee Worthy	Lee Axworthy / Emma Smith
				Miss Bertha Dillon	Dillon Axworthy / Miss Bertha C

Bye Bye Byrd

I have had particularly fond memories of Bye Bye Byrd since he came to the New York Free-For-All scene at Yonkers and Roosevelt in 1959 and dominated the action that year against the best pacers in the nation. At age 17, I was very impressed and he quickly became my favorite horse during the year in which I first became a harness racing fan. "Triple B," as he was known in the New York media and among fans at that time, was simply the best and was rewarded with Horse of the Year honors.

Knowing nothing about Bye Bye Byrd's pedigree, or of his stakes exploits as a two and three-year-old, I admired him for his tenacity, speed and "never say die" attitude on the racetrack. It wasn't until several years later that I realized I had been privileged to watch one of the sport's great racehorses for over a three-year period. I also understood later what his rich bloodlines meant to the sport then and how they have influenced many of today's superstars.

Bye Bye Byrd, bred and owned by Rex and Ethel Larkin, received his early lessons from the great trainer Tom Berry and was later sent to veteran Indiana trainer Don Taylor for racing. At two, Bye Bye Byrd was not a dominant colt, but he could hold his own against the best of them. At three, he fared better, winning 16 of 26 starts and setting a two-heat world record for three-year-olds. Near the end of his three-year-old season, the Larkins entrusted their star colt to the great Canadian horseman Clint Hodgins, who was a top trainer-driver on the New York circuit, to race in the rich Cane Pace at Yonkers. Bye Bye Byrd had the lead until the last few strides but was beaten by a head by Raider Frost. Bye Bye Byrd was then moved into the Hodgins stable to be readied for FFA racing in 1959.

The rest is history, and older fans and horsemen still remember the epic battles during the 1959, 1960 and 1961 seasons when Bye Bye Byrd took on the best week after week and made them know they were in a race. During the 1960 season, one of his greatest rivals was Adios Butler. That year, the great Adios Butler won 13 of his 17 starts on the way to his first Horse of the Year title. "The Butler" and "Triple B," engaged in several stirring contests and it was Bye Bye Byrd who handed Adios Butler three of his four defeats that season. And, in 1961, it was Adios Butler who equalled Bye Bye Byrd's half-mile track record of 1:57.4 which he set as a four-year-old in 1959.

Bye Bye Byrd set or equalled 12 world records during his career and retired as the sport's leading money-winning Standardbred. He also won major events at one and one-quarter and one and one-half miles. His regular driver Clint Hodgins was once quoted, "I think maybe Bye Bye Byrd was the gamest horse I ever drove. I won three heats with him at Springfield, Illinois on a Grand Circuit program one hot afternoon with each mile under two minutes."

At the end of his racing career, the Larkins decided to stand Bye Bye Byrd at his birthplace, their Poplar Hill Farm in Lexington, Kentucky, beginning with the 1962 breeding season. Unfortunately, Mr. and Mrs. Larkin, returning from a meeting of the Hambletonian Society in New York, died in a plane crash in November of 1965. This was after Bye Bye Byrd's first crop had raced.

A Chicago bank handled the affairs of the Larkins' Estate and they ultimately struck a deal with Hempt Farms' owner Max Hempt to sell Bye Bye Byrd. Hempt was very happy to obtain such an up-and-coming stallion for his Pennsylvania farm. Hempt then syndicated Bye Bye Byrd for $7,500 per share and the stallion went on to a long and fruitful career at Hempt Farms. Bye Bye Byrd died in 1980 at the age of 25.

Sire Line

Bye Bye Byrd is a grandson of the great stallion Volomite and is one of those who were able to extend that sire's male line a few more generations. Other modern-day Volomite line sires who fanned the flames of the male line for a time were Overtrick, Harold J. and Sampson Direct. Bye Bye Byrd passed the torch mainly through his sons Armbro Nesbit, Keystone Ore and Bye And Large. However, Bye

Race Record Highlights

At 2
- **1st** Illinois State Fair S. (three heats)
  Meadow Lands Farm S.
  two ITPHA S.
- **2nd** heat of Two Gaits Farm S.
  ITPHA S.
  Illinois Fair S.
- **3rd** heat of Fox S.
  heat of Two Gaits Farm S.

At 3
- **1st** Geers S.
  Great Mid-West S.
  Horseman Futurity
  Illinois State Fair S.
  Matron S.
  heat of Little Brown Jug Trial
  two ITPHA S.
- **2nd** Cane Futurity
  heat of Little Brown Jug Preview
- **3rd** two heats of American-National S.
  heat of Little Brown Jug Preview

At 4
- **1st** National Pacing Derby
  Good Time Pace
  two HTA Paces
  American-National S.
  New England Pacing Derby

At 4 (continued)
  two Transamerica Paces
- **2nd** National Championship Pace

At 5
- **1st** International Pace
  Good Time Pace
  National Pacing Derby
  leg of American Pacing Classic
  Illinois State Fair S.
- **2nd** International Encore
- **3rd** leg and Final of American Pacing Classic

At 6
- **2nd** International Pace
  National Championship Pace
  Richelieu International
- **3rd** Good Time Pace

Honors
At 4, voted Horse of the Year
At 3, set world record for two heats
At 4, set world record on half-mile track
Set or equalled 12 world records
Retired as leading money-winning Standardbred ever

Bye Bye Byrd

Photo courtesy of Hempt Farms

Race Record

Year	Age	Starts	Wins	2nd	3rd	Earnings	Record
1957	2	17	6	5	2	$ 26,967	p,2,2:01
1958	3	26	16	4	3	65,334	p,3,1:57.4
1959	4	20	14	4	0	212,433	p,4,1:57.4h
1960	5	25	11	7	2	187,612	p,T1:56.1
1961	6	13	3	4	2	61,911	
		101	50	24	9	$554,257	p,T1:56.1

Bye Bye Byrd

Bye Byrd's branch of the male line has now died out with no major commercial sires at stud.

The only remaining branch of the Volomite male line continuing to do well is the one that runs through Direct Scooter and his good son Matt's Scooter (see their chapters). Perhaps Matt's Scooter will leave a commercial son to carry on the great Volomite male line.

Bye Bye Byrd was a son of the good Volomite racehorse and stallion Poplar Byrd p,1:59.3 ($69,300) who was bred and owned by the Larkins and went to stud at their Poplar Hill Farm in 1950 for a fee of $400. Poplar Byrd was an excellent racehorse and was the leading money-winning two-year-old pacer of 1946 with $28,498. His wins included the Fox S., Little Pat S., McMahon Memorial and DuQuoin Fair S. At three, Poplar Byrd's trainer Tom Berry became incapacitated and the colt also suffered some problems. After being taken over by trainer-driver Wayne "Curly" Smart, Poplar Byrd won a pair of stakes at Lexington that fall.

At four, Poplar Byrd was again at the top of his game and won the Goshen FFA Pace, Dan Patch S., Single G. Classic, Directum I S., American S. and Stallion S. His trademarks were quick brushes of speed, courage and stamina against some of the nation's best pacers. He showed the same qualities at five and was then retired following the 1949 season.

Poplar Byrd's dam was the world champion filly Ann Vonian p,2,2:02½; 3,2:01¼ by Grattan At Law. She had set a two-heat record for two-year-old pacing fillies which stood from 1939 to 1949. With this pedigree, Poplar Byrd certainly had the right to become a nice sire. He had a decent career at stud, with Bye Bye Byrd being a great performer along with 1968 Triple Crown winner Rum Customer p,3,1:56 ($1,001,548) who never made an impact as a sire. Others of note were Fly Fly Byrd p,4,1:58.2 ($244,601), the filly Balenzano p,3,2:00 ($182,643) and the good mare Reba Byrd p,1:58.3 ($132,149). Like his son Bye Bye Byrd, Poplar Byrd made much more of an impact as a broodmare sire with such credits as Whata Baron, Kawartha Eagle, Lantern, Adios Cleo, Oil Strike and others.

Maternal Line

Bye Bye Byrd has one of the more interesting maternal pedigrees of any of the older pacing stallions. His dam, Evalina Hanover p,1:59.2 ($12,420) did not take a record until she was seven years old in 1953 and won only eight races during her career. However, she was about as blue-blooded as a horse could be at the time she retired. Evalina Hanover's sire was the great champion Billy Direct p,4,T1:55 who was the fastest harness horses of all time when his daughter left the track. Evalina Hanover's dam was Adieu p,2,T2:04¼ who happened to be a full sister to the racing champion, and possibly greatest sire ever, Adios p,T1:57½.

Evalina Hanover was owned by the Larkins and bred in 1954 to their young stallion Poplar Byrd. In the spring of 1955, Evalina Hanover's first foal was Bye Bye Byrd. She later produced four other 2:00 performers, but none of them was near the class of Bye Bye Byrd. One of her other sons, Egyptian Dancer p,3,Q1:58.2 ($4,425), a son of Overtrick, later became a very successful stallion in Illinois and many of his daughters are still producing good offspring.

The prolific speed heritage in Evalina Hanover's genes showed up in Bye Bye Byrd as a youngster and again through one of Bye Bye Byrd's full sisters, Evalina Lobell, who is the dam of the former two-year-old world champion Kawartha Eagle p,2,1:55.3 ($271,711). However, other than this flash of brilliance there was nothing much of championship caliber and this particular branch of the Maggie Gaines maternal family is not one of today's major speed producers.

Progeny of Note

Bye Bye Byrd began his stud career on a very positive note when his first four crops produced a number of stars. His first crop included Silent Byrd and Fashion Tip and his second featured the stars Meadow

Paige, Nardin's Byrd and Armbro Hardy. Batman, Bye And Large and Bye Bye Pat headed the third group and Bye Bye Sam the fourth. Bye Bye Byrd had 14 2:00 credits from these early crops and no other sire had as many at that stage of his career. As a result, Bye Bye Byrd began to attract even finer mares to his court.

There have been many star sons and daughters of Bye Bye Byrd through the years, but he was primarily noted as a colt sire. Several of his daughters were outstanding stakes winners and many went on to great careers in the broodmare ranks. However, it is Bye Bye Byrd's sons who were the major stars. His biggest money-winning son was Armbro Nesbit p,3,1:56 ($625,964) from a mare by Capetown (a pacing son of the great trotting sire Hoot Mon). He was an outstanding stakes and FFA horse who later became a stallion at Hanover Shoe Farms before his death at an early age. Armbro Nesbit daughters have done well as broodmares with his most famous credit as a broodmare sire being world champion Beach Towel p,3,1:50 ($2,570,357). His daughters have also produced such stars as T.K'.s Skipper p,T1:49.2 ($1,000,025) and Dictionary p,4,1:52.4 ($868,981).

Another great son of Bye Bye Byrd is Keystone Ore p,3,1:55.2 ($563,072) who was voted 1976 Horse of the Year after winning 22 of 33 starts, including the Little Brown Jug, and setting a world record on a half-mile track. He also went on to a career as a stallion, with limited success, and also has several good broodmare sire credits, including Stout p,4,1:49.4 ($1,093,983), Biba Fra p,4,1:50 ($342,908), Hometown Spirit p,1:50 ($131,448), Keystone Tad p,1:50.3 ($162,340) and Direct Flight p,4,1:51 ($825,052).

Other $500,000 winners for Bye Bye Byrd were Eastern Skipper p,3,1:56.2h ($563,072), Keystone Smartie p,3,1:57.4 ($534,340) and Nardin's Byrd p,3,1:59h ($507,391). Bye Bye Byrd sired a number of other performers who were well-remembered both for their stakes ability and later for being powers in the FFA ranks. These would include Miami Beach p,1:58 ($447,117), Bye Bye Max p,4,1:57.4 ($417,910), Batman p,3,1:58 ($378,649), Meadow Paige p,3,T1:55.2 ($363,877) and Bye Bye Sam p,4,1:57f ($299,566). His fastest of six 1:55 credits was Spare Hand p,1:53.4 ($199,746). Bye Bye Byrd's richest daughter was Keystone Memento p,3,T1:59.2 ($221,725).

Another Bye Bye Byrd son with some success at stud was Bye And Large p,3,1:58.3h ($160,725) whose best performer was the fast Justin Passing p,3,T1:53.2 ($806,348). However, like Armbro Nesbit with Beach Towel as a broodmare sire credit, Bye And Large will go down in history as the sire of the dam of the wonderful ironhorse Riyadh p,1:48.4 ($2,763,527). Thus, Bye Bye Byrd has three sons with 1:50 broodmare sire credits.

Let's take a look at some of the pedigree crosses at work with Bye Bye Byrd's top performers. Armbro Nesbit is inbred 3x3 to Adios and his sister Adieu, 3x4x5 to Volomite and 4x4 to Hal Dale. Keystone Ore and Keystone Smartie (both from Tar Heel mares) have similar setups with the addition of a 3x3 cross to Billy Direct. Nardin's Byrd is 3x4 to Volomite, 4x3 to Hal Dale and 4x4 to Napoleon Direct (the sire of Billy Direct). Bye Bye Max has an older pedigree, being inbred 3x3 to Volomite along with 4x4 crosses to Peter Volo and Napoleon Direct. Other Bye Bye Byrd stars with the 3x3 cross to Adios and his sister are Albert's Star p,3,1:56.4 ($324,198) and Say Hello p,2,1:55.4 ($189,257).

At this point, I would be remiss if I did not say more about Say Hello. He was one of the top two-year-old stars of 1977 but came back poorly at three and was winless in nine starts. However, he was well thought of and breeders were looking for a son of Bye Bye Byrd for stud duty. Say Hello was syndicated among some top breeders, received books of well-bred mares, but then, unfortunately, went on to become one of the most colossal failures among modern stallions. It seemed as though he could not even sire average performers and his daughters, unlike many other sons of Bye Bye Byrd, seem rather hopeless as broodmares. I've rarely seen anything like this from a horse who went to stud having pedigree, performance and opportunity. Say Hello is bred 3x3 to Adios and his sister, 3x5x5 to Volomite and 3x4 to Billy Direct. Ah, the great mysteries of breeding!

There are a number of other successful inbred 3x2 crosses appearing among Bye Bye Byrd's best sons. That cross is to Adios and his sister Adieu and appears in the pedigrees of Batman, Meadow Paige, Keystone Ponder p,1:58.3f ($349,498) and Bye And Large.

Analysis

During the apex of his stud career, Bye Bye Byrd was the leading money-winning sire for the 1973 and 1974 seasons. He is influential in that he appears in the first three generations of the sires Niatross, On The Road Again, Beach Towel, Armbro Cadet, Kiev Hanover and stallion newcomer Silver Almahurst. He also appears twice in later generations of Precious Bunny and Jenna's Beach Boy.

There was a period during the late 1970s through the mid-1980s, after Bye Bye Byrd's daughters began producing racehorses, when breeders were very hot on the trail of Bye Bye Byrd mares for their broodmare bands. They were being sold privately, retired from tracks and claimed from races since it was evident Bye Bye Byrd was moving up as a successful broodmare sire. In fact, Bye Bye Byrd was always competitive with Tar Heel (one year finishing second to that venerable leader), Bret Hanover and Meadow Skipper in the money-winning broodmare sire category.

Bye Bye Byrd ended his stallion career, which spanned the years from 1962 through the foals of 1981, with his offspring winning over $31,000,000 with 158 in 2:00 and 95 $100,000 winners. His broodmare credits are still rising and his daughters have produced over 830 2:00 performers as this is written, ranking him eighth on the all-time 2:00 broodmare sire list. Keep in mind, also, that Bye Bye Byrd was never bred to the huge numbers of mares seen by today's most popular stallions. His 19 crops of foals averaged just 57 per year with a high of 80 born in 1969.

As a broodmare sire, Bye Bye Byrd was particularly prolific when his daughters were bred to Albatross line stallions. Obviously, the premier credit for this cross is Niatross p,3,T1:49.1 (by Albatross) along with Hot Lead p,4,1:49.3 ($1,327,862) (by Jaguar Spur - son of Albatross) and Silver Almahurst p,1:49.4 ($1,091,024) (by Nihilator - grandson of Albatross). These three are sub-1:50 million-dollar winners. Other top performers by Albatross from Bye Bye Byrd mares are Kiev Hanover p,3,1:50.1 ($610,179), Keystone Sanford p,3,1:53.2 ($519,722) and the top mare Jef's Eternity p,1:54.4 ($569,802) who is the dam of the great filly Immortality p,3,1:51 ($1,614,939).

In the case of Hot Lead, his dam is the Bye Bye Byrd mare J.M. Valinda p,4,T1:58, who is inbred 3x3x4 to Adios and Adieu. Perhaps the extra dose of this blood is the key to his success. When added to the blood of his sire Jaguar Spur, Hot Lead's pedigree reads as follows: 5x4x4x4x5 to Adios and 4x5 to the three-quarter sisters Vibrant Hanover (grandam of Albatross) and Veda Hanover (grandam of Henry T. Adios). That's a pretty good concentration of extremely strong genes.

Bye Bye Byrd's daughters also clicked well with many other Meadow Skipper line stallions and hit the jackpot with two million-aires sired by French Chef - Amity Chef p,3,1:51.1 ($1,372,683) and Frugal Gourmet p,3,1:51.3 ($1,349,560). On The Road Again p,4,1:51.4 ($2,819,102), one of the sport's toughest performers, is by Happy Motoring from a Bye Bye Byrd mare. Spiked Byrdie, a Bye Bye Byrd daughter, is the only pacing mare to have produced two milion dollar winning offspring, the aforementioned Silver Almahurst and Division Street p,1:52.3f ($1,222,352) (by Most Happy Fella). Other former notable champions from Bye Bye Byrd mares include Super Clint p,3,1:54 ($208,923) (by Super Wave) and Jade Prince p,2,1:54.1 ($569,247) (by Meadow Skipper).

While examining the pedigrees of many of Bye Bye Byrd's broodmare credits I especially noticed that many of his top-producing daughters were from mares sired by Billy Direct line stallions such as Tar Heel, Thorpe Hanover and Direct Rhythm. Evalina Hanover, Bye Bye Byrd's dam, was by Billy Direct and there seems to be an affinity for the return of his blood to Bye Bye Byrd offspring. In addition, the dams of other excellent Bye Bye Byrd producers were sired by Adios and several of his sons, such as Henry T. Adios, Dancer Hanover and Bullet Hanover. Again, if we look at Bye Bye Byrd's dam Evalina Hanover we see that her dam was a full sister to Adios and the return of that Adios blood was extremely successful.

With Evalina Hanover's pedigree, being by Billy Direct from a sister to Adios, she was genetically set up to provide multiple common crosses to Bye Bye Byrd's offspring, since both Billy Direct and Adios were the top sires of their era and their daughters would appear in the court of Bye Bye Byrd. So genetically, historically and geographically, Bye Bye Byrd should have had many sons and daughters which would be "inbred" with 2x3, 3x3 and 3x4 crosses to Adios, his sister Adieu and Billy Direct. Add into that mix the fact that Bye Bye Byrd was also a grandson of the great sire Volomite which placed him in the third generation of Bye Bye Byrd's offspring. Volomite blood was still around in the 1960s and 1970s and there were many Bye Bye Byrd offspring linebred to Volomite.

Looking at the pedigrees of some of Bye Bye Byrd's best producing daughters, there are obviously going to be some strong links to Adios and Billy Direct through the blood of his dam Evalina Hanover. I have noted above the example of Hot Lead's dam J.M. Valinda. Here are some more examples: Spiked Byrdie (dam of Silver Almahurst and Division Street) is 3x3 to Adios/Adieu, 3x4 to Billy Direct and 3x4 to Volomite. Keystone Sandra (dam of Kiev Hanover) is inbred 3x2 to Adios/Adieu as is Hush A Bye (dam of Amity Chef) and Oui Oui Byrd (dam of Jade Prince p,2,1:54.1). Keystone Mist (dam of Windshield Wiper p,3,T1:53.2) and St. Patrick's Morn (dam of Super Clint p,3,1:54) are 3x3 to Adios/Adieu.

Don't think, however, that Bye Bye Byrd always needed the extra cross to Adieu's great brother Adios to impart to his daughters. Three of Bye Bye Byrd's all-time best broodmare sire credits are Niatross, On The Road Again and Jef's Eternity. Niagara Dream (dam of Niatross) has a 4x4 cross to the old foundation sire Peter Volo as her closest. Bye Bye Mollie (dam of On The Road Again) has no common ancestors in her first four generations and her closest cross is a 5x5 to the historic sire Guy Axworthy. Time Goes Bye (dam of Jef's Eternity) is bred 3x4 to Volomite, 4x3 to Hal Dale and 4x4 to Peter Volo.

As you can see, inbred or outcrossed, Bye Bye Byrd daughters were able to do it all. He is a strength in a male or female pedigree and so are some of his sons, particularly Keystone Ore. Bye Bye Byrd was a great one on the track and as a stallion; one only needs to see his blood in the pedigree of Niatross to realize that fact.

Bye Bye Byrd

Photo courtesy of Hempt Farms

Leading Progeny by Bye Bye Byrd

Fastest

Spare Hand, h, p,1:53.4 $199,746
Armbro Breton, g, p,1:54 $210,128
Nesbit Two, h, p,1:54.1 $284,721
Keystone Sixty, h, p,4,1:54.2 $276,845
Keystone Sceptre, h, p,1:54.3 $181,388
Keystone Scamp, h, p,4,1:54.4 $83,167
Keystone Sherlock, h, p,1:55.1 $142,815
The Iron Byrd, h, p,4,1:55.1 $114,855
Keystone Ore, h, p,3,1:55.2 $563,072
Meadow Paige, h, p,3,T1:55.2 $363,877

Richest

Armbro Nesbit, h, p,3,1:56 $625,964
Eastern Skipper, h, p,3,1:56.2h $600,164
Keystone Ore, h, p,3,1:55.2 $563,072
Keystone Smartie, h, p,3,1:57.4 $535,340
Nardin's Byrd, h, p,3,1:59h $507,391
Miami Beach, g, p,1:58 $447,117
Bye Bye Max, h, p,4,1:57.4 $417,910
Batman, h, p,3,1:58 $378,649
Meadow Paige, h, p,3,T1:55.2 $363,877
Keystone Ponder, h, p,1:58.3f $349,498

Bye Bye Byrd, *Bay Horse, 1955*
p, 2, 2:01; 3, 1:57.4; T1:56.1 ($554,272)

Poplar Byrd, 1944 p, T1:59.3 $69,300	Volomite, 1926 3, 2:03¼ $32,649	**PETER VOLO**, 1911 4, 2:02	Peter The Great, 1895 4, 2:07¼	Pilot Medium	**HAPPY MEDIUM** Tackey
				SANTOS	Grand Sentinel Shadow
			Nervolo Belle, 1906	Nervolo	Colbert Nellie D
				Josephine Knight	Betterson Mambrino Beauty
		Cita Frisco, 1921	San Francisco, 1903 2:07¾	Zombro	McKinney Whisper
				Oniska	Nutwood Wilkes Bay Line
			Mendocita, 1899	Mendocino	Electioneer Mano
				Esther	Express Coliseum
	Ann Vonian, 1937 p, 3, 2:01¼ $4,974	Grattan At Law, 1922 p, 4, 2:16¼h	Grattan Royal, 1908 p, 2:06¼	Grattan	Wilkes Boy Annie Almont
				Mona	Robert McGregor Jenny Bryan
			Daisy At Law, 1902 p, 2:12¼h	Heir At Law	Mambrino King Estabella
				Daisy Rysdyk	Royal Rysdyk
		Margaret Vonian, 1928 p, 2:05	Favonian, 1918 T2:01¾	J Malcolm Forbes	**BINGEN** **SANTOS**
				Allie Watts	General Watts Allie Allerton
			Margaret C. Brooke, 1919 p, 2:11¾	Baron Brooke	Justice Brooke Fruition
				Maud G	Prince Roi Dolly G
Evalina Hanover, 1946 p, 1:59.2 $12,420	Billy Direct, 1934 p, 4, T1:55 $12,040	Napoleon Direct, 1909 p, 1:59¾	Walter Direct, 1900 p, 2:05¾	Direct Hal	Direct Bessie Hall
				Ella Brown	Prince Pulaski Jnr Fanny Brown
			Lady Erectress	Tom Kendle	Erector Winnie Davis
				Nelly Zarro	Hal Pizarro Bay Tom Mare
		Gay Forbes, 1916 p, 2:07¾	Malcolm Forbes, 1904	**BINGEN**	May King Young Miss
				Nancy Hanks	**HAPPY MEDIUM** Nancy Lee
			Gay Girl Chimes, 1911 T2:28¼h	Berkshire Chimes	**CHIMES** Berkshire Belle
				Miss Gay Girl	Gay Boy Electric Belle
	Adieu, 1938 p, 2, T2:04¼	Hal Dale, 1926 p, 6, 2:02¼	Abbedale, 1917 p, 2:01¼	The Abbe	**CHIMES** Nettie King
				Daisydale D.	Archdale Mrs. Tmolus
			Margaret Hal, 1914 p, 2:19½h	Argot Hal	Brown Hal Lady Wildflower
				Margaret Polk	John R. Gentry Stella Hal
		Adioo Volo, 1930 p, 3, 2:05h	Adioo Guy, 1910	Guy Dillon	Sidney Dillon By Guy
				Adioo	Guy Wilkes By By
			Sigrid Volo, 1921 p, T2:04	**PETER VOLO**	Peter The Great Nervolo Belle
				Polly Parrot	Jersey B B Lady Maud C

Cam Fella

He is known simply as "The Pacing Machine." Ask any harness racing fan the identity of that horse and most will be able to tell you it's Cam Fella. I doubt there has ever been a tougher and more durable Standardbred than Cam Fella. His racetrack exploits so impressed fans, and horsemen, that his 1997 North American tour prompted thousands of people to recall their own special memories of Cam Fella. Now retired from both the racetrack and stallion duties, Cam Fella is one of the Standardbred representatives at the Kentucky Horse Park in Lexington, where he is visited by people from around the world. We could not have chosen a finer representative for our breed.

Cam Fella is legendary both as a racehorse and a sire. Very few have achieved the absolute pinnacle of the sport in both categories. Cam Fella might have achieved even more had it not been for a cruel stroke of fate: several years ago he was stricken with testicular cancer and his breeding activities had to be curtailed. In 1997, he was gelded in order to save his life. Fortunately for harness racing, Cam Fella regained his health and is now a great ambassador for the sport.

The saga of Cam Fella began when he was bred by Wilfred Cameron of Washington, Pennsylvania, who owned his dam, the Bret Hanover mare Nan Cam, whom he bred to Most Happy Fella. Due to a family tragedy, Cameron was forced to sell the mare in foal and, later, the yearling Cam Fella was sold at public auction.

Cam Fella was purchased as a yearling for $19,000 by Canadian trainer-driver Doug Arthur at the Tattersalls Sale in Lexington, Kentucky, on October 2nd, 1980. The youngster was the first horse in the ring during the seventh and final session of the Tattersalls Sale that year. Other than being sired by Most Happy Fella, his pedigree page was very unimpressive, hardly worth a second glance. The $19,000 Cam Fella fetched at the sale was mostly a testament to the lofty status of his sire Most Happy Fella. In addition to his less than blueblood pedigree, Cam Fella was small and was a ridgling (one testicle undescended).

At two, Doug Arthur brought Cam Fella along conservatively. In his first qualifying race, on August 11, 1981, at Greenwood Raceway, he made a break and he also made breaks in two of his first four parimutuel starts. Cam Fella had only one win in his first five parimutuel starts from mid-August through early November. However, he was beginning to show some speed and come-from-behind ability since he did not leave very fast from the gate. In his last six starts of the season, Cam Fella came into his own and showed some flashes of the brilliance which was to come. He won the $19,000 Valedictory Series Final at Greenwood in 2:00.2 after being parked out three-quarters of a mile. In previous legs of the Series, Cam Fella was second three times, but was twice placed back for interference. Another time, he won in 2:03.

Trainer Pat Crowe and owners Norm Clements and Norm Faulkner had been interested for weeks in the possible purchase of Cam Fella. Later, they made an agreement with Doug Arthur for the $140,000 purchase price. It seemed like a pretty strong price for a two-year-old who had a record of 11 3-3-3 and earnings of only $17,588. But Cam Fella was showing weekly improvement and ended his season on a very impressive note.

Three weeks after his purchase, Cam Fella was shipped to New Jersey to race at The Meadowlands where he won impressively in 1:58.4 in his first start as a three-year-old. The owners were offered $250,000 for him but turned it down. He then had three wins as favorite in the Hopeful Series at Yonkers before shipping back to The Meadowlands for another pair of wins, including a leg of the New Faces Series. Cam Fella went back to Yonkers to take the Hopeful Series Final followed by two more Meadowlands wins in a leg and the New Faces Series Final. Heavily favored in all of his starts, Crowe and Cam Fella usually left the gate conservatively, letting things settle down. Cam Fella was usually in front by the half and winning easily.

After wreaking devastation upon his opponents at The Meadowlands, Cam Fella was shipped coast-to-coast for the Spring

Race Record Highlights

At 2
- **1st** Valedictory Series Final
- **2nd** leg of Valedictory Series
- **3rd** leg of Valedictory Series

At 3
- **1st** Cane Pace
  Messenger S.
  Confederation Cup
  Queen City S.
  Prix d'Ete
  New Faces Series Final and two legs
  Hopeful Series Final and three legs
  Mohawk Sophomore Championship
  Monticello Classic Elimination
  Two legs of Spring Championship Series
- **2nd** Monticello Classic
  Simcoe S.

At 4
- **1st** two legs of World Cup Series
  U.S. Pacing Championship
  Frank Ryan Memorial
  Summer Pacing Championship
  Driscoll Series Final and two legs

At 4 (continued)
  Graduate Series Final and leg
  Ontario Jockey Club S.
  Canadian Pacing Derby
  American-National Maturity
  Stewart Fraser Memorial
- **2nd** four legs of Graduate Series
- **3rd** leg of World Cup Series

Honors

Voted Horse of the Year at three and four

Cam Fella

Photo by Ronni Nienstedt
Courtesy of Stonegate Farms

Race Record

Year	Age	Starts	Wins	2nd	3rd	Earnings	Record
1981	2	11	3	3	3	$ 17,588	p,2,2:00.2f
1982	3	33	28	2	0	879,723	p,3,T1:54.4
1983	4	36	30	4	2	1,144,056	p,4,1:53.1
		80	61	9	5	$2,041,367	p,4,1:53.1

Championship Series at Los Alamitos in California. He won his first two legs in 1:56.2 and 1:58.4 and was now undefeated in 11 starts for the year. However, in the rich $300,000 Final of the Series, disaster struck at the three-quarter pole when Cam Fella stepped into the sulky of the horse in front of him while racing fifth and trying to get into contention for the stretch drive. He did not go down and was uninjured, but finished eighth in the race.

Shipping back to Canada after the California trip, Cam Fella had a few weeks off. Then he won at Mohawk before being returned to The Meadowlands to see if he would be competitive with that season's top colts which included No Nukes, McKinzie Almahurst, Hilarion, Icarus Lobell, Temujin, Trenton and Merger. Cam's first race back at The Meadowlands was uncharacteristic in that he showed no pace and finished fourth. But being the resilient sort, Cam Fella bounced back two weeks later to win the Cane Pace Elimination and Final, even though he was not the favorite in each heat. Cam had proven he could take on the top three-year-olds.

In preparing Cam Fella for the Cane Pace, Crowe had trained him in 1:55 at The Meadowlands the prior week. Later, Crowe was quoted, "I don't know if there's ever been a horse trained that fast, but the way he did it told me we had a great horse. He wasn't done at the end of the mile by any means." That training effort convinced the owners that paying the $25,000 Supplemental Fee to enter Cam Fella in the Cane was a prudent investment. The return of $154,000 proved them correct.

In one of the biggest disappointments of the year for his owners and trainer, Cam Fella finished seventh in his Meadowlands Pace Elimination after being parked out first over to the three-quarters. He ran out of gas on the final turn and the next morning an examination revealed he had been hampered by a lung infection which had affected his breathing.

Cam was given a couple of weeks off and then returned to win the Queen City S. at Greenwood in 1:56f. He followed that with a win in the Monticello Classic Elimination but was then a distant second in the Final after being parked out every step of the way from the outside post eight. Following that defeat, Cam Fella was to win 11 of his next dozen starts, his only loss being by a nose to Icarus Lobell in the Simcoe S. Final. Cam swept through the Confederation Cup, Prix d'Ete and Simcoe S. Elimination. He later time-trialed at The Red Mile in Lexington in 1:54, won an Invitational there in 1:54.4 and ended his season with wins in the Messenger S. (for another $25,000 Supplemental Fee), Mohawk Sophomore Championship and Provincial Cup - the last two in 1:55.4 over the five-eighth mile tracks at Mohawk and Windsor.

Cam Fella ended his three-year-old season just as he started it: sound, solid, dependable and on a winning streak. For his efforts - 28 wins from 33 starts and earnings of $879,723 - Cam Fella was voted 1982 Horse of the Year by the overwhelming margin of 164 to 48 over the aged pacing star Genghis Khan. Cam Fella had won two legs of the pacing Triple Crown, the Cane and the Messenger, but was not eligible for the Little Brown Jug.

At four, the reigning Horse of the Year had to face the best older pacers in North America and he got off to a rather slow start. After qualifying twice at The Meadowlands in February in 1:57.2 and 1:56.2, Cam Fella raced in a $35,000 Meadowlands Open pace and was upset by Midas Almahurst and J.D.'s Buck. He had the lead in the stretch, but succumbed by a neck at the wire to finish third. He was given a month off and after he qualified back he finished second twice, at Brandywine and Freehold, in legs of the Graduate Series. His losses were only by a half-length and a neck, but Cam Fella had not come up a winner in his first three seasonal starts.

Cam Fella then won two legs of the Graduate Series before finishing second in another to Perfect Out. In his next start, Cam turned the tables on Perfect Out by finishing a nose in front of his rival, but was then disqualified and set back to second. A week later, Cam suffered another setback in the one and one-eighth mile leg of the World Cup

Series when he was third by three-quarters of a length to Perfect Out after pacing a journey from post 13 and outside every step of the way. Thus, in his first eight starts, Cam Fella had but two wins.

But the disappointments soon ended. It was as if the tough trip in the first leg of the World Cup served as a wake-up call for Cam Fella. He won the next one and one-half mile leg from post 11 and the final leg in 1:55 from post 10 after being parked out to the stretch. The old Cam Fella was back and tougher than ever.

The World Cup wins began a streak of 28 consecutive victories which took Cam Fella all over North America in major FFA events. His streak was threatened just a couple of times - he survived a 1:53.1 dead-heat with Walt Hanover at The Meadowlands after a brutal first over trip and later hung on by a measured half-length to the fast-closing Miller's Scout at Roosevelt Raceway. The 1:53.1 mile was Cam Fella's lifetime record and it was taken in one of his toughest races.

Cam Fella was not just beating up on average competition - the top pacers in the nation tried him at every turn, including Miller's Scout, Perfect Out, Armbro Aussie, J.D.'s Buck, Jef's Eternity, Soky's Atom, Mr. Dalrae and Coal Harbor. All were genuine Free-For-Allers with several having over $1,000,000 in earnings.

Cam Fella won with all kinds of different strategies - front end, come from behind, brush for the lead at the half, parked out all the way, etc. - it simply did not matter. He just did what he had to do to get to the front by the finish line. He traveled all over the United States and Canada for almost an entire year and drew legions of fans everywhere he went. Cam was the "people's horse" and they loved him for his courage and tenacity. Cam Fella's soundness was incredible; an example of this came in the penultimate race of his career at Pompano Park in early December. Cam had the lead parked out on the outside when the field hit the first quarter in a very fast :27.1. He then came home in :28.3 for a measured one-length win.

When all was said and done, Cam Fella had earned another Horse of the Year trophy by virtue of winning 30 of his 36 starts with earnings of $1,144,056. Many long-time harness racing observers felt then, and still feel now, that Cam Fella is perhaps our sport's greatest pacer, greater even than Niatross, Nihilator and Albatross. It's always difficult to compare horses of different eras, but Cam Fella was special. He had an indomitable will to win regardless of the speed, distance or adversity thrown at him. In my opinion, he is the toughest horse I have ever seen on the racetrack.

At three, Cam Fella had raced from January through November, and had actually raced continuously since the previous August. At four, he raced from February through December. Cam Fella's owners knew the value of promoting their horse and Cam received plenty of press coverage in the United States and Canada. He even had a fan club which would follow him from race to race and be allowed to participate in winner's circle ceremonies. Members had Cam Fella buttons and sometimes as many as two hundred fans would show up at a track to see their equine idol.

As a testament to Cam Fella's racetrack ability, here are some quotes from outstanding drivers of some of his competitors:

John Campbell - "I've never seen a horse do what Cam Fella has done. His most amazing asset, to me, is his durability; his ability to withstand the shipping, the change in track-to-track atmosphere. It wears other horses down, but he seems to thrive on it."

Buddy Gilmour - (drove Miller's Scout to 17 consecutive losses to Cam Fella) - "He only does what he has to do, but he always does it. He's just got a bigger heart than any other horse."

Dr. John Hayes - "It's the intangibles. I've seen him extended, used, pushed hard and looking ready to be beaten. Then it's like kicking a beehive. The tougher it gets for him, the more determined he gets."

And Cam's trainer-driver Pat Crowe has stated, "He just likes to win. Has to win. Has to get there first."

Cam Fella was syndicated for $4,000,000 during his four-year-old season and was retired to stud at Ed Freidberg's Jef's Standardbred Country Club in New Jersey for a stud fee of $15,000. Later in his career, he was transferred to Robert Tucker's Stonegate Farm in New Jersey where he stood his final years until forced into retirement.

Cam Fella

Sire Line

A prime representative of one of today's great pacing sire male lines, Cam Fella is a son of Triple Crown winner and sire of sires, Most Happy Fella p,3,T1:55 ($419,033) who is a son of the breed-changing sire Meadow Skipper. Most Happy Fella has been the most prolific of all Meadow Skipper's sons in terms of providing his own male line descendants to carry on the great Meadow Skipper line. In addition to Cam Fella and his sons, Most Happy Fella is the sire of top stallion Tyler B, grandsire of No Nukes and On The Road Again, and great-grandsire of Jate Lobell, Western Hanover and Die Laughing.

The Albatross and French Chef branches of the Meadow Skipper line are trying to find line-extenders, but it still appears the Most Happy Fella branch will be dominant.

Cam Fella is also trying to establish his own branch of this line through his own sons. Camtastic, Goalie Jeff and Precious Bunny have had limited success thus far, while the first crops from Presidential Ball and Cambest showed promise in 1997. The sons and daughters from Cam's Card Shark's first crop will race in 1998. Perhaps the brightest light among Cam Fella's stallion sons is Camluck who has had much success in Canada. And there are plenty of other Cam Fella sons with foals still to race.

With the Abercrombie male line moving forward at a rapid pace through his sons Artsplace and Life Sign, it will be very interesting to see how the Abercrombie-Most Happy Fella scenario plays out over the next decade. It should be fascinating and we'll most likely continue to see a steady stream of great and faster performers. If we can only breed into them half the soundness and toughness of Cam Fella, we'll really have something special.

Cam Fella's male line traces back through Most Happy Fella to Meadow Skipper to Dale Frost - a son of the great sire Hal Dale. On his maternal side, Cam Fella's grandam is a daughter of Dale Frost. Thus, Cam Fella's closest common pedigree cross is the 3x3 relationship to Dale Frost. However, if you look back one more generation, you will see what is probably the real strength in Cam Fella's pedigree - the 4x4x4x4 cross to Hal Dale. He has that cross through his sire, his dam's sire and the sires of both of his grandams. I have not come across any other stallion with Hal Dale in these exact same positions in a pedigree; Cam Fella's pedigree seems to be rather unique in that respect.

Maternal Line

Cam Fella was the second foal from the undistinguished Bret Hanover mare Nan Cam p,2:05.1f ($11,390). His second dam was the Dale Frost mare Nan Frost p,3,2:06.3f ($1,607) who had even fewer credentials. At that point, Nan Frost had four winners from six foals, with the fastest being the Bret Hanover son Cambret p,4,1:59.2 ($28,088). None of her three other foals won over $19,000. Cam Fella's third dam was Mynah Hanover p,2:05.2h whose fastest performer was the Good Time mare Good Little Girl p,2,2:03.4 ($13,705).

Nan Cam was a member of the family most commonly known as Belle Mahone. This family has had its share of fine horses over the years, but the branch leading to Nan Cam was one of its weakest.

Even today, with the success of Cam Fella and the upgraded breedings of the females in the family, there is still not much showing in the way of top horses. Cam Fella was individually gifted in a number of areas but this has not been remotely duplicated with others in the maternal family. This is certainly a case of the individual rising to levels far above the general ability of the family.

However, if you examine the pedigrees of some of the great stallions over the years, you will find plenty of these situations where a diamond is mined from a seemingly ordinary family. Genetics can always fool you and you never know which of the vast combinations of genes will get together to produce a horse like Cam Fella.

Progeny of Note

Cam Fella has established himself as one of the greatest pacing sires in history. After finishing second in the money-winning sires category in 1992 and 1994, Cam Fella rose to the top in 1995 and was third in 1996 and fifth in 1997 among pacing sires. He also ranks as the seventh leading money-winning pacing sires of all time, which is remarkable considering that his first crop only raced eleven years ago in 1987. To date, Cam Fella has sired five $2,000,000 winners and 12 $1,000,000 winners to lead both categories. He is also the leading sire of 1:50 pacers with 11.

The reason Cam Fella ranks so high in all of these categories is that he sired world class performers, able to dominate their peers and find a way to win the big races. Let's take a look at some of Cam Fella's great sons and daughters - several of which have their own chapters in this book. And, he's even sired eight daughters with earnings over $400,000.

Presidential Ball p,3,1:50 ($3,021,363) is Cam Fella's richest performer and was voted Two- and Three-Year-Old Pacer of the Year. At two, he won the Metro S. and L.B. Sheppard Final. Presidential Ball came back at three to win the two $1,000,000 races, the Meadowlands Pace and North America Cup along with a number of other major events. He retired as the leading single-season money winner of all time. Presidential Ball is now a stallion and his first crop had some impressive performers.

Cam's Card Shark p,3,1:50 ($2,498,204) was voted Horse of the Year at three and won the Meadowlands Pace, North America Cup and Messenger S. He also set a record for single-season earnings. The first crop of Cam's Card Shark will race in 1998.

Precious Bunny p,3,1:49.4 ($2,281,142) was also voted Horse of the Year at three and was the first horse to win two $1,000,000 events in the same year - the Meadowlands Pace and the North America Cup. He also won the Little Brown Jug and set a single-season earnings record. Precious Bunny has established himself as a good sire and was recently moved from New York to Canada where he could become even more impressive.

Camtastic p,4,T1:49.3 ($2,117,619) was a world champion at two and three and voted Pacer of the Year at two. He won the Breeders Crown at two and three and a heat of the Little Brown Jug. Goalie Jeff p,3,1:51.2 ($2,003,439) won the Breeders Crown, Little Brown Jug, North America Cup and Prix d'Ete at three and was voted Three-Year-old Pacer of the Year. Both of these stallions have had limited success, although Camtastic seems to be a sire of really outstanding older mares.

Village Connection p,1:51h ($1,620,056) was a half-mile track expert and a top performer in stakes and FFA events. He is standing his first season at stud in 1998. Village Jiffy p,1:50 ($1,527,683) won the Breeders Crown at two and four and was a top performer for four years. His oldest foals are yearlings in 1998.

Cambest p,T1:46.1 ($1,458,110) is the fastest Standardbred of all time and was a top stakes and FFA performer. His first crop raced in 1997 and showed promise.

Carlsbad Cam p,3,1:51 ($1,124,482) won the Meadowlands Pace and his oldest foals are four in 1998. Armbro Operative p,4,1:50 ($1,012,712) won the Little Brown Jug and Breeders Crown at three and the Breeders Crown at four. He stands his first season at stud in 1998. Camluck p,T1:48.4 ($1,003,260) is Cam Fella's second fastest record performer and was a Breeders Crown winner at four. His oldest foals are four in 1998 and based upon the early results he appears to be capable of siring world-class performers.

The above is only a brief look at the million-dollar winners of Cam Fella. He has scores of other top stakes performers and another Little Brown Jug winner in Fake Left p,3,1:51.2 ($314,417). Of Cam Fella's daughters, the mare Ellamony p,1:50.3 ($1,425,285) is his fastest and richest. She is a multiple world champion and, at three, equalled the all-age record for mares. She was voted Three-Year-Old Pacing Filly of the Year in 1993 and Older Pacing Mare of the Year in 1995. Other standouts among Cam Fella's daughters are Camourous p,1:51.2 ($806,333), Cammie's Lady p,1:51.2 ($765,108), world champion and Two-Year-Old Pacing Filly of the Year C.R. Daniella p,4,1:52 ($638,851), Cam's Exotic p,2,1:54f ($618,585) and Cinnamon Reel p,4,1:52.4 ($552,392), to name only his half-million dollar winners.

Analysis

Ironically, Cam Fella's richest performer, Presidential Ball, is the only one in the $1,000,000 list with a dam by a non-mainstream sire - Mountain Skipper p,T1:56.1. He is by Dale Frost from a mare by a stallion named Bulldog who is a full brother to the immortal trotting great Greyhound. Thus, Presidential Ball has an additional Dale Frost cross through a sire other than Meadow Skipper and is 5x5x3 to Dale Frost.

The Cam Fella cross with B.G.'s Bunny mares has worked wonders and five of Cam's 17 richest performers have that cross. Being a son of Albatross, B.G.'s Bunny is an extension of the Cam Fella/Albatross cross which has also worked so well. Five of Cam Fella's six richest sons are from mares with B.G.'s Bunny and/or Albatross blood. And you can extend the list even further with other mares by Albatross and Niatross; 21 of Cam Fella's 32 richest performers have mares with Albatross blood in their first or second generations - it's just a golden cross, one that has worked for years.

With Cam Fella being bred to so many mares with Meadow Skipper blood back in their second or third generation, it is not surprising to see all the 3x4 Meadow Skipper linebred crosses among Cam Fella's best sons and daughters. Those from Albatross mares, and other sons of Meadow Skipper, have 3x3 crosses to that stallion. What is interesting about the success of the Cam Fella/B.G.'s Bunny cross is that it provides a 3x4 cross to Bret Hanover since Cam Fella is from a Bret Hanover mare, as is B.G.'s Bunny.

Ellamony, Cam Fella's greatest daughter, is from a Race Time mare and is inbred 3x3 to Meadow Skipper. What is also interesting is that she is the only one of Cam Fella's very top performers who has a multiple cross to two broodmares - she is 4x3 to the full sisters Maxine's Dream and Dream Girl. Maxine's Dream is the grandam of Most Happy Fella and Dream Girl is Ellamony's great-grandam.

Before discussing Cam Fella as an up-and-coming broodmare sire, I want to bring to your attention another of those strange pedigree aberrations which show up upon careful examination. I've mentioned the Meadow Skipper, Albatross and B.G.'s Bunny influence with Cam Fella and how it is responsible for most of his top performers. However, there is another factor at work which has nothing to do with Meadow Skipper; rather, it concerns the lack of Meadow Skipper blood in mares bred to Cam Fella.

Until 1998, Cam Fella's two fastest, not richest, performers, both of which possess time-trial records, were Cambest p,T1:46.1 and Camluck p,T1:48.4. Ironically, neither of their dams has any Meadow Skipper blood. Cambest is from a Harold J. mare who is from an Adios Vic mare; Camluck is from a Striking Image mare who is from a Truluck mare. I will not pretend to understand this, or its significance, I just note it as a point of interest. It will be interesting to see how these two stallions, without the multiple Meadow Skipper crosses, compare as sires with all of the other Cam Fella sons who have the inbreeding and linebreeding to Meadow Skipper. In 1998, Pacific Fella p,1:48.2z ($653,351) paced to his fast record. He is inbred 3x3 to Meadow Skipper.

Like all other great sires, Cam Fella will eventually go on to become a great broodmare sire. History tells us so and there is no reason to think differently - especially after reviewing the early results from Cam's daughters. Cam Fella's young daughters already have 146 in 2:00, with 20 in 1:55.

Again, geography plays somewhat of a role in the success of particular stallions and Cam Fella is no exception. He stood in New Jersey and there are plenty of Cam Fella mares in the eastern states. When Beach Towel went to stud in New Jersey with great credentials, it was only natural for breeders to look to him for their good Cam Fella mares. The cross obviously worked because it has produced the great world champion Jenna's Beach Boy p,4,1:47.3 ($1,972,172) and the top stakes filly Paige Nicole Q p,3,1:52 ($712,801), along with Beach Romeo p,3,1:54.2.

Some other outstanding performers from Cam Fella mares are Oye Vay p,3,1:50.3 ($969,493) (by Albatross), Binding Offer p,4,1:51.1 (by Easy Goer), Raleigh Fingers p,4,1:51.2 ($239,534) (by Albert Albert), Direct Bill p,3,1:51.3 (by Direct Scooter), Earl's Court Road p,4,1:51.4 (by On The Road Again), Papa Lou p,1:52.3 (by Walton Hanover), and the list goes on.

One thing I have noticed is that Cam Fella mares seem to do very well with sons of Abercrombie, such as Albert Albert, Laag, Topnotcher, Kentucky Spur, Curragh and Dare You To. He also appears to be matching well with sons of No Nukes.

Cam Fella thrilled many fans fifteen years ago on North America's racetracks, and then his sons and daughters did the same. Cam was, and still is, a legend in his time. His 1997 North American tour brought out thousands of fans to greet this great champion and he always conducted himself as a "gentleman." The highlight of the tour was his appearance in front of over 50,000 fans at the Little Brown Jug in Delaware, Ohio. I spent a good portion of the day around Cam's stall watching the fans greet him, be photographed with him, and tell Norm Clements and Pat Crowe about their wonderful memories of Cam Fella.

Crowe was planning to jog Cam Fella once around the track for the fans and have him pace quickly down the stretch in front of the grandstand. But what happened was even better. Cam had been acting great and was in terrific shape for an 18-year-old horse. It seemed as if he wanted to "show off" in front of the fans. I asked Crowe how fast he thought Cam could pace a half-mile at his age and he replied: right around one minute. That would have been quite an accomplishment, but what happened brought a gasp from the crowd and then a long, standing ovation. Cam was acting so well on the track that Crowe let him out a notch and Cam Fella paced one time around the Delaware oval in :57 flat!

It was a demonstration that Cam Fella could still show the speed, courage and fortitude, at his advanced age, that he had shown throughout his career. He was, and is, a true champion.

Cam Fella

Photo courtesy of The Horseman and Fair World

Leading Progeny by Cam Fella

Fastest
Cambest, h, p,T1:46.1 $1,458,110
Pacific Fella, h, p,1:48.2z $653,341
Camluck, h, p,T1:48.4 $1,003,260
Camtastic, h, p,4,T1:49.3 $2,117,619
Cam Terrific, h, p,4,1:49.3 $592,594
Precious Bunny, h, p,3,1:49.4 $2,281,142
Village Jove, h, p,3,1:49.4 $278,125
Presidential Ball, h, p,3,1:50 $3,021,363
Cam's Card Shark, h, p,3,1:50 $2,498,204
Village Jiffy, h, p,1:50 $1,527,683

Richest
Presidential Ball, h, p,3,1:50 $3,021,363
Cam's Card Shark, h, p,3,1:50 $2,498,204
Precious Bunny, h, p,3,1:49.4 $2,281,142
Camtastic, h, p,4,T1:49.3 $2,117,619
Goalie Jeff, h, p,3,1:51.2 $2,003,439
Village Connection, h, p,1:51h $1,620,056
Village Jiffy, h, p,1:50 $1,527,683
Cambest, h, p,T1:46.1 $1,458,110
Ellamony, m, p,1:50.3 $1,425,285
Carlsbad Cam, h, p,3,1:51 $1,124,482

Cam Fella, Bay Horse, 1979
p, 2, 2:00.2f; 3, T1:54; 4, 1:53.1 ($2,041,367)

Most Happy Fella, 1967 p, 3, T1:55 $419,033	Meadow Skipper, 1960 p, 3, 1:55.1 $428,057	**DALE FROST**, 1951 p, 1:58 $204,117	**HAL DALE**, 1926 p, 6, 2:02¼	**ABBEDALE**	The Abbe / Daisydale D.
				Margaret Hal	Argot Hal / Margaret Polk
			Galloway, 1939 p, 2:04½h $5,294	Raider	**PETER VOLO** / Nelda Dillon
				Bethel	David Guy / Annotation
		Countess Vivian, 1950 p, 3, 1:59 $43,262	King's Counsel, 1940 p, 6, 1:58 $44,930	**VOLOMITE**	**PETER VOLO** / Cita Frisco
				Margaret Spangler	**GUY AXWORTHY** / Maggie Winder
			Filly Direct, 1941 p, 3, 2:06¾h $6,299	**BILLY DIRECT**	Napoleon Direct / Gay Forbes
				Calumet Edna	**PETER THE BREWER** / Broncho Queen
	Laughing Girl, 1961 p, 4, 2:04h $19,546	Good Time, 1946 p, 1:57.4 $318,792	**HAL DALE**, 1926 p, 6, 2:02¼	**ABBEDALE**	The Abbe / Daisydale D.
				Margaret Hal	Argot Hal / Margaret Polk
			On Time, 1938 p, 3, 2:03½h $1,472	**VOLOMITE**	**PETER VOLO** / Cita Frisco
				Nedda Guy	**GUY AXWORTHY** / Nedda
		Maxine's Dream, 1954 p, 2, T2:00 $36,557	Knight Dream, 1945 p, 3, T1:59 $76,973	**NIBBLE HANOVER**	Calumet Chuck / Justissima
				Lydia Knight	**PETER THE BREWER** / Guy Rosa
			Maxine Abbe, 1937 p, 4, 2:05h	**ABBEDALE**	The Abbe / Daisydale D.
				Maxine Direct	Walter Direct / Vernie Wilkes
Nan Cam, 1971 p, 5, 2:05.1f $11,390	Bret Hanover, 1962 p, 4, T1:53.3 $922,616	Adios, 1940 p, T1:57½ $33,329	**HAL DALE**, 1926 p, 6, 2:02¼	**ABBEDALE**	The Abbe / Daisydale D.
				Margaret Hal	Argot Hal / Margaret Polk
			Adioo Volo, 1930 p, 3, 2:05h	Adioo Guy	Guy Dillon / Adioo
				Sigrid Volo	**PETER VOLO** / Polly Parrot
		Brenna Hanover, 1956 p, 3, T2:01 $21,946	Tar Heel, 1948 p, 4, T1:57 $119,148	**BILLY DIRECT**	Napoleon Direct / Gay Forbes
				Leta Long	**VOLOMITE** / Rosette
			Beryl Hanover, 1947 p, 2, T2:02 $29,076	**NIBBLE HANOVER**	Calumet Chuck / Justissima
				Laura Hanover	The Laurel Hall / Miss Bertha Worthy
	Nan Frost, 1966 p, 3, 2:06.3f $1,607	**DALE FROST**, 1951 p, 1:58 $204,117	**HAL DALE**, 1926 p, 6, 2:02¼	**ABBEDALE**	The Abbe / Daisydale D.
				Margaret Hal	Argot Hal / Margaret Polk
			Galloway, 1939 p, 2:04½h $5,294	Raider	**PETER VOLO** / Nelda Dillon
				Bethel	David Guy / Annotation
		Mynah Hanover, 1950 p, 2:05.2h $44,184	Ensign Hanover, 1943 p, 4, 1:59.4 $81,070	**BILLY DIRECT**	Napoleon Direct / Gay Forbes
				Helen Hanover	Dillon Volo / Helen Dillon
			Betty Mahone, 1935 p, 2:03¼h $5,942	Corporal Lee	**PETER VOLO** / Lydia Lee
				Belle Mahone	Oliver Evans / Roxie

Cam's Card Shark

"He's the easiest top horse I've ever had to drive", said Hall of Fame driver John Campbell about Cam's Card Shark, in a *Hoof Beats* article. "He can do it all. He can leave. He can come from behind." Anyone who has seen Cam's Card Shark race knows Campbell is right. This horse could do it all, and many times had to do it all, in order to find a way to win. He was one gutsy performer on the racetrack.

Bred by Edward Freidberg's Jef's Standardbred Country Club, Cam's Card Shark was purchased privately in the January of his yearling season by New York City horse owner Jeffrey Snyder. Trainer Mickey McGivern was given the colt and prepared him for his two-year-old season, which began with a qualifying race at Saratoga in which he finished second and was timed in 2:05.3. The colt then competed in three $200 baby races at Saratoga, finishing second in all of them. He was timed in 2:06.1, 2:05.2 and 2:01.3. In the middle race Cam's Card Shark flashed some speed with a :28.4 closing quarter, and his speed was confirmed the following week when he closed again in :28.2 after a much faster mile.

Cam's Card Shark was then sent to The Meadowlands for a baby race in mid-June, which he won handily in 1:59, with a final quarter in :28. After that the colt developed inflammation soreness known as "bucked shins" and was away from the races for a period of seven weeks. He came back to win a qualifier in 1:59.2. But it was now the middle of August, Cam's Card Shark had competed only in baby races and qualifiers and won only $387. Sent back to Saratoga to race in two conditioned events, the colt survived a parked out trip to finish third and was timed in 1:58.3 - a gritty performance by a youngster who had been out of action for nearly two months. The next week, he was a 10-length winner at Saratoga in 1:58.2, which proved he was worthy of entering the stakes scene.

In his first two attempts at stakes racing, Cam's Card Shark competed in two New Jersey Sires S. events at Garden State Park, winning the first in 1:55.2 and the second in 1:56. It was those performances which once again showed the character and "never say die" attitude of this colt. In one of those races, he was parked out first over all the way and yet still pulled away in the stretch. It was an eye-opening performance for any youngster. A week later, he finished third in an Elimination for the Lou Babic Memorial at Freehold after being parked out three-quarters of a mile. In the $200,000 Babic Memorial Final on October 9th, Cam's Card Shark won in a sharp 1:55.4.

The $300,000 Breeders Crown was to be raced at Freehold two weeks later. Cam's Card Shark had been recognized and was considered one of the serious contenders. In fact, he went off as third choice at post time. During the race, Cam's Card Shark was interfered with in the first turn by Rayson Hanover, as a result of which he lost some ground and had to settle in sixth at the quarter. He later followed cover, went three wide down the backstretch and was still three wide on the final turn. However, the colt had too much ground to make up and Expensive Scooter cruised to a five-length victory over Sable Matters, with Cam's Card Shark just missing second.

Cam's Card Shark ended his two-year-old season with a sixth place finish in the Presidential S. Elimination, not qualifying for the Final, and taking third in the Governor's Cup Elimination and $550,000 Final. He ended his season with $233,490 in earnings and was first, second or third in 13 of his 14 starts while being reined by nine different drivers. It was a fine season for him, but not one to give a hint of the greatness he would show at three.

During the winter, Jeffrey Snyder moved Cam's Card Shark to the Bill Robinson stable to prepare for a full stakes campaign. Robinson was quoted in *Hoof Beats*, "We knew when we got him that he had a chip in his knee. It was small, though, and you only noticed it the day after he trained or sometimes in the first couple of steps he took out of the stall. But by the time he hit the track, he had worked it out." The colt opened his season in late March with a 1:57.1 qualifying win at Pompano Park. A week later, he won a Pompano conditioned event easily in 1:55 and then was shipped north to The Meadowlands for the Berry's Creek Elimination and Final. With John Campbell as his regular driver, Cam's Card Shark exploded upon the scene, winning his Elimination in 1:51.4 and the $305,500 Berry's Creek Final in 1:51

Race Record Highlights

At 2

1st Lou Babic Memorial Final
two New Jersey Sires S.

3rd Breeders Crown Final
Governor's Cup Final and Elimination
Lou Babic Memorial Elimination

At 3

1st Meadowlands Pace Final and Elimination
North America Cup Final
New Jersey Classic Final and Elimination
Messenger S.
Art Rooney P.
Berry's Creek Final and Elimination
James Dancer Memorial
Adios S. Final and Elimination
Miller Memorial Final and Elimination

2nd Burlington S.
North America Cup Elimination

Honors
Voted Horse of the Year in 1994
Set record for earnings in a single season

Cam's Card Shark

Photo by Monica Thors

Race Record

Year	Age	Starts	Wins	2nd	3rd	Earnings	Record
1993	2	14	5	3	5	$ 233,490	p,2,1:55.2
1994	3	18	15	2	0	2,264,714	p,3,1:50
		32	20	5	5	$2,498,204	p,3,1:50

flat. In the Final, the colt had to be patient since he had post nine and was fifth until the field hit the backstretch. Campbell then took him off the rail and he rocketed three-wide around the field to take a commanding lead around the final turn and go on to win by almost three lengths over favored Falcon's Future and Pacific Rocket.

This was just the beginning for Cam's Card Shark. He then swept the Miller Memorial Elimination in 1:54.3 and the $197,112 Final in 1:50.3 over Rosecroft's five-eighth mile track - just missing Riyadh's world record of 1:50.1 set a year earlier. Then it was on to the New Jersey Classic for a win in his Elimination and a 1:51 score in the $500,000 Final. At this point, Cam's Card Shark was undefeated in his seven seasonal starts and looked invincible, since he had several moves during a race and had a lightning fast brush of speed. However, all good things come to an end and for Cam's Card Shark it happened on the home turf of his trainer Bill Robinson - Canada's Woodbine track. The first loss was to Pacific Rocket in a division of the Burlington S. in which Cam had the lead but lost by a head at the wire. A second loss came the following week in a North America Cup Elimination, when he was caught in the stretch by Magical Mike after leading all the way.

The colt's luck changed for the rich $1,000,000 North America Cup Final. He drew the rail and had the lead in a fast :26.3 first quarter. But Pacific Rocket, a horse that could not be intimidated, then took the lead after being parked out for the first quarter. He was in front at the half in :55.2 and three-quarters in 1:23.3, which gave Cam's Card Shark the perfect pocket trip. With no other serious challengers, the two colts battled down the stretch with the fresher Cam's Card Shark pulling away by a length and one-half to win the big race in 1:51.4.

The North America Cup began another seven-race winning streak for Cam's Card Shark in which he exploited every race situation in order to win. Front-running tactics, coming from behind and being parked out were all the same to this colt since all he knew how to do was respond and win. He took the $342,595 Messenger S. at Rosecroft in 1:51 after sitting fourth the entire mile and getting up in time for a half-length win over Falcon's Future. A week later, in a Meadowlands Pace Elimination, Cam's Card Shark was third to the quarter, pulled and went to the outside to grab the lead by the three-quarters and held on for a nose win over Magical Mike in 1:50.1. In the $1,000,000 Meadowlands Pace Final, Cam's Card Shark and Campbell took control of the race just past the quarter and won easily over Historic and Magical Mike in 1:50, with a final quarter sprint in :26.3.

Cam's Card Shark looked so invincible at this point that the $377,430 Art Rooney Memorial at Yonkers Raceway was held as a non-wagering event. The pace was frantic from the start as Sable Matters and Keystone Luther both left quickly from posts one and two and were challenged on the outside for the early lead by Pacific Rocket who had left from post five. Pacific Rocket finally got to the front but paid the price of a :26.3 quarter over the Yonkers half-mile track. Meanwhile, Campbell had Cam's Card Shark sitting fourth on the rail as the front-enders sorted themselves out. Once things settled down just prior to the half, as Pacific Rocket attempted to slow the pace, Cam's Card Shark took to the outside, swept past his rivals and was in front at the half in :55.2 and three-quarters in 1:24. He came home an easy four-length winner in 1:52 over Pacific Rocket. At The Meadows, Cam's Card Shark made easy work of the Adios S., going wire-to-wire in 1:50.4 and 1:51.1 in his Elimination and the Final. The fractions of the Final showed his versatility: he paced the first quarter in :26.3 and the last quarter in :26.2.

However, the Cane Pace two weeks later showed Cam's Card Shark was not unbeatable. The colt was barred from the wagering since he had been so dominant, but no one hands out the purse checks until the race is run. Driver Ken Holliday had the top pacer Falcon's Future leaving from post three while Cam's Card Shark and Campbell were going from post five. Holliday was determined to leave and never look back. He left like a comet and was on top at the first quarter in :27, with Cam's Card Shark parked out second and Pacific Rocket on the rail in third. Falcon's Future hit the half in :57, with Cam still parked out and the three-quarters in 1:25.2 with Cam in the same situation. Falcon's Future was sharp that night as he paced home in :28 as Cam began to falter a bit in the stretch. Falcon's Future was the surprise winner in 1:53.2 with Cam's Card Shark finishing fifth, three lengths behind the winner. It was a shocker of a result and a precursor of later problems for Cam's Card Shark.

The following week, on September 3rd, Cam's Card Shark was back to his old feats and wired the $274,960 James B. Dancer Memorial field in 1:53.2. But he was not completely sound. With the Little Brown Jug coming up on September 22nd, Robinson wanted the colt fresh and so entered him in a qualifier on September 13th at Freehold. Pacific Rocket was also in the race and won in 1:55.3 with Cam's Card Shark second, three lengths behind. Tongues began wagging about Cam's Card Shark's fitness for the Little Brown Jug since it was known he had a nagging bone chip problem in his left knee. The Robinson camp was quiet about the matter.

On Jug day, the big crowd was anticipating a great race but there was still much speculation about whether Cam's Card Shark was sound and whether he would even race. During the warmups, Cam did not look good and Campbell and Robinson could be seen in earnest discussion. Speculation was rampant that the colt would be scratched, but as the field went to the gate for the Elimination, Cam was out there with the others. But just as the field began to line up behind the starting gate, Campbell suddenly pulled Cam's Card Shark back and took him off the track. There was a big gasp from the 54,000 in attendance and then it was announced that Cam's Card Shark would not race. Trainer Robinson later explained that his horse had to deal with troublesome knees and a sore shin. "John said he did not want to go with him," Robinson said. "He's the man. When John Campbell tells you not to race a horse, you don't race him. He knows this horse better than anybody." Then Robinson said, "He's finished. He's going to Hanover."

Sire Line

What can I say about Cam Fella that has not already been said by others? He was simply one of the greatest of all time, both as racehorse and as a sire, and there are very few in the history of the sport who can equal such prowess.

Cam Fella is the most courageous horse I have ever seen on a racetrack. He just refused to be beaten. Many of his sons have been blessed with extreme speed and a few have also exhibited the tenacity and will to win possessed by their sire. Only time will tell which of Cam Fella's sons will be those to carry on for "The Pacing Machine." Certainly Cam's Card Shark exhibited many of his sire's best traits.

You can read more about Cam Fella in his chapter.

Maternal Line

Cam's Card Shark comes from the maternal family known as Macketta or Maud (by Trombone). This family has several major branches and they seem to be improving over time, especially in this one particular branch that includes Cam's Card Shark. Through 1966, the family had only six 2:00 performers, but now has around 100 or more.

The B.G.'s Bunny mare Jef's Magic Trick p,2,2:02f ($28,340) is the dam of Cam's Card Shark and she was stakes-placed in the New Jersey Sires S. at two, being timed in 1:59.2. This mare has been an incredible producer with six sub-1:55 performers and five $200,000 winners among her nine winners from 10 foals. In addition to producing a Horse of the Year, her daughter Michelle's Jackpot p,2,1:54.4f ($548,975) (by Artsplace) was voted Two-Year-Old Pacing Filly of the Year in 1996.

In addition, Cam's Card Shark has an outstanding full brother in Cam's Magic Trick p,3,1:52.4f ($469,899) who is standing at stud in Ohio, and another fast full brother in Cam's Trickster p,3,1:52.2 ($59,350) who has been exported to New Zealand. Make no doubt about it, the Cam Fella-Jef's Magic Trick cross works!

But this mare has also proved she can do it without Cam Fella, which means, to me, that she is a very prepotent mare. Jef's Magic Trick produced Direct Current p,1:54.2 ($378,403) (by Direct Scooter), Feel The Wind p,2,1:54.3 (by Storm Damage), Britt's Best p,3,Q1:56.1 ($221,381) (by Troublemaker) and Twist In The Wind p,4,1:57.3 (by Storm Damage).

Taking a look at the rest of the female line, Cam's Card Shark's grandam is the noted stakes and Invitational winner Meadow Trick p,2:00.1h ($124,549) by Overtrick. She was a long-wearing and tough mare and those traits, combined with the same from Cam Fella, could account for Cam's

Card Shark's toughness. In addition to that star's dam, Meadow Trick also produced $100,000 winners Jef's Rick p,4,1:57.1f ($124,133) (by Whata Baron) and Jef's Eclipse p,3,1:57.2 ($102,950) (by Meadow Skipper) and the Cam Fella-sired pair of Sweet N Legal p,1:57.2f and Just Camelot p,3,1:58.4h.

The stallion Overtrick may be playing a significant part in the success of this cross. His daughters proved to be outstanding broodmares and were particularly effective when bred to Albatross. Jef's Magic Trick is the result of a son of Albatross being crossed with an Overtrick mare. Another interesting example of crossing Cam Fella with mares carrying Overtrick blood is the fastest Standardbred ever, Cambest p,T1:46.1 ($1,458,010), whose third dam is by Overtrick

The third dam of Cam's Card Shark is the Direct Rhythm mare Meadow Maine p,4,T2:01.3 ($33,974) who was a nice stakes filly in her day. She produced some decent racehorse types and the family traces back through several other mares, most of whom produced the hard-hitting types rather than the major speed-demon stakes winners. The latter quality seems to have originated with the dam of Cam's Card Shark and this is one of the reasons I am confident he will be a successful sire. Whether it comes from B.G.'s Bunny, Albatross or Overtrick, something happened genetically to give Jef's Magic Trick exceptional power, which she is passing on, in terms of racing performance, to many of her offspring. If Cam's Card Shark can pass on that "lightning in a bottle," he should do very well.

Analysis

Cam's Card Shark has stood at stud at Hanover Shoe Farms' New Jersey division and has had access to top broodmares from Hanover and many other major breeders. In fact, Cam was bred to 183, 160 and 143 mares in his first three seasons. He should have every chance to excel as a stallion and is one of several top sons of Cam Fella that are expected to make a future impact on the breed.

Like Precious Bunny, Cam's Card Shark is from a B.G.'s Bunny mare, which puts Albatross in his third generation and the fourth in any of his foals. Therefore, a breeder with an Albatross mare can still go to Cam's Card Shark. The resulting foal will have a 4x2 cross to Albatross, which could be very effective. Mares by sons of Albatross should also work, and have done so already for Precious Bunny, since two of his best fillies, Lady Buns and Before Sunrise are both from Sonsam (son of Albatross) mares. Big Towner, Abercrombie and Keystone Ore mares have also been very effective with Precious Bunny and this could serve as a guide to what will work best with the similarly bred Cam's Card Shark.

From a pedigree standpoint, Cam's Card Shark is linebred 3x4 to both Meadow Skipper and Bret Hanover and is 4x4x5 to Dale Frost. In addition to mares by Albatross, this stallion would seem to be a very good fit for most mares, except those by Cam Fella and B.G.'s Bunny, unless you really favor inbreeding. Daughters from most of the popular and leading broodmare sires would offer comfortable linebred crosses and the presence of Overtrick in the bottom part of Cam's Card Shark's pedigree adds another interesting aspect. Foals by Cam's Card Shark from No Nukes mares would have a 3x4 cross to Most Happy Fella; many Abercrombie, Big Towner and Direct Scooter mares would provide an outcross; foals from Bret Hanover mares would be 4x5x3 to that stallion; and foals from Tyler B mares would be inbred 3x3 to Most Happy Fella. Niatross, Sonsam and Nihilator mares would give another dose of Albatross blood.

As you can see, Cam's Card Shark has a pedigree providing breeders with choices of inbreeding, linebreeding or outcrossing. He is very versatile in that respect and it will be interesting to see which crosses work best, compared to other sons of Cam Fella.

Cam's Card Shark sold 112 yearlings at the end of 1997 fall sales for an average of $17,757. Included in that group were two colts for $100,000 each, another for $82,000 and two fillies for $85,000 and $82,000. They were very well received by trainers and owners and the Cam's Card Shark two-year-olds will have every opportunity for success in 1998.

Cam's Card Shark, Bay Horse, 15.2 Hands, 1991
p, 2, 1:55.2; 3, 1:50 ($2,498,204)

Sire/Dam	2nd Gen	3rd Gen	4th Gen	5th Gen	6th Gen
Cam Fella, 1979 p, 4, 1:53.1 $2,041,367	Most Happy Fella, 1967 p, 3, T1:55 $419,033	**MEADOW SKIPPER**, 1960 p, 3, 1:55.1 $428,057	DALE FROST, 1951 p, 1:58 $204,117	HAL DALE Galloway	ABBEDALE / Margaret Hal Raider / Bethel
			Countess Vivian, 1950 p, 3, 1:59 $43,262	KING'S COUNSEL Filly Direct	VOLOMITE / Margaret Spangler BILLY DIRECT / Calumet Edna
		Laughing Girl, 1961 p, 4, 2:04h $19,546	Good Time, 1946 p, 1:57.4 $318,792	HAL DALE On Time	ABBEDALE / Margaret Hal VOLOMITE / Nedda Guy
			Maxine's Dream, 1954 p, 2, T2:00 $36,557	KNIGHT DREAM Maxine Abbe	NIBBLE HANOVER / Lydia Knight ABBEDALE / Maxine Direct
	Nan Cam, 1971 p, 5, 2:05.1f $11,390	**BRET HANOVER**, 1962 p, 4, T1:53.3 $922,616	ADIOS, 1940 p, T1:57½ $33,329	HAL DALE Adioo Volo	ABBEDALE / Margaret Hal Adioo Guy / Sigrid Volo
			Brenna Hanover, 1956 p, 3, T2:01 $21,946	TAR HEEL Beryl Hanover	BILLY DIRECT / Leta Long NIBBLE HANOVER / Laura Hanover
		Nan Frost, 1966 p, 3, 2:06.3f $1,607	DALE FROST, 1951 p, 1:58 $204,117	HAL DALE Galloway	ABBEDALE / Margaret Hal Raider / Bethel
			Mynah Hanover, 1950 p, 2:05.2h $44,184	Ensign Hanover Betty Mahone	BILLY DIRECT / Helen Hanover Corporal Lee / Belle Mahone
Jef's Magic Trick, 1979 p, 2, 2:02f $28,340	B.G.'s Bunny, 1974 p, 3, 1:54 $215,192	Albatross, 1968 p, 4, 1:54.3f $1,201,470	**MEADOW SKIPPER**, 1960 p, 3, 1:55.1 $428,057	DALE FROST Countess Vivian	HAL DALE / Galloway KING'S COUNSEL / Filly Direct
			Voodoo Hanover, 1964	Dancer Hanover Vibrant Hanover	ADIOS / The Old Maid TAR HEEL / Vivian Hanover
		Bret's Romance, 1968 p, 4, 2:02f $13,967	**BRET HANOVER**, 1962 p, 4, T1:53.3 $922,616	ADIOS Brenna Hanover	HAL DALE / Adioo Volo TAR HEEL / Beryl Hanover
			Knight's Embassy, 1951	KNIGHT DREAM Miss Reed	NIBBLE HANOVER / Lydia Knight Bert Abbe / Four D McKinney
	Meadow Trick, 1968 p, 6, 2:00.1h $124,549	Overtrick, 1960 p, 3, 1:57.1h $407,483	Solicitor, 1948 p, 3, T1:57.2 $102,109	KING'S COUNSEL Jane Reynolds	VOLOMITE / Margaret Spangler Scotland / Jane Revere
			Overbid, 1954 p, 2, T2:05.4 $3,524	HAL DALE Barbara Direct	ABBEDALE / Margaret Hal BILLY DIRECT / Norette Hanover
		Meadow Maine, 1955 p, 4, T2:01.3 $33,974	Direct Rhythm, 1948 p, T1:56.1 $171,802	BILLY DIRECT Rhythm	Napoleon Direct / Gay Forbes Guy Abbey / Lyric
			Medios, 1949 p, 2, 2:09h $2,700	ADIOS Fuzzette Henley	HAL DALE / Adioo Volo Peter Henley / Fuzzette

Cambest

There are many titles associated with horses in harness racing: world, seasonal and divisional champions; and there are honors based on age, gender, gait and size of track. But there is only one horse that can be called "the fastest Standardbred of all time." Today, that horse is Cambest p,T1:46.1 ($1,458,110).

In addition to sheer speed, there are other qualities which set certain horses apart from their contemporaries. But under today's extreme speed racing conditions, few of them maintain that edge for long. Many of the best only race at two and three; a few put in seasons as four-year-olds. Some don't even make it back after racing at the top levels as two-year-olds. Any horse who can compete against the best in the business for four consecutive years, winning over $200,000 in each season, is very special. Cambest was that kind of racehorse - fast, sound, tough and long-lasting.

Cambest, who was originally named Gulf Shore, was bred by Courtney and Elizabeth Foos of Pennsylvania and Donald Geiger and John Sanford of Texas. He was the third foal from his dam and sold for $40,000 at the 1989 Kentucky Standardbred Select Yearling Sale to Dan Altmeyer and Jack Piatt of Pennsylvania. Trained during his first two seasons by Altmeyer, Cambest began his career by winning a baby race on May 24, 1990, in 2:00.1, with Altmeyer in the sulky. The colt led wire-to-wire and came home in a sparkling :27.4. A week later, Altmeyer drove him to his first parimutuel win in 1:59.3, coming from fourth at the half. For the rest of the season, and with the exception of one start, Dave Rankin would be his regular pilot. Altmeyer recalled, "He was especially good-looking as a two-year-old. He wasn't a big two-year-old, but he had a long stride and always kept his neck tucked a little to make him look proud."

Cambest won his third start in 2:00.3 before beginning his stakes career in the Hopeful S. Elimination at Buffalo. He went wire-to-wire and won by a nose in 1:59.3 over that half-mile track and hopes were high for his chances in the rich $190,000 Hopeful Final. In that race, Cambest had the lead parked out to the quarter in :28.2 and was still ahead by a neck in mid-stretch. However, he grudgingly yielded to He's Discreet and lost by a neck. Cambest came back a winner at Rosecroft in a Potomac S. division in a fast 1:55.2. Then it was on to the Niatross Eliminations at The Meadowlands, where he finished third to Die Laughing and did not qualify for the Final. He came back two weeks later to win his Woodrow Wilson Elimination in 1:55 flat.

The $1,043,500 Woodrow Wilson Final turned out to be a tough race for Cambest. He left very fast from post eight and was on top by the first quarter in a rapid :27 before yielding the lead in the :55.1 half. The early effort and some poor luck took its toll. As the field turned for the homestretch, Cambest was locked in, on the rail, which is where he finished, six lengths behind the victorious Die Laughing. He was timed in 1:53.2. Cambest then responded with a string of four consecutive victories in the Garden State S., two New Jersey Sires S. and the Lou Babic Memorial Elimination - all over Freehold's half-mile track. His fastest time was 1:56.1.

Based on these performances, Cambest was the heavy choice to win the $216,775 Babic Final, but he was again the victim of some poor racing luck. Leaving from post six, Cambest was forced three wide for the entire first quarter although he finally put his nose in front as the field passed that marker in :28. He continued on the front end right to the wire and was just nipped by a nose in 1:56.2 by Nuclear Legacy. Cambest came back to win the New Jersey Sires S. Final at Garden State Park in 1:54, and then took a Presidential S. Elimination at Rosecroft in 1:54.3.

After racing mostly on the front end in his other races, Cambest was taken off the early pace after leaving from post seven in the $298,345 Presidential S. Final. He had raced fourth most of the mile and was still three lengths from the leaders as the field turned for home. Cambest and Rankin found racing room, but came up a length short of the winning Die Laughing. Cambest's last race of the year was four

Race Record Highlights

At 2

1st Potomac S.
Garden State S.
New Jersey Sires S. Final at Garden State Park
Hopeful S. Elimination
Woodrow Wilson Elimination
Lou Babic Memorial Elimination
Presidential S. Elimination
two New Jersey Sires S. at Freehold

2nd Hopeful S. Final
Lou Babic Memorial Final
Presidential S. Final

3rd Niatross S. Final

At 3

1st New Jersey Classic Elimination

2nd Cane Pace
Terrapin S.
North America Cup Consolation
Meadowlands Pace Consolation

At 3 (continued)

New Jersey Sires S. at Garden State Park
leg of George Morton Levy Series

At 4

1st William Haughton Memorial

3rd leg of Driscoll Series

At 5

1st William Haughton Memorial
Lake Erie P.
Presidential Series Final and two legs
Nicole Hudock Memorial
Graduate Series P. at Blue Bonnets

2nd Graduate Series Final
George Morton Levy Series Final

3rd Tricentennial P.
leg of Driscoll Series

Honors

Fastest Standardbred of all time

Cambest

Photo by Tony Leonard
Courtesy of The Horseman and Fair World

Race Record

Year	Age	Starts	Wins	2nd	3rd	Earnings	Record
1990	2	18	12	3	1	$ 360,522	p,2,1:54
1991	3	22	3	5	0	295,008	p,3,1:53
1992	4	26	11	6	3	249,930	p,4,1:52.4h
1993	5	28	16	6	2	552,650	p,T1:46.1
		94	42	20	6	$1,458,110	p,T1:46.1

Cambest

weeks later in the Breeders Crown, but he was never a factor and finished eighth behind Artsplace.

In spite of these setbacks, Cambest still had a very successful rookie season, winning 12 of his 18 starts and banking $360,522 for his owners. In a highly competitive two-year-old colt division, Cambest ranked number five in earnings behind Artsplace and Die Laughing (who both earned over $1,000,000), June's Baby and Tooter Scooter.

Coming back as a three-year-old, Cambest was thrust against one of the best ever groups of colts, which included Artsplace, Die Laughing and Precious Bunny. All were great racehorses and have become successful sires. Cambest opened his season in impressive fashion with a win at The Meadows in 1:53.2 after posting opening fractions of :26 and :55. His first stakes event was a week later in a New Jersey Classic Elimination, which he won handily in 1:53 with a final quarter in :26.1. However, Cambest had no luck at all in the $500,000 New Jersey Classic Final, beginning with the draw for post positions. He drew number 10 and was never really in the hunt. He moved up to fifth on the final turn but was never able to make contact with the leaders and the race was won by Die Laughing over Precious Bunny.

Cambest then had to tangle with Artsplace in a division of the Terrapin S. at Rosecroft. He finished second in 1:52.1 after challenging Artsplace for the last quarter. The North America Cup Elimination was next and Cambest was parked out in a :27.4 third quarter and faded in the stretch to miss qualifying for the rich Final. This was followed by a fifth place finish to Artsplace in a Meadowlands Pace Elimination and a second to Miss Easy in the Meadowlands Pace Consolation. The colt found the winner's circle again at The Meadows in 1:53.1 in an Invitational event.

Unfortunately, the remainder of his year was spent chasing the big guns, with his best finish a good second to Silky Stallone in the $523,190 Cane Pace at Yonkers. But even though Cambest won only three races as a three-year-old, he still earned $295,008. Bill O'Donnell said about Cambest in a *Hoof Beats* interview, "He was a little aggressive as a three-year-old, but Danny (Altmeyer) plugged his ears later in the year, and that made a big difference. That was the problem with Cambest - when he got churned up, you couldn't calm him down. When Cambest was a four-year-old, Freddie Grant trained him and raced him with earplugs. He was aggressive in his first start or two, but after that, he was nice to drive."

Prior to his four-year-old season, Cambest was sold to Daniel Kramer, Denim Stable and David Cytrynbaum and placed with trainer Fred Grant. Bill O'Donnell drove him during his first nine starts at Freehold and The Meadowlands, with Walter Case taking over later, when Cambest raced mostly at Yonkers. Cambest had an excellent year winning 11 of 26 starts and earning nearly $250,000. His wins included the $150,000 William Haughton Memorial and numerous FFA events. He also took a new half-mile track record with a 1:52.4 score at Yonkers, in which he went wire-to-wire with an opening quarter in :27.4 and a closing one in :28.

Cambest was even better as a five-year-old, winning 16 of 28 starts and earning $552,650 for his owners. His wins included the William Haughton Memorial, Lake Erie P., two legs and Final of the Presidential Series and the Nicole Hudock P. He maintained top form all year, starting the season with a six-race winning streak and ending it by winning five of his last seven starts. Cambest won in 1:51.4 on the Blue Bonnets five-eighth mile track and 1:52.3 over Northfield's half-mile surface and twice in that time on the same size track at Yonkers. He also won in 1:51.2 at The Meadowlands after coming from ninth at the half.

Of course, the highlight of Cambest's year, and of his career, was his world record time trial at Springfield, Illinois, on August 16, 1993 at 3:20 p.m. at Illinois State Fairgrounds. It was 90 degrees with high humidity and a slight breeze - this was the setting for Cambest's epic mile of :26.1, :51.4; 1:19 1:46.1, with the individual quarters timed in :26.1, :25.3, :27.1 :27.1. This made Standardbred history and is a record which could be around for awhile.

The Hall of Famer, O'Donnell, who was in the sulky for the historic time trial takes us through the event, "It wasn't a perfect day for a time trial, but Cambest was perfect. I started him slowly in the first eighth and let him build up speed to the quarter in :26.1. He was slipping a little bit going down the backstretch, so I shut him down a touch before we got to the half in :51.4. The prompter was so far behind us that he didn't help Cambest at all. Someone asked me about the prompter afterwards and I said, 'Prompter, what prompter?'. Past the half, I had so much hold of him that he thought he was done. I could feel him go to the right a little bit. So I spoke to him and away he went. He was an incredibly fast horse. He came the final quarter in :27.1 and, in fact, he kept going right past the wire. He went way down around the turn. He was really good that day. For sheer speed, this horse has it like no other."

The record Cambest broke was the 1:48.2 shared by Matt's Scooter in a September, 1988, time trial at The Red Mile and Staying Together in a race victory at The Meadowlands in 1993. "I knew he could go that fast," said trainer Fred Grant, a perception shared by O'Donnell, who said of Cambest, "For a short piece of ground, he was the fastest horse I ever sat behind."

Several weeks before Cambest's time trial, Hanover Shoe Farms had reached an agreement with the owners regarding his future stud career. They had been impressed by his speed, soundness and longevity at the highest levels. Unfortunately, the elation of Cambest's connections over his success was soon to be tempered.

The bad news came in September. According to two blood-gas tests, Cambest had elevated levels of bicarbonate prior to the Senior Jug on September 19th at Delaware, Ohio. As a result, trainer Fred Grant received a fine and suspension. Cambest won the race in 1:52.1, but was later disqualified and forfeited the purse. In a post-race statement, Grant was visibly upset and denied any knowledge of the horse being "milkshaked," the term used for a mixture that includes bicarbonate of soda, which is believed to retard the buildup of lactic acid in muscles, which causes fatigue. Grant said, "The horse gets a lot of vitamins, a lot of carbohydrates and everything in his feed everyday. Maybe something stuck in there. I have no idea."

Dr. Richard Sams, director of the Ohio Racing Commission laboratory at Ohio State University tried to explain the situation. He was quoted in a Horseman & Fair World article, "An elevated value means some alkaline substance has been administered to the horse. It doesn't necessarily mean that bicarbonate itself has been administered. It doesn't mean the horse has been milkshaked. It doesn't matter how you administer one of these alkaline substances, whether it's a milkshake or whether it's in the feed. You still get the same result."

Cambest's blood was not analyzed at Springfield on the day of his world record time trial.

Several weeks after Cambest's problems and the controversy over the Delaware, Ohio race, Hanover Shoe Farms announced it would not stand him at stud. Hanover issued the following statement, "Notwithstanding the continuing high regard and respect we have for the integrity of the owners and the trainer of Cambest, due to the circumstances involved and in consideration of the negative public perceptions surrounding the incident which occurred before the Senior Jug on Sunday, September 19, 1993, Hanover Shoe Farms has decided not to stand Cambest." A week later, the owners of Cambest and Meg Nichols Leavitt's Walnut Hall Ltd. farm announced the horse would stand at stud at that farm's Lexington, Kentucky, location for the very reasonable stud fee of $2,500.

Ironically, Cambest reunited Walnut Hall Ltd.'s president Alan Leavitt with bloodlines he developed at his Lana Lobell Farm decades ago through Cambest's second dam, Pebble Lobell, and third dam, Pert Lobell.

Cambest

Sire Line

Cambest is, obviously, the fastest record son of the great sire Cam Fella, who is profiled in his own chapter. The pedigree of Cambest is somewhat different than the other top sons of Cam Fella in that there is no Meadow Skipper blood in his maternal line. All of Cam Fella's other major sons at stud, except for Presidential Ball and Camluck, have Meadow Skipper maternally. It will be interesting to see how these sires fare compared to the others.

Maternal Line

Cambest comes from a maternal family which is extremely deep and one of the most outstanding in the sport. It is known by various names, most commonly for the root mare Medio and also as the Miss Bertha C. family. There are numerous branches, both trotting and pacing, with scores of quality performers

I tend to think that some of Cambest's longevity is the result of the breeding in his immediate maternal family. Cambest's dam was a fast, hard-hitting type of mare by Harold J., who was a sire noted for producing that type of performer. His second dam was by Adios Vic, who sired racehorses of a similar persuasion. The sire of his third dam was Overtrick, who was a noted broodmare sire. Thus Cambest is the product of an extreme speed sire, who was one of the gamest horses ever, and a maternal heritage of toughness.

Cambest's dam, Oxford Mary Ann p,2,2:04.1f; 3,1:58.4f; 4,1:56.3h ($102,762) has produced seven faster than 1:59. In addition to Cambest, she is the dam of Power Right p,4,1:53.1 ($117,951) (by Albatross), Jack Clayton p,1:54.3 ($123,492) (by Niatross), Oxford Fella p,3,1:56.1 (by Cam Fella), Denmaster p,4,1:54.1f-'98 (by Dragon's Lair), English Tutor p,2,Q1:56.3 (by Cam Fella) and the mare Courtalisa p,3,1:58.1 (by Sonsam) who is the dam of two fast performers in Our Commitment p,4,1:52 ($323,049) (by Frugal Gourmet) and Cam's Paragon p,3,1:52.3 (by Cam Fella).

The grandam of Cambest is Pebble Lobell p,3,2:04.1f ($10,345) who has quietly produced 10 2:00 performers, the fastest being Kendal Lasso p,4,1:54.3 (by Coal Harbor) and richest the mare Oxford Penny p,1:56.1 ($221,448) (by Scarlet Skipper). None of Pebble Lobell's 10 winners took a record faster than 2:01.3 at two, nor were they Grand Circuit type performers. They were good, hard-hitting older raceway performers. The same holds true for Cambest's third, fourth and fifth dams; they produced just average performers and nothing much in the way of two and three-year-old speed.

Since Oxford Mary Ann was able to produce fast two-year-olds sired by Cam Fella, Albatross, Dragon's Lair and Sonsam, I suspect Harold J. p,4,1:57.4f ($159,179) may have been a strong influence in her pedigree. Harold J. had the breeding to be a top trotter but was a pacer. His sire is Worthy Boy and his dam the Scotland mare Lady Scotland, who produced several good pacers and had three daughters who established exceptional pacing lines. Harold J. is a full brother to Breath O Spring p,3,T2:10, who is the dam of world champions and good pacing sires Storm Damage p,3,1:53.2 ($659,296) and Race Time p,3,1:57 ($486,955). Another half-sister, Hodge Podge p,4,2:02.2h (by Hodgen), was a stakes winner and the dam of Prelude Lobell, one of the sport's great broodmares in the 1970s and 1980s.

In addition to Cambest, Harold J. has two other 1:52 broodmare sire credits. His daughter Happy Trick is the dam of Righteous Bucks p,3,1:52.2 ($673,938) (by Scarlet Skipper), Tidewater Trick p,1:52 ($238,111) (by Nero) and Pai Hui p,4,1:52.2 ($190,772) (by George Allen). And the Harold J. mare J.D. Betty is the dam of the ultra-tough performer J.D.'s Buck p,4,1:54.3 ($1,156,532) (by Adios Vic) and Tough Hombre p,4,1:51.3f ($631,656) (by Albatross). Harold J. never really got the respect he deserved, but now has nearly 400 2:00 broodmare sire credits. And his trotting heritage has shown up since he has six 2:00 broodmare sire credits for trotters, including $500,000 winner Free Token 1:56f and Turnpike Token 4,1:54.3 ($128,135). The lesson here is, don't underestimate the power of Harold J. in a pedigree.

Analysis

Cambest is linebred 4x4 to both Adios and Dale Frost - the two stallions that have established the most successful pacing branches of the modern era. He gets both of his Dale Frost crosses though Cam Fella. However, the link to Adios is through two of that stallion's greatest sons, Bret Hanover and Adios Vic. The latter handed Bret four of his six career defeats and was known for his incredible closing kick.

Oxford Mary Ann, Cambest's dam, had no common crosses in her first four generations. One interesting link is that she is 4x5 to the half-sisters Alma Lee and Jane Reynolds, the latter being the dam of Solicitor - the sire of Overtrick. Alma Lee is the grandam of Harold J.'s sire Worthy Boy, and Harold J. and Overtrick linked up to produce many top performers.

With the structure of Cambest's pedigree, he can be bred to the daughters of all modern-day sires except his own sire Cam Fella and, perhaps, Most Happy Fella and Harold J. mares - unless you want a foal inbred 3x2 to those stallions. Other than these, daughters of all other popular stallions fit him in a variety of ways, giving him access to all types of mares in the genetic pool. There also will not be any shortage of Cambest sons and daughters to help prove this young stallion. He was bred to 863 mares during his first four seasons at stud and will have every chance to make an impact.

Cambest

Photo courtesy of The Horseman and Fair World

Leading Progeny by Cambest

Fastest

Casino Winner, h, p,3,1:51.3 $36,689
Invader Hall, g, p,3,1:52.1 $78,755
Sonuva Best, h, p,3,1:52.3 $27,332
Color Me Best, g, p,3,1:52.4 $29,165
Springtime Romeo, h, p,3,1:52.4 $17,425
Ludwigpanbeethoven, h, p,2,1:53.1 $123,192
Cam Knows Best, h, p,3,1:53.2h $104,410
Best Mood, h, p,3,1:53.3 $78,386
Hoosier Favorite, h, p,3,1:54.1 $18,265
Trini's Best, h, p,3,1:54.1 $18,250

Richest

Ludwigpanbeethoven, h, p,2,1:53.1 $123,192
Happy To Be Best, m, p,3,1:55.4f $114,064
Cam Knows Best, h, p,3,1:53.2h $104,410
Invader Hall, g, p,3,1:52.1 $78,755
Best Mood, h, p,3,1:53.3 $78,386
Astronomer's Hall, m, $41,881
Casino Winner, h, p,3,1:51.3 $36,689
Getaway Hall, g, p,3,1:55.3h $35,488
Camie Kalo, m, p,2,1:54.3 $31,033
Something Windy, m, p,2,1:59h $30,386

Cambest, Brown Horse, 1988
p, 2, 1:54; 3, 1:53; 4, 1:52.4h; 5, T1:46.1 ($1,458,110)

Cam Fella, 1979 p, 4, 1:53.1 $2,041,367	Most Happy Fella, 1967 p, 3, T1:55 $419,033	Meadow Skipper, 1960 p, 3, 1:55.1 $428,057	**DALE FROST**, 1951 p, 1:58 $204,117	HAL DALE	**ABBEDALE** Margaret Hal
				Galloway	Raider Bethel
			Countess Vivian, 1950 p, 3, 1:59 $43,262	**KING'S COUNSEL**	**VOLOMITE** Margaret Spangler
				Filly Direct	**BILLY DIRECT** Calumet Edna
		Laughing Girl, 1961 p, 4, 2:04h $19,546	Good Time, 1946 p, 1:57.4 $318,792	HAL DALE	**ABBEDALE** Margaret Hal
				On Time	**VOLOMITE** Nedda Guy
			Maxine's Dream, 1954 p, 2, T2:00 $36,557	Knight Dream	**NIBBLE HANOVER** Lydia Knight
				Maxine Abbe	**ABBEDALE** Maxine Direct
	Nan Cam, 1971 p, 5, 2:05.1f $11,390	Bret Hanover, 1962 p, 4, T1:53.3 $922,616	**ADIOS**, 1940 p, T1:57½ $33,329	HAL DALE	**ABBEDALE** Margaret Hal
				Adioo Volo	Adioo Guy Sigrid Volo
			Brenna Hanover, 1956 p, 3, T2:01 $21,946	**TAR HEEL**	**BILLY DIRECT** Leta Long
				Beryl Hanover	**NIBBLE HANOVER** Laura Hanover
		Nan Frost, 1966 p, 3, 2:06.3f $1,607	**DALE FROST**, 1951 p, 1:58 $204,117	HAL DALE	**ABBEDALE** Margaret Hal
				Galloway	Raider Bethel
			Mynah Hanover, 1950 p, 2:05.2h $44,184	Ensign Hanover	**BILLY DIRECT** Helen Hanover
				Betty Mahone	Corporal Lee Belle Mahone
Oxford Mary Ann, 1980 p, 4, 1:56.3h $102,762	Harold J., 1959 p, 4, 1:57.4f $159,179	Worthy Boy, 1940 3, 2:02¼ $25,688	**VOLOMITE**, 1926 3, 2:03¼ $32,649	Peter Volo	**PETER THE GREAT** Nervolo Belle
				Cita Frisco	San Francisco Mendocita
			Warwell Worthy, 1932 3, 2:03¼	Peter The Brewer	**PETER THE GREAT** Zombrewer
				Alma Lee	Lee Worthy Jane Revere
		Lady Scotland, 1943	Scotland, 1925 T1:59¼	Peter Scott	**PETER THE GREAT** Jenny Scott
				Roya McKinney	McKinney Princess Royal
			Spinster, 1930 4, T2:05	Spencer	Lee Tide Petrex
				Minnetonka	Belwin The Miss Stokes
	Pebble Lobell, 1973 p, 3, 2:04.1f $10,345	Adios Vic, 1962 p, 3, 1:56.3 $455,896	**ADIOS**, 1940 p, T1:57½ $33,329	HAL DALE	**ABBEDALE** Margaret Hal
				Adioo Volo	Adioo Guy Sigrid Volo
			Miss Creedabelle, 1952 p, 4, 2:01.3 $23,688	Jimmy Creed	Frisco Forbes Virginia Grattan
				Belle Grattan	Dexter Worthy Iola Grattan
		Pert Lobell, 1966 p, 2, 2:05.3f	Overtrick, 1960 p, 3, 1:57.1h $407,483	Solicitor	**KING'S COUNSEL** Jane Reynolds
				Overbid	**HAL DALE** Barbara Direct
			Preview Hanover, 1961	**TAR HEEL**	**BILLY DIRECT** Leta Long
				Poppy Hanover	**NIBBLE HANOVER** Bertha Hanover

Camluck

Camluck was a $70,000 yearling at the 1988 Kentucky Standardbred Select yearling sale in Lexington. His background and looks merited the high price. He was a handsome, if somewhat smallish, dark bay colt by Cam Fella, and his dam was the world champion and multiple stakes-winning filly Lucky Lady p,3,1:55, a daughter of former world champion Striking Image p,2,1:55.

Camluck was unraced as a two-year-old due to an OCD lesion, but matured at three into a top stakes colt late in his sophomore campaign. His first major stakes win came in trainer Bob McIntosh's favorite event, the Provincial Cup at Windsor Raceway. That score, in 1:52.4f, became his three-year-old mark. He earned $267,878 at three, and was stakes-placed on a number of occasions, including a strong second (in track record time) to Beach Towel in the American-National at Sportsman's Park. At four, he became a genuine FFA'er, with his major accomplishment a rain-soaked score in the Breeders Crown Aged Pace over a good track at Ladbroke at The Meadows in 1:52.4f for Mike Lachance. Camluck also nabbed the Fraser Memorial at Edmonton in 1:53.4 and paced in 1:50.3 at Lexington during the Grand Circuit meet for John Campbell. He also had FFA scores at Mohawk, Greenwood, Hazel Park and Sportsman's at four, a season in which he had nine wins and earned more than $400,000.

At five, in 1992, Camluck earned an additional $324,694, winning ten times, and sending his earnings past the $1 million mark. His fastest race win was a 1:51 score at Garden State Park in the fall of that year, and he was a menacing second to stablemate Artsplace in the Senior Jug at Delaware that season. The Delaware performance earned him a try against the fence at Lexington for Mike Lachance, and Camluck responded with a T1:48.4 effort that placed him among the fastest horses in the history of the breed. Lachance is convinced that Camluck could have gone faster and admits to under-estimating the horse's strength. "I think he could have beaten 1:48," Lachance has said. "He surprised me with how strong he was."

Camluck is one of eight sub-1:50 credits for Cam Fella, his legendary sire, and his third fastest behind world champion Cambest's T1:46.1 mark and Pacific Fella's p,1:48.2z-'98. Camluck's earnings peaked at just over $1 million, and he entered the stud in 1993 at Seelster Farms in Lucan, Ontario. He bred 179 mares in his first crop. "Camluck is a very good-looking dark horse," trainer Bob McIntosh reported. "He was kind of small as a two-year-old, but he developed into a big, grand-looking horse who is over 16 hands. He is a nice cross physically, because you can see the Cam Fella influence in his dark color and gait, and also the presence of his dam, who is by Striking Image, in his physical appearance and substance. The white markings come from his dam."

Sire Line

As noted, Camluck is a son of Cam Fella, and grandson of Most Happy Fella in an emerging sire line that traces directly to Meadow Skipper. Most Happy Fella, in fact, has provided three distinct branches of his siring family. First, there are those tracing from Cam Fella; second is another branch which traces from Most Happy Fella's son Oil Burner to No Nukes, and then to such horses as Jate Lobell and Western Hanover. A third branch of the Most Happy Fella clan comes through Tyler B to Dragon's Lair, Magical Mike and Tyler's Mark. Being a part of the huge Meadow Skipper dynasty certainly gives any young horse with opportunity a major advantage.

The Cam Fella division of the Most Happy Fella line has provided much of the siring power among pacers in the past decade, with a whole slew of champions, including such noted powers as Presidential Ball, Precious Bunny, Cam's Card Shark, Camtastic, Goalie Jeff, Village Jiffy, Village Connection, Cambest, Beastmaster, Fake Left and Pacific Fella, among the best offspring.

Camluck would appear to have the siring power to be deemed the best young son of Cam Fella in the stud. His first few crops have produced exceptional colts and fillies who have dominated the

Race Record Highlights

At 3
- **1st** MacFarlane Memorial
  Provincial Cup Final
  Motor City P. Elimination
- **2nd** American-National S.
  Motor City P. Final
  Provincial Cup Elimination
- **3rd** Tompkins-Geers S.

At 4
- **1st** Breeders Crown Final
  Stewart Fraser Memorial
  FFA events
- **2nd** Breeders Crown Elimination
  Frank Ryan Memorial
  Senior Jug

At 5
- **1st** FFA events
- **2nd** Molson Series P.
  Senior Jug
  Stewart Fraser Memorial
- **3rd** Breeders Crown
  American-National S.
  leg of Graduate Series

Camluck

Photo by Monica Thors
Courtesy of Seelster Farms

Race Record

Year	Age	Starts	Wins	2nd	3rd	Earnings	Record
1990	3	22	7	3	1	$267,878	p,3,1:52.4f
1991	4	22	9	4	1	410,688	p,4,1:50.3
1992	5	25	10	4	3	324,694	p,T1:48.4
		69	26	11	5	$1,003,260	p,T1:48.4

Camluck

Ontario Sire Stakes, and even occasionally stepped out of Ontario to compete effectively along the Grand Circuit. His son from his first crop, Northern Luck p,3,1:49.1, was the fastest three-year-old in North America in 1997. While the other sons of Cam Fella have principally been noted as good filly sires, Camluck appears to have the siring power to produce exceptional colts as well.

Maternal Line

Much of Camluck's physical presence, as we have seen, can be attributed to his dam, the brilliant world champion mare, Lucky Lady p,2,1:58.1; 3,1:55, a lifetime winner of $591,857. The smallish daughter of Striking Image p,2,1:55 was a superb race-filly, winning 16 times at two and three at the very highest levels of her division for trainer Dick Hogan. Her major triumphs came in the Meadowlands features that year, as she captured both the Tarport Hap and the Mistletoe Shalee stakes. She was, like her son, an aggressive, dominant filly whose broodmare credits besides Camluck show her real merit. Her other foals include Cam's Lucky p,4,1:53.2f ($247,353), Cam's Fortune p,1:54.2 ($196,584) and Lucky Cam p,3,1:52.2. Camluck's sister, Lucky We Met, has two sub-1:55 female credits, including the good 1997 two-year-old Very Fast Cass p,2,1:54.

Lucky's Lady mother is the Truluck matron, Just Our Luck, a mare with three other 1:55 credits besides Lucky Lady. Truluck p,2,1:57.2, a son of Torpid, is a horse forgotten by history, but it should be noted here that he was a genuine stakes star himself as a two-year-old, winning the Fox Stake for George Sholty and racing on even terms (particularly at two) and three in the same crop that included Most Happy Fella and Columbia George, two of the toughest race-colts of all time.

Progeny Of Note

Camluck's early success in the stud has made him the star of the Ontario siring scene. Well-patronized from the very beginning, he has bred an average of nearly 160 mares in each of his first six seasons at stud. His fastest offspring to date is the Tattersalls Pace winner Northern Luck p,3,1:49.1 ($907,974), now a young Kentuckiana Farms (New Jersey division) sire. Camluck's other leading offspring include the sensational co-1996 Canadian Horse of the Year, the filly champion Whenuwishuponastar p,3,1:53.4 ($578,752). He also has D.M. Dillinger p,3,1:51.3 ($407,704) and Daylon Tempo p,4,1:53.2 ($353,451) among his best get to date.

His 1997 two-year-olds included the multiple stakes-winning filly Stonebridge First p,2,1:56.1f ($250,190) and the late-developing colt Northern Dynasty p,2,1:53.1 ($196,466).

Although he is a young horse, Camluck has already achieved a considerable reputation as a quality sire. He is clearly one of the most successful young sons of Cam Fella currently at stud with offspring old enough to race.

Analysis

Camluck has made an instant impact on the pacing sire scene as a result of his first two excellent crops of colts and fillies.

Being based in Ontario, Canada, Camluck is working with somewhat of a different gene pool than most of the American-based stallions and this can easily be seen when looking at the sires of the dams to whom he has been bred. Daughters of stallions such as Striking Force, Super Wave, River Rouge, Kawartha Skipper, Coal Harbor, Penn Hanover, Senor Skipper, Dallas Almahurst, Tarport Count, Horton Hanover and Threefold are not commonly found south of the Canadian border.

However, Camluck has made the best of this situation and those sires listed above are the broodmare sires of some of his best performers to date. Of Camluck's 38 fastest sons and daughters, 30 are from daughters of different broodmare sires which would seem to indicate that Camluck does not need a specific type of cross in order to be successful. He has sired good horses from many average broodmare sires and maternal families.

This is not to say that Camluck has not had his share of mares by the glamour sires and from good maternal families. He has, and has done well with those also. Listed among the broodmare sires of his top performers are Big Towner, Albatross, Bret Hanover, No Nukes, Abercrombie, Sonsam, Nero, Nihilator and Race Time.

Northern Luck, Camluck''s sub-1:50 and $900,000 winning son, is from the good Big Towner mare Town Sweetheart p,3,1:57.3f ($63,210) who has also produced Bear Dance p,2,1:53 ($312,163) (by Presidential Ball) and V.P. Finance p,4,1:52.2f ($502,163) (by Abercrombie). Town Sweetheart has been an outstanding producer and her son by Camluck is her best.

Mares by Big Towner appear to be an excellent cross for Camluck since three have already produced 1:55 performers by him. Big Towner is also the sire of the second dam of Daylon Tempo p,4,1:53.2-'98 ($353,451). Sonsam mares are responsible for two sub-1:54 performers and Abercrombie also has two in the 1:55 list.

Another sire which seems to be having some influence on Camluck's best horses is the Meadow Skipper son Smog who is the sire of the second dams of D.M. Dilinger p,3,1:51.3 ($407,704) and Northern Dynasty p,2,1:53.1 ($196,466). Smog stood in Canada for many years and there are plenty of Smog mares in Ontario. One daughter of Smog is the granddam of D.M. Dilinger and Northern Dynasty - the good Canadian stakes winner Silver Wraith p,3,2:00.4f ($132,448). Her great Kawartha Skipper daughter Silver Reign p,3,1:55.4f ($766,871) is the dam of Northern Dynasty and her other top daughter Misty Silver p,4,1:57.3f ($410,848) is the dam of D.M. Dilinger.

Sonsam mares have had some early success with Camluck as shown by the top filly Whenuwishuponastar p,3,1:53.4 ($578,752) and Dean Douglas p,3,1:52.4.

Overtrick also shows up frequently as the sire of the second dam of Camluck's better horses as shown by Glenmount Willy p,4,1:52.4, Weston Seelster p,3,1:54.2, Stonebridge First p,2,1:56.1f and Super Trooper p,2,1:59.2.

Looking at the common pedigree crosses in Camluck's best sons and daughters, we see Meadow Skipper and Bret Hanover duplicated in the first four generations many times. Northern Luck is 4x4 to Meadow Skipper and 4x5x4 to Bret Hanover. D.M. Dilinger is 4x3 to Strike Out (son of Bret Hanover), 4x4 to Meadow Skipper and 4x5x4 to Bret Hanover. By Xample p,3,1:52 ($326,775) is 3x4 to Most Happy Fella and 4x5x3 to Meadow Skipper. Glenmount Willy is closely bred 3x3 to Most Happy Fella and 4x5 to Bret Hanover. Another with the 3x3 Most Happy Fella cross is Twin B Fabio p,3,1:54f. It must also be noted that Camluck fillies are also excellent racehorses since they represent five of his 10 highest money winners. Camluck's very best filly, Whenuwishuponastar, is bred 4x4x4 to Meadow Skipper and 4x5x4 to Bret Hanover.

Camluck's own pedigree shows the closest common cross to be 3x4 to Bret Hanover and 4x4 to Dale Frost.

Camluck seems to be a rising star in the stallion ranks and has now drawn larger books of higher quality mares. Perhaps the best is yet to come.

Camluck

Photo by Monica Thors
Courtesy of Seelster Farms

Leading Progeny by Camluck

Fastest

Northern Luck, h, p,3,1:49.1 $907,974
D. M. Dilinger, h, p,3,1:51.3 $407,704
By Xample, h, p,3,1:52 $326,775
Uptown Weezie, g, p,3,1:52.2 $54,789
Glenmount Willy, g, p,4,1:52.4 $103,169
Sean Douglas, g, p,3,1:52.4 $91,840
Galyn Mack, g, p,3,1:53 $103,402
Northern Dynasty, h, p,2,1:53.1 $196,466
Any Excuse, h, p,4,1:53.2 $31,067
Coal Luck, h, p,3,1:53.2 $98,480

Richest

Northern Luck, h, p,3,1:49.1 $907,974
Whenuwishuponastar, m, p,3,1:53.4 $578,752
D. M. Dilinger, h, p,3,1:51.3 $407,704
Daylon Tempo, m, p,4,1:53.2 $353,451
By Xample, h, p,3,1:52 $326,775
Stonebridge First, m, p,2,1:56.1f $250,190
Northern Dynasty, h, p,2,1:53.1 $196,466
Sammie's Cammi, m, p,3,1:54.3f $168,379
Super Trooper, h, p,2,1:57.2 $118,012
Cam Boo Angel, m, p,3,1:53.4f $109,144

Camluck, Bay Horse, 1987
p,3 1:52.4f; 4,1:50.3; 5, T1:48.4 ($1,003,260)

Cam Fella, 1979 p, 4, 1:53.1 $2,041,367	Most Happy Fella, 1967 p, 3, T1:55 $419,033	Meadow Skipper, 1960 p, 3, 1:55.1 $428,057	**DALE FROST**, 1951 p, 1:58 $204,117	**HAL DALE** — **ABBEDALE** / Margaret Hal
				Galloway — Raider / Bethel
			Countess Vivian, 1950 p, 3, 1:59 $43,262	**KING'S COUNSEL** — **VOLOMITE** / Margaret Spangler
				Filly Direct — **BILLY DIRECT** / Calumet Edna
		Laughing Girl, 1961 p, 4, 2:04h $19,546	Good Time, 1946 p, 1:57.4 $318,792	**HAL DALE** — **ABBEDALE** / Margaret Hal
				On Time — **VOLOMITE** / Nedda Guy
			Maxine's Dream, 1954 p, 2, T2:00 $36,557	**KNIGHT DREAM** — **NIBBLE HANOVER** / Lydia Knight
				Maxine Abbe — **ABBEDALE** / Maxine Direct
	Nan Cam, 1971 p, 5, 2:05.1f $11,390	Bret Hanover, 1962 p, 4, T1:53.3 $922,616	Adios, 1940 p, T1:57½ $33,329	**HAL DALE** — **ABBEDALE** / Margaret Hal
				Adioo Volo — Adioo Guy / Sigrid Volo
			Brenna Hanover, 1956 p, 3, T2:01 $21,946	**TAR HEEL** — **BILLY DIRECT** / Leta Long
				Beryl Hanover — **NIBBLE HANOVER** / Laura Hanover
		Nan Frost, 1966 p, 3, 2:06.3f $1,607	**DALE FROST**, 1951 p, 1:58 $204,117	**HAL DALE** — **ABBEDALE** / Margaret Hal
				Galloway — Raider / Bethel
			Mynah Hanover, 1950 p, 2:05.2h $44,184	**ENSIGN HANOVER** — **BILLY DIRECT** / Helen Hanover
				Betty Mahone — Corporal Lee / Belle Mahone
Lucky Lady, 1980 p, 3, 1:55 $591,857	Striking Image, 1974 p, 2, 1:55 $56,028	Strike Out, 1969 p, 3, 1:56.3h $454,064	Bret Hanover, 1962 p, 4, T1:53.3 $922,616	**ADIOS** — **HAL DALE** / Adioo Volo
				Brenna Hanover — **TAR HEEL** / Beryl Hanover
			Golden Miss, 1954 p, 4, 2:02.1h $64,471	**ENSIGN HANOVER** — **BILLY DIRECT** / Helen Hanover
				Miss Pluto Scott — McKinney Scott / Ludene Pluto
		Reflection, 1964	Painter, 1955 p, 2, 2:01 $53,740	**TAR HEEL** — **BILLY DIRECT** / Leta Long
				Pretty Hanover — **NIBBLE HANOVER** / Easter Hanover
			Way Wave, 1958 p, 3, 1:58 $105,555	**GOOD TIME** — **HAL DALE** / On Time
				Fullsway — **KING'S COUNSEL** / Dell Frisco
	Just Our Luck, 1976	Truluck, 1967 p, 2, 1:57.2 $313,058	Torpid, 1954 p, 2, 1:58 $187,358	**KNIGHT DREAM** — **NIBBLE HANOVER** / Lydia Knight
				Torresdale — **ABBEDALE** / Calumet Cream
			Monel, 1959 p, 2, 2:03 $9,929	**TAR HEEL** — **BILLY DIRECT** / Leta Long
				Miracle Byrd — Poplar Byrd / Gardenia Hanover
		Drexel Sue, 1970	Adios Boy, 1951 p, 2, T1:58.3 $129,859	**ADIOS** — **HAL DALE** / Adioo Volo
				Carrie Castle — Bonnycastle / Crystal Gleam
			Belle Of Easton, 1952	Cardinal Prince — Peter Potempkin / Lillian L
				Jo Ann Hal — **HAL DALE** / True Athlone

Dexter Nukes

Dexter Nukes has been making a name for himself at the Armstrong Bros. breeding farm in Ontario, Canada, and is now a successful stallion following his career as an excellent racehorse. The fact that he is a son of the top sire No Nukes adds to his credentials and his attractiveness to breeders.

Dexter Nukes was bred by Lana Lobell Farms and Erba Stables and sold for $70,000 at the Lana Lobell 1987 yearling sale. His original name was Valhalla Lobell and he was the second foal and first colt from his dam. Owners Thomas and Mildred Dexter promptly changed the name of their new acquisition to Dexter Nukes. Thomas Dexter usually used the moniker "Dexter" in the names of most of his horses. He had owned horses for many years and was 87-years-old when he purchased Dexter Nukes.

At two, Dexter Nukes was trained by Dick Thomas and started in a baby race at The Meadowlands on May 14, 1988, which indicated he was ready early. However, the colt finished sixth and was timed in 2:03.3 with a final quarter in :28.3. This was to be his only start as a youngster since it was later found he fractured a coffin bone during the race. He was operated on to remove a bone chip and then turned out for several months.

Coming back at three for new trainer George Gilmour, Dexter Nukes was a different animal. He was ready early and qualified at Pompano Park in mid-January by winning in 2:03. He proceeded to win his first four starts by open lengths, coming from behind in three and going wire-to-wire in the fourth. The latter was his fastest time, 1:56.3, with an opening quarter of :28.2 and a closing one in :28.1. He was a star in the making.

The colt threw in a "clunker" in his next start and finished last, timed in 1:59.4. Two weeks later, he resumed his winning ways and began a five-race winning streak at Pompano Park, including two legs and the Final of the Pompano Beach Series and then working his way up to the Invitational ranks. At this point of the season, he had won nine of 10 starts and was headed to The Meadowlands.

Dexter Nukes' first two Meadowlands appearances brought him back to reality and made one wonder if he could successfully compete against the "major league" stakes colts. In two New Jersey Sires S., Dexter Nukes was fourth and third but he had outside post positions each race and was raced three-wide much of the way. His regular driver to that point had been the very capable Bruce Ranger but it was then decided that John Campbell should try the colt.

Campbell won his first New Jersey Sires S. drive with Dexter Nukes in 1:54.1. A week later, Bill O'Donnell drove the colt to a second place finish in the $100,000 New Jersey Sires S. Final, losing by only a neck to Land Fire after being three-wide for the second half in a very impressive race. This was the wake-up call Dexter Nukes needed and with Campbell in the sulky, he then proceeded to win seven of his next eight races, becoming the talk of the Meadowlands and the industry.

He won his New Jersey Classic Elimination in a brilliant 1:52.2 and the $500,000 Final in 1:53.2 on a windy, rainy night. Owner Thomas Dexter, 89 years old at the time, said, "I think this is the best horse I've had. I owned two others that were good (Skipper Dexter and Dexter Hanover), but this one's the best. I just didn't think I'd have to wait this long to get such a good one."

A week later, Dexter Nukes suffered a tough loss by a nose to Hit The Bid after cutting the entire race to the last step and pacing his final quarter in :26.4. He rebounded to win five consecutive races, including the Historic Cup, his Meadowlands Pace Elimination in 1:51.3 over Goalie Jeff and the $852,000 Meadowlands Pace Final in 1:51.3. In that great event, Dexter Nukes left from post seven and had the lead in the first turn, passing the quarter in :27. He and Campbell were able to get away with a :57.1 middle half and he just coasted home in :27.2 to win by over three lengths from Casino Cowboy. After the race, Campbell said, "He can really fire out of there. I gave him a little breather to the half, but he's a bit lazy and I didn't want to slow him down entirely. Once we got to the top of the stretch, I knew he wasn't going to be caught."

The Gaines Memorial was next and Dexter Nukes went two heats for the first time, winning in 1:53.2 and 1:52.3. A week later, he faced four-year-olds in a Meadowlands Open and was third behind T.K.'s Skipper and Camtastic. It was then up to Blue Bonnets in Montreal for

Race Record Highlights
At 3

1st Meadowlands Pace Final and Elimination
Gaines Memorial Final and Elimination
New Jersey Classic Final and Elimination
Jersey Cup
Historic Series
Prix d'Ete Elimination
Freestate Invitational
Pompano Beach Series Final and two legs
New Jersey Sires S.
2nd New Jersey Sires S. Final
3rd Messenger S. Elimination
New Jersey Sires S.

Dexter Nukes

Photo courtesy of Armstrong Bros.

Race Record

Year	Age	Starts	Wins	2nd	3rd	Earnings	Record
1988	2	1	0	0	0		
1989	3	27	19	2	3	$1,027,620	p,3,1:51.3
		28	19	2	3	$1,027,620	p,3,1:51.3

the Prix d'Ete, where Dexter Nukes won his Elimination wire-to-wire in 1:55. However, in the Final in which he was the heavy favorite, he made a break at the start and wound up fifth behind the winning Goalie Jeff.

Dexter Nukes was then preparing for the Messenger S. at Freestate Raceway and he won an Invitational in 1:54.3. But, in the Messenger Elimination, he finished a disappointing third to Sandman Hanover and was scratched from the Final due to a sore foot. This was the last race of his career. Dexter Nukes had won 19 of 27 starts at three with earnings of $1,027,620. It would have been a stellar performance by any colt, but since he was a son of the hot sire No Nukes, it made him especially valuable as a stallion prospect.

Sire Line

Dexter Nukes is a linebred Meadow Skipper stallion being 4x3 to that stallion. His dam is 3x3 to Dale Frost through Meadow Skipper and Fulla Napoleon. Since his sire is the very successful No Nukes, Dexter Nukes' connections, along with many North American breeders, are hoping he will be able to successfully carry on the No Nukes branch of the Most Happy Fella and Meadow Skipper male line.

Maternal Line

Dexter Nukes' dam Viking Princess p,2,2:00.1f; 3,T1:56 ($133,434) was a well-performed daughter of Albatross who won two legs and the Final of the Perfecta Series at two and was stakes-placed at two and three. She is a full, three-quarter- or half-sister to Outstanding Stock p,1:55.1 ($128,848) (by Niatross), Happy At Last p,3,1:56.3 ($135,753) (by Most Happy Fella), Emporium p,2,1:56.4 (by Sonsam), Caliope p,3,1:57.3 (by Sonsam) and Viking Fury p,1:58.1 ($197,999) (by Albatross).

Viking Princess has also produced more than just Dexter Nukes. She clicked with Matt's Scooter for Viking Terror p,1:52.4 ($336,005) and with No Nukes for Vignette Childer p,3,1:56.2 ($139,849) who was her first foal. Other Viking Princess offspring are Viking Renegade p,4,1:54 (Beach Towel), Viking Vengeance p,2,Q1:58.3f (No Nukes), Viking Temptress p,2,1:59.1h (Jate Lobell), Viking Sorceress p,2,1:59.1f (No Nukes) and Joseph Lobell p,3,1:59.2h (No Nukes).

The daughters of Viking Princess have also produced fast pacers. Vignette Childer has linked well with Matt's Scooter to produce Wrestling Matt p,2,1:52.2, Mattman p,2,1:53.3, Matturity p,3,1:54.3 and Will It Matter p,3,1:58-'98. Dexter Lobell, another full sister to Dexter Nukes, is the dam of Union Depot p,3,1:52 (Laag), It Matters p,4,1:54.4 (Matt's Scooter) and Ask A Lawyer p,2,1:54f (Dragon's Lair).

Viking's Princess' full sister, Chestnut Hill p,2,2:03.2 ($1,110) is the dam of the stakes winner Casino Gambler p,3,1:54.1 ($275,381) (by No Nukes) and another full sister, Viking Treasure p,3,2:12.3f ($1,165) is the dam of world champion and 1992 Three-Year-Old Pacing Filly of the Year So Fresh p,3,1:53 ($803,794) (by Laag), Kilburn p,3,1:52.3 ($249,117) (by Laag), Take The Points p,4,1:54.4 ($184,780) (by Fortune Teller), Serious Fun p,4,1:57f ($181,215) (by Flight Of Fire) and three other sub-1:57 performers.

This family is a prime example of how a good pedigree can overcome a mediocre racing record. The two full sisters mentioned above, Chestnut Hill and Viking Treasure, won only $2,275 between them and yet they both produced big winners. Many breeders, including me, tend to believe that good bloodlines can overcome a lack of racing ability. History shows there have been many more top horses from average or non-record mares with good pedigrees than from fast mares with poor pedigrees. Of course, you will want to avoid getting the worst of both worlds - breeding poorly-bred mares with no performance records. That's just asking for disaster.

Dexter Nukes' grandam is the mare Bacall p,3,2:05.2f ($6,417) by Fulla Napoleon p,3,1:57.1. Like Meadow Skipper, her sire Fulla Napoleon was a son of Dale Frost. Fulla Napoleon was an excellent colt performer at two and three. In fact, he was the Two-Year-Old Pacing Colt of the Year for 1967 and the runner-up to Rum Customer in his division at three. However, he did not make much of an impact as either a sire or as a broodmare sire.

We now look at his fifth dam, Bonnie Butler p,3,T2:03 ($10,307) by the great sire Volomite. Bewitch Hanover was her only 2:00 performer, but Bonnie Butler is also the dam of the Billy Direct mare Debby Hanover p,4,2:13.1h ($1,550) who gave us one of the sport's all-time great pacers - two-time Horse of the Year and Triple Crown winner Adios Butler p,4,T1:54.3 ($509,875). And the Butler's full sister Adios Governess is the dam of the top pacer and reasonably successful sire Governor Skipper p,3,1:54 ($1,039,756).

Back in his fifth and sixth generations, Dexter Nukes also has multiple crosses to some great broodmares - The Old Maid and Barbara Direct through different sires.

As you can see, there is a lot of class in Dexter Nukes' maternal family which is known by the name of Crazy Jane. However, for modern-day purposes the name should really be the maternal family of Bonnie Butler since except for two minor branches it is her descendants which make up the vast majority of the family.

Progeny of Note

Dexter Nukes has sired a number of top racehorses, including Grand Circuit and Ontario Sires S. winners. They are led by She's A Great Lady p,2,1:53.3; 3,1:51.1; 4,1:50.4 ($973,382). This mare was stakes filly at two and three and was the season's champion on all size tracks at three in addition to being voted Three-Year-Old Pacing Filly of the Year. She was also the leading money-winning pacing filly as a result of big wins in the Mistletoe Shalee S., Fan Hanover S., Nadia Lobell S., Scarlet O'Hara S. and Cinderella S. At four, she was brilliant and set world records of 1:51 on both half-mile and five-eighths mile tracks. Her half-mile track record of 1:51 at Delaware, Ohio, ties her as the fifth fastest ever on that size track, regardless of sex. She's A Great Lady also won the Breeders Crown and Milton S. at four and was voted Aged Pacing Mare of the Year. She lived up to her name and was really something special.

Another Dexter Nukes superstar is She's A Great Lady's full brother The Big Dog p,2,1:51.3; 3,1:50.2 ($809,261) who set a world record for youngsters and was voted Two-Year-Old Pacing Colt of the Year. His big wins came in the Governor's Cup Final and the Niatross P. The Big Dog experienced foot problems at three but is ready to race again at four as this is written.

Duke Of Abby p,2,1:54.4f; 3,1:52.3f; 1:51.3-'98 ($790,197) is another rich performer for Dexter Nukes, a multiple Canadian stakes winner at two and three in addition to a win in the Motor City P.

The fastest offspring of Dexter Nukes is Armbro Maestro p,2,1:59.2f; 3,1:52; 1:49.2 ($506,241) whose 1:49.2 was a world record for older geldings. Another fast and rich performer is Delayed Decision p,2,1:55.3f; 3,1:52.3f; 4,1:52 ($427,832). A pair of $300,000 winning Dexter Nukes daughters are Eftimia p,3,1:53.3; 4,1:52 ($380,867) and Mystic Music p,2,1:58.1f; 3,1:55 ($323,329). The colt Real Profit p,2,1:57.2h; 3,1:52 ($265,601) became the fastest horse in Ontario Sires S. history with his 1:52 score in 1995. Dexter Nukes also has a nice three-year-old filly racing in the middle of the 1998 season by the name of Armbro Rosebud p,3,1:53.3f-'98 ($597,301) who was a major stakes winner of over $500,000 at two.

At press time, Dexter Nukes had a flurry of 1:50 activity - Duke Of Abby p,1:49.3-'98, The Big Dog p,4,1:49.3-'98 and Armbro Pluto p,4,1:50. He now ranks only behind Cam Fella as a sire of 1:50 performers.

Analysis

As this chapter is written, Dexter Nukes has completed his ninth breeding season and has five full crops of foals at the races, not including his 1998 two-year-olds. Dexter Nukes has proven to be a very popular stallion in Ontario and his first eight breeding seasons saw him bred to over 1,200 mares - a high of 190 in 1995 and a low of 132 in 1992.

To date, Dexter Nukes has 236 2:00 performers from his 408 starters and they have earned a total of $17,260,143 at the races. He has sired five $500,000 winners, 38 $100,000 winners and 64 in 1:55 - a very good record for a young sire.

He also seems to be a good sire of fillies. Eight of his 16 richest performers are female as well as three of his ten fastest. In addition, 17 of his 38 $100,000 winners are female. Of course, his leading money winner, She's A Great Lady, is a mare.

I examined the six-generation pedigrees of Dexter Nukes' richest and fastest performers to see if there were any special pedigree cross situations among his top horses. The first, obvious point is that his two best horses, She's A Great Lady and The Big Dog are brother and sister. And, they are one of the best brother-sister combinations in the history of the sport. But they are not alone. Armbro Rosebud has a full brother in Armbro Morning p,3,1:54.4f ($147,399). Eftimia has a fast full brother in Ariva Dexter p,3,1:53, and Armbro Pluto p,3,1:52.3 ($226,791) and Armbro Ocular p,4,1:53.2 are brother and sister. Duke Of Abby also has a good brother in Dexter Doug p,4,1:53.3. It seems that when a mare hits well with Dexter Nukes it can happen again.

What is very strange, and perhaps it is just because of the excellence of Miss Donna Mayo (dam of She's A Great Lady, The Big Dog, etc.) is that Dexter Nukes' three richest performers are from mares by Silent Majority and his son Abercrombie.

The presence of several broodmare sires was evident in the best horses. Big Towner, Tyler B, Armbro Omaha and Bret Hanover showed up frequently and Bret Hanover's son Strike Out and grandson Legal Notice were also observed. Another factor seemed to be the presence of Bye Bye Byrd in the second or third generations of mares bred to Dexter Nukes. Shadow Wave also showed up frequently in the fourth and fifth generations of pedigrees. Mares with these bloodlines would seem to be the best candidates for Dexter Nukes.

Of course, most of Dexter Nuke's top horses had a 5x4x3 cross to Meadow Skipper simply due to his own pedigree and the proliferation of Meadow Skipper line mares in the breeding ranks.

Eftimia has an interesting maternal cross in that her dam is inbred 3x2 to the full Direct Rhythm sisters Skippy Rhythm and Patricia Rhythm. The dam of Mystic Music is linebred 3x4 to the half-brother and sister Meadow Skipper and Countess Adios. The dam of Real Profit is inbred 2x4 to Adios. The fast Min Nuke p,1:51.4 ($254,144) is linebred 4x3 to the full brother and sister Overtrick and My Finesse. Joyce Seelster p,1:53.3 ($241,708) is 3x3 to Albatross. Master Nukes p,1:52.3 has a dam bred 3x3 to the full brothers Bret Hanover and Baron Hanover and Armbro Moody p,4,1:52.4 has a dam bred 3x3 to the mares Brenna Hanover (dam of Bret Hanover) and Berinda Hanover.

For you owners of Dexter Nukes mares looking for prospective stallions, a hint of what may work is the success the sisters of Dexter Nukes have been having with Matt's Scooter and Laag. I also think that Abercrombie and his top sons will be good matches for Dexter Nukes mares along with Big Towner and his sons. With Dexter Nukes having no Bret Hanover, Abercrombie, Direct Scooter or Gene Abbe blood, and the Meadow Skipper crosses being back in his third and fourth generation, the only limitations for his daughters would be No Nukes and his sons, unless you wanted to try a little 2x3 breeding to that stallion.

Dexter Nukes looks to be a stallion on the rise and his next couple of crops to the races will be the result of his early success and higher quality mares. He's already proven he's capable of producing world-class performers and his future appears bright.

Leading Progeny by Dexter Nukes

Fastest
- Armbro Maestro, g, p,1:49.2 $506,241
- The Big Dog, h, p,3,1:50.2 $809,261
- She's A Great Lady, m, p,4,1:50.4 $973,382
- Duke Of Abby, g, p,1:51.3 $790,197
- Min Nuke, g, p,1:51.4 $267,434
- Delayed Decision, h, p,4,1:52 $427,832
- Eftimia, m, p,4,1:52 $380,867
- Real Profit, h, p,3,1:52 $265,601
- Kate's Nuke, h, p,4,1:52 $107,020
- Jaydexter, m, p,3,1:52.2 $169,140

Richest
- She's A Great Lady, m, p,4,1:50.4 $973,382
- The Big Dog, h, p,3,1:50.2 $809,261
- Duke Of Abby, g, p,1:51.3 $790,197
- Armbro Rosebud, m, p,3,1:53.3f $597,301
- Armbro Maestro, g, p,1:49.2 $506,241
- Delayed Decision, h, p,4,1:52 $427,832
- Eftimia, m, p,4,1:52 $380,867
- Mystic Music, m, p,3,1:55f $323,379
- Dallas Dex, m, p,4,1:54 $295,104
- Joyce Seelster, m, p,1:53 $285,968

Dexter Nukes, Bay Horse, 16½ Hands, 1986
p, 3, 1:51.3 ($1,027,620)

No Nukes, 1979 p, 3, T1:52.1 $572,430	Oil Burner, 1973 p, 4, 1:54.2 $535,541	Most Happy Fella, 1967 p, 3, T1:55 $419,033	**MEADOW SKIPPER**, 1960 p, 3, 1:55.1 $428,057	**DALE FROST** Countess Vivian	**HAL DALE** / Galloway **KING'S COUNSEL** / Filly Direct
			Laughing Girl, 1961 p, 4, 2:04h $19,546	**GOOD TIME** Maxine's Dream	**HAL DALE** / On Time Knight Dream / Maxine Abbe
		Dottie Shadow, 1968	Shadow Wave, 1955 p, 3, 1:56.3 $91,931	**ADIOS** Shadow Grattan	**HAL DALE** / Adioo Volo Silent Grattan / Peacedale
			Diana Streak, 1949 p, 4, 1:58.4 $9,250	Red Streak Diana Mite	Pegasus Pointer / Isabel Abbe **VOLOMITE** / Diana Dyer
	Gidget Lobell, 1974 p, 3, 2:00.3f $14,829	Overtrick, 1960 p, 3, 1:57.1h $407,483	Solicitor, 1948 p, 3, T1:57.2 $102,109	**KING'S COUNSEL** Jane Reynolds	**VOLOMITE** / Margaret Spangler Scotland / Jane Revere
			Overbid, 1954 p, 2, T2:05.4 $3,524	**HAL DALE** **BARBARA DIRECT**	Abbedale / Margaret Hal **BILLY DIRECT** / Norette Hanover
		Gogo Playmate, 1967	**TAR HEEL**, 1948 p, 4, T1:57 $119,148	**BILLY DIRECT** Leta Long	**NAPOLEON DIRECT** / Gay Forbes **VOLOMITE** / Rosette
			Gogo Playtime, 1957 p, 6, 2:02.4h $50,687	**GOOD TIME** Dell Siskiyou	**HAL DALE** / On Time Siskiyou / Elsie Truax
Viking Princess, 1979 p, 3, T1:56 $133,434	Albatross, 1968 p, 4, 1:54.3f $1,201,470	**MEADOW SKIPPER**, 1960 p, 3, 1:55.1 $428,057	**DALE FROST**, 1951 p, 1:58 $204,117	**HAL DALE** Galloway	Abbedale / Margaret Hal Raider / Bethel
			Countess Vivian, 1950 p, 3, 1:59 $43,262	**KING'S COUNSEL** Filly Direct	**VOLOMITE** / Margaret Spangler **BILLY DIRECT** / Calumet Edna
		Voodoo Hanover, 1964	Dancer Hanover, 1957 p, 4, T1:56.4 $87,746	**ADIOS** **THE OLD MAID**	**HAL DALE** / Adioo Volo Guy Abbey / Spinster
			Vibrant Hanover, 1960	**TAR HEEL** Vivian Hanover	**BILLY DIRECT** / Leta Long Guy McKinney / Guesswork
	Bacall, 1972 p, 3, 2:05.2f $6,417	Fulla Napoleon, 1965 p, 3, 1:57.1 $582,461	**DALE FROST**, 1951 p, 1:58 $204,117	**HAL DALE** Galloway	Abbedale / Margaret Hal Raider / Bethel
			Sarah Napoleon, 1947 p, 2:04.4h $20,790	Royal Napoleon Sara Van	**NAPOLEON DIRECT** / Jane Hall Clever Hanover / Toddling Van
		Behold Hanover, 1968 p, 2, 2:11.2h $1,200	Gamecock, 1959 p, 3, T1:57.2 $111,410	**TAR HEEL** Terka Hanover	**BILLY DIRECT** / Leta Long Nibble Hanover / **THE OLD MAID**
			Bewitch Hanover, 1962 p, 2, 1:59.3 $40,459	Bullet Hanover Bonnie Butler	**ADIOS** / **BARBARA DIRECT** **VOLOMITE** / Ruth Abbe

Die Laughing

Good looking, fast and rich are all words that can be used to describe Die Laughing. This representative of the prolific No Nukes/Albatross cross accomplished something during his two-year racing career that put him in select company with the great Nihilator - as the only two horses to win $1,000,000 or more in each season at both two and three years of age.

Bred by Robert Waxman of Ancaster, Ontario, Die Laughing was a great-looking yearling and sold for $82,000 at the 1989 Kentucky Standardbred Select Yearling Sale in Lexington. The successful purchasers were Martin Granoff's Val D'or Farm of New Jersey and the Chasanoff family's Alnoff Farm of New York. Trained by Jerry Silverman, Die Laughing was a major star at two, winning eight of his 12 starts and earning $1,142,322. However, Die Laughing was overshadowed by Artsplace who won $38,000 more and set a world record of 1:51.1 on a five-eighth mile track. Die Laughing finished second to Artsplace in the year end balloting for divisional honors.

At two, Die Laughing won his first two qualifying races in early July at The Meadowlands in 2:00.2 and 1:58, with final quarters in :27 and :27.1. He was ready early and had blazing speed. Driven by Richie Silverman, Jerry's son, Die Laughing was parked out first over in his first parimutuel start and finished second by a head in 1:56.2. His stakes season began with a Niatross S. Elimination win in 1:55.3 followed by an overpowering three and one-half length win in the $365,600 Niatross S. Final at The Meadowlands. Die Laughing was then considered the favorite for the upcoming Woodrow Wilson, but in his elimination he had a setback, finishing second to Three Wizzards after leading into the stretch.

The $1,043,500 Woodrow Wilson Final was next and Richie Silverman had to show a lot of patience and faith in his colt's ability. Silverman knew there would be plenty of early speed in the race and decided not to leave fast with Die Laughing from post five. At the :27 quarter, he was ninth, almost 15 lengths behind the leader. The half brought him a little closer, but he was still ninth and more than 10 lengths from the front. Silverman launched his bid before the three-quarters, still in ninth position and seven lengths from the top. Around the final turn, Silver Almahurst hung game on the front fighting off all challengers, Die Laughing was flying on the far outside. He was still almost five lengths back in mid-stretch, but found further reserves and got up in the last stride for a rousing nose victory over Silver Almahurst. The time was a world record equalling 1:52.1. Die Laughing had paced his final quarter in :26 and his final three-quarters in 1:22.1 - a superlative effort by a horse of any age.

Driver Silverman said after the race, "I thought there would be some quick fractions out there, and I always felt my colt was better off the pace. I wanted to take back at the start." The senior Silverman added, "I knew he'd kick in at the top of the lane, but I didn't know if he'd get there."

The colt had a month off before qualifying at Lexington in late September and then winning an overnight event there in 1:54.2. As if to prove his Woodrow Wilson performance was no fluke, Die Laughing won the $153,000 International Stallion S. in an identical world record equalling time of 1:52.1, going wire-to-wire. The Presidential Pace Elimination (in which Die Laughing was the 2-5 favorite) and $298,345 Final at Rosecroft Raceway were next and he won them both on the front end in 1:54.2 over Artsplace and 1:54 over Cambest.

Die Laughing was next entered in the rich Governor's Cup at Garden State Park. He won his elimination in 1:54.3, but in the $655,600 Governor's Cup Final, although he was the 3-10 favorite and had the lead in deep stretch, he lost by a half-length in a head-to-head battle with Artsplace.

The two rivals would meet for the final time in 1990 in the $605,870 Breeders Crown at Pompano Park - a battle which most thought would decide the two-year-old divisional championship. This was not to be

Race Record Highlights

At 2

1st Woodrow Wilson Final
Niatross S. Final and Elimination
Presidential S. Final and Elimination
International Stallion S.
Governor's Cup Elimination

2nd Governor's Cup Final
Woodrow Wilson Elimination

At 3

1st Prix d'Ete
Messenger S.
New Jersey Classic
Meadowlands Pace Elimination
North America Cup Elimination
New Jersey Sires S.

2nd Oliver Wendell Holmes Elimination

3rd North America Cup Final
heat of Little Brown Jug

Honors

Equalled world record for two-year-olds

Photo by Monica Thors
Courtesy of Fair Winds Farm

Race Record

Year	Age	Starts	Wins	2nd	3rd	Earnings	Record
1990	2	12	8	3	0	$1,022,064	p,2,1:52.1
1991	3	15	7	2	2	1,142,322	p,3,1:51.1f
		27	15	5	2	$2,164,386	p,3,1:51.1f

Die Laughing

Die Laughing's night, even though he was the 3-5 favorite against Artsplace. In a race that is still talked about, Artsplace paced one of the most stunning miles ever seen, with fractions of :26.2, :53.2 and 1:23 before coming home in :28.1 to score a resounding win in a world record 1:51.1. The loser in this incredible show of speed was Die Laughing, who challenged Artsplace first over almost to the three-quarters before tiring and finishing well back in his final effort of the season. Richie Silverman commented, "John (Campbell) obviously knew that Artsplace was at his best tonight and he went out and proved it. John's horse was awesome tonight." No one was going to beat Artsplace that night and it cost Die Laughing divisional honors, even though in four races between the two colts that season the score was even.

Die Laughing started his three-year-old season with a New Jersey Sires S. win in 1:54 at The Meadowlands in mid-May. A week later, he was interfered with at the half in a New Jersey Classic Elimination and defeated by Cambest, although he still qualified for the Final. The colt came back strong in the $500,000 New Jersey Classic Final. He was parked out first over in a :26.4 first quarter from post six, but still got the lead and held on to win the rich event in 1:51.4 by a neck over the rapidly improving Precious Bunny. This turned out to be an especially good year for three-year-old colts as the division included Artsplace, Precious Bunny, Cambest, Silky Stallone, Three Wizzards and Easy Goer. There would not be any easy pickings in 1991.

After traveling to Greenwood Raceway in Canada, Dic Laughing won his North America Cup Elimination in 1:53.1 by an easy three lengths. However, in the $1,000,000 Final, he suffered a parked out first over trip although he still managed to finish third behind Precious Bunny and Start The Fire. The Meadowlands Pace was next and Die Laughing again won an Elimination in 1:51.1. Disaster struck in the $1,000,000 Final, though; he drew post nine and was never in the hunt. He was seventh at the half and then fell back to last in the second half while being distanced. He was obviously in distress that night, and after the race he was sent to the University of Pennsylvania's New Bolton Veterinary Center for an evaluation. A statement from the Silverman Stable said, "They could find little, if anything, wrong with him. He has a heart monitor strapped to him and he'll wear that for 24 hours. The results of the monitoring will be sent back to New Bolton and they'll study it. He's eating good and seems like himself otherwise." Two weeks later, Richie Silverman reported, "I've trained him some and it seems the heart problem was a fluke thing that happens once. He didn't need medication to help him get better."

Two weeks after the Meadowlands Pace disappointment the colt won a qualifying race in 1:53.2 with a final quarter in :26.2. Then he was second in an Elimination of the Oliver Wendell Holmes S., timed in 1:51.1. He was back!

Silverman and Die Laughing raced next in the $603,500 Prix d'Ete at Montreal's Blue Bonnets track and went wire-to-wire to score in 1:51.2 by three lengths over Complex Trooper with Artsplace finishing third. The colt wanted the front and paced his first quarter in :26.2 to keep any challengers at bay. He also won his next two races on the front end, including the $475,000 Messenger S. at Rosecroft in 1:51.1.

The Little Brown Jug was next on Die Laughing's schedule and he appeared to come into that race in great form with three consecutive wins. He was in the second Elimination and finished third, by only a neck, to Precious Bunny in a three horse photo which included Three Wizzards. But in the Jug Final, Die Laughing had post nine and could never seriously get into the hunt. He was fourth most of the way and then finished sixth - four and one-half lengths behind the winning Precious Bunny.

Die Laughing was then scheduled to race in the Bluegrass S. at Lexington, but was scratched sick. The Breeders Crown was coming up in late October at Pompano and the only race Die Laughing had, other than a qualifier, was a Pompano Invitational in which he finished second by a neck in 1:52.4 to Three Wizzards, who had gotten very sharp at the end of the year. Unfortunately for Die Laughing, the $357,406 Breeders Crown had a similar result. Die Laughing had the lead all the way, led by a length in mid-stretch but then tired to finish fourth with Three Wizzards again victorious. This was Die Laughing's final start and he ended that year with earnings of $1,022,064 from seven wins in 15 starts. His lifetime earnings from the racetrack was $2,164,386 and he retired as the eighth leading money-winning pacer of all time.

Sire Line

Die Laughing's sire is No Nukes, who has been a premier stallion for the last decade. It appears he could be a sire of sires, much like his grandsire Most Happy Fella and great-grandsire Meadow Skipper. Early sons of No Nukes achieving some early success at stud are Jate Lobell, Dexter Nukes and Western Hanover. You can read more about No Nukes in his chapter. Just like Dexter Nukes and Western Hanover, Die Laughing is from an Albatross mare and the No Nukes/Albatross cross has been very successful.

Maternal Line

Die Laughing's dam is the non-record Albatross mare Makin Smiles who has produced seven winners from seven foals with three sub-1:53 performers. In addition to her first foal Die Laughing, Makin Smiles is the dam of Go For Grins p,1:51.2-'98 ($302,003) (colt by Jate Lobell) and Giggle Box p,3,1:52.3 ($51,362) (filly by Jate Lobell) and two other sub-1:57 fillies by Jate Lobell. Since Jate Lobell is also a son of No Nukes, it's obvious Makin Smiles is nicking very well with that sire line.

The grandam of Die Laughing is the Shadow Wave mare Real Hilarious p,4,1:58.3f ($191,110) who set a world record of 2:00.2h for two-year-old pacing fillies and was voted divisional champion at two and four. Real Hilarious was an outstanding stakes and Invitational winner and went on to produce speed and class. Her top foals include Ludicrous p,1:51.3 ($318,795) (by Nihilator), Little Brown Jug heat winner Crosscurrent p,3,1:53.4 ($197,040) (by Most Happy Fella) and $1,000,000 Meadowlands Pace winner Hilarion p,3,1:54.1 ($775,114) (by Strike Out) among others. Her Meadow Skipper daughter Real Lace p,3,1:58.4 is the dam of stakes and FFA winner Instrument Landing p,1:52.4 ($616,543) and her Niatross daughter Spoiled Royal is the dam of stakes winner Big Brat p,2,1:53.1 ($402,177) (by Cam Fella).

Seascape, a mare by Painter p,2,2:01 (son of Tar Heel), and the third dam of Die Laughing, was an outstanding broodmare with eight in 2:00, including Justascape p,4,1:53.4 ($100,338), world champion Sherry Almahurst p,3,1:55.1 ($163,256), Hilarious Sister p,3,T1:58.3 and Shadow Star p,3,1:59.2f ($243,439). Seascape has a full sister named Reflection who is also a great producer, being the dam of three world champions, Ring Of Light p,1:52.1 ($623,160), Striking Image p,2,1:55 (the first 1:55 two-year-old) and Mirror Image p,1:56.2 ($636,345). In addition, one of Reflection's daughters, Sharper Image (by Strike Out) is the dam of the 1:50 performer Bright As Day p,4,1:50 ($397,513).

The dam of both Seascape and Reflection is the great Good Time filly Way Wave p,3,1:58 ($105,555) who was a stakes winner at two and three, including a heat of the 1961 Little Brown Jug against colts. She finished second in another heat and third in the raceoff to Henry T. Adios.

This is the outstanding maternal family known as Maud by Dr. Herr and goes back to top horses from the 1930s era. It is one of those families which has withstood the test of time and this particular branch is its strongest. If a strong maternal pedigree is an asset for a sire, Die Laughing can draw plenty of strength from his bottom line.

Progeny of Note

Die Laughing's fastest performer, Sports Town p,4,1:49.3 ($635,655) arrived in early June, 1997 at The Meadowlands. He was a very good colt at two (1:54f) and three (1:52) and has been second and third in some major events including seconds in the Breeders Crown Final at two and the Cane

Die Laughing

Pace Final at three. Another good colt is Ryan's Miracle p,3,1:50.4 ($268,935) who was also a fast 1:52.1 two-year-old with wins in the Smullin Memorial Final and the Niatross S.

The richest offspring of Die Laughing is Live Or Die p,2,1:51.4 ($728,264) who was a world champion at two and won the $600,000 Governor's Cup, American-National S., International Stallion S., Bluegrass S. and Breeders Crown Elimination, among other events. He was also second in the Woodrow Wilson Final and third in the Breeders Crown Final. Unfortunately, he was struck with a serious illness at three and has not been the same since. Die Loving p,2,1:55; 3,1:52 ($461,992) is Die Laughing's top filly and her two- and three-year-old stakes wins include the Kentucky Standardbred Sales Co. S., Champlain S., Tarport Hap S. and Lady Maud S. This filly was also second in the Breeders Crown Final at two. Diehard Fan p,2,1:56.3f; 3,1:54.1 ($211,345) is another filly of note and a stakes winner at two and three.

Analysis

Die Laughing is a linebred stallion who is 4x3 to Meadow Skipper and 4x3 to Shadow Wave. He was syndicated and went to stud with plenty of broodmare support and was bred to books of 185, 176 and 168 during his first three years at stud. He was bred to high-quality mares and has every right to become a top sire. His first crop of two-year-olds raced in 1995 and were successful, earning nearly $2,000,000 and including five in 1:55, 25 in 2:00 and four $200,000 winners. Included in this group was the colt Live Or Die who equalled the world record of 1:51.4 for youngsters. In addition, Die Laughing's fillies did very well.

His second crop, which raced in 1996, had 26 2:00 two-year-olds, but only two in 1:55 and not as many major stakes winners as the first crop. Some of the downturn can be attributed to the first crop of his archrival Artsplace making the racing scene and doing extremely well.

Now, as this is written, Die Laughing's oldest foals are five and his 1998 two-year-olds are making their debuts. The sons and daughters of Die Laughing seem to be going on and he has achieved his first sub-1:50 credit. Another one or two of his offspring look like they can join that elite club in the near future.

To date, Die Laughing's first three crops have earned over $8,700,000 with 41 in 1:55, 193 in 2:00 and 15 $100,000 winners.

The big question with this stallion is, can he come up with a couple of world class colts to solidify his position as a major stallion and make breeders take more notice? The 1998 racing season will be important for Die Laughing since above-average success can put him in the top group of pacing sires. He's knocking at the door, but so are several other stallions.

The impressive thing about Die Laughing is that he has shown the ability to work well, from a pedigree standpoint, with broodmares by a large number of different sires. He does not appear to need a certain pedigree "nick." Thus far, his 25 richest performers are from mares by 20 different stallions. If there is one trend which could appear, it's that Die Laughing does very well with Bret Hanover mares and those with Bret Hanover somewhere in their pedigree. That is to be expected since Bret is a major broodmare sire and does not appear in Die Laughing's pedigree. Another presence in Die Laughing's better horses is Big Towner in a mare's pedigree. He is the sire of the grandam of Sports Town, the dam of Die Nasty, and his son Walton Hanover is the sire of the dams of Diehard Fan and Grin Reaper p,4,1:53.3-'98. Of course, Big Towner is also a very strong and important broodmare sire.

In case you are looking for offspring from mares by Albatross, Die Laughing was bred to few, if any, since the cross for the resulting foal would be an inbred 3x2 to Albatross. But there are several 3x3 Albatross success stories through mares by his sons Niatross, Sonsam and B.G.'s Bunny.

Mares with Albatross/Big Towner or Big Towner/Albatross crosses would be very suitable and be even nicer with some Bret Hanover blood in the pedigree. And Die Laughing's fastest performer is from a Tyler B/Big Towner cross so you may want to try mares with Tyler B blood, which serves to double up on Most Happy Fella - giving a foal a 4x2 cross to that great stallion.

Looking at the pedigree crosses of some of Die Laughing's most successful offspring, we note that his two best, Sports Town and Live Or Die, are linebred 4x3 and 4x4 to Most Happy Fella. Die Laughing is, himself, a 4x3 cross to Meadow Skipper and with today's broodmares it is not hard to add more multiple Meadow Skipper crosses. For example, Ryan's Miracle is from a Meadow Skipper mare and is therefore 5x4x2 to Meadow Skipper.

As you will see in other stallion chapters in this book, I am a strong proponent of multiple crosses to Albatross and some of this appears to be working for Die Laughing. Since his dam is by Albatross, it puts that stallion in the third generation of any Die Laughing foal. Smile As You Go p,4,1:52 ($247,336) and his brother Live Love Laugh p,2,1:53.2 ($169,577) have a 3x3 cross to Albatross as does Aahm A Jokester p,1:51.2z-'98 and Such A Hoot p,3,1:53.2 ($168,679). Yankee Aspen p,2,1:54, an outstanding filly, is 3x4x4 to Albatross since her dam is bred 3x3 to that stallion.

Another interesting factor here is the stallion Shadow Wave, a son of Adios. Die Laughing has a 4x3 cross to Shadow Wave in his own pedigree and seems also to be working well with broodmares with Big Towner in their pedigree. Big Towner is by the outcross sire Gene Abbe and from a Shadow Wave mare - thus adding another cross back to Shadow Wave.

Since Die Laughing was bred to so many quality mares it stands to reason he should sire some world-class performers. The dams of Die Laughing's two fastest sons, Sports Town and Ryan's Miracle, are cases in point. The dam of Sports Town is multiple stakes winner Tyler Town p,3,1:54.1 ($783,093) and the dam of Ryan's Miracle is Jugette winner Watering Can p,3,1:54.2 ($219,757). Another top mare, Breeders Crown winner Caressable p,2,1:55.4 ($1,006,380) is the dam of Smile As You Go and Live Love Laugh. If Die Laughing shows he can sire the best foals that top mares like these produce, and also move up average broodmares, then he will be assured a successful career.

Die Laughing

Photo courtesy of the USTA

Leading Progeny by Die Laughing

Fastest

Sports Town, h, p,4,1:49.3 $635,655
Ryan's Miracle, g, p,3,1:50.4 $268,935
Naked Gunner, h, p,4,1:51.1 $146,154
L Dee's Jonathan, h, p,4,1:51.2 $310,129
Aahm A Jokester, g, p,1:51.2z $76,811
Live Or Die, h, p,2,1:51.4 $728,264
Die Loving, m, p,3,1:52 $461,992
Smile As You Go, h, p,4,1:52 $247,336
Laughasyougo, g, p,3,1:52.3 $153,195
You're The Top, g, p,3,1:52.3 $56,406

Richest

Live Or Die, h, p,2,1:51.4 $728,264
Sports Town, h, p,4,1:49.3 $635,655
Die Loving, m, p,3,1:52 $461,992
L Dee's Jonathan, h, p,4,1:51.2 $310,129
Ryan's Miracle, g, p,3,1:50.4 $268,935
Smile As You Go, h, p,4,1:52 $247,336
Die Nasty, h, p,2,1:53.4 $221,729
Diehard Fan, m, p,3,1:54.1 $211,345
Live Love Laugh, h, p,2,1:53.2 $169,577
Such A Hoot, h, p,3,1:53.2 $168,679

Die Laughing, Brown Horse, 15.3 Hands, 1988
p, 2, 1:52.1; 3, 1:51.1f ($2,164,386)

No Nukes, 1979 p, 3, T1:52.1, $572,430	Oil Burner, 1973 p, 4, 1:54.2 $535,541	Most Happy Fella, 1967 p, 3, T1:55 $419,033	**MEADOW SKIPPER**, 1960 p, 3, 1:55.1 $428,057	Dale Frost	**HAL DALE** / Galloway
				Countess Vivian	**KING'S COUNSEL** / Filly Direct
			Laughing Girl, 1961 p, 4, 2:04h $19,546	**GOOD TIME**	**HAL DALE** / On Time
				Maxine's Dream	Knight Dream / Maxine Abbe
		Dottie Shadow, 1968	**SHADOW WAVE**, 1955 p, 3, 1:56.3 $91,931	**ADIOS**	**HAL DALE** / Adioo Volo
				Shadow Grattan	Silent Grattan / Peacedale
			Diana Streak, 1949 p, 4, 1:58.4 $9,250	Red Streak	Pegasus Pointer / Isabel Abbe
				Diana Mite	**VOLOMITE** / Diana Dyer
	Gidget Lobell, 1974 p, 3, 2:00.3f $14,829	Overtrick, 1960 p, 3, 1:57.1h $407,483	Solicitor, 1948 p, 3, T1:57.2 $102,109	**KING'S COUNSEL**	**VOLOMITE** / Margaret Spangler
				Jane Reynolds	Scotland / Jane Revere
			Overbid, 1954 p, 2, T2:05.4 $3,524	**HAL DALE**	**ABBEDALE** / Margaret Hal
				Barbara Direct	**BILLY DIRECT** / Norette Hanover
		Gogo Playmate, 1967	**TAR HEEL**, 1948 p, 4, T1:57 $119,148	**BILLY DIRECT**	Napoleon Direct / Gay Forbes
				Leta Long	**VOLOMITE** / Rosette
			Gogo Playtime, 1957 p, 6, 2:02.4h $50,687	**GOOD TIME**	**HAL DALE** / On Time
				Dell Siskiyou	Siskiyou / Elsie Truax
Makin Smiles, 1984	Albatross, 1968 p, 4, 1:54.3f $1,201,470	**MEADOW SKIPPER**, 1960 p, 3, 1:55.1 $428,057	Dale Frost, 1951 p, 1:58 $204,117	**HAL DALE**	**ABBEDALE** / Margaret Hal
				Galloway	Raider / Bethel
			Countess Vivian, 1950 p, 3, 1:59 $43,262	**KING'S COUNSEL**	**VOLOMITE** / Margaret Spangler
				Filly Direct	**BILLY DIRECT** / Calumet Edna
		Voodoo Hanover, 1964	Dancer Hanover, 1957 p, 4, T1:56.4 $87,746	**ADIOS**	**HAL DALE** / Adioo Volo
				The Old Maid	Guy Abbey / Spinster
			Vibrant Hanover, 1960	**TAR HEEL**	**BILLY DIRECT** / Leta Long
				Vivian Hanover	Guy McKinney / Guesswork
	Real Hilarious, 1970 p, 4, 1:58.3f $191,110	**SHADOW WAVE**, 1955 p, 3, 1:56.3 $91,931	**ADIOS**, 1940 p, T1:57½ $33,329	**HAL DALE**	**ABBEDALE** / Margaret Hal
				Adioo Volo	Adioo Guy / Sigrid Volo
			Shadow Grattan, 1943 p, 4, 2:07.1h $2,555	Silent Grattan	Grattan Royal / Silent T
				Peacedale	**ABBEDALE** / Miss Dorothy Dillon
		Seascape, 1965	Painter, 1955 p, 2, 2:01 $53,740	**TAR HEEL**	**BILLY DIRECT** / Leta Long
				Pretty Hanover	Nibble Hanover / Easter Hanover
			Way Wave, 1958 p, 3, 1:58 $105,555	**GOOD TIME**	**HAL DALE** / On Time
				Fullsway	**KING'S COUNSEL** / Dell Frisco

Direct Scooter

The saga of Direct Scooter is one of those pleasant horse racing stories in which little was expected and much was achieved.

Sickly and green as a two-year-old, Direct Scooter was sold in the K.D. Owen consignment at the 1978 Harrisburg sale. Owen, an oil man from Houston, Texas, bred Direct Scooter, his sire Sampson Direct and owned his grandsire Sampson Hanover. Owen also owned Direct Scooter's dam and her sire, the great trotter Noble Victory.

At two, Direct Scooter had been bothered by a lingering throat infection. Trainer Warren Cameron, son of Hall of Famer Del Cameron, was attracted by the colt's compact build and planned to bid up to $12,000 for his client Stanley Zupnick of Maryland who was looking for a racehorse. Other bidders had seen the colt train well, however, and the bidding went up to $21,000 before Zupnick became the new owner. After the purchase, Zupnick offered shares to his other partners, Dr. Max Fischer and Ruth Fogel of Washington, D.C., and Dr. George Orlove of Virginia.

Direct Scooter began his three-year-old season, and racing career, in a $2,200 Maiden race at Liberty Bell Park. In mid-April of 1979, he won a qualifier in 2:07.4, also at Liberty Bell, and then swept easily through his first three starts, the fastest win in 2:02.3. In his next start he suffered his first defeat when he was interfered with and made a break. He came back a week later to win in 1:59.1 at Liberty Bell.

Moving on to better things, and staked to just a few events, Direct Scooter raced in conditioned races at The Meadowlands, winning his first six starts at that mile track and moving up to the Open ranks. His winning streak was now at seven, the last of which was in a rapid 1:54.2 - just two-fifths of a second outside the world record for three-year-olds at the time. In addition, most of his wins had been by open lengths after gaining the lead just before or after the half.

Direct Scooter then had two second place finishes (being placed eighth for interference in one). He then came back to record two of his most impressive wins of the year. The first came at The Meadowlands on August 3 in a $20,000 Open event for three- and four-year-olds. Leaving from post seven, Direct Scooter was still fourth on the outside at the half and third at the three-quarters before finally getting to the rail on the final turn and opening up two lengths on the field in the stretch. He won by a head in 1:55.1 with the final quarter in :28.2 after being parked out most of the mile.

A week later, at Roosevelt Raceway on a sloppy track, Direct Scooter proved again he had plenty of guts. Leaving from post six, he was fourth on the outside at the half and made his move to the front first over on the outside at the three-quarters. His attempt for the lead was thwarted and he fell back over two lengths in the stretch. But being a fighter, he came back in the final stages to win going away by two lengths in another eye-opening effort.

Direct Scooter's first stakes engagement came a week after the Roosevelt race, in the two-heat Confederation Cup at Flamboro Downs. He went into this race with 12 wins from 15 starts and was the heavy favorite to win his Elimination. Drawing post seven on the half-mile track, Direct Scooter's lack of gate speed left him at a disadvantage against the top colts and he had to work out an outside trip. Cameron had him third at the top of the stretch, but he could only get to within a neck of the winning General Star at the wire. In the Final, he was interfered with at the start and was never in the hunt, finishing eighth.

A week later, in the rich Prix d'Ete at Blue Bonnets Raceway in Montreal, Direct Scooter continued to attract trouble, suffering interference while moving up from sixth at the half. This took him completely out of the race.

The colt returned to the more friendly confines of Liberty Bell Park, where he easily won two FFA events over older horses and then won three more at Yonkers - the fastest in 1:57.3 and each time overcoming long parked out trips. Direct Scooter then suffered through three races of "seconditis" at Yonkers, Hazel Park and Windsor against older FFA horses. Later, he raced in the $200,000 George Morton Levy P. at

Race Record Highlights

At 3
- **1st** L.K. Shapiro P.
  three legs of American Pacing Classic Series
- **2nd** American Pacing Classic Series Final
  heat of Confederation Cup

At 4
- **1st** Canadian Derby
  American-National Maturity
  Hanover S.
  Final of Graduate Series
  four legs of Graduate Series
  Cornell Memorial
  U.S. Pacing Championship
- **2nd** two legs of Driscoll Series
  Long Island Invitational
  Mohawk Gold Cup
  Clark Invitational
- **3rd** Driscoll Series Final

Honors

At four, set world record on five-eighth mile track

At four, set record for single-season earnings by older horse

At four, voted Aged Pacer of the Year

Direct Scooter

Painting by Richard Stone Reeves
Courtesy of The Horseman and Fair World

Race Record

Year	Age	Starts	Wins	2nd	3rd	Earnings	Record
1979	3	32	21	6	0	$298,162	p,3,1:54
1980	4	28	15	6	2	502,289	
		60	36	12	2	$800,451	p,3,1:54

Direct Scooter

Roosevelt and finished fourth after leaving from the second tier and having severe traffic problems. It was then off to Hollywood where "the Scooter" became a star again!

Direct Scooter ended his three-year-old season at Hollywood Park where he raced five times, winning four, and making quite a name for himself. His first effort there was a wire-to-wire 1:57.1 win in the $100,000 L.K. Shapiro S. He paced a final quarter in :27.3 after being parked out to the first quarter in :28.2 before getting to the front. He then swept through three $25,000 legs of the American Pacing Classic Series against older horses in a track record 1:54 and then in 1:55.1 before winning the one and one-sixteenth mile leg in 2:03.3, which was just two-fifths of a second slower than Adios Vic's world record for the distance. His 1:54 win tied him with five others as the second fastest three-year-old colt ever.

There was disappointment, however, in the one and one-eighth mile Final. Direct Scooter had the lead in the stretch, but succumbed to the older Flight Director by a head at the wire.

Direct Scooter was not a good gate horse and only had the lead at the quarter four times in his 32 starts at three. But he had quite a brush of speed and was on top by the three-quarters in nearly half his starts. He ended his three-year-old season with 21 wins from 32 starts and earnings of $298,162 - a super year for a colt who, at the beginning of 1979, had been unknown and green.

Coming back to the races at four, Direct Scooter had a solid season in which he won 15 of 28 starts, earning $502,289 which set a record for earnings by an older pacer. He opened his season in March with two losses to Armbro Splurge at The Meadowlands but then went on a streak of nine consecutive victories,. including the $122,500 Graduate Series Final at The Meadowlands, $100,000 National Pacing Derby at Roosevelt, two Meadowlands Invitationals, four legs of the Graduate Series at Freehold, Windsor, Mohawk and Brandywine and the Cornell Memorial at Freehold.

Direct Scooter then suffered four consecutive defeats in three legs and the Driscoll Series Final at The Meadowlands; three of those losses were by only a neck, including the Final. Later, Direct Scooter won the $100,000 Canadian Pacing Derby, the U.S. Pacing Championship and American-National Maturity at Sportsman's Park, the Hanover S. and the Blue Bonnets Challenge Cup.

Driven in all but one race by his trainer Warren Cameron, Direct Scooter was voted Aged Pacer of the Year for 1980. His fastest wins for the year were a pair of 1:54.2 miles on the five-eighth mile surfaces of Brandywine and Windsor, which were world records for four-year-old pacers. Only three-year-olds Storm Damage, Niatross and Hot Hitter had paced faster over that size track at the time.

Direct Scooter ended his career with a record of 36 wins from 60 starts and earnings of $800,451. He was clearly a viable stallion prospect and was syndicated, with Walnridge Farm of Cream Ridge, New Jersey, as his new home. Having an interesting disposition, Direct Scooter always wanted attention from people. He would turn over his water bucket and feed tub if he did not get that attention. Cameron said in a *Hoof Beats* article during the Scooter's four-year-old season, "He's such a good-feeling guy that if you give him some days off, he raises hell."

Sire Line

Direct Scooter and his sons have become the only viable continuation of the Volomite male line during the last couple of decades in North America. Direct Scooter's link to Volomite is through his sire, Sampson Direct, and grandsire, Sampson Hanover, who was a son of the great Volomite. In fact, Direct Scooter is a 3x4 cross to Volomite since his dam's sire, Noble Victory, is a grandson of Volomite through Victory Song.

Three other pacing stallion branches have evolved from the Volomite male line during the second half of the twentieth century, but none has had the staying power of Direct Scooter. The strongest attempt was by the top stallion Bye Bye Byrd, who was a grandson of

Volomite through his sire Poplar Byrd. Bye Bye Byrd had a number of sons at stud which fanned the flames for a while, but none was able to produce a son to carry on this branch of the family. Bye Bye Byrd's sons Keystone Ore, Armbro Nesbit and Bye And Large did well for a time, but their sons did not carry on. However, Keystone Ore and Armbro Nesbit are excellent broodmare sires.

Overtrick was a great-grandson of Volomite through Solicitor and King's Counsel, but he also did not produce a son to extend the line. Overtrick was a decent sire in the U.S. before being exported, and his daughters went on to be good producers.

The other Volomite-line sire to find a niche was Harold J. through his sire Worthy Boy - a son of Volomite. Harold J. was a good sire of racehorses, but could not produce many top stakes performers. Again, his daughters have done well in the broodmare ranks and he is the sire of the dam of the all-time fastest Standardbred Cambest p,T1:46.1 ($1,458,110). Worthy Boy worked both sides of the street by siring good trotters and good pacers. His major achievement is being the sire of the great Star's Pride who went on to become one of the greatest trotting sires in the history of the sport - if not the greatest.

Volomite blood is powerful and has been a strong factor in Standardbred pedigrees for two-thirds of a century. He's like a modern-day Hambletonian and when you trace any pacer or trotter's pedigree back a few generations, you are likely to find several crosses to Volomite.

Maternal Line

Direct Scooter is from the maternal family known as Nelly, which has produced high-class trotters as well as pacers. Some of its most famous trotters are Delmonica Hanover, her daughter Delmegan and Speedy Count. Other stars are Noble Florie, Noble Gal, Anders Favorite, Nordin Hanover, world champion Nan's Catch and her great daughter Moni Maker 4,1:52.2 ($2,600,000) and winner in 1998 of Sweden's Elitlopp Trot.

This maternal family is not high in numbers, but it has concentrated quality and is moving forward at a rapid clip. Speedy Count was the first 2:00 trotting credit for this family in 1964 and the next one did not appear until 1974 with Noble Florie, followed a year later by Buckeye Count and Delmonica Hanover. That's a pretty late start for a family which now ranks as one of the strongest among current trotting maternal families.

On the pacing side, the first 2:00 pacer for the Nelly family was Cleopatra Hanover in 1960. There was then a 16-year gap before the now forgotten 2:00 pacers Satellite Hanover and Gumboots in 1976. Direct Scooter was only the sixth 2:00 pacing credit for the Nelly family and it is now his branch of this family which appears to be the only one moving forward on the pacing side.

Direct Scooter's Noble Victory dam Noble Claire forgot her trotting heritage and was a pacer, winning three races at two, taking a record of 2:04 and being stakes-placed. She produced 16 foals during her career as a broodmare, the first at four and the last at the advanced age of 24. She was always bred to pacers and was owned during most of her career by Hanover Shoe Farms and bred to their top stallions.

Now, Noble Claire is tied with nine other pacing broodmares with 11 2:00 credits - second on the all-time list of leading broodmares. In addition to Direct Scooter, Noble Claire is the dam of Nappie Hanover p,3,1:54 ($168,031) (by Albatross), Nobelee Hanover p,3,T1:54.4 ($100,025) (by Albatross) and Norcross Hanover p,3,1:54.4h (by Albatross) to name only her 1:55 performers.

Progeny of Note

Direct Scooter was popular right from the start and has bred well over 100 mares each breeding season since the beginning of his career. He reached a high of 227 during the 1986 season, and ten years later, during the 1996 season, still bred 104. Direct Scooter sons and daughters have earned over $74,500,000 and he currently ranks as the sixth leading money-winning pacing sire of all time. He also ranks sixth on the all-time list of pacing sires of $100,000 winners and third behind only Albatross and No Nukes as a 2:00 sire with his 871 credits. This is some pretty strong company for an unusually bred "outcross" sire to be keeping, but which only goes to affirm that we need some outcross sires in Standardbred pacing blood. Direct Scooter is a perfect example, as is Big Towner who has been equally successful. And Big Towner has a dose of Adios blood in his third generation which Direct Scooter does not.

Direct Scooter's best performer is, of course, the great Matt's Scooter p,3,T1:48.2 ($2,944,591) - a world champion and the fastest standardbred of all time when he took his record in 1988. Direct Scooter has proven he is capable of siring extreme speed with the best of them; he is one of only five sires to have three or more 1:50 credits and he ranks behind only Cam Fella and Abercrombie in 1:51 credits.

Matt's Scooter, as you can read in his own chapter, was a great three-year-old and then came back even better at four to win Horse of the Year honors in 1989. Matt's Scooter has also gone on to become an excellent sire and should carry on the Direct Scooter sire line as an extension of the Volomite male line.

Another top son of Direct Scooter is In The Pocket p,3,T1:49.3 ($1,537,473) who won the rich Governor's Cup at two and was a world champion at three. He, too, has gone on to a bit of success as a stallion and is dividing his time between two continents. He stands at stud in North America during the spring and "down under" during our fall and winter. Although not getting anywhere near the quality mares bred by Matt's Scooter, In The Pocket has shown some promise of carrying on this sire line.

Strong Clan is Direct Scooter's other 1:50 credit. He won in that time during 1997 and has earnings of $663,377. Direct Scooter has also sired two other winners of over $900,000, Easter Sun Hanna p,1:52 ($930,481) and Expensive Scooter p,3,1:51 ($910,846) who won the Breeders Crown at two.

Direct Scooter is a master sire of two-year-olds who can set world records on a half-mile track. In 1992, Easter Sun Hanna won in 1:54.1h, which equalled the world record set by Tooter Scooter and WRH in 1990 - all sons of Direct Scooter. Also, in 1990, Direct Scooter's son Deal Direct won in 1:51.4 to become the fastest two-year-old colt in the sport at that time. A year before, the two-year-old Direct Scooter son O K Bye set a half-mile track world record of 1:54.3h. It seemed the Direct Scooter sons "owned" this world record category for a time.

Other good money winners by Direct Scooter are Direct Flight p,4,1:51 ($825,052), Armbro Global p,4,1:52.2 ($771,177), Scoot Outa Reach p,4,1:51.4 ($757,436), Scoot Herb p,1:54.3 ($616,563) and the mare Trimtex p,4,1:54.3f ($604,914).

Direct Scooter is not a noted filly sire, but there have been some nice exceptions. In addition to Trimtex, there are Red Head p,1:55.1 ($372,240), Village Jig p,3,1:56f ($342,505) (now a double 1:50 producer), Motivation p,3,1:52.3 ($300,847) and Terrie Letsgo p,3,1:53.1 ($296,505), for example. Motivation is Direct Scooter's fastest daughter and there are 49 males in front of her on the list.

Analysis

At stud, Direct Scooter was promoted as being an outcross stallion for just about all pacing mares from the popular bloodlines. For once, the promise of a heavily promoted stallion was largely fulfilled.

Take a look at the six-generation pedigree for Direct Scooter in this chapter. His sire, Sampson Direct p,4,T1:56 ($137,486) was bred to be a pacer and was a good one in his day. However, except for champion pacer and excellent sire Billy Direct being the sire of the dam of Sampson Direct, the rest of Sampson Direct's family, as we have seen, was all trotting - and good trotters, too.

While it is not surprising that Direct Scooter went on to become an outstanding pacer since he had good bloodlines and both his sire and dam preferred the pace, it is interesting that he's had such a profound impact on the Standardbred breed. Even though he was publicized and promoted as being a new "outcross" sire, many top breeders were very skeptical and it took a while for them to warm up to Direct Scooter. Here is a stallion who really did it on his own and earned his way into pacing sire history. Whichever genes made Direct Scooter a top racehorse and sire, he had them in spades.

Looking at Direct Scooter's pedigree, we see that he has the following common crosses - 3x4x6 to Volomite, 5x3 to Scotland and 4x5x5 to Peter Volo. There does not appear to be anything unusual about these crosses that would provide a hint to the reason for Direct Scooter's success. However, he does have a rather "old" pedigree by today's standards when you notice both Volomite and Scotland appearing as close as his third generation. They are foals of 1926 and 1925, respectively.

Doing the same exercise for some of Direct Scooter's contemporaries, and major competition, we find Cam Fella's two oldest relatives in the third generation being foals of 1940 and 1946; No Nukes' two oldest were both foals of 1948, and current pacing sire sensation Artsplace's are 1952 and 1958. What this shows is that Direct Scooter had the ability to skip generations and sire at a level beyond his place in the stallion timetable. Other great sires with a similar ability are Albatross and Big Towner as pacing stallions, and Speedy Crown and Super Bowl as trotting sires.

It has only been the last generation of pacing sires which has effectively been able to remove Direct Scooter from the listings of the current top sires. And they are at least two generations further removed from Hambletonian than is Direct Scooter. I'm not saying that Direct Scooter is one of the all-time great pacing sires, but he certainly merits respect for what he has accomplished against his peers. After all, his offspring have raced against those of Meadow Skipper, Bret Hanover, Albatross, Abercrombie, Cam Fella, No Nukes, Niatross, Tyler B and Big Towner, to name a few top sires.

Obviously, it is well known that Direct Scooter's major shortcoming is with his fillies. His sons far out-perform his fillies. In fact, the Direct Scooter Syndicate even acknowledged this fact, biting the bullet and setting a lower stud fee for Direct Scooter fillies than for his colts. It was simply a fact of life that Direct Scooter fillies were not of the same caliber as his colts and this was reflected in the prices paid for the females at every yearling sale. But he did sire some very nice fillies and several owners got themselves "bargains" at the sales.

What may have helped get Direct Scooter noticed, as it did for No Nukes, Oil Burner and B.G.'s Bunny, was the availability of the New Jersey mile tracks at The Meadowlands and Garden State Park, over which his offspring could race. No Nukes and Direct Scooter proved to be top sires in the long run, while the fast miles by early offspring of Oil Burner and B.G.'s Bunny may have led breeders to believe these stallions were better sires than history later proved. But Direct Scooter has stayed the course and sired some wonderful performers over the years.

Let's take a look at some of the pedigree crosses for Direct Scooter's best performers. Direct Scooter has 35 winners of $300,000 or more and Meadow Skipper was prominent in his three richest. Matt's Scooter and Easter Sun Hanna are both from Meadow Skipper dams and In The Pocket is from a Tar Heel mare whose dam is by Meadow Skipper. This makes perfect sense since Direct Scooter, being an outcross sire, was supposed to have clicked with mares by Meadow Skipper and his sons. In fact, 28 of the 35 dams of Direct Scooter's $300,000 winners were by Meadow Skipper line sires. Of the other five, two were mares by Warm Breeze, two by Keystone Ore and one by Tar Heel.

The presence of Most Happy Fella blood was very strong. It appeared in the dam or second dam of seven of the 19 richest offspring. Albatross mares, and those by his son B.G.'s Bunny also did extremely well with Direct Scooter. The success with B.G.'s Bunny mares is a prime example of a stallion being helped along simply by his geographic location. B.G.'s Bunny is the result of Albatross on a Bret Hanover mare and he is an excellent broodmare sire. There were many B.G.'s Bunny daughters owned in the New Jersey, New York and Pennsylvania areas and the cross was a natural one, throwing the combined blood of Albatross and Bret Hanover to Direct Scooter. Two other sires whose presence in the pedigrees of Direct Scooter's best performers was obvious are Shadow Wave and Overtrick.

A fine example of the affinity Direct Scooter had for the B.G.'s Bunny cross is that three full sisters by B.G.'s Bunny from the Shadow Wave mare Resourceful - Bloodstock's Bunny, Areba Bunny and Cunning Bunny - are the dams of world champion Tooter Scooter p,2,1:54.1h; 3,1:51.1 ($567,400), Brace Yourself p,4,1:52.4 ($392,362) and Armbro Maneuver p,3,1:50.2 ($389,850). They are all full brothers-in-blood with this relationship. The Meadow Skipper mare Meadow Good Miss also has a trio of top performers by Direct Scooter in world champion Easter Sun Hanna p,2,1:54.1h, 3,1:52.3; 1:52 ($930,481); All Star Hanna p,3,1:50.3 ($341,419) and Big Brother Hanna p,4,1:52.4 ($316,837). Direct Scooter is another sire who was able to turn out multiple top racehorses from particular mares.

It's too bad that the ascendancy of No Nukes daughters as broodmares has coincided with the lowering of commercial the appeal of Direct Scooter. He's probably not getting enough good No Nukes daughters to make a difference at this stage of his career. I say this because No Nukes combines the blood of many of the sires which have worked best with Direct Scooter - Most Happy Fella, Meadow Skipper, Shadow Wave, Overtrick and Good Time. Some examples of Direct Scooter with No Nukes mares are Sharp Attack p,4,1:50.4 ($160,656), Seth Jay p,3,1:51.3 and Crystal Eros p,3,1:56.2h ($255,256). No Nukes mares are also nicking well with Direct Scooter's great son Matt's Scooter.

Sons of No Nukes are doing well with Direct Scooter mares as shown by Mo Gumbo p,3,1:51.2 ($251,444) (by Nuclear Legacy), Rustler Hanover p,3,1:52-'98 ($713,431) (by Western Hanover) and Yankee Finesse p,3,1:53 ($110,663) (by Western Hanover).

Direct Scooter is now making his mark as a broodmare sire and has joined Albatross, Bret Hanover and Meadow Skipper as the only sires whose daughters have produced three or more performers in 1:50 or faster. Those stars are Village Jove p,3,1:49.4 ($253,657) (by Cam Fella), Pacific Rocket p,4,1:50 ($2,333,401) (by Albert Albert) and Village Jiffy p,1:50 ($1,527,613) (by Cam Fella). Village Jove and Village Jiffy are full brothers from the excellent Direct Scooter mare Village Jig p,2,1:56; 3,1:56f ($342,505).

Another top performer from a Direct Scooter broodmare is the former fastest female ever in a race - Sweetgeorgiabrown p,4,1:50.1 ($257,323) (by Jate Lobell - a son of No Nukes). Direct Scooter mares have done well with a variety of sire lines, including Cam Fella, Big Towner sons and grandsons Towner's Big Guy (Clint Black p,4,1:51.3 $137,000) and Totally Ruthless (the mare Nines Wild p,4,1:52 $253,121) and Albatross.

Direct Scooter has also done extremely well when his daughters are bred to Abercrombie and his sons. These crosses have produced world champion Pacific Rocket and Pacific Missile p,3,1:51.4 ($205,535) (by Albert Albert); Armbro October p,3,1:53.3 ($122,935) (by Armbro Emerson); the filly Diamond Dawn p,3,1:54.2 ($343,875) (by Laag); Sweetheart Final winner On Her Way p,2,1:54.2 ($533,423) (by Abercrombie) and Pacific Lightning p,3,1:52.1 (by Artsplace).

As you can see, Direct Scooter is already the broodmare sire of world champions, a two-time Breeders Crown winner, the former co-fastest racing mare ever, a Sweetheart S. winner and two millionaires. His daughters are still plentiful both on the track and as youngsters and I suspect they will continue to be excellent broodmare prospects. This is ironic for a sire whose daughters were so maligned as racehorses. But it appears the old adage holds true - "blood will tell."

Leading Progeny by Direct Scooter

Fastest
Matt's Scooter, h, p,3,T1:48.2 $2,944,591
In The Pocket, h, p,3,T1:49.3 $1,537,473
Strong Clan, h, p,1:50 $663,377
Direct Command, g, p,4,1:50.2 $221,006
Armbro Maneuver, h, p,3,1:50.2 $423,710
All Star Hanna, h, p,3,1:50.2 $417,679
Stoneridge Scooter, h, p,3,1:50.4 $592,100
General Cochran, g, p,1:50.4 $216,495
Sharp Attack, g, p,4,1:50.4 $160,656
Expensive Scooter, h, p,3,1:51 $910,846

Richest
Matt's Scooter, h, p,3,T1:48.2 $2,944,591
In The Pocket, h, p,3,T1:49.3 $1,537,473
Easter Sun Hanna, h, p,1:52 $930,481
Expensive Scooter, h, p,3,1:51 $910,846
Direct Flight, h, p,4,1:51 $825,052
Armbro Global, h, p,4,1:52.2 $771,177
Scoot Outa Reach, h, p,4,1:51.4 $757,436
Strong Clan, h, p,1:50 $663,377
Scoot Herb, h, p,1:54.3 $616,583
Trimtex, m, p,4,1:54.3f $604,914

Direct Scooter, Bay Horse, 15.3 Hands, 1976
p, 3, 1:54 ($800,451)

Sampson Direct, 1957 p, 4, T1:56 $137,486	Sampson Hanover, 1947 p, 4, T1:56.4 $28,708	**VOLOMITE**, 1926 3, 2:03¼ $32,649	**PETER VOLO** 4, 2:02	**PETER THE GREAT** — Pilot Medium / Santos
				Nervolo Belle — Nervolo / Josephine Knight
			Cita Frisco, 1921	San Francisco — **ZOMBRO** / Oniska
				Mendocita — Mendocino / Esther
		Irene Hanover, 1930 4, T2:01	**DILLON AXWORTHY**, 1910 3, 2:10¼	**AXWORTHY** — Axtell / Marguerite
				Adioo Dillon — Sidney Dillon / Adioo
			Isotta, 1917 3, 2:09¼h	**PETER THE GREAT** — Pilot Medium / Santos
				The Zombro Belle — **ZOMBRO** / The American Belle
	Dottie Rosecroft, 1945 p, 4, 2:05.2 $7,735	Billy Direct, 1934 p, 4, T1:55 $12,040	Napoleon Direct, 1909 p, 1:59¾	Walter Direct — Direct Hal / Ella Brown
				Lady Erectress — Tom Kendle / Nelly Zarro
			Gay Forbes, 1916 p, 2:07¾	Malcolm Forbes — Bingen / Nancy Hanks
				Gay Girl Chimes — Berkshire Chimes / Miss Gay Girl
		Beams Hanover, 1935 p, 3, 2:07¾h	Calumet Chuck, 1929 2, 2:04	Truax — **GUY AXWORTHY** / Hollyrood Nimble
				Sumatra — **BELWIN** / Sienna
			Lexington Maid, 1925 2, T2:17	**PETER VOLO** — **PETER THE GREAT** / Nervolo Belle
				Fruity Worthy — **AXWORTHY** / Fruition
Noble Claire, 1969 p, 2, 2:04 $5,557	Noble Victory, 1962 4, 1:55.3 $522,391	Victory Song, 1943 4, 1:57.3 $73,859	**VOLOMITE**, 1926 3, 2:03¼ $32,649	**PETER VOLO** — **PETER THE GREAT** / Nervolo Belle
				Cita Frisco — San Francisco / Mendocita
			Evensong, 1925 2, T2:08¾	Nelson Dillon — **DILLON AXWORTHY** / Miss Pierette
				Taffolet — **GUY AXWORTHY** / Taffeta Silk
		Emily's Pride, 1955 3, T1:58 $130,751	Star's Pride, 1947 5, 1:57.1 $140,969	Worthy Boy — **VOLOMITE** / Warwell Worthy
				Stardrift — Mr. McElwyn / Dillcisco
			Emily Scott, 1941 4, T2:04¼ $9,805	**SCOTLAND** — Peter Scott / Roya McKinney
				May Spencer — Spencer / Guyellen
	Scotch Claire, 1953 2, T2:06 $1,595	**SCOTLAND**, 1925 T1:59¼	Peter Scott, 1909 T2:05	**PETER THE GREAT** — Pilot Medium / Santos
				Jenny Scott — Bryson / Aetna
			Roya McKinney, 1911 4, T2:07½	**MCKINNEY** — Alcyone / Rosa Sprague
				Princess Royal — Chimes / Estabella
		Abbey Claire, 1945	Guy Abbey, 1925 3, 2:06¾	**GUY AXWORTHY** — **AXWORTHY** / Lillian Wilkes
				Abbacy — The Abbe / Regal McKinney
			Jean Claire, 1922 2, T2:08¾	**BELWIN** — **MCKINNEY** / Belle Winnie
				Honeymoon H — John A. McKerron / Rosa L

Dragon's Lair

Dragon's Lair scored one of the most stunning upsets in harness racing history when he handed Nihilator his only defeat as a two-year-old in the Breeders Crown at The Meadows. The race was on national television and Dragon's Lair became an instant celebrity in the harness racing community.

He later went on to win over $1,000,000 during his career - actually, during his two careers. Dragon's Lair was retired to stud after his three-year-old season, but had fertility problems and could only get a few mares in foal. After missing his four-year-old season, Dragon's Lair came back to race at five and six, winning over $200,000 each year. At seven, he was tried again as a stallion and found to be fertile. Now, Dragon's Lair has a successful stallion career to add to his racing credentials.

Dragon's Lair was originally named Santee Hanover since he was bred by Hanover Shoe Farms of Pennsylvania. After being sold for $43,000 as a yearling at the Harrisburg Sale, the colt's name was changed to Dragon's Lair. He was purchased by Harvey Heller and Gary Kornfeld, along with Jeff Mallet, who was the colt's trainer and driver. All were from Pennsylvania and raced at The Meadows.

The 1984 season showcased a number of top two-year-olds, headed by Nihilator, who won over $1,300,000, and Praised Dignity, who won nearly $1,200,000. Among the colts, Broadway Express and Witsend's Wizard won over $450,000, as did Dragon's Lair. This was a very strong crop of youngsters.

Dragon's Lair made his career debut on May 29, 1984, at The Meadows in a baby race and won easily in 2:02. A week later, in a Pennsylvania Sires S. at Pocono Downs, he won in 1:57.4 after starting from the second tier and being ninth at the half. Jeff Mallet recalled, "When I pulled him out at the half, he just circled the field and won in 1:57.4. That was a track record, and it was only June 8th, and it was his first start. I thought he would never go that fast again." Mallet added, "When I was pulling him up after the race, a tractor came out on the track and Dragon tried to kick the tractor. I was amazed he was so playful after that kind of mile."

Dragon was second two weeks later in a conditioned race at The Meadows, racing his last half in :56.4. He then embarked on a four-race winning streak which included victories in Pennsylvania Sires S. at Liberty Bell and The Meadows and a division of the Prix de l'Avenir at Blue Bonnets in Canada. One of these wins, in another race at The Meadows, was a world record performance over a five-eighth mile track, which the colt paced in 1:55.4. Dragon was then second in the Arden Downs S. at The Meadows after running a slight temperature following the race in Canada. He then had another four-race winning streak, including the Hanover Colt S. and two more Pennsylvania Sires S.

Mallet had Dragon's Lair primed for the rich Breeders Crown on October 12th at The Meadows, in which he would face the undefeated division leader Nihilator - a colt who had already stamped himself as one of the greatest of all time. "Since I knew there was a good chance he'd have to go two heats, I started training him extra heats well in advance of the race," said Mallet.

This Breeders Crown turned out to be a race for the ages. There were two eliminations held the same night as the Final. Dragon's Lair and Nihilator both drew in the first Elimination, which turned out to be a hard-fought battle. Mallet had Dragon cut the mile but, although he came home in :27.3, Nihilator was just a hair faster and got up in time for a head victory in a world record 1:54.3. In the other Elimination, Pershing Square defeated Broadway Express.

In the $579,375 Breeders Crown Final, Mallet wanted the lead with his colt but had to fight a battle with the Tommy Haughton-driven Pershing Square, who had similar designs. Dragon's Lair finally prevailed after being parked out in a scorching :26.3 first quarter. Mallet said, "Tommy Haughton was yelling, 'Take the hole, Jeff'. I didn't want to drop in the hole because I knew that Nihilator would

Race Record Highlights

At 2

1st Breeders Crown
 Hanover Colt S.
 Prix de l'Avenir
 five Pennsylvania Sires S.

2nd Breeders Crown Elimination
 Arden Downs S.

At 3

1st Messenger S. Elimination
 Pennsylvania Sires S.

2nd Messenger S. Final
 Battle of Brandywine Final

3rd North America Cup Elimination
 Battle of Brandywine Elimination

Aged

1st George Morton Levy Series Final (twice)
 On The Road Again P.
 two legs of George Morton Levy Series
 Mohawk Gold Cup

2nd leg of Molson Series

Honors

Set world record for two-year-olds on five-eighth mile track

Dragon's Lair

Photo by Tony Leonard
Courtesy of Walnut Hall

Race Record

Year	Age	Starts	Wins	2nd	3rd	Earnings	Record
1984	2	14	11	3	0	$ 454,899	p,2,1:54.1f
1985	3	12	5	3	2	201,448	
1987	5	17	8	3	0	211,783	p,1:51.3
1988	6	23	6	4	1	217,187	
		66	30	13	3	$1,085,317	p,1:51.3

Dragon's Lair

pop right out of the third spot and trap me. I knew that I couldn't come first over against these good colts. So, I went to the front." He added, "Once I got to the front, his next quarter was paced in 30 seconds. You can rate him very easily."

Dragon's Lair picked up the pace again with a :28.3 third quarter and took a two-length lead into the stretch. Nihilator pulled out and was initially gaining some ground, but then he tired and Broadway Express came up to nose him out for the second spot. Dragon's Lair crossed the finish line in 1:54.1 to regain the world record for two-year-olds and become a hometown hero at The Meadows.

Apparently there is never a dull moment with Dragon's Lair. Mallet related a story about what happened to the colt following the big Breeders Crown victory and the end of his season. "We turned Dragon's Lair out and he proved to be quite a jumper," said his trainer. "He jumped over fences at Meadow Lands Farm and then we turned him out at Greensburg and he jumped a fence and trotted off into the woods. There were five people looking for him, calling, 'Dragon! Dragon!' Finally, he came out of the forest himself."

By most standards, Dragon's Lair's figures would indicate he had a good year at three since he won five of his 12 starts and earned over $200,000. However, he was not the same horse that he had been at two. Dragon began his season with a 1:56.2 win in a Meadows Invitational, coming home in only :30.1 to defeat Keystone Famous by a neck. Next, he finished a tired third in his Battle of Brandywine Elimination and was second to Pershing Square in the Final the following week. Things looked better after a 1:58.4 win at Yonkers and a 1:55.4 win in his Messenger S. Elimination at Roosevelt. After leading all the way in the Messenger Final, Dragon was nipped at the wire by a head by Pershing Square. Dragon followed the Messenger with a third place finish in his North America Cup Elimination and was then given five weeks off.

Returning in mid-August, Dragon won a Pennsylvania Sires S. in 1:54.3. It was his best effort of the year. A week later, he made a break at the start from post eight, was parked out all the way and finished fifth in the Cane Pace. A week after that, he made another break at Pocono Downs while on the lead in a Pennsylvania Sires S. After being off another five weeks, Dragon returned to win a Pennsylvania Sires S. at The Meadows and a week later ended his disappointing season with a second place finish at Garden State Park.

Dragon's Lair was then syndicated and stood his first season at stud at Almahurst Farm in Kentucky. He received a good book of mares for the 1986 breeding season, but he had fertility problems and could only get a few mares pregnant. From 79 mares bred that season, only seven foals were born.

Since Dragon's Lair was no longer considered a commercial sire prospect, he returned to the races in 1987 when he was a five-year-old. A year away from the races seemed to have cured any ills he might have had and he returned in fine form. Now owned by the Dragon's Lair Syndicate, he was driven in all but one start by John Campbell. Dragon won three qualifying races at The Meadowlands in 1:58, 1:57 and 1:54.3 in preparation for his first start. He opened his season with three straight wins including a 1:51.3 victory at Vernon Downs which turned out to be his lifetime record. In that mile, Dragon's Lair opened up with a :25.4 first quarter and closed with a :27.2 final quarter.

For the year, Dragon's Lair won eight of his 17 starts, including the $105,000 Mohawk Gold Cup and the $100,000 On The Road Again P. at Yonkers.

Dragon's Lair came back the following year to win over $200,000 once again, with FFA wins at Roosevelt, Yonkers and The Meadowlands. His big win was in the $145,000 George Morton Levy Series Final, in which he also pushed his career earnings over the $1,000,000 mark.

However, Dragon's Lair's efforts were not confined only to the racetrack during 1988. He was tried again in the breeding shed and test bred to seven mares, from which four foals resulted the following spring. Dragon's Lair was officially retired from the races at the end of the 1988 season.

Sire Line

Dragon's Lair is one of the sires attempting to extend the male line of the top racehorse and sire Tyler B. Most Happy Fella is the sire of Tyler B and has been the Meadow Skipper son with the most success in producing sons which are good sires. His son Cam Fella has at least a half-dozen sons who may have an impact on the breed and his grandson No Nukes also looks like he will be a sire of sires.

Tyler B's best son as a stallion has been Dragon's Lair and he is closely followed by Tyler's Mark. Another son, Cole Muffler, who is a full brother to Dragon's Lair, had an excellent first crop in 1996 including two sub-1:53 two-year-olds and he could bear watching. It is worth noting that all of these sons of Tyler B are from Race Time mares, as is Magical Mike, whose first yearlings sold in 1997. In fact, Tyler's Mark and Magical Mike have dams which are full sisters - making the two stallions full brothers in blood. Another close relationship among these sires is that the grandam of Dragon's Lair is by Tar Heel, while the grandam of Tyler's Mark and Magical Mike is by O'Brien Hanover, a son of Tar Heel. Other Tyler B sons which have had some success at stud are Franz Hanover and Dignatarian.

You can read more about Tyler B in his chapter.

Maternal Line

Dragon's Lair has one of the finest modern day maternal families; it has produced plenty of extreme speed and high earning horses. Originally known as the family of Medio, it is more commonly known today as the family of Miss Bertha C. or Miss Bertha Dillon.

This maternal family has a number of successful branches and that which led to Dragon's Lair is one of the best. The key mare here is Sandy's Sable p,2,2:00.1 ($17,451), a daughter of Race Time, who is the dam of Dragon's Lair. She has been one of the all-time great broodmares in the history of the sport. From 14 foals, Sandy's Sable's credits include four in 1:55, eight in 2:00, one $1,000,000 winner and three $600,000 winners. In addition to Dragon's Lair, Sandy's Sable is also the dam of Bruce's Lady p,3,1:53.3 ($772,607), Cole Muffler p,3,1:53.3f ($682,380), Michael's Dragon p,1:54.4($131,836), Sandpiper Hanover p,1:56.4 ($94,271), Sandbea Hanover p,3,T1:58.2, Sable Hanover p,3,T1:58.4 ($27,092) and Sanrema Hanover p,2,1:59.3 ($63,974). Bret Hanover is the sire of Sable Hanover and Sandpiper Hanover, while Tyler B is the sire of all the other sons and daughters of Sandy's Sable.

All seven daughters of Sandy's Sable have been 2:00 producers. Some of the top stars from these mares are Call For Cash p,3,1:51 ($213,863), Mattduff p,3,1:51.2 ($362,024) and Sablevision p,3,1:53.1 ($379,777) (from Sable Hanover); Nuclear Legacy p,3,1:52 ($556,122) (from Sandia Hanover); and Scooter Hanover p,3,1:52 ($216,755) (from Sandbea Hanover).

The granddaughters of Sandy's Sable are carrying on the family tradition and are also excellent producers. Some of their credits include His Mattjesty p,3,1:51 ($993,881), I Saw Him First p,3,1:51.1 ($532,732), Sable Matters p,3,1:52.2 ($370,023), King Of Pain p,3,1:52.4, Lady Mattingly p,3,1:53 ($107,615) and Sanabelle Island p,3,1:52.2 ($637,577).

Progeny of Note

Dragon's Lair has shown he can sire speed and class from his four full crops which have raced. Thus far, 84% of his foals have been starters and 67% of his starters have won in 2:00 or faster. Dragon already has 248 in 2:00, not including his 1998 two-year-olds, 70 in 1:55, 2 in 1:50 and 47 $100,000 winners.

Stand Forever p,4,1:49.2h ($694,472) is Dragon's Lair's most outstanding performer. He set a world record for the fastest time ever on a half-mile track; he won the Tattersalls S. and the John Simpson S. at three and was an Open class winner at four. Island Glow p,1:50 ($608,174), the other 1:50 credit for Dragon's Lair, won a heat of the

Dragon's Lair

Little Brown Jug and Gaines Memorial at three and later was a successful Open class pacer.

Top fillies are also part of Dragon's Lair's success story and his best are Electric Slide p,3,1:52.4 ($908,792) and Armbro Nest p,4,1:50.4 ($674,821). Electric Slide won the Breeders Crown at two; the Jugette Final and Nadia Lobell S. were among her major wins at three. Armbro Nest was a solid performer at two, three and four and her wins included a heat of the Jugette and the Roses Are Red Final. In addition, Armbro Nest was second in the Breeders Crown Finals at two and three.

Bonnie And Clyde p,2,1:53.4 ($501,138) was a top two-year-old colt for Dragon's Lair and Doc's Girl p,3,1:53.4 ($411,890) was an excellent filly. Another very fast filly is Gabrielle p,4,1:51 ($139,376). Another Dragon's Lair colt with a Little Brown Jug heat victory is Powerful Structure p,3,1:52.2 ($196,359). Dragon's Lair had a pair of excellent two-year-old colts in 1997 - Dragon Again p,2,1:52.3; 3,1:51.3-'98 ($193,245) and Holy Dragon p,2,1:53.2h who set a world record for two-year-olds on a half-mile track and died in a race accident two weeks later.

From a speed stand point, some other fast Dragon's Lair performers are Longport p,3,1:50.4 ($171,793), Stone Dragon p,4,1:50.4-'98 ($377,677), Jet Lair p,4,1:51.2-'98 and the mare Fimbrethil p,4,1:51.4-'98.

Analysis

As mentioned earlier in this chapter, only seven foals were produced from Dragon's Lair's first season as a stallion due to his fertility problems. But they made such an impressive showing during the 1989 season that breeders wanted to go to Dragon's Lair if his fertility ever improved - which it did later.

From those seven foals, six raced at two and three took sub-1:59 records. Six of the seven ultimately took 2:00 records. Among that group was the ill-fated Talon Almahurst, who was a very impressive colt who won his first five starts, including a 1:54.3 win in the Goshen Cup. He then finished second in his Woodrow Wilson Elimination and would have been one of the major favorites for the Final. But in a sad twist of fate, he died before the Wilson and deprived Dragon's Lair of a possibly great two-year-old. Also in that first small crop were the stakes-winning fillies Royalty Almahurst and Temptres Almahurst.

Dragon's Lair turned the same kind of trick with his second small crop of just four foals which were sired when he was bred to only seven mares while he was still racing in 1988. From those four foals came two 1:58 two-year-olds in 1991: L P G and Marie Elaine. The Dragon looked like he definitely was trying to be a sire.

In 1989, his first year off the racetrack, Dragon's Lair bred 23 mares which resulted in 14 foals. Ten of those raced, with seven taking 2:00 records. Among those youngsters were the stars Bonnie And Clyde, Dragon Revrac and Smoke Robertson - all sub-1:56 youngsters.

The numbers of mares bred, and Dragon's Lair's fertility, continued to increase and he was quickly becoming a rising young stallion at his new home, Walnut Hall Farm of New York. His list of mares bred rose as follows: 23, 69, 91, 124 and then stayed in the 101 to 125 range from 1993 through 1997.

Dragon's Lair fillies have fared well at the races and should not be discounted at the sales. To date, 18 of his 47 $100,000 winners are female and there are many high-class performers. I suspect they will also have a very good residual value as broodmare prospects. One thing you may want to consider when breeding mares sired by Dragon's Lair is that his sisters and several of their daughters have worked especially well with Direct Scooter and his sons Matt's Scooter and In The Pocket. This may indicate a "nick" for these bloodlines and it could be an interesting cross for future generations.

The closest cross in Dragon's Lair own pedigree is an inbred 3x3 to Tar Heel. He is also 4x3 to Good Time and 4x4 to Adios. Meadow

Skipper is in his third generation of the male line and he has plenty of Hal Dale and Volomite blood - just what a good pacing sire needs. He's also a product of the very prolific Tyler B/Race Time cross.

With Meadow Skipper appearing only in the fourth generation of Dragon's Lair's foals from the standpoint of the male line, he was open to mares by that stallion and many of his great sons and grandsons. And with his dam being a Race Time/Tar Heel cross, Dragon's Lair is able to be bred to most mares by today's popular young sires.

His pedigree pattern has worked well for producing offspring linebred 3x4 or 4x4 to Meadow Skipper and the vast majority of his best racehorses have those crosses. There are some interesting situations, however. Niatross and his son Nihilator are the sires of the dams of six of Dragon's Lair's 10 richest offspring - five from Niatross mares. And his two richest, Electric Slide and Stand Forever, are both from Niatross mares whose dams are by Adios line sires. Taking this another step, seven of the 10 richest sons and daughters of Dragon's Lair have dams sired by Albatross line stallions - Albatross, Niatross, Sonsam, and Nihilator.

Another interesting observation is that 15 of Dragon's Lair's 20 richest performers have dams with sub-1:59 records - five of them below 1:55. It is clear that the best horses come from the best mares, again giving validity to the old saying, "breed the best to the best and hope for the best."

Look at the Dragon's Lair speed department. Of his eight fastest sons and daughters, five are from dams sired by sons of Albatross - three by Niatross and two by Sonsam. In fact, the dams of his two fastest daughters are by Sonsam, so you may want to look for Dragon's Lair fillies from good Sonsam mares. In this case, we are talking about the Dragon's Lair daughters Armbro Nest p,4,1:50.4 ($674,821) and Gabrielle p,4,1:51 ($139,371) whose dams are the excellent racemares La Toya p,3,1:54.3 and Conquered Quest p,3,1:52.4.

Only a couple of Dragon's Lair's best horses have unusual pedigree structures and one is the 1:50 performer Island Glow. He is inbred 3x3 to Race Time and linebred 3x4 to Most Happy Fella. In addition, Island Glow is 4x4x5x5 to both Good Time and Tar Heel. But the interesting cross is that he is also 3x4 to the great producing three-quarter-sisters Tarport Cheer and Tarport Kathy - another example of success by crossing back to outstanding females.

The second cross to note was that of Stone Dragon p,4,1:50.4-'98 ($377,677) who is inbred 3x3 to the full brother and sister Race Time and Touch Of Spring. His other pedigree crosses are 4x4x5x4 to Tar Heel, 5x5x4x4 to Adios and 4x4 to Good Time.

Mares by No Nukes, who is from the same Most Happy Fella sire line, are also doing well with Dragon's Lair and I have seen this same Most Happy Fella situation with other sires as well. Another cross worth watching is that with mares by Big Towner and his sons.

Dragon's Lair appears to be a sire ready to break out and produce a truly great horse. He's had plenty of good ones and has a wide genetic pool with which to work. Perhaps even better days are still ahead.

Dragon's Lair

Photo courtesy of The Horseman and Fair World

Leading Progeny by Dragon's Lair

Fastest

Stand Forever, h, p,4,1:49.2h $694,472
Island Glow h, p,1:50 $608,074
Armbro Nest, m, p,4,1:50.4 $674,821
Longport, h, p,3,1:50.4 $171,793
Stone Dragon, g, p,4,1:50.4 $377,677
Gabrielle, m, p,4,1:51 $239,376
Jet Lair, h, p,4,1:51.2 $80,211
Park Lane Comet, h, p,3,1:51.2 $135,325
Resurgent Dragon, h, p,3,1:51.3 $266,256
Dragon Again, h, p,3,1:51.3 $193,245

Richest

Electric Slide, m, p,3,1:52.4 $908,792
Stand Forever, h, p,4,1:49.2h $694,472
Armbro Nest, m, p,4,1:50.4 $674,821
Island Glow h, p,1:50 $608,074
Bonnie And Clyde, h, p,2,1:53.4 $501,138
Doc's Girl, m, p,3,1:53.4 $411,890
Stone Dragon, g, p,4,1:50.4 $377,677
Dragon So, m, p,4,1:52.4 $296,470
Peter's Dragon, h, p,2,1:54.3 $283,951
Smoke Robertson, h, p,3,1:54.4f $275,012

Dragon's Lair, Bay Horse, 1982
p, 2, 1:54.1f; 1:51.3 ($1,085,317)

Tyler B, 1977 p, 3, 1:55.1 $687,388	Most Happy Fella, 1967 p, 3, T1:55 $419,033	Meadow Skipper, 1960 p, 3, 1:55.1 $428,057	Dale Frost, 1951 p, 1:58 $204,117	**HAL DALE**	**ABBEDALE** Margaret Hal
				Galloway	Raider Bethel
			Countess Vivian, 1950 p, 3, 1:59 $43,262	King's Counsel	**VOLOMITE** Margaret Spangler
				Filly Direct	**BILLY DIRECT** Calumet Edna
		Laughing Girl, 1961 p, 4, 2:04h $19,546	**GOOD TIME**, 1946 p, 1:57.4 $318,792	**HAL DALE**	**ABBEDALE** Margaret Hal
				On Time	**VOLOMITE** Nedda Guy
			Maxine's Dream, 1954 p, 2, T2:00 $36,557	Knight Dream	**NIBBLE HANOVER** Lydia Knight
				Maxine Abbe	**ABBEDALE** Maxine Direct
	Tarport Cheer, 1966 p, 3, 2:08.3f	**TAR HEEL**, 1948 p, 4, T1:57 $119,148	**BILLY DIRECT**, 1934 p, 4, T1:55 $12,040	Napoleon Direct	Walter Direct Lady Erectress
				Gay Forbes	Malcolm Forbes Gay Girl Chimes
			Leta Long, 1940 p, 4, 2:03¾ $9,321	**VOLOMITE**	Peter Volo Cita Frisco
				Rosette	Mr. McElwyn Rose Scott
		Meadow Cheer, 1956 p, 2, 2:05h $16,083	**ADIOS**, 1940 p, T1:57½ $33,329	**HAL DALE**	**ABBEDALE** Margaret Hal
				Adioo Volo	Adioo Guy Sigrid Volo
			Betty G., 1946 p, 4, 2:13.3h $292	Wilmington	Bert Abbe Miss Saginaw
				Betty Crispin	Crispin Gold Girl
Sandy's Sable, 1974 p, 2, 2:00.1 $17,451	Race Time, 1961 p, 3, 1:57 $486,955	**GOOD TIME**, 1946 p, 1:57.4 $318,792	**HAL DALE**, 1926 p, 6, 2:02¼	**ABBEDALE**	The Abbe Daisydale D.
				Margaret Hal	Argot Hal Margaret Polk
			On Time, 1938 p, 3, 2:03½h $1,472	**VOLOMITE**	Peter Volo Cita Frisco
				Nedda Guy	Guy Axworthy Nedda
		Breath O Spring, 1953 p, 3, T2:01.1 $3,144	Worthy Boy, 1940 3, 2:02½ $25,688	**VOLOMITE**	Peter Volo Cita Frisco
				Warwell Worthy	Peter The Brewer Alma Lee
			Lady Scotland, 1943	Scotland	Peter Scott Roya McKinney
				Spinster	Spencer Minnetonka
	Carolonda, 1965	**TAR HEEL**, 1948 p, 4, T1:57 $119,148	**BILLY DIRECT**, 1934 p, 4, T1:55 $12,040	Napoleon Direct	Walter Direct Lady Erectress
				Gay Forbes	Malcolm Forbes Gay Girl Chimes
			Leta Long, 1940 p, 4, 2:03¾ $9,321	**VOLOMITE**	Peter Volo Cita Frisco
				Rosette	Mr. McElwyn Rose Scott
		Adios Onda, 1959	**ADIOS**, 1940 p, T1:57½ $33,329	**HAL DALE**	**ABBEDALE** Margaret Hal
				Adioo Volo	Adioo Guy Sigrid Volo
			Onda Hanover, 1952 p, 2, 2:02.3 $24,755	**NIBBLE HANOVER**	Calumet Chuck Justissima
				Ormonde Hanover	Dean Hanover Norma Hanover

Falcon Almahurst

Falcon Almahurst was a success story for his popular and charismatic owners Charles and LaVerne Hill who owned Hill Farms in Hilliard, Ohio, as well as the Scioto Downs racetrack. They took the gamble of purchasing the highest priced yearling of the 1976 sales in the hopes of having an outstanding son of Meadow Skipper who would win lots of money and then stand at stud.

They were right on both counts.

The yearling Falcon Almahurst was entrusted to Hall of Fame trainer-driver Bill Haughton and they were a fine match. At two, Falcon Almahurst won two "baby races" at Brandywine in 2:04.2f and 2:01.1f, followed by a record 1:59 victory at The Meadowlands. He raced only six times that season, winning his first three races and coming in second in the Hanover-Hempt S. and Arden Downs S. However, Falcon's earnings were only $12,380, hardly an auspicious start for a $150,000 colt. But he was impressive enough to have been ranked number five at 1:54.1 on the 1978 Experimental Ratings.

Following his second place finish in the Arden Downs S., Falcon Almahurst was away from the races for a month after injuring a stifle. Trainer Haughton had commented, "He threw a stifle at The Meadows just training one day. When we got him right again, and it looked like we were going to be alright, I brought him up to Hazel Park for the Geers S. In the mud he got the damn thing out again, so we just stopped with him." Haughton added, "Falcon Almahurst's problem was one only time would take care of."

Haughton also felt Falcon Almahurst would be worth the high price paid. At the beginning of the colt's three-year-old season, Haughton commented, "Falcon Almahurst should not be at the top of the Experimental Ratings or anything at this point, but he might turn out to be the top colt by the end of the season." He added, "He was a beautiful training colt. Right from the start he was one of the more expensive colts of all-time who was really worth the money from the word go."

Falcon Almahurst did come back strong at three and it was only the great sophomore season of Abercrombie that kept Falcon from winning divisional honors. He finished second in the balloting to Abercrombie and even garnered some votes for Pacer of the Year. Falcon had won eight of his 22 starts and earned $388,396 for the season in addition to setting an all-age world record of 1:55.2 on a half-mile track and pacing to a 1:52.2 time-trial at Lexington to become the fastest three-year-old in the sport's history.

Falcon's season began with a 1:58.2 Kentucky Sires S. win at Lexington with catch driver George Sholty in the sulky. The victory was then followed by six consecutive defeats with trainer Haughton back in the sulky. During that period, Falcon was second in the Cane Pace Final and in the Hanover-Hempt S. Falcon had drawn poorly in three of those races and suffered parked out trips; he also made a break while on the lead in the stretch at Yonkers.

Being the master trainer that he was, Haughton got Falcon Almahurst back on track and the colt won eight of his last 16 starts and only finished more than three lengths back only once in his losing efforts. In seven head-to-head battles, Falcon defeated Abercrombie only twice, but one of his victories was in the Meadowlands Pace and the other in the first heat of the Little Brown Jug - the two major three-year-old stakes races of the year.

Falcon had bounced back from his losing streak by winning a heat of the Gaines Memorial and he was second in the Final. A week later, it was time for the $560,000 Meadowlands Pace - the richest race ever at the time and certainly a race in which the Hills could pay for their investment in the colt and have a ready-made stallion in the process. Had Falcon Almahurst known of his responsibilities that night he could not have been more awesome. He drew post nine in his $140,000 Elimination and Haughton left easily, letting the traffic settle in front of him. Falcon was fifth on the outside at the quarter but moved quickly to the front in a :28.1 second quarter to take the lead to the half in :56. He held off all challengers and went on to a three-length 1:54.2 win over Armbro Tiger.

Race Record Highlights

At 2

2nd Hanover-Hempt S.
      Arden Downs S.

At 3

1st Meadowlands Pace
      Tattersalls S.
      heat of Little Brown Jug
      Jug Preview
      Kentucky Sires S.

2nd Cane Pace
      Gaines Memorial Elimination
      Hanover-Hempt S.
      heat of Prix d'Ete

3rd Little Brown Jug Elimination

Honors

Set record as fastest pacer on a half-mile track
Set record as fastest three-year-old pacer on a mile track

Falcon Almahurst

Photo by Tony Leonard
Courtesy of The Horseman and Fair World

Race Record

Year	Age	Starts	Wins	2nd	3rd	Earnings	Record
1977	2	6	3	2	0	$ 12,380	p,2,1:59
1978	3	22	8	6	2	388,396	p,3,T1:52.2
		28	11	8	2	$400,776	p,3,T1:52.2

Falcon Almahurst

The Meadowlands Pace Final, for a $280,000 purse, was tougher because of the presence of Abercrombie and Flight Director. Falcon was once again unlucky in the draw and left from post eight. Haughton was confident of his colt and used a similar strategy in this heat, being a parked out fourth at the :28.1 first quarter. He then made a move again for the front and was carried on the outside far longer. Falcon was the parked out leader as the field passed the half in :56 and he finally got to the front on the backstretch. Around the final turn and into the stretch, Falcon Almahurst opened up a few eyes and a few lengths and went on to win by two in a brilliant 1:55.2 performance with Abercrombie taking second and Flight Director third.

Falcon then lost four consecutive heats in the Adios S. and Prix d'Ete. In three of those heats he was parked out most of the way since he was now a "marked man" and the horse to beat. True to his character, Falcon rebounded in the Jug Preview at the Hills' home track of Scioto Downs, winning in 1:55.2 two weeks prior to the Little Brown Jug.

In the Jug, Falcon's owners and trainer experienced both exhilaration and disappointment. Falcon drew the rail for his Jug Elimination and Haughton took full advantage with a front-end win in 1:55.2 - the fastest mile ever paced over a half-mile track by a pacer of any age, which made the partisan Delaware, Ohio, fans very happy. Abercrombie was a length and one-quarter back in second place with Flight Director third.

Happy Escort had won the first Elimination for driver Bill Popfinger in 1:57.2 and Falcon Almahurst was made the heavy choice in the next heat. If either Falcon or Happy Escort were to win, the Jug would be over. But the race, true to the dramatic traditions of the Jug, came up with another surprise. Flight Director caught the leading Falcon Almahurst in the stretch and went on to win over League Leader with Falcon falling back to third. Falcon had earlier used his energy to park out Abercrombie through fractions of :28.3, :56.2 and 1:26.1 while setting up the race for the late-closing horses.

This result meant that there would be a three-horse raceoff between Falcon, Happy Escort and Flight Director. In the raceoff, Joe O'Brien had Flight Director on top early, followed by Happy Escort with Haughton sitting third with Falcon Almahurst. Popfinger then made a surprise early move to go around Flight Director and take the lead. He held on to win over Flight Director with Falcon finishing two lengths behind in third. Although Falcon lost the big prize that day, he did take home a world record and added to his growing credentials as a stallion prospect while earning the respect of watchful breeders.

A week after the Little Brown Jug, Falcon Almahurst showed up at The Red Mile in Lexington for an attempt to lower his personal 1:54.2 lifetime record. Haughton had the colt primed and he paced through fractions of :28.1, :56 and 1:24.4 to the three-quarter pole. During the final quarter, Falcon really dug in and came home in :27.3 for a 1:52.2 mile - the fastest ever for a three-year-old, by a full second, and the second fastest mile of all time behind only Steady Star's 1:52 time-trial at four.

Falcon Almahurst's final career start came in the Tattersalls Pace at Lexington, which he won in a courageous three-heat effort. Falcon won the first heat in 1:55.2 by two lengths over Flight Director and then that colt came back to nip him at the wire by a head in 1:57.2 in the second heat. The two colts returned for a raceoff in which Haughton and Falcon followed Flight Director for the entire mile until the final steps of the long stretch when Falcon thrust his nose in front at the wire to win in 2:00.2 with a final quarter in :27.1.

Falcon Almahurst had proved his speed, stamina and courage and was now a fine stallion prospect. He was always a horse who drew attention on the racetrack due to his outstanding appearance and the distinctive way he raced - with his head held higher than today's top pacers, who go low-headed. His racing career finished, Falcon headed for the Hill Farms and the next successful chapter of his career.

Sire Line

Falcon Almahurst is another top stallion in the long line of Meadow Skipper sons. However, his pedigree cross is a bit different than most other Meadow Skipper sons due to the close proximity of trotting blood, as you will see in the next part of this chapter. It must also be pointed out that Falcon Almahurst is the fourth fastest son of Meadow Skipper.

In the production of 2:00 pacers, and in earnings by his offspring, Falcon Almahurst ranks as one of the better sons of Meadow Skipper, behind only Albatross, Most Happy Fella and Nero. He is also in the list of the top 2:00 sires of all time, ranking ninth. And now, Falcon Almahurst is moving up in the ranks of pacing broodmare sires; he was ranked number 12 in 1996 and number 11 in 1997 in the all-age category.

For more about Falcon's sire Meadow Skipper see his chapter.

Maternal Line

The maternal family of Falcon Almahurst is the well-known and respected family known as Lizzie Witherspoon, which has produced world-class performers at both the pacing and trotting gaits. This particular branch of the family should be more commonly known as that of Isotta. Nero, Seahawk Hanover, Sampson Hanover and "down under" sire star Holmes Hanover are a few male representatives of this maternal family on the pace.

The trotting side of the family has such famous names as world champion Nevele Pride, world champion filly Impish and her long list of stakes-winning descendants, Noble Gesture, Duke Rodney, Carlisle and Kimberly Kid to name only a few.

Falcon Almahurst was the very first foal from his Shadow Wave dam Ingenue p,2,T2:01.4; 3,1:58.3 ($37,818) who won several stakes at three, including the Hanover-Hempt S., Niagara Filly S., Tennessee P. and Breeders Filly S. Ingenue was an excellent producer with nine winners from her 12 foals, and Falcon Almahurst was her fastest and richest performer. She is also the dam of the good stakes-winning fillies Robin Almahurst p,3,1:56.1 ($113,304) (by Meadow Skipper) and Lark Almahurst p,2,1:57 ($227,553) (by Albatross) in addition to Condor Almahurst p,4,1:52.4 ($50,684) (by Nihilator) and Baracuda Almahurst p,3,1:55.3 (by High Ideal) among others.

Ingenue's two top fillies have both produced good stakes winners themselves. Robin Almahurst is the dam of Sumkinda Wonderful p,3,1:52 ($200,180), Falcon Bret p,1:55.1 ($297,062) and Wonderful Thing p,3,1:52.1 while Lark Almahurst is the dam of Fannie's Champ p,3,1:53.3 ($405,409).

There is trotting blood very close on Falcon Almahurst's bottom line since his grandam is the fast pacing filly I'm It p,2,T1:59.4 ($24,185). I'm It took her two-year-old record in 1960 and that placed her among the fastest half-dozen freshman pacing fillies in the sport's history at the time. The irony of I'm It is that she is sired by Rodney, one of the sport's leading trotting sires, and is from a Volomite mare who trotted. But this is about where this branch of the maternal family suddenly switched gaits.

In addition to producing the dam of Falcon Almahurst, I'm It had six 2:00 performers, including the hard-hitting world champion FFA performer Invincible Shadow p,1:56.1f ($252,069) (by Shadow Wave). The Shadow Wave link seems very important in tracing the success of this family. I'm It also had a High Ideal daughter named Impish Almahurst who is the dam of world champion Intruder Almahurst p,1:52.1 ($193,345) (by Keystone Ore). Another High Ideal daughter who is a very successful producer is Irene Almahurst who is the dam of Pilgrim's Patriot p,1:51.1 ($802,871) (by Niatross).

Regarding the trotting branch of this maternal family, it is interesting to note that Falcon Almahurst's third dam, Kimberly Mine 3,2:03 ($23,770) (by Volomite) is a full sister to trotting stakes winner and world champion Kimberly Kid 4,1:59 ($191,188). Falcon's fourth dam, the Mr. McElwyn mare Kimberly Hanover 2,2:08¾ ($11,592), finished tied for second-in-summary in the 1945 Hambletonian S. against Titan Hanover.

Kimberly Hanover, who is a half-sister to the good racehorse and sire Sampson Hanover p,4,T1:56.4, who was Volomite's fastest son, had a trotting daughter named Kimberly Rodney 3,2:05f ($17,811), by Rodney, who produced a top trotter in Nevele Diamond 3,1:58.3 ($220,559) when bred to trotting sire Nevele Pride, and a top pacing daughter Hope Diamond p,3,T1:59 ($57,852) when bred to pacing sire Henry T. Adios. It is Hope Diamond who later became the grandam of the outstanding exported sire Holmes Hanover who is a son of Albatross.

In any case, Falcon Almahurst was equipped with a very strong and high-quality maternal family and his first five dams were themselves good performers.

Progeny of Note

Falcon Almahurst has sired a number of excellent and fast stakes winners during his long career as a stallion, but the true standout is his daughter Stienam p,2,1:55.2; 3,1:53.4 ($1,355,474) who is one of the gamest and toughest mares I've ever seen. She was a multiple stakes winner at two and three and was voted Three-Year-Old Pacing Filly of the Year after winning the Breeders Crown, Tarport Hap S. and Adioo Volo S. among others. Her races against arch-rival Amneris are legendary.

At two, Stienam lost the Breeders Crown by a neck to Amneris after being caught in the final strides. A year later, Stienam got her revenge in the Breeders Crown by getting up at the end to defeat Amneris by a head in a stirring stretch battle in which these two fillies were five lengths in front of the rest of the field.

I have always felt that Stienam would be a great broodmare and produce a bevy of stars. To date, however, she has only six in 2:00 with her best being Patriot Stena p,4,1:52.3 ($130,740) and Stienam's Girl p,3,1:53.2 ($102,282). This is good production for an average mare, but not in keeping with Stienam's legacy and expectations. But her daughter Stienam's Girl (by Nihilator) has begun her broodmare career by producing a great filly - Stienam's Place p,2,1:53.4; 3,1:50.4 ($1,402,301). The Artsplace daughter has won the Sweetheart P. at two and the Breeders Crown, Mistletoe Shalee and Tarport Hap P. at three. She also set a world record for three-year-old fillies.

While on the subject of Falcon Almahurst fillies, Stienam has a sister named L'Eggins p,3,1:54.2 ($188,882) who was a stakes winner at two and three and set a world record.

Another major claim to fame for Falcon Almahurst is his son B. J. Scoot p,2,1:55.1f; 3,1:52.3h ($891,010) who won the 1988 Little Brown Jug to become first Ohio-sired horse to win the Jug in its home state. Ten years earlier, Falcon had almost accomplished that goal. Long-wearing and rich sons of Falcon Almahurst are Joss p,1:54.3 ($620,843) and Le Courrier p,4,1:53 ($478,319) who were Free-For-All stars for several years.

Falcon Almahurst is also no stranger to siring fast two-year-olds as evidenced by his son Raque Bogart p,2,1:52.1 ($453,500) who became a world champion at two. The fastest son of Falcon Almahurst surfaced when Izatiger paced in 1:51.1. His other sub-1:52 performers are Kyle's Falcon p,1:51.3 and Almahurst Stinger p,1:51.4 ($196,800).

Sons and daughters of Falcon Almahurst have dominated the Ohio Sires Stakes program since his first starters reached the track in 1982. For the last decade and a half, Falcon Almahurst sons and daughters have won countless races in the Ohio program and they are still doing well.

Analysis

During the last 19 breeding seasons, Falcon Almahurst has bred 100 or more mares 16 times. The three exceptions were when he bred 89 in 1993, 87 in 1996 and 66 in 1997. The earnings of his offspring total over $40,000,000 to date and Falcon has sired 84 in 1:55 and 554 2:00 performers. And as mentioned earlier, Falcon Almahurst's daughters are good enough producers to have already moved him into the top dozen pacing broodmare sires in the money-winning category.

My first impression while examining the bloodline links in Falcon Almahurst's best offspring was the very frequent presence of Good Time blood close up. For example, eight of Falcon's 23 richest performers have dams sired by sons of Good Time - four from Race Time mares and two each from Columbia George and Best Of All mares. Another good cross is with Bret Hanover blood as seven of the top 22 have dams by Bret Hanover and his sons High Ideal, Melvin's Woe and Flying Bret. In addition, there is another whose dam is sired by Baron Hanover - Bret's full brother.

Looking at the elite, the top 10 money winners, seven of those 10 have first or second dams sired by Good Time or his sons. This cross holds true in the speed category as well since five of the fastest eight and 11 of the fastest 25 have dams by Good Time or his sons.

Falcon Almahurst is also noted as a sire of good stakes fillies as well as colts. In addition to the great Stienam, there are Caramel Sundae p,4,1:54.2 ($352,349), Love To Shop p,3,1:56.3 ($212,144), Missy Almahurst p,3,1:56.4f ($196,559), Tango Almahurst p,4,T1:56.2 ($194,546) and L'Eggins p,3,1:54.2 ($188,882), among the more well known.

The only downside to Falcon Almahurst is that he appears unable to keep up with the modern-day speed explosion to the 1:50 level. He has two below 1:52 but most of his best are between 1:52 and 1:53.2. There are probably several reasons for this, the two most prominent being, first, his position as a first generation son of Meadow Skipper who has to compete against stallions three and four generations ahead of him; and, second, most of his foals never had the opportunity to race on the big mile tracks as do many of the New Jersey sires. A third reason is the quality of mares Falcon was bred to during his entire career. Yes, there were a few years following the success of his early crops when some major breeders sent mares to him; but, for the most part, the majority of his consorts were average at best. To his credit, he did a wonderful job in moving these mares up to a higher level.

Most of Falcon Almahurst's best sons and daughters had the types of crosses you would expect from his pedigree - 4x4 to Adios and 4x4x5x5 to Hal Dale. A couple of exceptions among his best include the 2x3 inbred cross of world champion Raque Bogart to Meadow Skipper. An interesting situation with Raque Bogart is that his dam Bola is a half-sister to Stienam and Joss. Thus the broodmare Margeaux and her daughter Bola have produced three of Falcon's five richest performers. Obviously, this cross works!

There is a very similar situation with another mare, Worthy Wick who is by Worthy Boy from a Scotland mare and whose second dam is by none other than the historic sire Guy Axworthy. These are pretty old bloodlines and Worthy Wick was born in 1961. Nevertheless, when bred to Falcon Almahurst she produced her best performer, Tres Grand Vitesse p,3,1:55.2h ($292,878). He was an outcross having no common ancestors in his first four generations his closest cross being 5x5x3 to the great sire Volomite. This old cross intrigued me so I delved further into Worthy Wick's own pedigree and what I found was quite interesting. Worthy Wick had extremely close and high-quality crosses in her bloodlines. First, she is inbred 2x2 to Volomite and his Guy Axworthy half-sister Lady Bird since Volomite's dam Cita Frisco is the dam of both. Secondly, Worthy Wick's sire Worthy Boy is inbred 3x3 to Peter The Great and 2x4 to the champion full brother and sister duo of Peter Volo and Volga E. Thus Worthy Wick possessed a strong concentration of some of the finest old bloodlines in Standardbred history.

When I turned from examining Falcon Almahurst's richest performers to his fastest, this Worthy Wick cross showed up again. The old mare's final foal was produced in 1984, when she was 23 years of age; it was a filly sired by the Albatross son Billy Dart. The filly, Dazzle Dart, never raced and was bred at two. Owned for several years by Hill Farms, Dazzle Dart was bred to Falcon Almahurst and produced the fast performers Dazzle Hill p,4,1:53.4 and Dazzler Hill p,1:54f. But, the best was yet to come. Dazzle Dart's 1994 foal by Falcon Almahurst is Kyle's Falcon p,3,1:51.3 who is his second all-time fastest record offspring.

The successful crosses of Margeaux and her daughter Bola with Falcon Almahurst, and Worthy Wick and her daughter Dazzle Dart with Falcon

Almahurst, would indicate there are certain broodmare "nicks" which work with sires; and you can often see it with mothers and daughters going to the same stallion.

Now, let's take a look at Falcon Almahurst as a broodmare sire. As this chapter is written, he has 557 2:00 broodmare sire credits from his daughters. His daughters seem to work well with several sire lines, especially Big Towner, No Nukes, Tyler B and with Abercrombie and his son Laag.

Some of the best horses from Falcon Almahurst mares are Ultimate Falcon p,1:47.4-'98 ($212,680) (Falcon Seelster) who paced the second fastest race mile in history on the new one-turn track at Colonial Downs in Virginia, Shadow Dance p,1:49.4 ($689,473) (Big Towner), Under Orders p,4,1:50.4 ($495,292) (Silent Majority), No Standing Around p,3,1:51 ($373,014) (Jate Lobell), Falcon's Scooter p,4,1:51.1 ($431,755) (Matt's Scooter), Fernbank Filly p,3,1:51.4 ($228,436) (No Nukes) and Crisp Sahbra p,3,1:52.3h ($447,195) (Towner's Big Guy).

Of course, another solid cross which is working extremely well, especially for Ohio breeders, is when Falcon Almahurst mares are taken to Ohio's hot sire Nobleland Sam who is a son of Sonsam. Nobleland Sam is a dominant sire in the Ohio program and there have been plenty of Falcon Almahurst mares in his 200-plus court during recent seasons. The result is the production of foals with the classic 4x3 linebred cross to Meadow Skipper. Some of the results of this cross are Indiana Sam p,4,1:51.4 ($285,918), Moonlight Sam p,3,1:52.2f ($299,978), Sonic Sam p,3,1:52.3, Cagey Jake p,4,1:53.2f and Sharpe Sam p,3,1:53.2, to name a few.

As you can see, Falcon Almahurst was, and is, an excellent sire and now an up-and-coming broodmare sire. I would not hesitate recommending a fast-record Falcon Almahurst mare with a good maternal family to any breeder. His bloodlines are versatile and can fit many of today's popular stallions.

Leading Progeny by Falcon Almahurst

Fastest
- Izatiger, h, p,1:51.1 $280,542
- Kyle's Falcon, h, p,3,1:51.3 $44,498
- Almahurst Stinger, g, p,1:51.4 $217,931
- Yo Eleven Lo, h, p,4,1:52f $199,199
- Raque Bogart, h, p,2,1:52.1 $453,500
- Soaring Falcon, h, p,4,1:52.1 $352,468
- H A's Pace Setter, h, p,4,1:52.2 $111,956
- B. J. Scoot, h, p,3,1:52.3h $891,010
- Hotrod Falcon, g, p,4,1:52.3h $177,640
- Kuzzin Kat, g, p,4,1:52.3 $161,488

Richest
- Stienam, m, p,3,1:53.4 $1,355,474
- B. J. Scoot, h, p,3,1:52.3h $891,010
- Joss, r, p,1:54.3 $620,843
- Le Courrier, h, p,4,1:53 $478,319
- Raque Bogart, h, p,2,1:52.1 $453,500
- Timothy Haymaker, h, p,4,1:56.3h $398,232
- Pearl's Falcon, h, p,4,1:54.2 $367,836
- Soaring Falcon, h, p,4,1:52.1 $352,468
- Caramel Sundae, m, p,4,1:54.2 $352,349
- Hilliard Hill, h, p,1:53.4 $344,237

Falcon Almahurst, Bay Horse, 1975
p, 2, 1:59; 3, T1:52.2 ($400,776)

Meadow Skipper, 1960 p, 3, 1:55.1 $428,057	Dale Frost, 1951 p, 1:58 $204,117	**HAL DALE**, 1926 p, 6, 2:02¼	ABBEDALE, 1917 p, 2:01¼	The Abbe	Chimes Nettie King
				Daisydale D.	Archdale Mrs. Tmolus
			Margaret Hal, 1914 p, 2:19½h	Argot Hal	Brown Hal Lady Wildflower
				Margaret Polk	John R. Gentry Stella Hal
		Galloway, 1939 p, 2:04½h $5,294	Raider, 1929 p, 1:59½	**PETER VOLO**	PETER THE GREAT Nervolo Belle
				Nelda Dillon	DILLON AXWORTHY Princess Nelda
			Bethel, 1926 p, 2:03	David Guy	GUY AXWORTHY Belle Zombro
				Annotation	Azoff Citation
	Countess Vivian, 1950 p, 3, 1:59 $43,262	King's Counsel, 1940 p, 6, 1:58 $44,930	**VOLOMITE**, 1926 3, 2:03¼ $32,649	**PETER VOLO**	PETER THE GREAT Nervolo Belle
				Cita Frisco	San Francisco Mendocita
			Margaret Spangler, 1918 p, 2:02¼	**GUY AXWORTHY**	Axworthy Lillian Wilkes
				Maggie Winder	Oratorio Clara Direct
		Filly Direct, 1941 p, 3, 2:06¾h $6,299	Billy Direct, 1934 p, 4, T1:55 $12,040	Napoleon Direct	Walter Direct Lady Erectress
				Gay Forbes	Malcolm Forbes Gay Girl Chimes
			Calumet Edna, 1931 p, 2:08½h	Peter The Brewer	PETER THE GREAT Zombrewer
				Broncho Queen	Empire Direct The Broncho
Ingenue, 1968 p, 3, 1:58.3 $37,817	Shadow Wave, 1955 p, 3, 1:56.3 $91,931	Adios, 1940 p, T1:57½ $33,329	**HAL DALE**, 1926 p, 6, 2:02¼	**ABBEDALE**	The Abbe Daisydale D.
				Margaret Hal	Argot Hal Margaret Polk
			Adioo Volo, 1930 p, 3, 2:05	Adioo Guy	Guy Dillon Adioo
				Sigrid Volo	**PETER VOLO** Polly Parrot
		Shadow Grattan, 1943 p, 4, 2:07.1h $2,555	Silent Grattan, 1921 p, T2:09¾	Grattan Royal	Grattan Mona
				Silent T	Silent Brook Agave
			Peacedale, 1936 p, 2, 2:17h $45	**ABBEDALE**	The Abbe Daisydale D.
				Miss Dorothy Dillon	DILLON AXWORTHY Zulu Belle
	I'm It, 1958 p, 2, T1:59.4 $24,185	Rodney, 1944 5, T1:57.2 $111,176	Spencer Scott, 1937 4, T1:57¼ $52,742	Scotland	Peter Scott Roya McKinney
				May Spencer	Spencer Guyellen
			Earl's Princess Martha, 1935 3, 2:01¾	Protector	**PETER VOLO** Margaret Arion
				Mignon	Lee Axworthy Mary Thomas S
		Kimberly Mine, 1949 3, 2:03 $23,770	**VOLOMITE**, 1926 3, 2:03¼ $32,649	**PETER VOLO**	PETER THE GREAT Nervolo Belle
				Cita Frisco	San Francisco Mendocita
			Kimberly Hanover, 1942 2, 2:08¾ $11,592	Mr. McElwyn	**GUY AXWORTHY** Widow Maggie
				Irene Hanover	DILLON AXWORTHY Isotta

Falcon Seelster

Falcon Seelster was a horse with extreme speed who could exhibit it on all size tracks. His record mile of 1:51 for three-year-olds on the half-mile track at Delaware, Ohio, still stands today, after a dozen years, and is one of the longest lasting pacing world records. Falcon Seelster's epic mile took place in a $4,000 Invitational event on the same afternoon that Nihilator won the Little Brown Jug in slower time. Falcon Seelster was so dominant in this mile that he won by over 20 lengths.

Tom Harmer, Falcon Seelster's trainer and driver, said, "On Little Brown Jug Day at Delaware, I thought we could break the world record, but I didn't think we would shatter it like we did." Harmer was not only impressed with Falcon Seelster's speed. "I call him a 'patented horse,'" said Harmer. "If you could draw a horse on paper and have it turn out, you would draw him. He does everything right that you ask him to do. He's very easy to drive and train."

A true speed machine, Falcon Seelster set or equalled 16 track records over various size tracks and finished first, second or third in 48 of 51 starts - a model of consistency. Unfortunately for Falcon Seelster, he was born the same year as Nihilator.

Falcon Seelster was bred by William Ryne and James Kruba of Pennsylvania and Howard Stern of New Jersey. He was sold for $12,500 as a yearling to Canadian ownership and again at three for $65,000 to Charles Day and the Ciara Stable. Following his three-year-old season, Falcon Seelster was syndicated by Castleton Farm.

At two, Falcon Seelster did not get started until late in the year, winning his first qualifier in Canada on October 6th in 2:11. Two weeks later, he won his parimutuel debut in 2:04.3 after being parked out every step of the way. A week later he was second by a neck in 2:04.4 after cutting the pace. These were his only two starts as a youngster, hardly the credentials you would expect from a colt who would set an amazing world record the following year.

Falcon Seelster was ready early at three and prepped at Pompano Park. He won five of his seven starts there from late January through early April (he was disqualified from a win in another) and lowered his record to 1:56.1. His preferred style was to race on the front end and he was winning by open lengths. The Pompano wins included a leg and Final of the Pompano Beach Series. The colt then travelled to Chicago's Maywood Park and won two of three starts, including a brilliant 1:54 effort with a come-from-behind final quarter in :27.4.

His stakes season began on May 25th at Sportsman's Park. Falcon Seelster was up to the task, winning the $102,000 American-National S. in 1:55.4 for regular driver and trainer Tom Harmer. A week later, Falcon Seelster travelled up to Calgary, Canada, and won the $200,000 Nat Christie Memorial in 1:53.3 over that five-eighth mile track. Following an Invitational win at Sportsman's Park, Falcon Seelster headed east to face the bearcats in the rich Messenger S. at Roosevelt Raceway. He dominated his Messenger S. Elimination to win by three lengths in 1:57. In the Messenger Final, however, Falcon Seelster raced in fourth position, parked out for three-quarters of a mile, and finished third behind Pershing Square and Dragon's Lair. Nihilator did not race in this event.

Back at Sportsman's Park, Falcon Seelster added two more wins in 1:54.4 and 1:55 and then finished an uncharacteristic sixth in special Invitational at Hinsdale Raceway. Falcon Seelster's next battle really put him in the spotlight. It was at The Meadowlands and was his first effort against Nihilator. Falcon and Harmer left from post four and sat second for much of the mile as Nihilator cruised to a world record 1:49.3 mile. Falcon Seelster finished just two lengths behind and was individually timed in 1:50 flat. A week later, in a three-year-old Open event at The Meadowlands, Falcon Seelster turned in a wire-to-wire 1:53 win.

Continuing his stakes schedule, Falcon Seelster raced in the $242,370 Slutsky Memorial at Monticello and, after leading all the

Race Record Highlights

At 3

1st Prix d'Ete
Provincial Cup
Cane Pace Elimination
Messenger S. Elimination
Nat Christie Memorial
American-National S.
Sophomore Pacing Championship
Pompano Beach Series Final and leg

2nd Cane Pace Final
Slutsky Memorial

3rd Messenger S. Final

At 4

1st George Morton Levy Series Final and two legs
leg of Presidential Series

2nd Presidential Series Final and two legs
leg of U.S. Pacing Championship
two legs of Graduate Series
leg of George Morton Levy Series

Honors

Set world records on half-mile and five-eighth mile tracks at three
Set or equalled 16 track records

Falcon Seelster

Photo by Larry Cohen
Courtesy of Castleton Farm

Race Record

Year	Age	Starts	Wins	2nd	3rd	Earnings	Record
1984	2	2	1	1	0	$ 325	p,2,2:04.3f
1985	3	31	24	4	1	843,470	p,3,1:51h
1986	4	18	11	6	0	277,250	
		51	36	11	1	$1,121,045	p,3,1:51h

way, lost in the final stride by a nose to the fast-closing Chairmanoftheboard in 1:55.4. A week later at Yonkers, the scene was the Cane Pace. Falcon Seelster won his $180,000 Elimination on the front end by seven lengths in 1:53.4 which broke the Yonkers track record previously held by On The Road Again. But the $240,000 Cane Pace Final was a replay of the Slutsky Memorial. Falcon Seelster again led every step of the way only to lose in the final stride by a nose to his nemesis Chairmanoftheboard in 1:55.1.

Falcon Seelster then went up to Canada and scored his richest win of the year in the $358,000 Prix d'Ete in 1:53.2 over the Blue Bonnets five-eighth mile surface. Leaving from post nine, Falcon was parked out third to the quarter and then assumed the lead. He went on to win by an impressive five lengths. Eleven days later, Falcon Seelster did his best imitation of a rocket as he sped around the Delaware half-mile oval through fractions of :27, :54.3 and 1:22.4 in his incredible 1:51 mile. The Little Brown Jug crowd was stunned by the time and the fact that the record has lasted a dozen years speaks to the magnitude of Falcon Seelster's accomplishment.

Falcon Seelster ended his three-year-old season with an eight-race winning streak which began with the Prix d'Ete and the record Delaware mile. He continued to win at Lexington, Maywood, Mohawk, Windsor, and Lewiston and ended his season with a 1:53.2 win at Pompano Park. Included among these wins were the Mohawk Sophomore Championship, the Provincial Cup and the Sunshine State Pace.

In that year, Falcon Seelster won 24 of his 31 starts and earned $843,470, which placed him third in earnings in the three-year-old pacing category behind Nihilator and Chairmanoftheboard. In addition, Falcon Seelster was second to Nihilator in the balloting for Three-Year-Old Pacer of the Year.

Originally scheduled to go to stud duty following his three-year-old season, Falcon Seelster's owners had a change of heart and decided to showcase him as a four-year-old. Beginning his season early again, in his first start Falcon Seelster was second to Lustra's Big Guy in a leg of the Presidential Series at The Meadowlands. He came back a week later to defeat that opponent and win the next leg in 1:55. After leading most of the way in the Final, however, Falcon Seelster faded to second in the stretch.

Falcon Seelster got back on the winning track with a victory at Pompano Park followed by two wins in legs of the George Morton Levy Series at Yonkers. He then lost twice to the eventual 1986 Horse of the Year Forrest Skipper at Freehold and Rosecroft, and twice more to Chairmanoftheboard and Twin B Playboy in the Levy Series. During that four-race losing streak, Falcon Seelster was second three times.

The four-year-old then redeemed himself with a seven-race winning streak which included the $119,000 Levy Series Final at Roosevelt in 1:55.2 - a remarkable effort after being parked out first over to the three-quarters before getting the lead. His other wins included FFA events at Maywood, Greenwood, Northfield, The Meadows and Sacramento; Falcon Seelster was certainly well-travelled in showing off his talents. He was especially sharp at The Meadows on July 4th, scorching that surface with a 1:51.3 mile - the fastest ever at that point over a five-eighth mile track.

During this period, there was a lot of "hype" about which was the better or faster horse - Falcon Seelster or the undefeated Forrest Skipper, who had won three times at The Meadowlands that year in 1:51.3 and time-trialed there in 1:50.3. By early August, Forrest Skipper had won all nine of his starts. His success had scared off so many opponents that only he and Falcon Seelster were entered in the $60,000 U.S. Pacing Championship race to be held at The Meadowlands on Hambletonian Day. This race then became a match race between the two horses.

Match races are notorious for strange things happening - both in Thoroughbred and Standardbred racing. Yes, sometimes the two horses will be nose-to-nose racing down the stretch; but there are also instances where one horse totally dominates the other, which would not happen if they were in a regular race against each other with others in the field. Under ordinary conditions, one would have reasonably expected a full-field race including Falcon Seelster and Forrest Skipper to be decided at the wire between these two top horses in the 1:51 range.

However, things were very different in this match race. Lucien Fontaine was driving Forrest Skipper and drew post position two; Tom Harmer had the rail with Falcon Seelster. Harmer used the rail to his advantage and got away quickly with Falcon Seelster to reach the quarter in :27.2 and the half in :54.2. Fontaine, though, was not content to just tuck in behind the leader. He had Forrest Skipper right alongside, challenging Falcon Seelster and racing on the outside losing ground. He believed he had the better horse and his strategy was to wear down Falcon Seelster. Harmer still had Falcon Seelster on top after five-eighths of a mile, but Forrest Skipper suddenly surged by on the outside and took the lead before the three-quarter pole, which was passed in 1:21.2.

Once he was passed, Falcon Seelster appeared to be all done and Forrest Skipper opened up a 12-length lead heading into the stretch, extending it to 16 lengths at the wire in an eased up 1:53.3. This impressive victory added to Forrest Skipper's stature, but hurt Falcon Seelster. In mid-September, six weeks later, Falcon Seelster won a qualifying race at Sportsman's Park in 1:57 and then went in a time-trial at Lexington in an effort to reduce his 1:51 record. The attempt failed. He reached the three-quarters in 1:23, but could only come home with a 1:54 mile. This was Falcon Seelster's last appearance on the racetrack before he began a new career as a stallion.

Sire Line

Falcon Seelster is one of the stallions attempting to keep the Bret Hanover branch of the Adios male line from extinction. The great Bret Hanover sired many sons who were tried as stallions and some of them such as Storm Damage, Strike Out, Warm Breeze, High Ideal and Seahawk Hanover attained a decent degree of success. Strike Out left two sons who had limited success, Legal Notice and Striking Image, but they never passed the torch.

The other Bret Hanover stallions mentioned have not left commercially successful sons. However, Warm Breeze (see his chapter) seemed to do the best with his son Falcon Seelster who appears to be the only viable Bret Hanover line stallion left in North America - and he was exported to New Zealand before his announced return to the United States as a dual-hemisphere stallion for the 1998 breeding season. Thus, it seems up to Falcon Seelster and his sons to carry the Bret Hanover male line into the future. Falcon Seelster's son, Falcon's Future p,3,1:51f ($1,054,761) appears to be the son with the most potential.

Bret Hanover, of course, is the greatest son of perhaps the sport's greatest sire, Adios. Today, the Adios line flourishes again through Abercrombie and his sons - especially Artsplace who seems to be taking the pacing breed to a new dimension, given the results of his first two crops. The Adios line seemed to be overwhelmed by the Meadow Skipper male line until the success of Abercrombie brought the Adios line back in full force. In addition to Artsplace, other good Abercrombie sons at stud are Life Sign, Albert Albert and Laag.

So, at this point in time, everything seems to rest on the shoulders of Falcon Seelster and his sons as to whether the Abercrombie branch of the Adios male line will be the only one to move forward into the twenty-first century.

Maternal Line

Falcon Seelster is the fourth foal, and second colt, from the Overtrick stakes-placed mare Fashion Trick p,2,2:01.3h; 3,2:04.4f; 1:59 ($62,227). To date, Fashion Trick has produced 15 foals, including, at 23 years of age, a 1995 foal. Among her foals are four in 1:55 and eight in 2:00 (four by Warm Breeze). Fashion Trick is a member of the prolific Jessie Pepper maternal family and she was the first 2:00 performer from her branch of this family.

Pacing sires Tar Heel and No Nukes are also from this maternal family. Trotting sires are also plentiful as we find Scotland, Hickory Pride, Hickory Smoke, Worthy Bowl and Guy Abbey listed.

In addition to Falcon Seelster, Fashion Trick is also the dam of Fantastic Seelster p,4,1:52.4 ($296,845), Nitro Fashion p,1:54.2 ($112,502), Breezy Fashion p,T1:55 and four others in 2:00. Fashion Trick's daughter Fran Seelster (by Threefold) is the dam of the good 1997 two-year-old Stonebridge First p,2,1:56.1f ($250,190) by Camluck. Other daughters of Fashion Trick have produced in 2:00, but nothing of real quality.

Fashion Trick's dam is the Adios Butler mare Meadow Child p,3,2:07h who produced only one good horse in Fashion Trick and another 2:01.1f performer from her six foals. The next dam is the non-record mare Midway Lady by Nibble Hanover 1:58¾. The maternal family goes back three more generations to the dam of the great trotting sire Scotland and the pacer Highland Scott p,1:59¼.

Progeny of Note

Falcon Seelster's ratio of 2:00 performers to starters is 63%, just so-so at today's speed levels. However, when he gets the good ones, they are really good. A case in point is the wonderful mare Shady Daisy p,2,1:54.4; 3,1:53.3h; 1:51 ($1,807,755) who raced from 1990 through 1995 and is the leading money-winning pacing mare of all time. Shady Daisy set world records for mares on all-size tracks and won the Breeders Crown for mares at ages four and six in addition to being voted Aged Pacing Mare of the Year at ages four, five and six. She was a class act and even held her own against the males.

The best son of Falcon Seelster is the fast Falcon's Future p,2,1:51.3f; 3,1:51f-1:51.4h ($1,054,761). You can tell by his record what kind of speed demon he was. Falcon's Future's 1:51.3 on a five-eighth mile track as a two-year-old was second only to Artsplace as the fastest freshman colt in history. Just like his sire, Falcon's Future was a half-mile track expert and won at Northfield in 1:51.4, less than a second slower than his sire's record. At two, Falcon's Future won eight of his 11 starts and came back at three to win 12 of 28 with victories in $100,000 events, including the Cane Pace, Nat Christie Memorial, MacFarlane Memorial and Cleveland Classic. Like his sire, Falcon's Future stands over 16 hands tall.

Some other top Falcon Seelster performers include Falcon Dakota p,1:50.3 ($923,981), Music Director p,1:51.1 ($796,593), Mantese p,1:52.4 ($528,349), Duke Duke p,3,1:52f ($533,048), who set a world record for three-year-old geldings on a five-eighth mile track, Dawn Q. p,3,1:51.3 ($392,671), Lightening Speed p,4,1:51($384,222), Trump Casino p,4,1:49.1 ($452,830) (Falcon Seelster's fastest offspring), Ultimate Falcon p,1:47.4z-'98 ($215,480), Nicholas T. p,4,1:50.2 ($168,170) and a number of other top performers.

Following a few relatively quiet years, Falcon Seelster had a good group of 1997 two-year-olds at the races, primarily due to the fact that there were 160 foals born to him in 1995 which gave him more of a chance to have a few stars. His 1997 two-year-old standouts included Two-Year-Old Pacing Colt of the Year Sealed N Delivered p,2,1:52.2; 3,1:51.3-'98 ($615,019) (winner of the $590,600 Governor's Cup Final), Mybrowneyedgirl p,2,1:53.1 ($451,732, winner of the $506,700 Three Diamonds Final), Shady Character p,2,1:53.3; 3,1:51.1-'98 ($417,836), Genuine Woman p,2,1:54.3 ($132,541), She's So Misty p,2,1:56.2 ($128,147) and I Married A Witch p,2,1:53.1 ($238,294).

To date, Falcon Seelster has sired the winners of nearly $30,000,000 with 377 in 2:00, 100 in 1:55 and 70 $100,000 winners.

Analysis

As this chapter is written, Falcon Seelster has had eight crops of foals which have raced and he has sired several truly outstanding sons and daughters. The main complaint about Falcon Seelster is that he has been inconsistent as a sire and this has been reflected in the prices buyers are willing to pay for his yearlings. From 1991 through 1997, Falcon Seelster yearlings have averaged between $9,691 and $15,014 and these averages have ranked him anywhere from 10th to 23rd among pacing sires. During the same period, the total earnings of his two- and three-year-old performers, considered a barometer of a stallion's current success, have ranked him from 10th to 20th among his peers.

As you can see, Falcon Seelster is a decent stallion but rated in the second tier among the large group of commercial pacing stallions. And, with each passing year, there is more competition from recently retired great pacers. Thus, a stallion needs to maintain a high ranking every year to ward off the new "young studs" and continue to get his share of top broodmares.

Following the 1995 breeding season, at the age of 13, Falcon Seelster was sold to the Nevele R Stud of New Zealand for stallion duty in that country. Although Falcon Seelster was seemingly overwhelmed by the competition in North America, he may have an opportunity to become a top stallion in New Zealand since the levels of speed are perhaps a second or two slower than in North America. In addition, the Australians and New Zealanders tend not to push their two-year-olds as hard and as early as we do, which could be another plus for Falcon Seelster. While he's had some top youngsters, his offspring appear to get better with age. In fact, two of his seven fastest horses, Falcon Dakota p,1:50.3 and Music Director p,1:51.1, both took lifetime records at the age of eight in 1997.

Falcon Seelster had what you could call a "comeback year" in 1997 with such two-year-old stars as Sealed N Delivered, Shady Character, Mybrowneyedgirl, Genuine Woman, She's So Misty and I Married A Witch. As a result, Falcon Seelster is standing at stud at Perretti Farm in New Jersey for the 1998 North American breeding season and will possibly return to New Zealand for their breeding season which begins when ours ends. It will be interesting to see if 1997 was another in Falcon Seelster's pattern of up-and-down years, or whether he can continue with more consistency.

The closest common cross in Falcon Seelster's pedigree is 3x4 to Adios since he is the great-grandsire on the paternal side and his son Adios Butler is the sire of Falcon Seelster's grandam. There are also several crosses to Hal Dale, and Falcon Seelster is 4x4x4x5 to that stallion. Falcon Seelster has no Meadow Skipper blood and went to stud positioned as an outcross sire for all the mares with crosses to Meadow Skipper - much like Big Towner and Direct Scooter when they went to stud.

The various pedigree crosses which have worked well for Falcon Seelster are interesting in that he seems to relish the application of more Adios blood. He has two crosses to Adios in his own pedigree and was bred to many mares with Adios blood in their pedigrees. As a result, most of Falcon Seelster's top performers show multiple fourth and fifth generation crosses to Adios. As with many other stallions, Good Time blood also appears to be another strong influence at work.

Two of Falcon Seelster's six richest performers, Music Director and Duke Duke, have no Meadow Skipper blood. This is a situation which showed up strongly with Big Towner as a sire. He had no Meadow Skipper blood and did very well with mares without that great sire's blood. However, the majority of Falcon Seelster best sons and daughters do have Meadow Skipper blood. Close crosses to Bret Hanover also seem to work well. Falcon Seelster is a grandson of Bret Hanover and mares with Bret Hanover blood have produced well with Falcon Seelster: Sealed N Delivered is 3x4 to Bret, Duke Duke 3x3 to Bret, Trump Casino 3x4 to Bret, Castleton Rowdy p,1:52.1 ($296,018) 3x4 to Bret and Manificent p,3,1:51.4 ($279,838) 3x4 to Bret, to name just a few.

Ultimate Falcon p,1:47.4z-'98 ($215,480) is a good example of a close sibling cross since he is inbred 3x3 to Bret Hanover and his full brother Baron Hanover.

Another pedigree cross which is working well, and I've noted the same thing at work for other stallions in this book, is crossing back to the mare Breath O Spring. That mare is the grandam of Warm Breeze (Falcon Seelster's sire) and also the dam of Race Time and Storm Damage among others. Manificent is inbred 3x3 to the full brother and sister Race Time and Touch Of Spring; Goalie Jess p,1:56.1f ($240,344) is inbred 3x2 to the half-sisters Touch Of Spring and Spring Rumpus (both daughters of Breath O Spring); Monsieur Mindale is inbred 3x3 to the Race Time and Touch Of Spring; and there are others.

Adios Butler is the sire of Falcon Seelster's grandam and when the blood of his sisters was returned to Falcon Seelster though mares some more good performers resulted with common crosses to Adios Butler's dam Debby Hanover. Falcon Dakota is linebred 4x3 to Adios Butler and his sister Adios Governess, Lightening Speed is 4x4 to the same cross; and Nicholas T. is 4x3 to the same duo.

In the case of Falcon Seelster's two best offspring, Shady Daisy is 4x4x4 to Good Time and 4x5x5 to Adios while Falcon's Future has no common ancestors in his first four generations. Sealed N Delivered is interesting in that his dam has three separate crosses to Meadow Skipper. Sandy Daisy has another close relative in the good 1998 Falcon Seelster three-year-old Shady Character p,3,1:51.1-'98 ($417,836) whose dam is a Sydney Hill half-sister to Shady Daisy.

Falcon Seelster has worked well with mares from a number of different sire lines. He has had particular success with Oil Burner mares which have produced Falcon's Future, Mantese p,1:52.4 ($528,349) and Super Seeled p,4,1:51.2 ($145,019). Albatross, Most Happy Fella and Big Towner mares have also been prominent with Falcon Seelster. But he has also sired top performers from mares by unheralded sires like Fortune Teller, Rorty Hanover, Hot Hitter, Troublemaker, Escort, True Duane, Royce, Rashad and Umbrella Fella, to name a few.

Many sires who have made a bit of a name for themselves often go on to make good broodmare sires. With Falcon Seelster's unique bloodlines and the racing success of many of his daughters, I suspect his daughters will do well as producers. Although most of Falcon Seelster's daughters are only now beginning to have foals of racing age, the early returns are promising. Two of his daughters have already produced Beach Bubbles p,2,1:52 (by Beach Towel), Nuclear Shock p,3,1:52.2 (by No Nukes) and Armbro Peregrine p,3,1:54.2 (by Jate Lobell).

Yes, Falcon Seelster has his niche among pacing sires and, while not at the top, he is certainly a worthy "blue collar" type stallion who can sire good performers.

Leading Progeny by Falcon Seelster

Fastest
- Ultimate Falcon, h, p,1:47.4z $215,480
- Trump Casino, h, p,4,1:49.1 $452,830
- Nicholas T, h, p,4,1:50.2 $168,170
- Falcon Dakota, g, p,1:50.3 $923,381
- Shady Daisy, m, p,3,1:51 $1,807,755
- Falcon's Future, h, p,3,1:51f $1,054,761
- Lightening Speed, h, p,4,1:51 $384,222
- Music Director, g, p,1:51.1 $796,593
- Shady Character, h, p,3,1:51.1 $417,836
- Escape For Now, g, p,4,1:51.2 $213,379

Richest
- Shady Daisy, m, p,3,1:51 $1,807,755
- Falcon's Future, h, p,3,1:51f $1,054,761
- Falcon Dakota, g, p,1:50.3 $923,381
- Music Director, g, p,1:51.1 $796,593
- Sealed N Delivered, h, p,3,1:51.4f $615,019
- Duke Duke, g, p,3,1:52f $533,048
- Mantese, h, p,1:52.4 $528,349
- Mybrowneyedgirl, m, p,2,1:53.1 $459,732
- Trump Casino, h, p,4,1:49.1 $452,830
- Shady Character, h, p,3,1:51.1 $417,836

Falcon Seelster, Bay Horse, 16.1 Hands, 1982
p, 2, 2:04.3f; 3, 1:51h ($1,121,045)

Warm Breeze, 1973 p, 4, 1:53.1 $254,168	Bret Hanover, 1962 p, 4, T1:53.3 $922,616	**ADIOS**, 1940 p, T1:57½ $33,329	**HAL DALE**, 1926 p, 6, 2:02¼	Abbedale	The Abbe Daisydale D.
				Margaret Hal	Argot Hal Margaret Polk
			Adioo Volo, 1930 p, 3, 2:05h	Adioo Guy	Guy Dillon Adioo
				Sigrid Volo	**PETER VOLO** Polly Parrot
		Brenna Hanover, 1956 p, 3, T2:01 $21,946	Tar Heel, 1948 p, 4, T1:57 $119,148	**BILLY DIRECT**	Napoleon Direct Gay Forbes
				Leta Long	**VOLOMITE** Rosette
			Beryl Hanover, 1947 p, 2, T2:02 $29,076	**NIBBLE HANOVER**	Calumet Chuck Justissima
				Laura Hanover	The Laurel Hall Miss Bertha Worthy
	Touch Of Spring, 1967 p, 2, T2:03 $480	Good Time, 1946 p, 1:57.4 $318,792	**HAL DALE**, 1926 p, 6, 2:02¼	Abbedale	The Abbe Daisydale D.
				Margaret Hal	Argot Hal Margaret Polk
			On Time, 1938 p, 3, 2:03½h $1,472	**VOLOMITE**	**PETER VOLO** Cita Frisco
				Nedda Guy	**GUY AXWORTHY** Nedda
		Breath O Spring, 1953 p, 3, T2:01.1 $3,144	Worthy Boy, 1940 3, 2:02½ $25,688	**VOLOMITE**	**PETER VOLO** Cita Frisco
				Warwell Worthy	**PETER THE BREWER** Alma Lee
			Lady Scotland, 1943	**SCOTLAND**	Peter Scott **ROYA MCKINNEY**
				Spinster	Spencer Minnetonka
Fashion Trick, 1972 p, 5, 1:59 $62,227	Overtrick, 1960 p, 3, 1:57.1h $407,483	Solicitor, 1948 p, 3, T1:57.2 $102,109	King's Counsel, 1940 p, 6, 1:58 $44,930	**VOLOMITE**	**PETER VOLO** Cita Frisco
				Margaret Spangler	**GUY AXWORTHY** Maggie Winder
			Jane Reynolds, 1938 4, 2:07h	**SCOTLAND**	Peter Scott **ROYA MCKINNEY**
				Jane Revere	**GUY AXWORTHY** Volga E
		Overbid, 1954 p, 2, T2:05.4 $3,524	**HAL DALE**, 1926 p, 6, 2:02¼	Abbedale	The Abbe Daisydale D.
				Margaret Hal	Argot Hal Margaret Polk
			Barbara Direct, 1947 p, 3, T2:00.4 $5,747	**BILLY DIRECT**	Napoleon Direct Gay Forbes
				Norette Hanover	**PETER THE BREWER** Helen Hanover
	Meadow Child, 1966 p, 3, 2:07h $7,088	Adios Butler, 1956 p, 4, T1:54.3 $509,875	**ADIOS**, 1940 p, T1:57½ $33,329	**HAL DALE**	Abbedale Margaret Hal
				Adioo Volo	Adioo Guy Sigrid Volo
			Debby Hanover, 1948 p, 4, 2:13.1h $1,550	**BILLY DIRECT**	Napoleon Direct Gay Forbes
				Bonnie Butler	**VOLOMITE** Ruth Abbe
		Midway Lady, 1952	**NIBBLE HANOVER**, 1936 1:58¾ $25,599	Calumet Chuck	Truax Sumatra
				Justissima	Justice Brooke Claire Toddington
			Midway, 1941	**VOLOMITE**	**PETER VOLO** Cita Frisco
				La Roya	**GUY AXWORTHY** **ROYA MCKINNEY**

French Chef

Few colts have ever had a two-year-old season like French Chef. Bred and owned by Norman Woolworth's Clearview Stable, French Chef retired as the fastest two-year-old in history on half, five-eighth and mile tracks. Handsome, fast, good-gaited and dominant, his major two-year-old victories came in the Kentucky Pacing Derby at Louisville Downs; the International Stallion and Meadow Lands Farm Stakes at The Red Mile; and the Goshen Cup at the Meadowlands. Winning 21 of 23 starts, he was voted Two-Year-Old Pacer of the Year, earning $278,599. He would have won much more, of course, had he won the Woodrow Wilson at The Meadowlands. However, he made a break in his elimination heat at the start and failed to qualify for the rich event. It was one of the few blemishes on a dominant, front-running freshman season for trainer-driver Stanley Dancer.

French Chef's season began in style. In the Hoosier Futurity at Indianapolis, Dancer sent French Chef right to the front in the second heat and he never looked back. The precocious colt paced fractions of :28.2, :56.4 and 1:25.1 to the three-quarters and then came home in :28.4 to finish his world record mile in 1:54. No other horse was within 20 lengths of French Chef. In his next start, French Chef equalled Whamo's 1:57.4 record for two-year-olds on a half-mile track. That record was later broken by Slapstick's 1:57.2 mile. French Chef then won in 1:56.1 over Scioto Downs' five-eighth mile track for another world record for youngsters.

After scoring his biggest win of the year in the $200,000 Kentucky Pacing Derby in 1:57.3 over Slapstick, Dancer said, "We would have got the record if I had just got to the colt. Having a top colt makes it easy to look good."

At three, French Chef did not return in top form, winning only three of 14 starts for Dancer, although he did capture an elimination of the Meadowlands Pace and the Oliver Wendell Holmes at The Meadowlands. The fact that he was the fastest freshman in history at the time he retired to Stoner Creek Stud is generally forgotten, since his stud career was full of peaks and valleys.

Sire Line

French Chef was a foal of 1978 and thus came along late in the career of his supersire Meadow Skipper. He was part of Meadow Skipper's 12th crop (the same as Adios winner Landslide) and near the end of Meadow Skipper's storied career, since the "sultan of Stoner Creek" produced only four crops after 1978. Besides Albatross, French Chef must be appraised as one of Meadow Skipper's best two-year-olds. He was certainly on a par with champions Nero and Jade Prince. French Chef's best offspring was the rugged Beach Towel, and the legacy of speed was fulfilled when Beach Towel sired the world champion racehorse Jenna's Beach Boy p,4,1:47.3. But for all of Meadow Skipper's greatness as a sire, the only sons of his to have lasting impacts are Albatross and Most Happy Fella.

Maternal Line

On his female side, French Chef is one of the best-bred horses ever to grace anyone's stallion barn, although his dam, La Pomme Souffle, was by trotting sire Nevele Pride. French Chef hails from the famed Minnehaha maternal family, one of the breed's largest and most successful. There are several successful internal branches of this family, and French Chef hails from one of its best strongholds, tracing directly from the noted Guy Abbey producer The Old Maid, a foal of 1945.

The Old Maid family includes trotting stars such as world champion Crevette, and Hambletonian winners Speed Bowl and Duenna; as well as pacing stars Thorpe Hanover, Dancer Hanover, Amneris, Frugal Gourmet, Cinnamon Reel and Shady Daisy. The maternal trail leading to French Chef came through Spinster Hanover, a 1952 daughter of The Old Maid's mating with Bill Gallon. Spinster Hanover founded both trotting and pacing branches of her family, since she is the second dam of Kentucky Futurity winner Filet Of Sole and world champion

Race Record Highlights

At 2
1st Kentucky Pacing Derby
Goshen Cup
International Stallion S.
Reynolds Memorial
Review Futurity
Arden Downs S.
Meadow Lands Farm P.
Count B. S.
Tom Hal S.
Battle of Saratoga
Blue Bonnets Grand Circuit S.
Hoosier Futurity
Kentucky Sires S.

At 3
1st Oliver Wendell Holmes P.
Battle of Brandywine Preview
Freehold Invitational
3rd Hanover Colt S.
heat of Adios S.

Honors
Voted Two-Year-Old Pacer of the Year
World champion at two over mile, half-mile and five-eighth mile tracks

French Chef

Photo by Tony Leonard
Courtesy of The Horseman and Fair World

Race Record

Year	Age	Starts	Wins	2nd	3rd	Earnings	Record
1980	2	23	21	0	0	$278,599	p,2,1:54
1981	3	14	3	1	2	92,846	
		37	24	1	2	$371,445	p,2,1:54

Crevette, and third dam of Hambletonian winners Speed Bowl and Duenna. Another daughter of Spinster Hanover, the Victory Song mare Brief Romance, produced the world champion two-year-old Brisco Hanover 2,1:57.

Spinster Hanover's 1965 daughter Pompanette, a daughter of Florican, leads us to French Chef. Pompanette's claims to fame are at both gaits. She produced the superb filly champions Filet of Sole and Crevette, as well as La Pomme Souffle, the dam of French Chef, and French Chef's full sister, Peach Melba, who in turn was the dam of the $1 million winner Kentucky Spur, a son of Abercrombie.

Regarding French Chef's maternal trotting heritage, Stanley Dancer said, "French Chef was terribly gaited at first. He acted like he wanted to trot, but he couldn't trot at all; just thought he could. He'd trot in hobbles for the longest time."

Progeny Of Note

French Chef's major claim to fame is as the sire of Beach Towel p,3,1:50 ($2,570,357), a horse who certainly ranks among the top racing pacers of all time. Beach Towel won 29 races at two and three, including 18 heats during his sophomore season when he triumphed in the Meadowlands Pace, Little Brown Jug, Prix d'Ete, Tattersalls Pace, Breeders Crown, Adios, American-National, Miller and Hayes Memorials.

But Beach Towel was not French Chef's only claim to fame. He also produced the Meadowlands Pace winner Frugal Gourmet p,3,1:51.3 ($1,349,560) and the fast Messenger winner Amity Chef p,3,1:51.1 ($1,372,683) as well as the Sweetheart winner Concertina p,3,1:55.1f ($814,509) (dam of North America Cup winner Arizona Jack p, 3,1:50.2 ($705,823)). French Chef accomplished a great deal from small books of mares. He stood at Stoner Creek Stud for eight seasons, from 1982 through 1989, and produced only a little over 400 foals, an average of just over 53 foals per year. His last American crop, foaled in 1990, included only 14 foals. Despite producing Beach Towel, Amity Chef and Frugal Gourmet, he fell out of favor with breeders and yearling buyers. French Chef did not produce the kind of long-barrelled, attractive horses which the market demanded. His Nevele Pride dam contributed to the fact that he produced some short-coupled, short-backed horses that were undesirable to buyers. He was subsequently exported "down under" where he became a siring success, only to die unexpectedly while still in his teens.

Analysis

French Chef has always been a very interesting horse to follow simply because of his pedigree pattern - in addition to his being a great colt performer and a son of the great sire Meadow Skipper. Since his dam is by the great trotter Nevele Pride, French Chef was kind of an outcross sire for many mares, and breeding pundits wondered how the trotting influence would affect the French Chef offspring.

In retrospect, French Chef has to be considered a decent sire since his offspring won over $19,000,000 from only eight North American crops and 171 of his 332 starters took 2:00 records. The main problem with French Chef seemed to be that his sons and daughters were in the "all or nothing" category. French Chef showed he was capable of siring such great racehorses as Beach Towel, Amity Chef and Frugal Gourmet, all million-dollar winners, but he was just not consistent enough to maintain commercial viability. He sired 14 $200,000 winners and 27 in 1:55 and his colts were far better than the fillies, aside from the top filly Concertina p,3,1:55.1f ($814,509).

The amazing aspect of French Chef's stallion career was his affinity for daughters and granddaughters of Bye Bye Byrd. The success of this cross is astounding and certainly gives support to the theory of sire line "nicks" for certain stallions. The French Chef/Bye Bye Byrd cross demonstrates this theory to the fullest degree. French Chef's four fastest performers are from Bye Bye Byrd mares or mares by his sons. And this can be extended to six of French Chef's seven fastest sons, as well as eight of the 11 fastest.

French Chef's three $1,000,000 winners all have this cross - Beach Towel is from an Armbro Nesbit (son of Bye Bye Byrd) mare while both Amity Chef and Frugal Gourmet are from Bye Bye Byrd daughters. Magic Formula p,4,1:52 ($315,873) and Gold Dust p,1:52.2 ($89,294) are both from daughters of the Bye Bye Byrd son Keystone Ore. Chef's Magic p,3,1:52.4f ($254,307) is from a daughter of the Bye Bye Byrd son Nardin's Byrd.

Another cross which worked well for French Chef was to Bret Hanover mares. However, there is a distinct difference in the speed potential of the Bye Bye Byrd and Bret Hanover crosses. The Bye Bye Byrd crosses produced 1:50, 1:51.1 and 1:51.3 million-dollar winners while the fastest Bret Hanover cross kicked in at the 1:54 level with four performers between 1:54 and 1:54.2. Bret Hanover's son High Ideal is the sire of the dam of French Chef's fifth richest performer, Dancing Master p,3,1:53.4 ($495,700) and Bret is the sire of the sixth richest, Souffle p,3,Q1:56.1 ($427,671).

Taking a look at some of the pedigree crosses, it is interesting to note the common sibling crosses in many of French Chef's best offspring. Beach Towel has no common crosses in his first four generations, but is 5x5x4 to Adios and his sister Adieu. Amity Chef is 4x4 to Hal Dale and 4x3 to Adios and Adieu since his dam was inbred 3x2 to that brother/sister combination. As was pointed out in his chapter, Bye Bye Byrd's second dam, Adieu, is the full sister to Adios which makes some of these crosses possible. Frugal Gourmet is 5x4x4 to Billy Direct and 4x2 to the half-sisters Spinster Hanover and Timely Hanover.

Magic Formula is inbred 2x4 to Meadow Skipper with a 4x4x4 cross to Adios and Adieu. Another closely bred to Meadow Skipper is Banquet Table p,1:52.1 ($319,840) who is 2x3 to that great stallion. Satellite p,3,1:53.4 ($65,565) is bred 4x3 to Billy Direct and 5x4x4 to the great brother and sister trotters Peter Volo and Volga E. Another with a common cross to top broodmares is the aforementioned Dancing Master who has a 5x4 cross to the half-sisters The Old Maid and Lady Scotland. Continuing with the sibling connections, Souffle has a 4x4x4 cross to Hal Dale along with 4x4 to the full brothers King's Counsel and Chief Counsel and a 5x5 cross to the half-brother and sister The King Direct and Calumet Edna.

French Chef seemed to do very well with certain aspects of pedigree crosses, mainly with Bye Bye Byrd and Bret Hanover, and when brother and sister connections appeared in pedigrees of his offspring. It's also interesting to note that Amity Chef and Frugal Gourmet were both capable of siring top horses, but like their sire, could not maintain that ability with consistency. The jury is still out concerning Beach Towel, but he seems to be having trouble coming up with another Jenna's Beach Boy or Paige Nicole Q. However, in Beach Towel's case, the sons and daughters of the best mares bred to him are now beginning to race and the situation may turn around.

French Chef mares have been decent broodmares but also seem to have the same "all or nothing" syndrome endured by their sire. Some top performers from French Chef daughters include Arizona Jack p,3,1:50.2 ($705,823) (by Abercrombie), No More Mr Niceguy p,1:51.3 ($212,209) (by Niatross), Tilly's Sam p,4,1:51.4f ($280,837) (by Nobleland Sam), Mountain Jackson p,3,1:52.2 ($83,914) (by Forrest Skipper), Cindy's Tootsie p,1:52.1 (by Nihilator), Monsieur Mindale p,1:52.4 ($233,395) and Frenchtown Lady p,1:53.3 ($170,295) (both by Falcon Seelster) and Noble Return p,3,1:53.1f ($22,211) and Noble Attack p,3,1:53.2f ($80,747) (both by Nobleland Sam). French Chef mares bred to the good Ohio sire Nobleland Sam have produced three of French Chef's eight fastest broodmare credits.

French Chef will always be remembered for his racing ability and his three outstanding sons. It's too bad he did not have a longer and more successful stallion career in North America before being exported "down under" for additional stallion duties.

French Chef

Photo courtesy of The Horseman and Fair World

Leading Progeny by French Chef

Fastest

- Beach Towel, h, p,3,1:50 $2,570,357
- Amity Chef, h, p,3,1:51.1 $1,372,683
- Frugal Gourmet, h, p,3,1:51.3 $1,349,560
- Magic Formula, g, p,4,1:52 $315,873
- Banquet Table, g, p,1:52.1 $319,840
- Gold Dust, h, p,1:52.2 $89,294
- Chef's Magic, h, p,3,1:52.4f $254,307
- Pianist, g, p,1:52.4 $230,719
- Armada, h, p,1:53.1 $193,127
- Dancing Master, h, p,3,1:53.4 $495,700

Richest

- Beach Towel, h, p,3,1:50 $2,570,357
- Amity Chef, h, p,3,1:51.1 $1,372,683
- Frugal Gourmet, h, p,3,1:51.3 $1,349,560
- Concertina, m, p,3,1:55.1f $814,509
- Dancing Master, h, p,3,1:53.4 $495,700
- Souffle, h, p,3,Q1:56.1 $427,671
- Banquet Table, g, p,1:52.1 $319,840
- Magic Formula, g, p,4,1:52 $315,873
- Mr Softee, h, p,1:54.2 $259,194
- Chef's Magic, h, p,3,1:52.4f $254,307

French Chef, Brown Horse, 1978
p, 2, 1:54 ($371,445)

Sire/Dam	2nd gen	3rd gen	4th gen	5th gen
Meadow Skipper, 1960 p, 3, 1:55.1 $428,057	Dale Frost, 1951 p, 1:58 $204,117	Hal Dale, 1926 p, 6, 2:02¼	Abbedale, 1917 p, 2:01¼	The Abbe — Chimes / Nettie King Daisydale D. — Archdale / Mrs. Tmolus
			Margaret Hal, 1914 p, 2:19½h	Argot Hal — Brown Hal / Lady Wildflower Margaret Polk — John R. Gentry / Stella Hal
		Galloway, 1939 p, 2:04½h $5,294	Raider, 1929 p, 1:59½	**PETER VOLO** — **PETER THE GREAT** / Nervolo Belle Nelda Dillon — **DILLON AXWORTHY** / Princess Nelda
			Bethel, 1926 p, 2:03	David Guy — **GUY AXWORTHY** / Belle Zombro Annotation — Azoff / Citation
	Countess Vivian, 1950 p, 3, 1:59 $43,262	King's Counsel, 1940 p, 6, 1:58 $44,930	**VOLOMITE**, 1926 3, 2:03¼ $32,649	**PETER VOLO** — **PETER THE GREAT** / Nervolo Belle Cita Frisco — **SAN FRANCISCO** / Mendocita
			Margaret Spangler, 1918 p, 2:02¼	**GUY AXWORTHY** — Axworthy / Lillian Wilkes Maggie Winder — Oratorio / Clara Direct
		Filly Direct, 1941 p, 3, 2:06¾h $6,299	Billy Direct, 1934 p, 4, T1:55 $12,040	Napoleon Direct — Walter Direct / Lady Erectress Gay Forbes — Malcolm Forbes / Gay Girl Chimes
			Calumet Edna, 1931 p, 2:08½h	**PETER THE BREWER** — **PETER THE GREAT** / Zombrewer Broncho Queen — Empire Direct / The Broncho
La Pomme Souffle, 1972 p, 2, 2:02 $1,475	Nevele Pride, 1965 4, T1:54.4 $873,350	Star's Pride, 1947 5, 1:57.1 $140,969	Worthy Boy, 1940 3, 2:02½ $25,688	**VOLOMITE** — **PETER VOLO** / Cita Frisco Warwell Worthy — **PETER THE BREWER** / Alma Lee
			Stardrift, 1936 2:03	**MR. MCELWYN** — **GUY AXWORTHY** / Widow Maggie Dillcisco — **SAN FRANCISCO** / Dilworthy
		Thankful, 1952 4, T2:03.2 $31,104	Hoot Mon, 1944 3, 2:00 $74,950	Scotland — Peter Scott / Roya McKinney Missey — **GUY ABBEY** / Tilly Tonka
			Magnolia Hanover, 1944 3, 2:13.1h $1,167	Dean Hanover — **DILLON AXWORTHY** / Palestrina Melba Hanover — Calumet Chuck / Isotta
	Pompanette, 1965 3, 2:05 $39,004	Florican, 1947 5, 1:57.2 $152,222	Spud Hanover, 1936 4, 2:03 $7,917	Guy McKinney — **GUY AXWORTHY** / Queenly McKinney Evelyn The Great — **PETER THE GREAT** / Miss De Forest
			Florimel, 1938 2, 2:03½ $16,594	**SPENCER** — Lee Tide / Petrex Carolyn — **MR. MCELWYN** / Harvest Gale
		Spinster Hanover, 1952 4, T2:00.4 $17,496	Bill Gallon, 1938 3, T1:59½ $45,939	Sandy Flash — **PETER VOLO** / Miss Bertha Dillon Calumet Aristocrat — Belwin / May W.
			The Old Maid, 1945	**GUY ABBEY** — **GUY AXWORTHY** / Abbacy Spinster — **SPENCER** / Minnetonka

Gene Abbe

Gene Abbe is a horse who has meant several things to harness racing. As a racehorse, he was a stakes and FFA performer during a five-year racing career. As a stallion, he has single-handedly saved an important branch of the Abbe pacing line. From a business standpoint, Gene Abbe was the first commercial stallion to use artificial insemination and this paved the way for the use of this method with more stallions.

We will first look briefly at Gene Abbe's racing career, which spanned the years 1946 through 1950 - an era of mostly low purses and one in which heat racing was prevalent for two- and three-year-olds and even in some top FFA events.

Gene Abbe was bred by Clint Lighthill of Ottawa, Ohio. He owned the fast, but temperamental, mare Rose Marie p,2:05h and bred her to Bert Abbe after she had produced the decent racehorse Joe C. Abbe p,2:08.4h. Gene Abbe was Rose Marie's fifth foal and the second by Bert Abbe.

Raced at two in 1946, Gene Abbe lost both heats in his first start but then won 14 consecutive heats in his next seven starts to end his season with a nice winning streak. Of course, this feat attracted attention and before the start of his three-year-old season, Gene Abbe was sold to Harry Short, a trainer-driver from Columbus, Ohio.

After winning 35 of his 53 starts at two and three, mainly on the Ohio Fair Circuit, Gene Abbe had to face tougher horses at four. He began a three-year odyssey which would take him from coast to coast and to Canada, racing against the nation's best Free-For-Allers and holding his own.

Gene Abbe was sold at the end of his four-year-old season at the Harrisburg sale to Charles Ruderman of New York for $11,500 - the highest priced aged horse sold there that year.

At five, and trained by Fred Parks, Gene Abbe was lame early in the year but made it back to the races in July and again battled his way up among the FFA leaders. He won nearly $21,000 and was sold at the end of the year in California for $15,500 to Mildred Knisley who had a nice racing stable.

Following his six-year-old season in 1950, Gene Abbe was retired to stud at Mrs. Knisley's new farm in Ohio. However, he was not aggressively promoted and had only 31 registered foals in his first four crops. Pickwick Farm owner Walter Michael took note of Gene Abbe's early success as a stallion, from his few foals to race, and purchased him for his own farm. There, Gene Abbe would get better mares and receive much more promotion as a stallion.

As already mentioned, Gene Abbe was a pioneer stallion in the use of artificial insemination. How did this come about? During the early 1960s, when Gene Abbe was standing stud in Pickwick Farms in Ohio, he was under the care of farm manager Hal Jones. Jones, long one of the sport's most respected farm managers who later managed Blue Chip Farm, Hanover Shoe Farm and Lana Lobell Farm, spoke of the Gene Abbe experience in a 1984 *Hoof Beats* article. He said that farm owner Walter Michael "was interested in the quantity of mares we bred, not necessarily the quality of the mares we bred." Jones continued, "He wanted to know how many mares a stallion was breeding, not how good they were."

So Gene Abbe was bred to 181 mares in 1961 through artificial insemination and other breeders suddenly developed more than a passing interest in the technique. Refinements were made through the years and today artificial insemination is commonplace. If only for that contribution, Gene Abbe has a place in Standardbred history.

Sire Line

Gene Abbe's male line was only five generations removed from the founding father Hambletonian through Bert Abbe-The Abbe-Chimes-Electioneer-Hambletonian.

Checking this male line, Gene Abbe's sire Bert Abbe had not sired a good stallion son until Gene Abbe came along. In addition, it appeared the male line descending from The Abbe would only be carried forward by his son Abbedale who sired Hal Dale - the stallion who gave us the lines leading to Adios, Meadow Skipper and Good Time.

But, Gene Abbe saved the day for this branch of The Abbe male line and his son Big Towner has been one of the sport's leading sires for a

Race Record Highlights

At 2

1st numerous Ohio Fair S.

At 3

1st numerous Ohio Fair S.

At 4

1st Goshen Grand Circuit S.

At 5

1st Downing Memorial P. (1½ miles)
Downing Memorial Preview (1½ miles)

2nd Saratoga Grand Circuit S.
Empire P.
Chicago Pacing Derby Final

3rd heat of Chicago Pacing Derby

At 6

1st Chicago Pacing Derby (1 1/16 miles)

2nd heat of Great Lakes P.

3rd heat of Chicago Pacing Derby

Gene Abbe

Photo courtesy of the USTA

Race Record

Year	Age	Starts	Wins	2nd	3rd	Earnings	Record
1946	2	16	14	0	1	$ 2,940	p,2,2:10¼
1947	3	37	21	6	4	8,884	p,3,2:03.4h
1948	4	40	6	9	6	6,815	
1949	5	26	5	6	5	20,888	p,T2:00.3
1950	6	32	3	6	3	11,712	
		151	49	27	19	$51,239	p,T2:00.3

Gene Abbe

number of years. In addition, Big Towner's sons Broadway Express and Walton Hanover have had some success. Another Gene Abbe son, Fortune Richie, has given us million-dollar winner Dorunrun Bluegrass who is now trying to become established as a sire. But it looks like the future of the Gene Abbe line now rests with the sons of Big Towner and the flame of that future is showing signs of flickering.

Gene Abbe's sire Bert Abbe p,1:59¼ was a fast horse in the 1920s and has an interesting pedigree. His second dam was a mare named Nelly Patch who was foaled in 1903, a daughter of the legendary great racehorse and "showman," Dan Patch.

This male line is very important to the Standardbred breed since it provides another outcross line for breeders. And it has been a very strong line since both Gene Abbe and his son Big Towner have produced great racehorses as well as top fillies who later went on to become exceptional broodmares.

Maternal Line

Gene Abbe never took a 2:00 record, nor did any member of his maternal family at the time he went to stud. Rose Marie, Gene Abbe's dam, traces back six generations to a mare named Kit who was foaled over 120 years ago. The rest of the pedigree is lost to the ages.

Rose Marie had 11 foals, nine of them taking records. Gene Abbe was by far the best, the next in line being Counsel Pick p,2:05h ($62,313). Rose Marie may be an indicator of the toughness of this family since she produced her last foal at the age of 25 - pretty late for a broodmare. Her son Gene Abbe also exhibited longevity. He was 34 years of age when he died in 1978 at Blue Chip Farms, where he is buried. He had been moved to Blue Chip Farms from Ohio several years earlier when he was already an "aging" stallion.

Gene Abbe had a half-sister named Sorpresa Rosa (by Direct Brewer) and her Baron Hanover daughter Baroness Betty Jo produced a couple of nice performers in Silver Similie p,1:57 ($224,762) and Betty Jo Chris p,1:59 ($193,869) - both by the Good Time son Chris Time. They broke the logjam and began the flow of 2:00 performers from this maternal family. However, it is still a very minor family and not doing particularly well.

Progeny of Note

Gene Abbe had one of the longest stud careers on record, standing commercially from 1951 through 1977. He sired a total of 1,073 foals with 871 starters for an excellent 81% starter ratio. His offspring won $26,784,061 on the racetracks with 42 taking marks of 2:00 or faster.

The largest number of foals from Gene Abbe's Ohio crops were 103, 108 and 127 from 1961 through 1963 respectively. Thereafter, his crops numbered mostly from 39 to 64 foals into his mid-twenties

In 1962, 1963 and 1964, Gene Abbe was second only to Adios on the money-winning pacing sire listing. He gained the top ranking for the first time in 1965 over Adios. I must point out that Gene Abbe had far more horses on the racetracks than Adios did at this point. However, this is not to diminish Gene Abbe's achievement of becoming the sport's leading money-winning sire during this period and remaining in the top group for years. Later, he would be among the leaders as a broodmare sire.

Gene Abbe sired 60 $100,000 winners during his stallion career. Two of his three top earners were the full brothers and major FFA stars of the early 1960s, Irvin Paul p,4,1:58.3f ($548,518) and Stephan Smith p,1:58.4h ($335,527). I grew up watching this pair compete at Yonkers and Roosevelt Raceways in New York when I first began following the sport. They were two tough customers on any size track - so typical of Gene Abbe and the type of horses he sired.

Ironically, those great brothers were two of only three living foals from Gene Abbe and the mare Edalena. When bred to four other stallions, and producing five foals, Edalena never produced any horse faster than 2:05.1. Her five foals had combined earnings totalling just over $28,000. In contrast, Irvin Paul and Stephan Smith totalled over $884,000. Talk about a stallion moving up a mare!

Of course, Gene Abbe's greatest son is Big Towner p,4,1:54.4 ($547,126 (see his chapter). Suffice to say here he was a tough racehorse in the mold of his sire and has become one of the truly outstanding stallions of the modern era. Gene Abbe was 30 years old when Big Towner was born and 31 years old when his other good siring son Fortune Richie p,3,2:00.1f ($179,902) was born. Age certainly did not seem to be a factor with Gene Abbe.

Another fast and hard-hitting son of Gene Abbe was Sly Attorney p,4,1:54.4 ($315,051). He is followed in the money-winning list by Blaze Pick p,1:59h ($297,677) who was a top racehorse, but today is more recognized as the sire of the dam of the great racehorse and top stallion Jate Lobell p,3,1:51.2 ($2,231,402).

Another top performer in the "golden era" of the mid-1960s in New York was Rex Pick who regularly did battle with the likes of Cardigan Bay in the FFA events. Rex Pick p,4,2:00.2h ($277,918) was another ultra-tough pacer who never knew the end of a mile. Still another was Leader Pick p,4,1:59.4 ($257,901).

The first horse to draw attention to Gene Abbe was Irish, who came from his initial crop. Irish p,2:00.2h ($227,728) was a top colt and later an outstanding FFA performer who raced in the mid- to late 1950s.

Gene Abbe's sons were far better on the track than his daughters, although the daughters later excelled as broodmares. His richest daughter is No Thru Traffic p,4,2:00.1 ($166,638); she and Poplar Wick p,2,1:59.3 ($100,151) were his only two $100,000 winners. Poplar Wick was also Gene Abbe's fastest daughter. His only other 2:00 females are Pine Needles p,3,1:59.4, Mary B. Good p,4,2:00, Gigi Blue Chip p,3,T2:00 and Honey B. Good p,4,T2:00.

Analysis

Gene Abbe was considered to be an outcross sire since he was from a different branch of The Abbe sire line and his dam certainly had no close-up ancestors which would limit breeders' choices. In fact, the closest common cross in Gene Abbe's pedigree does not come until the fifth generation when the George Wilkes son Onward appears once in Bert Abbe's pedigree and once in Rose Marie's pedigree.

Other common pedigree crosses in Gene Abbe's pedigree are the 4x6 to Bourbon Wilkes and 5x5 to the full brothers Nutwood and Pistachio. Basically, his pedigree was so non-mainstream he could have been bred to virtually any mare in North America, with the exception of daughters of Bert Abbe.

Gene Abbe did not get many mares by Adios, Good Time, Tar Heel and other top sires of his era. Most of his $100,000 winning and 2:00 performers came from daughters of sires like Attorney, Poplar Byrd, The Widower, Josedale Counterpoint, Cold Cash and others. However, when bred to the daughters of top sires Gene Abbe did very well, as would be expected.

As a broodmare sire, Gene Abbe's daughters have produced 350 in 2:00 and they've had quite a few major stars. His leading money-winning broodmare sire credit is the fine FFA performer Quite A Sensation p,3,1:53.3 ($1,085,068) followed by Boomer Drummond p,4,1:53.2 ($859,822).

Gene Abbe's most famous broodmare credit is the great racehorse, sire and broodmare sire Nero p,4,T1:55.1 ($528,208) and another Gene Abbe daughter produced the Little Brown Jug winner Happy Escort p,3,1:55.4 ($280,169).

Other stars of note are the tough, tough mare Meadow Blue Chip p,1:54.3 ($415,264), See You There p,1:53 ($339,523), Fitch p,1:53.1 ($209,117), Lola Jean p,1:53.4 ($304,245), Enlightening p,4,1:56.1f ($423,321), Strike Le Ru p,1:56.1 ($425,274) and Penn State p,1:58.4h ($494,194). And that is only scratching the surface.

The fastest male and female Gene Abbe broodmare credits, See You There and Lola Jean, are both sired by the Albatross son Good To See You. And the second richest performer, Boomer Drummond, is sired by Mariner - a full brother to Albatross. The Albatross influence worked well for extreme speed as it did for Gene Abbe's son Big Towner when he was bred to all those Albatross mares.

Meadow Skipper also clicked well with Gene Abbe mares as shown for example by Meadow Blue Chip, Nero and Skipa Napoleon p,4,T1:56.2.

Geography had a strong influence on Gene Abbe's career as a sire and as a broodmare sire. Due to the large number of Gene Abbe daughters in the Ohio area, many were bred to Baron Hanover (Bret Hanover's full brother)

Gene Abbe

when he later stood at Pickwick Farm. The cross was golden for Baron Hanover and the pair combined to produce dozens of outstanding performers.

Sometimes you come upon a factor which just leaves you shaking your head for an explanation. I was examining the pedigrees of the very best horses with which Gene Abbe was involved - both as a sire and as a broodmare sire - and noticed something interesting: the old sire Grattan Royal (Grattan-Mona) who was a foal of 1908 and was bred and last owned in Illinois. Grattan Royal sired three in 2:00, including the famous Grattan Bars p,1:59½ who won 37 of 39 starts during his career.

Well, it seems that Grattan Royal shows up in the pedigrees of the very best of Gene Abbe to a startling degree. Here are a few examples. Gene Abbe's most renowned broodmare credit is Nero and his dam is by Poplar Byrd whose dam Ann Vonian is by a son of Grattan Royal.

Big Towner, the greatest son of Gene Abbe, is from Tiny Wave, a mare by Shadow Wave whose dam Shadow Grattan is a granddaughter of Grattan Royal. In fact, Tiny Wave is bred 4x5 to Grattan Royal since she has crosses to him through both her sire and dam. Perhaps it's just circumstantial evidence, but did the extra cross to Grattan Royal make Big Towner the greatest of all the Gene Abbes?

There is more evidence in the matter. Poplar Wick, Gene Abbe's fastest daughter and one of only two $100,000 winning females, is from a Poplar Byrd mare and that sire's dam is a granddaughter of Grattan Royal. Gigi Blue Chip and Mary B Good, two of only five Gene Abbe 2:00 females, both have dams whose sire is a grandson of Grattan Royal.

Gene Abbe's son Fortune Richie who, like his sire in his early days, never had an opportunity to be bred to top mares but has sired plenty of quality, is from the mare Kathleen Grattan by Silent Grattan - a son of Grattan Royal.

One of Gene Abbe's top broodmare credits is the great mare Meadow Blue Chip and her dam is by The Widower whose dam is Widow Grattan by Grattan Royal.

These Grattan Royal crosses come from a variety of different sources - not just through a single strong sire or dam. That's why this incidence struck me and prompted further research - especially when I noted it was with the very best performers linked to Gene Abbe. Unfortunately, I don't know what it means from a genetic standpoint and probably will never know. All I can say is that if you believe in "nicks" in pedigrees, these are some prime examples.

In summary, Gene Abbe was one of those stallions who appeared to be ahead of his time, given his modest pedigree and his lack of opportunity with the sport's best mares until very late in his career. It's amazing what he did accomplish against some strong competition and he certainly rates as a legendary sire as far as the pacing breed is concerned. Let's hope one of Big Towner's sons can keep this line going.

Leading Progeny by Gene Abbe

Fastest
- Big Towner, h, p,4,1:54.4 $547,126
- Sly Attorney, h, p,4,1:54.4 $325,051
- Mark B Time, h, p,1:55.1 $216,219
- Happy Abbe, h, p,1:56 $235,716
- Rostokop, g, p,4,1:56.3 $78,215
- Abbe's Good Boy, g, p,4,1:57.1 $141,489
- Dopey Diesel, g, p,1:57.3 $128,161
- Mike Pick, h, p,1:58 $60,341
- Jim-Bar-Gene, h, p,4,1:58 $65,128
- Nelson Guy, h, p,3,T1:58.1 $189,711

Richest
- Irvin Paul, g, p,4,1:58.3f $548,518
- Big Towner, h, p,4,1:54.4 $547,126
- Stephan Smith, h, p,1:58.4h $335,527
- Sly Attorney, h, p,4,1:54.4 $325,051
- Blaze Pick, h, p,1:59h $297,677
- Rex Pick, g, p,4,2:00.2h $277,918
- Leader Pick, h, p,4,1:59.4 $257,901
- P B Abbe, h, p,1:59.3 $239,490
- Happy Abbe, h, p,1:56 $235,716
- Exalted Ruler, h, p,2:00.1h $230,393

Gene Abbe, Bay Horse, 1944
p, 2, 2:10¼h; 3, 2:04.3h; T2:00.3 ($51,239)

Bert Abbe, 1922 p, 1:59¼	The Abbe, 1903 p, 2:04	Chimes, 1884 3, 2:30¾	Electioneer, 1868	**HAMBLETONIAN 10** — Abdallah I / Charles Kent Mare
				Green Mountain Maid — Harry Clay / Shanghai Mary
			Beautiful Bells, 1872 2:29½	The Moor — Clay Pilot / Belle Of Wabash
				Minnehaha — Steven's Bald Chief / Nettie Clay
		Nettie King, 1887 4, 2:20¼	Mambrino King, 1872	Mambrino Patchen — **MAMBRINO CHIEF** / Rhodes Mare
				Belle Thornton
			Nettie Murphy	Hamblin Patchen
	Miss Ella H., 1913 p, 2:12¼	Mack H., 1909 2:29¼h	John A. McKerron, 1895	Nutwood Wilkes — Guy Wilkes / Lida W
				Ingar — Director / Anna Titus
			Wainscot, 1890	**ONWARD** — **GEORGE WILKES** / Dolly
				Hecla — **STRATHMORE**
		Nelly Patch, 1903	Dan Patch, 1896 p, T1:55¼	Joe Patchen — Patchen Wilkes / Josephine Young
				Zelica — Wilkesberry / Abdallah Belle
			Dun Daisy	
Rose Marie, 1927 p, 2:05h	Martinos, 1913 4, 2:12¼h	Cochato, 1903 3, 2:11½	Todd, 1899	Bingen — May King / Young Miss
				Fanella — Arion / Directress
			Castanea	Pistachio
				Lindora Wilkes
		Queen Audubon, 1905	Audubon Boy, 1897	J J Audubon — **ALCYONE** / Dolly Pomeroy
				Flaxy — **BOURBON WILKES** / Kit III
			Miss Nutonia, 1896	Nutwood — Belmont / Miss Russell
				Iona — **ALCYONE** / Jessie Pepper
	Lady Permilia, 1912 p, 2:12¼h	Coastman, 1888 p, 2, 2:08¼	**BOURBON WILKES**, 1875	**GEORGE WILKES** — **HAMBLETONIAN 10** / Dolly Spanker
				Favorite — Abdallah I / Lizzie Pebbles
			Albatross	Coaster — Caliban / Sal
				Calypso — **MAMBRINO CHIEF** / Senator Mare
		Virginia Alta, 1907	Anderson Wilkes, 1884	**ONWARD** — **GEORGE WILKES** / Dolly
				Magnet — **STRATHMORE** / Miss Kirksey
			True Lady, 1899	

Good Time

"The Mighty Mite" was a name Good Time acquired during his meteoric five-year career on the racetrack from 1948 through 1952. Due to his diminutive size, Good Time was usually viewed by the public as an underdog in a race, regardless of his stellar record, and the crowds loved him for his speed and courage.

Good Time retired as the leading money-winning Standardbred of all time, a two-time Horse of the Year (three years apart) and a multiple world champion. He is one of the sport's all-time great racehorses, and one of its legends, too. He also had a wonderful stud career at Castleton Farm in which he was a top sire and later a great broodmare sire. His genetic contributions to the pacing breed are still strongly felt to this day.

This is the story behind Good Time's birth. Prominent owner and businessman William Cane wanted to breed his mare On Time to Abbedale. However, he later changed his mind and asked to switch to Hal Dale if the mare had not gotten in foal to Abbedale on the first try. She had not and was later bred to Hal Dale. Thus was Good Time conceived. Cane, retiring early from a successful construction business, owned other top horses such as Walter Dear, McLin Hanover, Mighty Medium, Chestertown, Sam Williams and Cheer Up. Under Cane's ownership, Walter Dear was a Hambletonian winner. In addition, Cane owned Yonkers Raceway and Good Time Park, the one-mile track which hosted the Hambletonian for many years in Goshen, New York.

Cane sent the yearling Good Time to Frank Ervin to break and train. Ervin was one of the best, if not the best, trainers in harness racing history. His success spanned decades and reached a pinnacle with his three-year campaign of Bret Hanover. When Cane asked Ervin what he thought of the homebred Good Time, Ervin said, according to a 1984 *Hoof Beats* article, "He's so darn small I honestly don't think he's worth a quarter." Of course, once Good Time began blowing by Ervin's more highly regarded colts in training sessions, Ervin realized Good Time was going to be something special.

Ervin estimated that Good Time stood less than 13 hands high when he received him to break as a yearling. Early in his racing career Good Time measured 13.1 hands. When he entered stud, Good Time stood just over 14 hands. He was so small that the Houghton Sulky Co. made a special model for him.

But Good Time had a racing heart all out of proportion to his size. Ervin later said, "Good Time came along when I needed a great horse. And when the sport needed a great horse." Good Time set money-winning records at both two and three; was the first horse to win over $100,000 at two and three; retired as the leading money-winning Standardbred; became the first Standardbred to earn over $300,000; was the first pacer to win over $100,000 in a single season and the first pacer to race below 1:58. At Lexington, in 1951, Good Time broke the 1:58 race record held by Directum I since 1914 and tied by Billy Direct in 1937 and King's Counsel in 1946.

Later, after Ervin had raced Bret Hanover, he was constantly asked to compare Bret and Good Time. Ervin was very diplomatic about it and made several different comments at various times. "Great as they were," Ervin said, "I'd have to say the filly Good Counsel would be my choice. How she could turn it on, even when going a quarter in :28 or even a tick faster. She was from the first crop of foals by Good Time. She was a helluva filly and seemed to be able to turn it on no matter how fast we were going."

Another time Ervin was quoted, "I could not stand up before a group and say Bret Hanover was the greatest. He was the greatest in his era, and I know that in my heart. But when talking, my thoughts wander back to Good Time 18 years before. Eighteen years can make a lot of difference, and not trying to detract from Bret's greatness, I knew I was talking to a lot of people who had never seen Good Time, and to those who had forgotten him. I hadn't forgotten him. They were both truly great horses."

"Good Time meant a lot to the horse business," said Ervin on another occasion. "They'd pay attention to that little fellow in every town we'd go. He was so little, you know, and they probably felt sorry

Race Record Highlights

At 2
1st Little Pat S.
Fox S.
Ohio Standardbred S.
American-National S.
McMahon Memorial
Two Gaits Farm S.

At 3
1st Little Brown Jug
American-National S.
Geers S.
Matron S.
Review Futurity
Poplar Hill Farm S.

At 4
1st National Pacing Derby
(1½ miles)
Empire State P.

At 4 (continued)
Star Pointer P.

At 5
1st Mid-America P.
Chicago Pacing Derby
Wolverine P.
Downing Memorial Elimination

At 6
1st National Pacing Derby
(1¼ miles)
New England Derby
Chicago Pacing Derby
U.S. Harness Writers P.
(1½ miles)
Champion FFA P.
Parshall Memorial
Farewell P.
Almahurst Farm P.

Honors
Set world record on mile track
Set world records for 1½ and 1¼ miles
At 5, set world race record
At 6, set world record for two-heat race
At 3, voted Horse of the Year
At 6, voted Horse of the Year
Retired as the richest pacer of all time
Set several single-season earnings records

Good Time

Photo by Skeets Meadors
Courtesy of Castleton Farms

Race Record

Year	Age	Starts	Wins	2nd	3rd	Earnings	Record
1948	2	17	12	2	3	$ 46,433	p,2,2:02½
1949	3	19	15	2	1	58,766	p,3,1:58.4
1950	4	20	14	1	3	52,705	
1951	5	22	14	5	2	50,589	p,1:57.4
1952	6	33	23	4	2	110,299	
		111	78	14	11	$318,792	p,1:57.4

for him. But they didn't need to. When they'd spring that gate, he'd hold his own. He had the most rhythmic gait of any horse I've ever sat behind. He had to have a great gait, as small as he was, to go that fast." However, he did not like sloppy tracks and made several breaks over them.

Ervin also related a story about Good Time and The Little Brown Jug. Good Time was likely to be the heavy favorite for the Jug. However, he was struck down by a virus a couple of weeks prior to the big race. He trained the Sunday before the race in a dull 2:07. Other trainers knew of this and more entered than expected - 16 total. But in another show of strength, will and courage, Good Time shook off the virus to win the Jug. Ervin said later, "He forgot about his sickness, his dullness and all that as soon as I turned him the right way of the track. His ears came up and he went. I worried until he cooled out and his temperature stayed normal."

At one time or another during his racing career, Good Time defeated every horse he ever raced against, including Direct Rhythm, Tar Heel, Solicitor, Dudley Hanover, Scottish Pence and Prince Adios to name a few. Following the 1952 racing season, Good Time was retired to begin his stud career at Castleton Farm in Lexington, Kentucky. Frank Ervin purchased one-quarter of Good Time when he went to stud.

William Cane died in 1956 while the stallion was leased to Castleton Farm. Cane's holdings were dispersed at the sales arena at Keeneland Race Course and Good Time went to the auction block. Charles Hill of Ohio had the last bid at $116,000, but the lease agreement stated that Castleton could match the high bid and take the horse - which it did. Good Time continued to stand at Castleton Farm until his death at 31 years of age.

Sire Line

Good Time is one of the three great siring sons of the pivotal sire Hal Dale, the others being Adios (perhaps the greatest ever), and Dale Frost who is the sire of Meadow Skipper (and the same argument can be made for him). Although Good Time did not achieve the breed-changing status of those other Hal Dale sons, he was a very strong sire in his own right. Unfortunately, the male line from Good Time did not succeed at the highest levels into the modern era as did those from Adios and Meadow Skipper.

The best sons of Good Time at stud were Race Time, Best Of All and Columbia George. All three did well for a time, with Race Time the best, but were eventually surpassed by the exploding Adios and Meadow Skipper sons at stud. Of course, those stallions had access to multitudes of well-bred and good-performing Good Time broodmares which certainly helped them along. Today, among the sons of Good Time, Race Time seems to have had the most impact on the breed, and you can read more about his racing and breeding career in his chapter.

Maternal Line

Good Time's maternal family is known as Kathleen (or Ethelwyn) and is one which has shown extreme speed and class for decades. Good Time's branch of this maternal family is also that of the excellent sire Big Towner. On Time p,3,2:03½h ($1,472), the dam of Good Time, has produced some other top pacers in addition to Good Time. His full sister, Our Time p,2,2:02.3 ($50,227) was widely considered one of the nation's top fillies of her era and is still the only filly to have won the Fox S., as she did in 1949, which was also the year her famous brother was winning the Little Brown Jug. On Time also had another stakes-winning full sister to Good Time in My Time p,3,2:01.4 ($22,130).

On Time began her broodmare career on a great note with Good Time her very first foal, followed by Our Time, her second. She produced nine foals, all winners, though none of them came close to her initial pair. However, several of her daughters went on to become effective broodmares and branches of these maternal lines are still producing good pacers today. In fact, one of Our Time's granddaughters is the dam of the well-remembered and high-class world champion, stakes and FFA winner Whata Baron p,T1:53.3 ($502,320).

Good Time's grandam was a trotting mare named Nedda Guy 3,2:03½h ($14,318), who was a top mare in her day. She is a daughter of the outstanding world champion trotting mare Nedda T1:58¼ ($12,294), who won 23 of her 43 starts. One very interesting point to observe in Good Time's dam's pedigree is that she is bred 4x5 to a mare named Esther who was a Thoroughbred mare. Esther is the third dam of the great sire Volomite and the second dam of Atlantic Express, the sire of Good Time's grandam Nedda.

Frank Ervin once ranked Good Time's younger sister Our Time as one of the five best pacers he ever trained, the other four being Adios, Bret Hanover, Good Time and Good Counsel. She became the only filly ever to win the Fox S. Her brother Good Time had won the same stake the previous year. Our Time also set a world record of 2:02.3 for two-year-old fillies. In 1948, the same year her older brother Good Time was voted Horse of the Year for the first time, Our Time was the top two-year-old filly in the nation and won over $50,000 to become the highest money-winning two-year-old up to that time.

Progeny of Note
Good Time was never bred to the high numbers of mares which the top stallions see today. His two crops with the most foals were those of 1962 and 1963 with 54 and 57 respectively. These are very small crops by today's standards. Yet Good Time rose to the top and was competitive with the very best of his day. He sired 92 sons and daughters in the 2:00 list, the fastest being Hustling Time p,4,T1:55 from the great mare Stand By.

It was the money-winning category in which Good Time was truly a standout. His top performers are Best Of All p,4,1:56.2 ($549,074), Race Time p,3,1:57 ($486,955) - both of whom became outstanding sires - Timely Knight p,1:58.1f ($448,669), Crash p,3,1:55.1 ($399,485), Columbia George p,3,1:56 ($398,324) (like Best Of All, a long-time Hanover Shoe Farm stallion), Good Time Boy p,1:58.1f ($352,976), Good Bye Columbus p,1:58f ($327,555), Timely Napoleon p,1:58.3h ($310,785) and Rivaltime p,3,1:58 ($303,449).

Good Time's famous daughter Good Counsel p,2,1:58.1; 3,1:57 ($48,900) broke the two-year-old filly record on mile and half-mile tracks. And the half-mile track record was even faster than that for colts. She also set a world record as the fastest three-year-old in a race, regardless of gender, and the fastest ever for a filly or mare. At two, Good Counsel won 14 of 16 starts and came back at three to win four of five starts.

However, Good Time's fastest daughter is not Good Counsel but Gypsy Fortune p,3,1:56.4. Good Counsel come second, followed by the former world champion two-year-old filly Timely Beauty p,2,T1:57.1 ($115,265). Another speedy filly who went on to a great broodmare career is Way Wave p,3,1:58 ($105,555). The list of top Good Time fillies seems endless and a large percentage of his best racing daughters went on to do just as well in the broodmare ranks. Good Time's three richest daughters are Blossom Time p,2:01f ($181,612) (a full sister to Race Time), All Alert p,3,1:58 ($165,713) and Scotch Jewel p,3,1:58.4 ($165,671).

Never a stranger to siring Divisional Champions, Good Time's two-year-old colt credits include the full brothers Best Of All and Coffee Break along with Race Time. Scotch Jewel was a two-year-old filly champion. Race Time took colt honors again at three as did Scotch Jewel and later All Alert.

Analysis
Good Time was a very well-bred colt in his era, possessing the Hal Dale/Volomite cross. He had no common ancestors in his first four generations and, in fact, the main common ancestor in his entire pedigree is the Hambletonian son Electioneer to which Good Time has a 5x6x6 cross.

Many of today's important Standardbreds carry Good Time blood. Artsplace has Good Time as the grandsire of his second dam. No Nukes has a 4x4 cross to Good Time and his third dam is by Good Time. Jate Lobell is 5x5x3 to Good Time and his second dam is by Good Time. Western Hanover is 5x5x4 to Good Time. David's Pass and Village Jiffy are bred 4x4 to Good Time. The great mare Ellamony is linebred 3x4 to Good Time. Another great mare, Immortality, has a 5x5x4 cross to Good Time. The dam of Shady Daisy is inbred 3x3 to Good Time and Shady Daisy is 4x4x4 to him. Island Glow is 4x6x6x4 to Good Time. As you can see, Good Time

Good Time

certainly continues to exert an influence on today's pedigrees through his descendants.

Looking at the common pedigree crosses in some of Good Time's best sons and daughters, we find some very old crosses to the famous stallion Guy Axworthy who was a foal of 1902. He was 26 years old when Good Time's second dam was foaled and that explains some of this situation. Best Of All had a 4x6x5x4 cross to Guy Axworthy, Timely Knight was 4x5x4, Crash 4x4, Timely Beauty 4x4, Gypsy Fortune 4x4 and Way Wave 4x4 - all to Guy Axworthy. Inbreeding to Volomite also produced good results, such as the 3x3 crosses to Volomite for Race Time, Good Time Boy, Good Counsel, Hustling Time and Way Wave. Good Time's outstanding son Columbia George was inbred 3x3 to Abbedale.

There are a couple of other interesting points. Hustling Time, Good Time's fastest record son, has a third dam who is very inbred 3x2 to the great historic matron Emily Ellen, in addition to his 3x3 cross to Volomite. Another is the world champion filly Timely Beauty who has a 4x4 cross to the full brother and sister Peter Volo and Volga E. - both of whom were champions in their day.

As a broodmare sire, Good Time has been extremely strong. He has sired the dams of 428 in 2:00, and this mostly before the era of extreme speed and mile tracks. When bred to Bret Hanover, and other stallions carrying his blood, Good Time daughters have been outstanding. Good Time's fastest broodmare credits are Cue Light p,3,1:51.2 (by Strike Out - son of Bret Hanover) and Alert Move p,1:51.4 (by Bret Hanover). The world champion and good sire Warm Breeze p,4,1:53.1 is also by Bret Hanover from a Good Time mare, as are High Ideal p,3,T1:55.1 and the good mares Pam Ryan p,4,1:58.3f, Lyn's Beauty p,1:58.3, Princess Sam p,3,1:59.2 and Carolina Rhythm p,3,1:59.2. Little Brown Jug winner Hot Hitter p,3,1:54f is by Strike Out from a Good Time mare.

Of course, Meadow Skipper is another strong influence for Good Time mares if only for his great son Most Happy Fella p,3,T1:55 who is from the Good Time mare Laughing Girl. Thus, Good Time is also partially responsible for one of today's most dynamic sire lines.

Albatross, and his sons Niatross and Nihilator, are responsible for some of the faster broodmare credits for Good Time, as are some of Most Happy Fella's sons such as Tyler B and Precious Fella. Another top cross for Good Time daughters was Bye Bye Byrd.

These are some of the reasons Good Time has been held in such high esteem by veteran breeders and observers of the sport. Not only was he a unique racehorse, and a great crowd pleaser and ambassador for the sport, but Good Time's bloodlines have been kept alive through the decades by the quality of his offspring, his stallion sons and his producing daughters.

Leading Progeny by Good Time

Fastest
- Hustling Time, h, p,4,T1:55 $76,817
- Crash, h, p,3,1:55.1 $399,485
- Candid Camera, h, p,4,1:55.3 $129,621
- Columbia George, h, p,3,1:56 $398,324
- Best Of All, h, p,4,1:56.2 $549,074
- Fast Clip, h, p,3,1:56.3 $231,581
- Gypsy Fortune, m, p,3,1:56.4 $80,962
- Good Show, h, p,3,T1:56.4 $22,961
- Race Time, h, p,3,1:57 $486,955
- Coffee Break, h, p,3,1:57 $217,901

Richest
- Best Of All, h, p,4,1:56.2 $549,074
- Race Time, h, p,3,1:57 $486,955
- Timely Knight, h, p,1:58.1f $448,669
- Crash, h, p,3,1:55.1 $399,485
- Columbia George, h, p,3,1:56 $398,324
- Good Time Boy, h, p,1:58.1f $352,976
- Good Bye Columbus, h, p,1:58f $327,555
- Timely Napoleon, h, p,1:58.3h $310,785
- Rivaltime, h, p,3,1:58 $303,449
- Local Time, h, p,3,1:59.1 $281,427

Good Time, Bay Horse, 1946
p, 2, 2:02.1; 3, T1:58.4; 1:57.4 ($318,792)

Hal Dale, 1926 p, 6, 2:02¼	Abbedale, 1917 p, 2:01¼	The Abbe, 1903 p, 2:04	Chimes, 1884 3, 2:30¾	**ELECTIONEER**	Hambletonian 10 / Green Mountain Maid
				Beautiful Bells	The Moor / Minnehaha
			Nettie King, 1887	Mambrino King	Mambrino Patchen / Belle Thornton
				Nettie Murphy	Hamblin Patchen
		Daisydale D., 1908 3, 2:15¼	Archdale, 1897	Expedition	**ELECTIONEER** / Lady Russell
				Aline	Allie West / Coquette
			Mrs. Tmolus, 1901	Pactolus	Patronage / Buda
				Flaxey	
	Margaret Hal, 1914 p, 2:19½h	Argot Hal, 1903 p, T2:04¾	Brown Hal, 1879	**TOM HAL JNR**	Kittrel's Tom Hal / Julia Johnson
				Lizzie	John Nederland / Blackie
			Lady Wildflower, 1891	Duplex	Bay Tom Jnr
				Sally Ward	Bennett Chapman / Sweepstakes
		Margaret Polk, 1906	John R. Gentry, 1889 p, T2:00½	Ashland Wilkes	Red Wilkes / Daisy B
				Dame Wood	Wedgewood / Fancy
			Stella Hal, 1885	**TOM HAL JNR**	Kittrel's Tom Hal / Julia Johnson
				Dolly	Pat Malone / Old Bald
On Time, 1938 p, 3, 2:03½h $1,472	Volomite, 1926 3, 2:03¼ $32,649	Peter Volo, 1911 4, 2:02	Peter The Great, 1895 4, 2:07¼	Pilot Medium	Happy Medium / Tackey
				Santos	Grand Sentinel / Shadow
			Nervolo Belle, 1906	Nervolo	Colbert / Nellie D
				Josephine Knight	Betterson / Mambrino Beauty
		Cita Frisco, 1921	San Francisco, 1903 2:07¾	Zombro	McKinney / Whisper
				Oniska	Nutwood Wilkes / Bay Line
			Mendocita, 1899	Mendocino	**ELECTIONEER** / Mano
				ESTHER	Express / Colisseum
	Nedda Guy, 1928 3, 2:03½h $14,318	Guy Axworthy, 1902 4, 2:08¾	Axworthy, 1892 3, 2:15½	Axtell	William L / Lou
				Marguerite	Kentucky Prince / Young Daisy
			Lillian Wilkes, 1886	Guy Wilkes	George Wilkes / Lady Bunker
				Flora	Langford
		Nedda, 1915 1:58¼	Atlantic Express, 1908 T2:07¾	Bellini	Artillery / Merry Clay
				Expressive	**ELECTIONEER** / **ESTHER**
			Pleasant Thought, 1901 T2:21	Prodigal	Pancoast / Beatrice
				Extasy	Baron Wilkes / Ethelwyn

Jate Lobell

Jate Lobell compiled one of the best modern-day records of any Standardbred and retired as the third richest pacer of all time after just two seasons of racing. He was undefeated at two and was voted divisional champion each season he raced. Jate Lobell has also compiled an enviable record as a stallion.

Bred by Alan Leavitt's Lana Lobell Farm of New Jersey, Jate Lobell was purchased as a yearling for $20,000 by Joseph McCluskey of Battle Creek, Michigan, and trained by Mark O'Mara. Jate Lobell made his racing debut at Chicago's Maywood Park on June 18, 1986, winning by 18 lengths in 2:01.4. This was a signal of things to come: the average margin of victory in Jate Lobell's 15 wins at two was four and three-quarter lengths, including two 13-length wins in stakes races.

A week after his Maywood qualifier, Jate Lobell won over the same half-mile track in 1:58.4. He then won an overnight event at The Meadowlands in 1:57.4. His first stakes engagement came on August 2nd in the $100,000 Abe Lincoln S. at Maywood Park and Jate Lobell showed early that he was an awesome pacer. Drawing the rail for the first time, he made a break before the start and found himself sixth at the quarter and half. O'Mara took him to the outside and Jate was fourth in the stretch, only a couple of lengths from the leader. Finding racing room, Jate got up in time for a dramatic win by a neck in 1:58.3.

His next four races on the big mile tracks of Springfield and Indianapolis really showcased Jate's speed. In the Little Pat S. at Springfield, Jate won in straight heats of 1:53.3 and 1:55.3 by five and 13 lengths. At Indianapolis in the Fox S., Jate won his Elimination in 1:54.3 after taking the early lead, getting shuffled back, and then coming from fifth in the stretch to win by a length over Redskin. The second heat was all Jate Lobell. He grabbed the lead at the three-quarters and went on to a 1:54.1 win with a final quarter in :26.2.

Jate Lobell's next stop was Louisville Downs for the Kentucky Pacing Derby where he won his Elimination and Final, equalling Barberry Spur's world record of 1:55.2 for two-year-olds on a half-mile track and setting a two-heat record of 3:52.2. His Elimination win was not easy, however, as Jate was parked out to the half in :57.4 before finally getting the lead. He went on to win by a length and one-half in 1:57 over Marvel and Redskin. The $384,570 Kentucky Pacing Derby Final was a lot easier for O'Mara and Jate. They sat third most of the mile and powered home in :28.2 to win in the 1:55.2 world record-equalling time by two lengths over Simcoe Hanover.

Then it was back to Chicago for a 1:55.2 five-length win in the $106,200 American-National S. over Redskin. Jate Lobell's next stop was The Red Mile in Lexington, Kentucky, where he was bet down to 1-20 in each heat of the International Stallion S. Jate won his Elimination wire-to-wire over Marvel in 1:56 and came back to take the Final in 1:53, over a sloppy track, to become the second fastest two-year-old colt of all time and miss Nihilator's world record by only one-fifth of a second.

Heading north to New Jersey, Jate Lobell raced in the Lou Babic Memorial at Freehold and won his Elimination in 1:56. A week later, he ended his season with a three-length win in the $254,550 Babic Final. This was his fifteenth consecutive win during an undefeated season in which he won $585,804 and earned divisional honors. He was not eligible for the Breeders Crown that year.

In any other year, Jate Lobell might have won Horse of the Year honors, but Free-For-Aller Forrest Skipper was also undefeated in 15 starts and had more support among the voters. so Jate was second in the Horse of the Year balloting - an outstanding achievement for a two-year-old.

Before the three-year-old season got underway, Jate Lobell was syndicated for $12,000,000 by Tom Crouch of Kentuckiana Farms which also joined Joe McCluskey in ownership of the colt.

Race Record Highlights

At 2
1st International Stallion S.
Lou Babic Memorial
Abe Lincoln P.
Kentucky Pacing Derby
Fox S.
Review Futurity
American-National S.

At 3
1st North America Cup
Confederation Cup
New Jersey Classic
American-National S.
Prix d'Ete Elimination
New Jersey Futurity
five New Jersey Sires S.

At 3 (continued)
2nd Messenger S.
Prix d'Ete Final
Meadowlands Pace Elimination
Slutsky Memorial
Oliver Wendell Holmes Elimination
3rd Breeders Crown Final and Elimination

Honors
Voted Two-Year-Old Pacing Colt of the Year
Voted Three-Year-Old Pacing Colt of the Year
Equalled world record for two-year-olds on half-mile track
Set world record for two heats for two-year-olds on half-mile track

Jate Lobell

Photo by Monica Thors
Courtesy of The Horseman and Fair World

Race Record

Year	Age	Starts	Wins	2nd	3rd	Earnings	Record
1986	2	15	15	0	0	$ 585,804	p,2,1:53
1987	3	25	15	7	2	1,645,598	p,3,1:51.2
		40	30	7	2	$2,231,402	p,3,1:51.2

Jate Lobell

Coming back at three in 1987, Jate was rated number one on the Experimental Championship Ratings at 1:49. If achieved, that time would have made him the fastest harness horse of all time. That's the kind of respect Jate Lobell had after his great two-year-old season.

Jate began the year with two qualifying race wins in April at Pompano Park and The Meadowlands - both in 1:55.3. He opened his racing season with three easy wins in New Jersey Sires S. events at The Meadowlands with the fastest in 1:53.3. However, Jate Lobell met with his first career defeat in his nineteenth start at the hands of upstart Run The Table. The setting was the $200,000 New Jersey Sires S. Final. Jate Lobell had the rail and he held the lead to mid-stretch when Run The Table caught and passed him by a neck. The two battled down the stretch in a furious last eighth, but Run The Table prevailed by a length and one-half in 1:51, pacing his own final quarter in :26.4.

Getting back on the winning track, Jate Lobell won his next five starts, including a six-length win over Run The Table in the $500,000 New Jersey Classic in 1:51.2 which turned out to be his lifetime record. The rich North America Cup at Canada's Greenwood Raceway was included in this streak and Jate won his Elimination easily in 1:54.1. The $1,000,000 North America Cup Final was a nailbiter for Jate Lobell and his connections. He had the rail and was pacing nicely in front through fractions of :27.3, :55 and 1:23.2. He had just over a length lead in mid-stretch and looked comfortable until Frugal Gourmet made a run at him to the wire. It took the photo-finish camera to separate the two colts, but Jate Lobell prevailed by a nose in 1:52.3.

Two weeks later, Jate won the $353,700 American-National S. in 1:53 at Sportsman's Park for his 23rd career win from 24 starts. Jate then lost three consecutive races. He lost by a neck to Frugal Gourmet in a Meadowlands Pace Elimination and then drew post nine for the $902,500 Final. In that rich Final, Jate Lobell had the worst race of his life. He was tenth at the quarter and at the half and ninth by eleven lengths in the stretch. He finally found racing room, along with his best pace, but could only get up to seventh at the finish, four lengths behind the winning Frugal Gourmet. Jate had paced his final quarter in :26 flat, but his early dalliance cost him the race. Three weeks later, Jate Lobell was defeated again by Frugal Gourmet after setting the early fractions but tiring in the stretch.

The old Jate Lobell returned twelve days later for a 1:51.3 win in an Open event at Springfield. Just five days later, Jate raced in the Prix d'Ete at Blue Bonnets in Canada, winning his Elimination in 1:56.2. In the Final, he was second all the way and lost by a neck to his nemesis Frugal Gourmet in 1:54.1. The Confederation Cup at Flamboro Downs was next and Jate led wire-to-wire in both heats, winning his Elimination in 1:57 and the Final in 1:54.1.

After winning two New Jersey Sires S. at Freehold, Jate Lobell then endured another three-race losing streak in which he finished second each time. But the defeats were not for lack of effort. The first loss was in the $447,310 Messenger S. at Roosevelt Raceway. Leaving slowly from post eight, Jate was ninth at the quarter and half until he made a sweeping move to the lead on the outside at the three-quarter pole. But the big effort took its toll and Jate tired in the stretch, where he was caught by Redskin. In the Slutsky Memorial at Monticello the following week, Jate Lobell was second to Call For Rain in his Elimination and second to that colt again in the Final after being forced to go three-wide in the second half to get into contention.

Jate Lobell rebounded after these losses to win the New Jersey Futurity at Freehold in 1:56, on the last day of October. He was then made ready for the season-ending Breeders Crown which was to be raced in mid-November. Unfortunately, Jate Lobell was apparently tired after a long 25-race campaign, which did not auger well because he had to face the division's late season star Call For Rain along with Run The Table. In his Breeders Crown Elimination, Jate was sixth at the half. He worked his way up to third in the stretch only to fall back a bit, failing to challenge the leaders. Run The Table defeated Call For Rain by a neck with Jate Lobell another three lengths back in third place.

The Breeders Crown Final was Jate Lobell's last race and he was shuffled back and locked in until late in the stretch. Although he closed in :27.3, he still finished third, a length behind the winning Call For Rain and Run The Table. For the year, Jate Lobell won 15 of his 25 starts with earnings of $1,645,598 and earned Three-Year-Old Pacing Colt of the Year honors.

Sire Line

Jate Lobell is a son of No Nukes who is shaping up to become a sire of good sires. Jate has been his most successful son and others of note are Dexter Nukes, Die Laughing and Western Hanover. Since Jate Lobell is from the first crop of No Nukes, he helped establish that great stallion and is now making a name for himself.

No Nukes and Jate Lobell are from the Most Happy Fella sire line through his son Oil Burner. Most Happy Fella has been the most successful son of Meadow Skipper in terms of being able to carry on the male line through several more generations and Jate Lobell also has a number of sons who will try to extend the line.

When Kentuckiana Farms owner Tom Crouch was interviewed in the August, 1994, issue of *Hoof Beats*, he discussed the gait of Jate Lobell. "We know what Albatross has done for the breed, but that's not to say that Meadow Skipper didn't. Meadow Skipper started the evolution. And Jate Lobell was the first horse whom I'd seen since Albatross who again was changing the gait of our pacer," said Crouch.

He added, "Jate showed pure speed, and Lord only knows how fast he could go. He was a powerful horse, he got off the ground, and he stayed off the ground. He was big-gaited, he was handy, and he was very athletic. He was gaited completely different than No Nukes."

You can read more about No Nukes, Oil Burner and Most Happy Fella in their chapters.

Maternal Line

The maternal family of Jate Lobell is very interesting because it is an obscure family when compared to those that have hundreds of 2:00 performers. His maternal family is known as the O'Keefe Mare family and its first 2:00 credit did not appear until 1970. Even today, the only active branch is through Jate Lobell's dam J.R. Amy.

J.R. Amy was a non-record mare sired by the Gene Abbe son Blaze Pick p,1:59h who had only three in 2:00 from a small number of foals. Of course, Gene Abbe blood in a pedigree has never hurt any stallion, in my opinion. J.R. Amy was the only foal from her dam, the Good Time mare Good Time Minnie p,4,2:05.4 ($14,476). Jate's third dam was The Widower mare Minnewashta p,3,2:01 ($38,312) who was tough and compiled 40 wins during her career. The next dam is Minnehaha p,2:02¼ who was a good racemare in the mid-1930s.

Aside from the great production of J.R. Amy, there have been few other stars from this maternal family. Minnewashta produced Bye Bye Dannibyrd p,4,1:59.4 ($90,118) and her full sister, Lea, is the grandam of Bat Champ p,1:55.4f ($326,679). Beyond that, there is not much.

However, great producing mares sometimes come from strange sources and the dam of Jate Lobell is a good case in point. If you are a romantic, you can look at J.R. Amy's pedigree and say that the fountain of her ability to produce top pacers is Dan Patch. Dan Patch, you say? The harness racing legend of the early 1900s? How can that be?

Well, J.R. Amy can be traced back to Dan Patch through both her sire and dam. Her sire Blaze Pick is a grandson of Bert Abbe whose dam is a daughter of Nelly Patch - by Dan Patch. J.R. Amy's dam, Good Time Minnie, is a great-granddaughter of the mare Theda Patch who is also by Dan Patch. Thus, J.R. Amy has a 6x5 cross to Dan Patch in her pedigree. Obviously, that is stretching reality to think her success as a broodmare comes strictly from Dan Patch who had actually failed to produce anything of note during his career as a stallion. And the cross is so far back that it probably does not affect today's performers to a great degree. Still, it's an interesting sidelight to the story of J.R. Amy.

Jate Lobell

J.R. Amy was bred by J.R. Miller of Dutton, Ontario. She did not race and was bred at two to J.R. Bret, a son of Bret Hanover. Her very first foal was J.R. Decker p,4,1:55.4 ($172,279) who was a good Canadian stakes and FFA winner.

As a broodmare, J.R. Amy has produced 13 winners from 14 foals, including four in 1:55 and nine in 2:00. Besides Jate Lobell and J.R. Decker, her best performers have been Lake Hills Jeb p,2,1:54.2 ($340,953) (General Star), Jiffy Lobell p,3,1:54.3 ($56,674) (Oil Burner), One Price p,3,1:54.3 ($26,355) (Matt's Scooter), Jeanine Lobell p,3,T1:57.2 ($95,655) (J.R. Bret) and J.T. Lobell p,1:56.2f ($99,908) (No Nukes).

Seven of J.R. Amy's daughters have produced foals, but only a couple are dams of 1:55 performers. Her Slapstick daughter Jocelyn Lobell is the dam of More Stylish p,4,1:53.3 ($106,333) (No Nukes) and her Oil Burner daughter Jenny Lobell has produced Jay Lobell p,1:54.3f ($209,639) (Fortune Teller) and Jerome Lobell p,1:53.3 (Slapstick).

So Jate Lobell has an unusual maternal family, but one which has probably served him very well since it helps him link well with most daughters of today's top pacing stallions. And he is far enough removed from Most Happy Fella to permit him to be bred to daughters of stallions from his male line. Whatever factor gave J.R. Amy the ability to produce a horse like Jate Lobell seems to have been passed on to her greatest son. Perhaps she received the best genes from her two grandsires - Gene Abbe and Good Time - who are both all-time great sires.

Progeny of Note

If he had never sired anything else of note, Jate Lobell would have become well-known just as the sire of the truly great racehorse Riyadh p,1:48.4 ($2,755,427). This horse has been a standout from ages two through seven and is a multiple world record holder. He was the fastest older pacer on a mile track and also set a record of 1:49.1 on a five-eighth mile track. His major wins include the Cane P., Messenger S., Little Brown Jug Elimination, Meadowlands Pace Elimination and the U.S. Pacing Championship. As this is written, Riyadh ranks as the fifth fastest horse in a race and the sixth leading money-winning pacer of all time.

Jate Lobell also has three other $1,000,000 winners to his credit, David's Pass p,3,1:50.4 ($1,652,500), Gothic Dream p,3,1:50.4 ($1,528,671) and Village Jasper p,3,1:51 ($1,057,595). David's Pass won two $1,000,000 races in a single season - the North America Cup and the Meadowlands Pace, in addition to the Messenger S. and Adios S. Gothic Dream won the rich Metro S. and equalled the world record for two-year-olds in 1996 and won the $1,000,000 North America Cup in 1997. Village Jasper won 14 of 30 starts and over $1,000,000 at three with victories in the Breeders Crown and Confederation Cup.

Bo Knows Jate p,1:51.2 ($921,603) is another son of Jate Lobell who was a top young stakes performer and graduated to the FFA level. Broadway Jate p,1:51.2 ($912,976) is a stakes and FFA winner and more proof that the Jate Lobell offspring continue to improve with age. Safely Kept p,2,1:52.4 ($866,999) was a fast stakes-winning two-year-old and also won the $1,000,000 North America Cup. Speaking of the North America Cup, Jate Lobell won that $1,000,000 event in 1987 and his sons have also won it - in 1992, 1995 and 1997. Quite an accomplishment for any sire.

Kingsbridge p,4,1:51.2f ($693,569) scored a surprise win in the 1992 Breeders Crown for three-year-old colts; Megamind p,4,1:50.4-'98; ($611,474) is a major stakes winner at two and three, as was Adios S. winner Electric Yankee p,3,1:51.3f ($506,752).

Jate Lobell is able to sire prolific speed at two. America's Pastime p,2,1:51.4 ($455,832) was a good example of this when he equalled the world record in 1992 while winning the Woodrow Wilson Final. Other major two-year-old stakes winners for Jate are Metro S. winner Shipp's Saint p,3,1:54.1f ($480,555), Sheppard Memorial and

Kentucky Pacing Derby winner Caprock p,3,1:52.2 ($475,217) and Sheppard Memorial winner Armbro Mackintosh p,3,1:51.1 ($471,628) who is beginning to make a little noise as a sire.

Jate Lobell also has plenty of top fillies and they are headed by Hazelton Kay p,2,1:53.4f ($762,651) who was a Breeders Crown winner at two. Other good money-winning females are Classy River Gal p,4,1:52.4 ($530,628), Teen Talk p,3,1:52.2 ($442,607) and Low Places p,3,1:52.2 ($414,777). Jate also has fast fillies, in addition to rich ones, as attested to by his world champion daughter Sweetgeorgiabrown p,4,1:50.1 ($257,323) who is the former co-fastest female in a race. Loving Success p,3,1:51.3 ($287,012) is another speedy female.

Analysis

Ranking right with today's best pacing sires, Jate Lobell has been an outstanding success at stud. With his bookings never exceeding 136 mares in a single season, he has already sired the winners of over $43,000,000 from just seven full crops of racehorses. Jate always ranks among the top four pacing sires in terms of his offspring's money-winnings in both the all-age and two- and three-year-old categories and was the sport's leading sire of $100,000 winners in 1995 and 1996. Also in 1995, Jate Lobell was the sport's leading sire of two- and three-year-old money-winners with earnings of $4,874,031, higher than Cam Fella and No Nukes.

Jate Lobell's foals get to the races, as shown by his 89% of starters from foals. And once they get to the races, they are speedsters with 77% taking 2:00 records. In addition, over one-third of Jate Lobell's 2:00 performers have records of 1:55 or faster and he has sired over 100 $100,000 winners.

The closest common cross in Jate Lobell's pedigree is 5x5x3 to Good Time and he only has one cross to Meadow Skipper which appears in the fourth generation on his sire's side. Adios only appears once and way over in the fifth generation. Thus, Jate Lobell is very open to being bred to mares by most Meadow Skipper line stallions and certainly to daughters with Adios blood on both their male and female side. In fact, I would try to breed mares with as much Adios and Meadow Skipper blood as possible to Jate Lobell.

Now let's take a look at the pedigrees of some of Jate Lobell's best performers. First of all, I want to mention that the sire Ensign Hanover appears in the pedigrees of three of Jate Lobell's four $1,000,000 winners and his daughter Golden Miss appears in the pedigrees of eight of the 26 highest money-winners sired by Jate Lobell. This is significant since it represents a very strong "nick" of bloodlines. Another strong cross is that of mares with the blood of Bret Hanover and his sons which appeared close up in 19 of Jate Lobell's 50 $200,000 winners.

Looking at Jate Lobell's richest performers, the best is Riyadh and he has no common ancestors in his first four generations. His closest crosses are 5x4 to Billy Direct and 5x5 to Hal Dale. There is also a 5x4 cross to the full brother and sister Adios and Adieu. David's Pass is bred 6x6x4x4 to Good Time and Gothic Dream is 6x6x4x3 to Good Time. Village Jasper is 4x3 to Most Happy Fella. All three are $1,000,000 winners and do not have any close crosses by today's standards. There is a connection to the Ensign Hanover mare Golden Miss p,4,2:02.1h ($64,471) who was stakes-placed at two and three and a Fast Class winner in New York as an older mare. She is the grandam of Riyadh and the dam of Strike Out who is the sire of the dam of David's Pass. Ensign Hanover, a son of Billy Direct, is also the sire of the third dam of Gothic Dream and thus has an important connection to these three $1,000,000 winners.

Golden Miss also had several daughters who have gone on to become top producers and started other branches of the "Golden Miss family." The female descendants of Golden Miss have linked extremely well with Jate Lobell and produced many of his best sons and daughters.

Getting back to the pedigrees of Jate's best racehorses, Bo Knows Jate is 6x6x5 to Good Time; Broadway Jate is 5x2 to Meadow Skipper; Safely Kept is 5x3 to Meadow Skipper; Hazelton Kay is 5x4 to Meadow Skipper; Kingsbridge is 5x3 to Meadow Skipper and 4x3 to Overtrick; Megamind is 4x3 to Most Happy Fella and 4x4 to the half-sisters Meadow Cheer and Meadow Helene; Classy River Gal is 5x3 to Meadow Skipper and 4x4 to Good Time; Electric Yankee is 4x3 to Most Happy Fella and 5x4x4 to

Jate Lobell

Meadow Skipper; Armbro Mackintosh has no common ancestors in his first four generations; America's Pastime is 5x2 to Meadow Skipper; Sweetgeorgiabrown is 5x3 to Meadow Skipper and Swingin Single is 4x4 to Good Time and 6x3 to Adios.

That should give you a flavor of what is going on with Jate Lobell. As you can see, he is acting as an outcross sire to a large extent and the crosses you see are far different from those in the chapters of most other sires. This is largely due to his maternal family and also to the fact that his sire No Nukes is from an Overtrick mare. In years to come, I'm sure we will be seeing sons of Jate Lobell at stud who will be the sires of foals with 3x3 crosses to No Nukes through the daughters of some of that stallion's other sons. That could be an explosive speed cross.

Jate Lobell is a solid sire, works well with a large variety of bloodlines and has shown he can sire fast and durable performers. An obvious good cross is Jate Lobell with Abercrombie mares, which has already produced such standouts as Bo Knows Jate, Safely Kept, Village Jasper p,1:51 ($1,057,595) and Kettle Bee p,3,1:51 ($414,925). Jate has also crossed well with mares by Niatross and his sire Albatross. Niatross mares are the dams of Gothic Dream, Hazelton Kay and Everybodydancenow p,1:51.3 ($249,101), to name a few. Albatross dams have produced Kingsbridge, Classy River Gal, Low Places, Go For Grins p,1:51.2-'98 ($302,003), Caprock p,3,1:52.2 ($475,217) and Lookout Man p,3,1:51 ($253,323), among others.

Jate Lobell's prospects as a broodmare sire seem unlimited and his daughters are already in great demand. As this chapter is being written, Jate already has 50 2:00 credits as a broodmare sire, including Decor p,2,1:54 ($376,168) (by Artsplace), I'd Like To Win p,3,1:53.2f (by Signed N Sealed), Oranges p,4,1:52.4-'98 ($231,299) (by Precious Bunny), Timberton p,3,1:52.4-'98 (by Artsplace), Lipstick Don't Lie p,3,1:53.2-'98 (by Sportsmaster), Eyes Of An Angel p,3,1:53.3 ($224,861) (by Artsplace), Artist Stena p,3,Q1:54-'98 (by Artsplace), Stud Muffin p,3,1:54.2-'98 (by Matt's Scooter), Awesome Winner p,2,1:56.2f-'98 (by Signed N Sealed), Fox Valley Victory p,3,1:56 (by Incredible Finale), Toofunnyforwords p,3,1:54.1f ($125,925) (by Cam Fella) and Starter Hanover p,4,1:54.2f-'98 (by Walton Hanover).

Just as Jate Lobell has been very successful with Abercrombie mares, his daughters are having early success when bred to Abercrombie's great son Artsplace.

Yes, Jate Lobell is a top sire and has earned his ranking among today's best.

Leading Progeny by Jate Lobell

Fastest
- Riyadh, h, p,1:48.4 $2,763,527
- Sweetgeorgiabrown, m, p,4,1:50.1 $257,323
- Swingin Single, g, p,4,1:50.2 $252,222
- Mystical Prince, h, p,3,1:50.3 $353,293
- Kingdom Of The Sea, h, p,4,1:50.3z $66,280
- David's Pass, h, p,3,1:50.4 $1,652,500
- Gothic Dream, h, p,3,1:50.4 $1,522,421
- Megamind, h, p,4,1:50.4 $611,474
- Village Jasper, h, p,3,1:51 $1,057,595
- Kettle Bee, h, p,1:51 $414,295

Richest
- Riyadh, h, p,1:48.4 $2,763,527
- David's Pass, h, p,3,1:50.4 $1,652,500
- Gothic Dream, h, p,3,1:50.4 $1,522,421
- Village Jasper, h, p,3,1:51 $1,057,595
- Bo Knows Jate, h, p,1:51.2 $921,603
- Broadway Jate, h, p,1:51.2 $912,976
- Safely Kept, h, p,2,1:52.4 $866,999
- Hazelton Kay, m, p,2,1:53.4f $762,651
- Kingsbridge, h, p,4,1:51.2f $693,569
- Megamind, h, p,4,1:50.4 $611,474

Jate Lobell, Bay Horse, 1984
p, 2, 1:53; 3, 1:51.2 ($2,231,402)

No Nukes, 1979 p, 3, T1:52.1 $572,430	Oil Burner, 1973 p, 4, 1:54.2 $535,541	Most Happy Fella, 1967 p, 3, T1:55 $419,033	Meadow Skipper, 1960 p, 3, 1:55.1 $428,057	Dale Frost	**HAL DALE** Galloway
				Countess Vivian	**KING'S COUNSEL** Filly Direct
			Laughing Girl, 1961 p, 4, 2:04h $19,546	**GOOD TIME**	**HAL DALE** On Time
				Maxine's Dream	Knight Dream Maxine Abbe
		Dottie Shadow, 1968	Shadow Wave, 1955 p, 3, 1:56.3 $91,931	Adios	**HAL DALE** Adioo Volo
				Shadow Grattan	Silent Grattan Peacedale
			Diana Streak, 1949 p, 4, 1:58.4 $9,250	Red Streak	Pegasus Pointer Isabel Abbe
				Diana Mite	**VOLOMITE** Diana Dyer
	Gidget Lobell, 1974 p, 3, 2:00.3f $14,829	Overtrick, 1960 p, 3, 1:57.1h $407,483	Solicitor, 1948 p, 3, T1:57.2 $102,109	**KING'S COUNSEL**	**VOLOMITE** Margaret Spangler
				Jane Reynolds	Scotland Jane Revere
			Overbid, 1954 p, 2, T2:05.4 $3,524	**HAL DALE**	**ABBEDALE** Margaret Hal
				Barbara Direct	**BILLY DIRECT** Norette Hanover
		Gogo Playmate, 1967	Tar Heel, 1948 p, 4, T1:57 $119,148	**BILLY DIRECT**	Napoleon Direct Gay Forbes
				Leta Long	**VOLOMITE** Rosette
			Gogo Playtime, 1957 p, 6, 2:02.4h $50,687	**GOOD TIME**	**HAL DALE** On Time
				Dell Siskiyou	Siskiyou Elsie Truax
J.R. Amy, 1970	Blaze Pick, 1964 p, 5, 1:59h $297,677	Gene Abbe, 1944 p, T2:00.3 $51,239	Bert Abbe, 1922 p, 1:59¼	**THE ABBE**	Chimes Nettie King
				Miss Ella H.	Mack H Nelly Patch
			Rose Marie, 1927 p, 2:05h	Martinos	Cochato Queen Audubon
				Lady Permilia	Coastman Virginia Alta
		Susan Wayne, 1950 p, 2:04.3h $16,810	Orphan Wayne, 1947 2:09.4h $2,783	Worthy Boy	**VOLOMITE** Warwell Worthy
				Athlone's Princess	Athlone Guy Anna Bradford's Girl
			Miss Wayne Hal, 1940	**HAL DALE**	**ABBEDALE** Margaret Hal
				Worthy Petress	Lee Worthy Petress Binarion
	Good Time Minnie, 1962 p, 4, 2:05.4 $14,476	**GOOD TIME**, 1946 p, 1:57.4, $318,792	**HAL DALE**, 1926 p, 6, 2:02¼	**ABBEDALE**	**THE ABBE** Daisydale D.
				Margaret Hal	Argot Hal Margaret Polk
			On Time, 1938 p, 3, 2:03½h $1,472	**VOLOMITE**	Peter Volo Cita Frisco
				Nedda Guy	Guy Axworthy Nedda
		Minnewashta, 1952 p, 3, 2:01 $38,312	The Widower, 1935 p, 3, T1:59½ $19,983	**ABBEDALE**	**THE ABBE** Daisydale D.
				Widow Grattan	Grattan Royal I'm A Widow
			Minnehaha, 1932	Martinique	Dillon Axworthy The Miss Stokes
				Theda Patch	Dan Patch Thistle Bird

Jenna's Beach Boy

One of the most satisfying achievements for those involved in any form of horse racing is to see a "homebred," - a horse which the breeder keeps and races instead of selling - become a champion racehorse. For Lee and Linda DeVisser of Holland, Michigan, racing as the L. & L. DeVisser Partnership, Jenna's Beach Boy was everything they could hope for from a homebred - and more. At career's end, Jenna's Beach Boy retired as the fastest Standardbred ever in a race and the fastest on mile, five-eighth and half-mile tracks. He won 30 of 42 starts and earned $1,972,172 along the way.

Jenna's Beach Boy has set the standard for the sport in terms of absolute speed on the racetrack. It is a credit to the DeVissers that they had the courage to send Jenna's Beach Boy to the races as a four-year-old after turning down multi-million dollar offers for him following his great two- and three-year-old seasons. The sport was very fortunate to have a drawing card as popular and charismatic as the "Beach Boy" and he did not disappoint, turning in a series of spectacular efforts.

Jenna was trained from when he was a colt by Joe Holloway, who has trained horses for the DeVissers since 1986. After striking out on his own as a trainer during the 1988 racing season, Holloway has been very successful, with such credits as Mystical Maddy, She's A Great Lady, Tooter Scooter, Florida Jewel, McCluckey, Island Glow, Red Bow Tie and America's Pastime, to name just a few top horses in addition to Jenna's Beach Boy.

The DeVisser-Holloway combination has been particularly successful ever since Florida Jewel in 1990. That trotter improved greatly in the Holloway stable and went on to win FFA events at The Meadowlands, major races in Europe and finished third to Mack Lobell and Peace Corps in Sweden's Elitlopp. In 1996 the DeVisser-Holloway combination hit a jackpot rarely seen in a single season - two world champions: The mare She's A Great Lady, who set world records of 1:51 on both five-eighths and half-mile tracks, and Jenna's Beach Boy.

The name Jenna's Beach Boy was given to the colt in honor of the DeVisser's granddaughter, Jenna. This future champion was the first foal from his dam, but after she had attempted to kick him, Jenna was raised in a safer environment by a nurse mare.

Jenna's Beach Boy made his first lifetime start as a two-year-old on June 7, 1994, at The Meadowlands in a $1,000 baby race. He was driven by John Campbell, who was to be the driver for the colt's first eight trips to the post, including baby races. Jenna drew post seven and was still seventh at the three-quarter call. However, he paced home in :28 flat and closed to fourth, timed in 2:00.2. In his second baby race a week later, Jenna raced in the middle of the field until the three-quarters and then came home in :27.2 to finish second in a time of 1:57.3. He won his final baby race a week later in 1:57, getting up in the stretch for a head victory.

At this point, Jenna's Beach Boy looked like a decent colt, but there was no hint of the greatness that would follow. His first start in a New Jersey Sires S. race took place on June 29th. Jenna drew post ten and was sent off at betting odds of 12-1, the highest in his career. He left fast and had the early lead at the quarter but was then a victim of the famous "Meadowlands Shuffle" and found himself fifth on the rail and six lengths behind the leader in the stretch. He closed well to finish third and was timed in 1:56.2. In another New Jersey Sires S. event a week later, Jenna went off at odds of 9-2, sat third most of the mile and came home in a fast :27.2 to finish third, only a neck behind the winner, and timed in 1:53.4. He had shown dramatic improvement and looked more like an up-and-coming stakes colt.

On July 14th, Jenna's Beach Boy finally lived up to all expectations, pacing a tough mile on the outside until the stretch and then pulling away for a two and three-quarter length win in 1:54.4. It was a very impressive performance. The following week the $100,000 New Jersey Sires S. Final took place and Jenna's Beach Boy was second choice in the wagering. The colt left from post four and was still fourth past the half when Campbell made a three-wide move on the backstretch to get into contention. After a battle, Jenna grabbed a neck lead in the stretch but could not hold on to it and was passed by the fast-closing Sands A Flyin in 1:52.2. It was a tremendous effort on Jenna's part and the last time the colt would lose as a two-year-old.

Race Record Highlights

At 2

1st Breeders Crown Final and Elimination
Wayne Smullin Memorial Final and Elimination
New Jersey Sires S.

2nd two New Jersey Sires S.

3rd New Jersey Sires S. Final at The Meadowlands

At 3

1st Breeders Crown Final
New Jersey Classic Final and Elimination
Provincial Cup Final and Elimination
Miller Memorial Final and Elimination
Burlington S.
Rambling Willie Invitational
Meadow Skipper P.

At 3 (continued)

Magical Mike P.
New Jersey Sires S.

2nd Windy City S.

At 4

1st Breeders Crown
Driscoll Series Final and leg
Dan Patch Invitational
Senior Jug
U.S. Pacing Championship
leg of Graduate Series

Honors

Equalled world record for two-year-olds
Voted Two-Year-Old Pacing Colt of the Year
Voted Three-Year-Old Pacer of the Year
Set world record for three-year-olds on mile track
Voted Pacer of the Year at four
Set all-age world record for fastest race mile ever
Set world records on all size tracks at four

Jenna's Beach Boy

Photo courtesy of Monica Thors

Race Record

Year	Age	Starts	Wins	2nd	3rd	Earnings	Record
1994	2	12	7	2	2	$ 481,284	p,2,1:51.4
1995	3	16	14	2	0	1,031,793	p,3,1:48.4
1996	4	14	9	1	1	459,095	p,4,1:47.3
		42	30	5	3	$1,972,172	p,4,1:47.3

Jenna went on to win his final five starts, which included the $670,700 Breeders Crown Final and Elimination and the $138,084 Wayne Smullin Memorial Final and Elimination.

On August 5, Jenna easily won a Meadowlands overnight event for two-year-olds in 1:54.3. Two weeks later he won the Smullin Elimination at Rosecroft Raceway in 1:54.1 by seven lengths in his first race with Bill Fahy in the sulky. (John Campbell was committed to driving Cam's Card Shark in the Cane Pace on the same night.) In the Smullin Final, Jenna's Beach Boy showed some of his extreme speed by pacing a parked out first quarter in :26.4 from post seven, taking the lead and never looking back. He won the event by over three lengths in 1:53.3 and Bill Fahy became his regular driver.

Trainer Joe Holloway gave the colt some time off following the August 27th Smullin race as he was experiencing some allergy problems. In preparation for the Breeders Crown, Jenna qualified back at Garden State Park on September 24th in 1:54.3 and again on October 8th in 1:55.2.

That year, the Breeders Crown was held at Woodbine in Canada and the Eliminations were scheduled for October 20th. That meant Jenna's Beach Boy had only those two qualifying races during the seven-week period leading up to the Breeders Crown Elimination, which led to speculation about the colt's soundness. He was made second choice in the betting to Stand Alone, who looked very strong coming into the big race. In the race, Jenna and Fahy were parked out to the first quarter and then had the lead at the half. They yielded the front past the half and were third at the three-quarters, but later found racing room to blow by the field and win by two lengths in 1:52.4 over Stand Alone.

Still, the public was not convinced and Jenna was again made second choice to Stand Alone in the rich Breeders Crown Final. Longshot Only Pan took the early lead and hit the quarter in a fast :26.3 with Jenna's Beach Boy racing a parked out second after leaving from post eight. Stand Alone had a nice trip on the rail behind the battling front-end colts. Fahy and Jenna finally grabbed the lead and took the field to the half in :55.1. They passed the three-quarters in 1:23.1 with Only Pan fading and Stand Alone going to the outside to give chase to his arch-rival. However, Jenna had strength to spare and opened a two-length lead in the stretch which he expanded to four at the wire over Stand Alone with Dontellmenomore another five lengths back in third. The final time was a breathtaking 1:51.4 - equaling the fastest time ever recorded for a two-year-old pacing colt. Jenna's previous 1:53.3 victory over Rosecroft's five-eighth mile track tied him with Stand Alone as a Season's Champion.

So it was that Jenna's Beach Boy, a colt who lost two of his three baby races, wound up winning seven of his 12 starts - his last five coming consecutively - and earning $481,284 by season's end. He was voted Two-Year-Old Pacing Colt of the Year.

Coming back at three, Jenna's Beach Boy had a spectacular year, winning 14 of 16 starts, and earning $1,031,793. These figures would have been even more impressive had he not missed three months of racing from June 9th to September 16th - the heart of the stakes season. The last time was because he suffered a hairline fracture in the pastern bone of his right hind leg just prior to eliminations for the $1,000,000 North America Cup. He recovered so well from the injury that trainer Holloway considered entering the colt in the Meadowlands Pace on July 15th, but decided to give the injury more time to heal. This was not a good time for the DeVissers as Jenna's stablemate, No Standing Around, a $175,000 winter purchase, caught a debilitating virus which eventually caused his death.

Jenna's Beach Boy began his 1995 season by winning a qualifying race at The Meadowlands on April 7 in 1:54.4, with a final quarter in a rapid :26 seconds. A week later he won his first start in 1:54.2, closing in :26.2. In his next start, Jenna took on both three- and four-year-olds but after leading for most of a 1:50.3 mile, he was caught in the stretch and lost by a length to Cam Terrific. He was not to lose again until November 17th when Village Connection edged him out by a nose at the wire. This was after Jenna had recovered from a break at the start and led from the half until the last stride.

Following his defeat against the older horses, Jenna won five consecutive stakes, including the $165,404 Miller Memorial Final and Elimination, the $500,000 New Jersey Classic Final and Elimination and the $100,000 Burlington S. Then came the three-month layoff to heal from his injury.

Holloway eased Jenna back to the races carefully and was in the sulky to qualify him in 1:55.2 at Pocono Downs on September 1st and again on September 9 in a qualifier at Garden State Park, which he won in 1:53.3. The first actual race of Jenna's "second season" was a New Jersey Sire S. event at Garden State Park, in which Jenna proved unequivocally that he was back in top form. Jenna was parked out first over to the half in :55.4, gained the lead and took the field to the three-quarters in 1:24.3 and then sprinted home in :26.4 for an awesome 1:51.2 mile.

Not eligible for the Little Brown Jug due to a missed stakes payment as a yearling, Jenna went to Delaware, Ohio, and won an Invitational race against Riyadh and others in 1:52.1 in a wire-to-wire effort. It was then on to Lexington, Kentucky, where Jenna showed his true ability by winning the Meadow Skipper Pace on September 30th in 1:48.4, with fractions race veterans could hardly believe. Leaving from post six, Jenna and regular driver Bill Fahy had the lead at the quarter in :26.4, a 15-length lead at the :53 half (:26.1 second quarter) and sped to the three-quarter marker in an unheard of 1:19.4 (:26.4 third quarter). There was an audible gasp from the crowd at that point and Jenna kept motoring down the stretch to close his epic mile with a :29 final quarter. The 1:48.4 mile was the fastest ever by a three-year-old and the second fastest race mile in the history of harness racing.

Following this great effort, Jenna was given a week off. Two weeks later he qualified at Garden State Park and then won a conditioned race there a week later in 1:51.2. Next was the $605,000 Breeders Crown, at Woodbine in Canada, and Jenna won that race on the lead all the way in 1:52.4. This was on a very cold night with wind gusts of 35 miles per hour. Jenna's Beach Boy was looking good that night and was on the bit when the starting gate wings folded. Jenna took off and was at the first quarter in an astonishing :26. Driver Bill Fahy said after the race, "I planned on letting everyone kill themselves and just float to the front, but he had other things on his mind tonight."

Two weeks later came defeat in the Windy City S. but after that Jenna won his last three starts, in the Provincial Cup Final and Elimination and a Meadowlands Invitational, to end his three-year-old season. Jenna was crowned as Pacer of the Year for 1995, but could not match trotting filly C.R. Kay Suzie in the Horse of the Year voting.

Harness racing was blessed with the return of Jenna's Beach Boy for a four-year-old season as the gracious DeVissers chose to give something back to the sport and provide a standout box-office attraction for 1996.

Jenna's Beach Boy did his part and was voted Pacer of the Year, although his racing season was not without some surprises. Qualifying at Pompano Park in March, Jenna won in 1:53.3, but it was not until April 20th at Pocono Downs that he made his first start of the year. He was an easy winner, but a test later came back positive and he was disqualified. This was not exactly the way his connections wanted to begin the year. Holloway stated that when he trained Jenna for the first time after shipping from Florida he treated him with a medication to keep the horse from tying up. This treatment was eight days prior to the Pocono Downs race. Holloway said he had been told by veterinarians that the medication would be out of the horse's system in 96 hours. But this did not prove to be the case and the winner's share of the purse had to be forfeited, along with losing credit for another victory.

Of course, Jenna was unaware of all this and the following week won a leg of the Graduate Series at Mohawk raceway in 1:53.3, holding on by a nose over his tough rival Ball And Chain. Jenna's next three starts were at The Meadowlands and resulted in three surprising losses. The first was in an Invitational event when he lost by a half-length to L.V. Whiskers in 1:50.1. The following week, Jenna was the favorite in the $163,500 Graduate Series Final and made a break at the start. He later caught the field but had a long overland trip and finished ninth, six lengths behind victor Ball And Chain. "We tried a new bike on him and it didn't work," said driver Bill Fahy. "He got a little fired up and he just couldn't handle the first turn."

After a couple of weeks off, Jenna returned in an Invitational and got caught in a speed duel in which he was parked out to the quarter in :26.1 before taking the lead at the half in a lightning fast :53. He later gave up the lead, but held on for third in a 1:49.3 mile won by Riyadh.

During this period, after five starts, Jenna had just one official victory and $39,800 for his efforts. It was as if the nation's best aged pacers had said to him, "welcome to the big leagues, son." However, that was the end of his breaking in period as an older pacer. Jenna turned the tables on the others, winning seven of his last nine starts and setting world records on mile (1:47.3), five-eighth mile (1:49.2f) and half-mile tracks (1:49.3h) while increasing his 1996 bankroll to $459,095.

Following his third place finish to Riyadh, Jenna qualified in 1:51 and then defeated Riyadh and Ball And Chain in 1:49.3 in the Driscoll Series at The Meadowlands, with a final quarter in :26.3. The following week, in the $200,000 Driscoll Final, Jenna stayed off the front-end speed duel when Make A Deal beat him to the first quarter in :26.1, pacing on the outside from post ten. It was obvious Make A Deal would not be around at the finish, so driver Jack Moiseyev and Riyadh seized the opportunity to get the jump on Jenna. They powered to the front, reaching the half in :53.4, with Jenna sitting second on the rail. Riyadh paced a :26.3 third quarter to keep everyone at bay and took a length lead over Jenna into the stretch, with Ball And Chain another three lengths back in third. In a great stretch battle, Jenna passed Riyadh to prevail by a length in a world record 1:47.3 - the fastest race mile ever by a Standardbred.

Jenna was off the following week, after which it was on to Hoosier Park to win the Dan Patch Pace in 1:49.4. But just when it looked like he was going to roll on undefeated to the end of the year, he ran into a problem in the $244,000 American-National S. at Sportsmans Park. That track is known for its notorious first turn, which many out-of-town horses have trouble negotiating the first time. Jenna was another victim. Fahy said, "Jenna's Beach Boy was simply going too fast coming into the first turn and he couldn't handle it." Jenna did recover from the break, but had to go three-wide, eventually getting the lead at the three-quarters. But he could not hold on in a :27 final quarter and faded to eighth, with Chicago-based Falcon Dakota the race winner.

Back at The Meadowlands a week later, Jenna won the U.S. Pacing Championship in 1:49.3, in preparation for the following week's $300,000 Breeders Crown. In that race, the true Jenna was back and he won in 1:48.4. Thus, Jenna accomplished a tremendous feat, winning the Breeders Crown at two, three and four - the first pacer ever to do so.

But even the great horses get beaten and Jenna had probably the toughest trip of his life in the $267,750 Canadian Pacing Derby, just two weeks after his Breeders Crown triumph. Jenna had some bad luck at the post position draw when he got the outside post ten. Village Connection had the rail and protected his position with an incredible :25.4 first quarter, parking out Cam Terrific. Jack Moiseyev and Riyadh also wanted the lead and were three-wide in the first quarter, followed by Winning Goalie and Jenna's Beach Boy, both also three-wide. Riyadh cleared for the lead before the half in :54 with Jenna still three-wide and racing fifth. Riyadh went by the three-quarters in 1:21.4 with Jenna's Beach Boy now second and challenging Riyadh. In the stretch Riyadh had nearly a two-length lead at one point, but Jenna caught him and edged slightly ahead before yielding to the fast-closing Ball And Chain, who had enjoyed a perfect trip on the rail during the furious front-end struggle. Ball And Chain was the winner in 1:50.2, with Jenna finishing fourth, two lengths behind. However, this must have been his most courageous race ever and showed he was indeed a gritty as well as a fast pacer.

Many times after tough efforts like Jenna's in Canada, the champion horses come back with more great performances. Jenna was no exception. The last two races of his career resulted in world record performances: the 1:49.2f win at Rosecroft and the 1:49.3h win in the Senior Jug at Delaware, Ohio. Those miles were the first ever sub-1:50 performances on five-eighth and half-mile tracks. Thus, Jenna's Beach Boy ended his epic career with a flourish. He would enter the stallion ranks with even more impressive credentials and greater respect than he had after his first two racing seasons.

Sire Line

The only thing which might caution against predicting success for Jenna's Beach Boy is the fact that he is a grandson of French Chef p,2,1:54 ($371,445) - and that could be a bad rap. A great racehorse and a world champion two-year-old who won 21 of 23 starts, French Chef had better than average statistics as a sire, but was never really accepted as a major sire, even after the success of his millionaire sons Amity Chef p,3,1:51.1 and Frugal Gourmet p,3,1:51.3f. Neither of those stallions became successful at stud, which made breeders wonder about the French Chef male line in general. However, Jenna's Beach Boy is a son of French Chef's best son, Beach Towel p,3,1:50 ($2,570,357) who was a great champion on the racetrack. And Beach Towel has achieved far more success at stud, including siring 1:50 performers, than French Chef's other two outstanding sons.

Another interesting aspect of the pedigree of Jenna's Beach Boy is the trotting bloodlines from the dam of French Chef. His dam paced, but was sired by the great trotting champion Nevele Pride, from a broodmare by another great trotting champion, Florican. Trotting blood close up in great pacers is not unusual and can be found at the fastest levels. For example, the dam of Cambest, the fastest Standardbred of all time, is by Harold J. - a pacing sire with strong trotting bloodlines. Direct Scooter, certainly an outstanding sire of extreme pacing speed, has strong and close trotting blood. The dam of Niatross had much trotting blood, as did the maternal family of Nihilator. And those are just a few examples.

Being a great-grandson of Meadow Skipper, Jenna's Beach Boy has an opportunity at stud to accomplish several important things for the Standardbred breed. As many breeders already know, Meadow Skipper's greatest son, Albatross, has been having problems siring a son who will extend his line in North America. Perhaps it will be Ball And Chain, new at stud in 1997. His sons seem to be doing fine in Australia and New Zealand, but they are working with a very different gene pool. The Most Happy Fella branch of the Meadow Skipper line is doing well and looks like it will have successful sub-branches through Cam Fella, No Nukes and Tyler B.

Therefore, if Jenna's Beach Boy is commercially successful, he will help continue the French Chef branch of the Meadow Skipper sire line, which may have been saved by the success of Beach Towel. Don't forget, Meadow Skipper's influence is being more diluted with each passing generation and by the year 2000 he will appear in the fifth and six generations of many pedigrees.

Although he does not realize it, a lot rests on the shoulders of Jenna's Beach Boy concerning the future of a stallion line branch. If Jenna's Beach Boy is successful he could take the breed to even more incredible levels of speed.

Maternal Line

The maternal family of Jenna's Beach Boy can be traced way back to a mare named the Col. Morgan Mare, but the family is more commonly known as the Minnehaha or Thompson Sisters family. It is one of the strongest in the sport.

Jenna's Beach Boy is the first foal from the fast Cam Fella mare, Five O'Clock Cindy p,2,1:58.3; 3,1:54.4 ($116,375) who raced at two and three and was bred at four. Bred by Ed Freidberg's JEF's Standardbred Country Club and raced by the DeVissers, Five O'Clock Cindy was a $16,000 yearling at the 1988 Kentucky Standardbred Selected Yearling Sale. The DeVissers had purchased the filly for $50,000, on Holloway's advice, in the late spring of her two-year-old season after four baby races. In a *Hoof Beats* article, Lee DeVisser said, regarding Five O'Clock Cindy, "She was mean, bad-dispositioned and liked to nip and kick. We knew she was onery, but Joe liked her."

At two, Five O'Clock Cindy won $58,628 from her 14 starts, but had only one win and that in her next to last start of the year. However, she had seven seconds and three thirds in New Jersey Sires S. races and Early Closers at Freestate Raceway.

Five O'Clock Cindy was timed in 1:58.3 in her first parimutuel start at two and was very competitive; she only finished farther than two lengths behind the winner in three of her 14 starts. Her style at two was to come from behind and she showed closing quarters as fast as :27.4 after tough miles. In the 1989 $100,000 New Jersey Sires S. Final at The Meadowlands, Five

Jenna's Beach Boy

O'Clock Cindy was eighth, three-wide and over eight lengths behind the leader at the three-quarter pole. But she finished a rousing second by only a half-length in 1:56.2.

Unfortunately, Five O'Clock Cindy had only an abbreviated three-year-old season in 1990, winning four of 11 starts with earnings of $57,747 while taking a record of 1:54.4. She began her season early in order to race in the Meadowlands Late Closer events during February, March and April. She won a leg of the Jersey Girls Series and was second and third in legs of other series. In the New Jersey Sires S. events, Five O'Clock Cindy sparkled, winning her first by three lengths in 1:56.3, with Joe Holloway driving and the second in 1:54.4 by seven lengths, with John Campbell in the sulky. But just when she was at her best she was scratched lame from the $100,000 New Jersey Sires S. Final and that ended her racing career. The filly had kicked in a trailer while on the way to The Meadowlands and broken her hock. At three, Five O'Clock Cindy had developed more early speed - she was on top at the first quarter at Rosecroft in :27.1 parked out - she was versatile and also had a good closing kick.

The grandam of Jenna's Beach Boy is the Windshield Wiper mare Eyewash, who shows four winners from five foals. Jenna's third dam is the stakes winner Beloved Hanover p,2,2:01.3 ($43,432), a daughter of Adios, who is a full sister to world champion Bullet Hanover p,3,T1:55.3 ($132,578) and three-quarter-sister to the dam of world champions Overtrick p,3,1:57.1h ($407,483) and Overcall p,1:57.1f ($784,006). Although Eyewash and Beloved Hanover could be considered only average producers by today's standards, the roots of the family are deep.

From a pedigree cross standpoint, Five O'Clock Cindy is inbred 3x3 to Meadow Skipper and is also 4x6x3 to Adios and 4x4x4 to Dale Frost. In addition, she has a 5x4 cross to the half-brother and sister Ensign Hanover and Norette Hanover, son and daughter of the mare Helen Hanover.

Analysis

Jenna's Beach Boy is a classic linebred 3x4x4 to Meadow Skipper. His next closest common crosses are 4x5 to Bye Bye Byrd, 4x5x5x5 to Dale Frost, 6x4 to Tar Heel and 6x5x5x4 to Adios. In all, he has eight crosses to Hal Dale in his first six generations. With this type of pedigree, and with French Chef being his grandsire, Jenna's Beach Boy is set up very well to accommodate most of today's top pacing mares, except for those by Cam Fella and Beach Towel.

For example, a foal by Jenna's Beach Boy would have Meadow Skipper appearing only as close as the fourth generation on his male side, with the same holding true for Most Happy Fella. Jenna's Beach Boy would appear to be able to nick well with mares by No Nukes, Albatross, Abercrombie, Direct Scooter, Bret Hanover, Niatross, Nihilator, Big Towner, Tyler B., B.G.'s Bunny and Sonsam - all of whom are among today's leading pacing broodmare sires.

Jenna's Beach Boy had an incredible brush of speed that he could sustain and was also capable of making several moves during a race. He was able to come back from an injury, sustained his form over three years at the races, did not need a certain size track in order to perform at his best and took the sport to new levels of racing speed. He began his stallion duties at Carter Duer's Peninsula Farm in Kentucky for the 1997 breeding season and had a full book of quality broodmares. If ever a stallion has a chance to become successful, it is Jenna's Beach Boy.

Since his sire Beach Towel seems to be working very well with a variety of broodmare sires, I would suspect the same for Jenna's Beach Boy - especially with his pedigree pattern. Beach Towel also has a fondness for lots of Adios blood, which appears in the dams of many of his best performers. I think this will hold true for his son. Broodmares by Abercrombie and Bret Hanover could lead the way here as well as those by their best sons. In addition, Albatross mares bring out the best in any sire and his daughters are just about a sure thing to click with Jenna's Beach Boy.

As always in breeding matters, there are no absolutes. But Jenna's Beach Boy will certainly be given the proper chance for success at stud and may also extend another interesting branch of the Meadow Skipper sire line. If both he and Beach Towel are successful, breeders of the future will have even more choices.

Jenna's Beach Boy, Bay Horse, 16 Hands, 1992
p, 2, 1:51.4; 3, 1:48.4; 4, 1:47.3 ($1,972,172)

Beach Towel, 1987 p, 3, 1:50 $2,570,357	French Chef, 1978 p, 2, 1:54 $371,445	**MEADOW SKIPPER**, 1960 p, 3, 1:55.1 $428,057	**DALE FROST**, 1951 p, 1:58 $204,117	**HAL DALE**	Abbedale Margaret Hal
				Galloway	Raider Bethel
			Countess Vivian. 1950 p, 3, 1:59 $43,262	King's Counsel	**VOLOMITE** Margaret Spangler
				Filly Direct	**BILLY DIRECT** Calumet Edna
		La Pomme Souffle, 1972 p, 2, 2:02 $1,475	Nevele Pride, 1965 4, T1:54.4 $873,350	Star's Pride	Worthy Boy Stardrift
				Thankful	**HOOT MON** Magnolia Hanover
			Pompanette, 1965 3, 2:05h $39,004	Florican	Spud Hanover Florimel
				Spinster Hanover	Bill Gallon The Old Maid
	Sunburn, 1977 p, 2, 1:58.3 $52,216	Armbro Nesbit, 1970 p, 3, 1:56 $625,964	**BYE BYE BYRD**, 1955 p, 5, T1:56.1 $554,272	Poplar Byrd	**VOLOMITE** Ann Vonian
				Evalina Hanover	**BILLY DIRECT** Adieu
			Armbro Impel, 1965	Capetown	**HOOT MON** Margo Mite
				Dottie's Pick	**ADIOS** Pick Up
		Sunbelle Hanover, 1966	**TAR HEEL**, 1948 p, 4, T1:57 $119,148	**BILLY DIRECT**	Napoleon Direct Gay Forbes
				Leta Long	**VOLOMITE** Rosette
			Suave Hanover, 1959 p, 3, 2:03.3 $5,696	**ADIOS**	**HAL DALE** Adioo Volo
				Shy Ann	Cardinal Prince Bid Hanover
Five O'Clock Cindy, 1987 p, 3, 1:54.4 $116,375	Cam Fella, 1979 p, 4, 1:53.1 $2,041,367	Most Happy Fella, 1967 p, 3, T1:55 $419,033	**MEADOW SKIPPER**, 1960 p, 3, 1:55.1 $428,057	**DALE FROST**	**HAL DALE** Galloway
				Countess Vivian	King's Counsel Filly Direct
			Laughing Girl, 1961 p, 4, 2:04h $19,546	Good Time	**HAL DALE** On Time
				Maxine's Dream	Knight Dream Maxine Abbe
		Nan Cam, 1971 p, 5, 2:05.1f $11,390	Bret Hanover, 1962 p, 4, T1:53.3 $922,616	**ADIOS**	**HAL DALE** Adioo Volo
				Brenna Hanover	**TAR HEEL** Beryl Hanover
			Nan Frost, 1966 p, 3, 2:06.3f $1,607	**DALE FROST**	**HAL DALE** Galloway
				Mynah Hanover	Ensign Hanover Betty Mahone
	Eyewash, 1979	Windshield Wiper, 1973 p, 3, T1:53.2 $379,205	**MEADOW SKIPPER**, 1960 p, 3, 1:55.1 $428,057	**DALE FROST**	**HAL DALE** Galloway
				Countess Vivan	King's Counsel Filly Direct
			Keystone Mist, 1969	**BYE BYE BYRD**	Poplar Byrd Evalina Hanover
				Meadow Julia	Thorpe Hanover Julia Frost
		Beloved Hanover, 1962 p, 2, 2:01.3 $43,432	**ADIOS**, 1940 p, T1:57½ $33,329	**HAL DALE**	Abbedale Margaret Hal
				Adioo Volo	Adioo Guy Sigrid Volo
			Barbara Direct, 1947 p, 3, T2:00.4 $5,747	**BILLY DIRECT**	Napoleon Direct Gay Forbes
				Norette Hanover	Peter The Brewer Helen Hanover

Laag

Grey horses have always been very attractive and especially easy for the race-goer to spot. With his red harness and red shadow roll Laag was easily visible on the track. And he was so fast as he passed other colts he sometimes appeared to be a grey and red blur.

Laag earned the title "Fastest grey Standardbred of all time," an honor that was emphasized in the advertisements for stud services following his racing career. In a short time, it seemed there were grey Standardbreds everywhere - mostly due to the huge early popularity of Laag at stud, when he bred 201 and 192 mares during his first two seasons.

Another tribute to Laag's racing ability, and his popularity among the fans, was a limited edition of a collectible plastic model of Laag produced by the Breyer company - a world-famous name in the field of model horses. The only other Standardbred models they have ever released are of Adios, Niatross, Dan Patch and his sire Joe Patchen.

Laag was bred by Albert Adams, who loved grey horses and was, at the time, Executive Vice President of Almahurst Farm of Kentucky. Adams sold an interest to Earl and Geraldine Laviana of Pompano Beach, Florida and the colt, trained by Dick Farrington, raced in their names during his two-year career on the track. He was later syndicated for stallion duties.

The young grey colt began his racing career at Brandywine Raceway in a qualifying race on May 23, 1986. In a very inauspicious debut, he finished sixth and was timed in 2:06.2. However, one and one-half weeks later he came back to win another qualifier in 2:04 at the same track. Laag's first parimutuel race followed at Brandywine and he came home a winner in 2:02. It was then off to the Meadowlands to test the waters against the better freshmen. Laag passed his test with flying colors, winning a two-year-old overnight event in a scintillating 1:56.2 in mid-June with a final quarter in :27.4. He looked like a legitimate stakes colt and a coming star.

Laag's first stakes race was the Goshen Cup at The Meadowlands. This was the first occasion I saw the colt and over the years I have not forgotten his performance; he was one of the most impressive early-season youngsters I have seen. Leaving from post two, Laag was second at the quarter and then driver Bill O'Donnell took him to the front and never looked back. Laag had a three-length advantage at the top of the stretch and pulled away to a five-length win over Redskin in 1:55.3 with a fantastic sprint of :26.4 through the final quarter. He was now undefeated in his three starts and one of the most talked about two-year-olds in the nation.

But ten days later, at Rosecroft Raceway in the Potomac Pace, everything changed when Laag made a break while on a seemingly safe lead in the stretch. He continued to run through the remainder of the mile and finished fourth. The colt had injured himself and would not race again for over two months until he won a September 10th qualifier in 2:00 at Garden State Park. He was deemed ready for the International Stallion S and was shipped to Kentucky. Driven by Ron Waples, Laag left conservatively from post seven in the first heat and was still seventh at the half. Waples had him fourth on the outside on the backstretch and the colt flew through the stretch but missed by three-quarters of a length to Sticky Two Step. In the next heat, he had the lead at the half, but made a break and fell out of contention in a race won by divisional champion Jate Lobell, who was undefeated in 15 starts that year.

Laag's season was somewhat salvaged the following week at The Red Mile when he turned a lot of heads by scoring a fourteen-length win in 1:54 to become the fourth fastest two-year-old colt of the season. That was his last start of the year and he ended the season with four wins from his seven starts and earnings of $52,514. But Adams, Laviana and Farrington all knew the best was yet to come the following year.

The 1987 racing season proved to be the vindication for Laag in a very competitive year for colts. Jate Lobell and Frugal Gourmet both won over $1,000,000, followed by Run The Table's $904,022 and

Race Record Highlights

At 2

1st Goshen Cup

2nd heat of International Stallion S.

At 3

1st Tattersalls S. Final
Jug Preview
Jersey Cup
Meadowlands Pace Elimination
Prix d'Ete Elimination

2nd Meadowlands Pace Final
Oliver Wendell Holmes Elimination
North America Cup Elimination
Tattersalls S. Elimination

3rd Oliver Wendell Holmes Final

Honors

At three, set world record for dead heat win

Laag

Photo courtesy of The Horseman and Fair World

Race Record

Year	Age	Starts	Wins	2nd	3rd	Earnings	Record
1986	2	7	4	1	0	$ 52,514	p,2,1:54
1987	3	18	9	4	1	590,481	p,3,1:51.2
		25	13	5	1	$642,995	p,3,1:51.2

Laag

Laag's $590,481. However, Laag achieved several honors, the first being the season's fastest performer of any age on a half-mile track with his 1:53.4 score at Delaware, Ohio, and his world record setting 1:51.2 dead-heat with Jaguar Spur at The Red Mile in Lexington.

Laag qualified in mid-May at The Red Mile in 1:55.3 and a week later he served notice that he would be back among the elite winning his first seasonal start over the same track in 1:53.2. His first stakes engagement was in the Battle of Brandywine Elimination, in which he encountered traffic problems all the way to finish fifth and miss qualifying for the Final. He came back to win an overnight event at Brandywine the following week in 1:55.4 and then headed up to Canada for the Eliminations for the rich North America Cup at Greenwood.

Showing true grit in his Elimination, Laag had to make a long three-wide move at the half after being shuffled back to sixth at the quarter. He worked his way up to second, for driver Bill O'Donnell, but as he entered the stretch he was four lengths behind the leader. Full of pace, Laag closed the gap to just three-quarters of a length in the 1:54.4 mile, pacing his final half in about :55.3. It was a solid performance. But in the $1,000,000 North America Cup Final, Laag's luck was nothing but bad right from the draw. Drawing post nine, he was locked in fifth at the three-quarters and only managed to finish fourth behind Jate Lobell and Frugal Gourmet in a 1:52.3 mile. However, he did bring home a check for $80,000 for his owners.

After this setback it was back to The Meadowlands in preparation for another rich race, the Meadowlands Pace. Laag scored a big win in his division of the Jersey Cup with a three and three-quarter length win over Dictionary in a fast 1:51.3. Two weeks later, Laag showed he was in the best form of his career with a 1:52.1 win in his Meadowlands Pace Elimination. He was parked out third to the quarter and put his grey head in front, still parked out, at the half in :56.4. Once on top, Laag paced home in :55.2 after the tough first half, throwing in a :26.4 final quarter to win by over four lengths for O'Donnell.

The $902,500 Meadowlands Pace was next and Laag's luck changed; this time he drew the rail. Never quick out of the gate, Laag was immediately shuffled back as the result of a front-end speed duel and was eighth at the half, in the outside flow of horses. Still seventh in the stretch, and looking hopelessly out of the race, Laag found his best pace for O'Donnell and started to pick up horse after horse. But he ran out of racetrack and lost the big prize by a neck to Frugal Gourmet who won in 1:52. Laag paced his final quarter in :25.4, which showed the kind of speed he was capable of.

In the Cane Pace at Yonkers a week later, Laag was interfered with and then parked out the final three-quarters to finish fifth. The Oliver Wendell Holmes Pace was next at The Meadowlands. Laag took second in his Elimination, parked out all the way, and third in the Final - both to Run The Table.

Trainer Dick Farrington took over the reins for the remainder of the season. Laag won a Blue Bonnets Invitational in 1:53.4 over archrival Frugal Gourmet and then took an Elimination of the rich Prix d'Ete in 1:53.3, again over Frugal Gourmet, after being parked out first over to past the half. Laag was even made the odds-on favorite for the Prix d'Ete Final, but he made an uncharacteristic break at the start and was never in the race, which was won by Frugal Gourmet over Jate Lobell.

Laag then raced in the Little Brown Jug Preview at Scioto Downs and turned in another of his amazing performances. Even with the rail, Laag was a parked out fifth at the quarter, but he moved up to third with a three-wide move at the half, and was challenging for the lead on the outside at the three-quarters. He flashed home in the stretch to win in 1:54.1f.

Then, on Little Brown Jug day, a race for which Laag was not eligible, he raced on the same card at Delaware, Ohio, and set a season's record by winning in 1:53.4. This time was faster than any of the four Little Brown Jug heats contested that day. The Jug was won by Jaguar Spur who was to make history with Laag a week later at Lexington.

In a race never to be forgotten by those who witnessed it, Jaguar Spur and Laag engaged in two fantastic heats of the Tattersalls Pace. In the first heat, Laag was parked out to the half in :55.1 and finally got the lead. He had a short lead by a neck at the top of the stretch and he and Jaguar Spur battled the rest of the way head-to-head, with Jaguar Spur putting his head in front right at the wire in 1:51.3. As if that battle was not enough, these two colts came back and did it again. Laag was parked out to the quarter in :27.1 before grabbing the lead. The fractions were exactly the same for the first three-quarters as in the initial heat. This time, Jaguar Spur had a neck advantage at the top of the stretch and the two colts battled the entire distance again. They came home in :27, and the photo finish camera could not separate the two courageous warriors. The race was declared a world record 1:51.2 dead-heat. The Lexington crowd gave both colts a standing ovation.

Laag's career was now over. It had ended on a positive note, with three wins from his last four starts and the admiration of owners, trainers and breeders for his tenacity. As the saying goes, he was a "typical Abercrombie," which is quite a compliment to his toughness on the racetrack. Laag won nine of his 18 starts at three and 13 of 25 lifetime.

Sire Line

Laag and Armbro Emerson were the first two high-profile Abercrombie sons to stand at major breeding farms and their success led the way for many more to follow during the great rebirth of the Adios sire line. You can read more about Abercrombie in his chapter.

Maternal Line

The dam of Laag is the Meadow Skipper mare Tinsel, who only took a record of 2:05.3f and had earnings of $2,868. But she has been an excellent producer, including two $500,000 winners and four $250,000 winners. Not many mares have those credentials.

Tinsel's other top performers are all sons of High Ideal: Trim The Tree p,2,1:53.3 ($528,098), Christmas List p,1:54.2f ($277,041) and Avalanche p,1:55.2 ($263,341). She also has two High Ideal daughters who are 1:57 producers of raceway-type horses. Tinsel's best producing daughter is the Niatross mare Ballerina Girl, who is the dam of Broadway Spirit p,3,1:51.2 ($348,690) and Untamed Heart p,4,1:55 ($187,018).

I suspect Tinsel has some special genes in her makeup since she has produced at this top level. One hint of this may be that her dam Kathleen Grattan p,3,2:05.2f ($38,571), by Task Force, has also produced Fortune Richie 3,2:00.1f ($179,902) who is a son of Gene Abbe. That in itself is not so remarkable until you realize Fortune Richie is the sire of 14 in 1:55 and 67 in 2:00 from very little broodmare support. Most of his offspring have been bred by his owner Luel Overstreet of Kentucky, who names many of his foals with the surname Bluegrass. Fortune Richie's best son is Dorunrun Bluegrass p,1:49.4 $1,880,235, who is now a stallion at New York's Blue Chip Farms. Fortune Richie must have something special to sire a sub-1:50 performer - just as his half-sister Tinsel has.

Laag's maternal family is not one of the most well-known or glamorous in the sport. It is known as the family of Molly B. and its first 2:00 performer did not surface until 1966. Even today, this is not a very active or prolific maternal family although there is a branch, through Kathleen Grattan's half-sister Adios Dotty, which is starting to do well and produced a 1:49.3 performer in 1997 - the Die Laughing son Sports Town - as well as the fast Jessee Purkey p,1:51.4 ($531,325). So we know there are some speed genes lurking in this family just waiting to break loose.

Obviously, the great Meadow Skipper is the sire of Laag's dam so there is plenty of support in that location. The sire of Laag's grandam is the trotter Task Force, who only had a two-year-old record of 2:10.2h and won $4,420. He's a son of the good stallion Worthy Boy who sired both trotters and pacers. The rest of this maternal family gets pretty nondescript around the fifth generation.

Progeny of Note

Since Laag was syndicated well, and was a very fertile stallion, there

Laag

were plenty of broodmares sent to him right from the start. The numbers of mares bred to him during his first four seasons at stud at Almahurst Farm of New Jersey were 201, 192, 145 and 135, which guaranteed having a lot of racehorses at the tracks. When his first crop raced in 1991 and did very well, breeders flocked to Laag the next season, sending an astounding 308 mares to his court which resulted in a crop of 235 1993 foals.

As on the racetrack, Laag was up to the task. His first crop showed 25 in 2:00, earnings of over $1,000,000 and four $100,000 winners. Laag's initial crop established him as a sire of top fillies since it included So Fresh, Ghostly and Laag's Pleasure - three of his four $100,000 winners.

Laag followed up with more good crops, but his impact has been less over the past couple of years. However, Laag has an honor roll many sires would be proud to call their own, led by $1,000,000 winner Bilateral p,4,1:50.2 ($1,051,876) who won the Berry's Creek Series Final and Oliver Wendell Holmes P. at three and went on to become a top FFA performer. Laag also sired the 1995 Two-Year-Old Pacing Colt of the Year, A Stud Named Sue p,2,1:52.3; 3,1:52.2f ($992,519) whose major victories included the Woodrow Wilson P. and Metro S.

Darth Raider p,1:49.2 ($421,045) gives Laag a sub-1:50 credit and Ready To Rumble p,3,1:51 ($764,072) was a top performer at two, three and four. Jet Laag p,1:50.4z-'98 ($643,376) won the Lou Babic Memorial at two and the American-National S. at three, while the fast Reality Check p,4,1:50.4 ($352,542) has also been a Grand Circuit winner.

It is as a filly sire that Laag seems really to shine. Some of his standout females are world champion So Fresh p,3,1:53-1:53.3h ($803,794) who was voted Three-Year-Old Pacing Filly of the Year, won the Breeders Crown that year, and won 23 of 28 starts at two and three. Chippie's Ruler p,2,1:54.1f; 3,1:53.4 ($441,686) was voted Two-Year-Old Pacing Filly of the Year and won the Three Diamonds Final. Ghostly p,2,1:55; 3,1:53 ($414,600) was a major stakes winner at two and three and Kimmee Lyn p,2,1:51.4 ($78,411) was the co-fastest two-year-old of 1995 regardless of sex. And these are just a few of Laag's top fillies.

Laag also has two daughters starring in 1998 in Open Class events - Jules Jodoin p,1:51-'98 ($326,690) and Movie Star Laag p,4,1:51.2-'98 ($247,784). At his writing, Jules Jodoin has won 14 of her 18 1998 starts and has been a dominant mare.

Analysis

Laag has proven capable of siring world and divisional champions. He has also sired top fillies in addition to top colts, with 17 of his leading 38 money winners being female as well as 13 of his 38 fastest offspring. However, as well as he seems to have done, breeders always expect more and the number of mares bred to Laag has tapered off during the past few years. After he bred 308 mares in 1992, Laag had books of 256, 126 and 86 mares from 1993 to 1995. However, he rebounded with 142 in 1996, the year following the two-year-old exploits of A Stud Named Sue and Chippie's Ruler. Of course, there is always competition from new stallions and breeders wanting "the latest." But another factor is that according to some experts Laag should be siring even better horses due to the sheer numbers of mares bred to him.

Well, that's a tough argument but it can be answered. Part of the problem is that Laag may have been bred to too many mares for his own good. Whenever a stallion exceeds 150 mares, or probably 100 mares to be more realistic, the rule of diminishing returns comes into play. There are simply not enough top mares to spread around to all the good stallions available today and Laag has been bred to many inferior mares over the years. He certainly has proven capable of moving many of them up to a higher level, but he can't be expected to do that for the majority.

Another problem has been the acceptance of Laag in the yearling marketplace. His average has steadily decreased; again, this is due to the number of foals available and the quality of the dams of all those foals. He is a prime example of the law of supply and demand in the marketplace.

Laag can still sire very competitive performers - it's just that many owners and trainers have moved on to other stallions, looking for the next Albatross, Abercrombie or Cam Fella. Laag has already sired the winners of over $32,000,000, with 140 in 1:55, 491 in 2:00 and over 75 $100,000 winners, so he continues to be a marketable stallion. I also suspect his daughters will have a good chance to become top broodmares. Abercrombie will then appear in the third generation of Laag's daughter's foals and Meadow Skipper in the fourth generation. This gives Laag mares plenty of opportunities for Albatross, No Nukes, Bret Hanover, Direct Scooter, Big Towner and Cam Fella line stallions of the present and future. Given the number of Laag mares in the current Standardbred population, I think we'll be seeing plenty of grey horses in the future.

Looking at the pedigrees of some of Laag's best performers, the one that uniquely stands out is that of A Stud Named Sue, who appears, on the surface, to be a typical 3x4 linebred cross to Meadow Skipper. However, a deeper look shows he is actually bred 2x2 to the half-brothers Abercrombie and Bruce Gimble. Both stallions are sons of the Duane Hanover mare Bergdorf, Abercrombie being by Silent Majority and Bruce Gimble by Most Happy Fella. Bergdorf is also the grandam of Odds Against p,1:50.1 ($1,403,938). Laag, a son of Abercrombie, was bred to Rule Model, a daughter of Bruce Gimble, to produce A Stud Named Sue who is also bred 3x3 to Bergdorf. The inbreeding shown in this pedigree is a fine example of breeding back to a good female ancestor in addition to good male ancestors. A Stud Named Sue also has a lot of Knight Dream blood with a 5x6x5x5x5 cross to that stallion.

Laag's richest son is the $1,000,000 winner Bilateral, who is inbred 3x3 to Meadow Skipper. He also has Knight Dream blood, being 5x5x5 to Knight Dream and his full sister Marjorie Armstrong. Another similarity in the bloodlines of A Stud Named Sue and Bilateral is that dams of each are representatives of the Most Happy Fella/Poplar Byrd bloodlines cross.

So Fresh, the richest daughter of Laag with earnings over $800,000, is inbred 3x3 to Meadow Skipper and has a 4x4x4 cross to Dale Frost. Looking further down the list of Laag's highest money winners, we see that Ready To Rumble p,3,1:51 ($764,072), Jet Laag and Dust Devil p,1:52 ($432,209) are all 3x3 to Meadow Skipper and the top fillies Chippie's Ruler and Ghostly are 3x4 to Meadow Skipper. All of these good sons and daughters of Laag are inbred or linebred to Meadow Skipper.

Ironically, Laag's fastest offspring is Darth Raider at 1:49.2 and his dam has no Meadow Skipper blood. His dam is a mare by Adios Vic from a daughter of Patrick Song - a grandson of Volomite. Darth Raider's second dam, Victory Abbey, is inbred 2x3 to the full brothers Gay Song and Victory Song, both products of a great sire and a great dam, Volomite and Evensong. In addition to this cross, Victory Abbey is 4x4 to the full brother and sister Peter Volo and The Great Miss Morris and 3x4x4 to Volomite. Thus, Victory Abbey, a mare who was inbred to extremely prolific bloodlines, goes on to produce a daughter who is the dam of a 1:49.2 performer. This makes you want to believe in the saying "blood will tell" - even without the additional influence of Meadow Skipper in the dam's pedigree.

Another Laag offspring with an interesting pedigree, and one of his fastest, is Dixie Laag p,3,1:51 ($76,822) from the mare Dixie Clamp. She is inbred 3x3 to the full brothers Bret Hanover and Baron Hanover. Laag's two fastest females, Panhunter p,4,1:51.1 ($135,434), 3x4x4 to Meadow Skipper, and Kimmee Lyn p,2,1:51.4 ($78,811), 3x3 to Meadow Skipper, are more examples of how well the inbreeding to Meadow Skipper has worked.

Laag has been successful with daughters from a large variety of broodmare sires, but a few of his fastest have been from Niatross mares. In this vein, don't forget, as mentioned above, that Laag's best producing half-sister is by Niatross. It could be that this family is "nicking" with Niatross for extreme speed. To date, mares from 18 different broodmare sires have

Laag

produced Laag's 25 fastest performers, with Niatross, Albatross, Big Towner, No Nukes and Falcon Almahurst being the repeat sires. Albatross and Big Towner mares lead with three credits each. In the top 26 money-winning list of Laag performers, the leading broodmare sire is Big Towner with five credits. The Big Towner cross is interesting since it may point to another successful "nick," bearing in mind the aforementioned success of Dorunrun Bluegrass, who is a grandson of Gene Abbe and Big Towner is Gene Abbe's best son.

I also want to mention that Laag's son Admiral's Galley p,2,1:54.2 ($324,259) is the sire of a sub-1:50 performer in 1998 - Tulane p,1:49.2z-'98 from an Oil Burner mare.

In summary, Laag seems to be a better than average sire and certainly a viable son of Abercrombie. He has found his niche among pacing stallions and is still only 14 years old in 1998. He is now standing at Taylor Palmer's Boxwood Farm in New Jersey and getting a decent group of mares. He is a very versatile sire since he works well inbred to Meadow Skipper line mares and fits just about all broodmares by today's popular sires. I would expect mares with a Big Towner/Meadow Skipper cross to work very well with Laag. The fact that he can sire good fillies, along with top two-year-olds, also works to his advantage.

Leading Progeny by Laag

Fastest
- Darth Raider, g, p,1:49.2 $421,045
- Bilateral, h, p,4,1:50.2 $1,051,876
- So Excited, h, p,4,1:50.3 $123,264
- Reality Check, h, p,4,1:50.4 $352,542
- Jet Laag, h, p,1:50.4z $643,376
- Ready to Rumble, h, p,3,1:51 $764,072
- Jules Jodoin, m, p,1:51 $326,690
- Sakra Mania, h, p,4,1:51 $316,506
- Dixie Laag, g, p,3,1:51 $76,822
- Panhunter, m, p,4,1:51.1 $135,434

Richest
- Bilateral, h, p,4,1:50.2 $1,051,876
- A Stud Named Sue, h, p,3,1:52.2 $992,519
- So Fresh, m, p,3,1:53 $803,794
- Ready to Rumble, h, p,3,1:51 $764,072
- Jet Laag, h, p,1:50.4z $643,376
- Chippie's Ruler, m, p,3,1:53.4 $411,686
- Dust Devil, g, p,1:52 $432,209
- Darth Raider, g, p,1:49.2 $421,045
- Ghostly, m, p,3,1:53 $414,600
- Diamond Dawn, m, p,3,1:54.2 $378,278

Laag, Gray Horse, 1984
p, 2, 1:54; 3, 1:51.2 ($642,995)

Gen 1	Gen 2	Gen 3	Gen 4	Gen 5	Gen 6
Abercrombie, 1975 p, 4, 1:53 $984,391	Silent Majority, 1969 p, 3, 1:56.3 $362,369	Henry T. Adios, 1958 p, 6, 1:57 $706,833	Adios, 1940 p, T1:57½ $33,329	**HAL DALE**	**ABBEDALE** Margaret Hal
				Adioo Volo	Adioo Guy Sigrid Volo
			Greer Hanover, 1948 p, 3, 2:06.2h $6,482	**NIBBLE HANOVER**	Calumet Chuck Justissima
				Veda Hanover	**BILLY DIRECT** Vivian Hanover
		Hobby Horse Tar, 1964	Tar Heel, 1948 p, 4, T1:57 $119,148	**BILLY DIRECT**	Napoleon Direct Gay Forbes
				Leta Long	**VOLOMITE** Rosette
			Wilellen, 1955 p, 3, 2:04.2h $16,994	Wilmington	Bert Abbe Miss Saginaw
				Willola	Willglow Romola
	Bergdorf, 1967 p, 4, 2:03.3 $6,035	Duane Hanover, 1952 p, 4, 1:58 $280,288	Knight Dream, 1945 p, 3, T1:59 $76,973	**NIBBLE HANOVER**	Calumet Chuck Justissima
				Lydia Knight	**PETER THE BREWER** Guy Rosa
			Dorsh Hanover, 1932 4, 2:15½h	Dillon Axworthy	Axworthy Adioo Dillon
				Great Medium	Peter The Great Dorsch Medium
		Princess Best, 1959 p, 4, 2:07f	The Widower, 1935 p, 3, T1:59½ $19,983	**ABBEDALE**	The Abbe Daisydale D.
				Widow Grattan	**GRATTAN ROYAL** I'm A Widow
			Princess Chief, 1945 p, 2:07 $9,506	Chief Abbedale	**ABBEDALE** Marion Candler
				The Gay Princess	Crispin Princess Duffy
Tinsel, 1971 p, 3, 2:05.3f $2,868	Meadow Skipper, 1960 p, 3, 1:55.1 $428,057	Dale Frost, 1951 p, 1:58 $204,117	**HAL DALE**, 1926 p, 6, 2:02¼	**ABBEDALE**	The Abbe Daisydale D.
				Margaret Hal	Argot Hal Margaret Polk
			Galloway, 1939 p, 2:04½h $5,294	Raider	**PETER VOLO** Nelda Dillon
				Bethel	David Guy Annotation
		Countess Vivian, 1950 p, 3, 1:59 $43,262	King's Counsel, 1940 p, 6, 1:58 $44,930	**VOLOMITE**	**PETER VOLO** Cita Frisco
				Margaret Spangler	**GUY AXWORTHY** Maggie Winder
			Filly Direct, 1941 p, 3, 2:06¾ $6,299	**BILLY DIRECT**	Napoleon Direct Gay Forbes
				Calumet Edna	**PETER THE BREWER** Broncho Queen
	Kathleen Grattan, 1956 p, 3, 2:05.2h $38,571	Task Force, 1949 2, 2:10.2h $4,420	Worthy Boy, 1940 3, 2:02½ $25,688	**VOLOMITE**	**PETER VOLO** Cita Frisco
				Warwell Worthy	**PETER THE BREWER** Broncho Queen
			Thistledown, 1938	Guy Abbey	**GUY AXWORTHY** Abbacy
				Blue Heather	**PETER VOLO** Princess Gay
		Alice Grattan, 1937 p, 3, 2:07¾	Silent Grattan, 1921 p, T2:09¾	**GRATTAN ROYAL**	Grattan Mona
				Silent T	Silent Brook Agave
			Miss Alice Paul p, 2:11h	Ross K	Constenano Morning Glory
				Birdie B	Nicholas B Molly B

Life Sign

He's the horse who raced the most impressive mile in Little Brown Jug history. That's what most people would remember about Life Sign the racehorse. Or they might have visions of the dramatic photos of Life Sign, Riyadh and Presidential Ball finishing almost as a team in that 1993 Jug Final.

But, Life Sign is more than just a dramatic Jug winner. He would have been a great racehorse even without the Jug win. Life Sign had speed, stamina and an abundance of heart, as one might expect from a son of super-sire Abercrombie and the world champion mare Three Diamonds.

Life Sign was bred by George Segal's Brittany Farms of Versailles, Kentucky, which still owns him. Segal, a long-time horse owner, is a member of the Chicago Board of Trade and a director of the Hambletonian Society. In 1997, he was inducted into the harness racing Hall of Fame in Goshen, New York. Some of Segal's other major stars include Artsplace, Delinquent Account, Enroute, Leah Almahurst, Odds Against, Tucson Hanover and Western Hanover, to name just a few.

Life Sign was trained by Gene Riegle, Hall of Famer and winner of the Glen Garnsey Trainer of the Year award. A top trainer and driver since the 1950s, some of his stars over the years are Artsplace, Western Hanover, Troublemaker, Leah Almahurst, Nuclear Legacy, Silky Stallone, Arnie Almahurst and Life Sign's dam Three Diamonds.

At two, Life Sign made his racetrack debut on July 11 at The Meadowlands. In a qualifying race he finished second, timed in 2:00.2 and pacing his last quarter in :28. A week later, he won a qualifying race in 1:58 over the same track. Life Sign finished second in his first parimutuel start in a conditioned event after coming the last three-quarters on the outside from seventh. His first stakes race, in the Arden Downs S, resulted in a fifth place finish after having the early lead. On August 28, Life Sign won his first stakes event - a 1:56 score in the Hoosier Futurity at Indianapolis. He then went to Sportsman's Park and won the American-National S. by six lengths in a very impressive 1:54.1. He had served notice he was going to be a top colt.

Life Sign was then shipped to Canada for the Eliminations of the rich Metro S. at Mohawk and his first battle against the division's elite young pacers. Life Sign was a good second by a neck to Presidential Ball in his Elimination. Going off at odds of 10-1 in the $719,700 Metro S. Final, Life Sign left from post five and had to race on the outside, never getting close enough to challenge the leaders on a very foggy night. In a cavalry charge across the wire, Life Sign finished sixth and was placed fifth, only one and one-half lengths behind the winning Presidential Ball.

Two weeks later at the Red Mile in Lexington, Kentucky, Life Sign gained more fans with a win in the $113,100 International Stallion S. in 1:52.4. This was another race in which Life Sign showed his courage and grit. Leaving from post nine, driven by Bill Fahy, Life Sign was parked out fifth to the quarter and had gained the lead at the half, still parked out, in a very fast :54.3. He then dropped in on the rail and was third at the three-quarters and second midway through the stretch. In what later became his trademark, Life Sign reached down for more and came charging through the stretch to win by a length over Wilco's Kosby.

The $300,000 Breeders Crown at Pompano Park was next on Life Sign's schedule. The luck of the draw went against him and he left the gate from post seven. Fahy had worked him up to third on the outside at the half and a challenging second at the three-quarters before taking a brief lead in the stretch. Being parked out to the three-quarters in an unbelievable 1:23.3 had taken its toll, however, and Life Sign yielded to the fast-closing Village Jiffy in the stretch and finished second. He came back a week later to win a Presidential S. Elimination at Rosecroft in 1:54.3 after another overland journey, but finished third the next week in the Final after grabbing the lead at the half in another fast :55.1.

Life Sign had now gained respect and was being made the favorite in his races. The Governor's Cup was next at Garden State Park. Life Sign dropped his Elimination to Village Jiffy after leading all the way until the last few yards. But in the $537,800 Governor's Cup Final, Life Sign did what he was to do the following year for driver John

Race Record Highlights

At 2
- **1st** Governor's Cup Final
  International Stallion S.
  American-National S.
  Hoosier Futurity
  Presidential S. Elimination
- **2nd** Breeders Crown
  Governor's Cup Elimination
- **3rd** Presidential S. Final

At 3
- **1st** Little Brown Jug Final and heat
  Breeders Crown
  Art Rooney Memorial Final
  Cleveland Classic
  Meadowlands Pace Elimination
  Cane Pace Preview
  Burlington S.

At 3 (continued)
  MacFarlane Memorial
  Bluegrass S.
  Windy City P. Elimination
- **2nd** Meadowlands Pace Final
  Windy City P. Final
  James Dancer Memorial Elimination
  North America Cup Elimination
- **3rd** North America Cup Final
  James Dancer Memorial Final
  Cane Pace

Honors

Set two-heat world record on half-mile track at three

Life Sign

Photo courtesy of The Horseman and Fair World

Race Record

Year	Age	Starts	Wins	2nd	3rd	Earnings	Record
1992	2	13	5	4	2	$ 557,543	p,2,1:52.4
1993	3	22	13	6	3	1,354,911	p,3,1:50.3
		35	18	10	5	$1,912,454	p,3,1:50.3

Life Sign

Campbell. Life Sign and Campbell left cautiously from post four and were parked out fifth to the half in :56.2. The colt was still outside on the backstretch and was moving up to third when he encountered some interference. Once beyond that incident, Life Sign got rolling again and went right to the front, taking a one-length lead in the stretch and holding on by a nose in 1:53.1 over Bonnie And Clyde. This was the biggest payday of his year and his $557,543 in earnings placed him second behind Presidential Ball among two-year-old colts that season.

Coming back at three, Life Sign was expected to be a star and he did not disappoint. Gene Riegle's son Bruce drove Life Sign to two qualifying wins at Scioto Downs and was also in the sulky for Life Sign's next three races in Scioto Downs Invitational events. In his first start of the season, Life Sign met with a surprise defeat by the older Deadlock in 1:54.1. But the colt was back on track the next two weeks with victories in 1:52.4 and 1:52; in the latter he defeated Deadlock by over 11 lengths. It was now on to the stakes battles with John Campbell in the sulky for all of Life Sign's remaining starts.

Life Sign won a division of the Burlington S. in 1:53 at Greenwood after being parked out for the last three-quarters and winning going away by over three lengths. The Eliminations for the rich North America Cup were a week later; Life Sign finished second by a half-length to Beastmaster. In the $1,000,000 North America Cup Final, Life Sign went to the front just after the quarter and led the field into deep stretch where he was overpowered by Presidential Ball and The Starting Gate to finish third in the 1:51 mile. Another $1,000,000 race was coming up next and Life Sign won his Meadowlands Pace Elimination in a personal record 1:50.3 after again being parked out the last five-eighths. It seemed that with Life Sign, the tougher he was raced the more he responded. Racing on the outside, whatever the distance, did not seem to bother him at all.

In the Meadowlands Pace Final, Life Sign was fourth on the rail to the half and on the backstretch took to the outside to move up to third at the 1:21.4 three-quarters. He was almost three lengths from the leader at this point, but as he made up ground during the stretch he momentarily swerved and hooked wheels with Presidential Ball. Once free, he could only come within three-quarters of a length of the winning Presidential Ball at the wire in 1:50 flat. Presidential Ball defeated Life Sign again a week later in an Art Rooney Memorial Elimination; Life Sign raced second on the rail most of the trip and finished second. It probably was not a tough enough trip for the colt. In the $301,760 Art Rooney Memorial Final at Yonkers, Presidential Ball was again the front runner followed by Riyadh and Life Sign, who was third on the rail. Approaching the half, Campbell decided to go to the outside with Life Sign so he could be in a challenging position, letting Presidential Ball know he was there while locking Riyadh in on the rail. Life Sign was parked out the rest of the way, but he kept at Presidential Ball, wore him down and paced under the wire a length victor over Riyadh, with Presidential Ball holding on for third.

Life Sign then went to Ohio's Northfield Park for the $204,500 Cleveland Classic and overwhelmed the field with a 1:51.4 score over that half-mile track. A week later, he won in unusual fashion, going wire-to-wire at Yonkers in a Cane Pace Preview over Presidential Ball. The Cane Pace Final was another example of Life Sign's bad luck at the draw. He had post 11, in the second tier, and was parked out right from the start. Although he was second at the three-quarters, he finished third, behind Riyadh and Presidential Ball. Campbell put him on the front end again at Freehold for the James Dancer Memorial Elimination and Final. Life Sign was the heavy favorite in both. He led to deep stretch in both races, but lost the Elimination by a head to Ready To Rumble and the Final by less than a length to longshot Captain Pantastic.

Riegle gave the colt a week off and he came back fresh to begin a six-race winning streak. His first start back was a six-length win in the $100,000 MacFarlane Memorial at Hazel Park. Then it was off to Delaware, Ohio for the Little Brown Jug - and history.

Life Sign's dramatic Jug victory did not come over ordinary pacers. He defeated Presidential Ball in the first heat by three lengths and overcame that colt and Riyadh in the Jug Final. Life Sign's two 1:52

victories combined for a total of 3:44, which broke the former two-heat record by one and two-fifth seconds.

The first heat tested Life Sign's mettle. The rail horse Native Born and driver Walter Case Jr. were not willing to give up the lead to Life Sign without a fight. Native Born tore into the first turn at full speed with Life Sign second. Suddenly, John Campbell pulled Life Sign from the rail and sprinted for the lead, passing the quarter marker on the outside in a very quick :26.2. Presidential Ball followed this move and when Life Sign got to the rail Jack Moiseyev continued on to the front with Presidential Ball. No sooner had that colt gotten to the rail when Campbell and Life Sign were on the move again to retake the lead and pass the half in a dynamic :53.3.

Life Sign had a bit of a breather in the third quarter, and he was able to relax through a :29.2 quarter. He would need the respite since Village Jiffy, sitting first over from the half, was ready to make a challenging move. Life Sign was ready for the challenge and came home in :29 to score a resounding three-length win over Presidential Ball with Native Born another two lengths back. At the time, the 1:52 mile was a world record first heat on a half-mile track and the fastest mile in the history of the Little Brown Jug.

For the Jug Final, Riyadh, who had won his Elimination, drew the rail with Life Sign leaving again from post two. Driver Jim Morrill Jr. had Riyadh right on the gate and left alertly, as did Campbell with Life Sign. The two colts raced as a team through the first turn with Riyadh maintaining his slight advantage.

While Life Sign was trying for the lead, Jack Moiseyev and Presidential Ball moved over to the rail and closed the hole, followed by Ready To Rumble, leaving Life Sign high and dry on the outside. Campbell finally managed to briefly tuck in Life Sign before the :27 quarter, but it was only a short rest. As Captain Pantastic moved up from the rear, Campbell did not want to get locked in and pulled off the rail again at the three-eighths pole. "I knew it was going to be a long trip from there," said Campbell. "If I didn't think he would be close I wouldn't have moved him then."

At the :56 half, Life Sign was third, sitting first over outside of Presidential Ball who was on the rail right behind the leading Riyadh. Morrill and Riyadh then stepped up the pace with a :27.4 third quarter to pass that mark in 1:23.4. Life Sign was still there on the outside as Riyadh took a length and one-half lead into the stretch drive. Moiseyev, trying to find a way off the rail with Presidential Ball, later commented, "The way the race went, I thought Life Sign would curl up after that." But Life Sign was nowhere near finished and found further reserves to brush past Riyadh and cross the finish line with a half-length advantage. Riyadh was a neck ahead of Presidential Ball, who had found room on the inside. This resulted in a three-horse photo of truly great pacers involved in one of the most memorable races in harness racing history.

Earlier in the season, trainer Gene Riegle had compared Life Sign to Artsplace, which had surprised some observers. After the Jug, Riegle said, "I made a prediction earlier. I thought he was just as good a colt as Artsplace. I'm not going to take that back." In the winner's circle ceremony, driver John Campbell told the large crowd, "It was just an awesome performance. It wasn't great driving. It was a great horse. He just overcame a tough trip. He was phenomenal." Campbell has also noted, "Abercrombie's never cease to amaze me. They're just a phenomenal breed. They've got tremendous stamina....they carry their speed a long way."

Life Sign lived up to his new champion status two weeks after the Jug, winning the Bluegrass S. at The Red Mile in 1:53. Two weeks after that, the $300,000 Breeders Crown at Freehold featured another exceptional Life Sign performance. He was parked out first over most of the mile in fractions of :26.3, :55.3 and 1:24.2 before gaining a nose advantage in the stretch and going on to win by a neck over the fast-closing Beastmaster, with Presidential Ball and Riyadh finishing back.

Three weeks later, Life Sign easily won a Windy City S. Elimination at Maywood Park and was favored over Presidential Ball in the $350,000 Final. On that night, however, Presidential Ball had the rail and used it to full advantage. Campbell was content to sit second after leaving from post seven and try Presidential Ball in the stretch. Presidential Ball, with Jack Moiseyev, was allowed leisurely fractions in :27.4, :57.3 and 1:25.2 to the three-quarters. Life Sign was now on the outside and challenging all through the stretch, but could get no closer than a head at the finish.

Unfortunately for Life Sign and his connections, that defeat in the last start of his career may have cost him divisional honors. As the final tally was 144½ for Presidential Ball to 125½ for Life Sign. In Presidential Ball's favor were victories in the two $1,000,000 races of the season and $850,000 more in earnings than Life Sign. But these two colts were "this close" on the racetrack - Life Sign had defeated Presidential Ball five times that season and had lost to him on four occasions. It was a great rivalry.

Sire Line

Life Sign is another young sire making a move to continue the extension of the Adios sire line. Abercrombie, Life Sign's sire and a great-grandson of Adios, has been almost solely responsible for bringing this line back to life after it appeared to have been overwhelmed by the Meadow Skipper male line. Abercrombie has now had successful siring sons in Artsplace, Albert Albert and Laag, to name a few, and should keep moving forward.

Maternal Line

Very few stallions have gone to stud with a pedigree as strong as Life Sign. His dam was the result of the great Albatross/Bret Hanover cross. She was no ordinary mare. Life Sign's dam is the champion Albatross mare Three Diamonds p,2,1:56; 3,1:53.1 ($735,759). Three Diamonds was bred by Tom Crouch's Kentuckiana Farms and sold at the first Kentucky Standardbred Select Yearling Sale in 1980 for $100,000 to George Segal. She won 25 of her 31 lifetime starts, set world records on all-size tracks and was voted Two-Year-Old and Three-Year-Old Pacing Filly of the Year. At three, she won the Jugette, the filly companion event to the Little Brown Jug over the same track which later brought her son so much respect. Like Life Sign, Three Diamonds was trained by Gene Riegle.

Unfortunately, Three Diamonds died in March of 1995, at 16 years of age, from complications following the birth of a full brother to Life Sign.

Life Sign is not the only outstanding performer from Three Diamonds. She was bred to Big Towner and produced multiple stakes winner Threefold p,3,1:51.1 ($634,004) who has sired 26 $100,000 winners, 33 in 1:55 and 165 2:00 performers. By Matt's Scooter, Three Diamonds produced Lifetime Success p,3,1:52.2, and by Tyler B she had Trinity Lobell p,1:54.4 ($107,856). The final foal from Three Diamonds is a full brother to Life Sign named His Alibi p,3,1:53-'98. Three daughters of Three Diamonds old enough to have foals of racing age have produced stakes horses which include Market Report p,4,1:51.3f ($226,235) (by Jate Lobell), Forecast p,1:54.1h (by Big Towner) and Warrior For Peace p,4,1:53.1-'98 ($104,238) among others.

The grandam of Life Sign is the unraced Bret Hanover mare Ambiguity, who produced only five foals, four of whom were fillies and they were all good producers. Three Diamonds was, of course, Ambiguity's best offspring and she also had Either Or p,3,T1:57.1 (by Meadow Skipper) who is the dam of four sub-1:55 performers, including Neutrality p,3,1:52.2 ($633,349). Either Or's daughter Lady Has Arrived p,3,1:57.4 (by Safe Arrival) produced an outstanding horse in Arrive At Five p,4,1:50.1 ($866,259) (by Nihilator). A daughter by Abercrombie, Private Tears, is the dam of three sub-1:55 horses.

The third dam of Life Sign is the Knight Dream mare K. Nora, a full sister to the stakes and FFA winner Adora's Dream p,4,1:58.1h ($401,809). K. Nora was bred to Bret Hanover and produced the world champion Oxford Circus p,2,1:57.1 (six in 2:00), Tiger's Milk (10 in 2:00, including Tucson Hanover p,4,1:51.3 $1,072,623 by Albatross) and Angel Hair (seven in 2:00, dam of world champion Naughty But Nice p,3,1:54f $1,062,197 by Albatross and grandam of world champion Leah Almahurst p,3,1:52.3 $1,053,201 by Abercrombie).

Life Sign's maternal family is known as Miss Duvall and over the years there have been several distinct branches develop in this family, with the most successful being the branches through Adora (by Adios), Romola Hal (by The Senator) and Hobby Horse Tar (by Tar Heel). I also want to note that Silent Majority, the sire of Abercrombie and grandsire of Life Sign, is from another branch of this same maternal family.

During the thirty-something years that I have been closely following the pedigree and breeding aspect of harness racing, the Adora branch of this family has always intrigued me because so many of the performers have seemed precocious at a very early age. In addition, the family is getting better with age and continues to produce champions in every generation. It has also spread out and developed even more branches within this part of the family. The Adora family was developed several decades ago mainly through the efforts of the esteemed breeder William Shehan. Now, most of the major breeders are making sure they include this family's female descendants in their own breeding program. This is one solid maternal family and a big favorite of mine.

On a personal note, a favorite pacer of mine in 1962 was the Knight Dream son Adora's Dream who, as a three-year-old that season, came into the Messenger S. at Roosevelt Raceway undefeated. I got to the track early that night to make sure I could stake out a position right on the fence at the finish line to see Adora's Dream score a major victory. I was a young man, a big fan of harness racing, and I wanted to be close to the action. Adora's Dream had the lead in the stretch and looked like a sure winner until John Simpson and Thor Hanover came from out of nowhere, way out in the middle of the track, and got up right at the wire to nip Adora's Dream, with Lehigh Hanover also right there in the photo. The large crowd was stunned, no one more so than I, and Thor Hanover paid $144.00 to win.

From that point on, I began to follow the progress of Adora's Dream's sisters and other relatives and saw that family develop generation after generation until it became one of the best in the sport. This family seems to possess early speed along with toughness, a combination necessary to compete at the highest levels. In addition, it does not seem to favor colts or fillies and there have been a number of champions from each gender.

Analysis

Life Sign stood his first season at stud in 1994 at Tom Crouch's Kentuckiana Farm, for a fee of $7,500, and he has been immensely popular during his first four seasons. He bred 174 mares that first year, and during his next three seasons at stud, Life Sign bred 176, 180 and 184 mares.

The first crop of yearlings by Life Sign was very well received at the sales. Ninety-six colts and fillies averaged $32,414 to place him right behind established sires Cam Fella and Artsplace, and in front of such sires as No Nukes, Abercrombie, Jate Lobell, Precious Bunny and Matt's Scooter. Four of Life Sign's yearlings brought $100,000 or more.

Concerning crosses which may work best for Life Sign, we may get a hint by looking at Artsplace, who is also by Abercrombie from an Albatross mare. He seems to be working with mares from many different lines, including those from sons and grandsons of Albatross. Another stallion to examine is the Abercrombie son Albert Albert, whose dam is by Albatross and second and third dams by Bret Hanover and Knight Dream, the same as Life Sign. Albert Albert has sired some very nice offspring, his best being the $2,300,000 winner Pacific Rocket p,4,1:50 who is from a Direct Scooter mare. Albert Albert has also clicked well with mares by Bret Hanover, Albatross, Big Towner, No Nukes, Tyler B., Landslide and Niatross.

A mare by a son of Albatross, when bred to Life Sign, would have a foal with a 3x3 Albatross cross and it would be 3x4 with a grandson. I don't see any problem with that type of cross and, in fact, would try to plan one providing the individuals match up physically. Another good cross would be mares with the No Nukes/Albatross cross; there are plenty of good ones out there. I also think Big Towner, Direct Scooter and Tyler B mares will be very effective with Life Sign, as well as those with Bret Hanover blood.

Even though Life Sign's dam is a product of the Albatross/Bret Hanover cross, it would be far enough back in many cases for linebreeding to occur. Doubling up on that cross certainly would strengthen a pedigree. Cam Fella was tough and is noted for siring tough horses. Combining the courage of Life Sign and Cam Fella in a pedigree by using a mare with the prolific Cam Fella/Albatross cross is another way to go, and I think many breeders will try that cross as more Cam Fella mares are retired.

This analysis is being written following Life Sign's first crop racing in 1997 and in early 1998. To date, he has a fine 84% starters from his three-year-olds: 113 from 134 starters with 65 of those in 2:00. Life Sign's first crop has five $100,000 winners to date and 23 1:55 performers. He is off to a decent start, but nowhere near the exploit of Artsplace - another Abercrombie/Albatross stallion.

However, Life Sign has shown quite enough to merit a serious look as a potentially outstanding stallion for the future. Like Artsplace, he has been able to do a good job in siring stakes fillies since 14 of his 23 richest performers are females. In addition, 15 of his 38 fastest are fillies. Life Sign

Life Sign

has shown the ability to sire Grand Circuit type performers and there are now many racing in the major stakes.

Now let's take a look at the pedigree crosses for his top colts and fillies. Mares by No Nukes have been especially prolific with Life Sign - even more so than they are for Artsplace. To date, nine of Life Sign's 25 richest are from No Nukes mares with another pair from mares by his son, Jate Lobell. In fact, 18 of the 25 richest are from mares by Most Happy Fella line stallions. In the speed department, three of Life Sign's fastest sons and daughters are from No Nukes mares as are seven of the 22 fastest. This seems to be a very dynamic cross for Life Sign. Mares by Sonsam have also produced well in the speed department with the dams of two and grandams of two of the twenty fastest performers.

The filly Life Cycle p,2,1:53.4 ($209,746) is currently the richest Life Sign offspring and has some interesting pedigree crosses. Life Cycle's closest cross is 4x5x4 to Meadow Skipper and his half-sister Countess Adios. In addition, there is a 5x6x5x6x6x4x5 cross to Adios and a 5x6x6x5x4 to Tar Heel. That's a lot of Adios and Tar Heel blood - the former "golden cross." Life Cycle's second dam, Armbro Tequila, is inbred 2x3 to Adios. Armstrong Bros. farm became famous for its abundance of Adios mares in the 1960's and 1970's and they successfully practiced extensive inbreeding to that stallion.

Life Sign's richest and fastest son is Day In A Life p,3,1:51.2-'98 ($157,480) who is bred 4x4 to both Meadow Skipper and Bret Hanover. In fact, Life Sign's four richest colts have similar fourth generation crosses to Meadow Skipper and Bret Hanover - in some cases three crosses to each stallion. Lease On Life p,2,1:52.3 ($143,522) is 3x4 to Albatross and both Fit For Life p,2,1:53.3 ($125,273) and the filly L'Chaim p,3,1:55f-'98 ($114,627) are both inbred 3x3 to Albatross. Seven of the 11 richest Life Sign performers have either inbred 3x3 or linebred 3x4 crosses to Albatross. If you have a mare with Albatross blood, or are looking for a Life Sign yearling, try to find one with Albatross and Bret Hanover blood - it seems to be working very well for Life Sign as the same cross does with many other stallions.

As much as we have seen multiple crosses to Meadow Skipper, Albatross and Bret Hanover among Life Sign's richest performers, a little bit of the opposite is true in the list of his fastest offspring. Two of the four fastest, Bonanza Alert p,3,1:52.2-'98 and Signfeld p,3,1:53.1f-'98 have no common ancestors in their first four generations.

I found it very interesting that Life Sign is working well with mares from very different sires which are working the best with Artsplace and Albert Albert - another good Abercrombie/Albatross stallion. Both of those stallions have done very well with Big Towner mares and this has not shown up yet with Life Sign. Of course, it could be that he just has not bred many Big Towner mares; but, that cross seems to be worth a try since it has done so well with other Abercrombie sons.

Leading Progeny by Life Sign

Fastest
Day In A Life, h, p,3,1:51.2 $157,480
Bonanza Alert, g, p,3,1:52.2 $43,883
Lease On Life, h, p,2,1:52.3 $143,522
Sign Of Rain, m, p,3,1:53.1 $66,018
Signfeld, h, p,3,1:53.1f $11,010
Strong Life, h, p,3,1:53.2 $38,578
Cable Guy, h, p,3,1:53.3f $50,384
Fit For Life, h, p,2,1:53.3 $125,273
Life Cycle, m, p,2,1:53.4 $209,746
Almahurst Frontier, h, p,2,1:53.4 $25,180

Richest
Life Cycle, m, p,2,1:53.4 $209,746
Day In A Life, h, p,3,1:51.2 $157,480
Lease On Life, h, p,2,1:52.3 $143,522
Fit For Life, h, p,2,1:53.3 $125,273
L'Chaim, m, p,3,1:55f $114,627
Sultry Song, m, p,3,1:55.3 $88,809
House Of Fun, h, p,2,1:54.2 $78,685
Sign Of Rain, m, p,3,1:53.1 $66,018
Live The Life, h, p,3,1:54.2 $61,540
Polished Satin, m, p,3,1:54.2f $59,380

Life Sign, Bay Horse, 1990
p, 2, 1:52.4; 3, 1:50.3 ($1,912,454)

Abercrombie, 1975 p, 4, 1:53 $984,391	Silent Majority, 1969 p, 3, 1:56.3 $362,369	Henry T. Adios, 1958 p, 6, 1:57 $706,833	ADIOS, 1940 p, T1:57½ $33,329	HAL DALE	ABBEDALE Margaret Hal
				Adioo Volo	Adioo Guy Sigrid Volo
			Greer Hanover, 1948 p, 3, 2:06.2h $6,482	NIBBLE HANOVER	Calumet Chuck Justissima
				Veda Hanover	BILLY DIRECT VIVIAN HANOVER
		Hobby Horse Tar, 1964	TAR HEEL, 1948 p, 4, T1:57 $119,148	BILLY DIRECT	Napoleon Direct Gay Forbes
				Leta Long	VOLOMITE Rosette
			Wilellen, 1955 p, 3, 2:04.2h $16,994	Wilmington	BERT ABBE Miss Saginaw
				Willola	Willglow Romola
	Bergdorf, 1967 p, 4, 2:03.3 $6,035	Duane Hanover, 1952 p, 4, 1:58 $280,288	KNIGHT DREAM, 1945 p, 3, T1:59 $76,973	NIBBLE HANOVER	Calumet Chuck Justissima
				Lydia Knight	Peter The Brewer Guy Rosa
			Dorsh Hanover, 1932 4, 2:15½h	Dillon Axworthy	Axworthy Adioo Dillon
				Great Medium	Peter The Great Dorsch Medium
		Princess Best, 1959 p, 4, 2:07f	The Widower, 1935 p, 3, T1:59½ $19,983	ABBEDALE	The Abbe Daisydale D.
				Widow Grattan	Grattan Royal I'm A Widow
			Princess Chief, 1945 p, 2:07h $9,506	Chief Abbedale	ABBEDALE Marion Candler
				The Gay Princess	Crispin Princess Duffy
Three Diamonds, 1979 p, 3, 1:53.1 $735,759	Albatross, 1968 p, 4, 1:54.3f $1,201,470	Meadow Skipper, 1960 p, 3, 1:55.1 $428,057	Dale Frost, 1951 p, 1:58 $204,117	HAL DALE	ABBEDALE Margaret Hal
				Galloway	Raider Bethel
			Countess Vivian, 1950 p, 3, 1:59 $43,262	King's Counsel	VOLOMITE Margaret Spangler
				Filly Direct	BILLY DIRECT Calumet Edna
		Voodoo Hanover, 1964	Dancer Hanover, 1957 p, 4, T1:56.4 $87,746	ADIOS	HAL DALE Adioo Volo
				The Old Maid	Guy Abbey Spinster
			Vibrant Hanover, 1960	TAR HEEL	BILLY DIRECT Leta Long
				VIVIAN HANOVER	Guy McKinney Guesswork
	Ambiguity, 1972	Bret Hanover, 1962 p, 4, T1:53.3 $922,616	ADIOS, 1940 p, T1:57½ $33,329	HAL DALE	ABBEDALE Margaret Hal
				Adioo Volo	Adioo Guy Sigrid Volo
			Brenna Hanover, 1956 p, 3, T2:01 $21,946	TAR HEEL	BILLY DIRECT Leta Long
				Beryl Hanover	NIBBLE HANOVER Laura Hanover
		K. Nora, 1961 p, 3, 2:05.3h $5,749	KNIGHT DREAM, 1945 p, 3, T1:59 $76,973	NIBBLE HANOVER	Calumet Chuck Justissima
				Lydia Knight	Peter The Brewer Guy Rosa
			Adora, 1952 p, 3, 2:02.2h $53,893	ADIOS	HAL DALE Adioo Volo
				Nora Abbe	BERT ABBE Nora Adele

Magical Mike

Magical Mike spread his "magic" over two racing seasons during 1993 and 1994 and is now doing stallion service at Blue Chip Farms in New York. Two-Year-Old Champion, World Champion, Breeders Crown winner and Little Brown Jug winner are all part of Magical Mike's resume. Behind every horse there is a story and Magical Mike's is one of class, consistency and royal bloodlines.

Bred by Shadow Lane Farms, consisting of Tom Walsh, Jr., his son Tom Walsh III and George Stubbs, of New York, Magical Mike gained an additional owner in David McDuffee, of New Hampshire, in December of the colt's yearling season. The elder Walsh has owned Standardbreds for over 40 years and has had horses with the Haughton Stable since the early 1980s, first with Billy Haughton and then with that Hall of Famer's son Tom. Magical Mike was named by, and for, Tom Walsh Jr.'s grandson Michael Schnurr.

Magical Mike was a standout two-year-old and earned year-end honors for his division as well as equalling the 1:51.4 fastest mile ever paced by a two-year-old colt. Tom Haughton drove the colt in his career debut, a $500 baby race at The Meadowlands on May 26th in which he went wire-to-wire, coming home in :27.4 for a 2:01 victory. He then won another baby race two weeks later in 1:59.4, with Mike Lachance in the sulky. Haughton tried the colt in a Yonkers Raceway qualifier but he made a break at the start.

The fast Tyler B colt made a sparkling parimutuel debut at The Meadowlands on June 24th with a front-running 1:54.4 performance after being parked out from post seven during the first quarter. A week later, Magical Mike won the Historic-Goshen Cup after taking the early lead and then sitting in the pocket until the stretch, when he pulled out and won again in 1:54.4. With four weeks before the Woodrow Wilson Eliminations, Magical Mike won a qualifier in 1:58.4 and a two-year-old conditioned race in 1:54.1, which was his fifth win in five starts.

The Wilson Elimination, on July 30th at The Meadowlands, gave Magical Mike his first career defeat. He left slowly from the rail and was fourth at the quarter, later being parked out to the half and three-quarters. Expensive Scooter went on to score a one-length win over Magical Mike in 1:54.3. In the two-week gap between the Elimination and the $747,700 Wilson Final Magical Mike won another overnight event in 1:54.3 after being parked out to the half.

In the rich Woodrow Wilson Final, John Campbell was in the sulky and Magical Mike, despite his stellar record, went off at odds of almost seven to one. In an incredible display of class, Magical Mike overcame an extremely tough trip. Leaving from post six, he never saw the rail and Campbell was content to race him in sixth position in the outside flow for the first half, which was paced in a suicidal :54.3 after a front-end duel between Comedy Hour, Pacific Rocket and Million To One. The third quarter was backed down to :28 and Campbell made his move with Magical Mike, going three-wide on the backstretch to move into contention. Expensive Scooter, Pacific Rocket and favored Armbro Mackintosh were also on the move and there was a lot of congestion on the final turn. Expensive Scooter finally grabbed a short lead from Million To One. Campbell was still fifth and almost four lengths back in mid-stretch. Then, in a furious drive, Magical Mike found racing room, stretched out his stride and got up in time for a nose victory in the world record-equalling time of 1:51.4. A nose behind in second was 54-1 shot Sweet Dragon, who mirrored Magical Mike's move, with Armbro Mackintosh another half-length back in third. If there were ever any doubts about Magical Mike's tenacity, they were answered that night.

A week later at Freehold, Magical Mike finished fifth in a division of the Garden State S. after being parked out all the way. Tom Haughton then gave the precocious colt a week off and was in the sulky the following week at The Meadows, when Magical Mike scored an easy 1:54 Pennsylvania Sires S. win. Twelve days later, he won the Keystone Classic over the same track in 1:54.3 after racing on the outside to the three-quarters in 1:24 before taking the lead. At Lexington, the colt won over a sloppy track in 1:55.4. He was then given a couple of weeks rest prior to the Presidential S. Elimination at Rosecroft. Mike Lachance had the driving assignment and won his Elimination in 1:55.1, but was beaten in the Final a week later. "In the

Race Record Highlights

At 2

1st Woodrow Wilson S. Final
Governor's Cup Elimination and Final
Presidential S. Elimination
Bluegrass S.
Keystone Classic
Historic-Goshen Cup
Pennsylvania Sires S.

2nd Woodrow Wilson S. Elimination

At 3

1st Little Brown Jug
Breeders Crown
Oliver Wendell Holmes S.

At 3 (continued)

Jug Preview
heat of Tattersalls S.
North America Cup Elimination

2nd Meadowlands Pace Elimination
Adios S. Elimination

3rd Meadowlands Pace Final
North America Cup Final
James Dancer Memorial
Burlington S.

Honors

Equalled world record for two-year-old colts
Voted Two-Year-Old Pacing Colt of the Year

Magical Mike

Photo by Monica Thors

Race Record

Year	Age	Starts	Wins	2nd	3rd	Earnings	Record
1993	2	16	13	1	0	$ 769,408	p,2,1:51.4
1994	3	18	9	3	4	912,677	p,3,1:50.2
		34	22	4	4	$1,682,085	p,3,1:50.2

Magical Mike

Final of the Presidential," Lachance said, "Magical Mike was so aggressive in behind the gate that he flipped his soft palate. He paced to the front in :27.2, but I could hear him roaring, and I knew he was in trouble. He cut most of the mile, but stopped at the end. After that race, they tied his tongue out to the side and changed to an open bridle, and he was more manageable."

It was then on to Garden State Park for the Elimination and Final of the rich Governor's Cup with John Campbell again taking the reins. Magical Mike won his elimination easily in 1:55.3 and then took the $550,000 final by almost three lengths over Expensive Scooter and Cam's Card Shark.

When everything was tallied at the end of the year, Magical Mike had won 13 of his 16 starts and earned $769,408, including the season's two richest races for two-year-olds - the first horse to win both events. He was also a world champion. Not a bad season and certainly one which would give an owner winter dreams of standing in the winner's circle after the Little Brown Jug, the Breeders Crown and the Meadowlands Pace. After all, who could have predicted that Cam's Card Shark, who Magical Mike handled easily in both the Presidential and Governor's Cup races, would show such dramatic improvement and become a buzzsaw through the 1994 three-year-old pacing division?

Tom Haughton knew he had a champion and he brought Magical Mike back cautiously, winning three qualifiers, the last in 1:53.4, before entering the colt for his first seasonal start. The stakes are high in the three-year-old division. Not only are the purses lucrative, but there are usually offers in excess of a million dollars from breeding farms and syndicators at the end of the year for the top one or two colts. There is a lot of pressure, publicity and expectation in this division.

Magical Mike won his first three-year-old start in a resounding 1:51.2 in late May from post nine at The Meadowlands. But any dreams of an undefeated season evaporated two weeks later in the Burlington S. when Magical Mike was third behind Pacific Rocket and Cam's Card Shark. A week later, he turned the tables on Cam's Card Shark and won a North America Cup Elimination in 1:52.3 with a :27 second final quarter. However, in the $1,000,000 Final, driver Mike Lachance said he knew Magical Mike could not leave fast and decided not to battle on the front end. He raced in the outside flow and was still sixth and three-wide at the three-quarter pole. The colt was having trouble with the footing on the Woodbine track and closed to finish third behind new archrivals Cam's Card Shark and Pacific Rocket. Everyone now knew this was going to be a very competitive year in the three-year-old division.

Two weeks later, at The Meadowlands, Magical Mike finished fourth in a three-year-old Open after being parked out and interfered with in the stretch. His next two starts brought victories in the Elimination and Final of the Oliver Wendell Holmes S. - the final in 1:50.2, with a last quarter in :26.4. In the Adios S., Magical Mike was second in his Elimination to Historic and made an uncharacteristic break in the first turn to lose all chance in the Final. In early September, Cam's Card Shark handed Magical Mike another defeat in the James B. Dancer Memorial. At this point of the season, Magical Mike had earned over $430,000, but had won only four of his 12, starts although he was second and third in six others against the top colts in the nation.

But this did not match up to expectations that Magical Mike would be the top colt in the division. The champion two-year-old colt from the previous year, he had lost some of his glamour due to the exploits of Cam's Card Shark at three. However, in horse racing, sometimes another's misfortune opens doors. Word was out that Cam's Card Shark was suffering some physical problems. Haughton sent Magical Mike to Scioto Downs for the Jug Preview and named Mike Lachance as the colt's regular driver for the rest of the year. Magical Mike seemed his old self at the Jug Preview and won handily in 1:52.1 just 12 days prior to the Little Brown Jug. He was now primed for the big day and the Magical Mike camp was optimistic he would turn in a good performance.

Twenty-one horses were entered for the Jug, necessitating three Elimination divisions. Keystone Luther won his in 1:53.1 after Cam's Card Shark was a very late scratch. That great Cam Fella colt was not sound enough to go to the gate and this opened the door for Magical Mike. Lachance took his colt away quickly and sped to the first quarter in :26.4, a full second faster than Keystone Luther's first quarter in his win. Lachance recalled, "I really didn't have it in my mind to park Falcon's Future in this elimination heat, but when I warmed up Magical Mike I let him pace around the first turn a little and he was so good. Behind the gate, he was perfect. I was driving him with two fingers." He added, "When the starting gate closed, Magical Mike went into the first turn at Delaware like he'd been doing it all his life." When Falcon's Future came up on the outside, Lachance said to himself, "I'm in front. I'm here. And I'm gonna stay here." And stay there he did through fractions of :56.2, 1:25.1 and a final quarter of :27.4 to close out a 1:53 mile and win by four lengths over Historic and Witty Dragon. The other Elimination was won in a nice come-from-behind effort by Island Glow in 1:53.4, with favored Pacific Rocket making a break in the stretch.

In the $276,928 Jug Final, Lachance let Roger Hammer take the early lead with Keystone Luther but then grabbed the lead before the half. "At the half, I felt confident," said Lachance. "He was so good and he was so relaxed." Both Lachance and Haughton thought Magical Mike was stronger in the second heat than the first. The colt went on to win in 1:52.3 over Island Glow and Keystone Luther, earning the plaudits of 54,926 racing fans, the largest crowd ever for a harness race.

Owner Tom Walsh put it all in perspective after the Jug. Quoted in a *Hoof Beats* article he said, "He's had a tough season. He's drawn outside post positions and he's been racing against entries (three or four powerful colts from the Bill Robinson stable). We've had no luck all the way along. Everything worked out for us today, though. He's finally got all the recognition he deserves."

The Little Brown Jug was also a very emotional day for trainer Tom Haughton. The exhilaration of a big win in the Jug mingled with the memories of his late father, Billy, and brother, Peter. The legendary Billy Haughton had won five Little Brown Jugs and this was Tom's first - ironically, on the day which would have been his brother Peter Haughton's fortieth birthday.

Magical Mike was then sent to Lexington and finished second by three-quarters of a length to Armbro Maneuver after an almost impossible trip from post eleven in the second tier. The following week he won an Elimination of the Tattersalls S. in 1:50.4 but Haughton opted to keep Magical Mike out of the Final in order to rest him for the upcoming Breeders Crown two weeks later.

The $400,000 Breeders Crown at Garden State Park was the final race of Magical Mike's career. He was the heavy favorite and Lachance decided to race him from off the pace since he was leaving from post five and there were a lot of early speed horses on the inside. The strategy worked to perfection as Falcon's Future and Island Glow took turns on the lead and Magical Mike picked up cover from Keystone Luther before the three-quarter pole. Falcon's Future and Keystone Luther were fighting for the lead with Magical Mike waiting right behind to pick up the spoils - in this case, the Breeders Crown trophy. Lachance timed it just right and swept by the two leaders to win by a half-length in 1:51.3.

So Magical Mike's three-year-old season ended on a very positive note with five wins in his last six starts, including the majors - the Little Brown Jug and Breeders Crown. Not to mention, of course, another $475,000 in purses during a six-week period. And, as an extra bonus, a trip to Blue Chip Farms to begin a stallion career. For the 1994 season, Magical Mike won half of his 18 starts and banked another $912,677 for his owners to make his total career bankroll $1,682,085.

Sire Line

Magical Mike is one of the sires attempting to extend the line of the top racehorse and sire Tyler B. Most Happy Fella is the sire of Tyler B and has been the most successful of Meadow Skipper's sons in producing sons which are good sires. His son Cam Fella has at least a half-dozen sons who may have an impact on the breed, and his grandson No Nukes also looks as if he will be a sire of sires.

Magical Mike

Tyler B's best son as a stallion has been Dragon's Lair, closely followed by Tyler's Mark. Another son, Cole Muffler, who is a full brother to Dragon's Lair, had excellent crops in 1996 and 1997, including three 1:53 two-year-olds and he could bear watching. All of these sons of Tyler B are from Race Time mares, as is Magical Mike, and that is a point worth noting. In fact, Tyler's Mark and Magical Mike have dams which are full sisters - making those stallions full brothers in blood. Another close relationship among these sires is that the grandam of Dragon's Lair is by Tar Heel, while the grandam of Tyler's Mark and Magical Mike is by O'Brien Hanover, a son of Tar Heel. Other Tyler B sons which have had some success at stud are Franz Hanover and Dignatarian.

Maternal Line

Magical Mike is from the maternal family known as Lida and his branch is the most active and prolific. The key mare is the fourth dam Shy Ann, who was a daughter of Cardinal Prince. This branch of the family has produced early and extreme speed, including the sport's first 2:00 two-year-old filly Adios Betty p,2,T1:58.4 (by Adios) who is Magical Mike's third dam. Adios Betty is the dam of Tarport Lib p,3,1:56.2 ($144,146) who was a world champion three-year-old filly. Magical Mike's second dam, the O'Brien Hanover mare Tarport Martha, is a half-sister to the dam of Entrepreneur p,2,1:56.4, who was the world champion two-year-old colt for a short time. Trenton and Beach Towel are also extreme speed representatives of this family.

Closer up, the dam of Magical Mike is the Race Time mare Racing Date p,3,T1:57.2 ($18,865). She has produced four 1:56 performers from nine foals, two of them being top two-year-olds. Magical Mike has a full brother, Miles McCool p,2,1:53.2; 3,1:51.2f ($333,721) who won the Fox S. and a Woodrow Wilson Consolation at two and the Adios S. at three.

Racing Date is a full sister to the outstanding broodmare Dateable who has produced Historic p,3,1:51f ($1,334,861), Tyler's Mark p,3,1:51.3 ($289,997), Digger Almahurst p,2,1:52.1f ($371,866) and Seven O'Clock p,4,1:53.3 ($559,080), among others.

Analysis

The close pedigree relationships involving the Tyler B sons Magical Mike, Tyler's Mark, Dragon's Lair and Cole Muffler (meaning that Race Time and Tar Heel are prominent in their maternal lines) is unusual and, as such, may give us a clue to the kinds of broodmare crosses which may be effective for Magical Mike.

Tyler's Mark has worked well with daughters of a number of sires, but seems to be especially good with Bret Hanover mares and has also sired good performers from mares by Bret's sons Strike Out, Seahawk Hanover and Flying Bret. He's also worked well with granddaughters of Meadow Skipper.

Dragon's Lair, on the other hand, has really clicked with daughters and granddaughters of Albatross, especially those by Niatross. No Nukes' daughters have also been good producers with Dragon's Lair. While Cole Muffler has only two crops to examine at this writing, two of his three 1:53 two-year-olds are from daughters of Merger and Armbro Wolf - both sons of Albatross. The other is from a mare by Abercrombie.

Magical Mike is linebred 3x4 to Tar Heel, 4x3 to Good Time and 4x4 to Adios. He only has one cross to Meadow Skipper, which would appear in the fourth generation of his foals. Thus, Magical Mike certainly should be able to cross with mares with one or more crosses to Meadow Skipper. Even Meadow Skipper daughters would only give Magical Mike's foals a 4x2 cross to that stallion. Mares by No Nukes would produce foals with 3x4 crosses to Most Happy Fella, which should ensure a nice outcome.

A very popular stallion during his first three breeding seasons at Blue Chip Farms, Magical Mike was bred to books of 128, 170 and 128 mares. His first crop of yearlings sold in the fall of 1997 and 65 of them averaged $17,460 at the various sales with five of those yearlings selling for $50,000-$55,000 - three colts and two fillies. They looked good and seemed to get into the hands of several top trainers. Magical Mike deserves a chance and could be a hit.

Magical Mike, *Bay Horse, 16 Hands, 1991*
p, 2, 1:51.4; 3, 1:50.2 ($1,682,085)

Sire/Dam	2nd Gen	3rd Gen	4th Gen	5th Gen	6th Gen
Tyler B, 1977 p, 3, 1:55.1 $687,388	Most Happy Fella, 1967 p, 3, T1:55 $419,033	Meadow Skipper, 1960 p, 3, 1:55.1 $428,057	Dale Frost, 1951 p, 1:58 $204,117	HAL DALE	ABBEDALE Margaret Hal
				Galloway	Raider Bethel
			Countess Vivian, 1950 p, 3, 1:59 $43,262	King's Counsel	VOLOMITE Margaret Spangler
				Filly Direct	BILLY DIRECT Calumet Edna
		Laughing Girl, 1961 p, 4, 2:04h $19,546	GOOD TIME, 1946 p, 1:57.4 $318,792	HAL DALE	ABBEDALE Margaret Hal
				On Time	Volomite Nedda Guy
			Maxine's Dream, 1954 p, 2, T2:00 $36,557	Knight Dream	Nibble Hanover Lydia Knight
				Maxine Abbe	ABBEDALE Maxine Direct
	Tarport Cheer, 1966 p, 3, 2:08.3f	TAR HEEL, 1948 p, 4, T1:57 $119,148	BILLY DIRECT, 1934 p, 4, T1:55 $12,040	Napoleon Direct	Walter Direct Lady Erectress
				Gay Forbes	Malcolm Forbes Gay Girl Chimes
			Leta Long, 1940 p, 4, 2:03¾ $9,321	VOLOMITE	Peter Volo Cita Frisco
				Rosette	Mr. McElwyn Rose Scott
		Meadow Cheer, 1956 p, 2, 2:05h $16,083	ADIOS, 1940 p, T1:57½ $33,329	HAL DALE	ABBEDALE Margaret Hal
				Adioo Volo	Adioo Guy Sigrid Volo
			Betty G., 1946 p, 4, 2:13.3h	Wilmington	Bert Abbe Miss Saginaw
				Betty Crispin	Crispin Gold Girl
Racing Date, 1977 p, 3, T1:57.2 $18,865	Race Time, 1961 p, 3, 1:57 $486,955	GOOD TIME, 1946 p, 1:57.4 $318,792	HAL DALE, 1926 p, 6, 2:02¼	ABBEDALE	The Abbe Daisydale D.
				Margaret Hal	Argot Hal Margaret Polk
			On Time, 1938 p, 3, 2:03½h $1,472	VOLOMITE	Peter Volo Cita Frisco
				Nedda Guy	Guy Axworthy Nedda
		Breath O Spring, 1953 p, 3, T2:01.1 $3,144	Worthy Boy, 1940 3, 2:02½ $25,688	VOLOMITE	Peter Volo Cita Frisco
				Warwell Worthy	Peter The Brewer Alma Lee
			Lady Scotland, 1943	Scotland	Peter Scott Roya McKinney
				Spinster	SPENCER Minnetonka
	Tarport Martha, 1968 p, 2, 2:06.2f $1,009	O'Brien Hanover, 1955 p, 6, 1:59.2h $302,255	TAR HEEL, 1948 p, 4, T1:57 $119,148	BILLY DIRECT	Napoleon Direct Gay Forbes
				Leta Long	VOLOMITE Rosette
			Ormonde Hanover, 1943 3, T2:04¾	Dean Hanover	Dillon Axworthy Palestrina
				Norma Hanover	SPENCER Charlotte Hanover
		Adios Betty, 1951 p, 2, T1:58.4 $34,171	ADIOS, 1940 p, T1:57½ $33,329	HAL DALE	ABBEDALE Margaret Hal
				Adioo Volo	Adioo Guy Sigrid Volo
			Shy Ann, 1943	Cardinal Prince	Peter Potempkin Lillian L
				Bid Hanover	Sandy Flash Betty Blythe

Matt's Scooter

When you saw Matt's Scooter on the track, you just knew you would not forget his remarkable, long-reaching stride. He was impressive as a racehorse and is impressive as a sire.

Many still think of Matt's Scooter in terms of his epic 1:48.2 time-trial in which he broke the record set by Niatross. However, Matt's Scooter also won $2,944,591 and is the fourth leading money-winning pacer of all time. And, this was accomplished as a three- and four-year-old after winning only $20,000 at two.

Matt's Scooter was bred by Max Gerson of New York City and sold for $17,500 at the Fall Classic yearling sale held at The Meadowlands in 1986. Gerson also bred Matt's Scooter's dam, the Meadow Skipper mare Ellen's Glory. The yearling sale catalog page for Matt's Scooter was not impressive; he was the third foal from a non-record mare whose first two foals had not earned a penny at two and three. He sold for about $4,500 less than the average-priced Direct Scooter colts that fall. Until Matt's Scooter came along, this looked like just an average racehorse family with very little speed at two and three.

Purchased by Gordon and Illa Rumpel of Ontario, Canada, Matt's Scooter was given to Harry Poulton to train. He raced for the Rumpels at two and Charles Juravinski became a partner on the colt when Matt's Scooter was three.

At two, Matt's Scooter made only nine starts, the first of which - a parimutuel race at Greenwood on June 15, 1987 - resulted in a 2:00.3 victory. But Matt's Scooter did not show much gate speed and he was parked out for three-quarters in each of his next four races, all of which he lost. His best efforts were wins in two legs of a Series at Blue Bonnets in 1:58.1 and 1:59.2. He ended his short season with a second in the Series on August 15th.

When Matt's Scooter came back at three, he was third and second in his first two efforts in overnight events at Mohawk Raceway. He scored his first win on May 1st with a 1:56.4 effort at Windsor Raceway for Buddy Gilmour. Matt's first stakes race was an Elimination for the Windy City P. at Maywood Park. He finished second, parked out the final three-quarters and timed in 1:54.4. He was beginning to look like a stakes colt. In the $228,000 Windy City Final, Matt's Scooter was parked out first over again, but finished a game second by a half-length to Wealthy Skipper.

It was then on to The Meadowlands for the New Jersey Classic. In his Elimination he paced another solid effort, finishing second by a nose in 1:54 to Money Lender. Matt's Scooter became a star in the $500,000 New Jersey Classic Final when he grabbed the lead after the half for Gilmour and went on to win going away by five lengths over Armbro Global and Paladium Lobell in 1:52 with a final quarter in :27.1. A week later, there was disappointment at Greenwood when he finished fourth in an Elimination for the rich North America Cup.

The Meadowlands Pace Eliminations were three weeks later. Matt's Scooter survived a horrible trip from post eight which saw him eighth at the quarter, and ten lengths behind the leaders. Mike Lachance, who was on his first drive with the colt, rushed him up three-wide to get into contention at the half. The colt finally took over the lead after the half, and in spite of tiring in the stretch he held on to finish fourth and qualify for the Final.

The $1,039,000 Meadowlands Pace Final proved another showcase for Matt's Scooter and the start of a string of nine victories in his final 13 races at three. Lachance and Matt's Scooter left from post two. Lachance later recalled how the race unfolded: "Ever So Rich left fast (from the rail) and I just eased Matt's Scooter away. I probably could've gotten to the front right away, but I took it slow because I didn't want to rush Matt's Scooter to the quarter. I got to the front at the quarter. Matt's Scooter felt great. I was able to give Matt's Scooter a breather during the third quarter, which only went in 29 seconds. That got us to the three-quarters in 1:24.3 and I just urged Matt's Scooter a couple of times in the stretch and he came home in :27.3 to win by two lengths." That big 1:52.1 win over Camtastic and Armbro

Race Record Highlights

At 2
- **1st** two legs of Blue Bonnets Series
- **2nd** Blue Bonnets Series Final

At 3
- **1st** Meadowlands Pace
  Messenger S.
  Prix d'Ete
  Nat Christie Memorial
  Confederation Cup
  New Jersey Classic
  American-National S.
  two New Jersey Sires S.
- **2nd** Windy City S. Final and Elimination
  Slutsky Memorial
  New Jersey Classic Elimination
  Confederation Cup Elimination

At 4
- **1st** Breeders Crown
  Stewart Fraser Memorial
  Mohawk Gold Cup Final and Elimination
  U.S. Pacing Championship
  two legs of Molson Series
  Driscoll Series Final and two legs
  Cornell Memorial
  two legs of George Morton Levy Series
  two legs of Graduate Series
  leg of William Haughton Series
  On The Road Again P.
- **2nd** Battle of Lake Erie
  Graduate Series Final
  leg of Levy Series

Honors

Voted Three-Year-Old Pacing Colt of the Year
Voted Horse of the Year at four
Retired as the fastest Standardbred of all time
Leading money-winning Standardbred of 1988

Matt's Scooter

Photo by Monica Thors

Race Record

Year	Age	Starts	Wins	2nd	3rd	Earnings	Record
1987	2	9	3	1	2	$ 20,039	p,2,1:58.1f
1988	3	22	11	7	2	1,783,558	p,3,T1:48.2
1989	4	30	23	3	1	1,140,994	
		61	37	11	5	$2,944,591	p,3,T1:48.2

Matt's Scooter

Global proved Matt's Scooter belonged with the elite that year and brought his seasonal earnings to around $850,000. But that was only about the halfway point for Matt's Scooter that year. He proved to be a terror the remainder of the season and went on to win Three-Year-Old Pacing Colt of the Year honors.

Lachance drove Matt's Scooter for the rest of the year and was fortunate to be in that position. Matt's Scooter had already raced eight times at three before Lachance got to drive him. John Campbell had been scheduled to drive Matt's Scooter in the Meadowlands Pace but the colt drew into the same division as Chatham Light, a horse trained by Campbell's brother Jim. John Campbell opted to drive Chatham Light, which gave Lachance his chance with Matt's Scooter. "Matt's Scooter kept improving every week after that. He was sound and just kept getting stronger," said Lachance.

Two weeks after the Meadowlands Pace win, Matt's Scooter finished third in a non-stakes race at Greenwood but then came back to win the Nat Christie S. at Calgary in 1:54. The next rich event was the Prix d'Ete at Blue Bonnets. Matt's Scooter won his Elimination in 1:55 over B.J.'s Scoot and the Final in 1:54.4, over Runnymede Lobell and B.J.'s Scoot, after being parked out first over for three-quarters of a mile. The Confederation Cup was next at Flamboro Downs. Matt's Scooter was shuffled back to seventh at the top of the stretch, but managed to find racing room to finish second by a neck to Runnymede Lobell in the Elimination. He had a better trip in the Final and won in 1:55 by two lengths over B.J.'s Scoot.

Matt's Scooter then went back to New Jersey and won a New Jersey Sires S. at Garden State Park in 1:53.2 with a final quarter in :26.4. This was a week before one of the greatest achievements of his career. The colt was not eligible to the Little Brown Jug so he was sent to The Red Mile for a time-trial. Prior to the time trial, Lachance met with Poulton, Rumpel and Juravinski and asked, "How fast do you think this guy can go?" They had wanted to beat 1:50 and if he could pace faster than the 1:49.1 of Niatross that would be great. "I honestly didn't think that Matt's Scooter could pace in 1:48 and a piece, but I thought he could pace between 1:49 and 1:50," said Lachance.

Lachance talked about the famous time-trial in a *Hoof Beats* interview. The big event took place just a day after he had won the Little Brown Jug driving B.J.'s Scoot, so it was quite a couple of days for this Hall of Fame reinsman. "I was trying to go the half in :54, but he's such a good-gaited horse it didn't bother me we got there sooner," said Lachance. "When we passed the three-quarters, I started to push him. The more I pushed him, the more he responded. I'm sure that his last eighth was the fastest eighth of the whole mile. That's how strong he was." Matt's Scooter had two prompters in his time-trial and paced the final quarter in :27 to break Niatross' world record of 1:49.1, set eight years earlier. Matt's Scooter's fractions were :27.1, :53.3, 1:21.2 and 1:48.2 - a monumental effort in becoming the fastest Standardbred of all time!

Matt's Scooter lived up to his new title two weeks later when he won the $461,404 Messenger S. at Yonkers Raceway in 1:56.3 after being parked out the entire mile. However, bad luck plagued him a week later in the $329,000 Slutsky Memorial at Monticello Raceway. Leaving from post six, Matt's Scooter was interfered with after the start. Lachance said, "I got interfered with in the first turn and was pushed seven-wide. I had to stop Matt's Scooter to a dead walk. He was completely out of the race, but he still came back and was beaten by Albert Albert a neck in 1:55.2. Matt's Scooter was better on a big track than he was on a half-mile, but he was okay around a half-mile track."

The colt returned to winning form with an easy 1:53.1 win in a New Jersey Sires S. at Garden State Park and followed that with an impressive win over Albert Albert in the $384,500 American-National S. at Sportsmans Park. Matt's Scooter ended his three-year-old campaign with a surprising head loss to Concussion at Mohawk. But the year had been a huge success with 11 wins in 22 starts, earnings of $1,783,558, the world championship and divisional honors.

Like a true champion, Matt's Scooter came back even better as a four-year-old. He raced from March through November and won 23 of 30 starts for earnings of over $1,140,994 - a sparkling campaign by any standard. In addition, being the fastest horse ever made Matt's Scooter "a marked man" as every other driver and owner wanted to beat him. As a result, Matt's Scooter suffered many parked out trips but continued to show his speed and courage.

Matt's Scooter won six of his first seven starts, losing only to Jaguar Spur by a half-length. He then lost two races to Jaguar Spur, then finished first over that rival in the Battle of Lake Erie, but was disqualified. He later won 17 of his last 19 starts, including his final 10 in succession. His fastest win of the year was in 1:50.3 with a final quarter in a fast 26 seconds.

"Matt's Scooter is the greatest horse I've ever driven," said Lachance in a December, 1994, *Hoof Beats* interview. "I've never driven a pacer with as much high speed as Matt's Scooter had. Even back in the late 1980s, before the new bikes, I know he could have paced a quarter in 25 seconds. And he was the best gaited pacer I ever drove when he was in high gear."

Among the major victories for Matt's Scooter as a four-year-old were the Breeders Crown at Freehold in 1:53.2, Driscoll Series Final and the U.S. Pacing Championship. The reward for Matt's Scooter was Horse of the Year honors by a 176-71 margin over the star trotting filly Peace Corps. Then, with all of his honors, Matt's Scooter was off to stud at Peretti Farms of New Jersey and the beginning of a new career.

Sire Line

Matt's Scooter is the greatest son of the good sire Direct Scooter, who has done a remarkable job in saving the Volomite line of pacing sires. In fact, Direct Scooter is linebred 3x4 to Volomite and his dam was bred to be a trotter, being by the great trotting sire Noble Victory. But Direct Scooter was a world champion pacer at three and won over $800,000.

Direct Scooter has several sons at stud, but Matt's Scooter is far superior to the others, although In The Pocket is also showing signs of sire ability. Since Direct Scooter has no Meadow Skipper and Adios blood, and no Hal Dale blood at all for that matter, he has now been serving as an excellent outcross sire for a couple of generations of pacers. You can find out more about Direct Scooter in his chapter.

Maternal Line

The Meadow Skipper mare Ellen's Glory, Matt's Scooter's dam, is from the maternal family known as Molly Dillard. This is not a family noted for speedy young stakes horses, but rather for producing long-wearing and hard-hitting older pacers. Aside from Matt's Scooter, Ellen's Glory has produced in this fashion, as have her first and second dams.

Ellen's Glory has produced six winners from her first eight foals of racing age and they include, besides Matt's Scooter, Skip To Glory p,1:53 ($93,258) (by Warm Breeze), Born To Glory p,1:55f ($124,230) (by Falcon Seelster), Mountain Zephyr p,3,1:57.3 (Warm Breeze) and Glorious Mae p,3,1:58 (by Direct Scooter). Ellen's Glory is a full sister to Michael's Glory p,4,1:55.4 ($212,796) and three-quarter-sister to David's Comet p,1:58f ($109,334). She also has a three-quarter-sister by Most Happy Fella, who has produced two sons in 1:54.4f and 1:56f.

This is not the sort of maternal family from which you would expect a world champion such as Matt's Scooter to arise, but such are the ways of nature when it comes to horse breeding. The big question is whether Matt's Scooter will be able to continue to pass on the traits which made him a top horse. Ellen's Glory is linebred 3x4 to Hal Dale and that is the only Hal Dale blood in the pedigree of Matt's Scooter.

Progeny of Note

From Matt's Scooter's first five crops of racing age, not including his 1998 two-year-olds, 72% of his racing sons and daughters have taken 2:00 records. Another interesting statistic is that 87% of Matt's Scooter's foals have been starters - an excellent showing. Of course, you must take into consideration that many of Matt's Scooter's offspring have been racing over the mile tracks of The Meadowlands and Garden State Park since they are eligible for nomination to the New Jersey Sires S. Still, he has excellent figures.

Direct Scooter has been maligned over the years for not being a sire of good fillies and his stud fee was even adjusted lower for fillies. However, Matt's Scooter seems to be doing quite well in the filly department. In fact, his richest offspring is the top world champion daughter Mystical Maddy p,4,1:50 ($1,436,325) who won 19 of 21 starts and was voted Three-Year-Old Pacing Filly of the Year in 1996. Her major wins included the Breeders Crown, Nadia Lobell S. and Mistletoe Shalee S. She won divisional honors again at four. In 1993, Matt's Scooter's daughter Freedom's Friend p,2,1:53.1 ($637,622) won divisional honors at two and her big wins included the Sweetheart Final and the Three Diamonds Final.

On the colt side, His Mattjesty p,2,1:52.1f; 3,1:51 ($993,881) won over $800,000 in 1996 at two, including the Breeders Crown Final and the Matron S. His Mattjesty's Breeders Crown win made Matt's Scooter the only pacing stallion, thus far in the 1990s, to sire two Breeders Crown champions in a single year. Other good Matt's Scooter colts are Mattgilla Gorilla p,3,1:53.3f ($370,789) who won the Cane Pace at three, Sable Matters p,3,1:52.2 ($370,023) who won the Niatross P. and the Garden State S., Falcon's Scooter p,3,1:51.1 ($482,825) who won the New Jersey Classic, Mattduff p,3,1:51.2 ($362,024) who won the Matron S. at two and the Burlington S. at three, and Good News Scooter p,1:50.3 ($356,697).

Matt's Scooter suffered a setback when his good son Stand Alone p,2,1:52.4 ($333,337) died after winning eight of his 11 starts. Stand Alone had won the Niatross S., the Bluegrass S. and the International Stallion S., among others.

The sons and daughters of Matt's Scooter are well-represented on the Grand Circuit and are always factors in the New Jersey Sires S. events.

Analysis

Matt's Scooter is a breeding throwback of sorts since he has no common ancestors in the first four generations of his pedigree. His closest common crosses are 4x5x5x6 to Volomite, 4x5x5 to Billy Direct, 5x4x5 to Scotland and 4x5 to Hal Dale. The youngest of these four stallions is Billy Direct, who was foaled in 1934. Thus Matt's Scooter, like his sire Direct Scooter, is kind of an outcross sire. But the presence of Meadow Skipper in his pedigree makes most of Matt's Scooter's offspring inbred or linebred.

Breeding for a top performer from Matt's Scooter seems to be a simple exercise when you look at the facts and figures. Of the top 25 money-winners by Matt's Scooter all but three were bred 3x3 or 3x4 to Meadow Skipper. Two of the three which did not have that cross were bred 3x5 to Meadow Skipper. The only horse in this group whose dam did not have any Meadow Skipper blood was Mattalac p,1:52 ($321,926) whose dam is by Race Time from a Direct Rhythm mare.

The appearance of Race Time in a broodmare's pedigree seems to be an extremely helpful factor when breeding to Matt's Scooter. Four of his top seven money-winners have Race Time in the pedigree in addition to the Meadow Skipper crosses and the same extends to nine of the top 21 performers. This seems to be significant and worth noting.

Matt's Scooter has also crossed very well with females from Sandy's Sable's maternal family. Her daughter Sable Hanover has produced two $200,000 winners by Matt's Scooter; another daughter Sandbea Hanover has a $180,000 winner; and a granddaughter, Sable B., has produced a $370,000 winner. Four of Matt's Scooter's six richest performers are from mares by Most Happy Fella line sires, as are 12 of the top 25. Matt's Scooter had some excellent two-year-olds in 1997 and I want to point out that his five best were by the Most Happy Fella line stallions Tyler B, On The Road Again (2), No Nukes and Oil

Burner. The second dams of three of those five were by Bret Hanover line stallions. Another example of that cross is the 1998 speedster Nuke The Scoot p,3,1:51.1-'98 who is by No Nukes from a Bret Hanover mare. Another strong presence, of course, is Albatross since he appears as the sire of the dam, or second dam, in 10 of the 22 highest earners.

A female factor in several top performers is that of the great producing mare The Old Maid - a top modern-day foundation mare. Matt's Scooter's ill-fated son Stand Alone had a couple of interesting crosses in his pedigree. His dam is bred 3x4 to the full sisters Meadow Cheer and Meadow Addy (both daughters of the foundation mare Betty G.) and his grandam is bred 3x3 to the half-brothers Dancer Hanover and Thorpe Hanover - both sons of The Old Maid. Scoot To Power p,3,1:52.1f ($341,026) has a dam who is bred 3x3 to Dancer Hanover and his half-sister Terka Hanover - son and daughter of The Old Maid. Viking Terror p,1:52.4 ($336,005) has a dam who is bred 3x4 to Dancer Hanover and Terka Hanover. And Grand Lady p,3,1:52.4 ($235,571) has a dam who is bred to The Old Maid and her half-sister Lady Scotland - also a great broodmare.

I point this out so you can look for connections to The Old Maid in the pedigrees of mares you may be considering sending to Matt's Scooter. If you think the success of this connection is merely a coincidence, consider the fact that Race Time's second dam, Lady Scotland, is a half-sister to The Old Maid. It appears that The Old Maid's and Lady Scotland's dam Spinster has a certain "nick" with Matt's Scooter.

Mares by Matt's Scooter should be interesting broodmare prospects since they will have the Direct Scooter blood and, most likely, a dose or two of Meadow Skipper blood through their dams as well as through Matt's Scooter. Since his fillies perform well and are from mostly good maternal families, there is no reason to think they will not be successful as broodmares in future years. His oldest daughters are now seven and should start having foals of racing age in 1997 and 1998.

A final thought: You may want to breed a mare with a fast record to Matt's Scooter. Of course, these were the types of mares which were accepted to his court - nothing but the best. Thus far, 18 of Matt's Scooter's 20 richest performers are from mares with records of 1:58.4 or faster. But it should be noted that Matt's Scooter's richest foal, Mystical Maddy, and his second fastest, Computer Scooter p,4,1:50.2-'98 ($176,529), are from non-record mares.

Matt's Scooter

Photo by Monica Thors

Leading Progeny by Matt's Scooter

Fastest
Mystical Maddy, m, p,4,1:50 $1,436,325
Computer Scooter, h, p,4,1:50.2 $176,529
Good News Scooter, h, p,1:50.3 $356,697
Call For Cash, h, p,3,1:51 $213,863
His Mattjesty, h, p,3,1:51 $993,881
Matt Russian, g, p,1:51.1 $168,052
Falcon's Scooter, g, p,3,1:51.1 $482,825
Rock Blaster, g, p,3,1:51.1 $105,145
Mr Mikey, g, p,4,1:51.1 $132,520
Nuke The Scoot, h, p,3,1:51.1 $33,370

Richest
Mystical Maddy, m, p,4,1:50 $1,436,325
His Mattjesty, h, p,3,1:51 $993,881
Freedom's Friend, m, p,2,1:53.1 $637,622
Falcon's Scooter, g, p,3,1:51.1 $482,825
Mattgilla Gorilla, h, p,3,1:53.3f $370,789
Sable Matters, h, p,3,1:52.2 $370,023
Mattduff, h, p,3,1:51.2 $362,024
Good News Scooter, h, p,1:50.3 $356,697
Scoot To Power, h, p,3,1:52.1f $341,026
Viking Terror, h, p,1:52.4 $336,005

Matt's Scooter, Bay Horse, 16 Hands, 1985
p, 2, 1:58.1f; 3, T1:48.2 ($2,944,591)

Sire/Dam	2nd Gen	3rd Gen	4th Gen	5th Gen	6th Gen
Direct Scooter, 1976 p, 3, 1:54 $800,451	Sampson Direct, 1957 p, 4, T1:56 $137,486	Sampson Hanover, 1947 p, 4, T1:56.4 $28,708	**VOLOMITE**, 1926 3, 2:03¼ $32,649	PETER VOLO	PETER THE GREAT / Nervolo Belle
				Cita Frisco	San Francisco / Mendocita
			Irene Hanover, 1930 4, T2:01	**DILLON AXWORTHY**	Axworthy / Adioo Dillon
				Isotta	PETER THE GREAT / The Zombro Belle
		Dottie Rosecroft, 1945 p, 4, 2:05.2 $7,735	**BILLY DIRECT**, 1934 p, 4, T1:55 $12,040	Napoleon Direct	Walter Direct / Lady Erectress
				Gay Forbes	Malcolm Forbes / Gay Girl Chimes
			Beams Hanover, 1935 p, 3, 2:07¾h	Calumet Chuck	Truax / Sumatra
				Lexington Maid	PETER VOLO / Fruity Worthy
	Noble Claire, 1969 p, 2, 2:04 $5,557	Noble Victory, 1962 4, 1:55.3 $522,391	Victory Song, 1943 4, 1:57.3 $73,859	**VOLOMITE**	PETER VOLO / Cita Frisco
				Evensong	Nelson Dillon / Taffolet
			Emily's Pride, 1955 3, T1:58 $130,751	Star's Pride	Worthy Boy / Stardrift
				Emily Scott	SCOTLAND / May Spencer
		Scotch Claire, 1953 2, T2:06 $1,595	**SCOTLAND**, 1925 T1:59¼	Peter Scott	PETER THE GREAT / Jenny Scott
				Roya McKinney	McKinney / Princess Royal
			Abbey Claire, 1945	Guy Abbey	GUY AXWORTHY / Abbacy
				Jean Claire	Belwin / Honeymoon H
Ellen's Glory, 1978	Meadow Skipper, 1960 p, 3, 1:55.1 $428,057	Dale Frost, 1951 p, 1:58 $204,117	**HAL DALE**, 1926 p, 6, 2:02¼	Abbedale	The Abbe / Daisydale D.
				Margaret Hal	Argot Hal / Margaret Polk
			Galloway, 1939 p, 2:04½h $5,294	Raider	PETER VOLO / Nelda Dillon
				Bethel	David Guy / Annotation
		Countess Vivian, 1950 p, 3, 1:59 $43,262	King's Counsel, 1940 p, 6, 1:58 $44,930	**VOLOMITE**	PETER VOLO / Cita Frisco
				Margaret Spangler	**GUY AXWORTHY** / Maggie Winder
			Filly Direct, 1941 p, 3, 2:06¾h $6,299	**BILLY DIRECT**	Napoleon Direct / Gay Forbes
				Calumet Edna	Peter The Brewer / Broncho Queen
	Gloria Barmin, 1968 p, 3, 1:59.2 $52,849	Greentree Adios, 1953 p, 2, 2:00.4 $31,897	Adios, 1940 p, T1:57½ $33,329	**HAL DALE**	Abbedale / Margaret Hal
				Adioo Volo	Adioo Guy / Sigrid Volo
			Martha Lee, 1937 p, 2:05½	Lee Harvester	Lee Axworthy / Willina H
				Ruth G	Peter G / Fanny McKerron
		Adept Hanover, 1960 p, 4, 2:04.3h $4,730	Tar Heel, 1948 p, 4, T1:57 $119,148	**BILLY DIRECT**	Napoleon Direct / Gay Forbes
				Leta Long	**VOLOMITE** / Rosette
			Arbutus Hanover, 1951	Dean Hanover	**DILLON AXWORTHY** / Palestrina
				Aida	Scotland / Aileen Arion

Meadow Skipper

Looking at the racing career of such a superior stallion as Meadow Skipper, one might expect to find clues indicating that the son of Dale Frost would become one of the most important pacing sires in the history of the breed. But there is little in Meadow Skipper's racing life that would really provide a clue to his future siring prowess.

He was not a dominant two-year-old. He won only $24,097 at two, despite 15 victories in 27 starts, many of them on Ohio fair tracks. His two-year-old mark, taken in 1962, was 1:59.4, as the future star raced for Delvin Miller.

Miller did not rate Meadow Skipper particularly highly as a two-year-old. He was not a competitive colt on the Grand Circuit so Miller sent him with groom/trainer Paul Crilly to race on the Ohio Fair circuit where he had more success. Later, Miller sent Foster Walker with a group of his horses. including Meadow Skipper, to race in California that fall. The plan was to send Meadow Skipper with that group, race him a few times, geld him and then have a good three-year-old to race the following year. Well, Meadow Skipper saved his stud career by racing well in California, taking his two-year-old record of 1:59.4 there. Driven by Joe Lighthill, he proved he was a better colt than Miller had originally thought. Miller then changed his mind about gelding Meadow Skipper. In 1962, only two pacing youngsters took 2:00 records, Meadow Skipper and his later archrival Overtrick.

Meadow Skipper spent the winter between his two- and three-year-old seasons in California and then won the Spring Sophomore Pace at Santa Anita at three. He was sent east where he won in 2:01.3 at Roosevelt in June and impressed Earle Avery so much that he called Norman Woolworth to recommend he try to purchase the colt from Hugh Grant. Woolworth acted on his advice and the result was that Meadow Skipper was sold during the spring of his three-year-old year, shortly before the Commodore Pace. The price has never been disclosed, but it was reported at the time to be in the vicinity of $150,000. Trained and raced by Earle Avery, Meadow Skipper won the Commodore Pace, and the rest, as they say, is history.

At three, he blossomed somewhat for Avery and Woolworth into a legitimate stakes star, but he was clearly not the best horse of his division. That honor fell to the handsome Solicitor colt Overtrick, and Meadow Skipper basically spent the year chasing his chief rival. Meadow Skipper did win the Cane Futurity (forerunner to the Cane Pace) in a Yonkers track record of 1:58.1h, and the Challenge Stakes at Scioto, and he was second to Overtrick in the Little Brown Jug. However, his most memorable battle with Overtrick, and his greatest victory, was in the first heat of the Poplar Hill Farm Pace at The Red Mile. It was in this race that he recorded his life mark of 1:55.1 - a world record for three-year-olds. Many horsemen referred to it as the greatest race they had ever seen. Overtrick and Diamond Sam traded the early lead and then Avery sent Meadow Skipper to the front. Meadow Skipper was on the engine and passed the half in :57.1 and the three-quarters in 1:26.1. Overtrick was the only serious challenger left and he came up to Meadow Skipper at the Red Mile tunnel. The two colts raced as a team down the stretch with Meadow Skipper never giving in and winning by a slim margin in an extremely game effort. He just refused to be beaten.

Meadow Skipper won $208,376 at three, winning 13 of 30 heats along the way.

It was not a dominant record, and nor was Meadow Skipper a dominant FFA star. As an aged horse, Meadow Skipper won only eight of 22 at four; and only two of seven at age five. His most important aged victory came in the 1¼ mile American Classic in California, and he was second in the Yonkers International and Realization Stakes, both at distances beyond a mile, those being the major aged events available in that era. Meadow Skipper is one of those horses who would have been improved by having more racing opportunity on mile tracks. Nearly all of the classic races of his era

Meadow Skipper

Race Record Highlights

At 2
- **1st** heat of Scioto Challenge S.
  multiple Ohio Home Talent S.
- **2nd** heat of Parshall Memorial
  two heats of Buckeye Futurity
  heat of Buckeye State S.
- **3rd** heat of Scioto Challenge S.

At 3
- **1st** Cane Futurity
  Commodore Pace
  Scioto Challenge S.
  Poplar Hill Farm S.
  Spring Sophomore S.
  Ville De Troit S.
  Governor's Cup
  heat of Director of Agriculture S.
- **2nd** heat of Little Brown Jug

At 3 (continued)
  Messenger S.
  Castleton P.
  Liberty Bell Early Closer
- **3rd** heat of Little Brown Jug
  two heats of Battle of Saratoga

At 4
- **1st** American Classic (1⅛ miles)
- **2nd** Realization S.
  April Star P.
- **3rd** Hi Lo's Forbes P.
  National Pacing Derby

At 5
- **1st** International Preview P.
  Washington Park FFA P.
- **2nd** Internationl Pace
- **3rd** American Pacing Classic

Honors
At three, set world record on mile track

Race Record

Year	Age	Starts	Wins	2nd	3rd	Earnings	Record
1962	2	27	15	6	2	$ 24,007	p,2,1:59.4
1963	3	30	13	8	6	208,376	p,3,1:55.1
1964	4	22	8	2	3	123,237	
1965	5	7	2	1	1	72,437	
		86	38	17	12	$428,057	p,3,1:55.1

Photo by Tony Leonard
Courtesy of The Horseman and Fair World

were on half-mile tracks, and the long-striding, often rough-going Meadow Skipper was clearly handicapped on the smaller ovals. The fact that several of his memorable successes, including his Lexington performance at three, and the American Classic victory at Hollywood Park as an aged horse, clearly showed his fondness for the bigger oval. Meadow Skipper's lifetime racing record includes 38 career victories in 86 starts, with earnings of more than $428,000.

Sire Line

Meadow Skipper was by far the most accomplished son of his sire, Dale Frost, whose total 2:00 production could be counted on a single pair of hands (he had only seven 2:00 offspring in an unspectacular stud career). No other son or daughter of Dale Frost ever achieved like Meadow Skipper, and the case could be made that Meadow Skipper was as important to the breed as any stallion that preceded him.

Like nearly every other contemporary pacing champion, Meadow Skipper traces in his male line to Hal Dale, and in fact is a grandson of the great patriarch. Hal Dale established three prominent sire lines through his sons, Adios, Good Time and Dale Frost. The Adios and Good Time lines enjoyed massive success in the 1950's and 1960's. The Adios line emerged through standouts like world champions Adios Butler and Bret Hanover, and the Good Time clan had memorable performers like Race Time, Best Of All and Columbia George. Then, in the late 1960's and early 1970's, the Dale Frost line emerged magnificently through Meadow Skipper. It was one of those unlikely curve balls that nature throws us once in a while.

Nearly every observer of the day thought the future of this sire line rested with Adios and his sons, or maybe even with Good Time's accomplished offspring. Almost no one chose Meadow Skipper as the catalyst of a new breed of North American pacer, but that is what he became. Meadow Skipper's get clearly remade the modern pacing horse into the exciting and speedy animal we have come to know today. The sire line he created through his sons Albatross and Most Happy Fella dominate pacing as few sires in history have. Grandsons of Meadow Skipper that do not trace through either Albatross or Most Happy Fella also account for such modern racing successes as Jenna's Beach Boy p,4,1:47.3 (a son of Beach Towel) and other successful sires, like the Canadian sensation Run The Table p,3,1:51, a son of Meadow Skipper's son Landslide.

Maternal Line

Christy Hayes owned Countess Vivian and had her booked to Adios for the 1959 breeding season. But Adios was bothered by laminitis problems that year and Delvin Miller made the decision to switch the mare to Dale Frost who was also standing at stud at his Meadow Lands Farm. However, he had a difficult time in convincing Hayes of the idea.

Meadow Skipper was foaled at Delvin Miller's Meadow Lands Farm on April 19, 1960. The name was a combination of Del Miller's farm and Christy Hayes' son Skip. Hayes died later that year and Countess Vivian, the foal she was carrying, and Meadow Skipper were sold to Hugh Grant of Pennsylvania - one of Miller's major owners.

Meadow Skipper's maternal background is interesting if for no other reason than the fact that like many accomplished horses he also had a talented female sibling. In Meadow Skipper's case, this was his Adios three-quarter sister Countess Adios p,3,1:57.3, a filly three years his junior who was one of the most successful racing fillies in the history of the breed. She was so good that at three she won two legs of pacing's Triple Crown, capturing both the Messenger and Cane Pace. She did not win the Little Brown Jug because she was ineligible for that classic, which was won by Bullet Hanover.

Countess Vivian is by King's Counsel p,1:58, one of the racing stars of the 1940's whose many memorable battles with Adios during their racing days are a unique feature of racing's archives. King's Counsel was a son of Volomite and was mated with the Billy Direct mare Filly

Direct p,3,2:06¾h to produce Countess Vivian p,3,1:59. Countess Vivian was herself a former world champion three-year-old race filly and stakes winner at both two and three. This is not a wide or deep family, by contemporary standards, but does include a number of current stars. The Abercrombie stallion Armbro Cadet, a leading Midwestern sire, traces directly to the same female line, as do the wonderful Canadian race fillies Heatherjeankillean p,1:53 and Ruthellenkillean p,3,1:53.2; the Little Brown Jug winner Armbro Omaha p,3,1:56.1; the $900,000 winner Take A Look p,1:54.1 and many other useful pacers, all tracing directly back to Countess Vivian.

Progeny Of Note

From his very first crop, Meadow Skipper went about rewriting the standards by which all other pacing sires would be judged. His first crop, foals of 1967, included the Triple Crown winner Most Happy Fella p,3,T1:55 ($419,033) and his second crop produced the wonder-colt Albatross p,4,1:54.3f ($1,201,470). In subsequent crops, he produced a slate of champion colts whose exploits vaulted Meadow Skipper to the pinnacle of the siring world. This group included the exciting colt star Nero p,4,T1:55.1 ($528,208), as good a two-year-old pacer as ever lived; the somewhat erratic Windshield Wiper p,3,T1:53.2 ($379,205); the Little Brown Jug star Governor Skipper p,3,1:54 ($1,039,756); the fabulously successful Ohio star Falcon Almahurst p,3,T1:52.2 ($400,776); the two-year-old phenomenom Scarlet Skipper p,3,1:56.2; General Star p,3,1:54.3; the aged sensation Genghis Khan p,1:51.4 ($983,467); the world champion Trenton p,3,1:51.3; Adios winner Landslide p,3,1:54.1; the multiple two-year-old world champion French Chef p,2,1:54; the millionaire Mr. Dalrae p,1:52.2; Triple Crown champion Ralph Hanover p,3,1:53.4 and Chairmanoftheboard p,3,1:53.2f ($1,341,823).

While Meadow Skipper's colts dominated the pacing classics, his daughters also graced many a winner's circle. His richest filly was the ill-fated Breeders Crown champion Naughty But Nice p,3,1:54 ($1,062,197), but no doubt his best racing daughter was the superb Handle With Care p,3,T1:54.2 ($809,689), whose two-year-old season saw her go undefeated. Meadow Skipper also had the world champion aged mare Tender Loving Care p,4,T1:52.3 and exquisite females like the diminutive Jugette winner Misty Raquel p,3,1:55.3 ($484,463) and aged star Green With Envy p,1:53.4 ($474,645).

Meadow Skipper stood for 16 seasons before his death from a heart attack in a paddock at Stoner Creek Stud in 1982. He was only 22 years old. His first crop were foals of 1967 and his last crop hit the ground in the spring of 1982. He was a magnificent-looking, dark brown horse whose get not only revolutionized the breed with their smooth motion and speed, but also provided good looks and soundness.

As a sire, he set new standards, creating bench marks of excellence that ushered in the modern pacing era, creating a siring dynasty that today dominates nearly all of North American pacing. Meadow Skipper was the first sire to produce the winners of $5 million in a single season, and when he died he was the leading 2:00 sire in all of the sport.

The late Stoner Creek Stud manager Tom Stewart was quoted, "Meadow Skipper was the perfect horse to be around. He was big, kind and gentle." Stewart added, "You work in this business all you life, and it's an honor to be around a horse like him."

Analysis

Meadow Skipper has done it all. There are very few stallions who have been great racehorses, great sires, great sires of sires and great broodmare sires. Meadow Skipper changed the Standardbred breed forever when his first crop raced nearly 30 years ago. His sons and daughters took the breed to a new level and their descendants continue to do the same.

Many sons of Meadow Skipper have been successful stallions, both nationally and in regional programs. The leaders are Albatross, Most Happy Fella, Nero, Falcon Almahurst, Governor Skipper, French Chef, Landslide and Windshield Wiper, among others. And, Meadow Skipper fillies and mares have been in demand for years by breeders.

Meadow Skipper

Meadow Skipper was the sport's leading money-winning sire from 1975 through 1978. He was overtaken by his sons Most Happy Fella in 1979 and 1980 and by Albatross from 1981 through 1984 and again in 1986. He still ranks among the top 10 pacing sires in career earnings ($66,640,376) and in $100,000 winners (184) and is the third leading 2:00 broodmare sire of all time.

Very few sires, if any, have had as many true all-time great sons and daughters as Meadow Skipper. He and Adios are the only two stallions to sire two pacing Triple Crown winners (Most Happy Fella and Ralph Hanover) and Meadow Skipper has also sired at least 16 divisional champion colts and fillies. At one point, his offspring virtually dominated the sport.

Meadow Skipper's list of great colts includes Albatross, Most Happy Fella, Nero, Ralph Hanover, Governor Skipper, French Chef, Falcon Almahurst and Genghis Khan. His top fillies include Naughty But Nice, Handle With Care, Misty Raquel, Green With Envy, Meadow Blue Chip, Roses Are Red and Tender Loving Care - and this is just scratching the surface.

Some sires seem to need certain breeding "nicks" to become successful while others are able to sire great performers from mares of varying bloodlines and racing ability. Meadow Skipper is a prime example of a stallion who could "move up" a mare and enable her to produce performers far beyond expectations. Nine of Meadow Skipper's ten fastest performers are from mares by different stallions, the only repeat broodmare sire being the Adios son Shadow Wave. Two other sires whose daughters had great success with Meadow Skipper are Bret Hanover and Thorpe Hanover. Granddaughters of Adios were especially good producers from Meadow Skipper as 13 of his 26 fastest colts and fillies are from daughters of Adios and his sons Bret Hanover, Shadow Wave, Queen's Adios, Henry T. Adios, Dancer Hanover and Adios Paul.

The same holds true for the pedigrees of Meadow Skipper's seven $1,000,000 winners. All show Adios or his sons involved as the sire of the dam or grandam. Much of the pedigree strength of Meadow Skipper's best performers comes from multiple crosses to Hal Dale, Billy Direct and Volomite. For example, among Meadow Skipper's successful stallion sons, Albatross is bred 3x4 to Hal Dale; Nero is 4x4 to Billy Direct and Volomite; Falcon Almahurst is 3x4 to Hal Dale and 4x4 to Volomite; Windshield Wiper is 3x5 to Hal Dale and 4x4 to both Billy Direct and Volomite and Slapstick is 3x4 to Hal Dale, 4x3 to Billy Direct and 4x4 to Volomite.

A colt and filly share honors as Meadow Skipper's fastest performers with his son Trenton and daughter Don't Dally both taking records of 1:51.3 as three-year-olds. Trenton is 3x4x5 to Hal Dale and 3x4 to King's Counsel while the filly is 3x4x5 to Hal Dale and 4x4 to Billy Direct. Genghis Khan, at 1:51.4, has no common ancestors in his first four generations since he is New Zealand bred from the top mare Robin Dundee.

Of Meadow Skipper's other $1,000,000 winners besides Albatross and Governor Skipper, the cross for Triple Crown winner Ralph Hanover is 3x4 to Hal Dale, 4x3 to Billy Direct and 4x4x5 to Volomite; Chairmanoftheboard is 3x4x5 to Hal Dale and 4x4 to the half-sisters Lady Scotland and The Old Maid; Land Grant is 3x4x4 to Hal Dale; Mr. Dalrae is 3x4 to Hal Dale and 4x4 to Volomite; and the filly Naughty But Nice is 3x4x5 to Hal Dale and 3x4 to Adios.

There are some other interesting aspects to certain crosses. Windshield Wiper has additional crosses of 4x4 to Adios and his sister Adieu and an inbred 2x4 cross to Dale Frost (Meadow Skipper's sire) and his half-sister Jackie Frost. Two top horses, Most Happy Fella and Governor Skipper, have inbred 3x3 crosses to Hal Dale. Both were excellent racehorses and Most Happy Fella was also a great sire.

Meadow Skipper was a sire not only of great males, but also of some of the sport's best ever fillies and mares. None who saw them will forget the performances of Handle With Care, Green With Envy, Naughty But Nice, Meadow Blue Chip, Don't Dally, Tender Loving Care, Misty Raquel, Roses Are Red and Watering Can. Both Naughty But Nice and Tender Loving Care have similar crosses - 3x4x5 to Hal Dale and 3x4 to Adios. Handle With Care is 3x5x4 to Hal Dale and 3x4 to King's Counsel which is a similar cross to Meadow Skipper's fastest son Trenton.

Today, we are interested primarily in Meadow Skipper as a broodmare sire but that will soon come to an end. His youngest daughters are 16 years old in 1998 and there are fewer than 200 of them under 20 years of age with many of those no longer in active production.

Meadow Skipper has been a spectacular broodmare sire, just as he was as a sire. His daughters have produced three sub-1:50 performers in Matt's Scooter p,3,T1:48.2, Call For Rain p,4,1:49.3 and Jet Jockey p,1:49.4. He also has eight $1,000,000 broodmare sire credits. To date, there are over 30 sub-1:52 horses from Meadow Skipper mares, including such stars as Storm Compensation p,1:50.3, All Star Hanna p,3,1:50.2, Native Born p,1:50.3, Dare You To p,1:50.4, Save Fuel p,1:51.1, Laag p,3,1:51.2, Brando Hanover p,3,1:51.3 and Tibet p,4,1:51.3.

Kentucky Spur p,3,1:52 Robust Hanover p,3,1:52.2, Pershing Square p,3,1:52.3, Leah Almahurst p,3,1:52.3, Incredible Finale p,4,1:53.2f, Totally Ruthless p,2,1:55.1f, Seahawk Hanover p,3,1:55.2 and Margie's Melody p,4,T1:55.4 (dam of Nihilator) are some other prime examples of Meadow Skipper broodmare credits.

Many breeding enthusiasts feel Meadow Skipper will go down in history as the greatest pacing sire of all time because of his domination of the breed during his peak years and for the continued success of his descendants - both male and female.

Meadow Skipper

Photo courtesy of the USTA

Leading Progeny by Meadow Skipper

Fastest
- Trenton, h, p,3,1:51.3 $88,639
- Don't Dally, m, p,3,1:51.3 $219,334
- Genghis Khan, h, p,1:51.4 $983,467
- Glen Almahurst, h, p,4,1:52.1 $452,619
- Mr Dalrae, h, p,1:52.2 $1,150,807
- Falcon Almahurst, h, p,3,T1:52.2 $400,776
- Rashad, h, p,4,1:52.3 $374,329
- Tender Loving Care, m, p,4,T1:52.4 $327,822
- George Allen, h, p,3,T1:53 $169,922
- Persistent, h, p,1:53 $212,188

Richest
- Ralph Hanover, h, p,3,1:53.4 $1,828,871
- Chairmanoftheboard, h, p,3,1:53.2f $1,341,823
- Albatross, h, p,4,1:54.3f $1,201,470
- Land Grant, h, p,3,1:56.1 $1,164,849
- Mr Dalrae, h, p,1:52.2 $1,150,807
- Naughty But Nice, m, p,3,1:54f $1,062,197
- Governor Skipper, h, p,3,1:54 $1,039,756
- Genghis Khan, h, p,1:51.4 $983,467
- Seatrain, g, p,1:55 $825,006
- Handle With Care, m, p,3,T1:54.2 $809,689

Meadow Skipper, Brown Horse, 1960
p, 2, 1:59.4; 3, 1:55.1 ($428,057)

Dale Frost, 1951 p, 1:58 $204,117	Hal Dale, 1926 p, 6, 2:02¼	Abbedale, 1917 p, 2:01¼	The Abbe, 1903 p, 2:04	Chimes	Electioneer / Beautiful Bells
				Nettie King	Mambrino King / Nettie Murphy
			Daisydale D., 1908 3, 2:15¼	Archdale	Expedition / Aline
				Mrs. Tmolus	Pactolus / Flaxey
		Margaret Hal, 1914 p, 2:19½h	Argot Hal, 1903 p, T2:04¾	Brown Hal	**TOM HAL JNR** / Lizzie
				Lady Wildflower	Duplex / Sally Ward
			Margaret Polk, 1906	John R. Gentry	Ashland Wilkes / Dame Wood
				Stella Hal	**TOM HAL JNR** / Dolly II
	Galloway, 1939 p, 2:04½h $5,294	Raider, 1929 p, 1:59½	Peter Volo, 1911 4, 2:02	**PETER THE GREAT**	Pilot Medium / Santos
				Nervolo Belle	Nervolo / Josephine Knight
			Nelda Dillon, 1920 p, 4, T2:08¾	Dillon Axworthy	**AXWORTHY** / Adioo Dillon
				Princess Nelda	Prince McKinney
		Bethel, 1926 p, 2:03	David Guy, 1915 3, 2:05¼	**GUY AXWORTHY**	**AXWORTHY** / Lillian Wilkes
				Belle Zombro	**ZOMBRO** / Belle Gibson
			Annotation, 1915 p, 2:18¼h	Azoff	**PETER THE GREAT** / Dolly Worthy
				Citation	Norvalson
Countess Vivian, 1950 p, 3, 1:59 $43,262	King's Counsel, 1940 p, 6, 1:58 $44,930	Volomite, 1926 3, 2:03¼ $32,649	Peter Volo, 1911 4, 2:02	**PETER THE GREAT**	Pilot Medium / Santos
				Nervolo Belle	Nervolo / Josephine Knight
			Cita Frisco, 1921	San Francisco	**ZOMBRO** / Oniska
				Mendocita	Mendocino / Esther
		Margaret Spangler, 1918 p, 2:02¼	Guy Axworthy, 1902 4, 2:08¾	**AXWORTHY**	Axtell / Marguerite
				Lillian Wilkes	Guy Wilkes / Flora
			Maggie Winder, 1906 p, 3, 2:06¼	Oratorio	Wilkes Boy / Canzonet
				Clara Direct	Direct / Miss Alcantara
	Filly Direct, 1941 p, 3, 2:06¾h $6,299	Billy Direct, 1934 p, 4, T1:55 $12,040	Napoleon Direct, 1909 p, 1:59¾	Walter Direct	Direct Hal / Ella Brown
				Lady Erectress	Tom Kendle / Nelly Zarro
			Gay Forbes, 1916 p, 2:07¾	Malcolm Forbes	Bingen / Nancy Hanks
				Gay Girl Chimes	Berkshire Chimes / Miss Gay Girl
		Calumet Edna, 1931 p, 2:08½h	Peter The Brewer, 1918 4, 2:02½	**PETER THE GREAT**	Pilot Medium / Santos
				Zombrewer	Zombro / Mary Bales
			Broncho Queen, 1916 p, 2:09¼h	Empire Direct	Direct Hal / Bessie Bonehill
				The Broncho	Stormcliffe / Linora

Most Happy Fella

Most Happy Fella has done it all. Not only was he a pacing Triple Crown winner, but he went on to become one of the sports most outstanding sires and founded a line of pacing sires which has risen to the top levels of the sport. In addition, he is one of the all-time great broodmare sires due to the success of his daughters as producers of champions.

Most Happy Fella was a member of his sire Meadow Skipper's first crop, as he was a foal of 1967. He injured a hock as a yearling, and was withdrawn from his breeder Stoner Creek Stud's annual yearling consignment to the Tattersalls auction in the fall of 1968. Stoner Creek instead sent the colt to Florida to have him broken by Hall of Famer Stanley Dancer. When the colt was put into a training sale at Pompano Park early that winter, it was Dancer who haltered the colt for $12,000. A big, rough-looking colt, Most Happy Fella was bothered throughout his career by the hock injury, which produced a somewhat rough-gaited style at both two and three. In fact, the young son of Meadow Skipper did not earn a sub-2:00 record at two, his freshman mark being only 2:01.3f. He earned only $31,794 at two, although he did win the American-National S., Arden Downs S., Batavia Colt S., Reading Futurity and Reynolds Memorial in 14 starts.

At three, however, Most Happy Fella emerged as the king of his division. Winning hard-driving victories in the Little Brown Jug, Cane Pace and Messenger, he completed a Triple Crown sweep, one of only eight pacers to do so. He also won the Adios, Shapiro, Matron, Orange County Cup, Reading Futurity and Canadian Grand Circuit stakes. Most Happy Fella was sold to Blue Chip Farm for $1,000,000 the day before the Little Brown Jug. He took his lifetime mark of p,3,T1:55 in a 1970 time trial at The Red Mile for Dancer. He won $387,239 at three, making his lifetime total $419,033 with 22 career victories. After being voted Pacer of the Year in 1970, he went to stud at Blue Chip Farms in New York.

During Most Happy Fella's stud career, his trainer/driver Stanley Dancer commented, "What a nasty horse he was to drive. You never knew when Most Happy Fella was going to make a break. He went with such a tight hobble, and he still felt like he was going to put in a step. I was surprised he was such a great sire. He sired some good-gaited horses."

Sire Line

The Most Happy Fella male line has proven to be the most dominant of all the Meadow Skipper sons, eclipsing even the great Adios. Most Happy Fella's son Cam Fella is a great sire and has at least a half-dozen sons who are positioning themselves as successors, including Precious Bunny, Presidential Ball, Cambest and Cam's Card Shark. Another Most Happy Fella son, Tyler B., was very successful in his own right and is the sire of Dragon's Lair, Tyler's Mark, Cole Muffler and 1998 first crop sire Magical Mike.

Happy Motoring gave us the good sire On The Road Again and other Most Happy Fella sons Precious Fella and Troublemaker did a decent job as stallions for a time. Then, of course, there is the Most Happy Fella son Oil Burner whose main claim to fame is being the sire of the great No Nukes who appears to have several strong candidates for continued siring stardom: Jate Lobell, Western Hanover, Dexter Nukes and Die Laughing.

Yes, the Most Happy Fella branch of the Meadow Skipper sire line seems very healthy right now and should continue to be successful well into the new century. In contrast, the Albatross branch may be nearing the finish line unless Ball And Chain and/or Silver Almahurst become successful sires. The French Chef branch of the Meadow Skipper line seems to rest with Beach Towel and his great son Jenna's Beach Boy while the Landslide branch is buoyed by the very successful Canadian stallion Run The Table.

While these other branches of the Meadow Skipper line seem to be taking forward steps with only a handful of stallions, the Most Happy

Race Record Highlights

At 2
1st American-National S.
Arden Downs S.
Batavia Colt S.
Reading Futurity
Reynolds Memorial
2nd Excelsior S.
Meadow Lands P.
Atlantic City Early Closer

At 3
1st Little Brown Jug
Cane Futurity
Messenger S.
Adios S.
L.K. Shapiro S.
Matron S.
Bullet Hanover S. Final
Orange County Cup
Best of All P.
Reading Futurity
Westchester S.

At 3 (continued)
Blue Bonnets Grand Circuit S.
Cardigan Bay P.
2nd Battle of Brandywine
Gaines Memorial
American Pacing Classic
heat of Adios S.
heat of Little Brown Jug
3rd Commodore P.
Hanover Colt S.
heat of Horseman Futurity

Honors
Triple Crown winner at three
Voted Pacer of the Year at three

Most Happy Fella

Photo courtesy of The Horseman and Fair World

Race Record

Year	Age	Starts	Wins	2nd	3rd	Earnings	Record
1969	2	14	6	4	0	$ 31,794	p,2,2:01.3f
1970	3	26	16	6	3	387,239	p,3,T1:55
		40	22	10	3	$419,033	p,3,T1:55

Fella branch has about a dozen candidates worthy of continuing this branch at a very high level in the sport.

Maternal Line

Much of Most Happy Fella's rough physical appearance can be attributed to his Good Time dam, Laughing Girl p,4,2:04h, a daughter of the Knight Dream matron Maxine's Dream p,2,T2:00. Laughing Girl was an unusually large mare to be by Good Time, whose foal type was generally small. The mare also produced two full brothers to Most Happy Fella, the exported Good Humor Man p,3,T1:58.4; and the stakes-winning Jolly Roger p,3,T2:00.4 before her early death.

Most Happy Fella is inbred to Hal Dale. Since he is by Meadow Skipper, a grandson of the great patriarch, and out of a mare by Good Time, a son of Hal Dale, this creates a 3x3 generation cross to Hal Dale. Like many of his contemporaries, Most Happy Fella thrived on a melding of blood from different branches of the Hal Dale sire line.

Progeny of Note

Most Happy Fella's first foals were born in 1972. This very initial offering included two of harness racing's greatest racing fillies, the multiple stakes winners Silk Stockings p,3,1:55.2 ($694,894) and her arch-rival Tarport Hap p,4,1:56.3f ($688,664). There was little to separate the two fillies, except their physical presence. Silk Stockings was a smallish, petite filly with a useful, quick brush that allowed her to get the jump on Tarport Hap, a big, strapping, rough-looking filly with great durability and strength. In 1973, Oil Burner p,4,1:54.2 ($535,431) came along. Oil Burner had been trained and driven by Stanley Dancer, but Dancer sold him as a three-year-old, and he quickly developed a reputation as one of the fastest pacers in history. Oil Burner, of course, would sire No Nukes, the legendary racehorse and speed-producing sire that founded the male line that today has led to successful racehorses and sires like Jate Lobell and Western Hanover.

After the initial success of the filly queens Silk Stockings and Tarport Hap, Most Happy Fella's stud career blossomed. His first crop of foals numbered only 53, but by 1976, his foal counts had improved dramatically. In that year, he produced 143 foals, followed by 171 in 1977. Most Happy Fella was earning a reputation as a great filly sire, but his first few crops did not produce a stellar colt. His 1976 crop included another good filly, the multiple stakes-winning Happy Sharon p,4,1:55.4 ($606,964), but his first top colt was just around the corner.

Tyler B was a foal of 1977 and thus was a contemporary of Niatross, one of the breed's most dominant colt performers. Tyler B never beat Niatross, but he did a lot for Most Happy Fella's reputation, getting a p,3,1:55.1 mark, with earnings of $688,644. It was clear that a top colt, maybe even a dominant performer, was on the way. It would be a couple more years before that colt hit the racetrack, but from Most Happy Fella's 146 foals in 1979 came one of the breed's greatest racehorses and biggest success stories. Cam Fella p,4,1:53.1 ($2,041,367) must be appraised as one of the finest racehorses ever produced. Although not a dominant two-year-old (he won only three races as a freshman), Cam Fella became a 28-race winner at three, and then won 30 times as a four-year-old, racing from early in the season to late in the fall. He was Horse of the Year in 1982 and 1983, one of the few two-time winners of that award. In his career, Cam Fella won 61 times in 80 starts, including 58 of 69 at three and four.

Most Happy Fella's subsequent crops included such other male stars as Doc's Fella p,4,1:54.1 ($1,267,059); Breeders Crown winner Troublemaker p,2,T1:54 ($1,112,103) and the rugged New York FFA star Division Street p,5,1:52.3f ($1,222,552). Then there was the Canadian champion Take A Look p,1:54.1f ($987,624); and the Meadowlands star Armbro Splurge p,1:55.2 ($602,327). Throughout his career, Most Happy Fella produced exceptional fillies, and his final crop of 1984 included the brilliant Armbro Feather p,1:51.3 ($1,454,927), his biggest money-winning female. Other notable sons of Most Happy Fella include his fastest offspring, the durable FFA star What's Next p,4,1:51.3 ($492,712); the world champion Armbro Aussie p,3,1:51.4 ($545,037); the world champion May Wine p,4,1:52.3 ($377,265) and the wonderful filly champion Toy Poodle p,3,1:53.4 ($434,793).

Most Happy Fella died at the age of 17 after breaking a leg in a pasture incident when he was spooked by a deer that entered his stud paddock at Blue Chip Farms. It was a huge loss for the industry, and for Blue Chip Farms. From only 13 crops he produced nearly 1,500 foals who won nearly $95 million, and he had more than 550 2:00 performers. His 1,221 starters averaged $77,000 in earnings.

Analysis

Most Happy Fella stands out as a sire of fast, tough and long-lasting racehorses and as a renowned broodmare sire. He and Albatross are Meadow Skipper's most outstanding stallion sons and each has made a major impact on the Standardbred breed. In addition, Most Happy Fella has done something that Albatross has found difficult; he has continued his successful sire line through several more generations of sons, grandsons and great-grandsons. He is a sire of sires and several of his sons seem to have the same capability.

There does not appear to be anything exceptional about Most Happy Fella's pedigree. He is inbred 3x3 to Hal Dale through his sire Meadow Skipper and his dam's sire Good Time. He also has crosses of 4x4x4 to Abbedale and 4x4 to Volomite.

The sport's leading money-winning sire for the 1979 and 1980 seasons, Most Happy Fella was runner-up to Albatross in this category from 1981 through 1984 and to his sire Meadow Skipper in 1978. He still ranks as the third leading money-winning pacing sire of all time with his offspring banking nearly $95,000,000. He is also second to Albatross in siring $100,000 winners.

Most Happy Fella has given us the great racehorse and sire Cam Fella as well as Tyler B, both of whom were excellent sires and are profiled in this book. In addition, there are other decent siring sons such as Oil Burner, Troublemaker, Precious Fella and Happy Motoring. Oil Burner gave us No Nukes who passed the torch to his primary sons Jate Lobell, Western Hanover, Dexter Nukes and Die Laughing. Happy Motoring is the sire of the very successful On The Road Again.

Of course, Cam Fella and Tyler B have also done their part in continuing the Most Happy Fella line. Cam Fella is responsible for Precious Bunny, Presidential Ball, Cambest, Camtastic, Goalie Jeff and the 1998 first crop sire Cam's Card Shark. It stands to reason, if the past is any indication, that one or more of the great Cam Fella sons will also continue this line. The same holds true for the sons of Tyler B since he is the sire of the successful Dragon's Lair, along with Tyler's Mark and the underrated Illinois sire Cole Muffler (Dragon's Lair's brother). In 1998, Magical Mike's youngsters make their racetrack debuts and perhaps he will emerge as Tyler B's most outstanding son at stud.

It is now clear that the Most Happy Fella male line is the dominant branch of the Meadow Skipper males with regard to successfully continuing this line. Other than those stallions already mentioned, there are two additional sires with the same potential - the Beach Towel son Jenna's Beach Boy (French Chef branch of Meadow Skipper) and Run The Table (Landslide branch of Meadow Skipper). However, I suspect the next great sires from this line will be sons or grandsons of No Nukes and Cam Fella. Some other Most Happy Fella sons who have achieved success are Denali, who dominated the California program for years, Dallas Almahurst, who was a good sire in Ontario, and Smooth Fella who achieved acclaim in New Zealand.

Among the top sons and daughters of Most Happy Fella, the main common cross is to Hal Dale - mostly in the fourth generation. Most Happy Fella clicked with a variety of broodmare sires, but the most successful were those from the Adios male line; the dams of 12 of his 20 fastest offspring are from the Adios male line. The most prominent of these is Bret Hanover who is responsible for five of this dozen. Other Adios line representatives are Silent Majority, Shadow Wave, Airliner and Adios Vic.

Bret Hanover is the sire of the dams of three of Most Happy Fella's four fastest performers - What's Next p,4,1:51.3, Armbro Feather p,1:51.3 and Scene Topper p,1:52.1 as well as other stars like Cam Fella and Troublemaker. In the money-winning department, Bret Hanover is the broodmare sire for three of Most Happy Fella's five $1,000,000 winners - Cam Fella, Armbro Feather and Troublemaker. The other two are Doc's Fella (Tar Heel mare) and Division Street (Bye Bye Byrd mare).

Tar Heel mares also had great success with Most Happy Fella and are responsible for such star sons as Tyler B., Doc's Fella, Armbro Aussie, Boone And Crockett and great daughters like May Wine, Silk Stockings, Tarport Hap and Happy Sharon. Tar Heel's good son Thorpe Hanover is the broodmare sire of the fillies Toy Poodle and Kris Messenger and colt Big Band Sound. Tar Heel also had success with Most Happy Fella as the sire of the grandams of top performers such as Division Street, What's Next, Take A Look, Happy Motoring, Midi A Semalu and Present Laughter.

The presence of other sires such as Bye Bye Byrd, Knight Dream, Shadow Wave and Scottish Pence were also noted in several of Most Happy Fella's best sons and daughters. Shadow Wave is especially interesting since he is the sire of the dams of both Oil Burner and Happy Motoring who sired their good sons No Nukes and On The Road Again.

Most Happy Fella is also very prominent as a sire of great fillies with seven $500,000 winners - Armbro Feather, Silk Stockings, Tarport Hap, Happy Sharon, Happy Lady, Midi A Semalu and Mistletoe Shalee. The first three of these are among the sport's all-time great females.

Now we'll take a look at some of the pedigree crosses among some of Most Happy Fella's stars. His fastest son, What's Next, is 4x3 to Tar Heel and 4x4x4 to Hal Dale. His dam is inbred 3x2 to Tar Heel and we've already seen Most Happy Fella's affinity for the Tar Heel connection. Armbro Feather and Armbro Aussie are 4x4x4 to Hal Dale as are Oil Burner, Silk Stockings, Tarport Hap, Big Band Sound, Happy Motoring, Midi A Semalu, Mistletoe Shalee and Denali, among others.

Cam Fella has a very interesting pedigree in that he is inbred 3x3 to Dale Frost and extremely linebred 4x4x4x4 to Hal Dale. The rich Division Street is 4x4x4 to Hal Dale, 4x4x5 to Billy Direct and an inbred 3x3 to the brother and sister Adios and Adieu. Take A Look has an interesting cross with his 3x3 to Countess Vivian who is the dam of Meadow Skipper (Most Happy Fella's sire).

The great mare Silk Stockings is 5x3 to Billy Direct, 4x4x4 to Hal Dale, 4x4 to the full brothers King's Counsel and Chief Counsel and 5x5 to the half-sisters Rose Scott and La Roya. Happy Sharon is 4x3 to Billy Direct, 4x3 to Knight Dream and 5x5 to Scotland and his full sister Rose Scott. Happy Motoring has five crosses to Hal Dale with his 4x4x4x5x4 and is also 4x4 to Knight Dream. Happy Lady has a similar 4x4 to Hal Dale and 4x4 to Knight Dream.

In the broodmare sire category, Most Happy Fella sparkles again and is currently in a battle for third place on the all-time list with his sire Meadow Skipper. To date they are only separated by 25 2:00 credits, with Most Happy Fella's daughters accounting for 1,562 2:00 performers at this writing. Only Albatross and Bret Hanover rank higher.

Most Happy Fella's daughters have long been among the most sought after in the breed and his youngest females are now 14 years of age. Most Happy Fella is the broodmare sire of such top performers as the sub-1:51 stars Mystical Maddy p,4,1:50 ($1,399,025), Without Reproach p,3,1:50 ($366,932), Ramblin Storm p,1:50.1 ($1,068,063),

Bilateral p,4,1:50.2 ($1,051,876), Vine Street p,3,1:50.2 ($356,600), Bullvon's Dream p,1:50.2 ($842,960), Road To The Top p,1:50.2 ($382,037), Prince Ebony p,1:50.3 ($909,774) General Cochran p,1:50.3 ($216,495), Bad Self p,1:50.4 ($355,371), Make Music p,4,1:50.4 ($403,651) and Apache Max p,3,1:51 ($275,865).

Also fast and rich are Keystone Raider p,4,1:51.1 ($946,914), Armbro Emerson p,4,T1:51.4 ($1,472,590), Scoot Outa Reach p,4,1:51.4 ($757,436), Cimarron p,1:51.4 ($878,904), Laughs p,3,1:52.1 ($1,383,172), Topnotcher p,4,1:52.3f ($1,340,840), Armbro Dallas p,3,1:52.3 ($1,401,201), the good Ohio sire Nobleland Sam p,3,1:53 ($451,417), Sweet Reflection p,3,1:53.1 ($1,004,639), Armbro Cadet p,4,1:53.2 ($693,392) and scores of others.

Most Happy Fella daughters are responsible for eight $1,000,000 winners, placing him behind only Bret Hanover and Albatross in that category. Just as Most Happy Fella did very well with mares by Adios line stallions, his daughters are doing equally well when bred to Adios line stallions. For example, millionaires Armbro Emerson, Armbro Dallas and Topnotcher are by Abercrombie as are Cimarron, Make Music, Armbro Omar p,4,1:51 and Armbro Cadet. Millionaire Ramblin Storm is by Storm Damage as are Vine Street and Safe Haven. Millionaire Bilateral is by Laag (Abercrombie son) as is Broad Grin p,3,1:51.4.

Abercrombie's sire, Silent Majority, is the sire of Laughs. The only two millionaire broodmare credits for Most Happy Fella which are not sired by Adios line stallions are Mystical Maddy (Matt's Scooter) and Sweet Reflection (Big Towner). Direct Scooter and his sons have also had success with Most Happy Fella mares as have Big Towner and his sons.

Another interesting point about Most Happy Fella's daughters is that three of them have produced extremely inbred top performers in Road To The Top p,1:50.2, Bad Self p,1:50.4, Traveling Man p,4,1:51.4, Vacationing p,1:52.4f ($562,405) and Tulsa Blue Chip p,1:53.1 ($465,456) - all by On The Road Again who is a grandson of Most Happy Fella. The common cross here is 3x2 to Most Happy Fella and it seems to be working well.

Any way you look at him, as a racehorse, sire, broodmare sire or sire of sires, Most Happy Fella has to be near the top of each list and will go down in Standardbred history as a monumental stallion.

Most Happy Fella

Photo courtesy of The Horseman and Fair World

Leading Progeny by Most Happy Fella

Fastest

Armbro Feather, m, p,4,1:51.3 $1,454,927
What's Next, h, p,4,1:51.3 $492,712
Armbro Aussie, h, p,3,1:51.4 $545,037
Scene Topper, h, p,1:52.1 $274,822
Division Street, g, p,1:52.3f $1,222,552
May Wine, m, p,4,1:52.3 $377,265
Deadly Fella, h, p,1:52.3 $343,044
Happy Chatter, h, p,1:53 $700,194
Boone and Crocket, h, p,1:53 $266,957
New York New York, h, p,1:53 $169,171

Richest

Cam Fella, h, p,4,1:53.1 $2,041,367
Armbro Feather, m, p,4,1:51.3 $1,454,927
Doc's Fella, g, p,4,1:54.1 $1,267,059
Division Street, g, p,1:52.3f $1,222,552
Troublemaker, h, p,2,T1:54 $1,112,103
Take A Look, h, p,1:54.1f $987,624
Happy Chatter, h, p,3,1:53 $700,194
Silk Stockings, m, p,3,1:55.2 $694,894
Nickylou, h, p,1:54.2 $694,747
Tarport Hap, m, p,4,1:56.3f $688,664

Most Happy Fella, Bay Horse, 1967
p, 2, 2:01.3f; 3, T1:55 ($419,033)

Meadow Skipper, 1960 p, 3, 1:55.1 $428,057	Dale Frost, 1951 p, 1:58 $204,117	**HAL DALE**, 1926 p, 6, 2:02¼	**ABBEDALE**, 1917 p, 2:01¼	The Abbe / Chimes, Nettie King Daisydale D. / Archdale, Mrs. Tmolus
			Margaret Hal, 1914 p, 2:19½h	Argot Hal / Brown Hal, Lady Wildflower Margaret Polk / John R. Gentry, Stella Hal
		Galloway, 1939 p, 2:04½h $5,294	Raider, 1929 p, 1:59½	**PETER VOLO** / **PETER THE GREAT**, Nervolo Belle Nelda Dillon / Dillon Axworthy, Princess Nelda
			Bethel, 1926 p, 2:03	David Guy / **GUY AXWORTHY**, Belle Zombro Annotation / Azoff, Citation
	Countess Vivian, 1950 p, 3, 1:59 $43,262	King's Counsel, 1940 p, 6, 1:58 $44,930	**VOLOMITE**, 1926 3, 2:03¼ $32,649	**PETER VOLO** / **PETER THE GREAT**, Nervolo Belle Cita Frisco / San Francisco, Mendocita
			Margaret Spangler, 1918 p, 2:02¼	**GUY AXWORTHY** / Axworthy, Lillian Wilkes Maggie Winder / Oratorio, Clara Direct
		Filly Direct, 1941 p, 3, 2:06¾h $6,299	Billy Direct, 1934 p, 4, T1:55 $12,040	Napoleon Direct / **WALTER DIRECT**, Lady Erectress Gay Forbes / Malcolm Forbes, Gay Girl Chimes
			Calumet Edna, 1931 p, 2:08½	**PETER THE BREWER** / **PETER THE GREAT**, Zombrewer Broncho Queen / Empire Direct, The Broncho
Laughing Girl, 1961 p, 4, 2:04h $19,546	Good Time, 1946 p, 1:57.4 $318,792	**HAL DALE**, 1926 p, 6, 2:02¼	**ABBEDALE**, 1917 p, 2:01¼	The Abbe / Chimes, Nettie King Daisydale D. / Archdale, Mrs. Tmolus
			Margaret Hal, 1914 p, 2:19½h	Argot Hal / Brown Hal, Lady Wildflower Margaret Polk / John R. Gentry, Stella Hal
		On Time, 1938 p, 3, 2:03½h $1,472	**VOLOMITE**, 1926 3, 2:03¼ $32,649	**PETER VOLO** / **PETER THE GREAT**, Nervolo Belle Cita Frisco / San Francisco, Mendocita
			Nedda Guy, 1928 3, 2:03½h $14,318	**GUY AXWORTHY** / Axworthy, Lillian Wilkes Nedda / Atlantic Express, Pleasant Thought
	Maxine's Dream, 1954 p, 2, T2:00 $36,557	Knight Dream, 1945 p, 3, T1:59 $76,973	Nibble Hanover, 1936 1:58¾ $25,599	Calumet Chuck / Truax, Sumatra Justissima / Justice Brooke, Claire Toddington
			Lydia Knight, 1929	**PETER THE BREWER** / **PETER THE GREAT**, Zombrewer Guy Rosa / **GUY AXWORTHY**, Rosa Lake
		Maxine Abbe, 1937 p, 4, 2:05h	**ABBEDALE**, 1917 p, 2:01¼	The Abbe / Chimes, Nettie King Daisydale D. / Archdale, Mrs. Tmolus
			Maxine Direct, 1918 p, 2:03¼	**WALTER DIRECT** / Direct Hal, Ella Brown Vernie Wilkes / Anderson Wilkes

Nero

At ages two and three, Nero was as exciting a racehorse as ever seen on the track. He had an air of invincibility about him and a special toughness when faced with adversity. As a stallion, his sons and daughters raced well during the early 1980s and Nero's stud fee kept climbing, reaching a high of $30,000 at one point. He sired a number of champions and his daughters were especially precocious.

But, like all good things, his high-flying years came to an end as more and more new stallions were retired during the free-spending 1980s and the competition from other great sons of Meadow Skipper simply overwhelmed Nero. Today, Nero is respected for his accomplishments and his career totals still rank him near the top ten of the all-time pacing sire list in terms of 2:00 performers and earnings of his offspring. As late as 1991, Nero was ranked sixth among the leading money-winning pacing sires of all time, behind only Albatross, Most Happy Fella, Meadow Skipper, Bret Hanover and Abercrombie. In addition, he has turned out to be a very solid broodmare sire and is moving up in that important category.

First, let's take a look a Nero as a racehorse. The Nero saga began when trainer Jim Crane placed an advertisement in the Wall Street Journal for new owners to invest in racehorses. It was a rather unorthodox approach for a harness racing trainer. A. Rene Dervaes, Jr., from Cheyney, Pennsylvania, answered the ad and agreed to invest with Crane. Nero was sold as a yearling and selected by Crane in the fall of 1973 at the Tattersalls sale for $20,000. The partnership consisted of Dervaes (75%), his friend and neighbor Jack Massau (15%) and Jim Crane (10%). Nero was bred by Mrs. W. H. Wyatt of Franklin, Tennessee.

The colt was put into training with Crane and five months before Nero's first start the trainer made the statement, "I have the best colt that I have ever dreamed of having." Months later, Crane's opinion proved prophetic as Nero won his first baby race at Brandywine Raceway in late June 1974 by 16 lengths in 2:03.1 with a final quarter in a dazzling :28.3. Crane then drove him to two more victories in overnight events at Rosecroft Raceway in 2:06.1 and 2:03.1 by eight and 14 lengths.

Nero's first stakes race was the L.B. Sheppard Memorial at Yonkers Raceway and Crane put Herve Filion up as the driver. The pair cruised to a 2:02.1 victory and Nero's stakes career was on its way. A week later, Nero won the Andy Kerr Memorial at Vernon Downs with Joe O'Brien, who was to be Nero's regular driver, in the sulky. Nero then swept through the Arden Downs S. and an Open event at Scioto Downs.

The prestigious $100,000 Fox S. at Indianapolis was next on the schedule for Nero and Dervaes and his partners flew there to watch the streaking colt on the big mile track. But an announcement was made before the race that Nero had been scratched. Dervaes rushed to the barn and found a groggy Nero being attended to. He had a large welt on his neck where someone had injected a near toxic dose of the drug Resperine, a tranquilizer made from snake root. This was almost a lethal dose, but Nero recovered. No one was ever arrested or charged in the incident, but Crane and Dervaes always had a guard posted with Nero thereafter. There was not even any wagering on the Fox S. that day; someone simply did not want Nero to win.

Showing his grit, Nero came back three weeks later to win the Ohio Standardbred Futurity and two heats of the Meadow Lands Farm S. at The Red Mile in Lexington. In the latter race, Nero won his heats in 1:57.1 and 1:56.2 to set a two-heat world record for two-year-olds.

At that point, Nero was undefeated in his 11 starts and a true harness racing star. His next engagement became a memorable one in harness racing lore. Nero won his heat of the International Stallion S. at The Red Mile in 2:00 and Alert Bret won his in 1:59.2. Nero had defeated Alert Bret in all three of their previous meetings and most observers expected him to do so again, although they anticipated a tough battle.

Race Record Highlights

At 2

1st L.B. Sheppard Memorial
Andy Kerr Memorial
Arden Downs S.
Hanover Colt S.
Meadow Lands Farm S.
Ohio Standardbred Futurity
heat of International Stallion S.

2nd International Stallion S. Final

At 3

1st Cane Futurity
Adios S.
Battle of Brandywine
Joe Neville Memorial
Chicagoan Pace
American-National S.
T.W. Murphy Memorial
Tattersalls S.
Gaines Memorial

At 3 (continued)

Scarlet & Gray S.
Jug Preview

3rd Matron S.

At 4

1st Invitational and FFA events
2nd U.S. Pacing Championship

Honors

Set world record for two heats by a two-year-old pacer
Voted HTA Two-Year-Old Pacer of the Year
Voted HTA Three-Year-Old Pacer of the Year

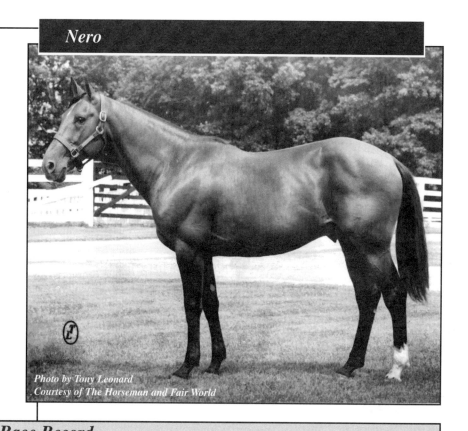

Nero

Photo by Tony Leonard
Courtesy of The Horseman and Fair World

Race Record

Year	Age	Starts	Wins	2nd	3rd	Earnings	Record
1974	2	14	13	1	0	$ 73,815	p,2,1:56.2
1975	3	28	18	1	1	328,643	p,3,1:55.2
1976	4	20	7	6	2	125,750	p,4,T1:55.1
		62	38	8	3	$528,208	p,4,T1:55.1

Nero

O'Brien and Nero immediately took the lead and passed the quarters in :27.3, :56.3 and 1:27.1, maintaining the lead into the stretch. Alert Bret, with driver Glen Garnsey, was challenging and had been on the outside for three-eighths of a mile, including the final turn. The two colts battled down the stretch with Nero on the inside and Alert Bret flying on the outside. About 100 yards from the finish, they were battling each other in tight quarters with Nero's sulky wheel getting jammed against the hubrail and scraping it all the way to the finish. Right at the wire, the wheel caught a wooden sign protruding from the rail and the impact caused Nero and driver Joe O'Brien to fall to the track in a nasty spill.

Alert Bret won the race by a short neck in 1:55.4 which was the fastest time ever for a two-year-old. To this day, horsemen still argue whether Alert Bret had crowded Nero into the rail and should have been disqualified, or if Nero was simply beaten at that point. The judges ruled there was no interference and Nero suffered his first and only defeat as a two-year-old. The win clinched USTA Two-Year-Old Pacer of the Year honors for Alert Bret with Nero winning similar honors from the Harness Tracks of America. Alert Bret had won 15 of 25 starts and earned over $40,000 more than Nero. However, he had beaten Nero in only one of four meetings.

Nero was pretty skinned up from the incident, and O'Brien had to be treated at a hospital for his injuries, but they came back eleven days later to win the Hanover Colt S. at Liberty Bell Park in 1:58.4. Nero's first season ended with 13 wins from 14 starts, earnings of $73,815 and a world record. Not bad for Rene Dervaes' first venture into horse racing as the result of reading an ad.

Following Nero's great season, trainer Crane ascribed the colt's success to "his way of going, his gait." Crane added, "He has the easiness of big, long easy strides that makes the horse completely. He wears no boots and just skips over the ground so easy that it is sort of a very relaxed, effortless way of going."

Nero was expected to be the top colt at three in 1975 and he did not disappoint. Nero won his first nine starts and 14 of his first 15 races. Nero's only defeat during that period was in a Northfield Park Invitational when Whata Baron defeated him in 1:58.4 when he was catch driven by Robert Williams. Except for Nero's first and last starts of the year, Joe O'Brien was in the sulky.

However, Nero was developing corns in his feet which caused stinging with every step on the track. Toward the end of the year, Nero's feet were hurting him and his racing attitude changed. O'Brien was quoted in a New York Times article, "I think the corns caused him to lose his concentration on racing late in the season. His feet were hurting and he just said the hell with it."

Nero's early wins at three included the Cane Futurity, Battle of Brandywine, Joe Neville Memorial, American-National S., Gaines Memorial, Adios S. and Scarlet & Gray S. Nero then finished only third in the Matron S. which was a sure indication that his feet were really a problem for him. He came back to win the Jug Preview but was not even a factor in his Little Brown Jug heat, finishing a very disappointing fifth to the winning Seatrain.

Little Brown Jug problems began for Nero in the post position draw when he drew into the second tier. His racing luck was also not good. Driver Joe O'Brien said after the race, "I was cut down on the first turn and had to go wide and the same thing happened on the last turn and we had to go wide again." He added, "And my colt was not as sharp as he had been earlier when he won the Cane Pace."

Nero went to Lexington after the Jug and won both heats of the Tattersalls S. over a sloppy track in 2:00.3 and 2:00. A week later over the same track, Nero won the Thomas W. Murphy Memorial. Just when it looked like he was back on track, and having won 31 of his 35 lifetime starts, Nero experienced more problems in two rich year-end races. In the Messenger S. at Roosevelt, Nero was parked out to the first quarter in a blistering :28 and then got locked in after he found a spot on the rail. He finally found racing room in the stretch, but still finished eighth, five lengths behind the winning Bret's Champ. Nero's final start of the season was in the L.K. Shapiro S. at Hollywood Park in California. He was the heavy favorite and had the lead at the top of the stretch. However, his feet were stinging badly and he fell back to sixth at the finish.

Though there were some disappointments, Nero's 18 wins from 23 starts, along with earnings of $328,643, earned him HTA's Three-Year-Old Pacer of the Year honors. The great filly Silk Stockings edged him out 90-87 in the USTA voting for Three-Year-Old Pacer of the Year honors. Alert Bret, Nero's arch-rival from a year earlier, had his own ailments and won only four of 13 starts for earnings of $37,815. He and Nero met four times, with Nero earning three wins and both colts being out of the money in the other race.

Nero came back to race as a four-year-old and was syndicated by Lana Lobell Farms owner Alan Leavitt for $3,600,000. Although Nero won $125,750, his season was a disappointment to his connections since he won only seven of 20 starts.

Racing mostly in Invitational and Free-For-All events, Nero traversed the country racing at ten different tracks from New York to California. He was still bothered by problems with corns in his feet which required constant attention. It seemed he was never 100% fit, but he still managed to time-trial in 1:55.1 and was a race winner in 1:55.2. Nero raced against a good group of Free-For-Allers and was defeated by the legendary Rambling Willie three times.

Nero ended his career with a win at The Meadowlands in 1:56.4, bringing his lifetime totals to 38 wins from 62 starts with $528,208 in earnings. He had done plenty to earn a place as a stallion at a major farm and his sire Meadow Skipper was flying high. Two other Meadow Skipper sons, Most Happy Fella and Albatross, were making names for themselves and Nero was the next logical great son of Meadow Skipper to be tried as a stallion.

Sire Line

Nero ranks as one of the leading three siring sons of the great stallion Meadow Skipper. The two in front of him are a pair of all-time great sires - Albatross and Most Happy Fella. All have chapters in this book. But Nero certainly did his part in expanding the greatness of Meadow Skipper, from the standpoint of both racehorse and stallion. Unfortunately, Nero did not leave a son who measured up anywhere near his own ability as a sire and the Nero branch of the Meadow Skipper male line is virtually extinguished.

Maternal Line

The maternal family of Nero is called Lizzie Witherspoon which has been responsible for top trotters as well as pacers - trotters such as world champions Nevele Pride, Impish, Noble Gesture and Duke Rodney, among others. In addition to Nero, the pacing branch is represented by Sampson Hanover, Falcon Almahurst, the outstanding "down under" sire Holmes Hanover, General Star, Mistletoe Shalee, Bardot Lobell and many more modern-day heroes.

Nero's dam is the Gene Abbe mare La Byrd Abbe who was a foal of 1964. Nero was her third foal and first colt. LaByrd Abbe produced 11 winners from 13 foals with seven in 2:00. However, most of her other foals were only ordinary, with the $35,027 earned by Marquess De Sade the highest amount earned by any of her produce other than Nero. Gene Abbe, as you will read in his chapter, excelled as both a sire and broodmare sire.

There are several full or half-sisters to Nero which have produced in 2:00, the best being his full sister Skipper's Romance p,3,T1:59.2 who is the dam of Messenger S., and Little Brown Jug heat winner Seahawk Hanover p,3,1:55.2 ($675,122) by Bret Hanover. She is also the dam of Seabert Hanover p,4,1:53.3 (by Tar Heel), Greater Love p,4,1:54f ($307,087) (by Big Towner) and Kawartha Tarson p,3,T1:55.1 ($117,880) (by Tar Heel). Greater Love is closely bred 2x3 to Gene Abbe since Big Towner is his best son.

None of the other daughters of La Byrd Abbe have produced up to expectations, although they have been quite adept at producing raceway-type performers. The fastest horse from Nero's immediate family is Cold Warrior p,1:51.2 ($150,723) who is by Nihilator from Sniffles Hanover - she by Big Towner-Skipper's Romance. Again, the Gene Abbe connection shows itself.

Nero

Nero's grandam is the Poplar Byrd mare Lanna Byrd p,4,2:07f who is the dam of the good Baron Hanover performer Town Leader p,4,1:56.4 ($256,427). Another connection here is that the biggest money winner in the family, Seahawk Hanover, is by Bret Hanover and Town Leader is by Baron Hanover - Bret's full brother.

Progeny of Note

Nero was on the stallion scene a long time and sired 1,365 starters from 1,715 foals. His last active year was in 1995 when he bred only eight mares. However, he was a hard worker during his first five years at stud when his foals numbered 139, 161, 152, 207 and 129. In 1980, Nero was bred to 269 mares! He was still being bred to over 100 mares as late as the 1990 breeding season. Nero spent the most productive part of his stallion career under the management of Lana Lobell Farms and it was during that period he made quite a name for himself and was bred to excellent mares.

As a stallion, Nero is the sire of 71 in 1:55, 540 in 2:00 and the winners of over $51,000,000. Nero's only $1,000,000 winner is Runnymede Lobell p,4,T1:51.2 ($1,615,125) who won the $1,043,000 North America Cup and the Cane Pace at three. Other big winners were Trutone Lobell p,3,1:54 ($847,945), Icarus Lobell p,3,1:53.3 ($836,802), the filly Armbro Dazzler p,2,1:55.4 ($577,915) who won the Sweetheart P., Great Nero p,1:54.1f ($555,849) and Apollo's Way p,3,1:56 ($502,536).

Nero was an especially good sire of fillies and sired a trio of "Two-Year-Old Pacing Fillies of the Year" in a four-year period - Areba Areba p,2,1:58 ($311,781) in 1980, Bardot Lobell p,2,1:54.4 ($300,906) in 1982 and De Buena Lobell p,2,1:55.4 ($393,230) in 1983. In 1982, Nero's daughter Tanzy Lobell p,4,T1:52.2 ($329,840) became the second fastest female in harness racing history just four days after Fan Hanover set the world filly record of T1:50.4. Six weeks prior to Tanzy Lobell's effort, the Nero daughter Bardot Lobell set a world record for two-year-old fillies when she time-trialed in 1:54.4. She also set a world record of 1:57 on a half-mile track in a race.

When his first crop raced in 1980 and did well, Nero ranked as the fifth leading pacing sire of two- and three-year-olds and had only one crop. When his second crop did equally well, Nero ranked third behind only Albatross and Meadow Skipper in this category, and was less then $100,000 behind Meadow Skipper. Nero had taken the sport by storm and was acknowledged as a successful stallion. The following year was much the same. The standings showed Albatross on top followed by Most Happy Fella with Nero above his sire Meadow Skipper in rankings dominated by that great stallion and his sons.

Analysis

The closest common crosses in Nero's pedigree are the 4x4 relationships to both Volomite and Billy Direct. An interesting relationship is that Nero's sire Meadow Skipper has a dam who is a product of the Volomite-Billy Direct cross and his dam, LaByrd Abbe also has a dam with the same Volomite-Billy Direct cross.

Looking at some of the most successful crosses working for Nero, daughters of sons of Adios produced eight of Nero's richest 14 performers and 11 of his top 20. Bret Hanover's daughters produced four, Adios Vic's three and there were two each from daughters of Airliner and Henry T. Adios. Another observation worth noting is that 10 of Nero's 21 richest performers were fillies.

In the speed department, daughters from sons and grandsons of Adios were still well-represented. However, Nero showed his versatility by siring fast performers from a wide variety of broodmare sire lines. Nero's 16 fastest performers, in 1:53.3 or faster, have the following broodmare sires in order of speed: Race Time, Scarlet Skipper, Columbia George, Colt Fortysix, Harold J., Tar Heel, Bret Hanover, Airliner, Airliner, Mighty Tide, High Ideal, Crash, Rush Hour, Most Happy Fella, High Ideal and B.G.'s Bunny. In fact, the dams of Nero's 21 fastest performers are by 17 different sires.

Another fact to note is that, while Nero's daughters ranked right up there with his colts in terms of making money, they were left behind a bit in the speed department. Tanzy Lobell's p,4,T1:52.2 ranks as the only female represented among Nero's 32 fastest performers. Other fillies begin to show up at the 1:54 to 1:55 level.

I examined the pedigrees of the top dozen money winners by Nero and found some interesting information. Nine of that dozen have a 4x4 cross to Hal Dale with two others being 4x5. The only one with no common cross in the first four generations was Tanzy Lobell from a Tar Heel mare. Most intriguing to me, however, was the close up presence of Adios in several of the mares which produced the best Nero offspring. The dams of Trutone Lobell, Armbro Dazzler and Adios S. winner Andrel p,3,1:53 ($392,560) are all inbred 2x3 to Adios. Andrel is even more interesting since he is inbred 2x3 to the half-brother and sister Meadow Skipper and Countess Adios, two of the sport's great race performers.

The presence of Bye Bye Byrd in a mare's pedigree also seemed to help Nero since both Trutone Lobell and Great Nero, two of Nero's five richest offspring, have that stallion as the sire of the second dam. Don't forget, Bye Bye Byrd's dam is a daughter of the full sister of Adios. So, in my opinion the Adios blood was a very important factor in the success of Nero's very best sons and daughters.

Nero's list of fastest performers showed a different trend. His second fastest horse is Eroticus p,4,1:51.3 ($177,105) from a daughter of Scarlet Skipper. Thus he is inbred 2x3 to Meadow Skipper and also has Bye Bye Byrd as the sire of his grandam. In addition, his dam is 3x4 to the full brother and sister Adios and Adieu. Yankee Kent, next at 1:51.3, is from a Colt Fortysix mare whose second dam is by Bye Bye Byrd. I hope I have convinced you that there is something to be said for the crosses of Adios and Bye Bye Byrd to Nero since they are present in his richest and fastest performers. If you have, or are looking for Nero broodmares, it would not be a bad idea to have those stallions in the pedigree.

Today, Nero ranks among the top 10 broodmare sires in the production of 1:51 pacers and is no stranger to extreme speed. Nero's daughters have already produced 16 1:52 performers and those mares are by 15 different sires. Some of his top broodmare sire credits are Danger Of Fire p,1:49.4 $616,251) (by Flight O Fire), Mr. Panman p,4,1:50.2 (by Niatross), Getting Personal p,3,1:50.4 (by Storm Damage), Ready To Rumble p,3,1:51 ($764,072) (by Laag), Don't Cross Cam p,3,1:51.1 (by Cam Fella), For The Children p,1:51.1 (by Storm Damage), Shannon Spirited p,1:51.2 (by Trenton), Tate Lobell p,1:51.2 (by Fortune Teller), K L's Sharpshooter p,4,1:51.2 (by Look Sharp), Sister Tami p,1:51.3 ($326,220) (by Nihilator), Sam Francisco Irv p,1:51.4 ($444,946) (by Armbro Aussie) Parson's Den p,4,1:51.4f-'98 (by Dragon's Lair), Mumbo King p,3,1:51.4-'98 (by Tyler's Mark), Nukester p,4,1:51.4 (by No Nukes) and Blatently Bald p,1:52 ($576,790) (by Abercrombie). Nero is also the sire of the grandams of two-time Breeders Crown winner Village Jiffy p,1:50 ($1,527,683), Woodrow Wilson winner Kassa Branca p,2,1:52.3 ($743,893) and Village Jove p,3,1:49.4.

The Bye Bye Byrd factor seems to work even for Nero broodmares. His daughters' fastest two performers are by Flight Of Fire and Niatross (the sire of Flight Of Fire). The sire of the dam of Niatross is Bye Bye Byrd. Enough said. Nero mares are also working especially well with Most Happy Fella line stallions and with Artsplace.

As you can see, Nero's daughters are capable of producing top pacers from almost any kind of sire and they are already responsible for 939 2:00 credits. After the 1997 racing season, Nero ranked a very respectable seventh on the all-time list of 2:00 broodmare sire credits among pacers. That put him in the company of Albatross, Bret Hanover, Meadow Skipper, Most Happy Fella, Tar Heel and Race Time - a very distinguished group.

Although Nero waned in the latter part of his career, he was always a popular sire and was one of the breed's stalwarts in his early days as a stallion. His quality has endured through time even though, like most stallions, he simply could not withstand the onslaught of the younger generations.

Nero

Photo courtesy of The Horseman and Fair World

Leading Progeny by Nero

Fastest

Runnymede Lobell, h, p,4,T1:51.2 $1,615,125
Watch Him Step, g, p,4,1:51.3 $183,947
Eroticus, g, p,4,1:51.3 $177,105
Yankee Kent, g, p,3,1:51.3 $59,216
Tidewater Nick, g, p,1:52 $242,669
Tanzy Lobell, m, p,4,T1:52.2 $329,840
Sometime Lobell, h, p,4,1:52.3 $374,030
Andrel, h, p,3,1:53 $392,560
Randolph Lobell, g, p,1:53.1 $245,848
Roman Pockets, h, p,4,1:53.1 $128,059

Richest

Runnymede Lobell, h, p,4,T1:51.2 $1,615,125
Trutone Lobell, h, p,3,1:54 $847,945
Icarus Lobell, h, p,3,1:53.3 $836,802
Armbro Dazzler, m, p,2,1:55.4 $577,915
Great Nero, h, p,1:54.1f $555,849
Apollo's Way, h, p,3,1:56 $502,536
Waverly Nero, h, p,1:57 $490,236
Nero's B B, h, p,1:55.2 $466,865
Kala Lobell, m, p,2,1:58.2 $463,287
J J's Cornell, h, p,1:54.3 $446,767

Nero, Bay Horse, 1972
p, 2, 1:56.2; 4, T1:55.1 ($528,208)

Sire/Dam	2nd Gen	3rd Gen	4th Gen	5th Gen	6th Gen
Meadow Skipper, 1960 p, 3, 1:55.1 $428,057	Dale Frost, 1951 p, 1:58 $204,117	Hal Dale, 1926 p, 6, 2:02¼	Abbedale, 1917 p, 2:01¼	THE ABBE	Chimes / Nettie King
				Daisydale D.	Archdale / Mrs. Tmolus
			Margaret Hal, 1914 p, 2:19½h	Argot Hal	Brown Hal / Lady Wildflower
				Margaret Polk	John R. Gentry / Stella Hal
		Galloway, 1939 p, 2:04½h $5,294	Raider, 1929 p, 1:59½	PETER VOLO	PETER THE GREAT / Nervolo Belle
				Nelda Dillon	Dillon Axworthy / Princess Nelda
			Bethel, 1926 p, 2:03	David Guy	GUY AXWORTHY / Belle Zombro
				Annotation	Azoff / Citation
	Countess Vivian, 1950 p, 3, 1:59 $43,262	King's Counsel, 1940 p, 6, 1:58 $44,930	VOLOMITE, 1926 3, 2:03¼ $32,649	PETER VOLO	PETER THE GREAT / Nervolo Belle
				Cita Frisco	San Francisco / Mendocita
			Margaret Spangler, 1918 p, 2:02¼	GUY AXWORTHY	Axworthy / Lillian Wilkes
				Maggie Winder	Oratorio / Clara Direct
		Filly Direct, 1941 p, 3, 2:06¾ $6,299	BILLY DIRECT, 1934 p, 4, T1:55 $12,040	Napoleon Direct	Walter Direct / Lady Erectress
				Gay Forbes	Malcolm Forbes / Gay Girl Chimes
			Calumet Edna, 1931 p, 2:08½h	Peter The Brewer	PETER THE GREAT / Zombrewer
				Broncho Queen	Empire Direct / The Broncho
La Byrd Abbe, 1964	Gene Abbe, 1944 p, T2:00.3 $51,239	Bert Abbe, 1922 p, 1:59¼	THE ABBE, 1903 p, 2:04	Chimes	Electioneer / Beautiful Bells
				Nettie King	Mambrino King / Nettie Murphy
			Miss Ella H., 1913 p, 2:12¼	Mack H	John A. McKerron / Wainscot
				Nelly Patch	Dan Patch / Dun Daisy
		Rose Marie, 1927 p, 2:05h	Martinos, 1913 4, 2:12¼h	Cochato	Todd / Castanea
				Queen Audubon	Audubon Boy / Miss Nutonia
			Lady Permilia, 1912 p, 2:12¼h	Coastman	Bourbon Wilkes / Albatross
				Virginia Alta	Anderson Wilkes / True Lady
	Lanna Byrd, 1958 p, 4, 2:07f $3,252	Poplar Byrd, 1944 p, T1:59.3 $69,300	VOLOMITE, 1926 3, 2:03¼ $32,649	PETER VOLO	PETER THE GREAT / Nervolo Belle
				Cita Frisco	San Francisco / Mendocita
			Ann Vonian, 1937 p, 3, 2:01¼ $4,974	Grattan At Law	Grattan Royal / Daisy At Law
				Margaret Vonian	Favonian / Margaret C. Brooke
		Lana Direct, 1945 p, 2:01.3 $32,584	BILLY DIRECT, 1934 p, 4, T1:55 $12,040	Napoleon Direct	Walter Direct / Lady Erectress
				Gay Forbes	Malcolm Forbes / Gay Girl Chimes
			Faith Hanover, 1938 p, 3, 2:12h	Sandy Flash	PETER VOLO / Miss Bertha Dillon
				Isotta	PETER THE GREAT / The Zombro Belle

Niatross

If you were to ask anyone in harness racing to name the top five racing pacers of all time, Niatross would almost certainly be included on virtually every survey. He raced only two years, but what a record he established! In just 39 lifetime starts, he compiled the best record as a colt performer in the history of the breed, winning 37 times. Bret Hanover, the horse closest to him in colt achievement, won 45 of 48 at two and three. Nihilator, Niatross' son, would win 32 of 35. Albatross, his sire, won 39 of 45 in his colt form. Beach Towel won 29 of 36. Jate Lobell won 30 of 40 at two and three.

Niatross' only two defeats came at three. The first was an infamous race at Saratoga, where he made a break late in the stretch and fell over the hubrail in a bizarre and inexplicable incident that miraculously left him unharmed. The second came in his very next start when he made a break in the elimination for the Meadowlands Pace, barely recovering to qualify for the final, which he subsequently won in dramatic fashion.

At two and three, Niatross was trained and driven by Clint Galbraith, a New York horseman whose long career would also feature the development of the pacing world champion Call For Rain. Galbraith owned Niatross originally with his breeder, the late Elsie Berger's Niagara Acres. At two, Niatross was undefeated, winning all 13 of his starts, including the Woodrow Wilson, Kentucky Pacing Derby, Hanover-Hempt, Pennsylvania Sire Stake at Liberty Bell, and the International Stallion and Meadow Lands Farm Stakes at Lexington. He was Harness Horse of the Year in 1979, and an interest in the colt was sold to a syndicate headed by Lou Guida who has been connected with many great pacers and trotters.

Niatross was Horse of the Year again in 1980, thundering through 26 starts, winning 24 and setting a single season earnings mark of more than $1.4 million. He swept through the Triple Crown, won the Meadowlands Pace, the Prix d'Ete, Reynolds Memorial, Battle of Brandywine, Oliver Wendell Holmes, Gaines Memorial, Hanover-Hempt, Dancer Memorial, Batavia Colt Stake and Hanover Colt Stake. He also won the American Pacing Classic and Shapiro Stakes near the end of his career over aged horses. He retired as the richest and fastest Standardbred ever, and set world records for the fastest race miles on mile (1:52.1) and half-mile tracks, the latter a 1:54.4h effort in winning the Little Brown Jug, the first sub-1:55 mile in the history of that great race. Thirty-five of Niatross' 37 wins were faster than 2:00.

Niatross is probably most celebrated for being the first sub-1:50 horse in the history of the breed in his momentous time-trial at The Red Mile in the early fall of 1980. His p,3,T1:49.1 effort capped an unprecedented and extraordinary career. He won most of his races in a commanding, front-running manner that was reminiscent of Bret Hanover's overpowering style. Niatross retired sound, and had he raced on, he certainly would have had an opportunity to lower the incredible world records he achieved at two and three. It is also important to note that Niatross' accomplishments came against a crop of colts considered to be one of the best in history. His two main rivals were the colt champions Storm Damage and Tyler B, both of whom were destined for stud careers of their own, and are also profiled in this book. Neither Storm Damage or Tyler B ever defeated Niatross, but they chased him on numerous occasions, providing stiff competition, as did others.

The only two horses to defeat Niatross were Trenton Time, a Race Time colt from Billy Haughton's stable who was the lucky horse that won the Saratoga stake the day Niatross went over the hubrail, and Bruce Gimble, the Most Happy Fella half-brother to Abercrombie, campaigned by Glen Garnsey. Bruce Gimble won that Meadowlands Pace elimination from which Niatross, after a backstretch break in stride, barely recovered. He was the last horse to defeat Niatross.

At the instigation of David Meirs III, the manager of Walnridge Farm in New Jersey, which is Niatross' present home, the big stallion toured North American tracks during the summer and fall of 1996 and 1997. As one of harness racing's greatest heroes, Niatross' appearances brought many old and new fans to the tracks and many recalled his racing exploits. This was a great public relations success for

Niatross

Race Record Highlights

At 2
1st Woodrow Wilson Pace
Kentucky Pacing Derby
Hanover-Hempt S.
Meadow Lands Farm S.
Pennsylvania Sires S.
International Sires S.

At 3
1st Little Brown Jug
Messenger S.
Cane Pace
Meadowlands Pace
Prix d'Ete
Reynolds Memorial
Battle of Brandywine
American Pacing Classic

At 3 (continued)
Oliver Wendell Holmes S.
Gaines Memorial
Hanover-Hempt S.
Dancer Memorial
Batavia Colt S.
Hanover Colt S.
L.K. Shapiro S.

Honors
Triple Crown Winner
Voted Horse of the Year at two and three
Retired as the fastest and richest Standardbred ever
Set single-season record for earnings
Set world record for the fastest race miles on mile and half-mile track

Photo courtesy of The Horseman and Fair World

Race Record

Year	Age	Starts	Wins	2nd	3rd	Earnings	Record
1979	2	13	13	0	0	$604,900	p,2,1:55.4
1980	3	26	24	0	0	1,414,313	p,3,T1:49.1
		39	37	0	0	$2,019,213	p,3,T1:49.1

harness racing, made even more so when Niatross made an appearance at the All-Star Cafe near Times Square in New York City.

Niatross was inducted into the Harness Racing Hall of Fame in 1997 and actually attended the dinner which was held at an outside tent at Goshen, New York's Harness Racing Museum. Calm and well-mannered, Niatross continues to be held in awe by fans and is a great ambassador for the sport.

Sire Line

Niatross is a direct descendant of the sport's most active pacing sire line, since he is the second fastest son of Albatross and grandson of Meadow Skipper, both also profiled in this book. Born in 1977, Niatross was a member of his sire's fourth crop of foals. His more than $2 million in earnings comprised nearly a third of the purse money won by Albatross' crop of 1977.

As a sire Niatross is Albatross' most accomplished son.

Maternal Line

Niatross' maternal background has always been the subject of discussion because his pedigree is so weak. True, he is out of a Bye Bye Byrd mare, and Bye Bye Byrd was one of our most successful broodmare sires, but the rest of the pedigree has less than memorable sires and has not left a big footprint. His dam, Niagara Dream p,4,2:07.2h was a modest race mare, but did produce, in addition to Niatross, the Grand Circuit-winning fillies Rosarium p,3,1:56.2 ($140,272) and Ellatross p,2,1:58.1 ($21,290), both full sisters to Niatross. Neither of those mares, however, has had much success as a broodmare, although Rosarium has four modest 2:00 credits. Niagara Dream was a full sister to the rugged Niagara Byrd p,2:00 ($103,133), and also produced the good Best Of All performers Minute Ms. p,3,1:58.2 ($54,762), Best Bizarre p,4,1:58.2 ($200,831) and Firebird's Best p,2,2:02.3f ($41,412). Niatross' second dam is the Scamp mare Scoot 2:05.2. Minute Ms. and Firebird's Best also had broodmare opportunities, but neither looks like the type to provide lasting success.

Niatross is out of a Bye Bye Byrd mare, a cross that was not particularly successful with Albatross. Of all of Albatross' most accomplished performers, only the fast Kiev Hanover p,3,1:50.1 and Collector's Piece p,4,1:51.3 are also from Bye Bye Byrd dams. Nearly all of Albatross' success came with mares from the Hal Dale line (Bret Hanover, Best Of All, etc.) and there is little of that in Niatross' maternal pedigree. The only link to Hal Dale in Niatross' maternal lineage is the fact that Bye Bye Byrd is a maternal grandson of the Hal Dale mare, Adieu, a sister to Adios.

Progeny Of Note

The siring career of Niatross is one of the most baffling mysteries in the annals of harness racing. Retired to stud after his amazing two-year racing career to the comfortable confines of the Castleton Farm stud barn in Kentucky, Niatross attracted many of the sport's most attractive broodmares from many of our leading breeders. Niatross was heavily patronized in Kentucky. There were 148 foals in the first crop; more than 200 in the second. After only his second year in the stud, when his first foals were only weanlings, the syndicate which then controlled the horse sent him to Pine Hollow Stud in New York, believing that the then-lucrative New York Sire Stakes would provide a much wider foundation for Niatross' future in the stud.

Meanwhile, the first crop of foals set records at the 1983 auctions, and that crop produced one of the most dominant colt pacers in history, the celebrated Nihilator p,3,1:49.3 ($3,225,653), also profiled in this book. That first crop also produced the splendid filly champion Semalu D'Amour p,3,1:54 ($880,187); Messenger winner Pershing Square p,3,1:52.3 ($812,277) (winner of a heat and second to Nihilator in a tight Jug final) and Oliver Wendell Holmes winner Handsome Sum p,3,1:52.2 ($281,193). The second crop featured another Little Brown Jug winner in the rugged and athletic Barberry Spur p,3,T1:50.2 ($1,634,017); Breeders Crown champions Caressable p,2,1:55.3 ($1,006,380) and Masquerade p,3,T1:53 ($598,542); as well as Matron winner Smartest Remark p,3,1:52.1 ($607,537); Goshen Cup winner Freight Saver p,3,1:52.2 ($593,409);

King Charles p,1:51.3 ($466,435); Cash Asset p,3,Q1:53.3 ($400,267) and American-National winner Southern Gentleman p,3,1:52.1 ($239,787). Seldom has any stud career begun with such a flourish.

However, after his move to New York, the quality of mares that Niatross received changed dramatically. Gone were the royally bred Bret Hanover mares which made up a high percentage of his book in Kentucky, a cross which produced consecutive Little Brown Jug champions in Nihilator and Barberry Spur. Since his move, Niatross has not produced a major stakes-winning colt performer. His lone successes are the precocious Chatham Light p,1:53.3 ($849,845); the ultra-consistent Ultra Jet p,1:51.1 ($756,571) and the top mares Miatross p,1:51.3 ($420,857) and Instant Rebate p,3,1:54.2f ($412,405). And those four performers, none of which had careers the equal of Nihilator or Barberry Spur, or even of the initial supporting casts, are the only true stars from some 12 crops of racing age that have been foaled since Niatross' removal from Kentucky.

It is hard to fathom such a decline in one of the breed's greatest racehorses and most successful young sires. The effect has been drastic: Niatross bred fewer than 40 mares during the 1997 breeding season, and has averaged fewer than 50 mares each season since 1994. In spite of this, however, his 1,500 offspring have won in excess of $55 million, and he has more than six hundred 2:00 credits, making him far and away the most successful son of his sire, Albatross. But ten of Niatross' 15 top money winners came from his first two crops. One is left to ponder what his stud career may have achieved had he remained in Kentucky.

Analysis

In all the years I have studied Standardbred breeding, the saga of Niatross stands out as the most dramatic turn-around I have ever seen by a major stallion. The flow of top horses just stopped as if a faucet of good genes had been turned off and replaced by one that produced average genes. When Niatross was moved to New York, and later New Jersey, from Kentucky, it almost seems as if an imposter took his place. Having seen the old boy at his various homes, I know that is not the case, but it illustrates the highs and lows of Niatross' stud career.

One positive aspect of the Niatross offspring seems to be that once they get to the races they stay there for years as shown by many of his fastest horses taking their lifetime records between the ages of five and nine. One, Rhett Almahurst p,1:53.4 ($309,174) took his best speed mark at 11 years of age and King Charles p,1:51.3 ($466,435) took his mark at age nine. Niatross has nine sub-1:52 performers, including the mares Miatross p,1:51.3 ($420,857) and Tululu p,4,1:51.3 ($154,294). And, speaking of females, two of Niatross' four richest performers are the mares Caressable p,2,1:55.4 ($1,006,380) and Semalu D'Amour p,3,1:54 ($880,187).

Taking a look at the pedigree crosses among Niatross' top offspring, there are two types which stand out - those with no common ancestors in the first four generations and those who are inbred 3x3 to Meadow Skipper. Another common thread is the multiple presence of Adios and his sister Adieu since Adios appears in the pedigrees of many mares and Adieu is the second dam of Bye Bye Byrd who is the sire of Niatross' dam.

The two best sons of Niatross, Nihilator and Barberry Spur, are both 3x3 to Meadow Skipper and from Bret Hanover mares. They also have the 5x5x3 cross to Adios and Adieu. The fast Smartest Remark has the same cross. Others with the 3x3 Meadow Skipper cross, but without the Adios connection, are Chatham Light, Freight Saver, King Charles, Miatross, No More Mr. Niceguy and Mr. Panman p,4,1:50.2 who is Niatross' third fastest performer behind Nihilator and Barberry Spur. In addition, eight of Niatross' 11 fastest performers are from mares by Adios line sires as well as seven of his 10 richest.

Pershing Square is the most inbred of the good Niatross sons as he is 3x2 to Meadow Skipper, 5x5x4 to Adios and Adieu and 5x5 to the full brothers King's Counsel and Blackstone. Semalu D'Amour also has interesting breeding as she has no common crosses in her first four generations but is 5x5x3 to Adios and Adieu. In addition, her third dam, Aileen, is inbred 3x2 to the great foundation mare Emily Ellen.

Other stars with no common pedigree crosses in the first four generations are Caressable, Pilgrim's Patriot, Casino Cowboy, Ultra Jet, Masquerade and Balanced Attack.

Niatross

Although Niatross has proven to be a puzzling sire, he has become an outstanding broodmare sire. Niatross daughters now have over 650 2:00 credits and they also include a million-dollar winner, Gothic Dream p,3,1:50.4 ($1,528,671) by Jate Lobell and eight $500,000 winners.

Niatross dams do very well in producing good fillies, as well as colts, and a few of the female stars are Coast p,3,1:52.1 ($247,917), Electric Slide p,3,1:52.4 ($908,792), Ghostly p,3,1:53 ($414,600) and Hazelton Kay p,2,1:53.4 ($762,651).

A sire who is working extremely well with Niatross mares is Dragon's Lair. His honor roll includes world champion half-mile track performer Stand Forever p,4,1:49.2h ($694,472), Pine Lane Comet p,1:51.2 ($126,995), Jet Lair p,4,1:52, Electric Slide p,3,1:52.4 ($908,792), Bonnie And Clyde p,2,1:53.4 ($501,138), Peter's Dragon p,2,1:54. ($282,701) and Smoke Robertson p,3,1:54.4f ($275,012).

There are also a few sire lines which seem to stand out above others for Niatross mares. No Nukes and his son Jate Lobell have had outstanding success with Niatross mares as have Abercrombie and his sons Laag and Albert Albert. On The Road Again is another who has sired good performers from Niatross mares as have many sires from the Most Happy Fella line.

Some of the other fast credits for Niatross mares are No Laughs p,1:50.1 ($182,885) and Nuclear Design p,1:50.4 ($357,326) (both by No Nukes), As Promised p,4,1:50.2 ($669,639) and Lusty Leader p,4,1:51.1 ($516,426) (both by Abercrombie) and Exotic Earl p,4,1:50.2 ($412,165) and Big Brat p,2,1:53.1 ($402,177) (both by Cam Fella). A few Laag performers from Niatross mares include Reality Check p,4,1:50.4 ($352,542), Panhunter p,4,1:51.1 ($135,434), Coalford Laag p,3,1:52.3 and Ghostly p,3,1:53 ($414,600).

Niatross mares have done well with a variety of sire lines and the list should also include Big Towner, along with Direct Scooter and his son Matt's Scooter. Even though some folks have disparaged Niatross in recent years because he became erratic in siring good performers, don't discount his daughters since they are proving to be excellent broodmares and are available at very reasonable prices. Perhaps this is a situation similar to that of Secretariat in the Thoroughbred business in that he was a great racehorse and there were high expectations of him as a stallion. He sired a few top horses, as did Niatross, but Secretariat has really made his mark as a great broodmare sire. Niatross may be in the process of doing exactly the same.

Leading Progeny by Niatross

Fastest
- Nihilator, h, p,3,1:49.3 $3,225,653
- Barberry Spur, h, p,3,T1:50.2 $1,634,017
- Mr Panman, h, p,4,1:50.2 $189,909
- Pilgrim's Patriot, h, p,1:51.1 $802,871
- Ultra Jet, h, p,1:51.1 $756,571
- King Charles, g, p,1:51.3 $466,435
- Miatross, m, p,1:51.3 $420,857
- No More Mr Niceguy, h, p,1:51.3 $211,809
- Tululu, m, p,4,1:51.3 $154,294
- Smartest Remark, h, p,3,1:52.1 $607,537

Richest
- Nihilator, h, p,3,1:49.3 $3,225,653
- Barberry Spur, h, p,3,T1:50.2 $1,634,017
- Caressable, m, p,2,1:55.4 $1,006,380
- Semalu D'Amour, m, p,3,1:54 $880,187
- Chatham Light, h, p,1:53.3h $849,845
- Pershing Square, h, p,3,1:52.3 $812,277
- Pilgrim's Patriot, h, p,1:51.1 $802,871
- Casino Cowboy, h, p,3,1:53.4 $802,445
- Ultra Jet, h, p,1:51.1 $756,571
- Smartest Remark, h, p,3,1:52.1 $607,537

Niatross, Bay Horse, 16 Hands, 1977
p, 2, 1:55.4; 3, T1:49.1 ($2,019,213)

Sire/Dam	2nd gen	3rd gen	4th gen	5th gen	6th gen
Albatross, 1968 p, 4, 1:54.3f $1,201,470	Meadow Skipper, 1960 p, 3, 1:55.1 $428,057	Dale Frost, 1951 p, 1:58 $204,117	**HAL DALE**, 1926 p, 6, 2:02¼	Abbedale	**THE ABBE** / Daisydale D.
				Margaret Hal	Argot Hal / Margaret Polk
			Galloway, 1939 p, 2:04½h $5,294	Raider	**PETER VOLO** / Nelda Dillon
				Bethel	David Guy / Annotation
		Countess Vivian, 1950 p, 3, 1:59 $43,262	King's Counsel, 1940 p, 6, 1:58 $44,930	**VOLOMITE**	**PETER VOLO** / Cita Frisco
				Margaret Spangler	**GUY AXWORTHY** / Maggie Winder
			Filly Direct, 1941 p, 3, 2:06¾h $6,299	**BILLY DIRECT**	Napoleon Direct / Gay Forbes
				Calumet Edna	Peter The Brewer / Broncho Queen
	Voodoo Hanover, 1964	Dancer Hanover, 1957 p, 4, T1:56.4 $87,746	Adios, 1940 p, T1:57½ $33,329	**HAL DALE**	Abbedale / Margaret Hal
				ADIOO VOLO	Adioo Guy / Sigrid Volo
			The Old Maid, 1945	**GUY ABBEY**	**GUY AXWORTHY** / Abbacy
				Spinster	**SPENCER** / Minnetonka
		Vibrant Hanover, 1960	Tar Heel, 1948 p, 4, T1:57 $119,148	**BILLY DIRECT**	Napoleon Direct / Gay Forbes
				Leta Long	**VOLOMITE** / Rosette
			Vivian Hanover, 1937	Guy McKinney	**GUY AXWORTHY** / Queenly McKinney
				Guesswork	**PETER THE GREAT** / Elsie Leyburn
Niagara Dream, 1964 p, 4, 2:07.2h $4,963	Bye Bye Byrd, 1955 p, 5, T1:56.1 $554,272	Poplar Byrd, 1944 p, T1:59.3 $69,300	**VOLOMITE**, 1926 3, 2:03¼ $32,649	**PETER VOLO**	**PETER THE GREAT** / Nervolo Belle
				Cita Frisco	San Francisco / Mendocita
			Ann Vonian, 1937 p, 3, 2:01¼ $4,974	Grattan At Law	Grattan Royal / Daisy At Law
				Margaret Vonian	Favonian / Margaret C. Brooke
		Evalina Hanover, 1946 p, 1:59.2 $12,420	**BILLY DIRECT**, 1934 p, 4, T1:55 $12,040	Napoleon Direct	Walter Direct / Lady Erectress
				Gay Forbes	Malcolm Forbes / Gay Girl Chimes
			Adieu, 1938 p, 2, T2:04¼	**HAL DALE**	Abbedale / Margaret Hal
				ADIOO VOLO	Adioo Guy / Sigrid Volo
	Scoot, 1946 2:05.2 $21,541	Scamp, 1939	**GUY ABBEY**, 1925 3, 2:06¾	**GUY AXWORTHY**	**AXWORTHY** / Lillian Wilkes
				Abbacy	**THE ABBE** / Regal McKinney
			Sweet Miss, 1935 3, T2:09½	**PETER VOLO**	**PETER THE GREAT** / Nervolo Belle
				True Charm	**GUY AXWORTHY** / Expressive Lou
		Doris Spencer, 1932	**SPENCER**, 1925 3, T1:59¾	Lee Tide	Lee Axworthy / Emily Ellen
				Petrex	**PETER THE GREAT** / Extasy
			Last Chance, 1922 3, 2:24¼	**PETER THE GREAT**	Pilot Medium / Santos
				Dorothy Axworthy	**AXWORTHY** / Dorothy

Nihilator

Defeated only three times in his 35 career starts, Nihilator, like his sire Niatross, was one of the breed's most commanding presences on the racetrack. Coming from Niatross' hotly anticipated first crop, Nihilator was a big, handsome, bay horse standing nearly 16 hands. He was an overpowering, aggressive racehorse whose style and speed also made him one of the most popular champions of the modern era.

Nihilator was bred in the Midwest by longtime Indiana breeder Robert Gangloff, and was sold privately as a yearling for $100,000 to a group headed by Lou Guida which would later become known as the Wall Street Stable. Nihilator was looked at, and selected for the investment group, by bloodstock agent Bob Boni, and was one of seven yearlings purchased by the investors, a group that also included future Messenger Stake winner Pershing Square.

Racing at two first for trainer Billy Haughton and then for driver Bill O'Donnell, Nihilator was a star from the moment he set foot on the training track in Florida. After his first baby race at The Meadowlands, he was everyone's choice for that year's Woodrow Wilson, and he did not disappoint. Racing from off the pace and thundering through the wire for Bill O'Donnell like he meant business, Nihilator won the Wilson in world record time of 1:52.4. This time was nearly three seconds faster than the stakes record, and is still among the fastest Wilsons in history. Nihilator's trainer Billy Haughton, who had probably trained more modern day stars than anyone, said after Nihilator's two-year-old season, "He is the greatest horse I've ever had, and the greatest horse anybody's ever had."

Nihilator won 12 of his 13 starts at two, winning $1,361,367. His sole defeat came at the hands of Dragon's Lair in the much-anticipated final of the 1984 Breeders Crown at The Meadows. That race has become legendary, not only for the overwhelming character of the victory by Dragon's Lair in world record time, but also as the scene of Nihilator's only defeat at two. In fact, the remarkable quality of that race did a lot to add credibility and build exposure for the Breeders Crown, then in its first year of operation.

Perhaps Nihilator's most impressive performance at two was posted in a heat of the International Stallion Stake at Lexington. He was parked the entire mile for O'Donnell, yet accelerated in the lane for a breath taking, going-away victory in 1:53.2. Many observers (not to mention his owners, trainer and driver) believe this may have been the best single performance in the horse's entire career. Nihilator also won the Goshen Cup at The Meadowlands, the Potomac and Baltimorean Series at Freestate, and a Kentucky Sire Stake at The Red Mile prior to the Grand Circuit meet.

Oddly, Nihilator was not voted Horse of the Year in 1984, an honor which fell to the world champion trotting filly Fancy Crown 3,1:53.4, winner of that year's Kentucky Futurity and Breeders Crown. Nihilator was, however, voted Pacer of the Year.

At three, Nihilator lost only twice in 22 starts, pushing his two-year total to 32 wins, and a record $3,225,653 (he is still the leading money-winning pacer in history). One of the defeats was to Marauder in a heat of the Adios and the other was to Armbro Dallas in the Pilgrim Stake at Garden State Park. His many three-year-old triumphs include the Meadowlands Pace, Little Brown Jug, Dancer Memorial, Jersey Cup, Terrapin, Homecoming Pace, Meadowlands Pace elimination, a heat of the Adios, and the Tattersalls at Lexington. He also became the fastest pacer in a race with a 1:49.3 clocking recorded on Hambletonian Day in 1985 at The Meadowlands in a match race with Falcon Seelster. That year he was voted almost unanimously Horse of the Year.

One of the most interesting stories in the Nihilator saga is that in the middle of his three-year-old season, after his 1:49.3 mile at The Meadowlands, he was shipped to Springfield for a time-trial, in an effort to lower the world record over the famed mile track of the Illinois State Fair. He was stabled in a nine-horse van that was

Race Record Highlights

At 2

1st Woodrow Wilson P.
International Stallion S.
Breeders Crown Elimination
Potomac P.
Goshen Cup
Baltimorian Series Final and leg
Kentucky Sires S.

2nd Breeders Crown Final

At 3

1st Meadowlands Pace Final and Elimination
Little Brown Jug
Breeders Crown
James Dancer Memorial

At 3 (continued)

Jersey Cup
Terrapin P.
Tattersalls P.
Homecoming P.
heat of Adios S.
Headline Brokers P.
Walt Whitman P.
Pilgrim Pace Elimination

2nd Pilgrim S. Final

Honors

Voted Two-Year-Old Pacer of the Year
Voted Horse of the Year at three
At two, set world record for two-year-olds on mile track
At three, set all-age world record for three-year-olds on mile track
At three, set all-age world record for two-heat race on mile track
At three, set all-age world record for two-heat race on half-mile track

Nihilator

Photo by Tony Leonard
Courtesy of The Horseman and Fair World

Race Record

Year	Age	Starts	Wins	2nd	3rd	Earnings	Record
1984	2	13	12	0	1	$1,361,367	p,2,1:52.4
1985	3	25	23	1	0	1,864,286	p,3,1:49.3
		38	35	1	1	$3,225,653	p,3,1:49.3

converted for his exclusive use. Persistent rains, however, wiped out any chance of the horse making a record attempt at Springfield, and instead he was sent to Du Quoin to attempt the same feat there some two weeks later. It is well-known that for some reason the Du Quoin track is much friendlier to trotters than pacers, and Nihilator was unsuccessful in his Du Quoin time trial, although it must be acknowledged that he had been unraced for nearly a month before his failed effort. However, following his month-long ordeal in Illinois Nihilator showed what kind of horse he was by promptly winning the Dancer Memorial, which was raced at Garden State Park that fall because of a fire at Freehold Raceway.

After the Dancer, Nihilator was sent to Delaware, Ohio for the most famous half-mile track of them all. This created some real drama. It was an intriguing situation because Nihilator had never before started on a half-mile track, and in fact had hardly ever trained over one, yet there he was facing the ultimate half-mile track test. Nihilator responded as might have been expected, pacing the fastest Little Brown Jug ever at the time in 1:52.1h. It is still the fourth fastest Jug in history. He beat one of the Jug's all-time best fields that day, including his razor-sharp stablemate Pershing Square, Dignatarian, Marauder and Broadway Express. It was a true indication of his greatness as a racehorse.

Nihilator was an aggressive, albeit hard-going horse who was only really good-gaited at extreme high speed. Like his sire, Niatross, he was a high-going horse. At a slower speed, Nihilator would rack along and be rough-gaited, but once O'Donnell put the hammer down, Nihilator would smooth out and become one of the slickest and most powerful champions in history. Nihilator was always an assertive horse, and much of the credit for his success as a racehorse must be attributed to trainer Haughton and driver O'Donnell, who worked hard to throttle and contain Nihilator's natural tendencies, and to mold him into one of the most luminous stars of the modern era. Under less capable handling, Nihilator's explosive speed and strength could have deserted him after his first few races.

Sire Line

Nihilator is a son of Niatross, grandson of Albatross, and great-grandson of Meadow Skipper, all profiled in this book. A foal of 1982, Nihilator was a member of the first crop of his sire.

Maternal Line

Nihilator's dam is the Bret Hanover mare Margie's Melody p,4,T1:55.4, a good race mare who won 12 times from two to four, and earned nearly $100,000, including a Kentucky Sire Stake win at Latonia. Nihilator was her first foal, and her dam was the Meadow Skipper mare Pretty Margie p,3,2:05.4f, a full sister to breeder Bob Gangloff's successful pacer Gay Skipper p,4,1:57.4 ($256,235). Pretty Margie also produced the Big Towner filly Goodmorningamerica p,3,1:54; Bret's Courage p,3,T1:55.2 ($246,687) and Incredible Bret p,3,1:56.1f ($242,844). A full sister to Pretty Margie, the Meadow Skipper mare Sassy Margie p,3,1:59f ($48,562), produced the Chicago star Bret's Avenger p,4,1:51.3 ($417,554) and the $200,000 winning full brothers Town Jester p,3,1:54.3f and Town Judge p,1:54.3f. Yet another sister of Pretty Margie with produce of note was Queen Margie, a non-record Meadow Skipper mare who is the dam of the successful Midwestern race horse and sire Incredible Finale p,4,1:53.2f ($1,165,508). Nihilator's third dam is the illustrious Storm Cloud matron Margie's Storm p,3,2:06, who from 11 foals produced six winners and founded a contemporary family that has one of the finest production records of any maternal clan in The Registry. Eight of her daughters became 2:00 producers. This is the Margaret Arion branch of the famed Mamie maternal family, a branch which also includes super trotting sire Valley Victory. Margaret Arion is the sixth dam of both Nihilator and Valley Victory, since her daughter Princess Peg founded the family leading to Valley Victory, and another daughter, Margaret Castleton, founded the family leading to Nihilator.

Yet another branch of the family produced the 1970's trotting star Killbuck Mary and the 1997 pacing star Gothic Dream. Of interest is the fact that Nihilator is the only colt that his dam Margie's Melody has ever produced, her next seven foals were all fillies, the last foaled in 1993.

Nihilator is inbred 3 x 3 to Meadow Skipper since he is three generations removed from Meadow Skipper along his sire line, and his dam's mother is also by Meadow Skipper. This was an excellent cross for Niatross as many of his champion offspring were inbred or linebred in a similar way. He is also linebred to Adios in that Albatross, his paternal grandsire, is out of a mare by Dancer Hanover, a son of Adios, and Nihilator is himself from a Bret Hanover mare, a cross that also produced Jug winner Barberry Spur. There is also a lot of trotting blood in this maternal pedigree, since Margie's Storm is a daughter of the Scotland stallion Storm Cloud, and all subsequent dams have trotting heritages. It should be remembered that Niatross has a proportion of trotting blood in his maternal pedigree, since his third dam is by the 1928 Kentucky Futurity winner Spencer. Nihilator's pedigree is an interesting mix of the inbred and linebred Hal Dale pacing line with a sire and dam with heavy concentrations of trotting blood in their maternal pedigrees.

Progeny Of Note

Nihilator foaled only six crops before succumbing to the after-effects of Potomac fever. His first crop was foaled in 1987 and included 141 foals from some of the finest modern pacing families. The primary first crop stars were Six Day War p,3,1:54.2 (t1:56.4h) and the fast Smiling Rebecca p,3,T1:52.1 ($153,909). Six Day War went on to become a double-gaited world champion. Nihilator's second crop, foals of 1988, included the fast aged star Silver Almahurst p,1:49.4 ($1,091,024) (although it should be noted that Silver Almahurst was second in the 1990 Woodrow Wilson); Start The Fire p,1:52.1 ($542,276) and Interpretor p,3,1:51.4 ($475,970). The foals of 1989, Nihilator's third crop, included the millionaire Shore Patrol p,3,1:51.2; the iron-tough, Breeders Crown-winning mare Swing Back p,1:51.1 ($917,262) and the fast Meadowlands star New Bucks p,1:49.3 ($311,721).

The 1990 foals continued a trend of continuous, but not spectacular production. The fastest and richest are the FFA stars Native Born p,1:50.3 (a $1 million winner) and Arrive At Five p,4,1:50.1 ($845,049), as well as Midwestern star Thirty G's p,1:51.3. In 1991, one of the foals who reached loftier heights than any of Nihilator's previous offspring was the p,3,1:51f Metro and Canadian Pacing Derby winner Historic, with more than $1.3 million earned. Historic and Breeders Crown two-year-old star Digger Almahurst p,2,1:52.1f are the only really legitimate male colt stars that Nihilator ever produced, and they are full brothers from the noted Race Time matron Dateable. The rest of his memorable offspring became successful older horses, earning major rewards at the raceway level. For example, New Bucks, a son of the Sonsam mare Candy Bucks, is Nihilator's fastest offspring with a 1:49.3 mark taken at The Meadowlands in 1995; he and world champion Silver Almahurst are the only sub-1:50 credits for Nihilator. To illustrate the point further, Nihilator's six fastest offspring all took their records as aged performers. Swing Back, the Breeders Crown winner of more than $900,000, is both the richest and fastest female daughter of Nihilator, and the only other rich, racing daughter is the attractive Sister Tami p,1:51.3 ($319,620), another which reached her peak form as an aged mare. Nihilator did not produce a two- or three-year-old racing filly of any note. He has produced four millionaires to date, Historic, Shore Patrol, Silver Almahurst and Native Born.

While Nihilator's exciting promise as a sire did not materialize, and his stud career was cut short by illness, he still produced the winners of more than $31 million including eight winners of over $500,000 and 26 winners of over $250,000. In addition, he has two sub-1:50 sons and 16 performers with records below 1:52. Of his 735 foals, nearly 600 were starters, a lifetime average of about $50,000 per starter. Nihilator produced five full crops, and one abbreviated crop from his last year at stud of only 37 foals. Because he was not a sire of explosive speed, and because he did not produce good race fillies, his stud career is generally viewed as a disappointment. However, his five full crops each averaged more than $6 million in earnings, and this places him among the most successful sires of his generation by comparison.

Nihilator

A horse of Nihilator's racing accomplishment always enters the stud with a heavy burden of expectation, as many of our greatest champions have discovered. The mission laid out for Nihilator was to produce a colt better than he was. Since he failed in that extremely difficult assignment, he has been judged much too harshly.

Although he never became the sire of extreme colt speed that everyone expected, his daughters have already become exceptional broodmares. There is no better example than the gifted Artsplace filly Stienam's Place p,3,1:50.4; world champion and Breeders Crown winner of more than $1 million. Stienam's Place is one of the most attractive, best-gaited and flawless racing fillies in history.

Analysis

As we have seen, Nihilator had an all too brief stallion career with only five full crops. However, not only did his offspring earn over $31,000,000, he also sired 368 2:00 performers from 580 starters, just over 63 percent. These are good statistics for any sire, but was basically in a "no-win" situation and even more was expected from him. Nihilator's impact on the sport's breeding history will have to come from the success of his daughters as producers. Early results show that they are already doing extremely well.

The common pedigree crosses for Nihilator are an inbred 3x3 to Meadow Skipper through his grandsire and granddam, 5x5x3 to Adios and his sister Adieu and 5x4 to Tar Heel. There is nothing especially unusual here except the presence of trotting blood on top and bottom in his third generation. The second dam of Niatross was a trotter and Nihilator's third dam was bred to be a trotter but paced.

Now, we will take a look at the pedigree crosses of his top horses and you may be a bit surprised at some of the results. The first thing I noted was the success Nihilator had when bred to mares with Albatross blood - that of his own grandsire. Four of Nihilator's 10 fastest performers are inbred to Albatross, as well as six of his top 25 fastest four being from Albatross mares and two from Sonsam mares.

The fastest son of Nihilator is New Bucks p,1:49.3 ($311,721) and his dam is by Sonsam (son of Albatross) giving him an inbred 3x3 cross to Albatross along with his 3x4 to Bret Hanover and 4x4x4 to Meadow Skipper. The fast Deadlock p,1:50.2 ($401,965) and Start The Fire p,1:52.1 ($542,276) are both from the Albatross mare Karril Hanover and are even more inbred to Albatross with 3x2 crosses to that great stallion in addition to their 4x4x3 to Meadow Skipper, 4x3 to Bye Bye Byrd and 4x5x5x4 to Adios and his sister Adieu. Two others with the very closely bred 3x2 cross to Albatross are Shore Patrol p,3,1:51.2 ($1,122,211) and Corsair p,3,1:52.2 ($104,351). Shore Patrol, in addition to the 3x2 Albatross cross is 4x4x3 to Meadow Skipper and 5x4x4 to the half brothers Dancer Hanover and Thorpe Hanover - both sons of the great mare The Old Maid. Corsair is from a full sister to Sonsam and has the 3x2 Albatross cross along with an inbred 3x3 to Bret Hanover and linebred 4x4x3 to Meadow Skipper. Another fast Nihilator son is Come Out Swinging p,1:50.4 ($255,742) with a 3x3 to Albatross and 4x4x4 to Meadow Skipper.

So, for extreme speed, we can readily see that the doubling up of crosses to Albatross has been successful for Nihilator and this has also worked for other sires. Albatross was a special and dynamic sire and having a few crosses to him would be a help in the speed department. Of course, the size and conformation of the sires and dams involved must be strongly considered so as not to get a small and fragile offspring. But, with the proper individuals, I see nothing wrong with this cross to Albatross.

Another good sire whose relatives seems to have an affinity with Nihilator is Bye Bye Byrd who is the sire of the dam of Nihilator's sire Niatross. Nihilator's second fastest performer and million-dollar winner Silver Almahurst p,1:49.4 ($1,091,024) is from a Bye Bye Byrd mare and bred 4x3 to that stallion as well has having 4x4 crosses to Meadow Skipper, Billy Direct and the brother and sister Adios and Adieu. I think Silver Almahurst has decent stallion potential and his offspring could dominate the Michigan Sires Stakes program when they start racing in 1998. Nihilator's third fastest performer also has a Bye Bye Byrd connection - that being Arrive At Five p,4,1:50.1 ($845,049) whose sire is the Bye Bye Byrd grandson Safe Arrival. Arrive At Five's crosses are 3x4 to Bret Hanover, 4x4x3 to Meadow Skipper and 4x4 to Bye Bye Byrd. The aforementioned Deadlock's second dam is by Bye Bye Byrd. Thus, three of Nihilator's four fastest performers all have Bye Bye Byrd blood.

Native Born p,1:50.3 ($1,000,000), Nihilator's newest millionaire in 1998, is inbred 4x4x2 to Meadow Skipper, 4x4 to Adios and 5x3 to Dancer Hanover. Historic p,3,1:51f ($1,334,861) is Nihilator's richest offspring and is from a Race Time mare. His common crosses are 4x4 to Meadow Skipper and 4x4 to Adios. Historic is from the excellent broodmare Dateable who also produced the top two-year-old Digger Almahurst p,2,1:52.1f ($371,866) by Nihilator.

Nihilator has also sired seven females in the 1:53 list, the fastest being the long-lasting Swing Back p,1:51.1 ($917,262) who took her record at age seven. Swing Back is from an Oil Burner mare and her pedigree crosses are 6x5x3 to Tar Heel, 4x4x4 to Meadow Skipper and 6x5 to the brother and sister Adios and Prashai. Another fast mare is Sister Tami p,1:51.3 ($318,120), who took her record at age six; she is from a Nero mare and is crossed 4x4x3 to Meadow Skipper. Smiling Rebecca p,3,T1:52.1 ($153,909) is 4x4x3 to Meadow Skipper and her dam is inbred 3x3 to Good Time.

Sons and daughters of Nihilator seem to stay on the track for long careers and many of his fastest performers have taken their lifetime marks at ages five, six and seven which may attest to their inherent soundness.

This sire line - Meadow Skipper to Albatross to Niatross to Nihilator - has been very prolific in siring top producing broodmares. Albatross and Meadow Skipper rank as numbers one and three on the all-time list while Niatross has been impressive and Nihilator equally so. The 1997 racing season was a landmark performance for Nihilator mares; they were the dams of divisional champions Stienam's Place p,3,1:50.4 ($1,402,301) and Sealed N Delivered p,2,1:52.2 ($570,329).

Stienam's Place is one of the greatest fillies in the history of the sport and she is by the top sire Artsplace. Her common pedigree crosses are 3x4 to Albatross, 4x5x5x4 to Meadow Skipper and 4x4 to Columbia George. Sealed N Delivered is by Falcon Seelster and has a 3x4 cross to Bret Hanover along with 5x5x3 to Meadow Skipper. The fast Magnetic Killean p,1:50.2-'98, by Run The Table, is Nihilator's fastest broodmare sire credit and has crosses of 3x5x5 to Meadow Skipper and 4x4 to Good Time. He also has Columbia George in his pedigree as his second dam is by that sire - the same as for the dam of Stienam's Place. Other top performers by Artsplace from Nihilator mares are Perfect Art p,3,1:51 ($557,853) who is 3x4 to Albatross and Tallulah Belle p,3,1:54f ($199,468).

Nihilator mares are doing extremely well with Abercrombie and his sons Artsplace and Laag. His daughters have also done well with Falcon Seelster and Direct Scooter. I expect that Nihilator mares will continue to get more exposure to the top stallions and will produce world class performers - two of whom we have already seen. Mares by Nihilator are readily available at very reasonable prices and should not be overlooked as top broodmare prospects.

Nihilator

Photo courtesy of The Horseman and Fair World

Leading Progeny by Nihilator

Fastest
- New Bucks, g, p,1:49.3 $311,721
- Silver Almahurst, h, p,1:49.4 $1,091,024
- Arrive At Five, h, p,4,1:50.1 $845,049
- Deadlock, h, p,1:50.2 $401,965
- Native Born, h, p,1:50.3 $1,000,000
- Come Out Swinging, h, p,1:50.4 $255,742
- Historic, h, p,3,1:51f $1,334,861
- Swing Back, m, p,1:51.1 $917,262
- Shore Patrol, h, p,3,1:51.2 $1,122,211
- Cold Warrior, h, p,1:51.2 $150,723

Richest
- Historic, h, p,3,1:51f $1,334,861
- Shore Patrol, h, p,3,1:51.2 $1,122,211
- Silver Almahurst, h, p,1:49.4 $1,091,024
- Native Born, h, p,1:50.3 $1,000,000
- Swing Back, m, p,1:51.1 $917,262
- Arrive At Five, h, p,4,1:50.1 $845,049
- Calypso Beat, g, p,1:52.1 $633,692
- Start The Fire, h, p,1:52.1 $542,276
- Six Day War, h, p,3,1:54.2 $493,962
- Interpretor, h, p,3,1:51.4 $475,970

Nihilator, Bay Horse, 1982
p, 2, 1:52.4; 3, 1:49.3 ($3,225,653)

Niatross, 1977 p, 3, T1:49.1 $2,019,213	Albatross, 1968 p, 4, 1:54.3f $1,201,470	MEADOW SKIPPER, 1960 p, 3, 1:55.1 $428,057	Dale Frost, 1951 p, 1:58 $204,117	HAL DALE	Abbedale / Margaret Hal
				Galloway	Raider / Bethel
			Countess Vivian, 1950 p, 3, 1:59 $43,262	King's Counsel	VOLOMITE / Margaret Spangler
				Filly Direct	BILLY DIRECT / Calumet Edna
		Voodoo Hanover, 1964	Dancer Hanover, 1957 p, 4, T1:56.4 $87,746	ADIOS	HAL DALE / ADIOO VOLO
				The Old Maid	GUY ABBEY / Spinster
			Vibrant Hanover, 1960	TAR HEEL	BILLY DIRECT / Leta Long
				Vivian Hanover	Guy McKinney / Guesswork
	Niagara Dream, 1964 p, 4, 2:07.2h $4,963	Bye Bye Byrd, 1955 p, 5, T1:56.1 $554,272	Poplar Byrd, 1944 p, T1:59.3 $69,300	VOLOMITE	PETER VOLO / Cita Frisco
				Ann Vonian	Grattan At Law / Margaret Vonian
			Evalina Hanover, 1946 p, 1:59.2 $12,420	BILLY DIRECT	Napoleon Direct / Gay Forbes
				Adieu	HAL DALE / ADIOO VOLO
		Scoot, 1946 2:05.2 $21,541	Scamp, 1939	GUY ABBEY	Guy Axworthy / Abbacy
				Sweet Miss	PETER VOLO / True Charm
			Doris Spencer, 1932	Spencer	Lee Tide / Petrex
				Last Chance	Peter The Great / Dorothy Axworthy
Margie's Melody, 1976 p, 4, T1:55.4 $94,303	Bret Hanover, 1962 p, 4, T1:53.3 $922,616	ADIOS, 1940 p, T1:57½ $33,329	HAL DALE, 1926 p, 6, 2:02¼	Abbedale	The Abbe / Daisydale D.
				Margaret Hal	Argot Hal / Margaret Polk
			ADIOO VOLO, 1930 p, 3, 2:05h	Adioo Guy	Guy Dillon / Adioo
				Sigrid Volo	PETER VOLO / Polly Parrot
		Brenna Hanover, 1956 p, 3, T2:01 $21,946	TAR HEEL, 1948 p, 4, T1:57 $119,148	BILLY DIRECT	Napoleon Direct / Gay Forbes
				Leta Long	VOLOMITE / Rosette
			Beryl Hanover, 1947 p, 2, T2:02 $29,076	NIBBLE HANOVER	Calumet Chuck / Justissima
				Laura Hanover	The Laurel Hall / Miss Bertha Worthy
	Pretty Margie, 1971 p, 3, 2:05.4f $3,033	MEADOW SKIPPER, 1960 p, 3, 1:55.1 $428,057	Dale Frost, 1951 p, 1:58 $204,117	HAL DALE	Abbedale / Margaret Hal
				Galloway	Raider / Bethel
			Countess Vivian, 1950 p, 3, 1:59 $43,262	King's Counsel	VOLOMITE / Margaret Spangler
				Filly Direct	BILLY DIRECT / Calumet Edna
		Margie's Storm, 1962 p, 3, 2:06 $4,529	Storm Cloud, 1954 2:00.4 $67,393	Scotland	Peter Scott / Roya McKinney
				Queen Nib	NIBBLE HANOVER / Silver Queen
			My Margie, 1955 3, T2:06.2	Mighty Song	VOLOMITE / Evensong
				Margaret Castleton	Guy Castleton / Margaret Parrish

No Nukes

Few two-year-old pacers have ever excited an entire industry the way No Nukes did in the spring of 1981. He was a big, black, handsome, good-gaited colt who had the look of a champion. The stir he created is interesting in light of the fact that he won only a single stake at two, that being the Goshen Cup in June at The Meadowlands. And he made only six starts as a freshman, winning four with one second, earning less than $50,000.

No Nukes was bred by William F. Brooks of Delaware and noted harness driver Ben Webster of New Jersey. The two shared ownership of the mare Gidget Lobell p,3,2:00.3f ($14,829) and bred her to the new stallion Oil Burner who was owned by Brooks and Webster. No Nukes was her first foal and sold at the 1980 Harness Breeders Yearling Sale at Liberty Bell Park in Philadelphia. The colt was purchased for $21,000 by Magna Stables and trainer Steve Demas with Webster also retaining part ownership.

Demas had a handful with No Nukes. At two, the horse's erratic behavior behind the gate for driver Ben Webster caused two recalls in the $1,760,000 Woodrow Wilson Final. He was subsequently removed from the betting but allowed to start. After making a poor start he showed his amazing speed. It is estimated by most observers that No Nukes paced his own middle half around :54 seconds, and three-quarters in under 1:23, to reach contention. But then he faded, surrendering to eventual winner McKinzie Almahurst in 1:56.1. No Nukes was a poor post horse the rest of his short racing life.

Following No Nukes' two-year-old season, Demas said, "He showed no signs of nervousness or being high-strung prior to his unfortunate incident in the post parade for the Wilson Pace. He got stirred up and it was just one of those things. Once he got fired up, he just wasn't going to settle down."

At three, Demas made a change in driver, bringing in the late Glen Garnsey. Demas reasoned that Garnsey's patient manner and gifted horsemanship could tame No Nukes' raw ability, and transform him into a useful and more productive horse. And to some extent, Garnsey's abilities did allow No Nukes to become a kinder, gentler pacer. He made 13 starts at three, winning six, including the Jersey Cup, a heat of The Adios, a Jersey Classic elimination, a Battle of Brandywine elimination and a heat of the Oliver Wendell Holmes. He was also second to Hilarion in the Meadowlands Pace final, and third in the Battle of Brandywine and Oliver Wendell Holmes finals. In most of his starts, Garnsey was under instructions not to send No Nukes charging from the gate. The plan that seemed to work best was for No Nukes to be taken off the gate, and then put into high gear after the first quarter. This tactic worked as best it could, although it often forced the speedy colt to move into some hot quarters, which exacted their toll late in the race. However, only a crafty drive from a then very young John Campbell behind Hilarion robbed No Nukes of victory in the Meadowlands Pace. He won $527,320 at three and took a p,3,T1:52.1 mark in a time trial at The Red Mile for Garnsey.

Glen Garnsey was quoted in a *Hoof Beats* interview, " Behind Striking Image, I'd have to say No Nukes was the fastest horse I ever drove. He got a reputation for doing things wrong, but he didn't want to be a bad horse. He did have problems, but if he wasn't a great horse, he couldn't overcome those problems. I think he'll be a great sire. He had wicked speed.

"Things seemed to happen to him. After he'd won a heat of the Adios S., he pulled a shoe leaving the final heat and made a break. Behind the gate, he'd get a little sideways and that time he just reached up and grabbed a shoe. After that race, I wanted Steve Demas who trained him to send him to Springfield. I think he might've beaten 1:50 out there. But, that never came off. In the Jug, he was hurting real bad and raced poorly."

For a horse who made only 19 career starts, and never won a single big race, No Nukes inspired the kind of admiration in horsemen that few horses have ever done. Many observers still feel that No Nukes

Race Record Highlights

At 2
- **1st** Goshen Cup
- **2nd** Woodrow Wilson Elimination

At 3
- **1st** Jersey Cup
  heat of Adios S.
  Jersey Classic Elimination
  Battle of Brandywine Elimination
  heat of Oliver Wendell Holmes S.
- **2nd** Meadowlands Pace
- **3rd** Battle of Brandywine Final
  Oliver Wendell Holmes Final

Courtesy of The Horseman and Fair World

Race Record

Year	Age	Starts	Wins	2nd	3rd	Earnings	Record
1981	2	6	4	1	0	$ 45,110	p,2,1:56.3
1982	3	13	6	1	2	527,320	p,3,T1:52.1
		19	10	2	2	$572,430	p,3,T1:52.1

was one of the fastest horses in history. His poor racing manners simply deprived him of the opportunity to fulfill his latent potential. Such was his luster that he went to stud at Lana Lobell Farm for a new syndicate which included many of the sport's top breeders. The syndication fee of $5,000,000, arranged by Lana Lobell Farm's Alan Leavitt when the colt was just a two-year-old, was the third highest price ever paid for a freshman Standardbred. Later in his life, No Nukes was moved to Demas' Upstream Farm, and then was moved again, ending up at Hanover Shoe Farms' New Jersey satellite farm, where he no doubt will complete his career.

Sire Line

No Nukes is a son of Oil Burner, and was from the first crop of his young sire. Interestingly enough, Oil Burner was from the first crop of his sire, Most Happy Fella, and Most Happy Fella had been a representative of Meadow Skipper's first crop. This rapid evolution of speed genetics seemed to reach its culminating point with No Nukes and his own, aggressive brand of raw speed excited breeders and trainers alike. However, No Nukes is the only major son of Oil Burner ever to reach any degree of siring success. His next best performer was the millionaire Energy Burner p,3,T1:53.1, and the only other high level performer was the fast Devil's Adversary p,3,1:54. No Nukes is a representative of one of the three successful branches of the Most Happy Fella siring dynasty. Oil Burner joined Tyler B and Cam Fella as sons of Most Happy Fella who founded their own specific sire lines.

Maternal Line

No Nukes has a very attractive and healthy maternal background. He is one of those rare siring stars who has a very good female pedigree. His dam is the Overtrick mare Gidget Lobell p,3,2:00.3f. Overtrick dams have had a few moments in the sun besides No Nukes. An Overtrick mare is the dam of Falcon Seelster p,3,1:51h, one of the breed's fastest horses. Another produced the world champion Trenton p,3,1:51.3. Overtrick himself was a contemporary of Meadow Skipper, and had the upper hand on his foe in nearly all their meetings. A son of Solicitor, Overtrick was an extremely attractive horse whose own stud career lacked any real pizzazz.

Besides No Nukes, Gidget Lobell has also produced the excellent stakes filly Peachbottom p,3,1:55.3 ($348,609), winner of the La Paloma at two and the Fan Hanover at three. Peachbottom, a full sister to No Nukes, was a big, attractive filly who later became an Armstrong Brothers broodmare, producing the good stakes fillies Crew Angel p,2,1:54.1f and Armbro Peachie p,2,1:55.4; 3,1:53. Another non-record full sister to No Nukes and Peachbottom, T M I, is the dam of the capable Abercrombie pacer Survivor Gold p,4,1:51 ($897,929) and the stakes-winning Sonsam filly Jollie Dame p,3,1:55.1 ($284,223).

No Nukes is a representative of the vast and auspicious Jessie Pepper maternal family, one of the oldest and brightest fountains of speed in all of harness racing, since Jessie Pepper's maternal pedigree can be traced back to the time of the Civil War. No Nukes' second dam is the Tar Heel mare Gogo Playmate, a foal of 1967, who produced no stars, but whose 15 foals included 13 winners. No Nukes' third dam is the Good Time mare Gogo Playtime p,2:02.4h, a half-sister to the 1950's Midwestern sire Rush Hour p,1:59.4. From there, we can trace No Nukes back to the 1921 Peter Scott mare Elsie Scott, a full sister to Scotland. Elsie Scott's mother Roya McKinney is one of the famed McKinney sisters that are responsible for the production of the Jessie Pepper family. Other noted stars in the same Roya McKinney branch of Jessie Pepper's family include such high-level stars as Tar Heel, Hickory Smoke, Hickory Pride, Armbro Flight, Armbro Goal, and the brilliantly fast Falcon's Future p,3,1:51f. No Nukes' third dam is a half-sister to the second dam of Falcon's Future.

Progeny Of Note

No Nukes was one of the most electrifying two-year-olds in history and his stud career has been marked by the production of early speed. His most successful sons and daughters have all been precocious freshmen, including the likes of Western Hanover p,3,1:50.4 ($2,546,647), Jate Lobell p,3,1:51.2 ($2,231,402), Die Laughing p,3,1:51.1f ($2,164,386) and Immortality p,3,1:51 ($1,614,939). We discussed earlier that there was a trend in this male line for early production since the sires all produced standout horses in their very first crops. No Nukes continued this phenomenal early production by producing Jate Lobell and Nadia Lobell p,3,1:53.4f ($1,007,119) in his very first crop. No Nukes has produced eight millionaire pacers including the group named above, as well as Jeremy's Gambit p,3,Q1:51.1 ($1,252,147), Lotta Soul p,1:50.2 ($1,052,015) and Dexter Nukes p,3,1:51.3 ($1,027,620). From this group has also come a remarkably successful group of young sires, including Western Hanover, Jate Lobell, Die Laughing and Dexter Nukes.

One of the major attributes of this sire line is the production of speed at two and three, and it is informative to note that of No Nukes' biggest money winners, all were either dominant or very successful young horses whose success and acclaim came at two and three. No Nukes has never been known as the sire of hard-hitting aged horses, since most of his get accomplish a great deal as young horses.

He has also been a very successful filly sire, following the example he set in his opening crop with Nadia Lobell. He also produced the Breeders Crown winner Immortality, first two-year-old filly to win $1 million and the brilliant Yankee Coed p,3,1:53.4 ($671,110). Yankee Coed was one of the few fillies to defeat her amazing contemporary Miss Easy.

For all of his early speed production, No Nukes has yet to sire a sub-1:50 performer, and this is a mystery given the proclivity of most of our top stallions to produce speed. But No Nukes is knocking on the door with eight 1:51 pacers, a list which includes such stars as the royally bred Make A Deal p,4,1:50.2 ($610,249) and the Meadowlands FFA star J C's Suprimo p,4,1:50.4 ($487,797). His fastest performer is Nuclear Siren p,3,1:50.1 ($417,744).

No Nukes has produced the winners of nearly $90 million through the end of 1997, including a spectacular 1988 crop which earned more than $15 million, a group headed up by the world champion Woodrow Wilson winner Die Laughing. He is also closing in on more than 1,000 2:00 performers, and his stud career must be appraised from almost any angle as fulfilling the potential inherent, but unfulfilled, in his enigmatic racing career.

Analysis

One of the great sires of the modern era, No Nukes, like Albatross, is known for siring exceptional early speed in both colts and fillies. He is an extension of the Most Happy Fella branch of the Meadow Skipper male line and he also appears to be the type of sire who is a successful sire of sires - much like his grandsire.

The only commercially high-level successful son of his sire Oil Burner, No Nukes has pedigree crosses of 4x4 to Good Time, 5x5x5x4x5 to Hal Dale, 5x4 to King's Counsel and 6x5x4 to Billy Direct. There was nothing in his pedigree which would have made one focus on No Nukes as a potentially great stallion. His Overtrick dam, Gidget Lobell p,3,2:00.3f, was just a nice filly who won $14,829 and her dam never earned a cent. No Nukes' third dam is Gogo Playtime p,2:02.4h who took her record at age six, won just over $50,000 and was just a good raceway type mare in the early 1960's.

The fourth dam of No Nukes is the 1941 Siskiyou mare Dell Siskiyou who is the dam of the stakes winner Rush Hour p,1:59.4 and also three daughters who were excellent producers. Rush Hour's full sister, Noon Rush by Brookdale, is the dam of world champion Speedy Pick p,1:58.4h ($397,633) who was a major FFA performer nationally in the late 1950's and early 1960's. Dell Siskiyou also had two daughters by Gold Worthy, Worthy Sis and Keystone Dixie, who both became top producers. Worthy Sis is the grandam of double-gaited world champion Speedy Romeo p,1:55.4 (t,4,1:59.2) ($492,114) and is the grandam of world champion Falcon's Future p,3,1:51f ($1,054,761). Keystone Dixie has nine in 2:00 headed by Keystone Rudolph p,1:52.4 ($293,088), Dixie Cheer p,4,1:54.3

and Sansom p,2,1:55.2. She is also the grandam of one of Oil Burner's best performers, Devil's Adversary p,3,1:54 ($558,141).

No Nukes has crossed well with a number of broodmare sires, but is especially prolific with mares by Albatross. This is certainly not a surprise when you consider the ability of both of these stallions to sire electrifying speed in their two- and three-year-olds. No Nukes on Albatross was a "no brainer" type of cross and it has produced fantastic results. Of the 25 $500,000 winners sired by No Nukes, 14 are from Albatross mares, including 8 of his ten richest and his eight millionaire sons and daughters. The only two No Nukes millionaires without Albatross or Meadow Skipper blood on the maternal side are Jate Lobell and Jeremy's Gambit. Both of these stars have no common ancestors in their first four generations with Jate's closest cross being 5x3 to Good Time.

Linebreeding to Meadow Skipper has been the key to No Nukes success as 17 of his top 25 money winners (68 percent) are linebred 4x3 to Meadow Skipper. Another interesting key, and one which we see so frequently among top horses, is having common crosses to siblings in the pedigree. Here are a few which have worked for No Nukes: his richest son, Western Hanover, is 4x3 to Meadow Skipper and 4x4 to the half-brother and sister Bullet Hanover and Overbid; Dexter Nukes is 4x3 to Meadow Skipper and also 4x5 to Bullet Hanover and Overbid and 4x5 to the half-brother and sister Dancer Hanover and Terka Hanover; Bomb Rickles p,4,T1:52.2 ($829,366) is 4x3 to Meadow Skipper and 4x5x5x4 to Tar Heel and his half-sister Adioleta.

Other similar sibling crosses include: Nuclear Flash p,1:52 ($767,603) who has a 4x3 cross to the half-sisters Gogo Playtime (No Nukes' third dam) and Keystone Dixie; Ticket To Heaven p,4,1:52 ($712,826) has no common ancestors in his first four generations, but his dam is bred 4x4 to the trotting world champion brother and sister Peter Volo and Volga E.

Interestingly, the only horse in the upper levels of the fastest and richest sons and daughters of No Nukes to have any inbreeding in his pedigree is the co-fastest performer, No Laughs p,1:50.1 ($182,885) who is inbred 3x3 to Most Happy Fella and is also 4x4x4 to Meadow Skipper and 4x4 to Tar Heel. Also at 1:50.1 is Nuclear Siren ($417,744) whose closest crosses are 4x3 to the great Adios son Shadow Wave. I must point out here that Shadow Wave has had a tremendous influence on the breed as a broodmare sire and his presence in the pedigrees of mares bred to No Nukes has paid dividends. Keep in mind that Shadow Wave is the sire of the dam of No Nukes' sire Oil Burner.

The Shadow Wave connection can be seen in Die Laughing who is 4x3 to both Meadow Skipper and Shadow Wave; Nuclear Design p,1:50.4 ($357,326) is 4x4x4 to Meadow Skipper and 4x5 to Shadow Wave, and J C's Suprimo's p,4,1:50.4 ($487,797) closest cross is 4x4 to Shadow Wave. Thus, three of No Nuke's seven fastest performers have common crosses to Shadow Wave in their pedigrees.

From the start, No Nukes has been an exceptional sire of fillies and those are headed by the millionaires Immortality and Nadia Lobell - two great stars. There may be another millionaire filly on the horizon as the No Nukes daughter Clover Hanover p,2,1:52.2 ($568,994) was a dominant force in the female division in 1997 at two.

The presence of Bret Hanover as the sire of the second dam of No Nukes' top performers is also noticeable, especially from mares with the Albatross/Bret Hanover cross. Mares by Niatross did not show up strongly in No Nukes' money-winning leaders, but two of his six fastest offspring are from Niatross mares. Good Time and his sons Race Time, Best Of All and Columbia George are also well-represented in the sire of the second dam position in many pedigrees.

As with most very successful stallions, No Nukes looks like he is also going to be an outstanding broodmare sire. He is already the sire of the dams of such top horses as Island Glow p,1:50 ($608,174) (by

Dragon's Lair). Island Glow is another fine example of breeding back to siblings. His pedigree crosses are as follows: 3x3 to Race Time, 3x4 to Most Happy Fella, 4x4 to Good Time and Tar Heel and an inbred 3x3 to the outstanding producers and three-quarter sisters Tarport Cheer and Tarport Kathy. This is truly a blue-blooded pedigree.

No Nukes is also the sire of the dams of Sharp Attack p,4,1:50.4 ($152,906) (by Direct Scooter), His Mattjesty p,3,1:51 ($986,251) (by Matt's Scooter), Katorzheniki p,4,1:51 ($391,251) (by Kiev Hanover), Matt Russian p,1:51.1 ($178,052) (by Matt's Scooter), Keep Your Pans Off p,4,1:51.1-'98 ($248,111) (by Abercrombie), the fast mare Camourous p,1:51.2 ($806,333) (by Cam Fella), Movie Star Laag p,4,1:51.2-'98 ($231,884) (by Laag), Yankee Cam p,4,1:51.3-'98 ($466,177) (by Cam Fella), Art In The Park p,3,1:52 ($495,164) (by Artsplace). Racing Fund p,3,1:52 ($599,217) (by Fundamentalist), Roses For Emma p,1:52 ($420,511) (by Albert Albert), Freedom's Friend p,2,1:53.1 ($637,622) (by Matt's Scooter) and Town Dreamer p,1:53.4 ($424,908) (by Towner's Big Guy), to name just a few.

A few of the sires who are doing exceptionally well with No Nukes mares are Matt's Scooter and his sire Direct Scooter, both New Jersey-based as is No Nukes; Abercrombie and his sons Artsplace, Laag, Life Sign and Albert Albert; and Cam Fella and Big Towner along with several of their sons.

No Nukes is now 19 years old, but is still holding his own against the onslaught of performers by the next two generations and some of his own descendants. His daughters are in high demand and the best are mostly owned by the top breeders in the sport. Yes, No Nukes has certainly lived up to his potential.

No Nukes

Photo courtesy of The Horseman and Fair World

Leading Progeny by No Nukes

Fastest
Nuclear Siren, h, p,3,1:50.1 $417,744
No Laughs, h, p,1:50.1 $182,885
Lotta Soul, h, p,1:50.2 $1,052,015
Make A Deal, h, p,4,1:50.2 $610,249
Western Hanover, h, p,3,1:50.4 $2,541,647
J C's Suprimo, h, p,4,1:50.4 $487,797
Nuclear Design, h, p,1:50.4 $357,326
Immortality, m, p,3,1:51 $1,614,939
Die Laughing, h, p,3,1:51.1f $2,164,386
Jeremy's Gambit, h, p,3,Q1:51.1 $1,152,247

Richest
Western Hanover, h, p,3,1:50.4 $2,541,647
Jate Lobell, h, p,3,1:51.2 $2,231,402
Die Laughing, h, p,3,1:51.1f $2,164,386
Immortality, m, p,3,1:51 $1,614,939
Jeremy's Gambit, h, p,3,Q1:51.1 $1,152,247
Lotta Soul, h, p,1:50.2 $1,052,015
Dexter Nukes, h, p,3,1:51.3 $1,027,620
Nadia Lobell, m, p,3,1:53.4f $1,007,119
Bomb Rickles, h, p,4,T1:52.2 $829,366
Silky Stallone, h, p,3,1:51.3 $785,323

No Nukes, Brown Horse, 1979
p, 2, 1:56.3; 3, T1:52.1 ($572,430)

Oil Burner, 1973 p, 4, 1:54.2 $535,541	Most Happy Fella, 1967 p, 3, T1:55 $419,033	Meadow Skipper, 1960 p, 3, 1:55.1 $428,057	Dale Frost, 1951 p, 1:58 $204,117	**HAL DALE**	**ABBEDALE** Margaret Hal
				Galloway	Raider Bethel
			Countess Vivian, 1950 p, 3, 1:59 $43,262	**KING'S COUNSEL**	**VOLOMITE** Margaret Spangler
				Filly Direct	**BILLY DIRECT** Calumet Edna
		Laughing Girl, 1961 p, 4, 2:04h $19,546	**GOOD TIME**, 1946 p, 1:57.4 $318,792	**HAL DALE**	**ABBEDALE** Margaret Hal
				On Time	**VOLOMITE** Nedda Guy
			Maxine's Dream, 1954 p, 2, T2:00 $36,557	Knight Dream	Nibble Hanover Lydia Knight
				Maxine Abbe	**ABBEDALE** Maxine Direct
	Dottie Shadow, 1968	Shadow Wave, 1955 p, 3, 1:56.3 $91,931	Adios, 1940 p, T1:57½ $33,329	**HAL DALE**	**ABBEDALE** Margaret Hal
				Adioo Volo	Adioo Guy Sigrid Volo
			Shadow Grattan, 1943 p, 4, 2:07.1h $2,555	Silent Grattan	Grattan Royal Silent T
				Peacedale	**ABBEDALE** Miss Dorothy Dillon
		Diana Streak, 1949 p, 4, 1:58.4 $9,250	Red Streak, 1941 p, 2:02 $49,856	Pegasus Pointer	Pegasus B Bally Pointer
				Isabel Abbe	Bert Abbe Virginia O
			Diana Mite, 1944	**VOLOMITE**	Peter Volo Cita Frisco
				Diana Dyer	**MR. MCELWYN** Fruity Volo
Gidget Lobell, 1974 p, 3, 2:00.3f $14,829	Overtrick, 1960 p, 3, 1:57.1h $407,483	Solicitor, 1948 p, 3, T1:57.2 $102,109	**KING'S COUNSEL**, 1940 p, 6, 1:58 $44,930	**VOLOMITE**	Peter Volo Cita Frisco
				Margaret Spangler	**GUY AXWORTHY** Maggie Winder
			Jane Reynolds, 1938 4, 2:07h	Scotland	Peter Scott Roya McKinney
				Jane Revere	**GUY AXWORTHY** Volga E
		Overbid, 1954 p, 2, T2:05.4 $3,524	**HAL DALE**, 1926 p, 6, 2:02¼	**ABBEDALE**	The Abbe Daisydale D.
				Margaret Hal	Argot Hal Margaret Polk
			Barbara Direct, 1947 p, 3, T2:00.4 $5,747	**BILLY DIRECT**	Napoleon Direct Gay Forbes
				Norette Hanover	Peter The Brewer Helen Hanover
	Gogo Playmate, 1967	Tar Heel, 1948 p, 4, T1:57 $119,148	**BILLY DIRECT**, 1934 p, 4, T1:55 $12,040	Napoleon Direct	Walter Direct Lady Erectress
				Gay Forbes	Malcolm Forbes Gay Girl Chimes
			Leta Long, 1940 p, 4, 2:03¾ $9,321	**VOLOMITE**	Peter Volo Cita Frisco
				Rosette	**MR. MCELWYN** Rose Scott
		Gogo Playtime, 1957 p, 6, 2:02.4h $50,687	**GOOD TIME**, 1946 p, 1:57.4 $318,792	**HAL DALE**	**ABBEDALE** Margaret Hal
				On Time	**VOLOMITE** Nedda Guy
			Dell Siskiyou, 1941	Siskiyou	Azoff Dolly McKinney
				Elsie Truax	Truax Elsie Scott

On The Road Again

In all the years I have been following harness racing there have been two pacers which have stood out in my mind as the toughest I've ever seen. They may not have been the fastest, but they had the most determination and grit. Those two horses are Cam Fella and On The Road Again; one a son and the other a grandson of Most Happy Fella. Neither are very big horses, but they must have hearts the size of watermelons.

On The Road Again won 44 of 61 races and earned $2,819,102. He retired as the second leading money-winning pacer of all time behind Nihilator and was as consistent as a horse could be on the racetrack. He was sound, long-wearing and had the will to win.

On The Road Again was bred by Anna and Sam Schulsinger of Brooklyn, New York, and purchased at the Garden State Mixed Sale in January 1982 for $10,000. At the time, he had just entered his yearling season and was the thirteenth foal from his dam Bye Bye Mollie who had not produced anything special to that point, nor did she later. The chestnut colt was from the first crop of the new sire Happy Motoring, a son of Most Happy Fella.

The young colt was the first yearling purchase ever made by owners Gordon and Illa Rumpel of Calgary, Alberta, Canada. They had previously owned just raceway stock. The new purchase was turned over to trainer Harry Poulton who was only 25 years old at the time.

On The Road Again turned out to be a precocious two-year-old and Poulton started him for the first time on June 24, 1983, in a non-betting race at the Calgary track. He was raced easily by Poulton in that start and finished third to the filly Reef Peace who was his stablemate. His first win was a week later in his first parimutuel start, timed in 2:04.1. He then won two legs of Calgary's Primary Series by 15 lengths and seven lengths - both in 2:01.4. In the $19,150 Primary Series Final, the colt went wire-to-wire, winning by 14 lengths in 2:00. He was driven by Fred Gillis in each of those Series efforts. Since there was not much opportunity in Western Canada for two-year-olds, On The Road Again was turned out after four wins from five starts. Poulton and Rumpel knew they had a star in the making. Trainer Poulton said after On The Road Again's great three-year-old season a year later, "After his two-year-old year, I thought he'd be competitive in the big races, get money, but I didn't expect him to do what he did. How could you predict something like that?"

Poulton had the three-year-old On The Road Again ready early and he won a qualifier in 2:03.1 at Calgary on the last day of February in 1984. He then won his first two starts at Northlands Park in Edmonton in 2:02.1 and 2:00.2. Entered into the Shelly Goudreau Memorial Series at Los Alamitos, On The Road Again began his relationship with driver Buddy Gilmour who drove him during the rest of his career. Gilmour is one of the all-time outstanding harness drivers and always gets the most from his horses without abusing them. He was the perfect fit for On The Road Again.

The colt swept through three $12,500 legs of the Goudreau Series, winning in 1:56.2, 1:56.3 and 1:56.2. In the last race he overcame a parked out second half trip to win by a half-length. The colt was the favorite for the $300,000 Goudreau Final. Leaving from post six, he was parked out to the first quarter, but gained the lead and was never headed as he dug in to hold off the closing rally of Guts by a nose with Armbro Cadet third in the 1:56 mile. This thrust On The Road Again into the national spotlight; it was the first glimpse of his toughness and tenacity while under pressure. The colt just refused to lose. At this point, On The Road Again was undefeated in his first six starts of the year.

He was then shipped to Chicago's Maywood Park and won his Windy City Pace Elimination by three lengths in 1:55.4. The $262,000 Final was to be his first defeat. Right before the start from post six, On The Road Again was shaking his head and the check rein came loose. Gilmour then elected not to leave fast with the colt and to race from behind after everyone else got settled. Traffic problems ensued and On

Race Record Highlights

At 2
- **1st** Calgary Pacing Series Final and two legs

At 3
- **1st** Meadowlands Pace
  - Cane Pace Final and Elimination
  - Confederation Cup
  - New Jersey Classic Final and Elimination
  - Shelly Goudreau Memorial Series Final and Elimination
  - Provincial Cup
  - Lucky Strikes P.
  - Prix d'Ete Elimination
  - Western Canadian Derby
  - Windy City S. Elimination
- **2nd** American-National S.
  - Meadowlands Pace Elimination
  - Windy City S. Final
  - Oliver Wendell Holmes S. Elimination
- **3rd** Oliver Wendell Holmes S. Final

At 4
- **1st** George Morton Levy Series Final and two legs
  - World Cup Final and two legs
  - leg of Graduate Series
  - leg of Driscoll Series
  - two legs of U.S. Pacing Championship
  - Challenge P.
  - Canadian Pacing Derby
  - Chesapeake P.
  - Stewart Fraser Memorial Final and Prep
  - Yonkers Fall Pacing Championship Final and leg
  - Mohawk Gold Cup
- **2nd** leg of Driscoll Series
  - Cornell Memorial
  - leg of Yonkers Fall Pacing Series
- **3rd** Breeders Crown
  - two legs of George Morton Levy Series

Honors
At three, voted Pacer of the Year
At three, set record for single-season earnings for a Standardbred
At four, equalled world race record for his age
At four, voted Aged Pacer of the Year

On The Road Again

Photo courtesy of Blue Chip Farms

Race Record

Year	Age	Starts	Wins	2nd	3rd	Earnings	Record
1983	2	5	4	0	1	$ 13,361	p,2,2:00f
1984	3	26	18	5	1	1,751,695	p,3,1:53.3
1985	4	30	22	4	3	1,054,046	p,4,1:51.4
		61	44	9	5	$2,819,102	p,4,1:51.4

On The Road Again

The Road Again never saw the rail. He was still sixth and looking for racing room midway through the stretch. Gilmour finally found an opening and hustled the colt up to second, but a length and one-half behind the winning Carl's Bird.

Still in Chicago a week later, On The Road Again was the favorite in the $175,000 American-National S. Drawing post six once again, as he had in four of previous five starts, he was parked out first over to the half in :57.1 before assuming the lead. The effort, however, took the sting out of him in the last few strides and he succumbed by a head to the fast-closing Farmstead's Fame in 1:56.1.

Shipped east, On The Road Again next raced in a three-year-old Invitational at Roosevelt. Coming from behind, he lost by a nose to Troublemaker. The Cane Pace was next at Yonkers. Rumpel made a supplemental payment to have his colt entered, and On The Road Again got back on the winning track with two impressive wire-to-wire wins, the Elimination in 1:56.4 and the Final, on the same night, also in 1:56.4 in a hard-fought head victory over Holmes Hanover. It was then on to the New Jersey Classic Eliminations at The Meadowlands, where On The Road Again won by three lengths from post nine in 1:54.4. The $460,000 New Jersey Classic Final was not an easy trip. The colt was parked out to the quarter, took the lead before the :55.4 half, gave it up again, and then battled back for a length win over Butler B G in 1:53.3.

On The Road Again was favored in his Meadowlands Pace Elimination and was hard used from post eight to get to the lead at the half in :55. He was shuffled back to third in the stretch, but came on again to finish second to Andrel by just a neck in 1:53. As always, he was prominent in the photo. The $1,293,000 Meadowlands Pace Final, still the richest in that series, was next and On The Road Again drew post 12, the second position in the second tier. In one of Buddy Gilmour's all-time great drives, he left patiently with the colt and was eighth on the outside at the first quarter. He followed the outside flow of horses to just before the half when he launched an aggressive three-wide move to get up to second and challenge for the lead. On The Road Again was on the lead on the outside at the three-quarters and held his position through the stretch to squeeze out a very impressive neck decision over Guts in 1:53.3. Trainer Harry Poulton was later quoted, "I thought his best race was the Meadowlands Pace - he went a long mile and hung in tough. That race meant the most to me."

After the Meadowlands Pace the colt was given a week off. Then he came back for the two-heat Oliver Wendell Holmes S. at the Meadowlands, in which he was defeated by Guts in his Elimination, and in the Final, by a half-length and by two lengths respectively. After another week off, On The Road Again won the $202,500 Confederation Cup at Flamboro Downs and followed that with a win in his Prix d'Ete Elimination at Blue Bonnets. However, in the Final he finished fifth, although he was only a length behind the winner, Butler B.G.

Returning to his home territory of Western Canada, On The Road Again won the $116,890 Western Canadian Derby by ten lengths at Northlands Park. The biggest disappointment of his three-year-old season came a week later in the $670,000 Breeders Crown at Northlands Park. On The Road Again was the even-money favorite in a race that also included Guts. Guts and On The Road Again had a great rivalry all year with the smaller On The Road Again racing in all kinds of different styles and the giant-sized Guts strictly a come-from-behind horse with a great closing kick. But things changed on this Breeders Crown night.

Guts regular driver Bill O'Donnell chose to drive Troublemaker, who had won the Messenger S. just a week before, and with Mickey McNichol substituting for him, race strategy went out the window. McNichol took Guts right to the front which surprised everyone, especially Gilmour and On The Road Again. They left from post seven and were fifth in the outside flow at the :27 first quarter. McNichol and

Guts slowed the pace down to a :30 second quarter toward the half and Gilmour had no choice but to go up to the front and challenge Guts. The two battled past the half before On The Road Again got to the front. Meanwhile, Troublemaker had been enjoying the cover of On The Road Again and had now moved into second place, challenging the leader while locking Guts in on the rail. On The Road Again began to tire in the stretch while Troublemaker went on to a three-quarter length win over Guts. On The Road Again finished fourth.

To show his spirit and will to win was not diminished, On The Road Again endured another transcontinental trip and was back at New York's Roosevelt Raceway for a $50,000 Invitational which he won by five lengths in 1:56. His last effort at three came at Canada's Windsor Raceway when he won the $105,000 Provincial Cup in 1:53.4 by two lengths over Guts. These last two performances were track records and showed the great form which Poulton was able to keep On The Road Again in during a season which lasted from February through October.

Of On The Road Again's eight losses during the season, six had been by one length or less - three of those by a head, a nose and a neck. He was used to close finishes: two of his wins were by a neck; two more by a nose and a head. He was one tough competitor. Hall of Famer Buddy Gilmour said, "He's the best three-year-old I've ever been fortunate enough to drive. He's tough and loves to race."

On The Road Again's earnings of $1,751,695 set a single-season record for a Standardbred. He had also won 18 of 26 starts, was voted Pacer of the Year over Nihilator and was second in Horse of the Year balloting to the trotting mare Fancy Crown. Not bad for a $10,000 early yearling purchase!

Coming back to the wars as a four-year-old, On The Road Again was no less intimidating. He had a great campaign with 22 wins from 30 starts and earnings of $1,054,046 while lowering his record to 1:51.4. During the same season in 1985, On The Road Again and Nihilator became the first two Standardbreds in history to record back-to-back million-dollar seasons.

At four, On The Road Again was again ready early and began his campaign with a win at Mohawk at the end of March. In the second start of the season he showed he had not lost any of his grit coming from behind to finish in a dead-heat with George S. in a leg of the Graduate Series at Rosecroft. A week later, he lost to that same horse by three-quarters of a length after being parked out every step of the way at Yonkers in a 1:55.3 mile.

A four-race winning streak was next before it was snapped by his old nemesis Guts by a neck at The Meadowlands with On The Road Again closing four lengths in the stretch and coming home in :26.2 in a 1:52.3 mile. Unfortunately, On The Road Again made the only break of his career in the $174,000 Driscoll Series Final at The Meadowlands when he was interfered with before the quarter. He recovered to take fifth, less than three lengths behind the winner. Longer distance was no problem as On The Road Again won the one and one-eighth mile World Cup Pace in 2:08.1 in what was to be the beginning of an eight-race winning streak. A week later, he won another World Cup event at one and one-half miles in 2:54.1. He also won the World Cup Final at one mile in 1:52.2 over Tuff Choice and Guts after having the lead at the half, being shuffled back to third in the stretch and then coming on again to win.

On The Road Again's winning streak went on to include the $145,000 George Morton Levy Series Final at Roosevelt in 1:55.2 and legs of the U.S. Pacing Championship at Roosevelt and The Meadowlands. He won the latter in a personal best of 1:51.4 which made him at the time the co-fastest four-year-old of all time. Also included in the winning streak was the $133,000 Blue Bonnets Challenge P. and a week later the $124,000 Canadian Pacing Derby at Greenwood. The streak ended with two second place finishes at Mohawk and Freehold before On The Road Again rebounded to win three of his next four races, including the $200,000 Stewart Frazer Memorial.

Following a second place defeat by a nose to Division Street at Yonkers after being parked out first over for three-quarters, On The Road Again won his final four starts of the year, including a leg and the $250,000 Yonkers Fall Pacing Championship Series Final. Just as he had been as a three-year-old, On The Road Again was always in the photo, even in defeat, as six of his eight losses at four were by one length or less with four of them by a neck or less.

On The Road Again was a perfect gaited pacer, standing 15.2, who wore no boots and loose 57-inch hobbles. A little insight into his personality comes from Sherri Poulton, the trainer's wife and On The Road Again's caretaker, who was quoted in a *Hoof Beats* article. Mrs. Poulton said, "He was just like a pet and loved to play catch with a towel. And, he'll pose forever as soon as he hears cameras clicking."

On The Road Again was voted Aged Pacer of the Year and was runner-up to Nihilator in the Horse of the Year and Pacer of the Year categories. Syndicated during his four-year-old campaign, On The Road Again was raced by Blue Chip Partners, The Road Group and Gordon and Illa Rumpel. He went to Blue Chip Farms in New York to stand at stud at the conclusion of his stellar racing career with great credentials.

Sire Line

On The Road Again is an excellent representative of the Most Happy Fella sire line - the most productive of the sons of Meadow Skipper. However, his success is from the unlikely source of his sire Happy Motoring p,3,1:56.2 ($538,495). Other Most Happy Fella sons are the more common fountains of greatness, such as Cam Fella, who has at least a half dozen commercial sons attempting to extend this sire line; Oil Burner, who gave us only No Nukes as a top sire, and whose sons are doing very well; and Tyler B who is trying to continue his line through sons Dragon's Lair, Tyler's Mark, Magical Mike, Cole Muffler and others.

Just as Oil Burner sired one son who became a great sire, Happy Motoring also has just one son who has done extremely well. Happy Motoring was an excellent racehorse and won the Cane Pace, Monticello Classic and Meadowlands Pace Elimination at three. In addition to On The Road Again, he had another million-dollar winner, Anxious Robby p,3,1:52.4 ($1,191,383) who was a stallion in Illinois with moderate success.

Maternal Line

The dam of On The Road Again is the unraced Bye Byrd Byrd mare Bye Bye Mollie. Bye Bye Byrd was an excellent broodmare sire and crossed extremely well with Meadow Skipper, his sons and grandsons.

On The Road Again was by far the best offspring Bye Bye Mollie ever produced, the next best being the Columbia George son S.A. Crest p,3,2:00.1h ($166,295). Four of her daughters produced 2:00 racehorses, but none were high-caliber stakes horses and few did much at two. This was not a family noted for precocious early speed.

Bye Bye Mollie's dam is the Gene Abbe mare Irish Mollie p,3,2:05.2h; T2:04.3 ($20,372) who produced the good Keystone Icy p,1:56.2 ($205,450) and Keystone Imp p,1:59.4f ($45,820) by Keystone Ore and his sire Bye Bye Byrd respectively. Again, Irish Mollie had five daughters who produced in 2:00, but nothing memorable in the way of well-known stakes winners. Irish Mollie is a full sister to the stakes winner and FFA star of the late 1950s Irish p,2:00.2h ($222,728) who ranked eleventh on the all-time money-winning list of pacers when he retired from racing in 1960.

The third dam of On The Road Again is the Doctor Rankin mare Shannon p,2:08 ($1,860). Her claim to fame is being a half-sister to Galloway p,2:04½h who is the dam of Dale Frost p,1:58 ($204,117) - sire of the great racehorse and stallion Meadow Skipper p,3,1:55.1 ($428,057). Bethel p,2:03 (by David Guy) is the next dam and On The Road Again has a 6x4 relationship to that mare. This maternal family is known as County House Mare and is not one of the deep families in the sport.

On The Road Again's first three dams were not particularly good producers of early speed, but he overcame that to a certain degree and sired plenty of fast two-year-olds. But he is noted more for his sons and daughters improving with age.

It seems On The Road Again was a true anomaly for this maternal family and I believe that the credit must go to Most Happy Fella. There is an interesting similarity here between Happy Motoring and Oil Burner, both siring one great son. Both of those sires are by Most Happy Fella from Shadow Wave mares. Perhaps each got one dose of all the best genes and funneled it into one son who also passed it on. Such are the mysteries of genetics!

Progeny of Note

Though past his prime as a top-level pacing stallion, On The Road Again has had a career of accomplishments to make any sire proud. His offspring have won over $45,000,000 from only nine crops through 1997. On The Road Again has sired three in 1:50, 28 in 1:52, over 140 in 1:55, 460 in 2:00 and 11 $500,000 winners at this writing. In addition, his oldest daughters are now just 11 years old and have already produced almost 100 2:00 performers.

Heading the list of the best On The Road Again sons and daughters is the great mare Delinquent Account p,2,1:54.1; 3,1:53.3; 4,1:52.1; 1:51.4 ($1,038,997). She was a world champion and her many stakes wins include the Breeders Crown at four. The three 1:50 performers to On The Road Again's credit are Catch A Flight p,4,1:49.4 ($501,785), Ash Blue Chip p,1:49.4 ($317,507) and Dr. Lecter Lobell p,1:50 ($494,846). Another of his big money winners just missing the 1:50 club is Silent Spring p,1:50.1 ($981,177) and a top mare who retired just shy of $1,000,000 in earnings is Sara Loren Rd p,1:53.4f ($963,768) who was a Jugette winner at three. Two others who flirted with the $1,000,000 mark were foals of 1987, as was Delinquent Account, and they are C.K.S. p,1:51.2 ($956,418) and Road Machine p,3,1:54.4h ($910,717). Road Machine won the rich Metro S. Final at two.

On The Road Again has a long roll of honor which includes other top winners such as That'll Be Me p,4,1:51.4f ($718,451), Shipps Schnoops p,3,1:51.4f ($658,123), Tibet p,4,1:51.3 ($653,680), Center Strip p,3,1:53.2h ($591,120) and Vacationing p,1:52.4f ($595,260), among his $500,000 winners.

Besides Delinquent Account and Sara Loren Rd, which represent two of his three richest foals, On The Road Again has sired his share of good fillies, although trainers will tell you they much prefer the On The Road Again colts. Other top fillies are Tarport Hap S. winner Tambourine p,4,1:54 ($413,160), Red Road p,4,1:53.3f ($285,541), Terri Terrific p,4,1:52.1 ($302,737), Lovin Yankee p,2,1:53 ($255,506), Le Mistral p,1:52.2 ($249,213), Home Again p,4,1:54.1 ($235,269) and Fatima p,3,1:52.2 ($218,850). On The Road Again's fastest record daughter surfaced in 1997, Thruway Hershey p,4,1:51 ($117,963).

Analysis

For years, the On The Road Again colts and fillies dominated the New York Sires S. program as well as making their presence felt in major Grand Circuit events. As late as 1989, On The Road Again's stud fee was a lofty $15,000 and in 1990 he bred 199 mares at a stud fee of $12,000. On The Road Again has always been a very popular stallion among breeders because his offspring get to the races and stay there. You will see many of his sons and daughters in the ranks of Invitational and Open events at racetracks throughout North America. They seem to stay sound and get better with age which are traits of both the Most Happy Fella sire line and of On The Road Again's maternal family.

On The Road Again has no common ancestors in his first four generations and his closest male line pedigree crosses are 5x4 to Billy Direct and 6x6x6x4 to Volomite. The most interesting cross in his pedigree is the 4x4 to the full brother and sister Adios and Adieu. On The Road Again picks up Adios as the grandsire of Happy Motoring's dam and Adieu as the grandam of his dam's sire Bye Bye Byrd. In any case, this is the closest cross in On The Road Again's pedigree and a fine example for those who believe in the linking of great full brothers and sisters in the middle of a pedigree.

Looking at the crosses which seemed to work best with On The Road Again, we find Bret Hanover at the top of the list since he is the sire of the dams of Delinquent Account and Silent Spring which are On The Road Again's two richest performers. Bret's son Warm Breeze is the sire of Road Machine, the fifth highest money winner. Bret Hanover also has a strong presence in the pedigrees of On The Road Again's three 1:50 performers. Warm Breeze is the sire of the dam of Ash Blue Chip; Sonsam, who is from a Bret Hanover dam, is the sire of Catch A Flight; and Dr. Lecter Lobell is from an Albatross mare and his second dam is by Bret Hanover.

As expected, Meadow Skipper mares have a strong presence since foals from that cross would have a 4x2 cross to that great stallion. On The Road Again is a grandson of Most Happy Fella and breeding back to that stallion also paid dividends. A foal by On The Road Again from a Most Happy Fella mare would be inbred 3x2 to that stallion, but enough breeders believed in the cross to make it work. Some examples of the 3x2 Most Happy Fella cross are Vacationing p,1:52.4f ($595,260), Tulsa Blue Chip p,1:53.1 ($476,849), Bad Self p,1:50.4 ($355,371) and Road To The Top p,1:50.2 ($384,487). The last two are among On The Road Again's seven fastest performers and their dams are both from mares by Tar Heel. One precautionary note, however, is that these examples all came to prominence as older horses and were not major stakes horses as youngsters.

Another interesting cross is the New Zealand-bred mare Smooth Millie p,1:53.4 with On The Road Again. She was a very fast older racemare and is a daughter of Smooth Fella - a son of Most Happy Fella who was exported and did very well. The cross for her On The Road Again offspring is an inbred 3x3 to Most Happy Fella and she has produced the good winners Bring 'Em p,1:54.1 (at the age of ten in 1997!) and Le Mistral p,1:52.2 ($249,213) (record at the age of six).

Other On The Road Again success stories have come from mares by Albatross and his sons Sonsam and Niatross. In fact, they are represented in eight of the top 25 money winners by On The Road Again.

The Meadow Skipper mare Chin Chin figures prominently in two of On The Road Again's best performers. Her Bret Hanover daughter Al Dente is the dam of his best offspring, Delinquent Account, and Chin Chin's Abercrombie daughter, Happy Bottom, is the dam of the fast Road Happy p,1:50.2 ($184,177). Delinquent Account is bred 4x3 to Meadow Skipper, as are many of On The Road Again's best offspring, and 5x3x5 to Adios. Her dam Al Dente has an interesting cross of her own. Al Dente is bred 2x4 to Adios and is also 3x3 to the Nibble Hanover full sisters Beryl Hanover and Odella Hanover. These two sisters are the grandams of 1964, 1965 and 1966 Horse of the Year Bret Hanover and 1973 Horse of the Year Sir Dalrae. So, Al Dente was inbred to a pair of mares with dynamite in their genes and produced a great horse herself.

Another Meadow Skipper mare with dual fast credits by On The Road Again is Bobbysocks who has produced Getabout p,4,1:51.3 ($242,139) and Hot Walker p,4,1:51.4 ($202,001). The dams of both of these producers are by sons of Adios.

My advice to breeders is that once you see On The Road Again works well with a particular mare, don't hesitate to take her back to him. Fine examples of this are the On The Road Again offspring of Breezie Skipper - Road Machine p,3,1:54.4h ($910,717) and Ash Blue Chip p,1:49.4 ($317,507) - the first his third richest performers and the second his co-fastest. In fact, the Most Happy Fella mare Tracy Blue Chip has produced four sub-1:55 performers by On The Road Again - all with the inbred 3x2 cross to Most Happy Fella.

As good a job as On The Road Again has done as a stallion, it does not look as if he will leave a son who will make any impact on the breed and extend this branch of the Meadow Skipper/Most Happy Fella line. I suspect, however, that On The Road Again will make a nice mark as a broodmare sire since he had some good fillies and was bred to quite a few blue-blooded mares during his stallion career. In addition, he adds some interesting bloodlines to his daughters' genetic make-up since his dam combines the cross of Bye Bye Byrd and Gene Abbe.

Some of the early results from his daughters have been promising, as shown by Athena Blue Chip p,1:50.3 ($457,118) who equalled Ellamony's world race record for mares in May 1996 only to see it broken by two-fifths of a second ten weeks later by Sweetgeorgiabrown. Other fast ones from On The Road Again mares are Orchard Street p,4,1:50.4 ($397,830) and Melina Mercouri p,3,1:51.1 ($151,198). These performers are sired by Goalie Jeff who is also a Most Happy Fella male line sire through his son Cam Fella. Thus, doubling up on Most Happy Fella with On The Road Again is working well for his daughters just as it did for him.

On The Road Again's greatest daughter, Delinguent Account, has also provided his best broodmare sire credit with the Breeders Crown winner Artiscape p,2,1:52.3 ($495,501) by Artsplace. If he comes back in 1998 in top condition, Artiscape has the potential to be one of the great colts.

Another broodmare credit from the Most Happy Fella male line is Showmethewayhome p,4,1:52.2 ($172,205) by Dragon's Lair, a Most Happy Fella grandson through Tyler B. Some other fast offspring from On The Road Again mares are Kurt And Brad p,1:52.3 ($150,813) (by Armbro Global), C Lulu Plein Truc p,4,1:54f ($212,792) (by Kiev Hanover), Lady Ann Mathew p,2,1:54.1 ($284,041) (by Matt's Scooter), Take Home The Gold p,3,1:54.3 ($170,576) (by Run The Table), Roadster Sahbra p,3,1:55f (by Towner's Big Guy), Allen Rd p,4,1:55 (by Direct Scooter) and Road To Pandalay p,2,1:55.3 ($158,223) (by Matt's Scooter). I also want to point out that Direct Scooter and two of his sons are on this short list, so that may be another cross worth watching and trying.

All in all, On The Road Again has had a very steady and solid stallion career. The only thing that stopped him from reaching the elite ranks is the lack of dominant two- and three-year-old super stars. If you want a solid racehorse and a reasonable chance at winning stakes, then On The Road Again is your ticket. And today he is at a very reasonable stud fee, given his accomplishments. At this stage of his career, On The Road Again is still capable of coming up with top performers, but I believe he will make a big name for himself as a broodmare sire.

On The Road Again

Photo courtesy of The Horseman and Fair World

Leading Progeny by On The Road Again

Fastest
- Ash Blue Chip, g, p,1:49.4 $318,822
- Catch A Flight, h, p,4,1:49.4 $501,785
- Dr. Lecter Lobell, g, p,1:50 $499,346
- Silent Spring, h, p,1:50.1 $981,177
- Road To The Top, g, p,1:50.2 $388,327
- Road Happy, g, p,1:50.2 $186,677
- Mob Scene, h, p,1:50.3 $363,368
- Bad Self, g, p,1:50.4 $355,371
- Vacationing, g, p,1:51 $608,586
- Thruway Hershey, m, p,4,1:51 $117,963

Richest
- Delinquent Account, m, p,1:51.4 $1,038,997
- Silent Spring, h, p,1:50.1 $981,177
- Sara Loren Rd, m, p,1:53.4f $963,768
- C. K. S., h, p,1:51.2 $956,418
- Road Machine, h, p,3,1:54.4h $910,717
- That'll Be Me, h, p,4,1:51.4 $725,471
- Shipp's Schnoops, h, p,3,1:51.4f $658,123
- Tibet, h, p,4,1:51.3 $653,680
- Vacationing, g, p,1:51 $608,586
- Center Strip, h, p,1:53.2h $591,120

On The Road Again, Chestnut Horse, 15.2 Hands, 1981
p, 2, 2:00f; 3, 1:53.3; 4, 1:51.4 ($2,819,102)

Happy Motoring, 1976 p, 3, 1:56.2 $538,495	Most Happy Fella, 1967 p, 3, T1:55 $419,033	Meadow Skipper, 1960 p, 3, 1:55.1 $428,057	Dale Frost, 1951 p, 1:58 $204,117	**HAL DALE**	**ABBEDALE** / Margaret Hal
				Galloway	Raider / **BETHEL**
			Countess Vivian, 1950 p, 3, 1:59 $43,262	King's Counsel	**VOLOMITE** / Margaret Spangler
				Filly Direct	**BILLY DIRECT** / Calumet Edna
		Laughing Girl, 1961 p, 4, 2:04h $19,546	Good Time, 1946 p, 1:57.4 $318,792	**HAL DALE**	**ABBEDALE** / Margaret Hal
				On Time	**VOLOMITE** / Nedda Guy
			Maxine's Dream, 1954 p, 2, T2:00 $36,557	**KNIGHT DREAM**	Nibble Hanover / Lydia Hanover
				Maxine Abbe	**ABBEDALE** / Maxine Direct
	Peaches N Cream, 1967 p, 3, 2:03.2h $22,966	Shadow Wave, 1955 p, 3, 1:56.3 $91,931	Adios, 1940 p, T1:57½ $33,329	**HAL DALE**	**ABBEDALE** / Margaret Hal
				ADIOO VOLO	Adioo Guy / Sigrid Volo
			Shadow Grattan, 1943 p, 4, 2:07.1h $2,555	Silent Grattan	**GRATTAN ROYAL** / Silent T
				Peacedale	**ABBEDALE** / Miss Dorothy Dillon
		Parisian Hanover, 1963 p, 2, 2:06.3 $2,923	Tar Heel, 1948 p, 4, T1:57 $119,148	**BILLY DIRECT**	Napoleon Direct / Gay Forbes
				Leta Long	**VOLOMITE** / Rosette
			Paris Hanover, 1959	**KNIGHT DREAM**	Nibble Hanover / Lydia Knight
				Precious Hal	**HAL DALE** / Treasure
Bye Bye Mollie, 1963	Bye Bye Byrd, 1955 p, 5, T1:56.1 $554,272	Poplar Byrd, 1944 p, T1:59.3 $69,300	**VOLOMITE**, 1926 3, 2:03¼ $32,649	Peter Volo	Peter The Great / Nervolo Belle
				Cita Frisco	San Francisco / Mendocita
			Ann Vonian, 1937 p, 3, 2:01¼ $4,974	Grattan At Law	**GRATTAN ROYAL** / Daisy At Law
				Margaret Vonian	Favonian / Margaret C. Brooke
		Evalina Hanover, 1946 p, 1:59.2 $12,420	**BILLY DIRECT**, 1934 p, 4, T1:55 $12,040	Napoleon Direct	Walter Direct / Lady Erectress
				Gay Forbes	Malcolm Forbes / Gay Girl Chimes
			Adieu, 1938 p, 2, T2:04¼	**HAL DALE**	**ABBEDALE** / Margaret Hal
				ADIOO VOLO	Adioo Guy / Sigrid Volo
	Irish Mollie, 1955 p, T2:04.3 $20,372	Gene Abbe, 1944 p, T2:00.3 $51,239	Bert Abbe, 1922 p, 1:59¼	The Abbe	Chimes / Nettie King
				Miss Ella H.	Mack H / Nelly Patch
			Rose Marie, 1927 p, 2:05h	Martinos	Cochato / Queen Audubon
				Lady Permilia	Coastman / Virginia Alta
		Shannon, 1942 p, 2:08 $1,860	Doctor Rankin, 1936	Scotland	Peter Scott / Roya McKinney
				Dorothy	**GUY AXWORTHY** / Dorothy Day
			BETHEL, 1926 p, 2:03	David Guy	**GUY AXWORTHY** / Belle Zombro
				Annotation	Azoff / Citation

Overtrick

Overtrick is considered by many to be one of the greatest pacers of all-time. He is also a top broodmare sire with over 600 2:00 credits. However, as great as he was a racehorse, Overtrick did not leave any major commercial sons to carry on his male line which descends from the legendary Volomite. But, he has been a tremendous influence in the bloodlines of some of today's top pacers and stallions.

Overtrick was owned and bred by Helen Buck of Far Hills, New Jersey, wife of mining magnate Leonard Buck. They owned Allwood Stables and had much success as owners and breeders during their years in harness racing. The Bucks' trotter, The Intruder, won the Hambletonian in 1956.

Trained and driven by Hall of Famer, John Patterson, Sr., Overtrick took on all comers and was fast, courageous and durable. He did not need a covered up trip to be at his best in a race. These traits were passed on to many of his top sons and daughters.

At two, Overtrick made an inauspicious career debut on May 30, 1962, at Goshen's Historic Track in New York. He finished seventh in an eight-horse race for a purse of $500. In his next start, almost a month later, Overtrick won his first race over the Goshen track in 2:07.1. His first stakes event was on July 4 at Goshen. He was sixth in the first heat of the Goshen Cup and did not come back for the second. His next start was the Excelsior S. at Monticello and Overtrick was a much-improved second to Majestic Hanover in 2:05.2. He now appeared to be a competitive stakes colt. However, he had only one win to show for his first four starts - hardly an impressive start for one who was to become Two-Year-Old Pacer of the Year.

He won nine of his next dozen starts, including the McMahon Memorial, Little Pat S., Ohio Standardbred Futurity and Meadow Lands Farm S., and defeated all challengers for the two-year-old title. Overtrick's fastest win was in 1:59.4 and he was brilliant on the big mile tracks during his mid-Western swing. Later, he became a noted half-mile track champion.

At three, Overtrick was the defending divisional champion. He opened his season with a disappointing sixth place finish in the Battle of Brandywine but, he was a resilient colt and came back to win 11 of his next 13 starts.

In one of his losses, Overtrick was defeated by Meadow Skipper in the $163,000 Cane Futurity at Yonkers Raceway. This loss prevented Overtrick from becoming a Triple Crown winner that year. Mrs. Buck had paid a $15,000 Supplemental Fee to gain entrance to the Cane but had poor luck in the draw when Overtrick drew post 12 in the second tier. However, Overtrick got away quickly behind the fast-leaving William Time. He was able to get to the rail with a minimum of effort as Meadow Skipper challenged for the early lead. Meadow Skipper was on top at the quarter.

Patterson took Overtrick off the rail in front of the grandstand the first time around and rocketed up to challenge the front-running Meadow Skipper. But Earle Avery would not give up the lead and Patterson was left parked out with Overtrick. The two great colts had seven lengths on the rest of the field as they turned for home, but Meadow Skipper hung tough and fought off another Overtrick challenge to win the race by three-quarters of a length in a track record equalling 1:58.4.

Overtrick was at his best in the Little Brown Jug at Delaware, Ohio, in September. He had lost to Meadow Skipper and Country Don in his previous two starts and in the first Jug heat Country Don was the 8-5 favorite followed by Meadow Skipper at 9-5 and Overtrick at 2-1 in close wagering.

In the first heat, the Marcel Dostie-driven Country Don took the early lead and sped to the three-quarters in an extremely fast 1:26.4 which took its toll on the colt. Meadow Skipper saw the rail briefly, but was parked out for a good portion of the mile. Meanwhile, after leaving from the second tier, Patterson sat coolly on the rail with Overtrick in fifth for much of the early pace and then followed cover in the outside flow during the second half. Overtrick swung three-wide through the final turn and passed Meadow Skipper to win by one and one-quarter lengths with Country Don fading back to third. The time was a startling 1:57.1 - an all-age world record over a half-mile track. Overtrick wound up setting seven world marks in the Jug that afternoon.

Having won the first heat, Overtrick earned the rail for the second.

Race Record Highlights

At 2
1st McMahon Memorial
Little Pat S.
Ohio Standardbred Futurity
Meadow Lands Farm S.
2nd Excelsior S.
Billy Direct S.
Washington Park S.

At 3
1st Little Brown Jug
Messenger S.
The Liberty Bell S.
Battle of Saratoga
Hanover-Hempt S.
Geers S.
Excelsior S.
Castleton P.
heat of Poplar Hill Farm P.

At 3 (continued)
2nd Cane Futurity
Adios S.
The Colonial P.
Poplar Hill Farm P.

At 4
1st Realization S.
International Pace (1½ miles)
Empire Pace (1¼ miles)
Dan Patch Encore P.
2nd Bye Bye Byrd P.
H T A Final
Dan Patch P.

Honors
At three, set eight world records
Voted Two-Year-Old Pacer of the Year
Voted Three-Year-Old Pacer of the Year

Overtrick

Photo courtesy of The Horseman and Fair World

Race Record

Year	Age	Starts	Wins	2nd	3rd	Earnings	Record
1962	2	16	10	3	0	$ 40,129	p,2,1:59.4
1963	3	23	16	4	0	208,833	p,3,1:57.1h
1964	4	11	8	3	0	158,521	
		50	34	10	0	$407,483	p,3,1:57.1h

In that heat, Patterson used the rail to his advantage and Overtrick was in front every step of the way, winning by two lengths over Country Don with Meadow Skipper taking third. The time 1:57.3 for a combined two-heat world record of 3:54.4.

At the Red Mile in Lexington the following week, Overtrick hooked up with Meadow Skipper again in an epic mile. The event was the Poplar Hill Farm P. for a purse of only $4,100, but the race turned out to be a 1:55.1 world record for three-year-olds. There was only a four-horse field and the race was clearly between Overtrick and Meadow Skipper. The two colts raced head-to-head down the stretch and Meadow Skipper prevailed at the wire, even though driver Earle Avery lost his whip in the stretch. Meadow Skipper had become the three-year-old world record holder on a mile track. In the second heat, Overtrick got revenge, leading all the way to win in 1:57.4 with a final quarter in an incredible :26.2.

In early November, Overtrick clinched divisional honors with an easy and impressive three-length win in the $146,324 Messenger S. at Roosevelt. He led wire-to-wire and scored over archrivals Meadow Skipper, who had to overcome an early break, and Country Don in 2:00.4.

When Overtrick raced as a four-year-old FFA pacer in 1964, he had to contend with a new arrival to North America - the great New Zealand champion Cardigan Bay who later went on to become the sport's first million-dollar winner under the training and driving of Stanley Dancer. The rivalry between the young American champion Overtrick and the older foreign champion was greatly "hyped" by the New York press and the harness racing publications. A match between the two became a track publicity director's dream.

It took place at Yonkers Raceway, which sponsored the $50,000 International Pace a distance of one and one-half miles. Four of America's best, Overtrick, Henry T. Adios, Adora's Dream and Rusty Range were to meet Cardigan Bay and Great Credit of New Zealand and Country Don and Adios Mir of Canada. A crowd of 35,128 turned out at Yonkers that night to watch the favored Overtrick take early command after leaving from the rail for John Patterson. Meanwhile, Stanley Dancer had Cardigan Bay racing easily in fourth and did not make a move off the rail until the field was at the one-mile marker. Overtrick was able to get away with slow fractions and passed the mile in a leisurely 2:05.4.

Patterson knew the Cardigan Bay challenge was coming and let Overtrick open up to his real speed. Cardigan Bay, however, showed he was an equal of the American champion by staying with Overtrick on the outside as the duo paced the final half in a rapid :58. But it was Overtrick who won the event by a diminishing neck. That great final half showcased two wonderful champions. Overtrick's perennial rival Country Don was third.

There was interest among fans and horsemen for a rematch between Cardigan Bay and Overtrick and that came to fruition later at Yonkers in the $25,000 Dan Patch Pace and the $25,000 Dan Patch Encore Pace. Those turned out to be two of harness racing's most memorable and dramatic races.

Driven by Vernon Dancer, substituting for his brother Stanley, Cardigan Bay used his magnificent brush of speed to get up in time in the final stride for a nose victory in 1:58.1 in front of Overtrick for a new Yonkers track record. Overtrick had started from the outside post eight with Cardigan Bay just inside him from post seven.

The following week, the Dan Patch Encore matched the two champions again. Cardigan Bay surprised everyone by taking the early lead after being parked out to the quarter in :28.2. He continued on the lead to the half in :59.2 with Overtrick moving up on the outside - exactly the reverse of their previous meetings. The two were head-to-head at the 1:29 three-quarters and after the turn Cardigan Bay had a neck lead in mid-stretch. But the game Overtrick was not done and found the strength and courage for a last surge which took him to the wire by a nose over Cardigan Bay in 1:59.1.

Lana Lobell Farm's Alan Leavitt syndicated Overtrick as a stallion and he stood at that Pennsylvania Farm from 1965 through the 1974 breeding season. When it became obvious Overtrick was not siring great horses, he was sold to Australian interests. Later, as Overtrick's daughters began producing racehorses, he became a noted broodmare sire.

Sire Line

Overtrick's sire, Solicitor p,2,2:03.2; 3,T1:57.2 ($102,109), was a talented colt and a world champion at two and three. He was raced by Del Miller during the same years that he two other top three-year-olds in his barn - Tar Heel and Direct Rhythm. Tar Heel defeated Solicitor in the 1951 Little Brown Jug. The owner of Tar Heel and Solicitor, W. N. Reynolds, died just 10 days prior to the Little Brown Jug and both colts subsequently went to auction. Hanover Shoe Farm purchased the pair - $125,000 for Tar Heel and $100,000 for Solicitor. Solicitor was a highly respected racehorse. However, this did not translate into success as a stallion and except for Overtrick he was ultimately a failure.

Overtrick's great-grandsire is the legendary Volomite whose pacing male lines have given us several top broodmare sires over the generations, including Bye Bye Byrd, Armbro Nesbit, Direct Scooter, Worthy Boy and Harold J. If the direct male line is to survive into the next century it will likely be due to the efforts of Direct Scooter and his sons Matt's Scooter and In The Pocket.

The closest common cross in Overtrick's pedigree is an old one, being 4x4 to Guy Axworthy through Solicitor, 4x6 to Peter Volo and 5x5x5x5 to Peter The Great. Overtrick was eight generations removed from Hambletonian.

Maternal Line

The maternal line of Overtrick is very strong, a branch of the well-known Minnehaha family. Overtrick's first five dams are 2:00 producers, and this includes mares foaled from 1927 to 1954 - quite an accomplishment in that era. Overtrick's dam is Overbid p,2,T2:05.4, a stakes-placed daughter of Hal Dale from the Billy Direct mare Barbara Direct. Thus, Overbid is a three-quarter sister to the former world champion two and three-year-old pacer, and Little Brown Jug winner, Bullet Hanover p,2,1:57; 3,T1:55.3 ($132,578).

Overbid produced eight winners from 11 foals and Overtrick was not her only great performer. It's quite unusual for a mare to produce two horses which have truly earned the label "great." Overtrick's half-brother, sired by the Hoot Mon son Capetown, is Overcall p,1:57.1f ($784,006) who was a top colt at two and three and later a multiple FFA champion with world records to his credit. In 1969, Overcall was voted Pacer of the Year by virtue of his 21-race undefeated campaign. He was tried at stud, but never made a major impact as a sire or broodmare sire.

Another fast performer in close proximity to Overtrick from this maternal family is the long-wearing Prince Ebony p,1:50.3 ($909,771) (by the Albatross son Conquered). Prince Ebony is from a Most Happy Fella daughter of My Finesse p,3,2:06.4f, a full sister to Overtrick. The pedigree crosses which combined to produce Prince Ebony - Albatross and Most Happy Fella - also worked wonders with Overtrick mares. Extratrick, another full sister to Overtrick, produced the world champion Albatross daughter Helen's Deal p,2,1:57.2 ($113,189).

Progeny of Note

Overtrick stood at stud in the United States for ten seasons before moving to Australia. He sired the winners of over $22,000,000 with one in 1:55 and 81 in 2:00. His fastest performer was the late-developing Free-For-Aller Shadyside Trixie p,1:54.3 ($255,223) and his next fastest was the good Andy Lobell p,1:55.2 ($336,417).

Sons of Overtrick tended to stay on the track for long careers and, as a result, 63 of them became $100,000 winners along with only five fillies. Overtrick was definitely a better sire of colts than fillies, but his daughters have gone on to fine broodmare careers. Overtrick's richest sons are Mr. Overnite p,1:57.1f ($400,902), Right Over p,1:57.3f ($398,455), Andy Lobell and Adelweiss Rainbow p,4,1:58.1h ($308,695). His richest daughter is Maggie Lobell p,1:58.4 ($180,258) followed by the tough as nails Rebel Lu p,2:00.1f ($160,304). They are the only two females among Overtrick's top 46 performers with earnings of $130,000 or more. From a speed standpoint, there is only one female among Overtrick's 32 fastest performers and she is Summa Cum p,1:57.1 - later to become the dam of Primus p,3,1:54 ($278,442).

Overtrick's legacy is clearly through his daughters. Four of them have individually produced the winners of over $1,000,000 and two other daughters are knocking at the door, having produced the winners of over $940,000. Two daughters of Overtrick have produced individual million-dollar winners: Fashion Trick with Falcon Seelster p,3,1:51h ($1,121,045) and Keystone Sandal with Sandy Bowl 4,T1:54.1 ($1,299,199). The latter is unusual in that he is a trotter. Keystone Sandal wanted to trot, took a trotting record of 4,T2:00.2, and was bred to trotters when retired. She has now produced six 2:00 trotters from sires such as Super Bowl, Nevele Pride, Arndon and Cumin.

Top broodmare sire credits continue to mount for Overtrick and there are some very famous names on the list. Obviously, there is Falcon Seelster who is still the fastest pacer on a half-mile track as a three-year-old; L V Whiskers p,1:49.3 ($349,273) is Overtrick's fastest broodmare credit; there is world champion Trenton p,3,1:51.3 (sired by Overtrick's great rival Meadow Skipper), Gold Coast Rocky p,1:51.2 and dozens of others in 1:55 or faster.

However, there is one broodmare credit for Overtrick which will always keep his name in front of breeders - he is the sire of the dam of the great stallion and top racehorse No Nukes p,3,T1:52.1 ($572,430). No Nukes (see his chapter) appears to be siring sons who will carry on his blood (and Overtrick's) for decades to come. Overtrick's presence may not end with the No Nukes line. Perhaps Falcon Seelster's son Falcon's Future will become a good sire. Also, keep in mind that Overtrick is the sire of the grandam of 1994 Horse of the Year and Hanover Shoe Farm stallion Cam's Card Shark whose first crop of foals will race in 1998.

Another observation is that Overtrick's daughters are capable of producing excellent racing fillies and mares, as shown by the exploits of Turn The Tide p,3,1:53.2 ($860,993), Saccharum p,4,1:53.3 ($805,295), Desperate Lady p,3,1:54.1 ($387,707), Peachbottom p,3,1:55.3 ($348,609), Future Fame p,3,1:56.4 ($239,496) and Keystone Wallis p,2,1:55.3f ($618,256).

Analysis

As expected when he went to stud, Overtrick was bred to plenty of mares by Adios and his sons and they produced many of his better sons and daughters. However, Overtrick's top three money-winning sons are from daughters of Goose Bay, Right Time and Nibble Hanover. But seven of his next nine in earnings are from daughters of Adios and his sons Airliner, Adios Senator and Meadow Gene.

Overtrick mares have produced very well with Albatross and his sons such as Niatross and Sonsam. The Most Happy Fella line stallions have been very successful with Overtrick mares, as shown by L V Whiskers (Armbro Aussie) and No Nukes, Gold Coast Rocky and Peachbottom (all by Oil Burner). Another good cross has been with Bret Hanover line stallions and there have been top performers by Warm Breeze, Trim The Tree, Committeeman, High Ideal and Storm Damage.

Leading Progeny by Overtrick

Fastest
- Shadyside Trixie, g, p,1:54.3 $255,223
- Andy Lobell, h, p,1:55.2 $336,417
- Painter Lobell, h, p,1:56 $159,052
- Little Startrick, h, p,3,T1:56.1 $91,326
- Neat Trick, g, p,1:56.4 $265,262
- Spiked Boots, h, p,1:56.4 $159,827
- Justassuming, h, p,1:57f $136,928
- Mr Overnite, h, p,1:57.1f $400,902
- Over Burden, h, p,1:57.1f $126,978
- Native Rocket, h, p,1:57.2f $289,674

Richest
- Mr Overnite, h, p,1:57.1f $400,902
- Right Over, h, p,1:57.3f $398,455
- Andy Lobell, h, p,1:55.2 $336,417
- Adelweiss Rainbow, h, p,4,1:58.1h $308,695
- Native Rocket, h, p,1:57.2f $289,674
- Adover Lobell, h, p,1:59.4h $287,873
- Keystone Atlas, g, p,1:58 $287,338
- Currituck Star, h, p,1:57.3f $276,530
- Neat Trick, g, p,1:56.4 $265,262
- Shadyside Trixie, g, p,1:54.3 $255,223

Overtrick, Bay Horse, 1960
p, 2, 1:59.4; 3, 1:57.1h ($407,483)

Sire/Dam	2nd gen	3rd gen	4th gen	5th gen
Solicitor, 1948 p, 3, T1:57.2 $102,109	King's Counsel, 1940 p, 6, 1:58 $44,930	Volomite, 1926 3, 2:03¼ $32,649	**PETER VOLO**, 1911 4, 2:02	PETER THE GREAT — Pilot Medium / Santos
				NERVOLO BELLE — Nervolo / Josephine Knight
			Cita Frisco, 1921	San Francisco — **ZOMBRO** / Oniska
				Mendocita — Mendocino / Esther
		Margaret Spangler, 1918 p, 2:02¼	**GUY AXWORTHY**, 1902 4, 2:08¾	Axworthy — Axtell / Marguerite
				Lillian Wilkes — Guy Wilkes / Flora
			Maggie Winder, 1906	Oratorio — Wilkes Boy / Canzonet
				Clara Direct — Direct / Miss Alcantara
	Jane Reynolds, 1938 4, 2:07h	Scotland, 1925 T1:59¼	Peter Scott, 1909 T2:05	PETER THE GREAT — Pilot Medium / Santos
				Jenny Scott — Bryson / Aetna
			Roya McKinney, 1911 4, T2:07½	McKinney — Alcyone / Rosa Sprague
				Princess Royal — **CHIMES** / Estabella
		Jane Revere, 1920 2, 2:06¾	**GUY AXWORTHY**, 1902 4, 2:08¾	Axworthy — Axtell / Marguerite
				Lillian Wilkes — Guy Wilkes / Flora
			Volga E., 1913 3, 2:04½	PETER THE GREAT — Pilot Medium / Santos
				NERVOLO BELLE — Nervolo / Josephine Knight
Overbid, 1954 p, 2, T2:05.4 $3,524	Hal Dale, 1926 p, 6, 2:02¼	Abbedale, 1917 p, 2:01¼	The Abbe, 1903 p, 2:04	CHIMES — Electioneer / Beautiful Bells
				Nettie King — Mambrino King / Nettie Murphy
			Daisydale D., 1908 3, 2:15¼	Archdale — Expedition / Aline
				Mrs. Tmolus — Pactolus / Flaxey
		Margaret Hal, 1914 p, 2:19½h	Argot Hal, 1903 p, T2:04¾	Brown Hal — **TOM HAL JNR** / Lizzie
				Lady Wildflower — Duplex / Sally Ward
			Margaret Polk, 1906	John R. Gentry — Ashland Wilkes / Dame Wood
				Stella Hal — **TOM HAL JNR** / Dolly
	Barbara Direct, 1947 p, 3, T2:00.4 $5,747	Billy Direct, 1934 p, 4, T1:55 $12,040	Napoleon Direct, 1909 p, 1:59¾	Walter Direct — Direct Hal / Ella Brown
				Lady Erectress — Tom Kendle / Nelly Zarro
			Gay Forbes, 1916 p, 2:07¾	Malcolm Forbes — Bingen / Nancy Hanks
				Gay Girl Chimes — Berkshire Chimes / Miss Gay Girl
		Norette Hanover, 1939 p, 2:09.1h $1,587	Peter The Brewer, 1918 4, 2:02½	PETER THE GREAT — Pilot Medium / Santos
				Zombrewer — **ZOMBRO** / Mary Bales
			Helen Hanover, 1927 p, 2:04¾	Dillon Volo — **PETER VOLO** / Miss Bertha Dillon
				Helen Dillon — Dillon Axworthy / Miss Pierette

Pacific Rocket

He was called "the Iron Horse" due to his durability and the fact that he hardly ever missed a week of racing. Pacific Rocket was a very typical Abercrombie-type performer - tough, sturdy and fast, never knowing the end of a mile. Sired by Albert Albert, a son of the great Abercrombie, Pacific Rocket's career may serve as a harbinger of things to come from the Abercrombie line offspring.

As a youngster, Pacific Rocket was precocious, winning his first two starts in qualifying races on June 3rd and June 10th at Gaitway Farm in New Jersey. Driven by his trainer, driver and part owner Ed Lohmeyer, Pacific Rocket was timed in 2:00.3 and 1:57.2. A week after the second race, an interest in the colt was sold to the prominent Canadian owner Peter Heffering. Although Lohmeyer was a majority owner and a highly-regarded trainer, he agreed to turn the colt over to Heffering's trainer Bill Robinson, who had a stable full of top colts for the major stakes.

Pacific Rocket was the favorite in his first New Jersey Sires S. race at The Meadowlands a week later, but he came up flat and finished a well-beaten fourth. Catello Manzi was in the sulky, and he became Pacific Rocket's regular driver during his two-year-old season. The following week, Pacific Rocket was his old self, cutting the fractions in the Historic-Goshen Cup, only to lose by a half-length to Magical Mike in a rapid 1:54.4. Returning to the New Jersey Sires S. races, Pacific Rocket dominated the next two events by five lengths and three lengths in 1:54.1 and 1:55.3. The $100,000 New Jersey Sires S. Final was another super showcase for Pacific Rocket. Even though he left from the outside post ten, he was on top at the quarter in :27.3 and led the rest of the way to win in 1:53.3 with a final quarter in a devastating :26.3.

The Woodrow Wilson Elimination was next on Pacific Rocket's schedule and the colt had a tough trip, being parked out at the half in :55.3. But he came back to finish second to Million To One, who won in 1:52.4. Since there were two weeks until the Wilson Final, Pacific Rocket raced in the Niatross S. at The Meadowlands and was second to Armbro Mackintosh. The $747,700 Woodrow Wilson Final was next on the agenda and Manzi left quickly from post four to gain the lead on the outside at the quarter in :27.3. There was a lot of activity in the second quarter with Million To One going to the outside to grab the lead at the half in :54.2 after a breathtaking :26.4 second quarter. Expensive Scooter dropped in behind him leaving Pacific Rocket third on the rail.

Million To One paced the third quarter in :28, hitting that station in 1:22.2 with Expensive Scooter challenging second on the outside, forcing Pacific Rocket to go three-wide to get into contention. While making the big move, Pacific Rocket was impeded a bit but found his pace again. Million To One tired at the head of the stretch and Expensive Scooter took a short lead by a head, but there were now horses coming from everywhere after laying off the torrid early fractions. Pacific Rocket had dead aim on Expensive Scooter, but could not hold off the charges from Armbro Mackintosh, Magical Mike and Sweet Dragon. Magical Mike roared down the stretch to get the lead and then held off Sweet Dragon by a short nose in a very exciting Wilson Final. Armbro Mackintosh held third by three-quarters of a length over the game Pacific Rocket who took fourth money. The race went in a world record equalling 1:51.4 with Pacific Rocket finishing in 1:52 - only a length behind the winner.

Pacific Rocket then went to Freehold for the Garden State S. and his first race over a half-mile track. He held the lead all the way to the closing yards when he yielded to several others. Armbro Mackintosh won in 1:55.4 and Pacific Rocket was fifth, but again only a length away from the winner. The colt's season ended on August 28th at Freehold in a New Jersey Sires S. when he made a break on the first turn and finished sixth. For the year, he had earned $190,521 in only 10 starts and had proven he could race with the best.

Hopes were high for Pacific Rocket's three-year-old season and he did not disappoint. In a season featuring such stars as Cam's Card Shark, Magical Mike, Falcon's Future, Historic, Lisheen and Hi Ho

Race Record Highlights

At 2
1st New Jersey Sires S. Final at The Meadowlands
two New Jersey Sires S.
2nd Woodrow Wilson S. Elimination
Niatross S.
Historic-Goshen Cup

At 3
1st Windy City S. Final and Elimination
Provincial Cup Final and Elimination
Burlington S.
North America Cup Elimination
New Jersey Classic Elimination
Berry's Creek P. Elimination
Woodbine Invitational
New Jersey Sires S.
2nd Breeders Crown
North America Cup Final

At 3, (continued)
Art Rooney Memorial
Cane Pace
James Dancer Memorial
Miller Memorial Final and Elimination
New Jersey Classic Final
Meadowlands Pace Elimination
3rd Messenger S.
Berry's Creek P. Final

At 4
1st Canadian Pacing Derby Final
U.S. Pacing Championship at The Meadowlands and Freehold
Dan Patch P.
Presidential Series Final and leg
two legs of Graduate Series
two legs of George Morton Levy Memorial Series

Honors

At four, set world record on five-eighth mile track
At four, equalled world record on half-mile track

Pacific Rocket

Photo by Monica Thors

Race Record

Year	Age	Starts	Wins	2nd	3rd	Earnings	Record
1993	2	10	3	3	0	$ 190,521	p,2,1:53.3
1994	3	27	11	11	2	1,418,325	p,3,1:50.4
1995	4	27	16	4	2	724,555	p,4,1:50
		64	30	18	4	$2,333,401	p,4,1:50

Pacific Rocket

Silverheel's, Pacific Rocket won $1,418,325 and was first, second or third in 24 of 27 starts. It was an outstanding season and his earnings placed him second behind Cam's Card Shark.

Like a typical Abercrombie-line horse, Pacific Rocket opened his season by winning his first two starts in April and closing it with five straight wins through December. His first start of the season was a 1:52.4 win at The Meadowlands and a week later he won the Berry's Creek Elimination in 1:53 over Falcon's Future. Then, in the Berry's Creek Final, the colt was a victim of interference in the stretch and was fourth but placed third. Jack Moiseyev was the driver in this race, as he was in all but one of Pacific Rocket's starts as a three-year-old in 1994.

The Miller Memorial was next and Pacific Rocket was second (by a nose) to Falcon's Future in the Elimination and second again in the Final to Cam's Card Shark. In the New Jersey Classic the colt won his Elimination in a fast 1:50.4, but was second again to Cam's Card Shark in the Final after being parked out first over during the last three-quarters. Pacific Rocket then won the Burlington S. in 1:51 over Cam's Card Shark and the North America Cup Elimination in 1:51.1.

The $1,000,000 North America Cup Final at Woodbine was next and Pacific Rocket left from post nine. He was third on the outside at the quarter and then gained the lead. He led into the stretch but then came the charge from arch-rival Cam's Card Shark, which took that colt to a length and one-half win over Pacific Rocket with Magical Mike taking third. In the Messenger S. a week later at Rosecroft, the script was the same. Pacific Rocket drew post ten, gained the lead at the quarter in :26.1, held it into the deep stretch but then finished third to Cam's Card Shark and Falcon's Future.

Pacific Rocket was now geared up for the Meadowlands Pace and was a good second (by a head) to Expensive Scooter in his Elimination after leading most of the race. In the Final, Pacific Rocket had an easier trip, racing second most of the way after having the early lead at the quarter. However, Cam's Card Shark was not to be denied and paced home a winner over Historic and Magical Mike, with Pacific Rocket taking fourth, but only two lengths behind the winner.

"Seconditis" kept plaguing Pacific Rocket in the Art Rooney Memorial, Cane Pace, New Jersey Sires S. and James Dancer Memorial. Twice he lost to Cam's Card Shark. He then had two weeks off before the Little Brown Jug, which turned out to be very disappointing day. Pacific Rocket made a break while pacing second in his heat and was eliminated from the Final. Three weeks after the Jug, Pacific Rocket won a New Jersey Sires S. at Freehold in 1:54 on the front end.

The Breeders Crown at Garden State Park was next on the schedule, and for this race Moiseyev and Pacific Rocket changed their strategy. Instead of racing in front, or near the front, the colt got away slowly from post six and was seventh from the quarter to the three-quarters following cover in the outside flow. As the field turned for home, Pacific Rocket was charging. He was fourth in mid-stretch and just missed catching Magical Mike by a half-length at the finish. He tried the same tactics a week later in the New Jersey Sires S. Final at Garden State, but ran into severe traffic problems and was second to Hi Ho Silverheel's.

That race was Pacific Rocket's last loss at three. He won the Windy City Elimination and Final at Maywood, wire-to-wire in 1:53.2 and 1:53. It was then on to Windsor for the Provincial Cup Elimination and Final, which he won in 1:53 and 1:52.3. Pacific Rocket ended his season with a win in the Woodbine Gold Cup. During his last twelve starts, the colt never finished lower than second and it was decided to bring him back to race at four.

Pacific Rocket stayed in training for Bill Robinson and packed in 27 starts from January 1 through December 22. He proved he was a gutsy and sound performer, racing through from April of his three-year-old season with just a week or two off now and then. He was driven in 15 of those starts by Jack Moiseyev, with Bill Gale, John Campbell, Brett Robinson and Tony Kerwood also taking turns in the sulky.

Pacific Rocket had a banner four-year-old season in 1995, winning 16 of 27 starts, pacing in 1:50 and leading the older pacers in earnings with $724,555. He was voted "Older Pacer of the Year" over Riyadh and Ball And Chain.

Pacific Rocket dropped his first decision of the year by a neck to Zero Inflation, but then won eight of his next 11 starts, including legs of the Graduate Series and Levy Series.

As the summer got hotter, so did Pacific Rocket. After a couple of losses, he went to Freehold and won the U.S. Pacing Championship in a world record 1:51.2 for older horses on a half-mile track. Following another loss, he put together four consecutive wins in 1:50.1 at Woodbine, 1:50.3f at The Meadows, his lifetime record 1:50 at Hoosier Park in the Dan Patch P. and 1:50.1 again at Woodbine. In the $135,000 U.S. Pacing Championship at The Meadowlands in August when he showed true grit in winning by a neck over Village Jiffy in 1:50. For a moment deep in the stretch, Village Jiffy had him headed, but Pacific Rocket came back like a true champion.

Pacific Rocket attained another world record a week later at The Meadows when he paced in 1:50.1. This was the fastest ever by an older pacer over a five-eighth mile track. In late August, Pacific Rocket won the $278,250 Canadian Pacing Derby Final in 1:50.1 at Woodbine. The following month, at the Breeders Crown at Northfield, Pacific Rocket made his last career start, and it was one of the few disappointments for his connections in 1995. He had the lead all the way until the final few steps when longshot That'll Be Me caught him at the wire in 1:52.4.

Sire Line

Pacific Rocket's sire is Albert Albert p,4,1:52 ($1,237,070), a world champion and multiple stakes-winning son of Abercrombie who is exquisitely bred and a sire of good, hard-hitting, extreme speed performers. He has sired good fillies as well as colts, which could be a sign Pacific Rocket will as well.

Albert Albert also has a very strong maternal family. His dam Lismore p,3,T1:57.2 ($150,309) has produced 10 in 2:00, including the four sub-1:53 performers Albert Albert, Lahar p,1:50.3 ($299,840), Curragh p,T1:51.4 ($509,740), Lisheen p,3,1:52.3 ($518,405) and Lisryan p,4,1:52.3f ($409,741) - all by Abercrombie. In addition, Lismore has produced six $250,000 winners.

You can read more about Albert Albert in his chapter. Also, refer to the chapter on Abercrombie, Pacific Rocket's grandsire, since the Abercrombie male line is seeking to make a place in history and Pacific Rocket is one of the early Abercrombie grandsons to stand at stud.

Maternal Line

The dam of Pacific Rocket is the Direct Scooter mare Flat Foot Fluzy who won $19,966 while being stakes-placed at two and timed in 1:57.3. She did not take a record. Flat Foot Fluzy was bred by Ed Lohmeyer, William Simon and John Van Kirk of New Jersey and raced by Lohmeyer and John Stoddard, also of New Jersey. An accomplished trainer and driver, Lohmeyer also dabbles in breeding and he retained Flat Foot Fluzy as a broodmare prospect following an injury during her last start at two. The filly raced just 11 times in 1989, but showed some class. She was bred at three to Albert Albert and Pacific Rocket was her first foal.

Flat Foot Fluzy's second foal, Pacific Missile p,3,1:51.4; 1:51.3-'98 ($254,990) was also by Albert Albert and was a fast stakes winner at two and three. Her third foal is the Artsplace colt Pacific Lightning p,2,1:55.4 and she has a 1998 three-year-old filly by Artsplace.

Quinella Blue Chip p,4,1:56.2 ($69,888), by the Most Happy Fella son Happy Motoring, is the second dam of Pacific Rocket and was stakes-placed at three and a marginal producer, her best foal being Greg's Miracle p,3,1:57.2 (by Primus). The third dam of Pacific Rocket is the good Bret Hanover mare Queen's Blue Chip p,2,T1:59.4 ($89,798) who was a multiple Grand Circuit stakes winner at two and three. She produced the very tough Most Happy Fella mare Happy Blue Chip p,4,T1:56.4 ($319,173) and three others in 2:00.

Pacific Rocket

The family goes back further, to the fourth dam Queenly Lorraine, who was a non-record daughter of Worthy Boy. However, she was a half-sister to the world champion two-year-old filly Timely Beauty p,2,T1:57.1 ($115,265), a Good Time filly who created a sensation with her 1:57.1 time trial at two in 1962, which made her the fastest two-year-old filly of all time. The maternal family here is the excellent one of Mambrino Beauty, more currently known as the Nervolo Belle family.

Flat Foot Fluzy is interesting in that she has no common ancestors within her first four generations. There is also much trotting blood in her pedigree since her sire Direct Scooter is trotting bred maternally through a Noble Victory mare and his sire line descends from Volomite. And Flat Foot Fluzy's third dam Queenly Lorraine also descends from a strong trotting family. In fact, she is bred 3x5x4 to the great full brother and sister combination of Peter Volo and Volga E. - both world champions of their era and Kentucky Futurity winners. Queenly Lorraine is also bred 3x2 to the half-sisters Alma Lee (dam of world champion trotter Rosalind T1:56¾) and Belvedere, grandam of trotting Triple Crown winner Scott Frost 1:58.3. As the saying goes, this maternal family "works both sides of the tracks" - trotting and pacing. I point this out because pedigree aficionados note that many strong pacing sires come from families with a close trotting heritage.

Analysis

Pacific Rocket's closest common cross is 4x4 to Bret Hanover and he also has a 4x5 cross to Meadow Skipper and 5x6x5x6x5 to Adios - which serves to put those prominent stallions pretty far back in the pedigrees of any of his foals. In addition, such modern sires as Albatross would be in the fourth generation of Pacific Rocket's foals on the male side, and Most Happy Fella would not show up until the fifth. Pacific Rocket can also be bred to daughters from other Abercrombie sons such as Laag, which would make the foal 3x3 to Abercrombie.

So with Pacific Rocket the breeder has many choices of inbreeding, linebreeding and outcrossing. I think Pacific Rocket will work with a large variety of broodmare sires, which should serve him well in his stud career. His sire and dam have shown they can both produce early and extreme speed and he can certainly be bred to mares with the same traits. For example, a No Nukes mare from an Albatross dam would have a foal by Pacific Rocket with a linebred 4x3 cross to Albatross with one of today's top pedigree crosses. Albatross mares to Pacific Rocket would produce a 4x2 cross to that great stallion, which should be very acceptable.

If you are looking for more of an outcross, try a mare by the excellent broodmare sire Big Towner whose second dam is by Tar Heel, Meadow Skipper, Bret Hanover, Race Time or Best Of All, for example. There are so many options with Pacific Rocket. In order to get many of those sires into a Pacific Rocket foal, a mare with a Dragon's Lair/Big Towner cross would do the trick since Dragon's Lair's pedigree contains Meadow Skipper, Most Happy Fella, Tar Heel, Race Time and Good Time.

Pacific Rocket was a very powerful performer and was consistent and impressive every year he raced. He was the kind of horse who never gave up and always fought to the finish. In that vein, mares by Cam Fella and On The Road Again, two similar types of racehorses who have sired tough, long-lasting performers, should also nick well with Pacific Rocket.

In 1996, Pacific Rocket stood his first season at stud in Pennsylvania and served 120 mares, which should give him a good start. He was moved to Tara Hills Stud in Ontario, Canada, for his second and third seasons and is drawing similar large books as he bred 124 mares in 1997. I have a good feeling about this stallion and will be quite surprised if he does not make an impact among pacing sires.

Pacific Rocket, Brown Horse, 1991
p, 2, 1:53.3; 3, 1:50.4; 4, 1:50 ($2,333,401)

Albert Albert, 1985 p, 3, 1:52.1 $1,237,070	Abercrombie, 1975 p, 4, 1:53 $984,391	Silent Majority, 1969 p, 3, 1:56.3 $362,369	Henry T. Adios, 1958 p, 6, 1:57 $706,833	**ADIOS**	**HAL DALE** Adioo Volo
				Greer Hanover	**NIBBLE HANOVER** Veda Hanover
			Hobby Horse Tar, 1964	**TAR HEEL**	**BILLY DIRECT** Leta Long
				Wilellen	Wilmington Willola
		Bergdorf, 1967 p, 4, 2:03.3 $6,035	Duane Hanover, 1952 p, 4, 1:58 $280,288	**KNIGHT DREAM**	**NIBBLE HANOVER** Lydia Knight
				Dorsh Hanover	**DILLON AXWORTHY** Great Medium
			Princess Best, 1959 p, 4, 2:07f $965	The Widower	Abbedale Widow Grattan
				Princess Chief	Chief Abbedale The Gay Princess
	Lismore, 1976 p, 3, T1:57.2 $150,309	Albatross, 1968 p, 4, 1:54.3f $1,201,470	**MEADOW SKIPPER**, 1960 p, 3, 1:55.1 $428,057	Dale Frost	**HAL DALE** Galloway
				Countess Vivian	King's Counsel Filly Direct
			Voodoo Hanover, 1964	Dancer Hanover	**ADIOS** The Old Maid
				Vibrant Hanover	**TAR HEEL** Vivian Hanover
		Bret's Romance, 1968 p, 4, 2:02f $13,967	**BRET HANOVER**, 1962 p, 4, T1:53.3 $922,616	**ADIOS**	**HAL DALE** Adioo Volo
				Brenna Hanover	**TAR HEEL** Beryl Hanover
			Knight's Embassy, 1951	**KNIGHT DREAM**	**NIBBLE HANOVER** Lydia Knight
				Miss Reed	Bert Abbe Four D McKinney
Flat Foot Fluzy, 1987	Direct Scooter, 1976 p, 3, 1:54 $800,451	Sampson Direct, 1957 p, 4, T1:56 $137,486	Sampson Hanover, 1947 p, 4, T1:56.4 $28,708	**VOLOMITE**	Peter Volo Cita Frisco
				Irene Hanover	**DILLON AXWORTHY** Isotta
			Dottie Rosecroft, 1945 p, 4, 2:05.2 $7,735	**BILLY DIRECT**	Napoleon Direct Gay Forbes
				Beams Hanover	Calumet Chuck Lexington Maid
		Noble Claire, 1969 p, 2, 2:04 $5,557	Noble Victory, 1962 4, 1:55.3 $522,391	Victory Song	**VOLOMITE** Evensong
				Emily's Pride	Star's Pride Emily Scott
			Scotch Claire, 1953 2, T2:06 $1,595	**SCOTLAND**	Peter Scott Roya McKinney
				Abbey Claire	Guy Abbey Jean Claire
	Quinella Blue Chip, 1981 p, 4, 1:56.2 $69,888	Happy Motoring, 1976 p, 3, 1:56.2 $538,495	Most Happy Fella, 1967 p, 3, T1:55 $419,033	**MEADOW SKIPPER**	Dale Frost Countess Vivian
				Laughing Girl	Good Time Maxine's Dream
			Peaches N Cream, 1967 p, 3, 2:03.2h $22,966	Shadow Wave	**ADIOS** Shadow Grattan
				Parisian Hanover	**TAR HEEL** Paris Hanover
		Queen's Blue Chip, 1969 p, 2, T1:59.4 $89,798	**BRET HANOVER**, 1962 p, 4, T1:53.3 $922,616	**ADIOS**	**HAL DALE** Adioo Volo
				Brenna Hanover	**TAR HEEL** Beryl Hanover
			Queenly Lorraine, 1959	Worthy Boy	**VOLOMITE** Warwell Worthy
				Lorraine	**SCOTLAND** Belvedere

Precious Bunny

After a two-year-old season in which he won only one of 14 starts and earned a mere $63,920, Precious Bunny took the harness racing world by storm at three when he set a single-season earnings record of $2,217,222 as a result of 20 wins from 25 starts. For his herculean efforts, Precious Bunny was awarded 1991 Horse of the Year honors.

Precious Bunny was bred by Alfred Ochsner of Cranbury, New Jersey, and was the first foal from his dam, Bunny's Wish. Ochsner owned Precious Bunny until late in his two-year-old campaign when he was sold to Peter Heffering for $125,000 and then given to top Canadian trainer Bill Robinson for conditioning.

At two, Precious Bunny was driven in all of his starts by Jody Stafford. The colt made his career debut on June 1, 1990, finishing third in a qualifying race at New Jersey's Gaitway Farm and winning another qualifier there a week later in 2:01.4. Eligible for the New Jersey Sires S., Precious Bunny won his first parimutuel start in a New Jersey Sires event at The Meadowlands in 1:57.2, with a final quarter in :27.2. He was a longshot at almost 15-1 odds.

However, that was Precious Bunny's only win at two. He finished third in the Historic-Goshen Cup, the New Jersey Futurity and a New Jersey Sires S., was timed in 1:55 on a mile track and 1:56.4 on a half-mile track, but could just not find the winner's circle in his remaining 13 starts of the year. Amazingly, he was charted on the lead in only two of his races.

Despite his setbacks, Precious Bunny had shown promise, and Pete Heffering took notice. Heffering's confidence was soon rewarded. At three, Precious Bunny was a totally different animal. He found early speed and was in front at the half in 20 of his 25 starts, and he also won three of the five races in which he was not in front at the half-way point.. The only major change Robinson made in the colt was a switch to a Kant-See-Back bridle to help the colt keep his mind on the race. In 1991, Precious Bunny won his first three starts as a three-year-old at Canada's Mohawk Raceway in 1:54.3, 1:54.4 and 1:56.3. He was then sent to The Meadowlands to compete in a New Jersey Sires S. in which he finished second to Nuclear Siren in 1:51.4. A week later, Precious Bunny proved he belonged with the big boys by winning a New Jersey Classic Elimination in 1:51.1 with a final quarter in :26.3. In the $500,000 New Jersey Classic Final at The Meadowlands, in which he was the favorite, Precious Bunny suffered some early setbacks. He was shuffled back to seventh by the quarter and was ninth at the half. Having to swing three wide to find racing room, Precious Bunny launched a long, overland trip and in a superlative effort just missed catching Die Laughing by a neck in 1:51.4. He then came back a week later to win a New Jersey Sires S. in 1:52.2.

Since Precious Bunny came to The Meadowlands, John Campbell had been his regular driver, but Campbell was committed to be the driver for Artsplace when that colt was ready to race. When the change came, it did not seem to put Precious Bunny at a disadvantage. During their three-year-old seasons, Precious Bunny defeated Artsplace three times and lost to him only once. Jack Moiseyev was then named Precious Bunny's regular driver and it turned out to be a great fit: the colt won 16 of his last 19 starts.

Moiseyev's first two drives with Precious Bunny resulted in wins in the $1,000,000 North American Pace Elimination and Final. These were followed by victories in the $1,000,000 Meadowlands Pace Elimination and Final. The last two races were the most difficult of the four. In the Meadowlands Pace Elimination, Precious Bunny left from post five and was interfered with a bit at the start. Moiseyev found himself sitting fourth at the quarter. Then he took to the outside at the half and Precious Bunny gained the lead shortly after, going on to win in 1:50.4 over Easy Goer. In the rich Meadowlands Pace Final, Precious Bunny left from post eight and was a parked out fifth at the quarter in :26.4 before setting sail for the lead, which he grabbed

Race Record Highlights

At 2
- **1st** New Jersey Sires S.
- **2nd** New Jersey Sires S.
- **3rd** Historic-Goshen Cup
  New Jersey Sires S.

At 3
- **1st** Little Brown Jug
  Meadowlands Pace Final and Elimination
  North America Cup Final and Elimination
  Adios S. Final
  Art Rooney Memorial
  Windy City S.
  Cleveland Classic
  Jug Preview
  New Jersey Classic Elimination
  three New Jersey Sires S.
- **2nd** Adios S. Elimination
  New Jersey Classic Final
  New Jersey Sires S.
- **3rd** heat of Provincial Cup

Honors

Voted Horse of the Year at three
At three, equaled world record on five-eighth mile track
At three, set single-season earnings record
First horse to win two $1,000,000 races in a season

Precious Bunny

Photo by Tony Leonard
Courtesy of Castleton Farm

Race Record

Year	Age	Starts	Wins	2nd	3rd	Earnings	Record
1990	2	14	1	2	3	$ 63,920	p,2,1:57.2
1991	3	25	20	3	1	2,217,222	p,3,1:49.4
		39	21	5	4	$2,281,142	p,3,1:49.4

while still outside at the half in :54.2. Once settled in on the rail, he threw a :27.2 third quarter at his rivals, followed by a final quarter in :28 to pace the fastest mile ever at night - 1:49.4. His margin of victory over Artsplace was two lengths. Precious Bunny had won over $1,000,000 in a 20-day period!

The colt then took his winning streak to seven with victories in the Art Rooney Memorial Elimination and Final at Yonkers. It was then on to the Adios S. at The Meadows and a loss to Artsplace in the Elimination. Precious Bunny challenged Artsplace after the half, but Artsplace prevailed in a world record 1:50.4 for a five-eighth mile track. An hour later, Precious Bunny got his revenge by equalling that record and winning the Adios Final by over three lengths.

The overwhelming favorite for the Cane Pace, Precious Bunny turned up sick and had to be scratched. Two weeks later, the colt won the Jug Preview at Scioto Downs in 1:52.3 and looked fit for the Little Brown Jug. And fit he was, turning in two wire-to-wire efforts in 1:54.1 and 1:55 to take the big pacing prize. The most vivid feature of that Little Brown Jug was the rocket-like start Precious Bunny showed in his Elimination victory. He accelerated so quickly with the starting gate that he had a two-length advantage before the field even hit the first turn. Later, dramatic photographs of the start would show just how fast he left the gate - there was Precious Bunny far in front with all the other starters in a row behind. Moiseyev commented, "I yelled at him, hit the wheel disk with the whip and he was ready to go." Precious Bunny was by the quarter in :27.

He followed the Jug win with triumphs in a New Jersey Sires S. at Garden State Park, the Cleveland Classic, a New Jersey Sires S. at Freehold and the Windy City Pace at Maywood Park. The last two races of Precious Bunny's career were losses in both heats of the Provincial Cup at Windsor. He appeared to be tired after a long and fantastic season.

The Horse of the Year balloting for 1991 turned out to be no contest. Precious Bunny received 270 of the 292 first place votes; his closest rival was the Hambletonian-winning trotter Giant Victory, with only 10 votes.

Sire Line

The fact that Precious Bunny is one of the greatest sons of Cam Fella makes breeders take note since Cam Fella is one of the best sires of all time. Cam Fella will have at least a half dozen good sons vying for honors as the top line extender and Precious Bunny is up there with the best of the others. Thus far, the Most Happy Fella sire line has been the dominant one from all the great sons of Meadow Skipper, and the Cam Fella branch is dueling with the sons of No Nukes and Tyler B for top honors. You can read more about Cam Fella in his chapter.

Maternal Line

Precious Bunny's dam is the good B.G.'s Bunny mare Bunny's Wish p,2,1:58.2 ($288,962) who was bred by the M.E.K. Stable of New Rochelle, New York, and raced by Al Ochsner, who bred her to Cam Fella to produce the subject of this chapter. Bunny's Wish was an excellent stakes filly at two, winning eight of her 15 starts, taking a record of 1:58.2 and earning $142,718, mostly in the New Jersey Sires S. Coming back at three, Bunny's Wish earned another $105,436 although she won only one of 15 starts. The filly was a consistent second seven times and timed in 1:55.3 on three occasions. She was second in three New Jersey Sires S. at The Meadowlands and the $100,000 Final, in addition to being second in the $125,000 Miss New Jersey S. Bunny's Wish raced a few times at four and again early in the season at five, after which she was bred to Cam Fella to produce her first foal, Precious Bunny.

The sire of Bunny's Wish, the Albatross son B.G.'s Bunny has become an excellent broodmare sire; his daughters have produced nearly 600 2:00 pacers. Included among this group, in addition to

Precious Bunny, are such standouts as Cam's Card Shark p,3,1:50 (by Cam Fella), Armbro Operative p,4,1:50 (by Cam Fella), Lorryland Butler p,1:50.1 (by Skip By Night), Armbro Maneuver p,3,1:50.2 (by Direct Scooter), Largo p,1:51 (by Cam Fella), Tooter Scooter p,3,1:51.1 (by Direct Scooter). B.G.'s Bunny mares have worked especially well with Cam Fella and Direct Scooter in the extreme speed category.

Bunny's Wish produced a Direct Scooter filly, Quick As Can Be p,3,1:56.2, the year after the birth of Precious Bunny. There was then a four-year gap until her next three foals in 1994, 1995 and 1996 - colts by Beach Towel and No Nukes.

The non-record Romeo Hanover mare Last Wish is the grandam of Precious Bunny and, in addition to Bunny's Wish, she is the dam of Ty Cobb p,1:56.3h ($104,775) by Hot Hitter. The next dam is the Bye Bye Byrd mare Bye Bye Time, who produced Dakota p,3,1:58.2 ($100,086) and Nevele Arrival p,1:59.1 ($376,704), both by Romeo Hanover.

This is the maternal family of Pickles and this branch has produced good, consistent horses for years. While the family has been responsible for some good raceway horses, there was no hint that anything like Precious Bunny would eventually arrive. Such are the mysteries of breeding!

Progeny of Note

From his first three crops of 88, 80 and 83 foals, Precious Bunny has sired two in 1:50, 35 in 1:55, one $1,000,000 winner and 21 $100,000 winners. His first crop has already earned over $6,000,000. It includes such standouts as Stout p,4,1:49.4 ($1,210,025), John Street North p,4,1:50.2-'98 ($746,207), Lady Buns p,3,1:52.4 ($504,899), Hare Hare p,4,1:51 ($638,364), Bahama Bunny p,3,1:52 ($454,661) and Cloudburst Hanover p,1:51.2-'98 ($301,760).

At three, Stout won the Confederation Cup Final and was second in the $1,000,000 Finals of the North America Cup and the Meadowlands Pace. John Street North was a winner of the $500,000 Breeders Crown at two and Miller Memorial at three. Lady Buns won the Champlain S. at two and was second and third in other major events. At three, she came back to win the $200,000 Fan Hanover Final. The Precious Bunnys were well-represented in stakes events all over North America; it was an excellent showing from his first crop.

Precious Bunny's 1996 two-year-olds were headed by the fillies Before Sunrise p,2,1:53 ($416,252) who won the $576,533 Breeders Crown and International Stallion S., and Paling Avenue p,2,1:54.1; 3,1:52.2f ($649,910) who won the Countess Adios S. and Breeders Crown Elimination. Snug Feeling p,4,1:52.4z-'98 ($304,853) was another top filly and winner of the Countess Adios S.

Analysis

Precious Bunny has certainly made his presence felt as a result of the success of his first three crops. As yet, though, there has not been a colt or filly which has shown his kind of dominance, but there are plenty of good ones. This son of Cam Fella seems to be able to sire top fillies as well as colts, as shown by the fact that four of eight and eight of 20 of his leading money winners are fillies.

As the pedigree crosses of his top performers show, Precious Bunny is clicking with a number of different sire lines. It is worth noting that three stallions account for six of his seven richest performers, two each from mares by Sonsam, Big Towner and Abercrombie. And of his seven richest, Albatross is a factor since the dams of two are by his son Sonsam, and Albatross is the sire of the grandam of the three other performers. This certainly is not surprising since Albatross is the all-time greatest broodmare sire and would not appear until the fourth generation of Precious Bunny foals on the sire's side of the pedigree. Therefore, foals from mares by Albatross would have a 4x2 cross; foals from Albatross sons, or with grandams by Albatross, a 4x3 cross to Albatross and mares with third dams by Albatross would produce foals with a 4x4 cross to Albatross. So, having Albatross anywhere in the bloodlines of a mare going to Precious Bunny gives the breeder plenty of versatility. In fact, seven of the 16 richest Precious Bunny offspring have Albatross as the sire of the second dam and thus a 4x3 cross to him.

Another point to note is the presence of Keystone Ore in the pedigrees of some of Precious Bunny's best horses. Keystone Ore, a son of Bye Bye Byrd, is the sire of the dam of Precious Bunny's $1,000,000 winner Stout, the sire of the dam of Harden p,1:50.1-'98 ($188,619) and the sire of the grandam of Explosive Bunny p,2,1:52.3 ($129,175). Abercrombie is also a sire whose daughters are working very well with Precious Bunny as evidenced by his daughter O.J. Almahurst producing the good brother and sister John Street North and Paling Avenue by Precious Bunny. Other nice ones from Abercrombie mares are Games p,4,1:53.2 ($121,329) and Dauntless Bunny p,4,1:50.1-'98 ($261,802).

The only popular broodmares which would not be a fit for Precious Bunny, due to inbreeding, would be those by Cam Fella, B.G.'s Bunny and Most Happy Fella.

Looking at the crosses at work with a few of Precious Bunny's best horses, eight of his 14 richest have a 4x3 cross to Albatross through his sons or daughters. Also, Precious Bunny's other 1:50 performer, B.J.'s Whirlwind p,4,1:50-'98 is from a No Nukes mare and is 4x3 to Albatross. Since Precious Bunny also has Bret Hanover in his pedigree through his sire and dam, there is plenty of opportunity to add more Bret Hanover blood, as so many modern mares have a cross or two to that great stallion.

Precious Bunny's own pedigree crosses consists of 3x4 to both Meadow Skipper and Bret Hanover, 4x4x5 to Dale Frost, 4x5 to Adios and Good Time and 5x4 to Dancer Hanover. As you can see, it is very hard not to have a foal with multiple crosses to these top stallions in the fourth generation and beyond. To date, there are only two of Precious Bunny's top performers with no common crosses in their first four generations - Bahama Bunny (Big Towner/Tar Heel mare) and Harden (Keystone Ore/Best Of All mare).

With only three full crops to examine, it is hard to predict the future of Precious Bunny (or, for that matter, any other stallion!), but he has shown consistency and the ability to sire stakes-winning colts and fillies. Like other sires, he's had plenty of good horses and is looking for the great one to put him over the top. His bookings have been limited by contract and he has bred between 112 and 127 mares during his first six seasons at stud. Most have been quality types due to his early stud fee of $9,000 and the number limitation. Precious Bunny should have every chance to become an outstanding sire.

Leading Progeny by Precious Bunny

Fastest
Stout, h, p,4,1:49.4 $1,210,025
B J's Whirlwind, h, p,4,1:50 $97,970
Dauntless Bunny, h, p,4,1:50.1 $261,802
Harden, h, p,1:50.1 $188,619
John Street North, h, p,1:50.2 $746,207
Hare Hare, h, p,4,1:51 $638,364
Flow Control, g, p,4,1:51 $199,738
Slug Of Jin, h, p,1:51.1 $253,992
Cloudburst Hanover, h, p,1:51.2 $301,760
Bahama Bunny, h, p,3,1:52 $454,661

Richest
Stout, h, p,4,1:49.4 $1,210,025
John Street North, h, p,1:50.2 $746,207
Paling Avenue, m, p,3,1:52.2f $649,910
Hare Hare, h, p,4,1:51 $638,364
Lady Buns, m, p,3,1:52.4 $504,899
Bahama Bunny, h, p,3,1:52 $454,661
Before Sunrise, m, p,2,1:53 $416,252
Snug Feeling, m, p,4,1:52.4z $304,853
Cloudburst Hanover, h, p,1:51.2 $301,760
Dauntless Bunny, h, p,4,1:50.1 $261,802

Precious Bunny, Bay Horse, 1988
p, 2, 1:57.2; 3, 1:49.4 ($2,281,142)

Sire/Dam	2nd Gen	3rd Gen	4th Gen	5th Gen	6th Gen
Cam Fella, 1979 p, 4, 1:53.1 $2,041,367	Most Happy Fella, 1967 p, 3, T1:55 $419,033	**MEADOW SKIPPER**, 1960 p, 3, 1:55.1 $428,057	**DALE FROST**, 1951 p, 1:58 $204,117	**HAL DALE**	**ABBEDALE** / Margaret Hal
				Galloway	Raider / Bethel
			Countess Vivian, 1950 p, 3, 1:59 $43,262	King's Counsel	**VOLOMITE** / Margaret Spangler
				Filly Direct	**BILLY DIRECT** / Calumet Edna
		Laughing Girl, 1961 p, 4, 2:04h $19,546	**GOOD TIME**, 1946 p, 1:57.4 $318,792	**HAL DALE**	**ABBEDALE** / Margaret Hal
				On Time	**VOLOMITE** / Nedda Guy
			Maxine's Dream, 1954 p, 2, T2:00 $36,557	**KNIGHT DREAM**	**NIBBLE HANOVER** / Lydia Knight
				Maxine Abbe	**ABBEDALE** / Maxine Direct
	Nan Cam, 1971 p, 5, 2:05.1f $11,390	**BRET HANOVER**, 1962 p, 4, T1:53.3 $922,616	**ADIOS**, 1940 p, T1:57½ $33,329	**HAL DALE**	**ABBEDALE** / Margaret Hal
				Adioo Volo	Adioo Guy / Sigrid Volo
			Brenna Hanover, 1956 p, 3, T2:01 $21,946	**TAR HEEL**	**BILLY DIRECT** / Leta Long
				Beryl Hanover	**NIBBLE HANOVER** / Laura Hanover
		Nan Frost, 1966 p, 3, 2:06.3f $1,607	**DALE FROST**, 1951 p, 1:58 $204,117	**HAL DALE**	**ABBEDALE** / Margaret Hal
				Galloway	Raider / Bethel
			Mynah Hanover, 1950 p, 2:05.2h $44,184	Ensign Hanover	**BILLY DIRECT** / Helen Hanover
				Betty Mahone	Corporal Lee / Belle Mahone
Bunny's Wish, 1982 p, 2, 1:58.2 $288,962	B.G.'s Bunny, 1974 p, 3, 1:54 $215,192	Albatross, 1968 p, 4, 1:54.3f $1,201,470	**MEADOW SKIPPER**, 1960 p, 3, 1:55.1 $428,057	**DALE FROST**	**HAL DALE** / Galloway
				Countess Vivian	King's Counsel / Filly Direct
			Voodoo Hanover, 1964	**DANCER HANOVER**	**ADIOS** / The Old Maid
				Vibrant Hanover	**TAR HEEL** / Vivian Hanover
		Brets Romance, 1968 p, 4, 2:02f $13,967	**BRET HANOVER**, 1962 p, 4, T1:53.3 $922,616	**ADIOS**	**HAL DALE** / Adioo Volo
				Brenna Hanover	**TAR HEEL** / Beryl Hanover
			Knight's Embassy, 1951	**KNIGHT DREAM**	**NIBBLE HANOVER** / Lydia Knight
				Miss Reed	Bert Abbe / Four D McKinney
	Last Wish, 1974	Romeo Hanover, 1963 p, 3, 1:56.1 $658,505	**DANCER HANOVER**, 1957 p, 4, T1:56.4 $87,746	**ADIOS**	**HAL DALE** / Adioo Volo
				The Old Maid	Guy Abbey / Spinster
			Romola Hanover, 1957 p, 3, T1:59 $18,104	**TAR HEEL**	**BILLY DIRECT** / Leta Long
				Romola Hal	**HAL DALE** / Romola
		Bye Bye Time, 1966	Bye Bye Byrd, 1955 p, 5, T1:56.1 $554,272	Poplar Byrd	**VOLOMITE** / Ann Vonian
				Evalina Hanover	**BILLY DIRECT** / Adieu
			High Time, 1955 p, 3, 1:59 $51,001	**GOOD TIME**	**HAL DALE** / On Time
				Peakie Hanover	Mr. McElwyn / Pauline Hanover

Presidential Ball

As this chapter is being written, there are only three pacers who have ever won over $3,000,000 - Nihilator, Artsplace and Presidential Ball. It is also not very common for a pacing colt to win divisional honors at two and come back to do the same at three - that's happened only 17 times in 44 years. Presidential Ball is therefore in some very select company, and deservedly so.

Trained by Canadian Bill Robinson, and owned by prominent Canadian owner Antonio Chiaravalle of Toronto, Presidential Ball burst on the scene in June of 1992 and won his first five career starts, all stakes events. After winning two legs of the Kindergarten Series at Greenwood in 2:00.3 and 1:57.1, Presidential Ball was sent to Yonkers for the L.B. Sheppard Memorial. In an awesome display in his Elimination, the colt made believers of everyone. He left from post eight for driver Jack Moiseyev and broke right at the start. Presidential Ball got back on stride and caught the field but was still eighth at the quarter and seventh at the half when he moved outside to make a run for contention. At the three-quarters, the colt was third and going three-wide around the last turn and into the stretch. He came flying down the stretch and got up in time to beat Cam's Magic Trick by a neck in an astonishing 1:56. A great performance by a pacer of any age!

In the $382,000 L.B. Sheppard Final, Presidential Ball was better behaved and was on the lead on the outside at the quarter in :27 after leaving from post four. He then gave up the lead and opted for a pocket trip to the stretch, where he regained the top and paced away from the field to win by over four lengths in 1:54.3 over Cam's Magic Trick again. His fifth consecutive win came in the Niatross S. at The Meadowlands in a 1:54.4 wire-to-wire effort. He looked invincible.

The Eliminations for the rich Woodrow Wilson S. at The Meadowlands were next and Presidential Ball was the most talked about competitor. However, his undefeated string ended in the Elimination, although it was not due to lack of effort. Leaving from post six, Moiseyev left conservatively and was seventh at the quarter. While making a move to the outside after the quarter, Presidential Ball was interfered with and lost a few lengths, after which he forced three wide to find pacing room in order to get into contention. He did this with a sweeping move on the backstretch to move up to third, but still five lengths behind the leaders. He finished third to Armbro Local and was timed in 1:53.4. Believe it or not, all this was done with a flat tire for the last seven-eighths of a mile!

Presidential Ball was made the 3-5 favorite in the $778,800 Woodrow Wilson Final and raced like a favorite should until the final strides. After gaining the lead on the outside from post eight in :27.1, Moiseyev was able to maintain the front end and was still on top as the field turned for home. Presidential Ball had a lead of just over a length in mid-stretch, but America's Pastime and Broadway Blue were flying on the outside. America's Pastime put his head in front right at the wire to win in a world record tying 1:51.4 over Broadway Blue with Presidential Ball finishing third, only a neck behind the winner in identical time.

Following that bitter loss, Presidential Ball came back to win the Garden State S. at Freehold in 1:54.3 and was then a surprising second a week later in an overnight event at Greenwood. The colt then won a division of the Nassagaweya S. in 1:54.4, followed by an Metro S. Elimination in 1:54.2 - both at Canada's Mohawk Raceway. Then in the $719,700 Metro S. Final, a race given a surreal effect by heavy fog, Presidential Ball went wire-to-wire to win by a neck over Bonnie And Clyde in 1:54.3. After the win, trainer Bill Robinson was asked how he compared Presidential Ball with another Robinson standout - Precious Bunny. "Precious Bunny had flashy speed; he could carry it a long way and didn't want anyone near him," Robinson said. "This guy doesn't seem to mind that. He races a lot like his sire (Cam Fella). Horses would get close to him but they couldn't seem to get past him."

The last race on Presidential Ball's two-year-old schedule was the Breeders Crown in late October at Pompano Park. The colt was given a two-week rest after the big Metro S. win and qualified at Pompano in an easy 1:55 mile a week before the Breeders Crown. Presidential Ball was the 4-5 favorite, but was saddled with post eight on Pompano's five-eighth mile track. He left alertly and followed the cover of Bonnie And Clyde who was going for the front. Fourth on the

Presidential Ball

Photo by Monica Thors

Race Record Highlights

At 2
- **1st** Metro S. Final and Elimination
  L.B. Sheppard Memorial Final
  Niatross S.
  Garden State S.
  Nassagaweya S.
  two legs of Kindergarten Series
- **3rd** Woodrow Wilson Final and Elimination

At 3
- **1st** Meadowlands Pace Final and Elimination
  North America Cup
  New Jersey Classic
  Windy City S.
  Provincial Cup
  Burlington S.

At 3 (continued)
  Miller Memorial Final
  Simcoe S.
  Art Rooney Memorial Elimination
  two New Jersey Sires S.
- **2nd** Messenger S.
  heat of Little Brown Jug
  Miller Memorial Elimination
- **3rd** Little Brown Jug Final
  Art Rooney Memorial Final

Honors
Voted Two-Year-Old Pacing Colt of the Year
Voted Three-Year-Old Pacing Colt of the Year
At three, set single-season earnings record

Race Record

Year	Age	Starts	Wins	2nd	3rd	Earnings	Record
1992	2	13	9	1	2	$ 799,197	p,2,1:54.2f
1993	3	25	17	5	2	2,222,166	p,3,1:50
		38	26	6	4	$3,021,363	p,3,1:50

outside at the quarter, Presidential Ball tried to brush to the front but was rebuffed by Bonnie And Clyde and settled into second. He was later locked in with Life Sign, Riyadh and Village Jiffy racing on the outside and he seemed to tire. He had no spark at the end of the mile and his last quarter was only :31.2. Upon being scoped after the race, Presidential Ball was found to have a viral infection, which would explain his poor performance. It was time to call it a season.

Presidential Ball's season long efforts, discounting his final start, were enough to earn him "Two-Year-Old Pacer of the Year" honors. He had nine wins in 13 starts and earnings of $799,197.

Coming back at three, Presidential Ball was again awesome, winning 17 of 25 starts with earnings of $2,222,166, which set a single season earnings record.

Presidential Ball won a qualifier at Pompano Park in 1:54 on April 23rd and had his first start a week later in the Miller Memorial Eliminations at Rosecroft. Jack Moiseyev was once again his regular driver. Just when it looked as if Presidential Ball was going to get an easy trip in his debut after racing second the entire mile, Vine Street flashed a :27 final quarter and beat Presidential Ball by a half-length. That was to be his last loss until the final day of July. He went on a 10-race winning streak beginning with the Miller Final in 1:50.3. This was followed by wins in the New Jersey Classic Elimination and Final, a New Jersey Sires S., Burlington S., North America Cup Elimination and Final, Meadowlands Pace Elimination and Final and a Cane Pace Elimination. These were some of the richest races of the season and Presidential Ball was at his best. He raced from behind, on the front end, made three-wide moves and multiple moves and won by an average of nearly two lengths.

His winnings were huge and accumulating rapidly. Presidential Ball won the $500,000 New Jersey Classic on May 29th and then at intervals of four weeks won the $1,000,000 North America Cup Final on June 26th and the $1,000,000 Meadowlands Pace Final on July 24th.

The North America Cup was a prime example of the kind of colt Presidential Ball was on the racetrack. Driven by Ron Waples from post eight, Presidential Ball was outside the entire mile and sixth at the half before making a sweeping three-wide move around the backstretch to get in a challenging position. He was still three lengths back in the stretch, but found the reserves to win by a half-length in 1:51 over The Starting Gate. Under pressure to win back-to-back $1,000,000 races, Presidential Ball responded with his lifetime best - a 1:50 mile in the Meadowlands Pace over Life Sign and Riyadh, with Jack Moiseyev back in the sulky. A week later, Presidential Ball defeated Life Sign again in a Cane Pace Elimination. Life Sign got revenge, however, in the Cane Pace Final when both he and Riyadh caught the front-running Presidential Ball in the stretch. Presidential Ball finished third, the only time all year he lost after having the lead at the half.

The three-year-old division had now gotten even more competitive with Life Sign and Riyadh showing they were capable of stepping right with Presidential Ball. After a win at Freehold in a New Jersey Sires S., Presidential Ball lost five of his next six starts to that dynamic duo, three to Life Sign and two to Riyadh, but never by more than three lengths. The key to beating Presidential Ball was not to let him get the lead and he was parked out all the way in the Art Rooney Memorial Elimination and Final events.

Sire Line
Presidential Ball was the third highest priced Cam Fella, at $75,000, to sell at the 1991 yearling auctions when he was sold at the Kentucky Standardbred Select Yearling Sale. Sons of Cam Fella may go on to start another branch of the Most Happy Fella sire line. You can read more about Cam Fella in his chapter.

Maternal Line
Presidential Ball was bred by George Avakian and Mark Berlin of New York and Elsa Goldstein of New Jersey and purchased by Tony Chiaravalle as a yearling. The dam of Presidential Ball, I Marilyn p,2,2:00.2; 3,1:57.2; 1:55.4 ($501,580) in an example of the "they can come from anywhere" theory. I Marilyn was bred by Paul Cray of New Hampshire and purchased as a yearling by Dr. Jerry Semer's Iris Acres and Marilyn Rogers, who raced her and then sold her at the beginning of her five-year-old season.

I Marilyn was a fast and tough mare who really earned her $500,000 bankroll. At two, she won New York Sires S. at Yonkers, Monticello, Buffalo and Syracuse and came back at three to win the same stakes at Yonkers, Monticello and Buffalo, along with the Breeders Filly S. at Vernon Downs. She won another New York Sires S. at four at Yonkers and raced against many of the nation's top mares at four and five. Presidential Ball was her first living foal - a filly by Cam Fella died early.

The reason I mention that good horses can come from anywhere is that I Marilyn is sired by Mountain Skipper and from a mare by White Mountain Boy - hardly well-known names among the more "fashionably" bred Standardbreds. However, Mountain Skipper was a stakes and Free-For-All winner and an extremely tough competitor who was voted Aged Pacer of the Year in 1973. Mountain Skipper had very little opportunity at stud, unlike another famous son of Dale Frost with Skipper in his name - Meadow Skipper. Mountain Skipper sired 30 2:00 pacers and three 2:00 trotters and is the sire of the dams of 38 2:00 pacers, including Presidential Ball.

Mountain Skipper's three 2:00 trotting credits bring to light a bit of trivia. Mountain Skipper's dam, Sadie Tass, was sired by a non-record son of Guy Abbey named Bulldog. He sired just a few horses with records and his claim to fame was being a full brother to the great Greyhound, who many still think was the greatest trotter in the sport's history.

Before I digress too far, I want to point out a little about Mountain Skipper since he could very well have been endowed with something special by Dale Frost, as was Meadow Skipper. Mountain Skipper's dam produced thirteen winners with her next fastest having records of only 2:04 and none of the others earning over $33,000. So, whatever Mountain Skipper had to make him a top horse did not, most likely, come down from his dam Sadie Tass.

We know that Presidential Ball's dam, I Marilyn, was an outstanding mare. Going back another generation, his second dam White Dawn p,2,2:04.3h; 3,2:00.2 ($180,723) was also a top mare and a multiple New York Sires winner at two, three and four. She was sired by the good racehorse White Mountain Boy p,4,T1:58.1, a son of Volomite. White Dawn produced seven fillies from her nine foals with I Marilyn being the best by far.

Progeny of Note

Presidential Ball's first crop had some impressive colts and fillies in 1997 and it will be interesting to see if they go in 1998 and if he can have another good crop of two-year-olds.

Heading Presidential Ball's first offering was the good colt Bear Dance p,2,1:53 ($312,163) who won the Nassagaweya S. and a Woodrow Wilson Elimination. he was also second in the rich Woodrow Wilson Final and the Niatross S. The top Presidential Ball filly was Presidential Lady p,3,1:54.f-'98 ($225,093) who won the Matron S. and Kentucky Standardbred Sales Co. S.

Four of Presidential Ball's five $100,000 winning two-year-olds from his first crop were fillies and the other three included Career Success p,3,1:53.2z-'98 ($154,458), Lush Limbaugh p,2,1:54.2 ($157,229) and Angel Be Great p,2,1:55.3 ($137,679). Another good filly was Something Persistent p,2,1:55h ($129,929).

Some of Presidential Ball's other stakes winning colts are Al For President p,3,1:52-'98 ($163,459), Browning Blue Chip p,2,1:53.3 ($54,201), Ryan's Way p,2,1:54.1 ($34,720), Chosen Fame p,3,1:53.2-'98 ($75,645), Inaugural Ball p,3,1:53.3f-'98 ($56,936) and Old Hickory p,3,1:54-'98 ($47,692). Presidential Ball's two- and three-year-olds are now in the early stages of the 1998 season and are making their presence felt. However, he still needs to sire the "big star" to get more notice.

Analysis

Presidential Ball is in a somewhat unique situation since his pedigree is so different than most other current top performers and sires. The closest common pedigree crosses for Presidential Ball are 4x4x3 to Dale Frost and 4x5 to Adios. He also has lots of Hal Dale blood with a 5x5x5x5x4x6 cross to that venerable stallion. The only commercial mares which a breeder may wish to exclude for purposes of avoiding inbreeding would be those by Cam Fella and his sire Most Happy Fella. Even though Presidential Ball has Bret Hanover in his pedigree, a Bret Hanover daughter would still only produce a foal which is bred 4x2 to him. As you can see, Presidential Ball's pedigree is very versatile, which could serve him well at stud.

Obviously, Albatross mares are those most likely to succeed with this stallion, as they do with all others. And there is the added attraction of the superb Cam Fella-Albatross mare success stories. If you do not have Albatross mares, try getting as much Albatross blood as possible to Presidential Ball - perhaps through a mare with a 3x3 cross to Albatross. There are plenty of those mares available and an example would be a Nihilator mare who is a daughter of a Sonsam mare.

Mares by other top broodmare sires, which are usually the daughters of the former leading sires, should also work and it would be nice if there was at least one dose of Albatross blood in the pedigree. One linking Albatross, No Nukes and Bret Hanover would be an excellent choice. Top broodmare sires like Big Towner, Abercrombie, Tyler B., Niatross, B.G.'s Bunny, Sonsam and Nihilator all have plenty of daughters which would match very well with Presidential Ball.

Looking at the pedigree crosses of Presidential Ball's top performers it is easy to see how his outcrossed maternal family influences these pedigrees. Instead of seeing a lot of 3x3 and 3x4 crosses to many different mainstream stallions, we are seeing primarily a 4x3 cross to Meadow Skipper as the closest common cross in most of Presidential Ball's foals.

For example, all seven of his current $100,000 winners are 4x3 or 4x4 to Meadow Skipper as the closest cross. In addition, two of those are also 4x4 to Bret Hanover. Another factor to watch is the strength of Albatross in a pedigree. For five of Presidential Ball's seven richest, Albatross is a major presence since he sired the dams of two of those performers, the second dams of two more and is the sire of B.G.'s Bunny who is the sire of the second dam of another.

Switching to Presidential Ball's speediest performers, we find that his 16 1:55 sons and daughters from dams by 12 different stallions which indicates he does not need to find certain "nicks" in the pedigrees. In this group, however, we find some crosses other than the 4x3 and 4x4 to Meadow Skipper as the closest. Chosen Fame is 3x4 to Most Happy Fella, 4x5x5 to Meadow Skipper and 4x4 to Bret Hanover; Browning Blue Chip is 4x2 to Bret Hanover and has a dam who is very inbred 3x2 to Tar Heel; and, Inaugural Ball is inbred 3x3 to Most Happy Fella.

Presidential Ball was a special racehorse and has the potential to be an exciting sire by offering a bit of an outcross pedigree. Hopefully he will be very successful and give the pacing ranks an infusion of new blood. This situation occurs every few generations and perhaps this is the time for Presidential Ball. With a total of 655 mares bred to him during his first four seasons at stud, Presidential Ball has proved very popular with breeders and should have every opportunity to prove himself as a stallion.

Leading Progeny by Presidential Ball

Fastest
Al For President, h, p,3,1:52 $163,459
Bear Dance, h, p,2,1:53 $312,163
Career Success, m, p,3,1:53.2z $154,458
Chosen Fame, h, p,3,1:53.2 $75,645
Browning Blue Chip, h, p,2,1:53.3 $54,201
Inaugural Ball, h, p,3,1:53.3f $56,936
Mr President, h, p,3,1:53.4 $20,052
Old Hickory, h, p,3,1:54 $47,692
Presidential Lady, m, p,3,1:54f $255,093
Ryan's Way, h, p,2,1:54.1 $34,720

Richest
Bear Dance, h, p,2,1:53 $312,163
Presidential Lady, m, p,3,1:54f $255,093
Al For President, h, p,3,1:52 $163,459
Lush Limbaugh, m, p,2,1:54.2 $157,229
Career Success, m, p,3,1:53.2z $154,458
Angel Be Great, m, p,2,1:55.3 $137,679
Something Present, m, p,2,1:55h $129,929
Chosen Fame, h, p,3,1:53.2 $75,645
Inaugural Ball, h, p,3,1:53.3f $56,936
Browning Blue Chip, h, p,2,1:53.3 $54,201

Presidential Ball, Brown Horse, 15.3 Hands, 1990
p, 2, 1:54.2f; 3, 1:50 ($3,021,363)

Sire/Dam	2nd Gen	3rd Gen	4th Gen	5th Gen	6th Gen
Cam Fella, 1979 p, 4, 1:53.1 $2,041,367	Most Happy Fella, 1967 p, 3, T1:55 $419,033	Meadow Skipper, 1960 p, 3, 1:55.1 $428,057	**DALE FROST**, 1951 p, 1:58 $204,117	**HAL DALE**	ABBEDALE / Margaret Hal
				Galloway	Raider / Bethel
			Countess Vivian, 1950 p, 3, 1:59 $43,262	King's Counsel	**VOLOMITE** / Margaret Spangler
				Filly Direct	**BILLY DIRECT** / Calumet Edna
		Laughing Girl, 1961 p, 4, 2:04h $19,546	Good Time, 1946 p, 1:57.4 $318,792	**HAL DALE**	ABBEDALE / Margaret Hal
				On Time	**VOLOMITE** / Nedda guy
			Maxine's Dream, 1954 p, 2, T2:00 $36,557	Knight Dream	**NIBBLE HANOVER** / Lydia Knight
				Maxine Abbe	ABBEDALE / Maxine Direct
	Nan Cam, 1971 p, 5, 2:05.1f $11,390	Bret Hanover, 1962 p, 4, T1:53.3 $922,616	**ADIOS**, 1940 p, T1:57½ $33,329	**HAL DALE**	ABBEDALE / Margaret Hal
				Adioo Volo	Adioo Guy / Sigrid Volo
			Brenna Hanover, 1956 p, 3, T2:01 $21,946	Tar Heel	**BILLY DIRECT** / Leta Long
				Beryl Hanover	**NIBBLE HANOVER** / Laura Hanover
		Nan Frost, 1966 p, 3, 2:06.3f $1,607	**DALE FROST**, 1951 p, 1:58 $204,117	**HAL DALE**	ABBEDALE / Margaret Hal
				Galloway	Raider / Bethel
			Mynah Hanover, 1950 p, 2:05.2h $44,184	Ensign Hanover	**BILLY DIRECT** / Helen Hanover
				Betty Mahone	Corporal Lee / Belle Mahone
I Marilyn, 1980 p, 5, 1:55.4 $501,580	Mountain Skipper, 1968 p, 5, T1:56.1 $304,376	**DALE FROST**, 1951 p, 1:58 $204,117	**HAL DALE**, 1926 p, 6, 2:02¼	ABBEDALE	The Abbe / Daisydale D.
				Margaret Hal	Argot Hal / Margaret Polk
			Galloway, 1939 p, 2:04½h $5,294	Raider	**PETER VOLO** / Nelda Dillon
				Bethel	David Guy / Annotation
		Sadie Tass, 1951 p, 2:11h $3,742	Bulldog, 1937	Guy Abbey	Guy Axworthy / Abbacy
				Elizabeth	**PETER THE GREAT** / Zombrewer
			Twilight June, 1943	Gayle The Great	Gaylworthy / Miss Volo E
				June Casco	Leon June / Sadie Casco
	White Dawn, 1969 p, 3, 2:00.2 $180,723	White Mountain Boy, 1946 p, 4, T1:58.1 $72,796	**VOLOMITE**, 1926 3, 2:03¼ $32,649	**PETER VOLO**	**PETER THE GREAT** / Nervolo Belle
				Cita Frisco	San Francisco / Mendocita
			Merry Bars, 1934 p, 2:04¼ $5,229	Grattan Bars	Grattan Royal / Polly Bars
				Silver Direct	Merry Direct / Halberta
		Little Mary C., 1963 p, 3, 2:08.3h $2,362	Adios Boy, 1951 p, 2, T1:58.3 $129,859	**ADIOS**	**HAL DALE** / Adioo Volo
				Carrie Castle	Bonnycastle / Crystal Gleam
			Wicomico Shamy, 1948 p, 2:07.1h $5,028	Cardinal Prince	Peter Potempkin / Lillian L
				Neshaminy	ABBEDALE / Dierker Direct

Race Time

Race Time was a "tough as nails" performer who had speed to burn. He was voted divisional champion each year he raced, from two through four. Physically Race Time did not appear to be anything special. He was not a big horse and was average-looking, but you knew you were seeing greatness once he was in full stride and mowing down the competition. He did that in 30 of his 43 lifetime starts while amassing nearly a half-million dollars in earnings.

Race Time was sold as a yearling for $19,000 to top trainer-driver Billy Haughton, but breeder Castleton Farm took him back when Haughton could not find owners who wanted the colt. Castleton gave the colt to Ralph Baldwin who trained and drove for the Castleton racing stable. The rest is history.

At two, Race Time won nine of his 12 starts, including victories in the Fox S., Geers S., McMahon Memorial and Two Gaits Farm S. He came back at three to win 11 of 14 starts, with wins in the American-National S., Adios S., Batavia Colt S., Cane Futurity, Messenger S., Review Futurity, Matron S. and Orange County Cup. Unfortunately for his connections, Race Time got sick just before the Little Brown Jug. He had a fever of 106 degrees and nearly died. Although he missed the Jug, he came back strong and won divisional honors once again.

Coming back at four, Race Time was a top FFA performer, winning 10 of 17 starts and earning over $225,000 while pacing to wins in the American-National Maturity, Realization S., Empire Pace, Overtrick Pace and five legs and the Final of the HTA Series.

Following the 1965 racing season Race Time was retired and sent to stud at Castleton Farm's new venture in Trenton, Florida. He later foundered and was moved to the main Castleton Farm in Lexington, Kentucky, where he spent the rest of his stud career. Race Time died from internal problems in 1979 at 18 years of age.

Sire Line

Race Time has turned out to be the most accomplished son of the great Good Time as a commercial stallion. He sired good racehorses and his daughters have been very successful as broodmares. However, like Good Time's other top sons who had the best chances at stud, Best Of All and Columbia George, none have left a top son to carry on this branch of the Hal Dale male line.

The best chance Race Time had to leave a successful son was probably through the world champion Temujin p,3,1:54.3h ($633,284) who was a son of the legendary mare Silk Stockings p,3,1:55.2 ($694,894) and had a nice racing career. If ever a stallion had the credentials to be a sire, it was Temujin. However, Temujin was very small of stature, which was common with the Good Time line, and perhaps that was a factor in his failure to be a top sire. But he stood at Lana Lobell Farms and he did have access to top mares for several years. Temujin was an excellent percentage sire and his sons and daughters got to the races - but he never sired the great horses a stallion needs to be commercially accepted.

You can read more about the great Good Time in his chapter.

Maternal Line

Race Time's maternal family is that of Minnehaha, one of the most prolific in the sport's history. The pedigree of Race Time contains a number of successful stallions and several are very close. For example, Race Time is a half-brother to the great racehorse and good sire Storm Damage p,3,1:53.2f ($659,296) (by Bret Hanover). Storm Damage was a world champion and the co-fastest two-year-old of 1979. Unfortunately, he was in the same crop as the incomparable Niatross and thus was only second best.

There are not very many broodmares who have produced more than one son who became a commercial success as a stallion, but Race Time's dam Breath O Spring p,3,T2:01.1 ($3,144) is one of them. Breath O Spring also produced a daughter named Touch Of Spring p,2,T2:03, a full sister to Race Time, and that mare is the dam of world champion Warm Breeze p,4,1:53.1 who was also a successful sire for a time. Like Storm Damage, he is a son of Bret Hanover.

Race Time's grandam is the Scotland daughter Lady Scotland who, in addition to producing Breath O Spring, is the dam of her full brother, the good sire Harold J. p,4,1:57.4f ($159,179) who has gained lasting fame as the sire of the dam of the fastest pacer ever, Cambest p,T1:46.1 ($1,458,110).

Race Record Highlights

At 2
1st Fox S.
Geers S.
McMahon Memorial
Two Gaits Farm S.

At 3
1st American-National S.
Adios S.
Batavia Colt S.
Cane Futurity
Messenger S.
Review Futurity
Matron S.
Orange County Cup

At 4
1st American-National Maturity
Realization S.
Empire Pace (1¼ miles)
Overtrick Pace
HTA Final and five legs

Race Time

Photo courtesy of The Horseman and Fair World

Honors

Voted Two-Year-Old Pacer of the Year
Voted Three-Year-Old Pacer of the Year
Voted Aged Pacer of the Year

Race Record

Year	Age	Starts	Wins	2nd	3rd	Earnings	Record
1963	2	12	9	1	0	$ 61,808	p,2,1:58
1964	3	14	11	3	0	199,292	p,3,1:57
1965	4	17	10	3	2	225,855	
		43	30	7	2	$486,955	p,3,1:57

Race Time

The great-grandam of Race Time is the Spencer mare Spinster 4,T2:05 who has top descendants on both the trotting and pacing gaits. In addition to being the dam of Lady Scotland, Spinster was bred to Guy Abbey and produced The Old Maid who became the dam of the pacing stars Dancer Hanover p,4,T1:56.4 ($87,746) (by Adios), Thorpe Hanover p,3,T1:58.2 ($130,804) (by Tar Heel) and Bachelor Hanover p,3,T1:59.2 ($209,021) (by Nibble Hanover). Dancer Hanover and Thorpe Hanover reached a certain degree of stallion success in North America and were especially good broodmare sires. Bachelor Hanover, after a short stud career in North America, was later an influential sire in New Zealand.

The Old Maid is also the fourth dam of the Meadow Skipper son French Chef p,2, 1:54 ($371,445) who was a racing champion and had some flashes of brilliance as a sire with Beach Towel p,3,1:50 ($2,570,357), Amity Chef p,3,1:51.1 ($1,372,683) and Frugal Gourmet p,3,1:51.3f ($1,349,560).

Progeny of Note

At stud, Race Time sired the winners of $37,555,359 from his 14 crops foaled between 1967 and 1980. His largest crop of foals was 104 in 1974 and his crop size averaged 66. One of Race Time's greatest strengths as a sire was that his offspring were sound and stayed sound for long careers on the track. Most improved with age and many took lifetime records at six, seven and eight years of age. And 86% of all his foals made it to the races - a very high figure.

Race Time sired 13 in 1:55, 217 in 2:00 and had 108 $100,000 winners. This is an excellent record when one remembers that most of his foals raced before the advent of The Meadowlands and the levels of speed we know today.

Race Time was the first sire to have two 2:00 two-year-olds in his first crop of foals and later (in 1972) became the first to have five 2:00 two-year-olds.

The leading money-winning son of Race Time was Dream Maker p,1:54.3 ($746,332) who later became a decent sire in Canada. He was a stakes winner at three and later a multiple FFA winner, including the U.S. Pacing Championship, Graduate Series Final and Provincial Cup, among other major victories.

Temujin p,2,1:54.4; 3,1:54.3h ($633,284) is Race Time's most famous son for two reasons. First, he drew immediate attention simply because he was the first foal from the superstar pacing mare Silk Stockings who was a legend in her time during the mid-1970s. Second, he lived up to expectations by setting a 1:56.1 world record for two-year-old colts on a half-mile track and was voted Harness Tracks of America (HTA) Two-Year-Old Pacer of the Year. Among his wins were the $200,000 Kentucky Pacing Derby and Fox S. At three, he became the fastest three-year-old ever on a half-mile track with a 1:54.3 clocking while winning a heat of the Little Brown Jug. As we have seen, Temujin went to stud at four, but never became a commercial success.

Lime Time p,1:54.1 ($609,270) was another world champion son of Race Time. He set a world record for older males on a half-mile track and was a stakes and FFA winner until he retired after his six-year-old season.

Other high money-winning sons and daughters of Race Time are Composite p,1:56.4 ($585,093), Trenton Time p,4,1:57 ($469,334), Jefferson p,1:58.2f ($361,378), Sailing Race p,1:59.2h ($353,916), Sugar Dust p,2,T1:57 ($340,121) and the top mares Missouri Time p,1:56.3f ($328,423) and Time O Nic p,T1:54.3 ($308,769).

Another world champion for Race Time was his son Ricci Reenie Time p,2,1:56.1 ($300,845) who was voted Two-Year-Old Pacing Colt of the Year in 1972. That season, Ricci Reenie Time won 11 of 15 starts, including the Fox S., Review Futurity, International Stallion S. and McMahon Memorial. He also became the fastest two-year-old colt in the sport's history with his 1:56.1 mile. At three, he came back to win the Adios S., Gaines Memorial and Little Brown Jug Preview. He, too, never made much of an impact as a sire.

Race Time's fastest offspring is Bandelier p,4,1:52.4 ($215,048) who won 13 of his 20 starts as a four-year-old in 1981, including the American-National Maturity.

Analysis

Race Time went to stud with a very important and close-up cross in his pedigree chart - he was inbred 3x3 to the great stallion Volomite. This cross was achieved in the following manner - Good Time's dam was a daughter of Volomite and Breath O Spring's sire, Worthy Boy, was a son of Volomite.

With his pedigree, Race Time was set up very well to receive the many top mares of that period with the Adios/Tar Heel and Tar Heel/Adios crosses which were so popular. There were also plenty of sons of Adios at stud and Race Time received many of their daughters. Another sire who shows up frequently in the pedigrees of the dams of Race Time's top performers is the great broodmare sire Knight Dream.

Now let's take a look at some of the pedigree crosses among Race Time's top performers. As expected, many of the mares bred to Race Time had crosses to Hal Dale line stallions. Thus we find dozens of Race Time's best offspring bred 3x4 to Hal Dale. Another strong influence was the blood of Volomite since Race Time was 3x3 to that stallion. There were so many mares with Volomite blood, at that time, it is not uncommon to find 4x4x4x4 and 4x4x4x5 crosses to Volomite among the best sons and daughters of Race Time.

Dream Maker was just 3x4 to Hal Dale with no other close common crosses. Temujin is interesting since he has a 2x4 cross to Good Time and is also 3x5x5x5 to Hal Dale. The close breeding to Good Time may be one of the factors accounting for his size - although neither his sire nor his dam were large horses. Another with a similar 2x4 cross to Good Time is Race Time's fastest daughter Enterprising who has the same 3x5x5x5 cross to Hal Dale and a heavy 4x4x6x6x5 cross to Volomite.

Race Time's third leading money winner, Lime Time, is 3x4 to Hal Dale, 4x4x5 to Volomite, 4x4 to Billy Direct and has an additional interesting cross - 3x3 to the half-sisters Lady Scotland and The Old Maid, both of which I mentioned earlier. Another good performer with a common cross to a top mare is Sailing Race who is 4x4x3 to Volomite and 4x4 to the full brother and sister Scotland and Rose Scott.

Bandelier, Race Time's fastest performer, is 3x4 to Hal Dale and 4x5 to Volomite and his half-sister Cita Worthy.

Today, we are concerned mostly about Race Time's daughters as producers. His youngest daughters are 18 years old in 1998 so you can see that most Race Time mares are past their prime production years. However, Race Time has had a profound influence on the pacing breed through his daughters. They have produced 974 2:00 performers, at this writing, which ranks Race Time as the sixth leading pacing broodmare sire of all time behind only Albatross, Bret Hanover, Meadow Skipper, Most Happy Fella and Tar Heel. That's pretty impressive company!

As you peruse this listing of top performers from Race Time mares you can see why he is held in such high esteem as a broodmare sire. Race Time's daughters have produced six millionaires - Misfit p,1:49.4 ($1,190,067) (by Abercrombie), Magical Mike p,3,1:50.2 ($1,682,085) (by Tyler B.), the great mare Ellamony p,1:50.3 ($1,425,285) (by Cam Fella), Historic p,3,1:51f ($1,334,861) (by Nihilator), Runnymede Lobell p,4,T1:51.2 ($1,615,125) (by Nero) and the successful sire Dragon's Lair p,1:51.3 ($1,085,317) (by Tyler B.).

That, in itself, would be quite a list. But there is more. Other familiar fast and rich performers from Race Time daughters are Reactor Lobell p,1:50.1 ($762,790) (by Slapstick), Echelon p,1:50.3 ($558,568) (by Slapstick), Miles McCool p,3,1:51.2f ($333,721) (by Tyler B.), Spectacle p,1:51.2 (by Albatross), Some Albert p,1:51.2 (By Albert Albert), Tyler's Mark p,3,1:51.3 (by Tyler B.), Don't Dally p,3,1:51.3 (by Meadow Skipper), Justin Passing p,3,T1:53.2 ($806,348) (by Bye And Large), Legal Notice p,3,1:53.3h (by Strike Out) and Cole Muffler p,3,1:53.3f ($682,380) (by Tyler B.). There are many more sub-1:55 performers and $100,000 winners; the list would cover several pages. This shows the kind of class Race Time's daughters have produced.

As an aside, it appears that Race Time blood continues to be influential through generations. Two examples are Race Time's appearance as the sire of the grandams of new stallions Ball And Chain p,1:49 ($1,435,390) and David's Pass p,3,1:50.4 ($1,652,500).

The stallion Tyler B (by Most Happy Fella) had tremendous success with Race Time mares - most notably Magical Mike and Miles McCool from the mare Racing Date p,3,T1:57.2 ($18,865). The Tyler B cross also worked wonders for Racing Date's full sister, Dateable, who is the dam of Tyler's

Mark and the mare Seven O'Clock. Dateable did not just do well with Tyler B., however; she is also the dam of the Nihilator duo Historic and Digger Almahurst p,2,1:52.1f ($371,866).

Race Time mares did exceptionally well when bred to Most Happy Fella line sires and have had top performers by Tyler B, Cam Fella, Troublemaker, Camtastic and No Nukes. Breeding Race Time mares to Niatross and his son Nihilator has also worked very well. One of the most prolific Race Time mares has been Sandy's Sable p,2,2:00.1 ($17,451) who is the dam of Dragon's Lair, Cole Muffler and Bruce's Lady - all by Tyler B. With Dragon's Lair already an accomplished sire, and his full brother Cole Muffler making noise in Illinois suggesting he wants to follow suit, there is something uniquely strong about this cross. Sandy's Sable also has several daughters who are beginning to produce 1:51 and 1:52 pacers.

I will conclude this chapter with the pedigree of a horse with a record of 1:50 and earnings of $608,074 before being exported "Down Under" for racing and breeding purposes. The horse is Island Glow by Dragon's Lair from the No Nukes mare Three Mile Island p,2,1:56.2f ($288,079). The second dam is the Race Time mare Racy Kathy.

Island Glow has a number of extremely interesting crosses, the closest being an inbred 3x3 to Race Time. I've mentioned earlier the crosses which seemed to have worked best with Race Time - Tyler B., Most Happy Fella, Adios and Tar Heel. Island Glow has all of them in abundance, plus multiples of two of the best maternal lines in the sport's history.

Here are Island Glow's pedigree crosses in addition to the 3x3 to Race Time: 3x4 to Most Happy Fella, 5x4x6x6x4 to Good Time, 4x4x5x5 to Tar Heel, 5x5x6x5 to Adios and at least a dozen crosses to Hal Dale. Of further significance is the 3x3 cross to the three-quarter sisters Tarport Cheer (Tar Heel-Meadow Cheer) and Tarport Kathy (Thorpe Hanover-Meadow Cheer). Another maternal cross is the 5x5 to the half-sisters Lady Scotland (Scotland-Spinster) and The Old Maid (Guy Abbey-Spinster).

Dragon's Lair, the sire of Island Glow, possesses much of the blood which has worked so well with Race Time. His sire Tyler B is by Most Happy Fella from the great broodmare Tarport Cheer who is the product of a Tar Heel/Adios cross. Sandy's Sable, the Race Time mare who is the dam of Dragon's Lair, is also from a mare with the Tar Heel/Adios cross.

Island Glow's dam, Three Mile Island, is by No Nukes who is a grandson of Most Happy Fella. Her dam is the Race Time mare Racy Kathy who is another product of the Tar Heel/Adios cross (although through Tar Heel's son Thorpe Hanover).

In any case, Island Glow's pedigree is a classic in that it not only doubled up on Race Time, but also with the crosses which worked best for Race Time: Most Happy Fella, Tar Heel and Adios.

Leading Progeny by Race Time

Fastest
Bandelier, h, p,4,1:52.4 $215,048
Lime Time, h, p,1:54.1 $609,270
Enterprising, m, p,3,1:54.2 $173,824
Dream Maker, h, p,1:54.3 $746,332
Temujin, h, p,3,1:54.3h $633,284
Time O Nic, m, p,T1:54.3 $308,769
Classic Tale, m, p,4,1:54.3 $132,903
Make Mine Sable, g, p,3,1:54.3 $50,741
Slipstream, h, p,1:54.4 $288,124
Shock Treatment, h, p,4,1:54.4 $107,928

Richest
Dream Maker, h, p,1:54.3 $746,332
Temujin, h, p,3,1:54.3h $633,284
Lime Time, h, p,1:54.1 $609,270
Composite, h, p,1:56.4 $585,093
Trenton Time, h, p,4,1:57 $469,334
Jefferson, g, p,1:58.2f $361,378
Sailing Race, h, p,1:59.2h $353,916
Sugar Dust, h, p,2,T1:57 $340,121
Missouri Time, m, p,1:56.3f $328,423
Time O Nic, m, p,T1:54.3 $308,769

Race Time, Bay Horse, 1961
p, 2, 1:58; 3, 1:57 ($486,955)

Good Time, 1946 p, 1:57.4 $318,792	Hal Dale, 1926 p, 6, 2:02¼	Abbedale, 1917 p, 2:01¼	The Abbe, 1903 p, 2:04	**CHIMES**	Electioneer Beautiful Bells
				Nettie King	Mambrino King Nettie Murphy
			Daisydale D., 1908 3, 2:15¼	Archdale	Expedition Aline
				Mrs. Tmolus	Pactolus Flaxey
		Margaret Hal, 1914 p, 2:19½h	Argot Hal, 1903 p, T2:04¾	Brown Hal	**TOM HAL JNR** Lizzie
				Lady Wildflower	Duplex Sally Ward
			Margaret Polk, 1906	John R. Gentry	Ashland Wilkes Dame Wood
				Stella Hal	**TOM HAL JNR** Dolly
	On Time, 1938 p, 3, 2:03½h $1,472	**VOLOMITE**, 1926 3, 2:03¼ $32,649	Peter Volo, 1911 4, 2:02	**PETER THE GREAT**	Pilot Medium Santos
				Nervolo Belle	Nervolo Josephine Knight
			Cita Frisco, 1921	San Francisco	**ZOMBRO** Oniska
				Mendocita	Mendocino Esther
		Nedda Guy, 1928 3, 2:03½h 14,318	**GUY AXWORTHY**, 1902 4, 2:08¾	Axworthy	Axtell Marguerite
				Lillian Wilkes	Guy Wilkes Flora
			Nedda, 1915 1:58¼	Atlantic Express	Bellini Expressive
				Pleasant Thought	Prodigal **EXTASY**
Breath O Spring, 1953 p, 3, T2:01.1 $3,144	Worthy Boy, 1940 3, 2:02½ $25,688	**VOLOMITE**, 1926 3, 2:03¼ $32,649	Peter Volo, 1911 4, 2:02	**PETER THE GREAT**	Pilot Medium Santos
				Nervolo Belle	Nervolo Josephine Knight
			Cita Frisco, 1921	San Francisco	**ZOMBRO** Oniska
				Mendocita	Mendocino Esther
		Warwell Worthy, 1932 3, 2:03¼	Peter The Brewer, 1918 4, 2:02½	**PETER THE GREAT**	Pilot Medium Santos
				Zombrewer	**ZOMBRO** Mary Bales
			Alma Lee, 1925 4, 2:04¾	Lee Worthy	**LEE AXWORTHY** Emma Smith
				Jane Revere	**GUY AXWORTHY** Volga E
	Lady Scotland, 1943	Scotland, 1925 T1:59¼	Peter Scott, 1909 T2:05	**PETER THE GREAT**	Pilot Medium Santos
				Jenny Scott	Bryson Aetna
			Roya McKinney, 1911 4, T2:07½	**MCKINNEY**	Alcyone Rosa Sprague
				Princess Royal	**CHIMES** Estabella
		Spinster, 1930 4, T2:05	Spencer, 1925 3, T1:59¾	Lee Tide	**LEE AXWORTHY** Emily Ellen
				Petrex	**PETER THE GREAT** **EXTASY**
			Minnetonka, 1922 T2:12¼	Belwin	**MCKINNEY** Belle Winnie
				The Miss Stokes	**PETER THE GREAT** Tillie Thompson

Run The Table

Run The Table has emerged as a nice stallion success story for the Canadian harness racing industry and the brothers Jack and Don McNiven who have spent decades in the business. Run The Table was a fast and rich racehorse, but when the major farms passed him by as a stallion prospect, the McNivens made their move and it has paid huge dividends.

Sold as a yearling for $40,000 at the 1985 Tattersalls Sale in Lexington, Kentucky, Run The Table was purchased by Martin Walsh, Howard and Joan Mann and Pat Baker. They sold him in March of his three-year-old season to the Dalona Stable of New Jersey which raced the colt during his three- and four-year-old campaigns. Run The Table was bred by Steve Stewart and Joseph Taylor, both of Lexington, Kentucky.

Run The Table is now owned by the McNiven's Killean Acres farm in Ingersoll, Ontario, Canada. They purchased him from Dalona Stable in January 1989 for the purpose of standing him at stud at their farm. The stallion was immediately popular with 155 mares being booked his first season.

Let's take a look at Run The Table as a racehorse. At two, the colt was trained by Hall of Famer Del Insko and won his first qualifying race wire-to-wire in 2:02.3 at The Meadowlands. He then finished fourth and fifth in the next two qualifiers but was timed in 1:59.2. The serious business of racing for purse money began on June 12, 1986 and Run The Table, driven primarily by Insko, was fourth in a New Jersey Sires S. A week later, in just his second lifetime start, Run The Table won the next New Jersey Sires S. in a very swift 1:55. He came back two weeks later to score again in 1:56.2.

But, those were to be Run The Table's only two wins for the year, although he was second in two more New Jersey Sires S. and the New Jersey Futurity. Run The Table was always competitive and three of his losses were by only a half-length. He was not a fast leaver from the gate which made his racing style that of a come-from-behind horse. However, Run The Table picked up checks in 13 of his 16 starts and ended his freshman season with over $90,000 in earnings.

Coming back early at three, Run The Table was third in a qualifying race at the end of January and made his first start at The Meadowlands the first week of February. He was second in his debut after being parked out for three-quarters. After finishing third in a leg of the New Faces Series, Run The Table finished sixth in his next start. During this period, the colt was purchased by the Dalona Stable and put under the care of trainer Jim Campbell - an excellent trainer and, yes, the brother of driver John Campbell.

Run The Table then turned the tables and won eight of his next ten races while moving up to the elite level of his three-year-old peers. This was a crop which included Jate Lobell, Call For Rain, Frugal Gourmet, Jaguar Spur, Laag and Redskin; it was a very deep year for good three-year-olds. Among his wins from February through July were a leg and the $107,000 New Faces Series Final, three legs and the $200,000 New Jersey Sires S. Final, New Jersey Classic Elimination and a Meadowlands Pace Elimination. After five consecutive wins, the colt was defeated by Jate Lobell in the $500,000 New Jersey Classic Final, finishing second.

While he was accomplishing these feats, Run The Table took his record of 1:51 while defeating Jate Lobell with a final quarter in :26.4. He had paced the last quarter of another race in :26.2 and also developed good gate speed. This last attribute enabled him to be a very versatile racehorse in that he could go wire-to-wire or race from behind. Many of his front-end winning efforts were by open lengths.

One of his absolute best performances came in a losing effort in the richest race of his career. The $902,500 Meadowlands Pace was the setting and Run The Table was saddled with post eight with much of the early speed drawing inside. John Campbell, the colt's regular driver since joining his brother's stable, eased Run The Table away from the gait and was content to race on the outside following the

Race Record Highlights

At 2
- **1st** two New Jersey Sires S. at The Meadowlands
- **2nd** New Jersey Futurity
  two New Jersey Sires S. at Freehold

At 3
- **1st** Oliver Wendell Holmes S. Final and Elimination
  Adios S. Final and Elimination
  Meadowlands Pace Elimination
  New Jersey Classic Elimination
  Little Brown Jug Preview
  Breeders Crown Elimination
  New Faces Series Final and Elimination
  New Jersey Sires S. Final at The Meadowlands
  three New Jersey Sires S. at The Meadowlands

At 3 (continued)
- **2nd** Breeders Crown Final
  New Jersey Classic Final
  Cane Pace Elimination
- **3rd** Meadowlands Pace Final

At 4
- **1st** leg of Driscoll Series
  New Jersey Sires S.
- **2nd** Driscoll Series Final
- **3rd** two legs of Molson Series

Honors
At three, set all-age two heat world record on mile track
At three, set world record for fastest second heat on a mile track

Run The Table

Photo by Monica Thors
Courtesy of Killean Acres

Race Record

Year	Age	Starts	Wins	2nd	3rd	Earnings	Record
1986	2	16	2	4	0	$ 90,021	p,2,1:55
1987	3	24	14	6	2	904,022	p,3,1:51
1988	4	18	4	3	3	177,010	
		58	20	13	5	$1,171,053	p,3,1:51

cover of the other outside flow horses. Run The Table raced sixth to the three-quarters when Campbell made his move on the final turn and sent him after the leaders. Run The Table was still fourth and a full six lengths from the leaders in the stretch when he turned on the afterburners and closed like a rocket on the outside to miss winning by a neck while taking third behind Frugal Gourmet and Laag in a 1:52 mile. He had to have paced home in :26 flat that night.

A week later in the Cane Pace Elimination, Run The Table uncharacteristically lost a two-length lead in the stretch to finish second. He was then scratched sick from the Final. After a two-week lay off he came back for a 1:51.1 five-length win at The Meadowlands in his Oliver Wendell Holmes P. Elimination. Run The Table was awesome that night. Coming back for the Final he won in 1:51.1 over Frugal Gourmet and Laag to gain some measure of revenge for the Meadowlands Pace defeat. The combined time was the fastest ever recorded for a two-heat race for horses of any age.

The Adios S. was next at The Meadows and Run The Table extended his streak to four with a 1:54 win in the Elimination and 1:53.2 in the Adios Final. The colt took his winning streak to five in the Jug Preview at Scioto Downs and then headed for Delaware, Ohio, and the Little Brown Jug.

Since the three-year-old pacing colt crop was so deep that year, 23 were entered in the Little Brown Jug which meant three divisions. As fate would have it, three of the best colts all drew into the same division: Frugal Gourmet, Jaguar Spur and Run The Table. Jaguar Spur had been beaten by Run The Table in both the Adios and the Jug Preview. Run The Table left from post four in his Jug Elimination and was fifth on the rail at the quarter. You can't sit too long in the Jug and Campbell soon made his move as did Frugal Gourmet. Run The Table was parked out the rest of the way and the day belonged to Jaguar Spur who held on for a 1:54 win with Run The Table only fourth and not qualifying for the Little Brown Jug Final. Jaguar Spur went on to win the Final.

In his next race, a late-September Lexington Early Closer, Run The Table was second to Call For Rain after tiring and losing five lengths in the stretch. It was time for a break. Campbell gave the colt a month off before qualifying him twice at Pompano Park to get ready for the year-ending Breeders Crown. The Elimination and Final were held the same night at Pompano. Run The Table won his Elimination in 1:53 over Call For Rain and Jate Lobell in an impressive front-running effort. In the rich Breeders Crown Final, he had the rail and was favored. Run The Table took the front-end route again and had a two-length lead in the stretch, but he could not hold on in the final strides and was overtaken by a head at the wire by the fast-closing Call For Rain with Jate Lobell taking third.

Thus ended a great three-year-old season for Run The Table in which he won 14 of 24 starts, was first, second or third in 23 of those races, set a world record, was the fastest horse of 1987 and earned $904,022. Not a bad year - especially against one of the best groups of colts ever.

Coming back at four, much was expected from Run The Table but he never seemed to get back to the great form he had at three. He easily won all four of his qualifying races in May, but it was only in his fifth parimutuel start that he found the winner's circle at The Meadowlands when he scored a win by a neck over Call For Rain. He won only three more races that season, including a leg of the Driscoll Series, a New Jersey Sires S. and Invitational event. Run The Table's earnings for the year were $177,010 and he ended his racing career with $1,171,053 on his card.

Run The Table had a nice career, but his unexceptional campaign at four, and the fact that he was a son of Landslide, did not make him the most attractive stallion prospect for the major farms. But that opened the door for Jack and Don McNiven.

Sire Line

Run The Table is a Meadow Skipper line sire through that great stallion's son Landslide p,3,1:54.1 ($162,835). A big, good-looking horse, Landslide was the highest priced yearling sold in the fall of 1979, purchased for $290,000 by Stonegate Farm's owner Robert Tucker of Glen Gardner, New Jersey. Tucker was looking for a stakes colt and a future stallion. He got both.

Landslide was injured and did not race at two. However, once he made his racing debut in late July of his three-year-old season, he made the harness racing world take notice. Trained and driven by Ed Lohmeyer, Landslide won the first start of his career in 1:56 - then the fastest debut mile in harness racing history. After just two starts, Landslide won the two-heat Adios S. at The Meadows. He then swept through the Review Futurity and Hayes Memorial at Springfield and DuQuoin before taking an Invitational event at Scioto Downs. Landslide liked the front end and was extremely tough once he got to the front.

Landslide went undefeated during his first nine starts and then suffered an interference break in an accident-marred heat of The Little Brown Jug. He was the odds-on favorite in his division. The colt then won a heat of the Tattersalls S. at The Red Mile in his lifetime best 1:54.1 and was second in the Final. Landslide won his next, and last, start in the T.W. Murphy Memorial at Lexington and ended his career with 11 wins from just 13 starts and earnings of $162,835.

Bringing excellent credentials to his new career as a stallion, the now syndicated Landslide was an interesting prospect due to his performance, his looks and the fact that his Tar Heel dam Hobby Horse Tar was also the dam of the great racehorse and decent sire Silent Majority p,3,1:56.3 ($362,269). Landslide stood the most active part of his career at New Jersey's Stonegate Farm and was well-received by breeders.

However, once the competition got hot and heavy in the New Jersey Sires S. program other stallions became more popular and Landslide's bookings, along with the quality of his mares, began to decline. But he has sired the winners of almost $29,000,000 with over 60 in 1:55, 347 in 2:00 and more than 75 $100,000 winners. Landslide mares also seem to be doing an excellent job as producers and he is credited with over 215 2:00 broodmare credits at this writing, including four 1:52 performers.

Run The Table is Landslide's best performer and by far his best son as a stallion. This is from just a handful of sons actively standing at stud. Landslide was an excellent sire of fillies, as well as colts, and nine of his 17 $250,000 winning offspring are female. Some of his top performers, in addition to Run The Table, are the mare Glenn's Super Star p,4,1:54.1 ($475,047), Dancercize p,4,1:53f ($435,773), Landslip Hanover p,3,1:54 ($396,270), the mares Shocking Secret p,3,1:54.1 ($378,088) and Walkin On Air p,3,1:55.4 ($370,970), and Barry's Choice p,1:52. ($322,682). Landslide's fastest performer is Doctor Gerson p,4,1:50.4 ($315,339).

The success of Run The Table is reminiscent of that of No Nukes and On The Road Again from their average sires Oil Burner and Happy Motoring in that there seemed to be a generation skip. But the Meadow Skipper sire line is so strong it is capable of most anything.

Maternal Line

Run The Table is not a sire with a glamour pedigree on his maternal side, although it is rapidly improving. His dam is the Best Of All mare Hustler's Best p,2,2:07.1h; 3,2:04.3h ($37,805) who was stakes-placed at two and a winner of two legs of the Hopeful Series at three. His second dam had a record of 2:06h and won $6,034 while producing Hustler's Boy p,1:56.4 ($206,095) in addition to Hustler's Best. Run The Table's third dam, Yankeetone, took a record of 2:09.3 and earned $3,393. Yankeetone produced two nice colts, however, Going Thru p,T1:58.2 ($323,102) (by Lehigh Hanover), who was second in a heat of the Little Brown Jug, and Popping Thru p,3,2:00.4h ($177,835) (by Best Of All) who was third in the L.B. Sheppard Memorial and a heat of the Adios S.

An interesting note is that Yankeetone's sire is the pacer Yankee Scott p,1:59.4 ($42,329) who was royally bred to be a trotter. His sire is the great Scotland and his dam is Yankee Maid, a winner of the Hambletonian and a half-sister to the great world champion and Hambletonian winner Greyhound.

Run The Table's dam Hustler's Best produced only four foals and all have made themselves known. Obviously, Run The Table is the fastest and richest performer from his dam, but she also produced Roman Lover p,4,1:54 ($160,161) who was second in the Prix de l'Avenir at two and also second in a heat of the North America Cup at three. Another foal is Scandal p,4,1:56.2 ($96,460) by Raven Hanover.

The only daughter from Hustler's Best is the unraced full sister to Landslide named Satan's Alley. She has already produced some top performers in Whiteland Trouble p,1:53h ($638,158) (by Troublemaker) and Whiteland Fella p,4,1:52.3 ($199,969) (by Cam Fella) in addition to five others in 2:00.

We never know from where the genes come which specify which horses will be great racehorses, and/or sires, but Run The Table must have gotten some of them from his ancestors. Regarding his first three dams, we find that the sire of his dam is the top racehorse and decent sire Best Of All, a son of great racehorse and great sire Good Time. The sire of Run The Table's second dam is Dancer Hanover who is a product of the wonderful cross of Adios and The Old Maid. It must be remembered that Dancer Hanover is also the sire of the dam of none other than Albatross. As always, blood will tell.

Run The Table is from one of the least known branches of the famous Jessie Pepper maternal family which has been a leader in the maternal family category for decades. Other branches have been responsible for such great sires as Tar Heel, No Nukes and the aforementioned Scotland. The good trotting sires Hickory Smoke and Hickory Pride are also from Run The Table's branch of the Jessie Pepper family, as is the great trotting mare Armbro Flight who is the dam of the successful stallion Armbro Goal. So the quality is there - you just have to mine the fields a bit to find it.

Progeny of Note

Run The Table has had six crops to the races as this chapter is written, not including his 1998 two-year-olds. He has succeeded beyond expectations and has made a name for himself in Canadian and U.S. stakes as well as becoming a powerful force in the rich Ontario Sires S. program.

To date, Run The Table has sired the winners of over $25,000,000 with 52 in 1:55, 305 in 2:00, four $500,000 winners and 61 $100,000 winners. With this success, Run The Table's stud fee had risen to $8,000 (Canadian) and he was the highest priced pacing stallion in Canada in 1997.

I mentioned earlier that Run The Table's first season at stud brought him 155 mares. The ensuing seasons showed a low of 103 mares in his third year all the way up to 220 mares during the 1995 season following the immediate success of his first two crops at the races.

Like his sire Landslide, Run The Table is a strong sire of fillies. Three of his four richest performers, Cathedra p,2,1:54.3; 3,1:52.3 ($733,789), Elegant Killean p,2,1:54.4f; 3,1:52.1 ($720,494) and Heatherjeankillean p,2,1:57.2f; 3,1:55f; 4,1:53.1 ($732,489) are all fillies. In addition, nine of his top 11 money winners, all with $300,000 or more in earnings, are female. Even in the speed department, five of his 14 fastest sons and daughters are fillies.

Run The Table's best female offspring is the filly Cathedra who won 14 of 16 starts at two and was a close third in balloting for two-year-old Pacing Filly of the Year in 1995. Cathedra won four Ontario Sires S. Gold events and the Canadian Breeders S. She was also a stakes winner at three, although not as dominant. Elegant Killean is another special filly who set world records at two and three for free-legged fillies since she was so smooth-gaited. This filly won nine of 16 starts at two and was even better at three, winning 14 of 16, including the Tarport Hap S. and Eliminations of the Fan Hanover S. and Nadia Lobell S. Heatherjeankillean won 12 of 19 at two, including four Ontario Sires S. Gold events, and went on to become an Open Class mare with a win in the Clare Series.

While Run The Table's fillies were dominating the Canadian stakes, his sons were not doing badly either. Rabbi Of Racing p,2,1:55.1; 3,1:52.4 ($737,208), his richest offspring, won 10 of 14 starts at two, including three Ontario Sires S. Gold races and Treecoscious p,2,1:56.1f; 1:52.4 ($496,432) won five of nine at two, including two Ontario Sires S. Gold.

Some other Run The Table stars in his rapidly expanding list are the fillies Reef The Table p,2,1:57.3f ($450,671), Jay's Table p,1:53 ($433,695), Tawnee Herbert p,2,1:57.4f, 3,T1:53.2 ($373,247), Ruthellenkillean p,2,1:56.1h; 3,1:53.2 ($391,998), who set a Canadian record on a half-mile track, Ever Running p,1:52.3-'98 ($334,813) and Debbielynnkillean p,2,2:00h; 3,1:55.4f ($333,767).

In the speed department, Run The Table's fastest performer is Magnetic Killean p,1:50.2-'98 ($178,566), followed by Goldenshot Killean p,1:51.3 ($309,047) and Twin B Reno p,4,1:51.3 ($212,848), Instant Offense p,3,1:52f ($237,623) and Superstar Killean p,3,Q1:52-'98 ($229,731).

Analysis

Run The Table is a very interesting stallion since he is by a Meadow Skipper son who has not sired any other successful stallion to date. In addition, his dam is a product of the Best Of All/Dancer Hanover cross which is also not a mainstream cross. Thus Run The Table is able to match very well with most broodmares and has been successful with a wide variety of bloodline crosses and mares with and without good racing or production records. He also seems to have the ability to "move up" mares by siring their best foals. These are all qualities to look for in a stallion and Run The Table seems to possess them. Detractors may say that his offspring are only successful in Canada, but I suspect they can excel in any arena if given the opportunity.

I examined the six-generation pedigree crosses of Run The Table's top performers and was not able to find too many common threads other than the fact that he likes plenty of Good Time blood in the dams of his offspring. Bret Hanover is also a significant factor since five of his eight richest offspring have Bret in the dam's pedigree - two through Legal Notice, two through High Ideal and one through Warm Breeze.

Cathedra is 3x4 to Meadow Skipper and 4x3 to Tar Heel, while Elegant Killean is 4x4 to Tar Heel as their closest common crosses. Heatherjeankillean has a 3x4 cross to the half-brother and sister Meadow Skipper and Countess Vivian. Rabbi Of Racing, Run The Table's richest son, is replete with eye-opening crosses. He is also 3x4 to the half-brother and sister Meadow Skipper and Countess Vivian, is 4x5x4 to Good Time and 4x4 to Good Time's full sister Our Time. His second dam is inbred 3x2 to Good Time and his sister Our Time. Another rich son, Treecoscious, is bred 4x4 to Good Time.

The most inbred of Run The Table's successful performers is the filly Reef The Table. She is inbred 2x2 to the half-brothers Landslide and Silent Majority, both sons of the mare Hobby Horse Tar; and she's 3x3 to Tar Heel. Another with an inbred cross is the mare Tawnee Herbert who is from a Meadow Skipper mare and, thus, inbred 3x2 to that great sire.

Another interesting sidelight is the appearance of Good Time's fine son Columbia George as the sire of the second dam in the listing of Run The Table's fastest performers. His fastest offspring, Magnetic Killean, is from a Nihilator mare who is from a Columbia George mare. Magnetic's dam is also a half-sister to the dam of the great mare Stienam and this indicates what Run The Table can do with top bloodlines. The fast Run The Table brother and sister, Moonlight Graham p,4,1:52.1f ($168,635) and Dawn's First Lady p,4,1:53 ($170,948) are from a Precious Fella mare who is from a Columbia George mare. Again, we see the Good Time connection.

Only time will tell, but Run The Table could be the real thing. He is off to a good start and the offspring of the best mares bred to him should race during the next two years. This will be the real test. He is an interesting sire and certainly a natural if you are racing in the Ontario program. And, I think he will make his presence felt in Grant Circuit events.

Run The Table

Photo courtesy of Killean Acres

Leading Progeny by Run The Table

Fastest
- Magnetic Killean, h, p,1:50.2 $178,566
- Goldenshot Killean, g, p,1:51.3 $309,047
- Twin B Reno, h, p,4,1:51.3 $212,848
- Instant Offense, h, p,3,1:52f $237,623
- Superstar Killean, h, p,3,Q1:52 $229,731
- Elegant Killean, m, p,3,1:52.1 $720,494
- Moonlight Graham, g, p,4,1:52.1f $168,635
- Take Home The Gold, g, p,4,1:52.2 $172,256
- Fancy Table, m, p,1:52.2 $125,838
- Cathedra, m, p,3,1:52.3 $733,789

Richest
- Rabbi Of Racing, h, p,3,1:52.4 $737,208
- Cathedra, m, p,3,1:52.3 $733,789
- Heatherjeankillean, m, p,4,1:53.1 $732,489
- Elegant Killean, m, p,3,1:52.1 $720,494
- Treecoscious, h, p,1:52.4 $496,342
- Reef The Table m, p,2,1:57.3f $450,671
- Jay's Table, m, p,1:53 $433,695
- Ruthellenkillean, m, p,3,1:53.2 $391,998
- Tawnee Herbert, m, p,3,T1:53.2 $373,247
- Ever Running, m, p,1:52.3 $334,813

Run The Table, Bay Horse, 16.2 Hands, 1984
p, 2, 1:55; 3, 1:51 ($1,171,053)

Sire/Dam	2nd Gen	3rd Gen	4th Gen	5th Gen	6th Gen
Landslide, 1978 p, 3, 1:54.1 $162,835	Meadow Skipper, 1960 p, 3, 1:55.1 $428,057	Dale Frost, 1951 p, 1:58 $204,117	**HAL DALE**, 1926 p, 6, 2:02¼	Abbedale	**THE ABBE** / Daisydale D.
				Margaret Hal	Argot Hal / Margaret Polk
			Galloway, 1939 p, 2:04½h $5,294	Raider	**PETER VOLO** / Nelda Dillon
				Bethel	David Guy / Annotation
		Countess Vivian, 1950 p, 3, 1:59 $43,262	King's Counsel, 1940 p, 6, 1:58 $44,930	**VOLOMITE**	**PETER VOLO** / Cita Frisco
				Margaret Spangler	**GUY AXWORTHY** / Maggie Winder
			Filly Direct, 1941 p, 3, 2:06¾ $6,299	**BILLY DIRECT**	Napoleon Direct / Gay Forbes
				Calumet Edna	**PETER THE BREWER** / Broncho Queen
	Hobby Horse Tar, 1964	Tar Heel, 1948 p, 4, T1:57 $119,148	**BILLY DIRECT**, 1934 p, 4, T1:55 $12,040	Napoleon Direct	Walter Direct / Lady Erectress
				Gay Forbes	Malcolm Forbes / Gay Girl Chimes
			Leta Long, 1940 p, 4, 2:03¾ $9,321	**VOLOMITE**	**PETER VOLO** / Cita Frisco
				Rosette	Mr. McElwyn / Rose Scott
		Wilellen, 1955 p, 3, 2:04.2h $16,994	Wilmington, 1938 p, 4, T1:59½ $7,988	Bert Abbe	**THE ABBE** / Miss Ella H.
				Miss Saginaw	Colonel Armstrong / Miss Adioo
			Willola, 1941 2:11¼h $299	Willglow	San Francisco / Worthy Spirit
				Romola	The Senator / May Dodge
Hustler's Best, 1974 p, 3, Q2:04.3h $37,805	Best Of All, 1964 p, 4, 1:56.2 $549,074	Good Time, 1946 p, 1:57.4 $318,792	**HAL DALE**, 1926 p, 6, 2:02¼	Abbedale	**THE ABBE** / Daisydale D.
				Margaret Hal	Argot Hal / Margaret Polk
			On Time, 1938 p, 3, 2:03½h $1,472	**VOLOMITE**	**PETER VOLO** / Cita Frisco
				Nedda Guy	**GUY AXWORTHY** / Nedda
		Besta Hanover, 1952	Knight Dream, 1945 p, 3, T1:59 $76,973	Nibble Hanover	Calumet Chuck / Justissima
				Lydia Knight	**PETER THE BREWER** / Guy Rosa
			Bertha Hanover, 1930 3, 2:08¾	Guy McKinney	**GUY AXWORTHY** / Queenly McKinney
				Miss Bertha Dillon	Dillon Axworthy / Miss Bertha C
	Hustling Thru, 1967 p, 3, 2:06h $6,034	Dancer Hanover, 1957 p, 4, T1:56.4 $87,746	Adios, 1940 p, T1:57½ $33,329	**HAL DALE**	Abbedale / Margaret Hal
				Adioo Volo	Adioo Guy / Sigrid Volo
			The Old Maid, 1945	Guy Abbey	**GUY AXWORTHY** / Abbacy
				Spinster	Spencer / Minnetonka
		Yankeetone, 1959 p, 4, 2:09h $3,393	Yankee Scott, 1950 p, 6, 1:59.4 $42,329	Scotland	Peter Scott / Roya McKinney
				Yankee Maid	**VOLOMITE** / Elizabeth
			Toneworthy, 1951 3, T2:04.2 $10,263	Worthy Boy	**VOLOMITE** / Warwell Worthy
				True Tone	Guy Day / Allegro

Shadow Wave

Few winners of the Little Brown Jug can lay claim to the fact that they were unraced at two. Shadow Wave was such a horse. The often unsound son of Adios laid claim to one of pacing's biggest prizes for trainer-driver Joe O'Brien in winning the 1958 Little Brown Jug. In the process, he defeated a talent-laden field that included Bye Bye Byrd, Thorpe Hanover, O'Brien Hanover and Harry's Dream, all major headliners of that era.

The lanky, attractive chestnut was bred by Castleton Farm and raced for Saul Camp of California, a longtime O'Brien patron and one of the leading Grand Circuit owners of that era (he also owned leading trotter Scott Frost--first winner of trotting's Triple Crown). Shadow Wave was easy to spot on the track, since he had four distinctive white stockings and a prominent blaze down the middle of his face. He also wore distinctive white sheepskin on his leather hobbles, and he cut quite a dashing picture as he rolled to 20 victories in his only season at the races.

Shadow Wave won his Little Brown Jug the hard way, circling the field from post position twelve in the opening heat, recording a 2:01 score over Thorpe Hanover and O'Brien Hanover. It remains one of the few occasions a Jug heat has been won from a second tier starting post.

Shadow Wave also captured the Reynolds Memorial and the American Pacing Classic at Hollywood Park during his three-year-old season, winning $91,881 in 31 starts. He also had two seconds and five thirds in his only year at the races. He took a mark of 1:56.3 and headed to stud duty at Almahurst Farm in Kentucky.

Sire Line

Shadow Wave was a son of Adios, and was from Adios' sixth crop. It should be remembered that Adios went to stud late (by contemporary standards) and was already 18 years old the year that Shadow Wave won the Jug. Adios never had a lot of foals, and what he accomplished with them was remarkable. Shadow Wave, a foal of 1955, was one of many sons of Adios that dominated North American pacing from the period beginning in 1952 and extending to the late 1960's, a period closed out by Adios' best son, the remarkable Bret Hanover, a foal of 1962.

Maternal Line

Shadow Wave's dam, Shadow Grattan p,4,2:07.1h, was by Silent Grattan p,T2:09¾, and the second dam was the Abbedale mare, Peacedale p,2,2:17h. Silent Grattan, the broodmare sire of Shadow Wave, had little impact on the breed overall, but had some other bright moments as well. His daughter Virginia Grattan is one of the breed's noted producers, as she was the dam of the good pacers Silent Byrd p,3,1:58 and Jimmy Creed p,T1:59.4. Virginia Grattan founded a maternal family of pacers still active in the late 1990's. Silent Grattan, a veritable modern unknown, was a 1921 son of Grattan Royal, a grandson of Wilkes Boy, and great-grandson of George Wilkes, one of the prominent early sons of Hambletonian whose male line produced the early pacing champions Dan Patch and Single G., but which has vanished from the modern pacing landscape. A branch of the George Wilkes siring family that produced trotting stars Florican, Songcan, Nearly Perfect and Sierra Kosmos is the only remnant of the once prominent George Wilkes legacy.

Progeny of Note

Shadow Wave, like his own sire, never had a lot of foals. In 14 years in the stud between 1960 and 1973, he sired but 524 foals, an average of just 37 foals per year. Despite this, his production record is a good one. He produced more than 400 starters and more than 350 were winners of some $15.1 million, an average of just over $36,000 per starter, which was good by the standard of 1960's purses. His notoriety came late in life, and nearly half his foals were produced in the last five years of his stud career. For example, he had 240 foals in his last three full crops, including 94 in 1970 and 91 in 1971. However, his last foals were produced in 1973.

Race Record Highlights

At 3

1st American Pacing Classic
　　Reynolds Memorial
　　Little Brown Jug
　　Messenger S. Consolation

2nd Matron S.

3rd Governor's Cup
　　Geers S.
　　leg of American Pacing Classic
　　heat of Reading Futurity

Honors

Set world record for three-year-old pacers

Photo courtesy of The Horseman and Fair World

Shadow Wave

Race Record

Year	Age	Starts	Wins	2nd	3rd	Earnings	Record
1958	3	31	20	2	5	$ 91,881	p,3,1:56.3
		31	20	2	5	$91,881	p,3,1:56.3

Shadow Wave

This late production record must be examined against his painfully slow start in the stud. In his first five years at stud, he had fewer than 70 foals! And no stars came from his early foals. His first accomplished pacer was the Chicago star Shady Counsel p,3,1:58.1 ($315,014), a foal of 1964, in Shadow Wave's fifth crop. His first major star, and his leading money-winning offspring, was the Canadian champion Super Wave p,1:57f ($481,370), a foal of 1966 from Shadow Wave's seventh crop. Springfield p,1:57.3 ($402,746), a full brother to Super Wave, followed a couple of years later. Shadow Wave then developed a reputation as the sire of tough, hard-hitting raceway horses, including the likes of Pacing Boy p,1:57.4f ($480,451), Ken's Shadow p,1:57.4f ($358,477) and Dangerous Wave p,2:00h ($325,375). One of his more exciting racing sons was the handsome Invincible Shadow p,1:56.1f ($252,069), winner, like his sire, of the American Pacing Classic at Hollywood Park. A little-known son, Shadow's Finale p,3,1:59.4f, sired the $1 million winner Incredible Finale p, 4,1:53.2f, now a siring star in Illinois.

Two of Shadow Wave's most noted racing fillies were Saucy Wave p,3,1:59.3h ($246,095) and Real Hilarious p,4,1:58.3f ($191,110), two major Grand Circuit stars of their era, who became solid broodmares in their own right. Saucy Wave's family includes the fast Cam Fella horse Exotic Earl p,1:50.2 ($618,585), who is from Saucy Wave's Niatross daughter Armbro Exotic. Real Hilarious founded the family that led to world champion Die Laughing p,3,1:51.1f ($2,164,386). Die Laughing is a son of No Nukes from Makin Smiles, an Albatross daughter of Real Hilarious. As a broodmare sire, Shadow Wave has produced more than 1,300 offspring, with nearly 450 2:00 credits. His most successful broodmare credit is that his daughter Tiny Wave produced Big Towner p,4,1:54.4, one of the quality sires of the 1980's and 1990's. Another important horse with a Shadow Wave dam was the quick Oil Burner p,3,1:54.4; 4,1:54.2 ($535,541), the sire of No Nukes.

Another noted daughter, and a mare appearing prominently in a number of high-profile pedigrees, is the modern-day foundation mare Shifting Sands, whose two daughters, Shifting Scene and Whispering Sands, founded a dynamic maternal family which has had great success in the 1980's and 1990's.

Analysis

One of the great sons of Adios, Shadow Wave excelled both on the racetrack and in the breeding shed. In addition, his bloodlines have carried forward successfully for generations and will continue to do so into the next century.

Shadow Wave died at 18 years of age and in his 12 full years at stud had over 90 foals just twice. For a stallion who had only 524 foals during his career, 80 percent of which were starters, Shadow Wave has made a solid impact on the Standardbred breed through his influence in the pedigrees of several of today's top stallions and through the successful broodmare production of many of his daughters.

When you consider that Shadow Wave is prominent in the pedigrees of such sires as No Nukes and his sons, Big Towner and his sons, Falcon Almahurst, On The Road Again and the good Illinois sire Incredible Finale, you can see his impact. In addition, new stallions like Armbro Operative, Falcon's Future, Northern Luck and Pacific Rocket also carry Shadow Wave blood and could be in the forefront of the next generation of top sires.

Shadow Wave sired 53 2:00 performers, during the years when that time meant something, and had 40 $100,000 winners to his credit. The closest common cross in Shadow Wave's pedigree is an inbred 3x3 to Abbedale who is the sire of the great stallion Hal Dale. Two of Shadow Wave's most outstanding performers were the full brothers Super Wave p,1:57f ($481,370) and Springfield p,1:57.3 ($402,746) who were bred 4x4 to Abbedale while their dam Savilla Song (by Victory Song) was inbred 3x3 to the great early sire Peter Volo. Shadow Wave's richest daughter is Saucy Wave p,3,1:59.3h and she is also 4x4 to Abbedale while her dam in linebred 4x4 to Peter Volo. Another top son of Shadow Wave with an interesting cross is Shadow Star p,3,1:59.2f ($243,439) who is 3x4 to Hal Dale and has a second dam inbred 3x3 to Volomite.

I am focusing on these connections to Peter Volo, his son Volomite and grandson Victory Song for a reason. During the 1960's, which represented most of Shadow Wave's stallion career, many of the mares available to stallions were from families which were just converting from trotting to pacing. Many of those were from sires who produced well with both gaits - Volomite, his sons Worthy Boy and Victory Song, Nibble Hanover, Dean Hanover and others. In fact, four of Shadow Wave's eight $250,000 winners were from trotting bred mares - two by Victory Song, one by Rodney and one by Dial. Extending this list to those 26 $150,000 winners, we see 10 of the 26 performers having dams by trotting sires.

Another thing to consider is that because Shadow Wave's sire, Adios, was the dominant stallion in the industry during the mid-1950's to the mid-1960's Shadow Wave could not have access to his daughters. Tar Heel mares were just becoming popular during the latter part of Shadow Wave's stud career and Gene Abbe mares were only beginning to make an impact. Considering this, you can see why Shadow Wave's top performers came from mares by sires like Victory Song, Diamond Hal, Scottish Pence, King's Counsel, H.D. Hanover, Dial, Rodney, Painter, Sampson Hanover, Lusty Song, Keystoner, Red Streak, Majestic Hanover, Empire Hanover and Waycross. Only Victory Song, King's Counsel and Rodney went on to renown as top broodmare sires. This points to the fact that Shadow Wave, like his sire Adios, was able to "move up" the mares to which he was bred.

There are a number of top horses who have two crosses to Shadow Wave within their first four generations. They include Die Laughing p,3,1:51.1f ($2,164,386), J C's Suprimo p,4,1:50.4 ($487,797), Nuclear Siren p,3,1:50.1 ($417,744) and Shadow Dance p,1:49.4 ($654,473).

Shadow Wave has had a second, and even greater, career as a broodmare sire. His daughters have produced over 445 2:00 performers, over 50 in 1:55 and seven $500,000 winners. Shadow Wave's two fastest broodmare credits are Ludicrous p,1:51.3 ($318,795) and Thirty G's p,1:51.3 ($265,013) - both sired by Nihilator. Also in the top five fastest is Condor Almahurst p,4,1:52.4 by Nihilator.

As expected, Shadow Wave's daughters had great success with Meadow Skipper and his sons. Shadow Wave mares clicked with Meadow Skipper to produce Falcon Almahurst p,3,T1:52.2 ($400,776) and his sister Robin Almahurst p,3,1:56.1 ($113,304) along with Rashad p,4,1:52.3 ($374,329). Most Happy Fella and Shadow Wave mares were an especially prolific pedigree cross and have sparked success for several generations. A few examples of this success story are Oil Burner p,4,1:54.2 ($535,541) (sire of No Nukes), Happy Motoring p,3,1:56.2 ($538,495) (sire of On The Road Again), Armbro Evita p,2,T1:56.4 ($310,161), Sammy Blue Chip p,1:53.3f ($459,307) and New York New York p,1:53 ($169,171).

With Shadow Wave mares Niatross sired Cash Asset p,3,1:53.3 ($400,267), Niafirst p,2,1:54.4 ($272,193) and Dazzle Almahurst p,3,T1:56.4. The other $500,000 winners credited to Shadow Wave broodmares are Meadowlands Pace winner Hilarion p,3,1:54.1 ($775,114) (by Strike Out); Midas Almahurst p,1:54.1 ($556,829) (by High Ideal); Big Towner p,4,1:54.4 ($547,129) (by Gene Abbe); Sweetheart S. winner Shannon Fancy p,2,1:55.4 ($589,583) and Apollo's Way p,3,1:56 ($502,536) (by Nero).

It is also interesting to note that when Shadow Wave mares were bred back to Adios-line stallions, there were success stories like Hilarion, Midas Almahurst and Siren Almahurst p,T1:55.4 (dam of No Nukes' co-fastest performer Nuclear Siren. All are inbred 3x3 to Adios.

As you can see, Shadow Wave's influence is great and has been so for several generations. If for nothing else, Shadow Wave would have had a place in history for siring the dams of such fine stallions as Big Towner, Oil Burner and Falcon Almahurst. He certainly has added strength to pedigrees and is a very positive influence.

Shadow Wave

Photo courtesy of The Horseman and Fair World

Leading Progeny by Shadow Wave

Fastest
- Invincible Shadow, h, p,1:56.1f $252,069
- Kay Wave, h, p,3,T1:56.1 $200,455
- Super Wave, h, p,1:57f $481,370
- Dart Almahurst, h, p,3,1:57.2 $56,312
- Springfield, h, p,1:57.3 $402,746
- Preston Almahurst, h, p,4,1:57.3f $286,277
- Shadow Dan, g, p,1:57.3 $176,117
- Castashadow, g, p,1:57.3 $169,235
- Gulliver, h, p,4,T1:57.3 $124,447
- Shadow Almahurst, h, p,T1:57.3 $100,871

Richest
- Super Wave, h, p,1:57f $481,370
- Pacing Boy, h, p,1:57.4f $480,451
- Springfield, h, p,1:57.3 $402,746
- Ken's Shadow, h, p,1:57.4f $358,477
- Dangerous Wave, g, p,2:00.2h $325,375
- Shady Counsel, h, p,3,1:58.1 $315,014
- Preston Almahurst, h, p,4,1:57.3f $286,277
- Invincible Shadow, h, p,1:56.1f $252,069
- Saucy Wave, m, p,3,1:59.3h $246,095
- Shadow Star, h, p,3,1:59.2f $243,439

Shadow Wave, Chestnut Horse, 1955
p, 3, 1:56.3 ($91,931)

Adios, 1940 p, T1:57½ $33,329	Hal Dale, 1926 p, 6, 2:02¼	**ABBEDALE**, 1917 p, 2:01¼	The Abbe, 1903 p, 2:04	Chimes	Electioneer Beautiful Bells
				Nettie King	Mambrino King Nettie Murphy
			Daisydale D., 1908 3, 2:15¼	Archdale	Expedition Aline
				Mrs. Tmolus	Pactolus Flaxey
		Margaret Hal, 1914 p, 2:19½h	Argot Hal, 1903 p, T2:04¾	Brown Hal	**TOM HAL JNR** Lizzie
				Lady Wildflower	Duplex Sally Ward
			Margaret Polk, 1906	John R. Gentry	Ashland Wilkes Dame Wood
				Stella Hal	**TOM HAL JNR** Dolly
	Adioo Volo, 1930 p, 3, 2:05h	Adioo Guy, 1910 p, 2:00¾	Guy Dillon, 1902 T2:21¼	**SIDNEY DILLON**	Sidney Venus
				By Guy	**GUY WILKES** **BY BY**
			ADIOO, 1895	**GUY WILKES**	**GEORGE WILKES** Lady Bunker
				BY BY	Nutwood Rapidan
		Sigrid Volo, 1921 p, T2:04	Peter Volo, 1911 4, 2:02	Peter The Great	Pilot Medium Santos
				Nervolo Belle	Nervolo Josephine Knight
			Polly Parrot, 1904 p, 2:13¼h	Jersey B B	Jersey Wilkes Blue Belle
				Lady Maud C	Chitwood Noretta
Shadow Grattan, 1943 p, 4, 2:07.1h $2,555	Silent Grattan, 1921 p, T2:09¾	Grattan Royal, 1908 p, 2:06¼	Grattan, 1887 2:13	Wilkes Boy	**GEORGE WILKES** Betty Brown
				Annie Almont	Hamlin's Almont Jnr Bandella
			Mona, 1887	Robert McGregor	Major Edsall Nancy Whitman
				Jenny Bryan	John Dillard II Old Den
		Silent T., 1913 2:10¾	Silent Brook, 1890 4, 2:16½	Dark Night	
				Jenny Clay	
			Agave, 1895 2:14¼h	**AXTELL**	William L Lou
				Nutilla	
	Peacedale, 1936 p, 2, 2:17h $45	**ABBEDALE**, 1917 p, 2:01¼	The Abbe, 1903 p, 2:04	Chimes	Electioneer Beautiful Bells
				Nettie King	Mambrino King Nettie Murphy
			Daisydale D., 1908 3, 2:15¼	Archdale	Expedition Aline
				Mrs. Tmolus	Pactolus Flaxey
		Miss Dorothy Dillon, 1920 p, 2, 2:17h	Dillon Axworthy, 1910 3, 2:10¼	Axworthy	**AXTELL** Marguerite
				Adioo Dillon	**SIDNEY DILLON** **ADIOO**
			Zulu Belle, 1906 p, 2:06¼	Petrigrew	
				Johannah Treat	

Sonsam

It is a rare horse who can run a single race in his career that is so memorable it sustains his presence in the minds of horsemen and observers for years afterwards. One of those horses is Sonsam.

The winning move he made in the 1979 Meadowlands Pace remains one of the most electric moments in the history of that great race, and certainly must rank near the top of anyone's list of the best performances ever. Sonsam was racing off the pace in the Meadowlands Pace final, and Hot Hitter and company were up front slugging it out through fast, early fractions. But Sonsam was impatient and wanted to go, and although he was in the outside tier, he was not advancing. Trainer-driver George Sholty decided, nearing the entry to the last turn, to give his exciting charge what he wanted. He boldly swung Sonsam three wide just past the half and rolled dramatically to the front in a sweeping, dynamic move that left the rest of the field and Meadowlands announcer Ed Gorman breathless. Sonsam then tacked on a :28 finishing panel to record a stakes record 1:53.2 mile. It was the kind of move seldom, if ever, seen in a major race; if you saw it, you would never forget it.

Sonsam was a foal of 1976, from the third crop of his sire, Albatross. An exciting, handsome and good-gaited two-year-old, Sonsam won 14 of 17 as a freshman, taking victories in such events as the Geers, Meadow Lands Farm, Almahurst Farm, a heat of the Fox Stake, a heat of the Review Futurity, a heat of the International Stallion Stake, and a Pennsylvania Sires at The Meadows. He was Two-Year-Old Pacer of the Year in 1978, racing for owner-breeders Barry and Irving Epstein. The Epsteins had bred the young champion, as he was from their stakes-winning Bret Hanover mare, Princess Sam p,3,1:59.1 ($76,665). His first year mark was 1:54.2 taken at The Red Mile in a performance where he clearly could have gone much faster. He had the kind of gait, power, presence and maturity seldom seen in two-year-olds. Sonsam was the fastest colt of his crop and was syndicated for $3,000,000 - the most expensive two-year-old of any breed at that time.

At three, Sonsam's thunderous Meadowlands Pace victory was added to scores in the Gaines Memorial, Hanover-Hempt and Battle of Brandywine before a sesamoid fracture sent him to the sidelines in mid-season. He won eight of only 14 starts at three, adding $573,456 to his freshman earnings to bring his two-year total past $820,000. When his season and career ended, there was much speculation about how fast he could have paced if the skeletal injury had not prematurely ended his career. It was clear to all that there was a lot of gas left in the can when he retired to stud duty at Pine Hollow Stud Farm in New York with a reputation as one of the fastest pacers yet produced.

Two of the sport's greatest trainer/drivers had special comments about Sonsam:

George Sholty said, "I always thought he could go in 1:50, but he never got there, so you can never tell. That might have come at Springfield, DuQuoin or Lexington, but he never made it that far." And Billy Haughton commented, "I'll never forget the night he circled those horses on the turn in the Meadowlands Pace. He went by them like they were standing still. I don't know if I ever saw a horse go by stakes colts that fast."

Sire Line

Sonsam is by Albatross, from the third crop of the top young sire of that day, and is a grandson of Meadow Skipper. The late 1970's and early 1980's were heady times for this sire line, as they came to dominate all of North American pacing, burying their contemporary sires in a wave of speed and power never before seen in the industry. For a brief time, Sonsam was the center of the wave.

Maternal Line

Part of Sonsam's attraction to breeders was the fact that he was not only a handsome, strong, good-gaited colt, but that he also possessed a royal maternal background. His dam was the stakes-winning Bret Hanover mare Princess Sam p,3,1:59.1 and he was from a Castleton

Race Record Highlights

At 2

1st Geers S.
Meadow Lands Farm S.
Almahurst Farm S.
heat of Fox S.
heat of Review Futurity
heat of International Stallion S.
Pennsylvania Sires S.

2nd Woodrow Wilson Pace
George M. Patchen S.

At 3

1st Meadowlands Pace
Gaines Memorial
Hanover-Hempt S.
Battle of Brandywine

2nd heat of Cane Pace
Battle of Brandywine Elimination
Meadowlands Pace Elimination

3rd heat of Adios S.

Honors

At three, set world record for three-year-old pacers on mile track

At two, voted Two-Year-Old Pacing Colt of the Year

Sonsam

Photo by Tony Leonard
Courtesy of The Horseman and Fair World

Race Record

Year	Age	Starts	Wins	2nd	3rd	Earnings	Record
1978	2	17	14	2	0	$246,648	p,2,1:54.2
1979	3	14	8	3	1	573,456	p,3,1:53.2
		31	22	5	1	$820,104	p,3,1:53.2

Sonsam

Farm family long noted for the production of quality pacers. This is the immediate family of the famed world champion pacing filly Good Counsel p,3,1:57, since Sonsam's second dam, Laurel Princess p,3,2:05.4 was a full sister to Good Counsel.

Princess Sam's first foal was the stakes-winning Albatross filly Mistral Sam p,3,T1:57 ($41,197), and Sonsam was her first colt. She also produced Samadhi, a non-record son of Meadow Skipper who, without much opportunity, sired the superb colt pacer Jake And Elwood p,4,1:50.4 ($2,273,187). Another sister to Sonsam, the ruggedly made Sonsamette p,3,1:58.2 ($16,111), also raced well. Princess Sam never came close to duplicating the superb quality of Sonsam in her 11 other foals. Only five of the 11 were by Albatross, and four of them were 2:00 performers. This family, once one of the strongest in the breed, is one of those maternal families that for some reason has fallen on hard times. There are no current, modern-day champions tracing their lineage to this immediate family, although it is the kind of class that certainly could reappear in a few generations.

Sonsam, like many of his successful contemporaries, featured the cross of a Bret Hanover mare on Albatross. This cross, one of the most dominant in the history of the breed, combined the gait and speed of the Albatross line with the power and physical quality of the Bret Hanover dams. Sonsam's pedigree is full of the blood of Hal Dale. Albatross is himself linebred to Hal Dale 3x4, and Princess Sam, the dam of Sonsam, is inbred 3x3 to Hal Dale. The resultant pedigree produced a 4x5x4x4 cross to Hal Dale in Sonsam's lineage, a forerunner of developments in the modern pacer which followed him.

Progeny of Note

Sonsam's stallion career began with as much excitement as any stallion of recent memory. First, there was the memory of his own unfulfilled potential as a racehorse. And, in 1982, when his first foals were yearlings, they created the kind of enthusiastic response from owners and trainers normally reserved for Horse of the Year types. Part of the warm response was because Sonsam produced such good-looking, mature yearlings. They really were handsome, even awesome. And when his first crop of two-year-olds produced the world champion filly Hit Parade p,2,1:53.4 and the Fox Stake winner Radiant Ruler p,2,1:54.4, Sonsam appeared headed for a successful stallion career that would finally fulfill the great promise that he had himself shown on the track.

Sonsam followed his strong opening act with more talent. His gifted son Marauder, a foal of 1982, raced against the mighty Nihilator. He even defeated Nihilator in a heat of The Adios, and subsequently won that great stakes event when Nihilator pulled out of the second heat. Marauder got a p,3,1:52.1f mark winning the Adios, and he earned $683,138.

The 1982 crop also produced The Denman p,4,1:52 ($468,927) and Discotheque p,3,1:52.4 ($346,075). The 1983 crop was topped by the now successful Ohio sire Nobleland Sam p,3,1:53 ($451,417). Subsequent crops featured his richest performer, the Fox Stake winner Till We Meet Again p,1:52.4 ($1,002,522) and his best filly star since Hit Parade in the sturdy Conquered Quest p,3,1:52.4 ($863,514); his fastest performer, the consistent Bullvon's Dream p,1:50.2 ($842,960), and Marvel p,1:54.2f ($596,795). There were other moments in the sun for Sonsam. He also produced the fast Courageous Legacy p,3,1:52.2 and the fast My Melissa p,3,T1:53.3.

Despite this good record of accomplishment, Sonsam's stud career lost the steam which had carried it through the first few years. He never bred big books of mares during his Pine Hollow days (his first foal crop that produced Hit Parade and Radiant Ruler included only 38 foals) and his foals began to develop a reputation for the same kind of skeletal injury that ended his career. Also, Sonsam was not a good breeder; his foal counts were never good compared with the number of mares bred. For example, he bred 108 mares in 1988 and produced a crop of but 59 foals the following spring. In the early 1990's, Sonsam completely fell out of favor with the leading breeders. In the final analysis, despite a solid record of accomplishment, siring the winners of nearly $34 million, he never delivered the big horse. As late as 1996, he bred only 22 mares.

Analysis

Sonsam entered stud service with as much hype as any stallion and was a year older than Niatross. Certainly, Sonsam was thought to be a great son of Albatross who would carry on that male line for his sire - just as Niatross was expected to do later.

Sonsam started off well, but his fall from popularity was precipitated primarily by fertility problems and then a lack of consistency in siring major performers. He's had plenty of stars during his stallion career, but, as with many outstanding horses, the expectations were too great. Now, Sonsam is making his mark as a broodmare sire as his daughters are producing fast and classy performers from a wide range of sires.

The pedigree of Sonsam is interesting in that he is linebred 4x3 Adios, 4x5x4x4 to Hal Dale, 4x4 to Tar Heel - three of the top sires of their era. In addition, Sonsam has two crosses to siblings: 4x4 to the full brothers King's Counsel and Chief Counsel and 5x5 to the half-brother and sister The King Direct and Calumet Edna. We will see later how many of Sonsam's best sons and daughters also have sibling crosses in their pedigrees.

The richest son of Sonsam is Till We Meet Again p,1:52.4 ($1,002,522) who is inbred 3x3 to Meadow Skipper and linebred 4x4 to both Good Time and Tar Heel. He has later sibling crosses of 5x5 to The Old Maid and Lady Scotland and 5x5x5 to King's Counsel and Chief Counsel. Another successful son with a very similar cross is the popular and excellent Ohio sire Nobleland Sam p,3,1:53 ($451,417) who is also 3x3 to Meadow Skipper, 4x4 to Good Time and 5x5x4 to the King's Counsel, Chief Counsel and Blackstone. Others inbred 3x3 to Meadow Skipper include Ahoy Captain p,4,1:53.4 ($430,031), the brothers Royal Majesty p,4,1:54 ($285,390) and First p,1:53.1 ($285,191) and Courageous Legacy p,3,1:52.2 ($183,670).

Sonsam is also an excellent filly sire with 11 of his daughters earning over $200,000. His richest female, Conquered Quest p,3,1:52.4 ($863,514) is bred 5x5x2 to Tar Heel and 4x4 to Volomite - the only one of Sonsam's top performers with that type of cross. Sonsam also "nicked" very well with multiple presences of Bret Hanover in a pedigree. Bullvon's Dream p,1:50.2 ($842,960) is inbred 3x3 to both Bret Hanover and Meadow Skipper; Marauder p,3,1:52.1f ($683,138) is bred 3x3 to the full brothers Bret Hanover and Baron Hanover; the filly Shop Till Ya Drop p,3,1:55.1 ($377,863) is 3x3 to Bret Hanover; and Pan Am Sam p,1:51.4 ($291,429) is 3x3 to Bret Hanover.

Common crosses to siblings show up quite often in the pedigrees of Sonsam's best horses. A good example is the full sister and brother combo of Hit Parade p,2,1:53.4 ($806,303) and Discotheque p,3,1:52.4 ($346,075) whose closest cross is 5x5x2 to Tar Heel along with 4x3 to the half-sisters Miss Tempo and Princess Counsel. This latter aspect is most interesting since their dam is from the same close maternal family of Sonsam. This cross works extremely well; Sonsam's fastest broodmare sire credit is New Bucks p,1:49.3 ($311,721) and he also has a 4x3 cross to Miss Tempo and Princess Counsel.

Sonsam is a very interesting broodmare sire. An examination of the pedigrees of his top broodmare credits indicates that Sonsam mares who are inbred are producing some of the best performers - along with the performers themselves being inbred. Here are some examples: New Bucks (mentioned above), Sonsam's fastest broodmare sire credit, is inbred 3x3 to Albatross and linebred 3x4 to Bret Hanover; Free Spender p,1:50.2 ($196,745) is 4x3 to Meadow Skipper, but his dam is inbred 3x2 to Meadow Skipper; Camtastic Dream p,1:50.4 ($339,192) is inbred 3x3 to Albatross and his dam is inbred 3x2 to Bret Hanover; the fast mare Armbro Nest p,4,1:50.4 ($674,821) is inbred 3x3 to Most Happy Fella and her dam is inbred 3x3 to Meadow Skipper.

The crosses above are present in four of the five fastest broodmare credits for Sonsam and I'm sure it is indicative of a certain pattern of success. The only horse in the top five without any inbreeding is Catch A Flight p,4,1:49.4 ($501,785) and he is linebred 4x4 to Meadow Skipper.

Here are the crosses for a few other top Sonsam broodmare sire credits: Diablo Cedarn p,4,1:51 is 3x3 to Tar Heel and 3x4 to Meadow Skipper; Art's Palace p,4,1:52.1-'98 is inbred 3x3 to Albatross and linebred 4x3 to Columbia George; Kassa Branca p,2,1:52.3 ($743,890) is 4x4x4 to Meadow Skipper and his dam is inbred 3x3 to Meadow Skipper; Lady Buns p,3,1:52.4 ($504,899) is 4x3 to Albatross as is Before Sunrise p,2,1:53 ($416,252) and the outstanding Canadian filly Whenuwishuponastar p,3,1:53.4 $578,752) is 4x4x4 to Meadow Skipper with a dam who is inbred 3x3 to Meadow Skipper.

As you can readily see, Sonsam broodmares seem to like multiple crosses of good blood up close to produce the best colts and fillies. This is a pattern worth considering when you are looking at Sonsam mares or their offspring.

Leading Progeny by Sonsam

Fastest

Bullvon's Dream, h, p,1:50.2 $842,960
Formal Invite, g, p,4,1:51.1 $65,542
Pan Am Sam, h, p,1:51.4 $291,429
The Denman, h, p,4,1:52 $468,927
Marauder, h, p,3,1:52.1f $638,138
Courageous Lady, h, p,3,1:52.2 $183,670
Klassy's Son, g, p,1:52.2 $140,789
Golden Triangle, h, p,1:52.3 $233,686
Armbro Jagger, g, p,3,1:52.3 $197,894
Molecular, g, p,4,1:52.3 $78,020

Richest

Till We Meet Again, h, p,1:52.4 $1,002,522
Conquered Quest, m, p,3,1:52.4 $863,514
Bullvon's Dream, h, p,1:50.2 $842,960
Hit Parade, m, p,2,1:53.4 $806,303
Marauder, h, p,3,1:52.1f $638,138
Marvel, h, p,1:54.2f $596,795
Crimson, g, p,4,1:54.4f $512,983
The Denman, h, p,4,1:52 $468,927
Nobleland Sam, h, p,3,1:53 $451,417
Ahoy Captain, g, p,4,1:53.4 $430,031

Sonsam, Brown Horse, 1976
p, 2, 1:54.2; 3, 1:53.2 ($820,104)

Albatross, 1968 p, 4, 1:54.3f $1,201,470	Meadow Skipper, 1960 p, 3, 1:55.1 $428,057	Dale Frost, 1951 p, 1:58 $204,117	**HAL DALE**, 1926 p, 6, 2:02¼	Abbedale	The Abbe Daisydale D.
				Margaret Hal	Argot Hal Margaret Polk
			Galloway, 1939 p, 2:04½h $5,294	Raider	**PETER VOLO** Nelda Dillon
				Bethel	David Guy Annotation
		Countess Vivian, 1950 p, 3, 1:59 $43,262	King's Counsel, 1940 p, 6, 1:58 $44,930	**VOLOMITE**	**PETER VOLO** Cita Frisco
				MARGARET SPANGLER	**GUY AXWORTHY** Maggie Winder
			Filly Direct, 1941 p, 3, 2:06¾ $6,299	**BILLY DIRECT**	**NAPOLEON DIRECT** Gay Forbes
				Calumet Edna	Peter The Brewer **BRONCHO QUEEN**
	Voodoo Hanover, 1964	Dancer Hanover, 1957 p, 4, T1:56.4 $87,746	**ADIOS**, 1940 p, T1:57½ $33,329	**HAL DALE**	Abbedale Margaret Hal
				Adioo Volo	Adioo Guy Sigrid Volo
			The Old Maid, 1945	Guy Abbey	**GUY AXWORTHY** Abbacy
				Spinster	Spencer Minnetonka
		Vibrant Hanover, 1960	**TAR HEEL**, 1948 p, 4, T1:57 $119,148	**BILLY DIRECT**	**NAPOLEON DIRECT** Gay Forbes
				Leta Long	**VOLOMITE** Rosette
			Vivian Hanover, 1937	Guy McKinney	**GUY AXWORTHY** Queenly McKinney
				Guesswork	Peter The Great Elsie Leyburn
Princess Sam, 1968 p, 3, 1:59.1 $76,665	Bret Hanover, 1962 p, 4, T1:53.3 $922,616	**ADIOS**, 1940 p, T1:57½ $33,329	**HAL DALE**, 1926 p, 6, 2:02¼	Abbedale	The Abbe Daisydale D.
				Margaret Hal	Argot Hal Margaret Polk
			Adioo Volo, 1930 p, 3, 2:05h	Adioo Guy	Guy Dillon Adioo
				Sigrid Volo	**PETER VOLO** Polly Parrot
		Brenna Hanover, 1956 p, 3, T2:01 $21,946	**TAR HEEL**, 1948 p, 4, T1:57 $119,148	**BILLY DIRECT**	**NAPOLEON DIRECT** Gay Forbes
				Leta Long	**VOLOMITE** Rosette
			Beryl Hanover, 1947 p, 2, T2:02 $29,076	Nibble Hanover	Calumet Chuck Justissima
				Laura Hanover	**THE LAUREL HALL** Miss Bertha Worthy
	Laurel Princess, 1963 p, 3, 2:05.4 $525	Good Time, 1946 p, 1:57.4 $318,792	**HAL DALE**, 1926 p, 6, 2:02¼	Abbedale	The Abbe Daisydale D.
				Margaret Hal	Argot Hal Margaret Polk
			On Time, 1938 p, 3, 2:03¼h $1,472	**VOLOMITE**	**PETER VOLO** Cita Frisco
				Nedda Guy	**GUY AXWORTHY** Nedda
		Princess Counsel, 1944 p, 2, T2:06¾	Chief Counsel, 1935 p, 3, T1:57¾ $24,784	**VOLOMITE**	**PETER VOLO** Cita Frisco
				MARGARET SPANGLER	**GUY AXWORTHY** Maggie Winder
			Miss Princess Laurel, 1935 p, 2:01	The King Direct	**NAPOLEON DIRECT** **BRONCHO QUEEN**
				Laurel Queen	**THE LAUREL HALL** Present Queen

Storm Damage

Bred and raised and sold as a yearling by Castleton Farm, Storm Damage seemed destined for a great career from the moment he sprang to his feet beside his royally bred dam Breath O Spring in 1977. He had the look of a champion. He was a big, ruggedly made horse much in the mold of his world champion sire Bret Hanover, and very much unlike his successful half-brother who preceded him, Race Time p,3,1:57. In fact, Castleton had two future stars in their paddocks along Ironworks Pike in Lexington at that time, since Tyler B was also foaled the same spring at the famed Kentucky breeding farm.

Sold as a yearling in 1978, Storm Damage was haltered for $70,000 by Michigan trainer Jerry Smith at Tattersalls. He had a solid two-year-old season in 1979, winning the Fox Stake for Billy Haughton, the Arden Downs, Battle of Saratoga and a Kentucky Sires Stake at Lexington. He also won a heat of the Review Futurity at Springfield and was second in the Matron at Wolverine in Michigan. Storm Damage was a big, attractive colt, a light bay in color, who developed into a dynamic pacer. That year, Storm Damage and Niatross were tied as the fastest colts of their division with 1:55.4 victories.

At three, Storm Damage further matured into a really important horse. Racing now for Hall of Famer Joe O'Brien, he set a world record for a five-eighth mile track of 1:53.2f, winning the Adios at The Meadows. He also won the Hayes Memorial at Du Quoin, a Matron division, two Kentucky Sires Stakes and a Meadowlands Pace elimination. Storm Damage won 11 times at three, and was second six times in a season which saw him win nearly $660,000. The only problem Storm Damage faced was that he was foaled the same year as the great Niatross, and in numerous encounters between the two horses, Storm Damage never defeated his arch-rival. He was six times second to the great pacer, in races such as the Meadowlands Pace, Little Brown Jug, Gaines Memorial and Oliver Wendell Holmes finals. It was a frustrating chase that nevertheless endeared Storm Damage to many observers because he was clearly a good horse who tried mightily.

Storm Damage was also one of the most successful racing sons of his sire, Bret Hanover, and with his royal pedigree, he returned to his breeder Castleton Farm for stud duty at their satellite New York farm.

Sire Line

Storm Damage was from the tenth crop of his illustrious sire Bret Hanover, and was therefore a grandson of the great Adios, continuing the success story enjoyed by this dynamic sire line. Both his sire and grandsire are profiled in this book.

Maternal Line

Storm Damage's female pedigree is one of the best in the sport. His dam, the Worthy Boy mare Breath O Spring, was 24 years old the spring she foaled him since she was a foal of 1953. Breath O Spring needs no introduction to most observers, since she is a member of the Lady Scotland branch of the vast Minnehaha maternal family. This is one of pacing's strongest maternal clans, as Breath O Spring produced not only Race Time, but also his full sister, Touch Of Spring, who was the dam of the world champion race horse and sire, Warm Breeze p,4,1:53.1. It is also a family noted for its female class. Another full sister to Race Time, the 1964 foal Charming Time, was the dam of the world champion filly Impatiens p,3,1:56, and is the second dam of the noted racing fillies Follow My Star p,4,T1:52.3 ($1,537,503) and So Cozy p,3,1:54.2 ($880,492). This is the same immediate maternal family that also produced the fastest pacing female in history, Caesar's Jackpot p,4,T1:49.4, still the only female to beat 1:50. A horse could hardly have a more royal pedigree.

Progeny of Note

Standing in New York with his get eligible to the rich New York Sire Stakes, Storm Damage's stud career began with strong support from most of the sport's leading breeders. Since his own sire Bret Hanover had become such a dominant broodmare sire, Storm Damage's daughters were pursued by the major breeders as well, who hoped they would become producing matrons for years to come.

Race Record Highlights

At 2
1st Fox S.
Battle of Saratoga
Arden Downs S.
Kentucky Sires S.
Matron S.
heat of Review Futurity
2nd heat of Fox S.
heat of Review Futurity

At 3
1st Adios S.
Hayes Memorial
Matron S.
two Kentucky Sires S.
Meadowlands Pace Elimination
heat of T.W. Murphy Memorial
2nd Meadowlands Pace Final
Oliver Wendell Holmes S.
Little Brown Jug
Gaines Memorial
Cane Pace
3rd Hanover-Hempt S.

Honors

Co-fastest two-year-old (with Niatross) of 1979
Set world record over five-eighth mile track

Storm Damage

Photo by Tony Leonard
Courtesy of Castleton Farm

Race Record

Year	Age	Starts	Wins	2nd	3rd	Earnings	Record
1979	2	14	7	2	3	$ 93,556	p,2,1:55.4
1980	3	22	11	6	1	565,740	p,3,1:53.2f
		36	18	8	4	$659,296	p,3,1:53.2f

Storm Damage

The star of Storm Damage's first crop, foals of 1982, was the $1 million winner Ramblin Storm p, 1:50.1 ($1,068,063), as tough and consistent a race horse as ever lived. While Ramblin Storm was excelling, Storm Damage came up with one of the most sensational pacers in history, the dazzling Call For Rain p,4,1:49.3 ($1,065,919), a foal of 1984 and thus from Storm Damage's third crop. Call For Rain is one of the finest race horses the breed has ever produced. A big, burly brute of a horse, Call For Rain raced with, and against, one of the most talented crops of three-year-olds in history, a group which included the likes of Jate Lobell, Laag, Frugal Gourmet and Jaguar Spur. Call For Rain won the Breeders Crown at both three and four, and swept through the tough Graduate Series legs and final. In the same crop as Call For Rain, Storm Damage also produced the two-year-old star Redskin p,2,1:55 ($1,865,702), still the leading money-winning two-year-old pacer in history. Storm Damage had already done something not even his own sire Bret Hanover could do, and that was to sire a $1 million winner. Storm Damage had three from his first three crops.

With such an auspicious beginning, Storm Damage's stud career looked to be fulfilling its exciting promise. Other good Storm Damage offspring were the top filly Storm Tossed p,4,1:53.4f ($969,244); the Grand Circuit winner Concussion p,4,1:54.1 ($780,362); aged Canadian star Soft Light p,4,1:52.3 ($691,220) and the accomplished NYSS star Kick Up A Storm p,3,1:54 ($687,936). In a later crop, Storm Damage produced the stakes colt Keystone Endeavor p,4,1:50 ($757,678). There were other good fillies, too, with Storm Damage proving to be a better sire of race fillies than his famous father. This list included Kittiwake p,1:54.3f ($554,206), Windy Answer p,3,1:54.4 ($531,645) and Electrical Express p,3,1:52.1 ($318,633). As late as 1992, Storm Damage was still breeding more than 200 mares a season.

However, soon after that, the breedings began to fall off precipitously. With the new wave of modern stallions that included Abercrombie and his sons, No Nukes and his sons, and Cam Fella's amazing rise to prominence, Storm Damage was shuffled out of the picture. After breeding more than 200 mares in 1992, his book fell off to less than 100 by 1994, and by 1997, he bred fewer than 40 mares.

Analysis

Storm Damage is a stallion with some of the oldest bloodlines still available for pacers and it is remarkable that he was able to keep up with sires who were several generations ahead. Storm Damage's sire was born in 1962 (Bret Hanover) and his dam in 1953 (Breath O Spring). As we have seen, his dam was 24 years old when she foaled Storm Damage. The second generation goes back even further when you see the dates of Adios (1940), Brenna Hanover (1956), Worthy Boy (1940) and Lady Scotland (1943).

The closest common crosses in Storm Damage's pedigree are 5x3 to Volomite and 5x4 to Peter Volo. To put this in perspective, the second generation dates for Jenna's Beach Boy are 1978, 1977, 1979 and 1979; for Pacific Rocket they are 1975, 1976, 1976 and 1981. So, in terms of pedigree, Storm Damage is three or four generations behind those sires.

Storm Damage has sired three million-dollar winners and 12 half-million dollar winners during his stud career. But time and more horse generations have passed him by and today he is only a marginal stallion. From the list of Storm Damage's 45 highest money winners, only one was foaled after 1991, the good 1992 filly Electrical Express p,2,1:52.1 ($318,633). As you can see, most of the Storm Damage stars, and there were plenty in his day, were foaled in the 1980's.

With no Meadow Skipper blood in his pedigree, Storm Damage was a natural for mares by Meadow Skipper and his sons and this held true with regard to the performance of his offspring. Of Storm Damage's 21 richest performers, 20 are from mares by Meadow Skipper and his sons. Ironically, Redskin p,2,1:55 ($1,865,702), the richest son of Storm Damage, he has no Meadow Skipper blood being from a Best Of All mare. Best Of All appears in four of Storm Damage's dozen richest sons and daughters. In addition to being the sire of the dam of Redskin, Best Of All is the sire of the grandams of Storm Prince p,1:53.1f ($580,139), Kittiwake p,1:54.3f ($554,206) and Windy Answer p,3,1:54..4 ($531,645) - the latter pair being two of Storm Damage's three richest fillies.

In the speed department, the dams of five of Storm Damage's seven fastest performers have a Meadow Skipper line or Tar Heel line cross. Keystone Endeavor p,4,1:50 ($761,928) is Albatross/Tar Heel, Vine Street p,3,1:50.2 ($356,600) is Most Happy Fella/Tar Heel, Storm Compensation p,1:50.3 ($492,220) is Meadow Skipper/Thorpe Hanover and the full brothers Getting Personal p,3,1:50.4 ($320,417) and For The Children p,1:51.1 ($166,488) are from a Nero/Thorpe Hanover mare. In all, 24 of Storm Damage's 25 fastest sons and daughters are from Meadow Skipper line mares; the only exception is Sun Damage p,1:52.1 ($175,688) who is from an Adios Vic mare.

Call For Rain p,4,1:49.3 ($1,065,919), the fastest son of Storm Damage, is from a Meadow Skipper/Bye Bye Byrd cross. He is bred 3x5 to Adios and his sister Adieu and 4x4 to Tar Heel and Hal Dale. Redskin is 4x4 to Hal Dale; Ramblin Storm 3x4 to Adios; the good mare Storm Tossed p,4,1:53.4f ($969,244) is 3x5 to Adios, 3x5x3 to the half-sisters Lady Scotland and The Old Maid, and her dam is inbred 3x2 to the half-brother and sister Dancer Hanover and Timely Hanover. Keystone Endeavor is 3x5x5 to Adios, 4x5x3 to Tar Heel and 3x5 to Lady Scotland and The Old Maid. The mare Windy Answer is 3x5 to Adios and 3x5 to Lady Scotland and The Old Maid - a cross which shows up quite often in the best of Storm Damage.

The good mare Kittiwake has a very interesting pedigree. She is 3x5 to Adios, 4x5x4 to Tar Heel and has additional crosses to top mares - 3x3 to the full sisters Brenna Hanover (dam of Bret Hanover, the sire of Storm Damage) and Buoyant Hanover; and 3x5 to Lady Scotland and The Old Maid. Thus, Storm Damage's three best females all have close crosses to exceptional sibling mares. Another fast performer with a similar cross is Storm Compensation who is 3x4 to Adios, 3x4 to Lady Scotland and The Old Maid and 3x4 to Dale Frost and his sister Jackie Frost. The fast brothers Getting Personal and For The Children are also 3x4 to Adios and 3x4 to Lady Scotland and The Old Maid.

As far as continuing the Bret Hanover male line, Storm Damage was a likely prospect to sire a few sons to carry it on, but this has not yet happened. The high hopes for Call For Rain fell flat when he was not successful at stud and Redskin was even less productive. It appears that Storm Damage's fast and well-bred son Vine Street will be the last hope for Storm Damage to continue his male line. Vine Street stands at stud in Michigan and his first crop will race in 1998.

Although much was expected from Storm Damage as a broodmare sire, he has yet to become a star in that arena. Daughters of Storm Damage have already produced over 500 2:00 performers, but have not been consistently turning out Grand Circuit stars and good, young colts and fillies. To date, the best broodmare sire credit for Storm Damage is likely to be the 1997 star filly Clover Hanover p,2,1:52.2 ($568,994) by No Nukes. She was voted Two-Year-Old Pacing Filly of the Year and could repeat this in 1998.

However, most of Storm Damage's fastest and richest broodmare credits have been with raceway type performers - not the stakes colts and fillies. But there is a certain pattern among his fastest broodmare credits - Storm Damage mares with close crosses to Adios seem to be his best producers. Multiple crosses to Adios were also prominent in the pedigrees of Storm Damage's best race horses.

For example, four of his five fastest broodmare sire credits have this cross. Richey Letsgo p,1:50.4 ($242,743) (by Abercrombie) is bred 4x4x4 to Adios and his Storm Damage mare is inbred 3x3 to Adios; Shogun Hanover p,4,1:51.4f ($419,374) (by Tyler B.) has the same cross - 4x4x4 to Adios with an inbred 3x3 to Adios' dam; Market Report p,4,1:51.3f ($216,525) (by Jate Lobell) has a dam who is very inbred 2x3 to Bret

Storm Damage

Hanover and 3x4 to Adios; and Prince Brian p,3,1:52f ($258,947) (by It's Fritz) is bred 3x3 to Meadow Skipper and has a Storm Damage dam who is 3x4 to Adios. If you are breeding or looking for Storm Damage mares, you may want one with this type of cross to Adios. Another inbred performer, although not to Adios, is Smicker p,4,1:52.1 (by Jate Lobell) whose dam is incestuously inbred 1x3 to the half-brothers Storm Damage and Race Time.

Storm Damage mares have done very well with Tyler B and may also work with some of his sons. Jate Lobell has also been very successful with these mares as have Abercrombie and No Nukes. Storm Damage mares are acceptable, but I think you need to be very selective with the individual and the pedigree.

Leading Progeny by Storm Damage

Fastest
- Call For Rain, h, p,4,1:49.3 $1,065,919
- Keystone Endeavor, h, p,4,1:50 $761,928
- Ramblin Storm, g, p,1:50.1 $1,068,063
- Vine Street, h, p,3,1:50.2 $356,600
- Storm Compensation, h, p,1:50.3 $492,220
- Getting Personal, g, p,3,1:50.4 $320,417
- For The Children, g, p,1:51.1 $166,488
- Safe Haven, h, p,1:51.2 $487,446
- Weather Related, g, p,3,1:51.2 $132,269
- Battle Damage, h, p,4,1:51.3 $253,947

Richest
- Redskin, h, p,2,1:55 $1,865,702
- Ramblin Storm, g, p,1:50.1 $1,068,063
- Call For Rain, h, p,4,1:49.3 $1,065,919
- Storm Tossed, m, p,4,1:53.4f $969,344
- Stormin Jesse, h, p,1:54h $808,344
- Concussion, g, p,4,1:54.1 $780,362
- Keystone Endeavor, h, p,4,1:50 $761,928
- Soft Light, g, p,4,1:52.3 $691,220
- Kick Up A Storm, h, p,3,1:54 $687,936
- Storm Prince, h, p,1:53.1f $580,139

Storm Damage, Bay Horse, 15.2 Hands, 1977
p, 2, 1:55.4; 3, 1:53.2f ($659,296)

Bret Hanover, 1962 p, 4, T1:53.3 $922,616	Adios, 1940 p, T1:57½ $33,329	Hal Dale, 1926 p, 6, 2:02¼	Abbedale, 1917 p, 2:01¼	The Abbe	CHIMES Nettie King
				Daisydale D.	Archdale Mrs. Tmolus
			Margaret Hal, 1914 p, 2:19½h	Argot Hal	Brown Hal Lady Wildflower
				Margaret Polk	John R. Gentry Stella Hal
		Adioo Volo, 1930 p, 3, 2:05h	Adioo Guy, 1910 p, 2:00¾	Guy Dillon	Sidney Dillon By Guy
				Adioo	Guy Wilkes By By
			Sigrid Volo, 1921 p, T2:04	**PETER VOLO**	PETER THE GREAT Nervolo Belle
				Polly Parrot	Jersey B B Lady Maud C
	Brenna Hanover, 1956 p, 3, T2:01 $21,946	Tar Heel, 1948 p, 4, T1:57 $119,148	Billy Direct, 1934 p, 4, T1:55 $12,040	Napoleon Direct	Walter Direct Lady Erectress
				Gay Forbes	Malcolm Forbes Gay Girl Chimes
			Leta Long, 1940 p, 4, 2:03¾ $9,321	**VOLOMITE**	PETER VOLO Cita Frisco
				Rosette	Mr. McElwyn Rose Scott
		Beryl Hanover, 1947 p, 2, T2:02 $29,076	Nibble Hanover, 1936 1:58¾ $25,599	Calumet Chuck	Truax Sumatra
				Justissima	Justice Brooke Claire Toddington
			Laura Hanover, 1931 2, T2:15¼	The Laurel Hall	PETER THE GREAT Baby Bertha
				Miss Bertha Worthy	LEE WORTHY Miss Bertha Dillon
Breath O Spring, 1953 p, 3, T2:01.1 $3,144	Worthy Boy, 1940 3, 2:02½ $25,688	**VOLOMITE**, 1926 3, 2:03¼ $32,649	**PETER VOLO**, 1911 4, 2:02	**PETER THE GREAT**	Pilot Medium Santos
				Nervolo Belle	Nervolo Josephine Knight
			Cita Frisco, 1921	San Francisco	**ZOMBRO** Oniska
				Mendocita	Mendocino Esther
		Warwell Worthy, 1932 3, 2:03¼	Peter The Brewer, 1918 4, 2:02½	**PETER THE GREAT**	Pilot Medium Santos
				Zombrewer	**ZOMBRO** Mary Bales
			Alma Lee, 1925 4, 2:04¾	**LEE WORTHY**	LEE AXWORTHY Emma Smith
				Jane Revere	Guy Axworthy Volga E
	Lady Scotland, 1943	Scotland, 1925 T1:59¼	Peter Scott, 1909 T2:05	**PETER THE GREAT**	Pilot Medium Santos
				Jenny Scott	Bryson Aetna
			Roya McKinney, 1911 4, T2:07½	**MCKINNEY**	Alcyone Rosa Sprague
				Princess Royal	CHIMES Estabella
		Spinster, 1930 4, T2:05	Spencer, 1925 3, T1:59¾	Lee Tide	LEE AXWORTHY Emily Ellen
				Petrex	PETER THE GREAT Extasy
			Minnetonka, 1922 T2:12¼	Belwin	MCKINNEY Belle Winnie
				The Miss Stokes	PETER THE GREAT Tillie Thompson

Strike Out

Breeder William Shehan was nearly an unknown when he bred his Ensign Hanover mare Golden Miss to Bret Hanover in 1968, the second year that Bret stood at Castleton Farm. Golden Miss had been a good race mare, winning 20 races and nearly $65,000 in an era when mares generally lacked the opportunity to earn substantial purse money. But with the emergence of Strike Out, who was the result of Golden Miss' mating with Bret, on the scene in early 1971, Bill Shehan would never again need an introduction in breeding circles.

Strike Out was from Bret Hanover's second crop and was voted Two-Year-Old Pacer of the Year after winning 14 of 19 starts for Canadian trainer and owner John Hayes, Sr. He earned $155,627 in those pre-Meadowlands days, taking major victories in the Fox Stake, Roosevelt Futurity, Hanover Colt S., Tom Hal, Reynolds Memorial, Count B Stake, Golden Blend and Florida Breeders.

At three, Strike Out won the Little Brown Jug, the Adios, the Battle of Saratoga, Prix d'Ete, Gaines, Tattersalls and Reynolds Memorial again. With 15 victories, he was again divisional champion of his year, setting a world record of 1:56.3h in winning the Little Brown Jug for trainer John Hayes and driver Keith Waples, both legends of Canadian racing.

Strike Out's aggressive speed was his forte, and his chestnut coat and flaxen mane made him the darling of racing fans all across North America. But after two years on the track, with earnings of more than $454,000, Strike Out retired to stud at Castleton Farm, the home of his famous sire.

Sire Line

Strike Out was from the second crop of his famed sire Bret Hanover, and was a grandson of the great Adios, both profiled in this book.

Maternal Line

Strike Out's pedigree has always fascinated. He is from an Ensign Hanover mare, and thus was linebred 4 x 3 to Billy Direct, since Ensign Hanover, the first Little Brown Jug winner, was by Billy Direct, and so was Tar Heel, the sire of Bret Hanover's dam. His immediate maternal family was not famous at the time, but has since become a modern-day foundation tribe which includes the likes of Malaysia, a half-sister to Strike Out, who is the dam of the incredible Riyadh p,1:48.4 ($2,565,477), winner of two legs of the 1993 Triple Crown and one of the fastest and most durable champions of the modern age. Golden Miss, a stakes-winning filly, from whom Strike Out inherited his gleaming chestnut coat, was also bred to Shadow Wave, himself a chestnut son of Adios, and winner of the Little Brown Jug. That mating produced a daughter named Shifting Sands and she, in turn, through her daughters Shifting Scene and Whispering Sands (both by Race Time) founded a very successful modern maternal family.

Progeny Of Note

Strike Out was neither a fertile horse nor a good breeder. He was never able to handle big books of mares, and his stud career suffered from the beginning. His first foals came in 1974 just at the onset of the Meadow Skipper era when the siring baton was being passed to the Dale Frost branch of the Hal Dale line, and his own sire line was pressured by the new competition.

Strike Out's first crop had only 55 foals, but it included two precocious freshman pacers. The first was the world champion Striking Image p,2,1:55, the first two-year-old in history to pace in 1:55. The second was the Michigan star Fulla Strikes p,2,T1:54.1 ($238,489). Strike Out came back in his 1975 crop with the good colt League Leader p,1:55.1 ($706,705) and his 1976 crop included the Little Brown Jug champion Hot Hitter p,3,1:54f ($963,574), plus a strong supporting cast including such stars as Alaskan Strike p,4,1:55.2 ($316,522), Striking Force p,4,T1:54.4 ($184,525) and the modestly successful Midwestern sire, Oil Strike p,3,T1:54.4 ($110,173).

In later years, despite small books that often numbered fewer than 30 foals, Strike Out assembled productive winners, including the

Strike Out

Photo courtesy of Castleton Farm

Race Record Highlights

At 2
1st Roosevelt Futurity
Fox S.
Hanover Colt S.
Hanover-Hempt S.
Tom Hal S.
Reynolds Memorial
Count B. S.
Golden Blend P.
Florida Breeders S.
2nd Arden Downs S.
Batavia Colt S.
Richelieu S.

At 3
1st Little Brown Jug
Adios S.
Battle of Saratoga

At 3 (continued)
Prix d'Ete
Best of All P.
Reynolds Memorial
Gaines Memorial
Tattersalls S.
Beaver S.
Castor S.
Florida Breeders S.
2nd Hanover-Hempt S.
Cane Futurity
Commodore P.
Battle of Brandywine
Matron S.
Adios S. Elimination
3rd Batavia Colt S.

Honors
Voted Two-Year-Old Pacer of the Year
Voted Three-Year-Old Pacer of the Year
Set world record for three-year-olds on half-mile track

Race Record

Year	Age	Starts	Wins	2nd	3rd	Earnings	Record
1971	2	19	14	3	0	$155,627	p,2,1:58
1972	3	25	15	6	1	298,437	p,3,1:56.3h
		44	29	9	1	$454,064	p,3,1:56.3h

Strike Out

quick Cue Light p,3,1:51.2 ($827,505), who was from a crop of but 22 foals. The world champion Legal Notice p,3,1:53.3h ($494,786) and the sturdy Ring of Light p,1:52.1 ($623,160) were part of a crop of 51 foals; and Meadowlands Pace champion Hilarion p,3,1:54.1 ($775,114) was from a crop of just 24 foals. It is a testament to Strike Out's overall quality that he has more than twenty 1:55 credits from fewer than 550 foals. Like the other sons of Bret Hanover, Strike Out was not a good filly sire. In fact, his fastest and richest female credit is Nite Strike p,1:56f ($300,047).

Strike Out's foals have won nearly $24 million, averaging nearly $55,000 per starter.

Analysis

I believe Strike Out was meant to be a top sire and carry on the Bret Hanover branch of the Adios male line; but he suffered from fertility problems. Strike Out had great quantities of sperm, but many were abnormal and this defect ultimately prevented him from getting quality mares. He was still used occasionally and bred eight mares in 1997 at 28 years of age. However, he has only produced 45 foals from 1987 through 1997; his highest number of foals in a single crop came in his second group with 63 foals in 1975. Strike Out died in 1998.

Strike Out appeared to be a sire on his way to glory when his first crop raced in 1976. Among this group was Striking Image p,2,1:55 ($56,028) and Fulla Strikes p,2,T1:54.1 ($238,489). However, he was unable to continue to produce at that level and although he has sired many outstanding performers during his career, Strike Out never made it to the upper echelon of pacing sires. He also had many sons who were tried as stallions and a few achieved limited success, such as Legal Notice, Striking Image, Hot Hitter, Oil Strike and Tyrant.

Little Brown Jug and Messenger S. winner Hot Hitter p,3,1:54f ($963,574) was Strike Out's richest and most dynamic performer and his pedigree shows the closest common cross being 4x3 to Hal Dale. Cue Light p,3,1:51.2 ($827,505), Strike Out's fastest and second richest son has the same 4x3 cross to Hal Dale and his dam is inbred 3x3 to the great sire Volomite - a cross we have seen many times among successful broodmares. Meadowlands Pace winner Hilarion p,3,1:54.1 ($775,114) is Strike Out's next richest performer and he is inbred 3x3 to Adios as is another fast son of Strike Out, Rained Out p,1:52.2 ($355,502). League Leader p,1:55.1 ($706,705) is linebred 3x4 to Adios as is the fast Baraka p,4,1:52.1 ($101,832).

Many of Strike Out's richest performers have 4x4 crosses to Hal Dale and several have no common ancestors in the first four generations. Fulla Strikes has an interesting pedigree cross since he is 5x3 to Volomite and 4x3 to the half-brother and sister Nelson Dillon and Fay Hanover. Fulla Strikes' dam, Mini Song, paced but is trotting-bred being by Victory Song (son of Volomite) from a Nibble Hanover mare. Striking Image, another champion Strike Out two-year-old, has a second dam who is inbred 3x3 to Volomite. Strike Out's second fastest performer is Ring Of Light p,1:52.1 ($623,160) and he is full brother to Striking Image. Thus, we see more strong connections to Volomite even among top two-year-old pacers.

Strike Out had good success with Good Time mares and both stallions stood at Castleton Farm. His two richest offspring, Hot Hitter and Cue Light, are both from Good Time mares and the brothers Striking Image and Ring Of Light have a second dam by Good Time. Legal Notice p,3,1:53.3h ($494,786), a Little Brown Jug heat winner, is from a Race Time (son of Good Time) mare as is Striking Sun p,4,T1:54.1 ($342,455). Keep in mind that Legal Notice is beginning to make his mark as a successful broodmare sire with such credits as Armbro Maestro p,1:49.2, Moffat Missy p,1:51.3, Superstar Killean p,3,1:52, Powerful Structure p,3,1:52.2, Heatherjeankillean p,4,1:53.1, Ruthellenkillean p,3,1:53.2 and Possessive Dragon p,2,1:54 to name just a few.

Unfortunately for Strike Out, it was only later in his career that he began to have access to mares by Albatross and other Meadow

Skipper sons and this delay certainly did not help his stallion career. Also, Strike Out was not a particularly top sire of fillies - only three of his top 36 winners of $150,000 or more are female.

Strike Out's daughters, though, have been generally successful as broodmares and have some fine credits. The richest performer from a Strike Out mare is the Meadowlands Pace, North America Cup and Messenger S. winner David's Pass p,3,1:50.4 ($1,652,500) who is by Jate Lobell. Strike Out's fastest broodmare credit is Bright As Day p,4,1:50 ($397,513) by Troublemaker and is inbred 3x3 to Bret Hanover - Strike Out's sire. Jate Lobell also checks in as the sire of Armbro Mackintosh p,3,1:51.1 ($471,638) and Pass N Jate p,3,1:52.4, so this looks like a very nice cross.

The four fastest, of over 430 2:00 broodmare credits for Strike Out, all come from Most Happy Fella line stallions - Troublemaker, Jate Lobell and Tyler's Mark. Other sires from this line who have also done very well with Strike Out mares are Tyler B (Ramsey Hanover p,1:51.4 $426,846) and Resonator p,4,1:53.1f ($659,985); Die Laughing (Your The Top p,3,1:52.3), Dexter Nukes (Armbro Moody p,4,1:52.4 and Fuzed p,1:53.4 $151,245). Abercrombie and his sons Laag, Kentucky Spur, Armbro Emerson also have fast performers from Strike Out mares.

Sonsam is the sire of the good filly Shop Till Ya Drop p,3,1:55.1 ($377,863), from a Strike Out mare, and she is inbred 3x3 to Bret Hanover. Sonsam also has Radiant Ruler p,2,1:54.4 ($199,666) from a Strike Out mare and Sonsam's son Prize Sarnel p,3,1:54 also has sired a top performer from a Strike Out mare - Master Shawn p,3,1:52.3 ($438,557).

Next to Storm Damage, Strike Out is probably Bret Hanover's next best siring son so don't worry about seeing his name in the pedigree of a broodmare or yearling that interests you.

Strike Out

Photo courtesy of Castleton Farm

Leading Progeny by Strike Out

Fastest
Cue Light, h, p,3,1:51.2 $827,505
Ring Of Light, h, p,1:52.1 $623,160
Baraka, h, p,4,1:52.1 $101,832
Rained Out, g, p,1:52.2 $355,502
Augie Donatelli, g, p,4,1:52.4 $100,859
Legal Notice, h, p,3,1:53.3h $494,786
Hot Hitter, h, p,3,1:54f $963,574
Muckalee Strike, h, p,1:54 $199,321
Mr Rodeo Drive, h, p,4,1:54 $394,788
Easy Hitter, h, p,4,1:54 $111,040

Richest
Hot Hitter, h, p,3,1:54f $963,574
Cue Light, h, p,3,1:51.2 $827,505
Hilarion, h, p,3,1:54.1 $775,114
League Leader, h, p,1:55.1 $706,705
Melvin's Strike, h, p,1:55.3 $684,397
Ring Of Light, h, p,1:52.1 $623,160
Legal Notice, h, p,3,1:53.3h $494,786
Joule, h, p,3,T1:54.4 $467,941
Strike Le Ru, g, p,1:55.4 $425,274
Mr Rodeo Drive, h, p,4,1:54 $394,788

Strike Out, Chestnut Horse, 1969
p, 2, 1:58; 3, 1:56.3h ($454,064)

Bret Hanover, 1962 p, 4, T1:53.3 $922,616	Adios, 1940 p, T1:57½ $33,329	Hal Dale, 1926 p, 6, 2:02¼	Abbedale, 1917 p, 2:01¼	The Abbe — Chimes / Nettie King Daisydale D. — Archdale / Mrs. Tmolus
			Margaret Hal, 1914 p, 2:19½h	Argot Hal — Brown Hal / Lady Wildflower Margaret Polk — John R. Gentry / Stella Hal
		Adioo Volo, 1930 p, 3, 2:05h	Adioo Guy, 1910 p, 2:00¾	Guy Dillon — Sidney Dillon / By Guy Adioo — Guy Wilkes / By By
			Sigrid Volo, 1921 p, T2:04	**PETER VOLO** — PETER THE GREAT / Nervolo Belle Polly Parrot — Jersey B B / Lady Maud C
	Brenna Hanover, 1956 p, 3, T2:01 $21,946	Tar Heel, 1948 p, 4, T1:57 $119,148	**BILLY DIRECT**, 1934 p, 4, T1:55 $12,040	Napoleon Direct — Walter Direct / Lady Erectress Gay Forbes — Malcolm Forbes / Gay Girl Chimes
			Leta Long, 1940 p, 4, 2:03¾ $9,321	Volomite — **PETER VOLO** / Cita Frisco Rosette — Mr. McElwyn / Rose Scott
		Beryl Hanover, 1947 2, T2:02 $29,076	Nibble Hanover, 1936 1:58¾ $25,599	Calumet Chuck — Truax / Sumatra Justissima — Justice Brooke / Claire Toddington
			Laura Hanover, 1931 2, T2:15¼	The Laurel Hall — **PETER THE GREAT** / Baby Bertha Miss Bertha Worthy — Lee Worthy / **MISS BERTHA DILLON**
Golden Miss, 1954 p, 4, 2:02.1h $64,471	Ensign Hanover, 1943 p, 4, 1:59.4 $81,070	**BILLY DIRECT**, 1934 p, 4, T1:55 $12,040	Napoleon Direct, 1909 p, 1:59¾	Walter Direct — Direct Hal / Ella Brown Lady Erectress — Tom Kendle / Nelly Zarro
			Gay Forbes, 1916 p, 2:07¾	Malcolm Forbes — Bingen / Nancy Hanks Gay Girl Chimes — Berkshire Chimes / Miss Gay Girl
		Helen Hanover, 1927 3, 2:04¾	Dillon Volo, 1920 4, T2:11½	**PETER VOLO** — **PETER THE GREAT** / Nervolo Belle **MISS BERTHA DILLON** — **DILLON AXWORTHY** / Miss Bertha C
			Helen Dillon, 1919 2, T2:08¼	**DILLON AXWORTHY** — **AXWORTHY** / Adioo Dillon Miss Pierette — **PETER THE GREAT** / Madam Thompson
	Miss Pluto Scott, 1934 p, 2:03½ $6,246	McKinney Scott, 1919	Peter Scott, 1909 T2:05	**PETER THE GREAT** — Pilot Medium / Santos Jenny Scott — Bryson / Aetna
			Diabla McKinney 3, 2:19	McKinney — Alcyone / Rosa Sprague Princess Annabel — Mambrino King / Annabel
		Lu Dene Pluto, 1928 T2:16	Peter Pluto, 1918 4, T2:05¾	**PETER THE GREAT** — Pilot Medium / Santos Nelle Worthy L — **AXWORTHY** / Miss Anna Jay
			Morganetta, 1919	Morgan Axworthy — **AXWORTHY** / Kinglyne Lady Wilina — The Hobo / Archie Girl

Tar Heel

As his name might indicate, Tar Heel was bred by North Carolina businessman W.N. Reynolds, a member of the famous family which founded the R.J. Reynolds Tobacco Co., and raced in Reynolds' stable for trainer-driver Delvin Miller at two, three and four. At two, the anything-but-handsome Tar Heel was a winner in 18 of 29 starts, winning $52,519 in post World War II money. At three, in 31 starts, he won 17 times, adding $66,630 with a time-trial mark of T1:57.2 taken for Miller at The Red Mile in the fall of 1951. He returned briefly to the races at four, but made only two starts, lowering his mark to T1:57. At two, the rugged son of Billy Direct and the royally bred Leta Long won the Little Pat, the Geers, American-National, Two Gaits Farm, Goshen Cup, Village Farm, and Lexington stakes as well as a heat of the Fox Stake. At three, he captured the Little Brown Jug, the American-National, the Review Futurity, Geers, Matron and a heat of the Horseman Futurity.

A big-headed, coarsely made horse who was not especially good-gaited, Tar Heel nevertheless was an effective half-mile track performer, as evidenced by his Little Brown Jug triumph. One of the racing scribes of his era commented on his gait by saying "It was hard to tell what he was doing, but we called it pacing." At the close of Tar Heel's career, the Reynolds Stable was dispersed at Tattersalls in the fall of 1952 and the young son of Billy Direct was purchased by Lawrence Sheppard for Hanover Shoe Farms along with Tar Heel's stablemate, the handsome Solicitor. Solicitor was by far the better-looking of the two horses, but Tar Heel was the one who made a sire. The roughly $200,000 that Sheppard spent to acquire Tar Heel and Solicitor was turned into millions for Hanover's operation.

Sire Line

Tar Heel is a son of the renowned world champion free-legged pacer Billy Direct p,T1:55 from a sire line that has nearly vanished from the modern racing landscape. Tar Heel is the only son of Billy Direct to make any impact as a sire in North America. In Australia and New Zealand, Billy Direct's son Garrison Hanover was a success.

Maternal Line

Tar Heel's dam was the Volomite mare Leta Long in one of the more productive branches of the Jessie Pepper maternal family, one of the breed's oldest and best-known maternal tribes. Leta Long was a 1940 daughter of the Mr. McElwyn mare Rosette, and that mare was a daughter of the 1921 Kentucky Futurity winner Rose Scott, a full sister to Scotland, and those two champions were offspring of the famed Roya McKinney, one of the trio of sisters responsible for nearly all the production in Jessie Pepper's family. In fact, Tar Heel's entire maternal background is trotting-bred, which is fascinating considering the significant impact he made on the modern pacer.

Tar Heel's half-brothers Keystoner p,1:57.4 ($128,291) (also a Little Brown Jug winner) and Meadow Pace p,3,1:59.3 ($160,390) were also excellent race horses, and Tar Heel's half-sister Adioleta p,3,2:00 was a Grand Circuit filly as well. This branch of the family has not had much success in the 1990's, and the last star from this immediate family was the 1983 Kentucky Pacing Derby winner Signed N Sealed p,2,1:56.1h; 3,Q1:55.4 ($311,902), whose grandam, Lady Leta, is a half-sister to Tar Heel.

Progeny Of Note

Tar Heel was a breeding farm and stud manager's dream, for he was the wonderful embodiment of a successful, fertile and manageable horse. His stud career spanned some 28 years and he never failed to deliver in the breeding shed, although it must be recognized that he never had big crops. For example, his first foals, born in 1954, numbered only 17, and his 1,368 foals in 28 years gave him an average of fewer than 50 foals a year. His biggest foal crop was in 1967 when he produced 91 foals, but he had only two other years when he had foal crops in excess of 80.

His biggest money winner was the gifted colt star Laverne Hanover p,3,1:56.3f ($868,557), a world champion two-year-old for Billy Haughton in 1968. Laverne was from Tar Heel's 13th crop, midway through his stallion career. The earliest star produced by Tar Heel was O'Brien Hanover p,1:59.2h ($302,225), a foal of 1955 in Tar Heel's

Race Record Highlights

At 2
- **1st** Little Pat S.
  Geers S.
  American-National S.
  Two Gaits Farm S.
  Goshen Cup
  Village Farm S.
  Lexington S.
  heat of Fox S.
  two Saratoga S.
- **2nd** heat of Fox S.
  heat of Two Gaits Farm S.
- **3rd** heat of Fox S.
  Knight Dream P.

At 3
- **1st** Little Brown Jug
  American-National S.

At 3 (continued)
- Review Futurity
  Geers S.
  Matron S.
  heat of Horseman Futurity
- **2nd** heat of Championship Stallion S.
  three heats of Horseman Futurity
- **3rd** heat of Championship Stallion S.

Honors

At three, set world record for three-year-olds on a half-mile track

At three, set world record for two-heat race on a half-mile track

Tar Heel

Courtesy of The Horseman and Fair World

Race Record

Year	Age	Starts	Wins	2nd	3rd	Earnings	Record
1950	2	29	18	4	3	$ 52,519	p,2,2:00.3
1951	3	31	17	7	1	66,630	p,3,T1:57.2
1952	4	2	0	0	0		p,4,T1:57
		62	35	11	4	$119,149	p,4,T1:57

Tar Heel

second crop, but it was clearly not until the 1960's that Tar Heel hit his stride. That is when he began to pick up matings with the many daughters of Adios, the siring star of that era. From those matings with Adios mares came not only Laverne Hanover, but also Otaro Hanover p,3,1:57h ($590,282); Kentucky p,3,1:57 ($497,270); the full brothers Isle Of Wight p,T1:56.2 ($493,514) and Nansemond p,4,1:56.1f ($448,436); Keystone Pat p,3,T1:55.3 ($389,522); Tempered Yankee p,4,1:58.2h ($305,349) and Sly Yankee p,3,1:59.3 ($255,357).

Tar Heel's best filly, a female any sire could be proud of, was the talented Hazel Hanover p,2,1:56.2 ($260,427), one of the few fillies good enough to start against the colts in the Woodrow Wilson at two, and later a broodmare star for Hanover Shoe Farms. Another of his successful race fillies was the black superstar Sunnie Tar p,3,1:56.4 ($223,617), one of the fastest pacing fillies ever to wear hobbles.

Tar Heel has less than 180 2:00 credits, a number which appears poor by contemporary standards, but it should be remembered that Tar Heel's stallion career was conducted largely in the pre-Meadowlands days when half-mile track racing for small purses was still the principal fare for pacers. Tar Heel had but two sub-1:55 credits in his entire career, both coming late in his siring life, and both as aged horses at The Meadowlands. Seabert Hanover p,4,1:53.3 has the honor of being Tar Heel's fastest while close behind is Finian Hanover p,1:54.2 ($344,361). While Tar Heel's foals may not have been fast, they did get to the races and did make money. Tar Heel's 28 crops earned nearly $40 million, with an extraordinary 1,119 starters from a total of 1,368 foals.

Tar Heel's broodmare credits would occupy another entire book, but suffice to say that in his career, and for many years after his death in the early 1980's, Tar Heel was the leading broodmare sire in the entire industry, setting records that would last a generation.

Analysis

By any standard, Tar Heel has gone down in history as one of the Standardbred breed's all-time great sires - both by the racing exploits of his sons and daughters and by the production of his daughters when they retired. During the height of his career, Tar Heel ranked at the top level as both a sire and broodmare sire.

The only failing in Tar Heel's stallion career was that he was unable to produce a long-term commercially successful son at stud to extend the sire line of Billy Direct which traces back to Hambletonian's son Dictator. This line is virtually extinct now in North America, but has met with more success in Australia and New Zealand. Tar Heel sons had a few opportunities to succeed and they were headed by Thorpe Hanover, Nansemond, Steady Beau and Gamecock. Thorpe and Nansemond never left any stallion sons of note, but Steady Beau gave us Steady Star who was the fastest Standardbred in history for a time with his 1:52 mile in 1971. That time was not eclipsed until Niatross' 1:49.1 in 1980. However, Steady Star became only a marginal sire and that ended the Billy Direct line at the top levels in North America.

Tar Heel sired a number of great performers but his best was probably the speedy Laverne Hanover p,3,1:56.3f ($868,557) who was the first two-year-old to pace in 2:00 on a half-mile track while winning 22 of 23 starts. He came back at three to win 21 of 28 starts, including the Little Brown Jug. He later became a FFA star and retired as the fourth leading money-winning pacer of all time while winning 61 of 98 starts. He was tried as a stallion but was not successful.

Another Little Brown Jug winner for Tar Heel was Nansemond p,4,1:56.1f ($448,436) who surprised the great Albatross in taking the Jug. Nansemond began his career with a bang; world champions Kawartha Eagle and Whatanut were in his first crop in addition to stakes winner Nat Lobell. The first crop of Albatross raced that same year and the two sires seemed pretty equal at that point. However, Albatross went on to achievements of historic proportions while Nansemond never duplicated his first crop and is now just another name in the record books.

Nansemond had a full brother who was just as good and an even better aged performer - Isle Of Wight p,T1:56.2 ($493,514). There were other full brothers, Richmond p,4,1:55.4f ($317,301), and

Southampton V. p,2,1:59.3f ($119,748) and a full sister Nancy Isle p,4,1:59.1f ($148,903) - all by Tar Heel from the great producing Adios mare Adios Scarlet p,4,2:03.4h.

Some other top performers by Tar Heel are Finian Hanover p,1:54.2 ($344,361), O'Brien Hanover p,1:59.2h ($302,255), Bengazi Hanover p,3,1:57.3f ($211,564), the great filly Sunnie Tar p,3,1:56.4 ($223,617) and Tar Boy p,1:58 ($220,064). Tar Heel's fastest offspring is Seabert Hanover p,4,1:53.3 ($97,468) from a Meadow Skipper full sister to Nero.

The cross with Adios mares was dynamite for Tar Heel. Some of his other top performers from those mares were Otaro Hanover p,3,1:57h ($590,282), Kentucky p,3,1:57 ($497,270), Keystone Pat p,3,T1:55.3 ($389,522), Tempered Yankee p,4,1:58.2h ($305,349) and Sly Yankee p,3,1:59.3 ($255,397). Tar Heel's richest daughter, Hazel Hanover p,2,1:56.2 ($260,427), and her full brother Hoot Hanover p,4,1:56.3 ($380,085) are from a mare by Henry T. Adios - a son of Adios. In fact, nine of Tar Heel's 14 richest sons, with earnings over $300,000, are from mares by Adios and his sons.

As a broodmare sire, Tar Heel ranks as one of the greatest of all time and a strong case could be made that he is absolutely the best. To date, his daughters have produced 1,326 2:00 performers which give him a rank just behind Albatross, Bret Hanover, Meadow Skipper and Most Happy Fella. However, raw statistics do not tell the full story since many Tar Heel mares produced these performers when the 2:00 mile was something special. Tar Heel's real ranking can only be seen when the overall quality of performers produced by his daughters is taken into account.

Tar Heel's list of broodmare credits is simply awesome. Not only do his daughters produce speed, but they also produce high-quality stakes performers who earn lots of purse dollars for their owners. And they have also produced some of the sport's all-time great performers.

Heading the list of Tar Heel's broodmare sire credits is, of course, the great Bret Hanover p,4,T1:53.3 ($922,616). Tar Heel daughters have also produced several million-dollar winners, including In The Pocket p,3,T1:49.1 ($1,537,473) (by Direct Scooter), Forrest Skipper p,3,1:50.3 ($1,044,650) (by Scarlet Skipper), Anxious Robby p,3,1:52.4 ($1,191,383) (by Happy Motoring), Triple Crown winner Ralph Hanover p,3,1:53.4 ($1,828,871) (by Meadow Skipper), Doc's Fella p,4,1:54.1 ($1,267,059) (by Most Happy Fella), Miller's Scout p,4,1:54.4f ($1,162,061) (by Tarport Effrat) and Praised Dignity p,2,1:56.4f ($1,194,715) (by Albatross).

Million-dollar winners is only one category in which Tar Heel mares excelled. Here are some of their less than million-dollar winning daughters who nonetheless are also among the sport's greatest ever filly performers - Cheery Hello p,3,1:52.3 ($869,619) (by Albatross), May Wine p,4,1:52.4 ($377,265) (by Most Happy Fella), Conquered Quest p,3,1:52.4 ($863,514) (by Sonsam), Hit Parade p,2,1:53.4 ($806,303) (by Sonsam), Silk Stockings p,3,1:55.2 ($694,894) (by Most Happy Fella), Happy Sharon p,4,1:55.4 ($606,964) (by Most Happy Fella), Tarport Hap p,4,1:56.3f ($688,664) (by Most Happy Fella), Bonjour Hanover p,3,1:57 ($226,821) (by Adios), Pammy Lobell p,4,T1:57.1 ($354,497) (by Airliner) and Romalie Hanover p,3,1:57.3f ($394,385) (by Dancer Hanover). This is an incredible list and, as you can see, many of the fillies were by the great sire Most Happy Fella.

Some of the other males of note from Tar Heel mares are Colt Fortysix p,3,1:50.3 ($232,538) (by Albatross), Armbro Aussie p,3,1:51.4 ($545,037) (by Most Happy Fella), Towner's Big Guy p,3,1:52.1f ($616,841) (by Big Towner), Coal Harbor p,4,1:52.3f ($465,620) (by Albatross), Lustra's Big Guy p,1:52.4 ($977,914) (by Big Towner), Royce p,4,1:53.4 ($437,177) (by Albatross), Landslide p,3,1:54.1 ($162,835) (by Meadow Skipper), Armbro Wolf p,3,1:54.1 ($869,987) (by Albatross), Holmes Hanover p,4,1:54.2 ($430,787) (by Albatross), Slapstick p,3,1:54.4 ($474,294) (by Meadow Skipper), Tyler B p,3,1:55.1 ($687,388) (by Most Happy Fella), Keystone Ore p,3,1:55.2 ($563,072) (by Bye Bye Byrd), Romeo Hanover p,3,1:56.1f ($658,505) (by Dancer Hanover), Armbro Omaha p,3,1:56.1 ($386,336) (by Airliner), Silent Majority p,3,1:56.3 ($362,369) (by Henry T. Adios) and Romulus Hanover p,3,1:57.1f ($485,000) (by Dancer Hanover).

More fast performers from Tar Heel mares are Tootie Roll p,4,1:51.1 ($164,884) (by Walt Hanover), Equitable p,4,1:51.4 ($370,705) (by Governor Skipper), Ms. Magic p,1:52.1f ($437,029) (by Temujin), Tanzy Lobell p,4,T1:52.2 ($329,840) (by Nero), to name just a few in the speed category.

Tar Heel

When the above listing of some of Tar Heel's greatest broodmare sire credits it is taken into consideration, it is difficult to assess whether Albatross, Meadow Skipper or Most Happy Fella are really superior to him in terms of quality. This is truly an all-star list and it may be unmatched.

Another aspect of Tar Heel's broodmare sire credits is that many of the males went on to relatively successful stud careers, including Bret Hanover, Tyler B., Silent Majority, Landslide, Holmes Hanover (down under), Slapstick, Precious Fella, Raging Glory, Peter Lobell and Bret Hanover's full brother Baron Hanover.

In addition, some of Tar Heel's daughters are among the greatest producers in the history of the sport including such broodmares Tarport Cheer (six $100,000 winners and perhaps the best ever), Romola Hanover (seven $100,000 winners and also a candidate for the best), Prelude Lobell (five $100,000 winners), Maryellen Hanover (five $100,000 winners), Brenna Hanover, Perna Hanover, Hobby Horse Tar (four $100,000 winners) and Hazel Hanover (four $100,000 winners).

There are several good horses inbred 3x3 to Tar Heel, but the most prominent example is the trio of Dragon's Lair p,1:51.3 ($1,085,317), Cole Muffler p,3,1:53.3f ($682,380) and Bruce's Lady p,3,1:53.3 ($772,602) all by Tyler B from the Race Time mare Sandy's Sable. Tar Heel is the maternal grandsire of both Tyler B and Sandy's Sable which provides the common cross in the third generation. Both Dragon's Lair and Cole Muffler are successful stallions.

Tar Heel won the Little Brown Jug in 1951 and his bloodlines have been prominent in that classic race ever since. Tar Heel's daughters have produced the Little Brown Jug winners Vicar Hanover (1964), Bret Hanover (1965), Romeo Hanover (1966), Laverne Hanover (1969), Armbro Omaha (1974), Keystone Ore (1976), Ralph Hanover (1983), and Colt Fortysix (1984). His sons Nansemond (1971) and Laverne Hanover (1969) have also won the Jug.

The pacing Triple Crown has been won by only eight horses, three of which are sons of Tar Heel broodmares: Bret Hanover, Romeo Hanover and Ralph Hanover. Horse of the Year honors have also been garnered by Tar Heel daughters with Bret Hanover (three times) and Forrest Skipper. Divisional champions have also been a strong category for Tar Heel daughters. Some of their champions, in addition to those already mentioned, are Laverne Hanover, Hazel Hanover, Silk Stockings, Keystone Ore, Armbro Omaha, Romulus Hanover, Cheery Hello, Romalie Hanover, Sunnie Tar, Royce, Isle Of Wight, Tarport Hap and Pammy Lobell.

There is more to tell, but I hope by now I have convinced you why Tar Heel ranks with the all-time greats as a stallion. Keeping in mind that all of these great horses mentioned above receive half of their genes from their dams, I believe Tar Heel has made an extremely strong genetic contribution to these horses and to the Standardbred breed.

Leading Progeny by Tar Heel

Fastest
Seabert Hanover, h, p,4,1:53.3 $97,468
Finian Hanover, h, p,1:54.2 $344,361
Kawartha Tarson, h, p,3,T1:55.1 $119,580
Keystone Pat, h, p,3,T1:55.3 $389,522
Richmond, h, p,4,1:55.4f $317,301
Matrix Hanover, h, p,4,1:55.4 $176,736
Serpico Hanover, h, p,1:56 $355,852
Nansemond, h, p,4,1:56.1f $448,436
Isle of Wight, h, p,T1:56.2 $493,514
Hazel Hanover, m, p,2,1:56.2 $260,427

Richest
Laverne Hanover, h, p,3,1:56.3f $868,557
Otaro Hanover, h, p,3,1:57h $590,282
Kentucky, h, p,3,1:57 $497,270
Penn State, h, p,1:57.4f $494,194
Isle of Wight, h, p,T1:56.2 $493,514
Nansemond, h, p,4,1:56.1f $448,436
Keystone Pat, h, p,3,T1:55.3 $389,522
Hoot Hanover, h, p,4,1:56.3 $380,085
Total Freight, g, p,1:57.4 $363,528
Serpico Hanover, h, p,1:56 $355,852

Tar Heel, Black Horse, 1948
p, 2, 2:00.3; 3, T1:57.2; 4, T1:57 ($119,148)

Billy Direct, 1934 p, 4, T1:55 $12,040	Napoleon Direct, 1909 p, 1:59¾	Walter Direct, 1900 p, 2:05¾	Direct Hal, 1896	Direct	**DIRECTOR** Echora
				Bessie Hall	Tom Hal Jnr Princess II
			Ella Brown, 1885	Prince Pulaski Jnr	Prince Pulaski Molly II
				Fanny Brown	Joe Bowers
		Lady Erectress	Tom Kendle	Erector	**DIRECTOR** Millie D
				Winnie Davis	Parkville Almont Jnr Mare
			Nelly Zarro	Hal Pizarro	
				Bay Tom Mare	
	Gay Forbes, 1916 p, 2:07¾	Malcolm Forbes, 1904	Bingen, 1893 2:06¼	May King	**ELECTIONEER** May Queen
				Young Miss	Young Jim Miss Mambrino
			Nancy Hanks, 1886 T2:04	**HAPPY MEDIUM**	Hambletonian 10 Princess
				Nancy Lee	Dictator Sophy
		Gay Girl Chimes, 1911 T2:28¼h	Berkshire Chimes 2:17¾	**CHIMES**	**ELECTIONEER** Beautiful Bells
				Berkshire Belle	**ALYCONE** Belle Brassfield
			Miss Gay Girl, 1904	Gay Boy	Allerton Hazelbud
				Electric Belle	Electricity Queen of Belair
Leta Long, 1940 p, 4, 2:03¾ $9,321	Volomite, 1926 3, 2:03¼ $32,649	Peter Volo, 1911 4, 2:02	**PETER THE GREAT**, 1895 4, 2:07¼	Pilot Medium	**HAPPY MEDIUM** Tackey
				Santos	Grand Sentinel Shadow
			Nervolo Belle, 1906	Nervolo	Colbert Nellie D
				Josephine Knight	Betterson Mambrino Beauty
		Cita Frisco, 1921	San Francisco, 1903 2:07¾	Zombro	**MCKINNEY** Whisper
				Oniska	Nutwood Wilkes Bay Line
			Mendocita, 1899	Mendocino	**ELECTIONEER** Mano
				Esther	Express Coliseum
	Rosette, 1933 2, 2:06 $4,222	Mr. McElwyn, 1921 T1:59¼	Guy Axworthy, 1902 4, 2:08¾	Axworthy	Axtell Marguerite
				Lillian Wilkes	Guy Wilkes Flora
			Widow Maggie, 1907 4, T2:24½	**PETER THE GREAT**	Pilot Medium Santos
				Maggie Onward	Onward The Widow
		Rose Scott, 1918 T1:59¾	Peter Scott., 1909 T2:05	**PETER THE GREAT**	Pilot Medium Santos
				Jenny Scott	Bryson Aetna
			Roya McKinney, 1911 4, T2:07½	**MCKINNEY**	**ALYCONE** Rosa Sprague
				Princess Royal	**CHIMES** Estabella

Tyler B

It was as if Tyler B was meant to be a star from the time he was foaled in the spring of 1977 at Castleton Farm. A full brother to the accomplished filly stars Tarport Hap p,4,1:56.3f ($688,664) and Tarport Crystal p,3,1:56.4. Tyler B was sold for $220,000 as a yearling at Tattersalls. Great things were expected from the strapping bay colt, on the racetrack and in the stud, and Tyler B delivered.

As a two-year-old, the son of Most Happy Fella-Tarport Cheer won the Geers, a Woodrow Wilson elimination and two New York Sires Stakes. Altogether in that year he won ten of his 21 starts, with a 1:57.4 mark. He was also third in the Fox Stake, behind Storm Damage, his Castleton-bred contemporary.

But it was not Storm Damage who provided Tyler B with his chief competition. That honor belonged to the extraordinary Niatross, one of the greatest race colts of any era. Tyler B never beat Niatross, but won more than $550,000 chasing him at three. He was remarkably consistent, with 23 on-the-board finishes in 27 starts. His most impressive win at three came in the Monticello Classic, and he was second to Niatross in both the Cane and Messenger, and third to him in the Meadowlands Pace final. Tyler B's 1:55.1 lifetime mark was taken at The Red Mile, winning the T.W. Murphy Memorial for Billy Herman. He retired to stud at Hanover Shoe Farms in 1980, having amassed nearly $700,000, with 18 wins from 48 career starts, and bred his first crop of mares in 1981.

The colt was trained by Delvin Miller for the Tyler B Stable.

Sire Line

Tyler B is a son of Most Happy Fella, and represents one of three successful extensions of the Most Happy Fella male line. The other branches of this immediate sire line are those leading through Most Happy Fella's son Oil Burner (No Nukes, et al) and a third line through Cam Fella and his sons.

Maternal Line

Tyler B is an impeccably bred horse; he represents some of the finest pacing genes available. His dam, the legendary Tar Heel matron Tarport Cheer, produced eleven 2:00 pacers, including the likes of Tyler B, his full sister Tarport Hap p,4,1:56.3f ($688,664) and his three-quarter sister Cheery Hello p,3,1:52.3 ($869,619). This immediate family, tracing directly to Delvin Miller's famed Betty G. family, also produced the world champion pacer Call For Rain and numerous other hard-knocking colt and raceway performers. An indicatation of the high esteem in which this family is held is the fact that Tyler B and Tarport Hap's full sister Laugh A Day is the highest-priced Standardbred yearling of all time, bringing a record bid of $625,000 at the 1983 Tattersalls sale.

Progeny Of Note

From Tyler B's first crop of foals came one of the most exciting young pacers in harness racing history, the oily-gaited Dragon's Lair p,1:51.3 ($1,085,317), winner of the 1984 Breeders Crown Two-Year-Old Pace championship in a legendary conquest of the great Nihilator. Tyler B's first crop also included the world champion and Breeders Crown winning filly Amneris p,2,1:53.1 ($974,141); the smallish but gifted Seven O'Clock p,4,1:53.3 ($559,080); the always contentious Dignatarian p,1:52 ($999,637) and the fast Franz Hanover p,1:52 ($371,656). It was a propitious start to an all-too-brief career.

The 1983 foals included the speedy Tyler's Mark p,3,1:51.3 ($289,100) (a successful Maryland stallion) as well as the good fillies Valentina p,2,1:56 ($708,325) and Angela Ty p,3,1:54.4 ($491,492). The 1984 crop included the world champion Rumpus Hanover p,2,T1:52.3 ($721,993); his 1985 crop produced the top stakes filly So Cozy p,3,1:54.2 ($880,492) and the seemingly indestructible Tyrannical p,1:52 ($410,422).

Tyler B stood at Hanover Shoe Farms for only ten years before his untimely death. The middle part of those ten years was characterized by solid production but without the benefit of a genuine star that he had so plainly led us to expect in his early years. We would have to wait until his last crop before Tyler B again produced the kind of colt that could dominate his division. That colt was the world champion two- and three-year-old Magical Mike p,2,1:52.1; 3,1:50.2; a lifetime

Race Record Highlights

At 2

1st Geers S.
  Woodrow Wilson P. Elimination
  two New York Sires S.
  Lexington Early Closer

2nd Arden Downs S.
  two heats of Fox S.

3rd Tom Hal S.
  New York Sires S.

At 3

1st Monticello Classic Final and Elimination
  Meadowlands Pace Elimination
  T.W. Murphy Memorial
  three New York Sires S.

2nd Cane Pace
  Messenger S.
  Miller Memorial
  Tattersalls S.
  Battle of Brandywine Elimination
  heat of T.W. Murphy Memorial

3rd Meadowlands Pace Final
  Batavia Colt S.
  Matron S.
  Hanover Colt S.

Tyler B

Photo courtesy of Hanover Shoe Farm

Race Record

Year	Age	Starts	Wins	2nd	3rd	Earnings	Record
1979	2	21	10	5	2	$136,513	p,2,1:57.4
1980	3	27	8	9	6	550,875	p,3,1:55.1
		48	18	14	8	$687,388	p,3,1:55.1

Tyler B

winner of more than $1.6 million. Magical Mike was a sensational race colt, equalling the world record at two in winning the Woodrow Wilson for trainer Tommy Haughton and catch-driver John Campbell, then coming back to win the Governor's Cup in the fall at Garden State Park. He is the only two-year-old to win both the sport's major mile track tests at two. He was Two-Year-Old Pacer of the Year.

At three, Magical Mike returned to top form, taking a world record second heat victory of 1:50.2 in the final dash of the Oliver Wendell Holmes at The Meadowlands for Jack Moiseyev. After that, he went to Delaware and won the Little Brown Jug, took a heat of the Tattersalls Pace at The Red Mile, and finished his career with an impressive come-from-behind score in the Breeders Crown at Garden State Park, all for Mike Lachance. It was a fitting send-off for his star-crossed sire.

As a broodmare sire, Tyler B quickly became a success, even though he produced only 540 daughters during his decade in the stud. But many were well-placed among the sport's leading breeders and their production record is already outstanding. Tyler B mares are already the dams of many prominent horses.

Tyler B produced the winners of nearly $64 million from but ten crops, with nearly 900 starters from just over 1,000 foals. His starters earned an outstanding average of nearly $78,000 each.

Analysis

The loss of Tyler B at 13 years of age was a blow to both Hanover Shoe Farm and to the sport in general. He was quite a sire, a great-looking horse, and a wonderful representative of the prolific Most Happy Fella male line. However, Tyler B's legacy continues to live on through several successful sons at stud such as Dragon's Lair, Tyler's Mark and Cole Muffler, and the anticipated success of the first crop of Magical Mike. In addition, Tyler B has become an excellent broodmare sire and his daughters continue to produce racing stars every year.

Tyler B has classic bloodlines of his own since he is by Most Happy Fella and from the Tar Heel mare Tarport Cheer who is one of the greatest broodmares of all time. The closest common crosses in Tyler B.'s pedigree are 5x3 to Billy Direct, 4x4x4 to Hal Dale an 5x5x4 to Volomite - all great stallions.

As a sire, Tyler B has produced two $1,000,000 winners in Magical Mike p,3,1:50.2 ($1,682,085) and Dragon's Lair p,1:51.3 ($1,085,317). Interestingly, both are from mares by Race Time with their grandams being by Tar Heel and his son O'Brien Hanover. Magical Mike is from Tyler B.'s final crop and Dragon's Lair is from his first. The first crop of Tyler B also produced his next two highest money winners, Dignatarian p,1:52 ($999,637) and the great filly Amneris p,2,1:53.1 ($974,141).

Tyler B had an affinity for Race Time mares and six of his 15 richest offspring are products of that cross from four different Race Time mares. Another very successful cross for Tyler B were mares by Steady Star; they produced three of his eight richest performers from three different mares.

A common denominator in the pedigrees of Tyler B.'s best sons and daughters is the presence of Tar Heel close up in these pedigrees. His 11 richest performers are all linebred 3x4 to Tar Heel with the exceptions of Dragon's Lair and his sister Bruce's Lady p,3,1:53.3 ($772,607) who are inbred 3x3 to that stallion. Fourth generation common crosses to Adios and Good Time are also very prominent in the best offspring.

Similar trends show up in the listing of Tyler B.'s fastest offspring. Biba Fra p,4,1:50 ($342,908) is Tyler B.'s only 1:50 performer and he is from a Keystone Ore mare with the second dam being by Race Time. And Race Time appears as the sire of the first or second dam in four of Tyler B.'s eight fastest sons. Bret Hanover is also a strong presence and appears as the sire of the dam or second dam of seven of the 14 fastest performers.

Biba Fra has a very interesting pedigree cross since his dam is inbred 3x3 to Meadow Skipper and his Adios half-sister Tarport Duchess. Tyler B's co-third fastest performer is the Fan Hanover son Bold Hope p,4,1:51.1 ($178,090) who is inbred 3x3 to Meadow

Skipper. Albatross and Meadow Skipper dams are also prominent in the production of speed from Tyler B's fastest sons and daughters.

Tyler B is also very well noted as a sire of great fillies such as the aforementioned Amneris and Bruce's Lady, along with So Cozy p,3,1:54.2 ($880,492), Tyler Town p,3,1:54.1 ($783,093), Valentina p,2,1:56 ($708,325), Seven O'Clock p,4,1:53.3 ($559,080) and Angela Ty p,3,1:54.4 ($491,492) among others.

Many Tyler B sons have been tried as stallions. Dragon's Lair and Tyler's Mark have been the most successful in the United States; Franz Hanover and Rumpus Hanover have achieved some success in Canada. I am particularly fond of the young Illinois stallion Cole Muffler p,3,1:53.3f ($682,380), a full brother to Dragon's Lair, who is off to a great start from his first two crops with 14 in 1:55, including a trio of 1:53 two-year-olds. Cole Muffler appears to be a sire with great potential but he is being limited by his access to mostly Illinois broodmares which, to be frank, do not rank among the industry's elite mares. This is because of Illinois' archaic and restrictive "Illinois Conceived and Foaled" rule. But Cole Muffler has done a great job with the mares he has been given and seems to have the rare ability to "move them up."

As might be expected from a sire whose achievements have been well above average, Tyler B is also an excellent broodmare sire and his daughters should continue to produce well for the next decade since about half of them are only 11 years old or younger.

Looking at Tyler B's best broodmare sire credits, we find that six of his 10 fastest credits come from Abercrombie line sires - three by Abercrombie, two by Laag and one by Kentucky Spur. In addition, many of Tyler B's other fast sub-1:55 credits are from mares by those sires and other Abercrombie sons such as Albert Albert, Artsplace and Life Sign. The Abercrombie son Kentucky Spur is interesting since he did not do very well as a commercial stallion, but he has "nicked" extremely well with Tyler B mares to sire horses like Zero Inflation p,4,1:51.1 ($481,893), Linebacker Spur p,1:52.1 ($142,308), Panhattan p,1:52.3 ($409,420) and Spurred On p,1:52.3 ($308,738) from four different Tyler B mares.

Direct Scooter and his sons Matt's Scooter and In The Pocket have also done very well with Tyler B mares. From them, Direct Scooter has sired Expensive Scooter p,3,1:51 ($910,846), I Saw Him First p,3,1:51.1 ($532,732), The Tang Man p,3,1:52.1 ($214,448) and other good performers. Matt's Scooter has done even better with Matt's Domino p,3,1:51.2 ($117,230), Scooter Hanover p,3,1:52 ($216,275), Mattnamara's Band p,2,1:52.2 ($241,221), Sable Matters p,3,1:52.2, Cape Matteras p,2,1:53.4 and the ill-fated Stand Alone p,2,1:52.4 ($333,337) who may have been a great one if not for his untimely death at two. Stand Alone had a very interesting pedigree; he was 3x4x4 to Meadow Skipper and his dam, Huricane Almahurst, was bred 3x3 to Meadow Skipper, 3x4 to the full sisters Meadow Cheer and Tarport Addy and 4x4 to the half-brothers Dancer Hanover and Thorpe Hanover. The Direct Scooter son In The Pocket is the sire of the fine mare Sanabelle Island p,3,1:52.2 ($600,077) from a Tyler B mare.

Tyler B.'s fastest broodmare sire credit is Sports Town p,4,1:49.3 ($628,655) by Die Laughing - also a Most Happy Fella line stallion. Breeding Tyler B mares back to stallions from his own sire line has worked very well as shown by Megamind p,3,1:51.3 ($582,174) (by Jate Lobell), Min Nuke p,1:51.4 ($267,434) (by Dexter Nukes), Luke's Rd p,3,1:52.2 ($264,511), Simulcast p,3,1:52.4 ($381,465) (by Jate Lobell), Pacific Dynasty p,3,1:53.2-'98 (by No Nukes) and Armbro Rosebud p,3,1:54.3f-'98 ($535,189) (by Dexter Nukes).

Of course, Albatross has also sired many top performers from Tyler B mares, including Noble Ability p,4,1:51-'98 ($285,133), Danny B. p,1:51.2 ($295,705), Sixty Six Spur p,4,1:51.4f ($219,263) and Cassanova Spur p,4,1:52.1 ($290,663).

Some of the other fast Tyler B broodmare credits are million-dollar winner Dontgetinmyway p,1:50.4-'98 ($1,060,281) (by Abercrombie), Broadcast p,4,1:51 ($185,822) (by Abercrombie), Sakra Mania p,4,1:51 ($316,506) (by Laag), Band Leader p,1:51.1 ($232,747) (by Abercrombie), Slick Pavement p,1:51.2 ($835,485) (by Walton Hanover) and Jessee Purkey p,1:51.4 ($521,335) (by Walton Hanover).

Tyler B may be gone, but he will certainly not be forgotten.

Tyler B

Photo courtesy of The Horseman and Fair World

Leading Progeny by Tyler B

Fastest
- Biba Fra, g, p,4,1:50 $342,908
- Magical Mike, h, p,3,1:50.2 $1,682,085
- Shogun Hanover, g, p,4,1:51.1f $418,534
- Pundit, g, p,4,1:51.1f $357,785
- Bold Hope, h, p,4,1:51.1 $178,090
- Miles McCool, h, p,3,1:51.2f $333,721
- Dragon's Lair, h, p,1:51.3 $1,085,317
- Tyler's Point, h, p,1:51.3 $432,916
- Tyler's Mark, h, p,3,1:51.3 $289,100
- Very Rare, m, p,4,1:51.3 $249,292

Richest
- Magical Mike, h, p,3,1:50.2 $1,682,085
- Dragon's Lair, h, p,1:51.3 $1,085,317
- Dignatarian, h, p,1:52 $999,637
- Amneris, m, p,2,1:53.1 $974,141
- So Cozy, m, p,3,1:54.2 $880,492
- Conditional, h, p,Q1:54.2 $851,758
- Arcane Hanover, h, p,1:52.1 $818,496
- Barely Visible, g, p,1:53.2 $805,434
- Tyler Town, m, p,3,1:54.1 $783,093
- Bruce's Lady, m, p,3,1:53.3 $772,607

Tyler B, Bay Horse, 16.1 Hands, 1977 p, 2, 1:57.4; 3, 1:55.1 ($687,388)					
Most Happy Fella, 1967 p, 3, T1:55 $419,033	Meadow Skipper, 1960 p, 3, 1:55.1 $428,057	Dale Frost, 1951 p, 1:58 $204,117	**HAL DALE**, 1926 p, 6, 2:02¼	**ABBEDALE**	**THE ABBE** Daisydale D.
				Margaret Hal	Argot Hal Margaret Polk
			Galloway, 1939 p, 2:04½h $5,294	Raider	**PETER VOLO** Nelda Dillon
				Bethel	David Guy Annotation
		Countess Vivian, 1950 p, 3, 1:59 $43,262	King's Counsel, 1940 p, 6, 1:58 $44,930	**VOLOMITE**	**PETER VOLO** Cita Frisco
				Margaret Spangler	**GUY AXWORTHY** Maggie Winder
			Filly Direct, 1941 p, 3, 2:06¾ $6,299	**BILLY DIRECT**	Napoleon Direct Gay Forbes
				Calumet Edna	**PETER THE BREWER** Broncho Queen
	Laughing Girl, 1961 p, 4, 2:04h $19,564	Good Time, 1946 p, 1:57.4 $318,792	**HAL DALE**, 1926 p, 6, 2:02¼	**ABBEDALE**	**THE ABBE** Daisydale D.
				Margaret Hal	Argot Hal Margaret Polk
			On Time, 1938 p, 3, 2:03½h $1,472	**VOLOMITE**	**PETER VOLO** Cita Frisco
				Nedda Guy	**GUY AXWORTHY** Nedda
		Maxine's Dream, 1954 p, 2, T2:00 $36,557	Knight Dream, 1945 p, 3, T1:59 $76,973	Nibble Hanover	Calumet Chuck Justissima
				Lydia Knight	**PETER THE BREWER** Guy Rosa
			Maxine Abbe, 1937 p, 4, 2:05h	**ABBEDALE**	**THE ABBE** Daisydale D.
				Maxine Direct	**WALTER DIRECT** Vernie Wilkes
Tarport Cheer, 1966 p, 3, 2:08.3f	Tar Heel, 1948 p, 4, T1:57 $119,148	**BILLY DIRECT**, 1934 p, 4, T1:55 $12,040	Napoleon Direct, 1909 p, 1:59¾	**WALTER DIRECT**	Direct Hal Ella Brown
				Lady Erectress	Tom Kendle Nelly Zarro
			Gay Forbes, 1916 p, 2:07¾	Malcolm Forbes	Bingen Nancy Hanks
				Gay Girl Chimes	Berkshire Chimes Miss Gay Girl
		Leta Long, 1940 p, 4, 2:03¾ $9,321	**VOLOMITE**, 1926 3, 2:03¼ $32,649	**PETER VOLO**	**PETER THE GREAT** Nervolo Belle
				Cita Frisco	San Francisco Mendocita
			Rosette, 1933 2, 2:06 $4,222	Mr. McElwyn	**GUY AXWORTHY** Widow Maggie
				Rose Scott	Peter Scott Roya McKinney
	Meadow Cheer, 1956 p, 2, 2:05h $16,083	Adios, 1940 p, T1:57½ $33,329	**HAL DALE**, 1926 p, 6, 2:02¼	**ABBEDALE**	**THE ABBE** Daisydale D.
				Margaret Hal	Argot Hal Margaret Polk
			Adioo Volo, 1930 p, 3, 2:05h	Adioo Guy	Guy Dillon Adioo
				Sigrid Volo	**PETER VOLO** Polly Parrot
		Betty G., 1946 p, 4, 2:13.3h	Wilmington, 1938 p, 4, T1:59½ $7,988	Bert Abbe	The Abbe Miss Ella H.
				Miss Saginaw	Colonel Armstrong Miss Adioo
			Betty Crispin, 1934 p, 2, T2:05¾	Crispin	**GUY AXWORTHY** Jean Claire
				Gold Girl	**PETER THE GREAT** May B

Western Hanover

Western Hanover was a tough and game colt who could always be counted on for a top effort, as shown by his record of 27 wins from 42 starts and only two placements lower than third. In 1992, he missed becoming the sport's eighth Triple Crown winner by just a nose in the 1992 Little Brown Jug Final. Western Hanover was retired as the fifth leading money-winning pacer of all time and was so highly regarded he began his stud career at Hanover Shoe Farm.

By going to Hanover, Western Hanover returned to his place of birth and to the management of the farm which had sold him for $105,000 as a yearling at the Harrisburg, Pennsylvania, sale in 1990. As a yearling, Western Hanover caught the eye of trainer Gene Riegle and long-time owner George Segal, who made the purchase. That same year, Riegle and Segal teamed up to campaign Artsplace to two-year-old pacing honors and earnings of over $1,000,000. Little did they know that lightning would strike again.

Not reaching the races until July 20th of his two-year-old season, Western Hanover began his career with a fourth place finish in a qualifying race at The Meadowlands and was timed in 1:57.1. A week later, he won a qualifier there in 1:56.4 by three lengths and the Riegle-Segal team knew they had a talented colt. Western Hanover then ventured up to Canada's Blue Bonnets track in Montreal and won a $139,500 division of the Prix de l'Avenir in 1:57 in his first official start. He followed that 12 days later with an impressive win in the New Jersey Futurity over Freehold's half-mile track in 1:57.4. Track size would not be a problem for Western Hanover.

He met with his first defeat a week later at Freehold when second in the Garden State S., but he came back to win a division of the Champlain S. at Mohawk in 1:55.4 after being parked out from the half and making a three-wide move on the backstretch. He had been driven in all of his starts to this point by John Campbell and his regular driver later became Bill Fahy. Following two losses to Cole Muffler, Western Hanover was a 26-1 longshot in the $716,000 Metro S. Final at Mohawk and finished a respectable third after being seventh at the half.

Getting braver with each start, Western Hanover returned to Freehold to win the Lou Babic Memorial Elimination and Final, surviving tough, parked out trips in each race. In the $205,350 Babic Final, Western Hanover was parked out first over to the half in :55.4 before finally taking the lead nearing the three-quarters in 1:25.1. Instead of tiring, the No Nukes colt found renewed strength and went on to win by seven lengths in 1:54.4. After this race, driver Bill Fahy commented, "He was a lot better than last week. He's still a little green but once he looked the other horse (Admiral's Galley) in the eye, he just kept on going. He still had some speed to spare at the end of the mile."

Western Hanover's luck was not so good in the Breeders Crown Eliminations two weeks later at Pompano Park when he drew post seven and never got in the hunt due to traffic problems. He finished fifth and did not qualify for the Final.

But as he usually did after a loss, Western Hanover rebounded quickly winning a Presidential Pace Elimination at Rosecroft in 1:54.3. Then he finished third in the Final after another rough, parked out journey from post nine. That was Western Hanover's last loss of the season as he came back to win the Governor's Cup Elimination and $584,300 Final at Garden State Park. His elimination was capped by a :26.4 final quarter when he paced away from the field to win by five lengths. In the Governor's Cup Final, the colt had another gritty performance. He was parked out first over to the half in :55.1, took the lead in the stretch and went on to win in 1:52.1 by over four lengths to end his successful season. The winning time equalled the fastest of the year for any two-year-old colt.

Western Hanover's eight wins from 14 starts and earnings of $697,332 were enough to earn him the title of Two-Year-Old Pacing Colt of the Year in a very close vote of 124½ for Western Hanover to 116½ for Sportsmaster.

Race Record Highlights

At 2
- **1st** Governor's Cup Final and Elimination
  Lou Babic Memorial Final and Elimination
  Prix de l'Avenir
  Champlain S.
  Presidential S. Elimination
  New Jerey Futurity
- **2nd** Garden State S.
  Metro S. Elimination
- **3rd** Metro S. Final
  Presidential S. Final
  Nassagaweya S.

At 3
- **1st** Messenger S.
  New Jersey Classic Final and Elimination
  Cane Pace
  heat of Little Brown Jug
  Windy City S. Final and Elimination

At 3 (continued)
  James Dancer Memorial Final and Elimination
  Provincial Cup
  Cleveland Classic
  Art Rooney Memorial Elimination
  Meadowlands Pace Elimination
  Terrapin S.
  two New Jersey Sires S.
- **2nd** Breeders Crown Elimination and Final
  Little Brown Jug heat and Final
  North America Cup Final
  Art Rooney Memorial Final
- **3rd** North America Cup Elimination

Honors
Voted Two-Year-Old Pacing Colt of the Year
Voted Three-Year-Old Pacing Colt of the Year

Western Hanover

Photo by Monica Thors
Courtesy of The Horseman and Fair World

Race Record

Year	Age	Starts	Wins	2nd	3rd	Earnings	Record
1991	2	14	8	2	3	$ 697,332	p,3,1:52.1
1992	3	28	19	7	1	1,844,315	p,3,1:50.4
		42	27	9	4	$2,541,647	p,3,1:50.4

Western Hanover

Coming back at three, Western Hanover was even stronger and was again awarded divisional honors as Three-Year-Old Pacing Colt of the Year. During his sparkling campaign, Western Hanover won 19 of 28 starts and earned $1,844,315.

One of Western Hanover's few losses occurred in an ignominious performance in his first start of the year. After two qualifying race wins, Western Hanover raced in a $7,500 Open event at Ohio's Scioto Downs. He was the 1-10 favorite and considered a "sure thing." With Bruce Riegle in the sulky, Western Hanover had the rail, raced third most of the mile and lost by a length to Mugshot Special in 1:55. That would be his last loss for over a month.

Driven again by Bill Fahy for the rest of the year, Western Hanover won his next four races including the $500,000 New Jersey Classic in 1:50.4, the Terrapin S. and a New Jersey Sires S. His first stakes loss came in a North America Cup Elimination at Greenwood with a third place finish. A week later, in the $1,000,000 Final, Western Hanover raced in an uncharacteristic fashion, taking the early lead and trying to go wire-to-wire. He was nailed in deep stretch by Safely Kept who went on to win in 1:53.1 with Western Hanover earning second prize of $250,000 - a disappointment for his connections.

Another million-dollar race was next on Western Hanover's schedule - the Meadowlands Pace. The colt turned in a solid performance in his elimination, winning in 1:51.4 after making a nice three-wide move on the backstretch. In the $1,000,000 Meadowlands Pace Final, Western Hanover finished seventh after an unfortunate race in which he was interfered with, had to race three wide for over a half-mile and was never seriously in contention. Crouch and Shipp's Purser were aiming for the same space on the rail in the first turn and Shipp's Purser suddenly went on a break, which scattered the trailing horses, including Western Hanover. A very disappointed Bill Fahy said after the race, "Whatever happened to cause Shipp's Purser to go offstride cost me all chance. It took me out of the race."

Western Hanover came back a week later to win an Art Rooney Memorial Elimination at Yonkers in a sparkling 1:52.4, but finished second by a half-length to Survivor Gold in the Final after a parked out three-wide move in the second half. The colt then went on a spree of six consecutive wins: the Cleveland Classic, Cane Pace Elimination and Final, the James Dancer Memorial Elimination and Final and the Messenger S. He won each event decisively and headed into the Little Brown Jug in the best form of his career. Since he had already won the Cane and Messenger stakes he was now in quest of the Triple Crown.

The 1992 Little Brown Jug had 22 horses entered and necessitated three Elimination divisions. Gamma Ray and Crouch both won their Eliminations. A 1-5 favorite in his Jug Elimination, Western Hanover had the early lead but yielded it and was then parked out first over, eventually losing by a neck to the surprisingly tough Fake Left. Then the first three finishers from each Elimination returned for a second heat. If any of the Elimination winners won this heat, the Jug would be over. Western Hanover would have none of that and turned in a courageous performance, turning the tables and scoring by a neck over Fake Left.

The four winners returned for a race-off. Western Hanover drew the rail and Fake Left left from post two. Fake Left was the faster of the two leaving the gate and got to the front with Gamma Ray first over and then Crouch as they passed the quarter in :27. Fake Left continued on the front through fractions of :55.4 and 1:25.2. In the stretch, Gamma Ray began to fade, giving room for Western Hanover to leave the rail and pace up to challenge Fake Left. Western Hanover gained with every stride, but Fake Left refused to give in and held off Western Hanover's bid by a scant nose at the wire. The Triple Crown bid was thwarted by mere inches.

Western Hanover then came back to win an Invitational at The Meadows and a New Jersey Sires S. at Garden State Park. The 1992 Breeders Crown was next on his schedule, at the Northfield Park half-mile track. Leaving from post seven in his Elimination, Western Hanover was parked out every step of the way but finished second to Survivor Gold after losing a shoe. In the Breeders Crown Final, Western Hanover was the favorite and looked to be having a good trip. He was third just before the half and then pulled out to go first over to challenge the leading Survivor Gold. He passed that colt in the stretch, took over the lead and looked like a winner. However, the 35-1 Kingsbridge had shadowed Western Hanover's move and had plenty of pace left in the stretch. He posted a major upset by getting to Western Hanover at the wire to win by a neck in 1:54.4. That tough defeat was the last of Western Hanover's career. He won both the Windy City Elimination and Final in 1:55 wire-to-wire fashion at Maywood Park and later closed out his racing days with back-to-back wins in the Provincial Cup at Windsor.

With just a little more luck, Western Hanover could have posted an even more amazing season. Remember that he was interfered with in the $1,000,000 Meadowlands Pace and did not earn a check and lost by only a nose in the Little Brown Jug Final and a neck in the Breeders Crown Final. This colt was a model of consistency all year and that's what earned him divisional honors for a second time.

Sire Line

Hanover Shoe Farms had been looking for a son of No Nukes to add to its stallion ranks and struck a deal with owner George Segal to purchase part of and stand Western Hanover at stud. No Nukes, of course, has been a premier sire for the last decade and looks like he could be a sire of sires, much like his grandsire Most Happy Fella and great-grandsire Meadow Skipper. Early sons of No Nukes achieving some success at stud are Jate Lobell, Die Laughing and Dexter Nukes. You can read more about No Nukes in his chapter.

Maternal Line

Western Hanover's dam is the Albatross mare Wendymae Hanover p,4,T1:57-1:57.4 who has also produced Wendy M. Hanover p,3,1:54 ($337,132) (by No Nukes) and Wendyann Hanover p,4,1:56.2 (by Big Towner) from five foals. His grandam is the Best Of All mare Wendy Sue Hanover who was one of the early mares to produce multiple sub-1:54 speed in Walt Hanover p,1:53.1 ($239,086) (by Albatross) and Walton Hanover p,3,1:53.2 ($802,741) (by Big Towner).

Walton Hanover, in my opinion, has always been a very underrated stallion. He was a top colt performer and over 72 percent of his racehorses have taken 2:00 records. His sons and daughters get to the races and he has shown the ability to sire extreme speed with his daughter Caesar's Jackpot p,T1:49.2 ($969,494) being the fastest mare ever. His son Hi Ho Silverheel's p,3,1:50.3 ($957,971) is one of the leading FFA pacer in North America as this is written. Walton Hanover has also had a $1,000,000 winner with his son Totally Ruthless.

The great-grandam of Western Hanover is Wendy Hanover p,3,T2:00.2, a mare by Bullet Hanover who was also an early sub-1:54 producer with Wellwood Hanover p,3,T1:53.1 ($253,191) (by Best Of All). Wendy Hanover is really the mare who started the great production in this maternal family (which is known as Delightful Martha) since the dams earlier in the pedigree produced mostly raceway type performers.

The third dam of Wendy Hanover is a mare named Easter Patch who is a daughter of Power Patch - considered one of the best sons of the legendary Dan Patch. A few other branches of this family are active, but the Wendy Hanover branch has far eclipsed all of them. This part of the family is doing so well, I suspect, because of the infusion of the blood of Adios, since Wendy Hanover is sired by a son of Adios. It's an illustration of the power of Adios in a pedigree.

Progeny of Note

Western Hanover's first two crops have stamped him as a sire on the rise and further proof that his sire No Nukes appears to be a good sire of sires. Siring a Triple Crown winner from a first crop is no small feat, but one that Western Hanover accomplished with his top son Western Dreamer p,4,1:49.2-'98 ($1,532,241) who won the Little Brown Jug, Cane Pace and Messenger S. along with other high profile stakes which earned him Pacer of the Year honors in 1997.

The first crop of Western Hanover has also featured such stakes standouts as Rambaran p,3,1:52.4f ($431,504), the top filly Western Azure p,4,1:51-'98 ($404,664), Miss Kitty Hanover p,3,1:51.4 ($300,909), the filly So Western p,3,1:52.3 ($257,384), Gifted Cowboy p,3,1:53.4f ($219,091) and Stampede Hanover p,4,1:50.3-'98 ($182,230), among many others.

Western Hanover's second crop also excelled and was headed by the top stakes colt Rustler Hanover p,3,1:52-'98 ($722,181) who won in 1:52.3 and earned over $600,000 at two. Western Hanover's top two-year-old filly in 1997 was Take Flight p,2,1:53.2 ($598,123) who won the Breeders Crown and nearly $600,000. Other good performers from Western Hanover's second crop are Take Down The Flag p,3,1:51-'98 ($212,419), Shotgun Scott p,3,1:51-'98 ($198,502), Western Ho p,3,1:55f-'98, the filly Western Slide p,2,1:57.3f and Mickey Black p,2,1:53.1 to name a few.

Analysis

Western Hanover will have every chance to be a success for several reasons. First, he was bred to 842 mares during his first five seasons with a high of 192 in 1996, which followed the successful selling of his first crop of generally good-looking yearlings at the fall sales and the good early training reports. Another reason for optimism is that Western Hanover had the top-notch Hanover Shoe Farms broodmares available, as well as the support of a number of other breeders with excellent mares. If he does not make it as a sire, it will not be for lack of opportunity.

Looking at Western Hanover's pedigree, his closest cross is a linebred 4x3 to Meadow Skipper. He is also 5x5x4 to Good Time and 4x5 to Tar Heel. Another interesting cross is the 4x4 relationship to three-quarter brother and sister Bullet Hanover and Overbid.

Western Hanover is an obvious candidate for mares by sons of Albatross, which would put that stallion in a 3x3 position with Western Hanover sons and daughters. Nihilator, Niatross, B.G.'s Bunny and Sonsam have been successful sons of Albatross as broodmare sires. The absence of performers from mares by sons of Albatross is surprising; it may be that breeders did not want to go 3x3 or 3x4 to Albatross. But I suspect Western Hanover's best performers could come from that cross.

I also think a return of Most Happy Fella blood through the daughters of his best sons, such as Cam Fella and Tyler B., would be helpful. In addition, since Western Hanover has no Abercrombie or Bret Hanover blood, those are other good crosses.

Western Hanover's first crop, which raced at two in 1996, was very sharp early, producing 32 in 2:00 from 88 starters with earnings of over $1,200,000. Impressive as this is, it did not equal the first crop of Artsplace, whose youngsters earned nearly three times that of Western Hanover's two-year-olds. Artsplace also had 11 more 1:55 performers, but that could be because his foals were New Jersey Sires S. eligible, with many racing at the mile tracks of The Meadowlands and Garden State Park, while the Western Hanovers were Pennsylvania eligible and racing on five-eighth mile tracks.

A high percentage of the Western Hanover colts and fillies get to the races, 85% from his first two crops, which is a good sign, and Western Hanover also has several good fillies.

Currently, Western Hanover has sired one $1,000,000 winner, three $500,000 winners and 18 $100,000 winners. He also has a 1:50 performer and five in 1:51 or faster so he has proven he can sire both speed and class.

Looking at the leading money winning sons and daughters of Western Hanover, we find that four of the seven richest, as well as seven of the 18 $100,000 winners, are females. So, don't worry about Western Hanover fillies - they are doing just fine. I've also noted that 11 of the 21 richest performers have Bret Hanover or his sons as the sires of either the first or second dams. And, Abercrombie appears close up in the pedigrees of three of the four richest. Western

Dreamer's dam is by Panorama, a son of Abercrombie; Rustler Hanover's second dam is by Abercrombie and Rambaran's dam is by Abercrombie. The same situation holds true in the speed department with Western Dreamer the fastest followed by Stampede Hanover p,4,1:50.3-'98 whose dam is by Abercrombie (and a full sister to the great mare Anniecrombie) and Shotgun Scott p,3,1:51-'98 has a second dam by Abercrombie.

With the structure of Western Hanover's pedigree being 4x3 to Meadow Skipper as the closest cross, many of today's mares will add more Meadow Skipper blood to the foals sired by Western Hanover. This has shown up as many 5x4x3 Meadow Skipper crosses appear in his top racehorses. Triple Crown winner Western Dreamer is 5x4x4 to Meadow Skipper. However, there are a few exceptions. Rustler Hanover has no common ancestors in his first four generations and neither do Rambaran, Miss Kitty Hanover and Chief Marty p,3,1:51.2 ($122,409).

The good mare Western Azure is 4x2 to Most Happy Fella as her closest cross, but she also is the usual 5x4x3 to Meadow Skipper. So Western is 4x3 to Most Happy Fella and his dam is inbred 3x3 to Meadow Skipper. 1998 star Take Down The Flag has an unusual pedigree in that he is 3x4 to Sampson Hanover since his dam is a very inbred 2x3 to that stallion. Shotgun Scott is 3x4 to Albatross, a cross which I particularly like, and his dam is inbred 3x3 to Bret Hanover. Another with an interesting cross is the mare Danger Woman p,4,1:54.1-'98 ($158,298) who is 4x3 to Most Happy Fella and has an inbred dam 3x2 to Bret Hanover. Another with a close Albatross cross is Yankee Finesse p,3,1:53f ($112,263) who is 3x4 to Albatross and whose second dam is inbred 2x3 to Meadow Skipper.

Western Hanover has proven he can work well with a variety of different sires and shown by his top three performers being from dams by Panorama (Western Dreamer), Direct Scooter (Rustler Hanover) and Flying Bret (Take Flight). Western Hanover looks to be a stallion with a bright future and I'm sure he had a fine group of quality mares in his court during the 1998 breeding season given the success of his first two crops.

Western Hanover

Photo courtesy of The Horseman and Fair World

Leading Progeny by Western Hanover

Fastest
- Western Dreamer, g, p,4,1:49.2 $1,532,241
- Stampede Hanover, h, p,4,1:50.3 $182,230
- Western Azure, m, p,4,1:51 $404,664
- Take Down The Flag, h, p,3,1:51 $212,419
- Shotgun Scott, h, p,3,1:51 $198,502
- Western Spirit, h, p,4,1:51.1z $39,650
- Chief Marty, h, p,3,1:51.3 $122,409
- Miss Kitty Hanover, m, p,3,1:51.4 $300,909
- Rustler Hanover, h, p,3,1:52 $722,181
- Northwest, h, p,4,1:52f $148,471

Richest
- Western Dreamer, g, p,4,1:49.2 $1,532,241
- Rustler Hanover, h, p,3,1:52 $722,181
- Take Flight, m, p,2,1:53.2 $598,123
- Rambaran, r, p,3,1:52.4f $431,504
- Western Azure, m, p,4,1:51 $404,664
- Miss Kitty Hanover, m, p,3,1:51.4 $300,909
- So Western, m, p,3,1:52.3 $257,384
- Gifted Cowboy, h, p,3,1:53.4f $219,091
- Take Down The Flag, h, p,3,1:51 $212,419
- Shotgun Scott, h, p,3,1:51 $198,502

Western Hanover, Brown Horse, 15 Hands, 1989
p, 2, 1:52.1; 3, 1:50.4 ($2,541,647)

No Nukes, 1979 p, 3, T1:52.1 $572,430	Oil Burner, 1973 p, 4, 1:54.2 $535,541	Most Happy Fella, 1967 p, 3, T1:55 $419,033	**MEADOW SKIPPER**, 1960 p, 3, 1:55.1 $428,057	Dale Frost	**HAL DALE** Galloway
				Countess Vivian	**KING'S COUNSEL** Filly Direct
			Laughing Girl, 1961 p, 4, 2:04h $19,546	**GOOD TIME**	**HAL DALE** On Time
				Maxine's Dream	**KNIGHT DREAM** Maxine Abbe
		Dottie Shadow, 1968	Shadow Wave, 1955 p, 3, 1:56.3 $91,931	**ADIOS**	**HAL DALE** Adioo Volo
				Shadow Grattan	Silent Grattan Peacedale
			Diana Streak, 1949 p, 4, 1:58.4 $9,250	Red Streak	Pegasus Pointer Isabel Hanover
				Diana Mite	**VOLOMITE** Diana Dyer
	Gidget Lobell, 1974 p, 3, 2:00.3f $14,829	Overtrick, 1960 p, 3, 1:57.1h $407,483	Solicitor, 1948 p, 3, T1:57.2 $102,109	**KING'S COUNSEL**	**VOLOMITE** Margaret Spangler
				Jane Reynolds	Scotland Jane Revere
			Overbid, 1954 p, 2, T2:05.4 $3,524	**HAL DALE**	Abbedale Margaret Hal
				BARBARA DIRECT	**BILLY DIRECT** Norette Hanover
		Gogo Playmate, 1967	**TAR HEEL**, 1948 p, 4, T1:57 $119,148	**BILLY DIRECT**	Napoleon Direct Gay Forbes
				Leta Long	**VOLOMITE** Rosette
			Gogo Playtime, 1957 p, 6, 2:02.4h $50,687	**GOOD TIME**	**HAL DALE** On Time
				Dell Siskiyou	Siskiyou Elsie Truax
Wendymae Hanover, 1983 p, 4, T1:57 $8,887	Albatross, 1968 p, 4, 1:54.3f $1,201,470	**MEADOW SKIPPER**, 1960 p, 3, 1:55.1 $428,057	Dale Frost, 1951 p, 1:58 $204,117	**HAL DALE**	Abbedale Margaret Hal
				Galloway	Raider Bethel
			Countess Vivian, 1950 p, 3, 1:59 $43,262	**KING'S COUNSEL**	**VOLOMITE** Margaret Spangler
				Filly Direct	**BILLY DIRECT** Calumet Edna
		Voodoo Hanover, 1964	Dancer Hanover, 1957 p, 4, T1:56.4 $87,746	**ADIOS**	**HAL DALE** Adioo Volo
				The Old Maid	Guy Abbey Spinster
			Vibrant Hanover, 1960	**TAR HEEL**	**BILLY DIRECT** Leta Long
				Vivian Hanover	**GUY MCKINNEY** Guesswork
	Wendy Sue Hanover, 1972 p, 3, 2:05.1f $6,406	Best Of All, 1964 p, 4, 1:56.2 $549,074	**GOOD TIME**, 1946 p, 1:57.4 $318,792	**HAL DALE**	Abbedale Margaret Hal
				On Time	**VOLOMITE** Nedda Guy
			Besta Hanover, 1952	**KNIGHT DREAM**	Nibble Hanover Lydia Knight
				Bertha Hanover	**GUY MCKINNEY** Miss Bertha Dillon
		Wendy Hanover, 1966 p, 3, T2:00.2 $9,114	Bullet Hanover, 1957 p, 3, T1:55.3 $132,578	**ADIOS**	**HAL DALE** Adioo Volo
				BARBARA DIRECT	**BILLY DIRECT** Norette Hanover
			Wayblaze, 1949	**KING'S COUNSEL**	**VOLOMITE** Margaret Spangler
				Goldie Patch	Peter Nutonia Easter Patch

Index

A Stud Named Sue, 234-236
Aahm A Jokester, 161-162
Abbacy, 65, 85, 171, 201, 237, 259, 289, 297, 339, 353, 365
Abbe's Good Boy, 206
Abbey Claire, 171, 259, 327
Abdallah I, 12-13, 207
Abdallah Belle, 207
Abercrombie, 14, 16, 18-19, 23-33, **34-41**, 42, 47, 49, 52, 54, 60-61, 63, 66, 68, 71, 74-76, 79-80, 82, 89, 91, 98-100, 107, 124, 127, 134, 147, 154, 168-170, 180, 182, 186, 191, 198-199, 220, 228, 233, 235-238, 241-245, 250, 263, 273, 276, 281, 284, 288, 295, 300, 303, 312, 322, 325-327, 331-332, 338, 343, 368-370, 375, 387, 394-395
Above Board, 24
Acquired Skill, 27
Adam Lobell, 54-56
Adams, Albert, 230
Adelweiss Rainbow, 319-320
Adept Hanover, 259
Adiana Hanover, 55
Adioleta, 302, 378
Adioo, 40-41, 46, 51, 57, 111, 353, 359
Adioo Dillon, 41, 57, 65, 71, 79, 85, 101, 119, 129, 171, 187, 195, 237, 245, 259, 267, 297, 359, 365, 371, 377, 389
Adioo Guy, 41, 46, 51, 57, 65, 71, 79, 85, 93, 101, 111, 119, 129, 135, 143, 149, 155, 163, 179, 187, 195, 229, 237, 245, 251, 259, 289, 297, 305, 315, 333, 339, 353, 359, 365, 371, 377, 389, 397
Adioo Volo, 40-41, 46, 51, 57, 65, 71, 79, 85, 93, 101, 111, 119, 129, 135, 143, 149, 155, 163, 179, 184, 187, 195, 221, 229, 237, 245, 251, 259, 289, 297, 305, 315, 327, 333, 339, 353, 359, 365, 371, 377, 389, 397
Adios, 14, 16, 19-22, 33-41, **42-51**, 52-60, 62, 65, 67-68, 70-71, 73-75, 77-79, 82-83, 85, 87-89, 91, 93, 96-99, 101-102, 105-111, 114-117, 129, 131-132, 135, 141, 143, 149, 154-155, 159, 161, 163, 168, 176-177, 179, 182, 184-185, 187, 191, 193-199, 202, 204-205, 210-211, 218-221, 228-230, 233, 237, 242, 244-245, 247-248, 250-251, 255, 259, 262-265, 268-269, 271-273, 277-278, 280-281, 286-287, 289-291, 293-295, 297-299, 302, 305, 311-312, 315, 317-318,
320, 326-327, 329-333, 337, 339-344, 347-350, 353-354, 356-357, 359, 361-363, 365-374, 377, 380-381, 386-387, 389, 393, 397
Adios Betty, 22, 45-48, 89, 149, 250-251
Adios Boy, 45-46, 48, 54, 149, 339
Adios Butler, 16, 20-21, 33, 47-48, 50, 52-54, 105-106, 112, 153, 192-195, 262
Adios Cleo, 114
Adios Don, 47-48, 50, 106, 117, 318
Adios Dotty, 233
Adios Governess, 20, 153, 194
Adios Harry, 45-48, 50, 54, 105-106
Adios Marches, 106
Adios Mir, 318
Adios Onda, 179
Adios Paul, 264
Adios Scarlet, 381
Adios Senator, 320
Adios Vic, 16, 23, 33, 47-50, **52-57**, 104-106, 126, 140-141, 143, 166, 235, 272, 280, 369
Admiral's Galley, 23, 236, 390
Adora, 26, 242-243, 245, 318
Adora's Dream, 242-243, 318
Adover Lobell, 320
Aetna, 171, 321, 345, 371, 377, 383
Agave, 57, 101, 187, 237, 359
Ahlberg, 55
Ahoy Captain, 363-364
Aida, 259
Aileen, 287
Aileen Arion, 259
Airliner, 33, 48, 272, 280, 320, 381
Al Dente, 110, 312
Al For President, 337-338
Alaskan Strike, 372
Albaquel, 29
Albatross, 14, 16, 18-33, 38-39, 42, 45, 54-56, **58-65**, 68, 70-71, 75-80, 82, 85, 91, 97-99, 101-102, 107-110, 116, 123-124, 126-127, 134-135, 140, 147, 152, 154-156, 159-161, 163, 167, 169-170, 177, 183-185, 194, 196, 205, 207, 212, 217, 220, 227-228, 235-236, 242-245, 250, 257, 262-264, 266, 268, 271-273, 276, 279-281, 283-284, 286-287, 289, 292-295, 297, 301-302, 312, 319-320, 326-327, 330-333, 337-338, 343, 350, 356, 360, 362-365, 369, 374, 380-382, 387, 393-395, 397
Albert Albert, 16, 22, 24, 26, 28-32, 38-
40, 61, 63, **66-71**, 80, 115, 127, 170, 191, 230, 242-244, 254, 288, 303, 322, 325, 327, 343, 387
Albert T, 30, 70
Albert's Star, 115
Alcyone, 171, 207, 321, 345, 371, 377, 383
Alert Bret, 108, 276, 278-279
Alert Move, 110, 212
Alice Grattan, 237
Aline, 51, 57, 111, 213, 267, 321, 345, 359
Alison Sara, 24, 30
All Alert, 211
All Da Time, 28
All Star Hanna, 26, 169-170, 265
Allegro, 353
Allen Rd, 313
Allerton, 119, 383
Allie Allerton, 119
Allie Watts, 119
Allie West, 51, 213
Allison Wonderland, 27
Allwin Steady, 25, 82-84
Allwood Stables, 316
Alma Lee, 141, 143, 179, 195, 201, 251, 326, 345, 371
Almahurst Farm, 174, 209, 230, 234, 354, 360-361
Almahurst Frontier, 244
Almahurst Stinger, 184, 186
Almont Jnr, 359
Almont Jnr Mare, 383
Alnoff Farm, 156
Alpha Lobell, 55
Altmans, 37
Altmeyer, Dan, 136
Alycone, 383
Amazonia, 12
Ambiguity, 49, 242, 245
America's Pastime, 218, 220, 222, 334
American Eclipse, 12
American Freedom, 27
Amity Chef, 16, 89, 110, 116-117, 198-200, 227, 342
Amneris, 184, 196, 384, 386-388
Anders Favorite, 167
Anderson Wilkes, 101, 207, 275, 283
Andrel, 281-282, 308
Andy Lobell, 319-320
Angel Be Great, 337-338
Angel Hair, 49, 110, 242
Angela Ty, 384, 387
Angeliou, 69
Angie Girl, 91
Ann Vonian, 93, 114, 119, 206, 229, 283, 289, 297, 315, 333
Anna Bradford's Girl, 221
Anna Titus, 207
Annabel, 377
Annie Almont, 57, 119, 359
Anniecrombie, 38-40, 395
Annotation, 65, 85, 93, 129, 187, 201, 237, 259, 267, 275, 283, 289, 315, 339, 353, 365, 389
Anxious Robby, 310, 381
Apache Circle, 29, 97, 99
Apache Max, 29, 273
Apache's Fame, 88, 97
Apollo's Way, 280, 282, 357
Apt-To-Acres, 80
Arbutus Hanover, 259
Arcane Hanover, 388
Archdale, 41, 51, 57, 65, 111, 119, 187, 201, 213, 267, 275, 283, 321, 345, 359, 371, 377
Archie Girl, 377
Areba Areba, 55-56, 169, 280
Areba Bunny, 169
Arion, 101, 187, 207, 259, 292
Arion Lobell, 55-56
Ariva Dexter, 154
Arizona Jack, 26, 39-40, 198-199
Armada, 200
Armbro Alert, 19, 23, 26
Armbro Aussie, 23, 26, 29, 31, 55, 123, 271-272, 274, 281, 320, 381
Armbro Bramble, 82, 84
Armbro Breton, 118
Armbro Cadet, 39, 116, 263, 273, 306
Armbro Caprice, 27
Armbro Carmita, 28
Armbro Colleen, 30
Armbro Dallas, 39-40, 273, 290
Armbro Dazzler, 55-56, 280-282
Armbro Easy, 30
Armbro Emerson, 16, 29, 31-32, 38-40, 170, 233, 273, 375
Armbro Evita, 357
Armbro Exotic, 26, 356
Armbro Feather, 110, 271-272, 274
Armbro Flight, 300, 350
Armbro Georgia, 25
Armbro Global, 168, 170, 252, 313
Armbro Glossy, 27
Armbro Goal, 300, 350

Entries in bold face indicate featured sires

Armbro Hardy, 115
Armbro Harmony, 23
Armbro Impel, 93, 229
Armbro Intimate, 24
Armbro Jagger, 364
Armbro Local, 334
Armbro Mackintosh, 219-220, 246, 322, 375
Armbro Maestro, 20, 23, 153-154, 374
Armbro Maneuver, 26, 83, 169-170, 249, 331
Armbro Moody, 154, 375
Armbro Morning, 154
Armbro Nesbit, 14, 17, 23-24, 30, 33, 55, 89-91, 93, 112, 115, 118, 167, 199, 229, 319
Armbro Nest, 28, 176-178, 363
Armbro Obliging, 30
Armbro Ocelot, 54
Armbro October, 170
Armbro Ocular, 154
Armbro Oliver, 28
Armbro Ollie, 55-56
Armbro Omaha, 32, 48, 154, 263, 381-382
Armbro Omar, 30, 273
Armbro Ontario, 54-55
Armbro Operative, 25, 61, 82-83, 125, 331, 356
Armbro Other, 25, 39-40, 63
Armbro Ozark, 54-55
Armbro Peachie, 300
Armbro Peregrine, 194
Armbro Pluto, 22, 25, 153-154
Armbro Rally, 55
Armbro Rambler, 55
Armbro Rhythm, 55
Armbro Romance, 21, 24, 78
Armbro Rosebud, 153-154, 387
Armbro Splurge, 166, 270
Armbro Tequila, 244
Armbro Tiger, 180
Armbro Utrillo, 29
Armbro Vibrant, 55
Armbro Vienna, 55-56
Armbro Wolf, 62, 64, 250, 381
Armstrong, Elgin, 54
Armstrong, Ted, 54
Armstrong Bros., 48, 54, 107, 150-151, 244
Arndon, 320
Arnie Almahurst, 238
Arrive At Five, 25, 242, 293, 295-296
Art In The Park, 76, 78, 303
Art's Palace, 78, 364
Art's Secret, 78
Arthur, Doug, 120
Artillery, 213

Artiscape, 77-78, 110, 313
Artist Stena, 30, 220
Artistic Pleasure, 76, 78
Artsplace, 14, 16, 20, 23-25, 28, 30-32, 34, 37-40, 61-63, 66, 68, **72-79**, 97, 100, 107, 110, 124, 133, 138, 144, 156, 158, 160, 169-170, 184, 191-192, 211, 220, 238, 241-244, 281, 294-295, 303, 313, 325, 328, 330, 334, 387, 390, 394
Arturo, 77-78
As Promised, 25, 39-40, 288
Ash Blue Chip, 21, 24, 311-312, 314
Ashland Wilkes, 51, 57, 111, 213, 267, 321, 345, 359
Ask A Lawyer, 152
Astronomer's Hall, 142
At Point Blank, 28, 91-92
Athena Blue Chip, 27, 313
Athens Blue Chip, 27
Athlone Guy, 221
Athlone's Princess, 221
Atlantic Express, 211, 213, 275, 345
Attorney, 205-206
Au Revoir, 46
Audubon Boy, 101, 207, 283
Augie Donatelli, 376
Avakian, George, 336
Avalanche, 233
Avery, Earle, 260, 316, 318
Awesome Almahurst, 82-84
Awesome Winner, 220
Axtell, 41, 171, 213, 267, 321, 345, 359, 383
Axworthy, 41, 57, 63, 65, 71, 79, 85, 93, 101, 111, 117, 129, 171, 179, 185, 187, 195, 201, 212-213, 221, 237, 245, 251, 259, 267, 275, 283, 289, 297, 305, 315, 319, 321, 339, 345, 353, 359, 365, 371, 377, 383, 389
Azoff, 65, 187, 201, 267, 275, 283, 305, 315
B.G.'s Bunny, 16, 18, 24-26, 29, 32-33, 61-62, 68, 76-78, **80-85**, 91, 126, 133-135, 160, 169, 228, 280, 330-333, 338
B. J. Scoot, 68, 184, 186, 254
B J's Whirlwind, 22, 25, 332
Baby Bertha, 111, 371, 377
Baby Sitter, 20
Bacall, 152, 155
Bachelor Hanover, 342
Bad Bert, 28, 69-70
Bad Self, 28, 273, 312, 314
Bahama Bunny, 99, 331-332
Baker, E.J., 42, 46
Baker, Pat, 346

Balanced Attack, 287
Bald Chief, 207
Baldwin, Ralph, 340
Balenzano, 114
Ball And Chain, 20, 23, 60-62, 64, 109, 225-227, 268, 325, 343
Ballerina Girl, 233
Bally Pointer, 305
Ballycullun, 29
Band Leader, 387
Bandelier, 342-344
Bandella, 359
Banquet Table, 199-200
Banshee Hanover, 30
Baracuda Almahurst, 183
Baraka, 374, 376
Barbara Direct, 135, 143, 153, 155, 163, 195, 221, 229, 305, 319, 321, 397
Barbara's Vic, 23
Barberry Spur, 25, 30, 108-109, 214, 286-288, 293
Barbette, 57
Barby's Makentrax, 30
Bardot Lobell, 279-280
Barely Visible, 388
Barnes, Harold, 34
Baron Brooke, 119
Baron Hanover, 16, 19, 33, 48, 107, 154, 185, 193, 204-206, 235, 280, 363, 382
Baron Wilkes, 213
Baroness Betty Jo, 204
Barongale, 111
Barracuda Beach, 90, 92
Barry's Choice, 349
Bart Hanover, 107
Bartolomew Wilkes, 51
Bat Champ, 217
Batman, 115-116, 118
Battle Damage, 370
Bay Line, 119, 213, 383
Bay Tom Jnr, 51, 213
Beach The Clock, 90
Beach Towel, 16, 21, 23-25, 28, 31-32, 40, 66, 74, **86-93**, 115-116, 126, 144, 152, 194, 196, 198-200, 227-229, 250, 262, 268, 271, 284, 331, 342
Beams Hanover, 171, 259, 327
Bear Dance, 99, 147, 337-338
Beastmaster, 144, 240-241
Beatrice, 213
Beau Dexter, 107
Beautiful Bells, 51, 57, 101, 111, 207, 213, 267, 283, 321, 345, 359, 383
Beautiful Hanover, 107

Before Sunrise, 134, 331-332, 364
Behold Hanover, 155
Belle Brassfield, 383
Belle Gibson, 267
Belle Grattan, 57, 143
Belle Mahone, 20, 124, 129, 135, 143, 149, 333, 339
Belle Of Easton, 149
Belle Of Wabash, 207
Belle Thornton, 51, 101, 207, 213
Belle Winnie, 171, 345, 371
Belle Zombro, 65, 171, 187, 201, 259, 267, 275, 283, 315
Bellfounder, 12
Bellini, 213, 345
Belmont, 51, 207
Beloved Hanover, 228-229
Belvedere, 326-327
Belwin, 65, 111, 143, 171, 201, 259, 345, 371
Bengazi Hanover, 99, 381
Bennett Chapman, 51, 213
Bergdorf, 37, 41, 71, 79, 235, 237, 245, 327
Berger, Elsie, 284
Berinda Hanover, 154
Berkner, George, 80
Berkshire Belle, 119, 383
Berkshire Chimes, 111, 119, 171, 267, 321, 377, 383, 389
Berlin, Mark, 336
Berry, Tom, 112, 114
Bert Abbe, 14, 16, 41, 69, 71, 79, 85, 97, 101, 135, 179, 202, 204-205, 207, 217, 221, 237, 245, 251, 283, 305, 315, 327, 333, 353, 389
Bertha C., 111, 140, 175, 353, 377
Bertha Derby, 111
Bertha Dillon, 76, 107, 111, 175, 201, 283, 321, 353, 371, 377, 397
Bertha Hanover, 79, 143, 353, 397
Beryl Hanover, 71, 78, 85, 107, 110-111, 129, 135, 143, 149, 195, 229, 245, 297, 312, 327, 333, 339, 365, 371, 377
Bessie Bonehill, 267
Bessie Gilbert, 41
Bessie Hall, 119, 383
Bessie Louise, 57
Best Bizarre, 286
Best Mood, 142
Best Of All, 14, 16, 28-29, 33, 83, 98, 185, 210-212, 262, 269, 286, 302, 326, 330, 332, 340, 348-351, 353, 369, 373, 393, 397
Besta Hanover, 353, 397

Index

Bethel, 65, 71, 79, 85, 93, 129, 135, 143, 149, 155, 163, 179, 187, 201, 229, 237, 245, 251, 259, 267, 275, 283, 289, 297, 305, 310, 315, 333, 339, 353, 365, 389, 397
Betterson, 51, 119, 213, 383
Betty Blythe, 93, 251
Betty Brown, 359
Betty Crispin, 179, 251, 389
Betty G., 179, 251, 257, 384, 389
Betty Hanover, 107, 135, 143, 149, 229, 333, 339
Betty Jo Chris, 204
Betty Kellar, 69
Betty Lobell, 28
Betty Mahone, 129, 135, 143, 149, 229, 333, 339
Bewitch Hanover, 153, 155
Biba Fra, 22, 24, 115, 386-388
Bid Hanover, 93, 229, 251, 392
Big Band Sound, 272
Big Brat, 159, 288
Big Brother Hanna, 169
Big Bum, 102, 110
Big Elbert, 69
Big Guy, 30, 32, 97, 99-100, 170, 186, 190, 303, 313, 381
Big Timer, 94
Big Towner, 14, 16, 18-19, 21, 23-25, 28-33, 63, 66, 69, 76-78, **94-101**, 109, 134, 147, 154, 160-161, 167-170, 177, 186, 193-194, 202, 204-206, 210, 228, 235-236, 242-244, 273, 279, 288, 292, 303, 313, 326, 331-332, 338, 356-357, 381, 393
Bilateral, 26, 234-236, 273
Bill Gallon, 93, 196, 201, 229
Billy Dart, 185
Billy Direct, 14-15, 17, 19-21, 41, 47-48, 63, 65, 71, 79, 82, 85, 93, 109, 111, 114-117, 119, 129, 135, 143, 149, 153, 155, 163, 168, 171, 179, 187, 195, 199, 201, 208, 219, 221, 229, 237, 245, 251, 256, 259, 262, 264, 267, 272, 275, 280, 283, 289, 294, 297, 301, 305, 311, 315, 317, 319, 321, 327, 333, 339, 343, 353, 365, 371-372, 377-378, 380, 383, 386, 389, 397
Binding Offer, 127
Bingen, 57, 101, 111, 119, 171, 207, 267, 321, 377, 383, 389
Bingo Hanover, 99
Birdie B, 237
Bit Of Good News, 27

Black Jade, 23
Black Jin, 12
Blackie, 51, 213
Blackstone, 20, 287, 363
Blatently Bald, 281
Blaze Pick, 205-206, 217, 221
Blitzen Almahurst, 110
Bloodstock's Bunny, 169
Bloomingdale, 37
Blossom Time, 211
Blue Belle, 51, 57, 111, 359
Blue Bonnets, 74, 88, 106, 137-138, 150, 158, 164, 166, 172, 190, 197, 216, 232, 252-254, 269, 308-309, 390
Blue Chip Farms, 97, 202, 204, 233, 246, 249-250, 268, 271, 307, 310
Blue Chip Partners, 310
Blue Heather, 237
Bo Knows Jate, 40, 218-220
Bobbysocks, 312
Bogart, 184-186
Bola, 185
Bold Hope, 387-388
Bold Moment, 25
Bomb Rickles, 302, 304
Bonanza Alert, 244
Bond Street, 80
Boni, Bob, 290
Bonjour Hanover, 47-48, 50, 107, 381
Bonnie And Clyde, 176, 178, 240, 288, 334, 336
Bonnie Butler, 153, 155, 195
Bonnycastle, 48, 149, 339
Bonwit, 37
Boobtube, 30
Boomer Drummond, 205
Boone And Crocket, 272, 274
Boring, Chris, 66, 68, 106
Born To Glory, 255
Bourbon Wilkes, 101, 205, 207, 283
Bouvier, 28
Boxwood Farm, 236
Brace Yourself, 169
Brando Hanover, 265
Breath O Spring, 140, 179, 193-195, 251, 340, 343, 345, 366, 368, 371
Bree's Brief, 99
Breezie Skipper, 24, 312
Breezy Fashion, 192
Breezy Road, 27
Brenda Blue Chip, 26, 28
Brenna Hanover, 71, 85, 107, 111, 129, 135,

143, 149, 154, 195, 229, 245, 297, 327, 333, 339, 365, 368-369, 371, 377, 382
Bret Hanover, 14, 16, 18-28, 30, 32-33, 38-39, 46-50, 52, 54, 60, 62, 68-71, 78, 80, 82, 84-85, 91, 98, **102-111**, 116, 120, 124, 126, 129, 134-135, 141, 143, 147, 149, 154, 160-161, 169-170, 175, 185, 191, 193, 195, 199, 205, 208, 211-212, 218-219, 228-229, 235, 242-245, 250, 257, 262, 264, 272-273, 276, 279-281, 284, 286-287, 292-295, 297, 302, 312, 320, 325-327, 332-333, 337-340, 343, 351, 354, 360, 362-363, 365-366, 368-369, 371-372, 374-375, 377, 381-382, 386, 394-395
Bret's Avenger, 110, 292
Bret's Champ, 108, 279
Bret's Courage, 292
Bret's Knight, 80, 109
Bret's Romance, 68-69, 80, 82, 135, 327
Brief Romance, 198
Brien Hanover, 175, 250-251, 354, 378, 381, 386
Bright As Day, 21, 24, 159, 375
Bring 'Em, 312
Brisco Hanover, 198
Britt's Best, 133
Brittany Lauxmont, 26
Brittany Farms, 72, 238
Broad Grin, 273
Broadcast, 30, 387
Broadway Blue, 28, 63, 334
Broadway Express, 16, 97-100, 172, 174, 204, 292
Broadway Jate, 218-220
Broadway Spirit, 233
Brod, 69-70
Broglio, Lee, 94, 96
Broncho Queen, 65, 85, 93, 129, 187, 201, 237, 259, 267, 275, 283, 289, 353, 365, 389
Brookdale, 301
Brooks, William F., 298
Brown Hal, 51, 57, 65, 111, 119, 171, 187, 201, 213, 267, 275, 283, 321, 345, 359, 371, 377, 389
Browning Blue Chip, 337-338
Bruce Gimble, 29, 37, 235, 284
Bruce's Lady, 175, 344, 382, 386-388
Brunhilde Hanover, 28
Bryson, 171, 321, 345, 371, 377, 383
Buck, Helen, 316

Buck, Leonard, 316
Buckeye Count, 167
Buda, 51, 213
Bulen, Keith, 34
Bulldog, 126, 337, 339
Bullet Hanover, 16, 47-48, 50, 52, 54, 83, 117, 155, 228, 262, 269, 302, 319, 393-394, 397
Bullvon's Dream, 26, 273, 362-364
Bunny's Wish, 24, 83, 328, 330-331, 333
Buoyant Hanover, 369
Burnish, 23
Butler B G, 82, 84, 308
Buxton, Dick, 104
By By, 51, 57, 111, 359, 371, 377
By Guy, 46, 51, 57, 111, 119, 310, 359, 371, 377
By Xample, 147-148
Bye And Large, 14, 17, 23, 112, 115-116, 167, 343
Bye Bye Byrd, 14, 17, 19-21, 23-25, 33, 46, 62, 89, 93, 108, **112-119**, 154, 166-167, 198-199, 212, 228-229, 272, 281, 286-287, 289, 294-295, 297, 310-311, 313, 315, 317, 319, 331-333, 354, 369, 381
Bye Bye Dannibyrd, 217
Bye Bye Max, 115, 118
Bye Bye Mollie, 117, 306, 310, 315
Bye Bye Pat, 115
Bye Bye Sam, 115
Bye Bye Time, 117, 331, 333
Bye Columbus, 211-212
C. A. Connection, 28
C. K. S., 311, 314
C. R. Kay Suzie, 225
C Lulu Plein Truc, 313
Cable Guy, 244
Cadet, 39, 116, 263, 273, 306
Caesar's Jackpot, 20, 23, 55, 61, 63, 366, 393
Cafe Racer, 69-70
Cagey Jake, 186
Caliban, 207
Caliope, 152
Call For Cash, 29, 175, 258
Call For Rain, 20, 23, 88, 216-217, 265, 284, 346, 348, 368-370, 384
Calumet Aristocrat, 93, 201
Calumet Chuck, 41, 71, 79, 85, 111, 129, 171, 179, 195, 201, 237, 245, 259, 275, 297, 327, 353, 365, 371, 377, 389
Calumet Cream, 149

Calumet Edna, 65, 71, 79, 85, 93, 129, 135, 143, 149, 155, 163, 179, 187, 199, 201, 229, 237, 245, 251, 259, 267, 275, 283, 289, 297, 305, 315, 333, 339, 353, 363, 365, 389, 397
Calypso, 101, 207
Calypso Beat, 296
Cam Boo Angel, 148
Cam Fella, 14, 16, 18-19, 23-33, 38, 40, 42, 54-55, 63, 75-76, 78, 82-84, 91, 99, 102, 108, 110, **120-129**, 133-135, 140-141, 143-144, 146, 149, 153, 159, 168-170, 175, 219-220, 227-229, 235, 243, 249, 268, 270-272, 274, 281, 288, 300, 303, 306, 310, 313, 326, 330-334, 336-337, 339, 343-344, 350, 356, 368, 384, 394
Cam Knows Best, 142
Cam Terrific, 20, 23, 128, 224, 226
Cam's Card Shark, 16, 21, 24, 61, 82-83, 124-125, 128, **130-135**, 144, 224, 248-249, 268, 271, 320, 322, 324, 331
Cam's Catch, 26, 63
Cam's Coal, 29
Cam's Exotic, 125
Cam's Fortune, 146
Cam's Jewel, 63
Cam's Lucky, 146
Cam's Magic Trick, 24, 83, 133, 334
Cam's Paragon, 140
Cam's Trickster, 133
Cambest, 15-16, 19, 23, 55, 75, 124-126, 128, 134, **136-143**, 144, 156, 158, 167, 227, 268, 271, 340
Cambret, 124
Camden Caroline, 27
Cameron, Warren, 164, 166
Cameron, Wilfred, 120
Cami Whitestocking, 27
Camie Kalo, 142
Camluck, 16, 20, 23, 75, 99, 124-126, 128, 140, **144-149**, 192
Cammie's Lady, 82-83, 125
Camourous, 125, 303
Camp, Saul, 354
Campbell, Jim, 254, 346
Campbell, John, 72, 74-75, 77, 88, 123, 130, 133, 144, 150, 158, 174, 222, 224, 228, 240-241, 246, 248, 254, 298, 325, 328, 346, 386, 390
Camtastic, 16, 20, 23, 26-28, 31-32, 55, 61, 63, 66, 68, 124-125, 128, 144, 150, 252, 271, 344, 363
Camtastic Dream, 28, 363

Candid Camera, 212
Candy Bucks, 23, 293
Cane, William, 208, 210
Canzonet, 267, 321
Cape Horn, 48
Cape Matteras, 387
Capetown, 93, 115, 229, 319
Capital Spending, 52
Caprock, 219-220
Captain Courageous, 99
Captain Pantastic, 240-241
Captain Webster, 51
Caramel Sundae, 23, 185-186
Carlsbad Cam, 29, 63, 125, 128
Carolina Rhythm, 212
Cardigan Bay, 105-106, 205, 269, 318
Cardinal Prince, 48, 93, 149, 229, 250-251, 339
Career Success, 337-338
Caressable, 161, 286-288
Carl's Bird, 38, 308
Carlisle, 183
Carlsbad Cam, 29, 63, 125, 128
Caramel Sundae, 23, 185-186
Carolina Rhythm, 212
Carolonda, 179
Carolyn, 93, 201
Carrie Castle, 149, 339
Cartier, 25, 37
Case Jr., Walter, 241
Cash Asset, 287, 357
Casino Cowboy, 150, 287-288
Casino Gambler, 152
Casino Winner, 142, 152
Cassanova Spur, 387
Castanea, 101, 207, 283
Castashadow, 358
Castleton Farm, 35-36, 38, 103, 105, 110, 188-189, 208-210, 286, 329, 340-341, 354, 366-367, 372-374, 376, 384
Castleton Rowdy, 193
Castleton Spring, 25
Catch A Flight, 21, 24, 311-312, 314, 364
Cathedra, 350-352
Cedarwood Chips, 55-56
Celebrity Girl, 39
Center Strip, 311, 314
Central Park West, 98
Ceremony, 27
Chairmanoftheboard, 26, 190, 263-264, 266
Chamberlain, Wilt, 104
Chapman, John, 94, 96
Charles Kent Mare, 12, 207

Charlotte Hanover, 251
Charming T, 30
Charming Time, 366
Chasanoff, 156
Chatham Light, 254, 287-288
Cheer Up, 208
Cheers, 23, 25
Cheery Hello, 61-62, 381-382, 384
Chef's Magic, 199-200
Cherry Gentry, 41
Chestertown, 208
Chestnut Hill, 152
Chevy Chase A., 56
Chiaravalle, Antonio, 334
Chickasaw Brave, 27
Chief Abbedale, 23, 41, 71, 79, 237, 245, 327
Chief Counsel, 47, 199, 272, 363, 365
Chief Marty, 395-396
Childs, Marvin, 102
Chill Factor, 76
Chimes, 16, 41, 46, 51, 57, 65, 85, 93, 101, 111, 119, 171, 179, 187, 201, 207, 213, 221, 251, 259, 267, 275, 283, 289, 305, 315, 321, 345, 353, 359, 371, 377, 383, 389
Chin Chin, 312
Chippie's Ruler, 234-236
Chitwood, 51, 57, 111, 359
Choice Yankee, 55
Chosen Fame, 337-338
Chris Time, 204
Christine's Sister, 24
Christmas List, 233
Ciara Stable, 188
Cimarron, 39, 273
Cindy's Tootsie, 199
Cinnamon Reel, 125, 196
Cita Worthy, 343
Citation, 65, 187, 201, 267, 275, 283, 315
Claire Toddington, 41, 85, 111, 195, 275, 371, 377
Clara Direct, 65, 187, 201, 267, 275, 283, 321
Classic Tale, 344
Classy River Gal, 219-220
Clay Pilot, 207
Clearview Stable, 196
Clements, Norm, 120, 127
Cleopatra, 167
Clever Hanover, 155
Clint Black, 170
Cloudburst Hanover, 331-332
Clover Hanover, 302, 369
Coal Harbor, 62, 78, 123, 140, 146, 381
Coal Luck, 148

Coalford Laag, 288
Coast, 80, 202, 288, 320
Coaster, 101, 207
Coastman, 101, 207, 221, 283, 315
Cochato, 101, 207, 221, 283, 315
Coffee Break, 211-212
Cohiba Mary, 76, 78
Col. Morgan Mare, 227
Colbert, 51, 119, 213, 383
Cold Cash, 205
Cold Front, 47-48, 50
Cold Warrior, 279, 296
Cole Muffler, 76, 175, 250, 268, 271, 310, 343-344, 382, 386-387, 390
Colisseum, 119, 213, 383
Collector's Item, 30
Collector's Piece, 286
Colonel Armstrong, 41, 353, 389
Color And Light, 56
Color Me Best, 142
Color Striped, 29
Colt Fortysix, 23-24, 26-28, 31, 55, 61-62, 64, 99, 280-281, 381-382
Columbia George, 14, 16, 28, 33, 55, 76, 79, 83, 146, 185, 210-212, 262, 280, 295, 302, 310, 340, 351, 364
Come Out Swinging, 28, 63, 294, 296
Comedy Hour, 246
Committeeman, 320
Complex Trooper, 158
Composite, 342, 344
Computer, 83, 91
Computer Chip, 26
Computer Scooter, 26, 257-258
Concertina, 26, 198, 200
Concussion, 254, 368, 370
Conejo Chief, 30
Condor Almahurst, 183, 357
Conquered, 27, 61, 319
Conquered Quest, 30, 177, 362-364, 381
Constenano, 237
Coquette, 51, 213
Corporal Lee, 129, 135, 143, 149, 333, 339
Corsair, 294
Cory's Big Guy, 30
Counsel Pick, 204
Counselor Bret, 24
Count N Sheep, 109-110
Countess Adios, 39, 47-48, 50, 78, 154, 244, 262, 281, 331
Countess Vivan, 229
Country Beau, 84

Index

Country Don, 316, 318
County House Mare, 310
Courageous Lady, 364
Courageous Legacy, 362-363
Courtalisa, 140
Covert Action, 100
Crane, Jim, 276
Crash, 211-212, 280
Cray, Paul, 336
Crazy Jane, 153
Crevette, 196, 198
Crew Angel, 300
Crilly, Paul, 260
Crimson, 364
Crisp Sahbra, 186
Crispin, 41, 71, 79, 179, 237, 245, 251, 389
Crosscurrent, 159
Crouch, Tom, 214, 217, 242-243
Crowded, 27, 278
Crowe, Pat, 120, 123, 127
Crystal Eros, 170
Crystal Gleam, 149, 339
Cue Light, 212, 374, 376
Cullin Hanover, 61, 64
Cumin, 320
Cunning Bunny, 25-26, 169
Cupid's Flight, 27
Curragh, 39, 68, 80, 127, 325
Currituck Star, 320
Cynthiana, 97, 101
Cytrynbaum, David, 138
D.M. Dilinger, 147-148
D'Elegance, 29
Daisy At Law, 57, 101, 119, 283, 289, 315
Daisy B, 51, 213
Daisy Grattan, 57, 101, 283, 289, 315
Daisy Rysdyk, 57, 119
Daisydale D., 41, 51, 57, 65, 71, 79, 85, 93, 101, 111, 119, 129, 179, 187, 195, 201, 213, 221, 237, 245, 251, 259, 267, 275, 283, 289, 297, 305, 321, 339, 345, 353, 359, 365, 371, 377, 389
Dakota, 27, 192-194, 226, 331
Dallas Almahurst, 146, 271
Dallas Dex, 154
Dalona Stable, 346
Dame Wood, 51, 57, 111, 213, 267, 321, 345, 359
Damita Hanover, 28
Dan Patch, 14, 97, 101-102, 114, 204, 207, 217, 221, 223, 226, 230, 283, 317-318, 323, 325, 354, 393

Dancer, Stanley, 58, 105, 107, 196, 198, 268, 270, 318
Dancer Hanover, 16, 46-48, 50, 52, 54, 60, 62, 65, 68, 71, 79, 82, 85, 107, 117, 135, 155, 163, 196, 245, 257, 264, 289, 293-295, 297, 302, 327, 332-333, 342, 350-351, 353, 365, 369, 381, 387, 397
Dancercize, 349
Dancin' On Air, 29
Dancing Master, 199-200
Dandy Promise, 55
Dangarvon, 110
Danger Of Fire, 21, 24, 281
Danger Woman, 395
Dangerous Wave, 356, 358
Danny B., 64, 387
Dare You To, 27, 127, 265
Dark Night, 359
Dart Almahurst, 358
Darth Raider, 20, 23, 55, 234-236
Dateable, 29, 250, 293, 295, 343-344
Dauntless Bunny, 25, 40, 332
David Guy, 65, 85, 93, 129, 187, 201, 237, 259, 267, 275, 283, 289, 310, 315, 339, 353, 365, 389
David's Comet, 255
David's Pass, 28, 211, 218-220, 343, 375
Dawn Michelle, 26
Dawn Q., 192
Dawn's First Lady, 351
Day, Charles, 188
Day In A Life, 244
Daylon Falcon, 97
Daylon Tempo, 146-148
Dazzle Almahurst, 357
Dazzle Dart, 185
Dazzle Hill, 185
Dazzler Hill, 185
De Buena Lobell, 280
Deadlock, 26, 63, 240, 294-296
Deadly Fella, 274
Deal Direct, 72, 74, 168
Dean Douglas, 147
Dean Hanover, 93, 179, 201, 251, 259, 357
Debbielynnkillean, 351
Debby Hanover, 153, 194-195
Decor, 78, 220
Del's Fella, 29
Delayed Decision, 153-154
Delightful Martha, 393
Delila Bluegrass, 24
Delinquent Account, 77, 110, 238, 311-312, 314
Dell Frisco, 149, 163
Dell Siskiyou, 155, 163, 221, 301, 305, 397
Delmegan, 167
Delmonica Hanover, 167
Demas, Steve, 298
Denali, 30-32, 271-272
Deneen's Delight, 30
Denim Stable, 138
Denmaster, 140
Dennis, Jim, 52, 105-106
Dennis Seelster, 28
Dervaes Jr., A. Rene, 276, 278
Desperate Lady, 320
Devil's Adversary, 300, 302
DeVisser, Lee, 227
DeVisser, Linda, 222
Dexter, Mildred, 150
Dexter, Thomas, 150
Dexter Doug, 154
Dexter Hanover, 107, 150, 268, 271
Dexter Lobell, 152, 159
Dexter Nukes, 16, 18, 23-25, 28, 31-32, 40, 61, 63, 66, **150-155**, 159, 217, 268, 271, 301, 302, 304, 375, 387, 393
Dexter Worthy, 57, 143
Diabla McKinney, 377
Diablo Cedarn, 29, 364
Dial, 357
Diamond Dawn, 170, 236
Diamond Hal, 357
Diamond Sam, 260
Diana Dyer, 155, 163, 221, 305, 397
Diana Lynn Lobell, 24
Diana Mite, 155, 163, 221, 305, 397
Diana Streak, 155, 163, 221, 305, 397
Dictator, 13-15, 17, 380, 383
Dictionary, 115, 232
Die Laughing, 16, 24, 27-28, 31-32, 61, 63, 72, 74-75, 99, 124, 136, 138, **156-163**, 217, 233, 268, 271, 301-302, 304, 328, 356-357, 375, 387, 393
Die Loving, 160, 162
Die Nasty, 160, 162
Diehard Fan, 160, 162
Dierker Direct, 339
Digger Almahurst, 250, 293, 295, 344
Dignatarian, 24, 175, 250, 292, 384, 386, 388
Dillcisco, 93, 171, 201
Dillon Axworthy, 41, 48, 65, 71, 79, 101, 107, 111, 171, 187, 201, 221, 237, 245, 251, 259, 267, 275, 283, 321, 327, 353, 359, 377

Dillon Volo, 65, 85, 93, 129, 187, 201, 237, 259, 275, 283, 289, 321, 339, 353, 365, 377, 389
Dilworthy, 201
Dime A Dip, 25
Direct Bill, 127
Direct Brewer, 204
Direct Command, 26, 170
Direct Flight, 29, 115, 168, 170
Direct Hal, 111, 119, 135, 143, 149, 155, 163, 171, 179, 195, 221, 229, 251, 267, 275, 305, 315, 321, 333, 339, 377, 383, 389, 397
Direct Rhythm, 116, 134-135, 154, 210, 256, 319
Direct Scooter, 14-15, 17-19, 23-33, 40, 48, 63, 69, 83-84, 91, 100, 114, 127, 133-134, 154, **164-171**, 176, 193, 227-228, 235, 243, 252, 254-257, 259, 273, 288, 295, 303, 313, 319, 325-327, 331, 381, 387, 395
Director, 17, 207, 383
Directress, 207
Directum I, 114, 208
Discotheque, 362-363
Distant Thunder, 78
Division Street, 116-117, 270, 272, 274, 309
Dixie Cheer, 301
Dixie Clamp, 29, 235
Dixie Laag, 29, 235-236
Doc's Girl, 176, 178
Doc's Fella, 270, 272, 274, 381
Doctor Gerson, 28, 349
Doctor Rankin, 310, 315
Dodger Boy, 40
Dolly, 27, 207, 213, 321, 345, 359
Dolly G, 119
Dolly II, 51, 57, 111, 267
Dolly McKinney, 305
Dolly Pomeroy, 207
Dolly Spanker, 51, 207
Dolly Worthy, 267
Dome Patrol, 83-84
Don't Cross Cam, 281
Don't Dally, 264-266, 343
Dontellmenomore, 224
Dontgetinmyway, 29, 39-40, 387
Dopey Diesel, 206
Dora, 69
Doris Spencer, 289, 297
Dorothy Axworthy, 289, 297, 315

Dorothy Day, 315
Dorsch Medium, 41, 71, 79, 237, 245
Dorsh Hanover, 40-41, 71, 79, 237, 245, 327
Dorunrun Bluegrass, 16, 21, 24, 48, 75, 97, 204, 233, 236
Dottie Rosecroft, 171, 259, 327
Dottie Shadow, 155, 163, 221, 305, 397
Dottie's Pick, 47-48, 50, 93, 229
Doug Arthur, 120
Downing, Richard, 102
Dr. Herr, 159
Dr. Lecter Lobell, 22, 25, 63, 311-312, 314
Dragon Again, 176, 178
Dragon Revrac, 176
Dragon So, 178
Dragon's Lair, 16, 23-24, 27-32, 140, 144, 152, **172-179**, 188, 250, 268, 271, 281, 288, 290, 303, 310, 313, 326, 343-344, 382, 384, 386-388
Dream Away, 22, 25, 77-78
Dream Girl, 22, 126
Dream Maker, 26, 342-344
Drexel Sue, 149
Duane Hanover, 20, 37, 39-41, 71, 76-77, 79, 235, 237, 245, 327
Dudie Egmont, 57, 101
Dudley Hanover, 60, 210
Duenna, 196, 198
Duer, Carter, 228
Duke Duke, 24, 40, 153-154, 183, 192-194, 279
Duke Of Abby, 24, 153-154
Duke Rodney, 183, 279
Dun Daisy, 101, 207, 283
Duncan MacLeod, 76
Dust Devil, 235-236
Dynasty, 144, 146-148, 263, 300, 387
Earl's Court Road, 127
Earl's Princess Martha, 187
Easter Hanover, 149, 163
Easter Patch, 393, 397
Easter Sun Hanna, 168-170
Eastern Skipper, 115, 118
Easy Goer, 63, 74, 127, 158, 328
Easy Hitter, 376
Easy Lovin, 30
Easy Prom, 106
Echelon, 27, 343, 374
Echora, 383
Eclipse, 12, 134
Edalena, 204
Eftimia, 153-154
Egyptian Dancer, 33, 114

Eicarl's Apache, 69
Either Or, 182, 242, 262, 301
El Patron, 21, 24
Elda Belle, 25
Electioneer, 13-14, 16, 46, 51, 57, 101, 111, 119, 207, 211, 213, 267, 283, 321, 345, 359, 383
Electric Belle, 119, 383
Electric Slide, 176-178, 288
Electric Yankee, 83, 218-219
Electrical Express, 368
Electricity, 383
Elegant Albert, 29, 70
Elegant Killean, 350-352
Elizabeth L, 57
Ella Brown, 111, 119, 171, 267, 275, 321, 377, 383, 389
Ellamony, 27, 125-126, 128, 211, 313, 343
Ellatross, 286
Ellen's Glory, 23, 252, 255, 259
Elsie Leyburn, 65, 85, 289, 365
Elsie Scott, 300, 305
Elsie Truax, 155, 163, 221, 305, 397
Emily Ellen, 55, 212, 287, 289, 345, 371
Emily Scott, 171, 259, 327
Emily's Pride, 171, 259, 327
Emma Smith, 111, 345, 371
Emory Girl, 25
Empire Direct, 65, 187, 201, 267, 275, 283
Empire Hanover, 357
Emporium, 152
Energy Burner, 300
English Tutor, 104
Enlightening, 205
Enroute, 238
Ensign Hanover, 17, 129, 135, 143, 149, 219, 228-229, 333, 339, 372, 377
Enterprising, 343-344
Entrepreneur, 250
Epstein, Barry, 360
Epstein, Irving, 360
Equipoise, 7
Equitable, 381
Erba Stables, 150
Erector, 119, 383
Eroticus, 281-282
Ervin, Frank, 43-44, 102, 104, 107, 110, 208, 210-211
Escape Artist, 29
Escape For Now, 194
Escort, 80, 182, 194, 205
Essig, Joe, 34
Estabella, 119, 171, 321, 345, 371, 383

Esther, 119, 171, 211, 213, 267, 321, 345, 371, 383
Eternity, 29, 62, 116-117, 123
Ethelwyn, 210, 213
Etiquette, 25
Evalina Hanover, 93, 114, 116-117, 119, 229, 289, 297, 315, 333
Evalina Lobell, 114
Evans, Dr. Arthur, 37
Evans, Don, 106
Evelyn The Great, 93, 201
Even Odds, 66, 108-110
Evensong, 21, 171, 235, 259, 297, 327
Ever Running, 351-352
Ever So Rich, 252
Everglade Angie, 25
Evergreen Sandy, 28
Everybodydancenow, 220
Exalted Ruler, 206
Excited, 27, 236, 298, 300
Exotic Earl, 26, 288, 356
Expectation, 119, 248, 294
Expedition, 51, 57, 65, 111, 213, 267, 321, 345, 359
Expensive Lady, 29
Expensive Scooter, 29, 130, 168, 170, 246, 248, 322, 324, 387
Explosive Bunny, 332
Expressive, 213, 345
Expressive Lou, 289
Expresson, 104
Extasy, 213, 289, 345, 371
Exterminator, 12
Extratrick, 319
Extreme Velocity, 27
Eyes Of An Angel, 220
Eyewash, 228-229
Fahy, Bill, 224-225, 238, 390, 392
Faith Hanover, 283
Fake Left, 63, 125, 144, 392
Falcon Almahurst, 16, 23-25, 28-29, 32-34, 36, 76, 97, **180-187**, 236, 263-264, 266, 279, 356-357
Falcon Dakota, 27, 192-194, 226
Falcon Seelster, 16, 23, 26-27, 29, 31-32, 40, 97, 99, 107-109, 186, **188-195**, 199, 255, 290, 295, 300, 319-320
Falcon's Future, 29, 132-133, 191-192, 194, 249, 300-301, 320, 322, 324, 356
Falcon's Scooter, 186, 256, 258
Fan Hanover, 27, 61-62, 64, 108-109, 153, 280, 300, 331, 350, 387

Fanciful Hanover, 76
Fancy Boots, 69
Fancy Crown, 290, 309
Fancy Table, 352
Fanella, 101, 207
Fannie's Champ, 183
Fanny Brown, 119, 383
Fanny McKerron, 259
Fantastic, 192, 230, 233, 302, 330
Farlane Marg, 25
Farlane Star, 25
Farm Norah, 27
Farmer's Hostess, 97
Farmstead's Fame, 109-110, 308
Farmstead's Future, 28
Farrington, Dick, 230, 232
Fashion Tip, 114
Fashion Trick, 29, 191-192, 195, 319
Fast Clip, 212
Fatima, 311
Faulkner, Norm, 120
Favonian, 119, 283, 289, 315
Fay Hanover, 374
Fearless Raider, 25
Fedorov, 69-70
Feel The Wind, 133
Feree Hanover, 28, 100
Fernbank Filly, 186
Fiji Islander, 27
Filet Of Sole, 196, 198
Filion, Herve, 276
Filly Byrd, 83
Filly Direct, 65, 71, 79, 85, 93, 129, 135, 143, 149, 155, 163, 179, 187, 201, 221, 229, 237, 245, 251, 259, 262, 267, 275, 283, 289, 297, 305, 315, 327, 331, 333, 339, 353, 365, 389, 397
Fimbrethil, 176
Final Cheers, 25
Finian Hanover, 380-382
Firebird's Best, 286
First Lady, 351
Fischer, Dr. Max, 164
Fit For Life, 244
Fitch, 205
Fits Of Fun, 23
Five O'Clock Cindy, 23, 227-229
Flat Foot Fluzy, 24, 69, 325-327
Flaxey, 51, 57, 111, 213, 267, 321, 345, 359
Flaxy, 101, 207
Flight Director, 34, 36, 166, 182
Flight Of Fire, 21, 24, 152, 281
Flora, 107, 213, 267, 321, 345, 383

Florican, 83, 93, 198, 201, 227, 229, 354
Florida Jewel, 222
Florimel, 93, 201, 229
Florita Lobell, 30
Flow Control, 30, 332
Fly Fly Byrd, 114
Flying Bret, 16, 33, 108, 185, 250, 278, 395
Fogel, Ruth, 164
Follow My Star, 366
Follow Up, 93
Fondle, 28
Fontaine, Lucien, 94, 191
Foos, Courtney, 136
Foos, Elizabeth, 136
For The Children, 281, 369-370
For Your Eyes Only, 28
Forbidden Goal, 29
Forbidden Love, 29
Forbidden Past, 62, 64
Forecast, 242
Forever Sparkle, 28
Formal Invite, 364
Forrest Eden, 55
Forrest Skipper, 25, 27, 32, 55, 77-78, 190-191, 199, 214, 381-382
Fortune Richie, 16, 24, 97, 204-206, 233
Fortune Teller, 23, 152, 194, 218, 281
Foster Walker, 260
Four D McKinney, 71, 85, 135, 327, 333
Fout, Jeff, 72
Fox Valley Victory, 220
Foxy Windy, 30
Fran Seelster, 192
Frances San Francisco, 57, 101
Franz Hanover, 175, 250, 384, 387
Freddi Fearless, 25
Free Spender, 26, 39-40, 363
Free Token, 141
Freedom's Friend, 256, 258, 303
Freidberg, Ed, 123, 227
Freight Saver, 286-287
French Chef, 16, 24, 26, 89, 93, 109, 116, 124, **196-201**, 227-229, 263-264, 268, 271, 342
Frenchtown Lady, 199
Frisco Dale, 52, 57, 98, 101
Frisco Forbes, 52, 57, 143
Frugal Gourmet, 16, 89, 116, 140, 196, 198-200, 216, 227, 230, 232, 342, 346, 348, 368
Fruition, 119, 171, 318
Fruity Volo, 171, 259, 305

Fruity Worthy, 111, 171, 259
Full Of Love, 23, 26
Full Worthy, 57
Fulla Napoleon, 16, 33, 152, 155
Fulla Strikes, 372, 374
Fullsway, 149, 163
Fundamentalist, 303
Future Fame, 320
Fuzed, 375
Fuzzette Henley, 135
Fuzzy Chatham, 57
G. E.'s Karla, 55
G. E.'s Romanero, 55-56
G. P. Fancy, 29
Gabrielle, 30, 176-178
Gaitway Farm, 322, 328
Galbraith, Clint, 284
Gale, Bill, 75, 325
Gallant Fox, 12
Galleria, 25, 77-78
Galyn Mack, 148
Gamecock, 155, 380
Games, 332
Gamma Ray, 392
Gangloff, Bob, 292
Gardenia Hanover, 149
Gardner, Paul, 94
Garnsey, Glen, 34, 36, 74, 238, 278, 284, 298
Garnsey Stable, 34
Garrison Hanover, 378
Gay Boy, 119, 383
Gay Girl Chimes, 41, 65, 93, 111, 119, 171, 179, 187, 201, 251, 259, 267, 275, 283, 289, 305, 315, 321, 353, 371, 377, 383, 389
Gay Skipper, 292
Gay Song, 20, 235
Gayle The Great, 339
Gaylworthy, 339
Gee Gee Cam, 24
Gee Gee Digger, 21, 24
Gee Lee Hanover, 104
Geiger, Donald, 136
Gene Abbe, 14-16, 19, 33, 91, 94, 96-101, 154, 161, **202-207**, 217-218, 221, 233, 236, 279, 283, 310, 313, 315, 357
General Cochran, 28, 170, 273
General Ring, 26
General Star, 26-27, 100, 109, 164, 218, 263, 279
General Watts, 119
Genghis Khan, 122, 263-264, 266

Gentle Miss, 54
Genuine Woman, 192-193
George Allen, 140, 266
George Wilkes, 13-14, 51, 57, 101, 111, 205, 207, 213, 354, 359
Gerson, Max, 252
Getabout, 312
Getaway Hall, 142
Getting Personal, 28, 281, 369-370
Ghostly, 27, 234-236, 288
Ghostly Returns, 27
Giant Victory, 330
Gidget Lobell, 155, 163, 221, 298, 300-301, 305, 397
Gifted Cowboy, 394, 396
Giggle Box, 159
Gigi Blue Chip, 205-206
Gillis, Fred, 306
Gilmour, Buddy, 123, 252, 306, 308-309
Gilmour, George, 150
Glad Rags, 106
Glamour Goes On, 30
Gleeful George, 97
Glen Almahurst, 266
Glengate Farms, 70
Glenmount Willy, 147-148
Glenn's Super Star, 349
Gloria Barmin, 259
Glorious Mae, 255
Glory Meadow, 23, 30
Go For Grins, 159, 220
Goalie Jeff, 16, 26-29, 31-32, 61, 63, 124-125, 128, 144, 150, 152, 271, 313
Goalie Jess, 194
Gogo Playmate, 155, 163, 221, 300, 305, 397
Gogo Playtime, 155, 163, 221, 300-302, 305, 397
Going Thru, 349
Gold Coast Rocky, 320
Gold Dust, 199-200
Gold Girl, 179, 251, 389
Gold Worthy, 301
Golden Blend, 372-373
Golden Cross, 20-21, 48, 80, 126, 206, 244
Golden Miss, 149, 219, 372, 377
Golden Money Maker, 83
Golden Triangle, 364
Goldenshot Killean, 351-352
Goldie Grattan, 101
Goldie Patch, 397
Goldstein, Elsa, 336
Good Boy, 206, 211-212

Good Bye Columbus, 211-212
Good Counsel, 208, 211-212, 362
Good Humor Man, 270
Good Little Girl, 124
Good News Scooter, 27, 256, 258
Good Show, 212
Good Time, 14, 16, 21-22, 33, 38, 45, 52-53, 79, 83, 97, 99, 106, 109, 113, 124, 129, 135, 143, 149, 155, 159, 163, 168, 170, 176-177, 179, 185, 193-195, 202, 204-205, **208-213**, 217-221, 224, 229, 250-251, 262, 270-271, 275, 295, 300-303, 305, 315, 326-327, 332-333, 339-340, 343-345, 350-351, 353, 363, 365, 374, 386, 389, 394, 397
Good Time Boy, 211-212
Good Time Minnie, 217, 221
Good To See You, 205
Good Will Ambassador, 45
Goodmorningamerica, 292
Goose Bay, 79, 320
Gorman, Ed, 360
Gothic Dream, 28, 60, 218-220, 288, 293
Governess, 20, 153, 194
Governor Skipper, 16, 20, 23, 27, 47, 94, 110, 153, 263-264, 266, 381
Grand Sentinel, 51, 119, 213, 383
Grandpa's Ashley, 69
Grant, Fred, 138-139
Grant, Hugh, 260, 262
Grateful Vikar, 54
Grattan At Law, 57, 93, 101, 114, 119, 283, 289, 297, 315
Grattan Bars, 206, 339
Grattan Royal, 41, 54, 57, 71, 79, 101, 119, 163, 187, 206, 221, 237, 245, 283, 289, 305, 315, 339, 354, 359
Great Medium, 41, 71, 79, 237, 245, 327
Great Nero, 278-282
Great Spirit, 57
Greater Love, 279
Green Mountain Maid, 51, 101, 207, 213
Green With Envy, 263-265
Greenberg, Bob, 80
Greentree Adios, 259
Greer Hanover, 41, 71, 79, 237, 245, 327
Greg's Miracle, 325
Greyhound, 14, 42, 46, 102, 126, 337, 349
Grin Reaper, 160
Guesswork, 41, 65, 71, 79, 85, 155, 163, 245, 289, 297, 365, 397
Guida, Lou, 284, 290

Guinea Gold, 97, 101
Gulf Shore, 136
Gulliver, 358
Gumboots, 167
Guts, 164, 306, 308-309
Guy Abbey, 20-21, 65, 71, 79, 85, 93, 135, 155, 163, 171, 192, 196, 201, 237, 245, 259, 289, 297, 327, 333, 337, 339, 342, 353, 365, 397
Guy Castleton, 297
Guy Day, 315, 353
Guy Dillon, 41, 46, 51, 57, 65, 85, 93, 101, 111, 119, 129, 187, 195, 201, 237, 259, 275, 283, 289, 297, 339, 353, 359, 365, 371, 377, 389
Guy McKinney, 41, 60, 65, 71, 79, 85, 93, 111, 155, 163, 195, 201, 245, 259, 289, 297, 305, 315, 327, 353, 365, 397
Guy Rosa, 41, 71, 79, 85, 129, 237, 245, 275, 353, 389
Guy Wilkes, 51, 57, 111, 119, 207, 213, 267, 321, 345, 359, 371, 377, 383
Guyellen, 171, 187
Gypsy Fiddle, 25
Gypsy Fortune, 211-212
H A's Pace Setter, 186
H. D. Hanover, 357
Hal Pizarro, 119, 383
Halberta, 339
Halcyon, 61
Hamblin Patchen, 51, 101, 207, 213
Hamlin's Almont Jnr, 359
Hammer, Roger, 249
Handle With Care, 263-266
Handsome Sum, 286
Hanover Shoe Farms, 45, 58, 62, 96, 102, 108, 115, 134, 139, 167, 172, 300, 378, 380, 384, 393-394
Happily Involved, 23
Happy Abbe, 206
Happy At Last, 152
Happy Blue, 325
Happy Bottom, 26, 312
Happy Chatter, 274
Happy Escort, 182, 205
Happy Lady, 272
Happy Medium, 13-14, 17, 51, 119, 213, 383
Happy Motoring, 16, 97, 116, 268, 271-272, 306, 310-311, 315, 325, 327, 349, 357, 381
Happy Sharon, 270, 272, 381
Happy Tid Bit, 97
Happy To Be Best, 142
Happy Trick, 140
Harada, 110

Harden, 25, 332
Hardie Hanover, 98, 100
Hare Hare, 30, 99, 331-332
Harmer, Tom, 188, 191
Harold J., 14-15, 17, 23, 33, 55, 112, 126, 140-141, 143, 167, 227, 280, 319, 340
Harrods, 37
Harry Clay, 207
Harry's Dream, 354
Harvest Gale, 201
Harvey, Harry, 58
Harvey Heller, 172
Hasty Grand Slam, 27
Haughton, Bill, 180
Haughton, Peter, 249
Haughton, Tom, 246, 248-249
Hayes, Christy, 262
Hayes, Dr. John, 123
Hayes Sr., John, 372
Hazel Hanover, 380-382
Hazelbud, 383
Hazelton Kay, 219-220, 288
He's Discreet, 136
Heat Relief, 97
Heatherjeankillean, 263, 350-352, 374
Hecla, 101, 207
Hedgewood Boy, 46
Heffering, Peter, 322, 328
Heir At Law, 57, 119
Helen Dillon, 129, 321, 377
Helen Hanover, 129, 135, 143, 149, 195, 228-229, 305, 321, 333, 339, 377
Helen's Deal, 319
Heller, Harvey, 172
Hempt, Max, 45, 112
Henry T. Adios, 14, 16, 20, 37, 41, 47-50, 54, 60, 68, 70-71, 77, 79, 82, 107, 116-117, 159, 184, 237, 245, 264, 280, 318, 327, 381
Her Ladyship, 79
Here's A Quarter, 25, 99-100
Herman, Billy, 384
Hi Ho Silverheel's, 27, 40, 324, 393
Hickory Pride, 192, 300, 350
Hickory Smoke, 192, 300, 350
High Ideal, 16, 25, 32-33, 107-108, 183, 185, 191, 199, 212, 233, 280, 320, 351, 357
High Time, 333
Highland Scott, 192
Highly Promoted, 26, 40
Hilarion, 122, 159, 298, 357, 374, 376
Hilarious Sister, 159
Hilarious Way, 108

Hill, Charles, 210
Hill, Laverne, 180
Hill Farms, 180, 182, 185
Hill, Marie, 44
Hilliard Hill, 186
His Majesty, 42
His Mattjesty, 30, 175, 256, 258, 303
Historic, 29, 132, 248-250, 293, 295-296, 343-344
Hit Parade, 362-364, 381
Hit The Bid, 150
Hobby Horse Tar, 37, 41, 70-71, 79, 237, 242, 245, 327, 349, 351, 353, 382
Hodge Podge, 140
Hodgen, 55, 140
Hodgins, Clint, 112
Hogan, Dick, 146
Hojo, 29
Hold True, 28, 228
Holliday, Ken, 132
Holloway, Joe, 222, 224, 228
Hollyrood Nimble, 111, 171
Holmes Hanover, 21, 24, 62, 183-184, 279, 308, 381-382
Holy Dragon, 176
Holy Terror, 25
Home Again, 311
Hometown Spirit, 22, 24, 109, 115
Honest Truth, 39
Honey B. Good, 205
Honeymoon H, 171, 259
Hoopla, 26
Hoosier Favorite, 142
Hoot Hanover, 381-382
Hoot Mon, 83, 93, 115, 201, 229, 319
Hope Diamond, 184
Horton Hanover, 29, 146
Hostess, 97
Hot Hitter, 166, 194, 212, 331, 360, 372, 374, 376
Hot Lead, 24, 116-117
Hot Walker, 312
Hotrod Falcon, 186
House Of Fun, 244
Huricane Almahurst, 387
Hush A Bye, 117
Hustler's Best, 29, 349-350, 353
Hustler's Boy, 349
Hustling Thru, 353
Hustling Time, 99, 211-212
I Marilyn, 24, 336-337, 339
I Married A Witch, 192-193
I Saw Him First, 175, 387

I'd Like To Win, 220
I'm A Widow, 41, 71, 79, 221, 237, 245
I'm It, 183, 187, 363
Icarus Lobell, 122, 280, 282
Ideal Society, 24, 32, 62
Immortality, 29, 63, 116, 211, 301-302, 304
Impatiens, 366
Impish, 30, 183, 279
Impish Almahurst, 183
Impish Lobell, 30
In The Pocket, 15, 17, 20, 23, 44, 48, 86, 88-89, 168-170, 176, 246, 255, 319, 381, 387
Inaugural Ball, 337-338
Incredible Aussie, 29
Incredible Bret, 292
Incredible Finale, 32, 220, 265, 292, 356
Indiana Sam, 186
Infellable, 29
Infinite Wisdom, 27
Ingar, 101, 207
Ingenue, 183, 187
Insko, Del, 346
Instant Offense, 351-352
Instant Rebate, 76, 287
Instrument Landing, 159
Interpretor, 293, 296
Intruder Almahurst, 183
Invader Hall, 142
Invincible Shadow, 183, 356, 358
Iola Grattan, 57, 143
Iola Hal, 57
Iona, 101, 207
Irene Almahurst, 183
Irene Hanover, 171, 187, 259, 327
Iris Acres, 336
Irish, 205, 310
Irish Mollie, 310, 315
Irma Blue Chip, 28
Iron Horse, 322
Irvin Paul, 204, 206
Irving, Dana, 97
Isabel Abbe, 155, 163, 221, 305
Isabel Hanover, 397
Island Glow, 22, 24, 175, 177-178, 211, 222, 249, 302-303, 344
Isle Of Wight, 380, 382
Isotta, 171, 183, 187, 201, 259, 283, 327
It Matters, 152
It's Fritz, 370
Izatiger, 184, 186
J C's Suprimo, 28, 99, 301-302, 304, 357
J. D. Betty, 140

405

Index

J. D.'s Bret, 23
J. D.'s Buck, 54-56, 122-123, 140
J J's Cornell, 282
J. K. Outlaw, 30, 78
J. M. Valinda, 24, 116-117
J. N. Dynamic, 27
J. R. Amy, 217-218, 221
J. R. Bret, 218
J. R. Decker, 218
J. T. Lobell, 218
J J Audubon, 101, 207
J Malcolm Forbes, 57, 119
Jack And Elwood, 88
Jack Clayton, 140
Jackie Frost, 264, 369
Jackpot Albatross, 23
Jacsue Brooks, 28
Jade Prince, 28, 94, 116-117, 196
Jaguar Spur, 16, 20, 23-24, 30-31, 60, 62, 64, 108-109, 116, 232-233, 255, 346, 348, 368
Jake And Elwood, 25, 88, 362
Jambooger, 30
James, Bert, 58
Jamuga, 30, 78
Jane Hall, 155
Jane Revere, 135, 143, 155, 163, 195, 221, 305, 321, 345, 371, 397
Jane Reynolds, 135, 141, 143, 155, 163, 195, 221, 305, 321, 397
Jate Lobell, 16, 18, 23, 25-32, 40, 66, 76, 78, 97, 124, 144, 152, 159, 170, 186, 194, 205, 211, **214-221**, 230, 232, 242-244, 268, 270-271, 284, 288, 301-302, 304, 346, 348, 368-370, 375, 387, 393
Jay Lobell, 218
Jay's Table, 351-352
Jaydexter, 154
Jazz Singer, 26
Jean Claire, 41, 171, 259, 327, 389
Jeanine Lobell, 218
Jef's Eclipse, 134
Jef's Eternity, 29, 62, 116-117, 123
Jef's Magic Trick, 24, 133-135
Jef's Rick, 134
Jef's Standardbred Country Club, 123, 130, 227
Jefferson, 342, 344
Jenna's Beach Boy, 16, 19, 23, 86, 89-92, 116, 126, 196, 199, **222-229**, 262, 268, 271, 368
Jenny Bryan, 57, 119, 359

Jenny Clay, 359
Jenny Scott, 143, 171, 259, 321, 345, 371, 377, 383
Jeremy's Gambit, 301-302, 304
Jerome Lobell, 218
Jerri Lee, 26
Jersey B. B., 46, 51, 57, 83, 111, 119, 359, 371, 377
Jersey Wilkes, 51, 57, 111, 359
Jessee Purkey, 233, 387
Jessie Pepper, 191, 207, 300, 350, 378
Jet Jockey, 21, 24, 38-40, 265
Jet Laag, 29, 234-236
Jet Lair, 176, 178, 288
Jiffy Lobell, 218
Jimmy Creek, 48, 52, 57, 143, 354
Jo Ann Hal, 149
Jocelyn Lobell, 218
Joe Bowers, 383
Joe C. Abbe, 202
Joe Patchen, 101, 207, 230
Joel's David, 55
Joey T., 84
Johannah Treat, 359
John A. McKerron, 41, 101, 171, 207, 283
John Dillard II, 359
John Nederland, 51, 213
John R. Gentry, 46, 51, 57, 65, 111, 119, 187, 201, 213, 267, 275, 283, 321, 345, 359, 371, 377
John Street North, 26, 40, 331-332
Johnston, Alice, 86
Jollie Dame, 300
Jolly Roger, 270
Jones, Hal, 202
Josedale Counterpoint, 205
Josedale Dorcas, 44
Joseph Lobell, 152
Josephine Knight, 51, 57, 111, 119, 171, 213, 267, 321, 345, 359, 371, 383
Josephine Young, 207
Joss, 184-186
Joule, 376
Joy Hanover, 30
Joyce Seelster, 154
Jud's Choice, 25, 84
Jules Jodoin, 30, 234, 236
Julia Frost, 229
Julia Johnson, 51, 213
June Casco, 339
June's Baby, 138
Juravinski, Charles, 252

Just Camelot, 134
Just Doodlin, 26
Just Our Luck, 146, 149
Justabit Of Magic, 26
Justascape, 159
Justassuming, 320
Justice Brooke, 41, 85, 111, 119, 195, 275, 371, 377
Justin Passing, 17, 27, 115, 343
Justissima, 41, 71, 79, 85, 111, 129, 179, 195, 237, 245, 275, 297, 353, 365, 371, 377, 389
K. C. Three, 56
K J Alert, 26
K L's Sharpshooter, 281
K. Nora, 242, 245
Kala Lobell, 282
Karril Hanover, 26, 294
Kassa Branca, 27-28, 31, 281, 364
Kate's Nuke, 154
Kathleen, 210
Kathleen Grattan, 206, 233, 237
Katie, 51
Katorzheniki, 30, 303
Kawartha Eagle, 114, 380
Kawartha Skipper, 146-147
Kawartha Tarson, 279, 382
Kay Blue Chip, 26
Kay Wave, 358
Kazbek, 69-70
Keep Your Pans Off, 303
Keller, Charlie, 56
Kelly Miles, 55
Ken's Shadow, 356, 358
Kendal Lasso, 140
Kendal Missile, 26
Kenney, Charlie, 58
Kenney, John, 58
Kent, Charles, 12, 207
Kentuckiana Farms, 146, 214, 217, 242-243
Kentucky Prince, 213
Kentucky Spur, 16, 32, 38-40, 127, 198, 265, 375, 387
Kerwood, Tony, 325
Kettle Bee, 30, 40, 220
Key Prospect, 76
Keymona Rainbow, 29
Keystone Atlas, 320
Keystone Dixie, 301-302
Keystone Endeavor, 22, 24, 63, 368-370
Keystone Famous, 174
Keystone Flamingo, 25

Keystone Icy, 310
Keystone Imp, 310
Keystone Luther, 132, 249
Keystone Memento, 115
Keystone Mist, 117, 229
Keystone Native, 29
Keystone Ore, 14, 17, 24-25, 27-30, 32-33, 112, 115, 117-118, 134, 167, 169, 183, 199, 310, 332, 381-382, 386
Keystone Pat, 380-382
Keystone Ponder, 116, 118
Keystone Raider, 25, 100, 273
Keystone Rudolph, 301
Keystone Sandal, 320
Keystone Sandra, 25, 117
Keystone Sanford, 116
Keystone Scamp, 118
Keystone Sceptre, 118
Keystone Sherlock, 118
Keystone Sixty, 118
Keystone Smartie, 115, 118
Keystone Tad, 27, 115
Keystone Tulsa, 27
Keystone Wallis, 320
Keystoner, 357, 378
Kick Up A Storm, 368, 370
Kiev Hanover, 25, 30, 61-62, 64, 88-89, 116-117, 286, 303, 313
Kilburn, 152
Killbuck Mary, 60, 293
Killean Acres, 346-347, 352
Kimberly Hanover, 183, 187
Kimberly Kid, 183
Kimberly Mine, 183, 187
Kimberly Rodney, 184
Kimmee Lyn, 234-235
Kindly Hanover, 98
King Charles, 287-288
King Of Pain, 175
King's Counsel, 14, 17, 20-21, 42, 44-45, 48, 65, 71, 79, 85, 93, 129, 135, 143, 149, 155, 163, 167, 179, 187, 195, 199, 201, 208, 221, 229, 237, 245, 251, 259, 262, 264-265, 267, 272, 275, 283, 287, 289, 297, 301, 305, 315, 321, 327, 333, 339, 353, 357, 363, 365, 389, 397
Kingdom Of The Sea, 27, 220
Kinway Heather, 27
Knight Dream, 33, 37, 39, 41, 49, 71, 77, 79-80, 83-85, 109-110, 129, 135, 143, 149, 155, 163, 179, 221, 229, 235, 237, 242-243, 245, 251, 270, 272, 275, 305, 315, 327, 333, 339, 343, 353, 379, 397

Knight's Embassy, 71, 80, 85, 135, 327, 333
Kinglyne, 377
Kingsbridge, 218-220, 393
Kit, 28, 204, 207
Kittiwake, 368-369
Kittrel's Tom Hal, 51, 213
Klassy's Son, 364
Knight Caller, 25
Knight's Embassy, 71, 80, 85, 135, 327, 333
Knisley, Mildred, 202
Kornfeld, Gary, 172
Kramer, Daniel, 138
Kris Messenger, 272
Kruba, James, 188
Kurt And Brad, 313
Kuzzin Kat, 186
Kyle's Falcon, 184-186
L. V. Whiskers, 21, 23, 225, 320
L Dee's Jonathan, 27, 162
L Dee's Leslie, 27
L'Chaim, 244
L'Eggins, 184-185
La Byrd Abbe, 279, 283
La Paloma, 300
La Pomme Souffle, 93, 196, 198, 201, 229
La Roya, 195, 272
La Toya, 28, 177
Laag, 16, 23, 26-32, 39, 55, 100, 127, 152, 154, 170, 186, 191, **230-237**, 242, 265, 273, 281, 288, 295, 303, 326, 346, 348, 368, 375, 387
Laag's Pleasure, 234
LaByrd Abbe, 279-280
Lachance, Mike, 144, 246, 248-249, 252, 386
Ladalia Hanover, 76, 79
Ladalia's Girl, 76
Ladatross, 27
Lady Ann Mathew, 313
Lady Ashlee Ann, 55
Lady Bird, 185
Lady Bunker, 51, 57, 111, 213, 359
Lady Buns, 134, 331-332, 364
Lady Dunn, 51
Lady Erectress, 41, 65, 93, 111, 119, 171, 179, 187, 201, 251, 259, 267, 275, 283, 289, 305, 315, 321, 353, 371, 377, 383, 389
Lady Genius, 29
Lady Has Arrived, 25, 242
Lady Hathaway, 30
Lady Kacne, 76, 79
Lady Lunken, 79
Lady Mattingly, 175
Lady Maud C., 46, 51, 57, 111, 119, 359, 371, 377

Lady Nelson, 26
Lady Patchen, 51, 213
Lady Permilia, 101, 207, 221, 283, 315
Lady Russell, 51, 213
Lady Scotland, 20, 55, 140, 143, 179, 195, 199, 251, 257, 264, 315, 340, 342-345, 363, 366, 368-369, 371
Lady Wildflower, 51, 57, 65, 111, 119, 187, 201, 213, 267, 275, 283, 321, 345, 359, 371, 377
Lady Wilina, 377
Lahar, 27, 40, 63, 68, 80, 325
Lake Hills Jeb, 218
Laker's Fortune, 23
Lana Direct, 189
Lana Lobell Farm, 52, 86, 139, 202, 214, 300, 318
Land Fire, 150
Land Grant, 264, 266
Landess, Jerry, 34
Landslide, 16, 26, 28, 31-33, 37, 69-70, 82, 196, 243, 262-263, 268, 271, 348-351, 353, 381-382
Landslide Hustler, 29
Landslip Hanover, 349
Landy Hanover, 76
Langford, 213
Lanna Byrd, 280, 283
Lantern, 114
Largo, 29, 83, 331
Lark Almahurst, 183
Larkin, Ethel, 112
Larkin, Rex, 112
Last Chance, 289, 297
Last Wish, 331, 333
Laugh A Day, 384
Laughasyougo, 162
Laugher, 85
Laughing Girl, 20, 129, 135, 143, 149, 155, 163, 179, 212, 221, 229, 251, 270, 275, 305, 315, 327, 333, 339, 389, 397
Laughs, 25, 37, 273, 288, 302, 304
Launch Code, 30
Laura Hanover, 71, 85, 107, 111, 129, 135, 143, 149, 195, 245, 297, 333, 339, 365, 371, 377
Laurel Princess, 362, 365
Laurel Queen, 365
Lauxmont Royce, 23
Laverne Hanover, 29, 47, 378, 380, 382
Laviana, Geraldine, 230
Le Courrier, 184, 186
Le Mistral, 311-312
Lea, 217
Lead Me On, 30

Leader Pick, 205-206
Leading Edge, 30
League Leader, 182, 372, 374, 376
Leah Almahurst, 26, 38-39, 238, 242, 265
Leamlara, 25
Lease On Life, 244
Leavitt, Alan, 52, 86, 139, 214, 279, 300, 318
Leavitt, Meg Nichols, 139
Lee Axworthy, 111, 187, 201, 259, 289, 345, 371
Lee Harvester, 259
Lee Tide, 65, 143, 201, 289, 297, 345, 371
Lee Worthy, 107, 111, 143, 221, 345, 371, 377
Legal Notice, 16, 23, 109, 154, 191, 343, 351, 374, 376
Lehigh Hanover, 47-48, 50, 243, 349
Lemoyne Hanover, 76
Leon June, 339
Leonor, 85
Leslie Seahawk, 27
Leta Long, 41, 65, 71, 79, 85, 93, 111, 129, 135, 143, 149, 155, 163, 179, 195, 221, 229, 237, 245, 251, 259, 289, 297, 305, 315, 327, 333, 339, 353, 365, 371, 377-378, 383, 389, 397
Lexington Maid, 171, 259, 327
Lida, 89, 250
Lida W, 207
Life Cycle, 244
Life Sign, 16, 27, 38-40, 49, 61-63, 68, 75, 124, 191, **238-245**, 303, 336, 387
Lightening Speed, 29, 192, 194
Lighthill, Clint, 202
Lighthill, Joe, 260
Like To Win, 220
Lil Pod's Fiddle, 25
Lillian L, 93, 149, 251, 339
Lillian Wilkes, 57, 65, 171, 187, 201, 213, 267, 275, 283, 289, 321, 345, 383
Lime Time, 342-344
Lindora Wilkes, 101, 207
Lindsey's Bunny, 84
Linebacker Spur, 387
Linora, 267
Lipstick Don't Lie, 220
Lisheen, 39, 68, 80, 322, 325
Lismore, 27, 68, 71, 80, 82, 325, 327
Lisryan, 39, 68, 80, 325
Little Bighorn, 30
Little Mary C., 339
Little Startrick, 320
Little Steven, 26, 69-70
Live Love Laugh, 161-162
Live Or Die, 160-162

Live The Life, 244
Lives On Laughter, 97
Lizzie, 51, 57, 111, 213, 267, 321, 345, 359
Lizzie Pebbles, 207
Lizzie Witherspoon, 183, 279
Local Time, 212
Lohmeyer, Ed, 322, 325, 349
Lola Jean, 205
Longport, 28, 176, 178
Longshot Only Pan, 224
Look Sharp, 281
Lookin Fine, 26
Lookout Man, 29, 220
Loren Messenger, 27
Lorryland Butler, 25, 83-84, 331
Lotion, 89
Lotta Soul, 26, 63, 301, 304
Lottie Strathmore, 85
Love To Shop, 185
Lovin Yankee, 55, 311
Loving Care, 263-266
Loving Success, 30, 219
Low Places, 219-220
Lu Dene Pluto, 377
Lucky Cam, 23, 146
Lucky Lady, 23, 144, 146, 149
Lucky We Met, 146
Ludene Pluto, 149
Ludicrous, 159, 357
Ludwigpanbeethoven, 142
Lukan Hanover, 26
Luke's Rd, 387
Luren Lee, 26
Lush Limbaugh, 337-338
Lushkara, 23
Lustra's Big Guy, 99-100, 190, 381
Lusty Leader, 288
Lusty Song, 357
Lydia Hanover, 71, 79, 129, 135, 143, 149, 179, 237, 245, 251, 305, 315, 327, 333, 339, 353, 389, 397
Lydia Knight, 41, 71, 79, 85, 129, 135, 143, 149, 179, 237, 245, 251, 275, 305, 315, 327, 333, 339, 353, 389, 397
Lydia Lee, 129
Lydon, Mark, 58
Lyn's Beauty, 212
Lyric, 135
M. E. K. Stable, 330
Mable's Scooter, 30
Macadream, 69
Mack H., 85, 101, 207, 221, 283, 315

Index

Mack Lobell, 222
Macketta, 57, 133
Madam Thompson, 377
Maestro, 20, 23, 153-154, 374
Magee, Dave, 75
Maggie Gaines, 114
Maggie Onward, 383
Maggie Wilkes, 51
Maggie Winder, 65, 85, 93, 129, 187, 195, 201, 237, 259, 267, 275, 283, 289, 305, 321, 353, 365, 389
Maggie Yeaser, 51
Magic Formula, 199-200
Magic Touch, 26
Magic Trick, 24, 83, 133-135, 334
Magical Mike, 16, 26, 132, 144, 175, 223, **246-251**, 268, 271, 310, 322, 324, 343, 386, 388
Magna Stables, 298
Magnet, 101, 207
Magnetic Almahurst, 26
Magnetic Killean, 26, 295, 351-352
Magnolia Hanover, 93, 201, 229
Majestic Hanover, 316, 357
Majestic Lobell, 52
Major Edsall, 359
Make A Deal, 26, 40, 226, 301, 304
Make Mine Sable, 344
Make Music, 28, 273
Makin Smiles, 159, 163, 356
Malaysia, 23, 372
Malcolm Forbes, 41, 57, 65, 93, 111, 119, 171, 179, 187, 201, 251, 259, 267, 275, 283, 289, 305, 315, 321, 353, 371, 377, 383, 389
Mallet, Jeff, 172
Mambrino Beauty, 51, 119, 213, 326, 383
Mambrino Chief, 207
Mambrino King, 51, 57, 101, 111, 119, 207, 213, 267, 283, 321, 345, 359, 377
Mambrino Patchen, 101, 207, 213
Mamie, 60, 292
Mamie Foster, 51
Manificent, 193-194
Mann, Howard, 346
Mann, Joan, 346
Mano, 119, 213, 383
Manor Born, 27
Mantese, 192, 194
Manzi, Catello, 75, 322
Marauder, 25, 27, 91, 290, 292, 362-364
Mardi's Crown, 30

Margaret Arion, 101, 187, 292
Margaret C. Brooke, 119, 283, 289, 315
Margaret Castleton, 93, 292, 297
Margaret Parrish, 101, 297
Margaret Polk, 41, 51, 57, 65, 85, 93, 101, 111, 119, 129, 179, 187, 195, 201, 213, 221, 237, 251, 259, 267, 275, 283, 289, 297, 305, 321, 339, 345, 353, 359, 365, 371, 377, 389
Margaret Spangler, 20-21, 65, 71, 79, 85, 93, 129, 135, 143, 149, 155, 163, 179, 187, 195, 201, 221, 229, 237, 245, 251, 259, 267, 275, 283, 289, 297, 305, 315, 321, 333, 339, 353, 365, 389, 397
Margaret Vonian, 93, 119, 283, 289, 297, 315
Margeaux, 185
Margie's Melody, 23, 265, 292-293, 297
Margie's Storm, 292-293, 297
Margo Laporte, 29
Margo Mite, 93, 229
Marguerite, 41, 171, 213, 267, 321, 345, 359, 383
Marie Elaine, 176
Mariner, 205
Marion Candler, 41, 71, 79, 237, 245
Marjorie Armstrong, 83, 235
Mark B Time, 206
Marked Man, 26, 182, 255
Market Report, 242, 369
Markim's Pride, 83-84
Marmaduke Hanover, 27
Marquess De Sade, 279
Martha Lee, 259
Martinique, 221
Martinos, 101, 207, 221, 283, 315
Marvel, 214, 362, 364
Marvin Childs, 102
Mary B. Good, 205-206
Mary Bales, 267, 321, 345, 371
Mary Thomas S, 187
Maryellen Hanover, 382
Masquerade, 286-287
Massau, Jack, 276
Master Barney, 29
Master Miles, 29
Master Nukes, 154
Master Shawn, 375
Matrix Hanover, 382
Matt Russian, 258, 303
Matt's Domino, 387
Matt's Scooter, 14-15, 17, 19, 23, 25-27, 29-32, 63, 66, 68, 114, 139, 152, 154, 168-170, 176, 186, 218, 220, 242-243, **252-259**, 265, 273, 288, 303, 313, 319, 387
Mattalac, 256
Mattcheever, 27
Mattduff, 175, 256, 258
Mattgilla Gorilla, 256, 258
Mattman, 152
Mattnamara's Band, 387
Matturity, 152
Maud G, 119
Maxine Abbe, 129, 135, 143, 149, 155, 163, 179, 221, 229, 251, 275, 305, 315, 333, 339, 389, 397
Maxine Direct, 129, 135, 143, 149, 179, 251, 275, 305, 315, 333, 339, 389
Maxine's Dream, 22, 126, 129, 135, 143, 149, 155, 163, 179, 221, 229, 251, 270, 275, 305, 315, 327, 333, 339, 389, 397
May B, 370, 388-389
May Dodge, 41, 353
May King, 119, 207, 383
May Queen, 383
May Spencer, 171, 187, 259
May W., 201
May Wine, 30, 271-272, 274, 381
Maybe Today, 78
Maynard Hanover, 99
Mc Toodles, 28
McCluckey, 222
McCluskey, Joe, 214
McCool, 250, 343, 388
McDuffee, David, 246
McGivern, Mickey, 130
McIntosh, Bob, 75, 77, 144
McKinney Scott, 111, 143, 149, 171, 179, 187, 195, 201, 251, 259, 297, 305, 315, 321, 327, 345, 353, 371, 377, 383, 389
McKinzie Almahurst, 82-84, 122, 298
McLin Hanover, 208
McNamara, Leo C., 44
McNichol, Mickey, 308
McNiven, Don, 346, 348
McNiven, Jack, 348
Meadow Addy, 257
Meadow Blue Chip, 205-206, 264-265
Meadow Cheer, 179, 219, 251, 257, 387, 389
Meadow Child, 192, 195
Meadow Gene, 320
Meadow Good Miss, 26, 169
Meadow Helene, 219
Meadow Julia, 229
Meadow Lands Farm, 45, 52, 103, 113, 170, 176, 186, 218, 220, 242-243, **252-259**, 265, 273, 288, 303, 313, 319, 387
Meadow Maine, 134-135
Meadow Paige, 115-116, 118
Meadow Skipper, 14, 16, 18-24, 26-28, 30, 32-34, 38-39, 42, 45, 47-48, 52, 54, 58, 60, 62, 65, 69-71, 78-80, 82-85, 89, 91, 93, 96-100, 102, 107-110, 116, 124, 126, 129, 134-135, 140, 143-144, 147, 149, 152, 154-155, 159-161, 163, 169-170, 175, 177, 179-180, 183, 185-187, 191, 193-194, 196, 198-199, 201-202, 205, 210, 212, 217, 219-221, 223, 225, 227-229, 233, 235-237, 242, 244-245, 249-252, 255-257, 259, **260-267**, 268, 270-272, 275-276, 279-281, 283, 286-287, 289, 292-295, 297, 300-302, 305, 310, 312, 315-316, 318, 320, 326-327, 330, 332-333, 337-339, 342-343, 348-349, 351, 353, 357, 360, 362-365, 368-370, 372, 381-382, 387, 389, 393-395, 397
Meadow Trick, 133-135
Meadowlands Shuffle, 94, 222
Medio, 140, 175
Medios, 135
Megamind, 29, 218-220, 387
Meirs III, David, 284
Melba Hanover, 93, 201
Melina Mercouri, 313
Mellowood Abby, 24
Melvin's Strike, 25, 108, 376
Melvin's Woe, 108, 185
Mendocino, 119, 171, 213, 267, 321, 345, 371, 383
Mendocita, 65, 111, 119, 143, 171, 187, 201, 213, 259, 267, 275, 283, 289, 315, 321, 339, 345, 371, 383, 389
Mercury C, 57
Merger, 76, 122, 250
Merger's Cousin, 76
Merry Bars, 339
Merry Clay, 213
Merry Direct, 339
Miami Beach, 115, 118
Miatross, 40, 287-288
Michael, Walter, 202
Michael's Dragon, 175
Michael's Glory, 255
Michelle's Jackpot, 76, 78, 133
Mickey Black, 394
Midas Almahurst, 122, 357

408

Midi A Semalu, 272
Midnight Stalker, 25
Midway Lady, 192, 195
Mighty Medium, 208
Mighty Song, 297
Mighty Tide, 280
Mignon, 187
Mike Pick, 206
Miles McCool, 250, 343, 388
Militant, 25
Miller, Del, 45-46, 262, 319
Miller, Don, 104
Miller, J. R., 218
Miller's Aussie, 55
Miller's Scout, 123, 381
Millie D, 383
Million To One, 246, 322
Mimzy, 93
Min Nuke, 154, 387
Mini Song, 374
Minnehaha, 51, 101, 196, 207, 213, 217, 221, 227, 319, 340, 366
Minnetonka, 65, 85, 143, 179, 195, 201, 251, 289, 345, 353, 365, 371
Minnewashta, 217, 221
Minute Ms., 286
Miracle Byrd, 149
Mirror Image, 159
Misfit, 21, 24, 38-40, 343
Miss Adioo, 41, 353, 389
Miss Alcantara, 267, 321
Miss Alice Paul, 237
Miss Allison Plate, 29
Miss Anna Jay, 57, 377
Miss Bertha C., 111, 140, 175, 353, 377
Miss Bertha Dillon, 76, 107, 111, 175, 201, 283, 321, 353, 371, 377, 397
Miss Bertha Worthy, 85, 107, 111, 129, 195, 297, 365, 371, 377
Miss Creedabelle, 52, 57, 143
Miss De Forest, 201
Miss Donna Mayo, 24, 28, 154
Miss Dorothy Dillon, 101, 163, 187, 305, 315, 359
Miss Duvall, 242
Miss Easy, 49, 74, 110, 138, 301
Miss Ella H., 71, 85, 101, 207, 221, 283, 315, 353, 389
Miss Elvira, 23, 75-76, 79
Miss Gay Girl, 111, 119, 171, 267, 321, 377, 383, 389
Miss Gold Skipper, 26
Miss Kirksey, 207
Miss Kitty Hanover, 394-396
Miss Mambrino, 383
Miss Nutonia, 101, 207, 283
Miss Pierette, 171, 321, 377
Miss Pluto Scott, 149, 377
Miss Princess Laurel, 365
Miss Reed, 69, 71, 85, 135, 327, 333
Miss Russell, 51, 207
Miss Saginaw, 41, 71, 79, 179, 237, 245, 251, 353, 389
Miss Tempo, 363
Miss Volo E, 339
Miss Wayne Hal, 221
Missey, 93, 201
Missile, 26, 69, 170, 325
Mission Of Truth, 30
Mississippi, 24
Missouri Time, 342, 344
Missy Almahurst, 185
Mistral Sam, 362
Misty Bretta, 24
Misty Maiden, 71, 85
Misty Raquel, 263-265
Mitchell, Shirley, 34
Mitzi Eden, 79
Mo Gumbo, 170
Mob Scene, 27, 314
Moffat Missy, 374
Moiseyev, Jack, 226, 241, 324-325, 328, 334, 336, 386
Molecular, 364
Molly B., 233, 237
Molly Dillard, 255
Molly II, 383
Mona, 41, 57, 101, 119, 187, 237, 359
Monel, 149
Money Lender, 252
Moni Maker, 167
Monieson, Brian, 72
Monsieur Mindale, 194, 199
Moonlight Graham, 351-352
Moonlight Sam, 186
More Stylish, 218
Morgan Axworthy, 377
Morgan Mare, 227
Morganetta, 377
Morning Glory, 237
Morrill Jr., Jim, 241
Mossy, 25
Most Happy Fella, 14, 16, 18-19, 22, 24-30, 32-33, 37-39, 54, 56, 60, 78, 83, 97-99, 108-109, 116, 120, 124, 126, 129, 134-135, 141, 143-144, 146-147, 149, 152, 155, 159, 161, 163, 169-170, 175, 177, 179, 183, 194, 196, 212, 217-219, 221, 227-229, 235, 244, 249-251, 255-256, 262-264, **268-275**, 276, 279-281, 284, 288, 300-303, 305-306, 310-313, 315, 319-320, 325-327, 330, 332-333, 336-339, 343-344, 357, 363, 369, 375, 381-382, 384, 386-387, 389, 393-395, 397
Mostest Yankee, 55
Motivation, 168
Mountain Jackson, 199
Mountain Skipper, 24, 126, 337, 339
Mountain Zephyr, 255
Movie Star Laag, 234, 303
Mow The Lawn, 25
Mr Dalrae, 123, 263-264, 266
Mr McElwyn, 41, 65, 93, 111, 171, 179, 183, 187, 201, 251, 305, 333, 353, 371, 377-378, 383, 389
Mr Overnite, 319-320
Mr Panman, 26, 281, 287-288
Mr Dalrae, 123, 263-264, 266
Mr Mikey, 258
Mr Overnite, 319-320
Mr Panman, 26, 281, 287-288
Mr President, 338
Mr Rodeo Drive, 376
Mr Softee, 200
Muckalee Strike, 376
Mugshot Special, 392
Mulberry Street, 28
Mumbo King, 281
Music Director, 99, 192-194
Mustang Hanover, 24, 27
My Finesse, 154, 319
My Margie, 297
My Melissa, 362
My Time, 210
Mybrowneyedgirl, 192-194
Myhalia Hanover, 25
Mynah Hanover, 124, 129, 135, 143, 149, 229, 333, 339
Myrtle Direct, 24, 27
Myrtle Hanover, 30
Myrtle McKlyo, 57
Mystic Music, 153-154
Mystical Maddy, 25, 222, 256-258, 272-273
Mystical Mood, 27
Mystical Prince, 27, 220
Nadia Lobell, 63, 153, 176, 256, 301-302, 304, 350
Naked Gunner, 162
Nan Cam, 120, 124, 129, 135, 143, 149, 229, 333, 339
Nan Frost, 124, 129, 135, 143, 149, 229, 333, 339
Nan's Catch, 167
Nancy Hanks, 111, 119, 171, 267, 321, 377, 383, 389
Nancy Isle, 381
Nancy Lee, 119, 383
Nancy Whitman, 359
Nansemond, 15, 17, 33, 47, 58, 380, 382
Napa Valley, 26
Napoleon Direct, 17, 41, 65, 71, 79, 85, 93, 111, 115, 119, 129, 135, 155, 163, 171, 179, 187, 195, 201, 221, 229, 237, 245, 251, 259, 267, 275, 283, 289, 297, 305, 315, 321, 327, 353, 365, 371, 377, 383, 389, 397
Nappie Hanover, 167
Nardin's Byrd, 28, 115, 118, 199
Nardins Grand Slam, 27
Nat Lobell, 94, 380
Natalie Hanover, 79
Natchitoches, 76
Nate Hanover, 52
Native Amber, 54
Native Born, 27, 52, 241, 265, 293, 295-296
Native Leader, 56
Native Rita, 27, 52
Native Rocket, 320
Natrona Hanover, 52
Naughty But Nice, 49, 110, 242, 263-266
Nearly Perfect, 354
Neat Trick, 320
Nedda Guy, 79, 101, 129, 135, 143, 149, 179, 195, 211, 213, 221, 251, 275, 305, 315, 333, 339, 345, 353, 365, 389, 397
Nelda Dillon, 65, 85, 93, 129, 187, 201, 237, 259, 267, 275, 283, 289, 339, 353, 365, 389
Nelle Worthy L, 57, 377
Nellie D, 51, 119, 213, 383
Nelly Patch, 85, 101, 204, 207, 217, 221, 283, 315
Nelly Zarro, 111, 119, 171, 267, 321, 377, 383, 389
Nelson Dillon, 171, 259, 374
Nelson Guy, 206
Nero, 16, 24, 26, 28-29, 31-33, 55-56, 83, 140, 147, 183, 196, 205-206, 263-264, **276-283**, 295, 343, 357, 369, 381
Nero's B B, 33, 282
Nervolo Belle, 21, 51, 57, 65, 101, 111, 119, 143, 171, 187, 201, 213, 259, 267, 275, 283, 289, 315, 321, 326, 339, 345, 359, 371, 377, 383, 389

Index

Nesbit Two, 89, 118
Neshaminy, 339
Nettie Clay, 207
Nettie King, 41, 51, 57, 65, 85, 101, 111, 119, 187, 201, 207, 213, 221, 267, 275, 283, 315, 321, 345, 359, 371, 377
Nettie Murphy, 51, 57, 101, 111, 207, 213, 267, 283, 321, 345, 359
Neutrality, 242
Nevele Arrival, 331
Nevele Diamond, 184
Nevele Pride, 39, 89-91, 93, 183-184, 196, 198, 201, 227, 229, 279, 320
Nevele R Stud, 193
New Bucks, 20, 23, 63, 293-294, 296, 363
New York New York, 12, 52, 56, 66, 86, 94-97, 104, 106, 112, 125, 130, 156, 169, 176, 202, 204-205, 208, 219, 233, 238, 246, 252, 268, 270, 274, 278-279, 284, 286-287, 306, 309-311, 316, 318, 330, 336-337, 357, 360, 366, 384-385
Newt Lobell, 54-56
Nia Rita, 28
Niafirst, 357
Niagara Acres, 284
Niagara Byrd, 286
Niagara Dream, 23, 117, 286, 289, 297
Niajet, 23
Niatross, 16, 18-20, 23, 25-26, 28-29, 31-33, 37, 40, 60-62, 64, 76-77, 80, 102, 108, 116-117, 123, 126, 134, 136-137, 140, 152-153, 156-157, 159-160, 166, 169, 177, 183, 199, 212, 220, 227-228, 230, 233, 235-236, 243, 250, 252, 254, 256, 270, 281, **284-289**, 290, 292-295, 297, 302, 312, 320, 322-323, 334-335, 337-338, 340, 344, 356-357, 363, 366-367, 380, 384, 394
Nibble Hanover, 40-41, 47-49, 71, 79, 85, 107, 109-111, 129, 135, 143, 149, 155, 163, 179, 192, 195, 237, 245, 251, 275, 297, 305, 312, 315, 320, 327, 333, 339, 342, 353, 357, 365, 371, 374, 377, 389, 397
Nicholas B, 237
Nicholas T., 26, 192, 194
Nick's Fantasy, 22, 24
Nickylou, 274
Nicole Q., 90-92, 126, 199
Nihilator, 16, 19-20, 23-33, 40, 52, 60-61, 63, 66, 77-78, 88, 100, 108-109, 116, 123, 134, 147, 156, 159, 172, 174, 177, 183-184, 188, 190, 199, 212, 214, 227-228, 242, 265, 279, 281, 284, 286-288, **290-297**, 306, 309-310, 334, 338, 343-344, 351, 357, 362, 384, 394
Nines Wild, 170
Nite Strike, 374
Nitro Fashion, 192
No Control N., 26
No Feathers, 29
No Laughs, 25, 288, 302, 304
No More Mr. Niceguy, 199, 287-288
No No Yankee, 34
No Nukes, 14, 16, 18-19, 24-26, 28-33, 38, 40, 63, 66, 75-76, 78, 98-99, 122, 124, 127, 134, 144, 147, 150, 152, 154-156, 159, 163, 167, 169-170, 175, 177, 186, 192, 194, 211, 217-221, 227-228, 235-236, 243-244, 249-250, 256-257, 268, 270-272, 281, 288, **298-305**, 310, 320, 326, 330-332, 338, 344, 349-350, 356-357, 368-370, 384, 387, 390, 393, 397
No Standing Around, 29, 186, 224
No Thru Traffic, 205
Nobelee Hanover, 167
Noble Ability, 25, 387
Noble Adios, 47
Noble Claire, 167, 171, 259, 327
Noble Feeling, 25
Noble Florie, 167
Noble Gal, 167
Noble Gesture, 183, 279
Noble Return, 199
Noble Victory, 164, 166-167, 171, 255, 259, 326-327
Nobleland Sam, 31-32, 186, 199, 273, 362-364
Noon Rush, 301
Nora Abbe, 245
Nora Adele, 245
Norahtross, 29
Norcross Hanover, 167
Nordin Hanover, 167
Noretta, 51, 57, 111, 359
Norette, 135, 155, 163, 195, 221, 228-229, 305, 321, 397
Norette Hanover, 135, 155, 163, 195, 221, 228-229, 305, 321, 397
Norma Hanover, 52, 179, 251
Norma Ruth Hanover, 52
Norris, 51
Northern Dynasty, 146-148
Northern Luck, 23, 99, 146-148, 356
Norvalson, 267

Nuclear Design, 28, 288, 302, 304
Nuclear Flash, 302
Nuclear Legacy, 136, 170, 175, 238
Nuclear Shock, 194
Nuclear Siren, 25, 301-302, 304, 328, 357
Nude Beach, 68, 91
Nuke The Scoot, 257-258
Nukester, 281
Nutilla, 359
Nutwood Wilkes, 51, 101, 119, 207, 213, 383
O'Brien, Joe, 182, 276, 278, 354, 366
O'Brien Hanover, 175, 250-251, 354, 378, 381, 386
O'Donnell, Bill, 75, 77, 88, 138, 150, 230, 232, 290, 308
O'Keefe Mare, 217
O'Mara, Mark, 214
O. J. Almahurst, 26, 332
O K Bye, 83, 168
Ochsner, Al, 330
Odds Against, 25, 37, 96, 235, 238
Odella Hanover, 78, 110, 312
Ogden Lobell, 110
Oil Burner, 16, 23, 29, 32-33, 55, 83, 97, 144, 155, 163, 169, 194, 217-218, 221, 236, 268, 270-272, 295, 298, 300-302, 305, 310-311, 320, 349, 356-357, 384, 397
Oil Strike, 114, 372, 374
Old Bald, 51, 213
Old Den, 359
Old Hickory, 337-338
Oliver Evans, 129
Olympia, 21, 97, 99, 101
Ombre Rose, 29
On Her Way, 39, 170
On The Road Again, 16, 18, 21, 24-28, 30-33, 63, 77, 99, 110, 116-117, 124, 127, 173-174, 190, 253, 256, 268, 271-273, 288, **306-315**, 326, 349, 356-357
On Time, 21, 37, 79, 97, 99, 129, 135, 138, 143, 149, 155, 163, 175, 179, 195, 208, 210, 213, 221, 229, 251, 275, 305-306, 315, 333, 339, 344-345, 353, 365, 389, 397
On Your Toes, 28
Onda Hanover, 179
One If By Pan, 69-70
One More Kiss, 23
One Price, 218
Oneinamillion N, 24
Oniska, 119, 171, 213, 267, 321, 345, 371, 383
Only Pan, 90, 224

Onward, 101, 205, 207, 383
Ooh's 'N Aah's, 69-70
Oranges, 220
Oratorio, 65, 187, 201, 267, 275, 283, 321
Orchard Beach, 42
Orchard Street, 28, 313
Oreo Byrd, 29
Orlove, Dr. George, 164
Ormonde Hanover, 179, 251
Orphan Wayne, 221
Otaro Hanover, 380-382
Oui Oui, 117
Our Commitment, 140
Our Time, 210-211, 351
Outstanding Stock, 152
Over Burden, 320
Overbid, 83, 135, 143, 155, 163, 195, 221, 302, 305, 319, 321, 394, 397
Overcall, 26, 28, 228, 319
Overstreet, Luel, 233
Overtrick, 14, 17, 23, 29, 33, 55, 112, 114, 133-135, 140-141, 143, 147, 154-155, 163, 167, 169-170, 191, 195, 219-221, 228, 260, 300-301, 305, **316-321**, 340-341, 397
Owen, K. D., 164
Oxford Circus, 242
Oxford Fella, 23, 140
Oxford Mary Ann, 23, 140-141, 143
Oxford Penny, 140
Oye Vay, 27, 62, 64, 127
P B Abbe, 206
Pace Setter, 186
Pacific Devil, 70
Pacific Dynasty, 387
Pacific Fella, 23, 99, 126, 128, 144, 170
Pacific Lightning, 170, 325
Pacific Missile, 69, 170, 325
Pacific Rocket, 16, 22, 24, 39, 69-70, 132-133, 170, 243, 246, 248-249, **322-327**, 356, 368
Pacific Sunshine, 69-70
Pacing Boy, 356, 358
Pactolus, 51, 57, 111, 213, 267, 321, 345, 359
Pai Hui, 140
Paige Nicole Q., 90-92, 126, 199
Painter, 149, 159, 163, 357
Painter Lobell, 320
Paladium Lobell, 252
Palestrina, 201, 251, 259
Paling Avenue, 40, 331-332
Palma Lobell, 26

Palmer, Taylor, 236
Palmetto Dear, 23
Pam Ryan, 212
Pammy Lobell, 381-382
Pan Am Sam, 363-364
Pancoast, 213
Panhattan, 387
Panhunter, 235-236, 288
Panorama, 23, 395
Papa Lou, 127
Paper Boy, 106
Paragon, 140
Paris Hanover, 315, 327
Paris Song, 23, 28
Parisian Hanover, 315, 327
Park Lane Comet, 178
Park Place, 30, 77-78
Parker, Rupe, 44
Parks, Fred, 202
Parkville, 383
Parshall, Doc, 45
Parson's Den, 55, 281
Pass, 28
Pass N Jate, 375
Pat Malone, 51, 213
Patchen Wilkes, 51, 101, 207
Patricia Rhythm, 154
Patrick Song, 235
Patriot Lobell, 55
Patriot Stena, 184
Patronage, 51, 54, 213
Patterson Sr., John, 316
Pauline Hanover, 333
Peace Corps, 222, 255
Peace Of Art, 78
Peacedale, 101, 155, 163, 187, 221, 305, 315, 354, 359, 397
Peach Melba, 198
Peachbottom, 300, 320
Peaches N Cream, 315, 327
Peacock, Cecil, 34
Peakie Hanover, 333
Pearl's Falcon, 186
Pebble Lobell, 139-140, 143
Pegasus B, 305
Pegasus Lobell, 55-56
Pegasus Pointer, 155, 163, 221, 305, 397
Peninsula Farm, 228
Penn Hanover, 146
Penn State, 205, 382
Perette Hanover, 29
Perfect Art, 30, 77-78, 295

Perfect Out, 122-123
Perfect Profile, 30
Perfidia, 28
Perky Mindy, 55
Perna Hanover, 382
Perretti Farm, 193
Pershing Square, 172, 174, 188, 265, 286-288, 290, 292
Pert Lobell, 139, 143
Peter G, 259
Peter Henley, 135
Peter Lind, 38
Peter Lobell, 28, 54-56, 382
Peter Mcklyo, 57
Peter Nutonia, 397
Peter Pluto, 377
Peter Potempkin, 93, 149, 251, 339
Peter Scott, 111, 143, 171, 179, 187, 195, 201, 251, 259, 297, 300, 305, 315, 321, 327, 345, 353, 371, 377, 383, 389
Peter The Brewer, 41, 65, 71, 79, 85, 93, 129, 143, 179, 187, 195, 201, 229, 237, 245, 251, 259, 267, 275, 283, 289, 305, 321, 345, 353, 365, 371, 389
Peter's Dragon, 178, 288
Peters, Elizabeth, 58
Petite Pan, 69-70
Petress Binarion, 221
Petrex, 65, 143, 201, 289, 297, 345, 371
Petrigrew, 359
Physically Race, 340
Pianist, 200
Piatt, Jack, 136
Pick Up, 36, 93, 229, 232, 249, 380
Pickles, 331
Pickwick Farm, 202, 206
Picture Me Gone, 27
Pilgrim's Patriot, 183, 287-288
Pilot Burns, 85
Pilot Medium, 17, 41, 51, 57, 65, 111, 119, 171, 213, 267, 289, 321, 345, 359, 371, 377, 383
Pindari Way A., 56
Pine Hollow Stud, 286, 360
Pine Lane Comet, 288
Pine Needles, 205
Pirate Skipper, 77-78
Pistachio, 101, 205, 207
Pleasant Surprise, 39, 46
Pleasant Thought, 213, 275, 345
Pleasure Seeker, 49
Polished Satin, 244
Polly Bars, 339

Polly Parrot, 41, 46, 51, 57, 65, 85, 101, 111, 119, 129, 187, 195, 297, 359, 365, 371, 377, 389
Pompanette, 93, 198, 201, 229
Popfinger, Bill, 182
Poplar Ann, 39
Poplar Byrd, 14, 17, 39, 93, 114, 119, 149, 167, 205-206, 229, 235, 280, 283, 289, 297, 315, 333
Poplar Hill Farm, 112, 114, 209, 260-261, 317-318
Poplar Wick, 205-206
Popping Thru, 349
Poppy Hanover, 143
Possessive Dragon, 374
Poulton, Harry, 252, 306, 308
Poulton, Sherri, 310
Powder, 24
Power Beach, 90
Power Bunny, 84
Power Patch, 393
Power Right, 140
Powerful Structure, 176, 374
Praised Dignity, 26, 29, 31, 40, 62, 64, 172, 381
Prashai, 295
Precious Bunny, 16, 21, 24-26, 30-31, 40, 61, 74-75, 82-83, 99, 116, 124-125, 128, 134, 138, 144, 158, 220, 243, 268, 271, **328-333**, 334
Precious Fella, 16, 27, 32-33, 109, 212, 268, 271, 351, 382
Precious Hal, 315
Prelude Lobell, 55, 140, 382
Present Laughter, 272
Present Queen, 365
Presidential Ball, 16, 21, 24, 99, 124-126, 128, 140, 144, 147, 238, 240-242, 268, 271, **334-339**
Presidential Lady, 337-338
Preston Almahurst, 358
Pretty Hanover, 149, 163
Pretty Margie, 292, 297
Preview Hanover, 143
Primus, 319, 325
Prince Adios, 45-47, 210, 370
Prince Brian, 370
Prince Ebony, 27, 273, 319
Prince McKinney, 267
Prince Pulaski, 119, 383
Prince Pulaski Jnr, 119, 383
Prince Roi, 119
Prince Royce, 66
Princess II, 383
Princess Annabel, 377

Princess Best, 38, 41, 71, 79, 237, 245, 327
Princess Chief, 38, 41, 71, 79, 237, 245, 327
Princess Counsel, 362-363, 365
Princess Duffy, 41, 71, 79, 237, 245
Princess Gay, 41, 71, 79, 237, 245, 327
Princess Martha, 187
Princess Nelda, 65, 187, 201, 267, 275, 283
Princess Pacific, 26
Princess Peg, 292
Princess Pete, 41
Princess Royal, 65, 143, 171, 259, 321, 345, 371, 383
Princess Sam, 212, 360, 362, 365
Private Ritual, 27
Private Tears, 242
Prize Sarnel, 375
Prodigal, 213, 345
Promised Princess, 25
Protector, 97, 101, 187
Proud Albert, 26, 69-70
Proudfoot Farms, 66
Pundit, 388
Que B., 83-84
Que Tal, 45
Queen Audubon, 101, 207, 221, 283, 315
Queen Margie, 292
Queen Nib, 297
Queen Of Belair, 383
Queen's Adios, 264
Queen's Blue Chip, 325, 327
Queenly Lorraine, 326-327
Queenly McKinney, 65, 85, 201, 289, 353, 365
Quick As Can Be, 331
Quinella Blue Chip, 325, 327
Quite A Sensation, 205
Rabbi Of Racing, 350-352
Race Time, 14, 16, 22, 24-27, 29, 33, 39, 69, 83, 108-109, 126, 140, 147, 175, 177, 179, 185, 193-194, 209-212, 250-251, 256-257, 262, 280-281, 284, 293, 295, 302-303, 326, **340-345**, 366, 370, 372, 374, 382, 386
Racing Date, 26, 250-251, 343
Racy Heart, 25
Racy Kathy, 344
Radiant Ruler, 362, 375
Raffi, 110
Raging Glory, 23, 30-31, 97, 382
Ragtime Band, 69
Raider Frost, 47, 112
Rain Proof, 23
Rained Out, 374, 376
Rake It In, 29

411

Raleigh Fingers, 69-70, 127
Ralph Hanover, 32, 76, 78, 263-264, 266, 381-382
Rambaran, 394-396
Ramblin Storm, 25, 272-273, 368-370
Ramsey Hanover, 375
Randolph Lobell, 282
Ranger, Bruce, 150
Rankin, Dave, 136
Rapidan, 51, 57, 111, 359
Raque Bogart, 184-186
Rashad, 26, 194, 266, 357
Raven Hanover, 350
Raycer Thad, 90, 92
Rayson Hanover, 28, 100, 130
Razzle Hanover, 28
Reactor Lobell, 25, 343
Ready Donut, 24
Ready To Rumble, 29, 234-236, 240-241, 281
Real Artist, 77-78, 100
Real Hilarious, 159, 163, 356
Real Lace, 159
Real Profit, 153-154
Reality Check, 28, 234, 236, 288
Reba Byrd, 114
Reba Hanover, 79
Rebel Lu, 319
Red Bow Tie, 20, 23, 97, 222
Red Chatham, 57
Red Head, 168
Red Medium, 41
Red Road, 311
Red Streak, 155, 163, 221, 305, 357, 397
Red Wilkes, 51, 213
Redskin, 214, 216, 230, 346, 368-370
Redskin Rocky, 68
Reef Peace, 306
Reef The Table, 351-352
Reflection, 149, 159
Refreshing Touch, 69, 80
Regal McKinney, 65, 171, 289
Remmen, Larry, 86
Remmen, Ray, 86, 88
Reservoir, 28
Resonator, 375
Respectfully Yours, 28
Resurgent Dragon, 27, 178
Rex Pick, 105, 205-206
Reynolds, W.N., 319, 378
Reynolds Stable, 378
Rhett Almahurst, 287
Rhodes Mare, 207

Ricci Reenie Time, 342
Richey Letsgo, 28, 369
Richmond, 380, 382
Riegle, Bruce, 72, 392
Riegle, Gene, 72, 74-75, 238, 240-242, 390
Right Over, 319-320
Right Tie, 54
Right Time, 100, 320
Righteous Bucks, 140
Ring Of Light, 159, 374, 376
Rippling River, 24
Rita Almahurst, 25
Rita Belle, 52
Rivaltime, 37, 104, 211-212
River Rouge, 146
Riyadh, 20, 23, 115, 132, 218-220, 225-226, 238, 240-241, 325, 336, 372
Road Happy, 26, 312, 314
Road Machine, 311-312, 314
Road To Pandalay, 313
Road To The Top, 26, 273, 312, 314
Roadster Sahbra, 313
Robert McGregor, 57, 119, 359
Robin Almahurst, 183, 357
Robin Dundee, 264
Robinson, Bill, 130, 132, 249, 322, 324, 328, 334
Robinson, Brett, 325
Robust Hanover, 265
Rock Blaster, 258
Rockapella, 30
Rodney, 183-184, 187, 279, 357
Rogers, Marilyn, 336
Romalie Hanover, 381-382
Roman Lover, 350
Roman Pockets, 282
Romeo Hanover, 331, 333, 381-382
Romola, 41, 71, 79, 237, 245, 333, 353
Romola Hal, 242, 333
Romola Hanover, 333, 382
Romola Lobell, 27
Romulus Hanover, 381-382
Rooney, Tim, 80
Rorty Hanover, 194
Rosa L, 171
Rosa Lake, 41, 85, 275
Rosa Sprague, 171, 321, 345, 371, 377, 383
Rosalind T1, 326
Rosarium, 286
Rose Marie, 101, 202, 204-205, 207, 221, 283, 315
Rose Scott, 20, 41, 65, 93, 111, 179, 251, 272,
305, 343, 353, 371, 377-378, 383, 389
Rosellen Hanover, 30
Rosenfeld, Seth, 86, 89
Roses Are Red, 52, 176, 264-265
Roses For Emma, 69-70, 303
Rosette, 41, 65, 71, 79, 85, 93, 111, 129, 155, 163, 179, 195, 221, 229, 237, 245, 251, 259, 289, 297, 305, 315, 353, 365, 371, 377-378, 383, 389, 397
Ross K, 237
Rostokop, 206
Roxie, 129
Roya McKinney, 55, 111, 143, 171, 179, 187, 195, 201, 251, 259, 297, 300, 305, 315, 321, 327, 345, 353, 371, 378, 383, 389
Royal Arms, 26
Royal Majesty, 363
Royal Napoleon, 155
Royal Rysdyk, 119
Royalty Almahurst, 176
Royce, 23, 33, 62, 66, 89, 194, 381-382
Ruderman, Charles, 202
Rule Model, 235
Rum Customer, 114, 152
Rumpel, Gordon, 252, 254, 306, 308, 310
Rumpel, Illa, 252, 306, 310
Rumpus Hanover, 384, 387
Run The Table, 16, 26, 29, 31-32, 37, 216-217, 230, 232, 262, 268, 271, 295, 313, **346-353**
Runnymede Lobell, 66, 68, 254, 280, 282, 343
Rush Hour, 280, 300-301
Rustler Hanover, 170, 394-396
Rusty Range, 318
Ruth Abbe, 155, 195
Ruth G, 259
Ruthellenkillean, 263, 351-352, 374
Ryan's Miracle, 28, 160-162
Ryan's Way, 337-338
Ryne, William, 188
Rysdyk, William, 12
S. A. Crest, 310
Sable B., 256
Sable Hanover, 29, 175, 256
Sable Matters, 130, 132, 175, 256, 258, 387
Sablevision, 175
Sabra Almahurst, 30
Saccharum, 320
Sacramento, 190
Sadie Casco, 339
Sadie Tass, 337, 339
Safe Arrival, 25, 242, 295

Safe Haven, 273, 370
Safely Kept, 40, 218-220, 392
Sailing Race, 342-344
Sakra Mania, 30, 236, 387
Sal, 207
Sally Lind, 38
Sally Ward, 51, 57, 111, 213, 267, 321, 345, 359
Sam Francisco Irv, 281
Sams, Dr. Richard, 139
Samadhi, 25, 362
Sammie's Cammi, 148
Sammy Blue Chip, 357
Sampson Direct, 17, 24, 27, 30, 112, 164, 166, 168, 171, 259, 327
Sampson Hanover, 14-15, 17, 84, 104, 164, 166, 171, 183, 259, 279, 327, 357, 395
Samshu Bluegrass, 37
San Francisco, 41, 57, 65, 101, 111, 119, 143, 171, 187, 201, 213, 259, 267, 275, 283, 289, 315, 321, 339, 345, 353, 371, 383, 389
Sanabelle Island, 175, 387
Sandbea Hanover, 175, 256
Sandia Hanover, 175
Sandman Hanover, 98-100, 152
Sandpiper Hanover, 175
Sands A Flyin, 22, 24, 90, 92, 109, 222
Sandy Bowl, 320
Sandy Daisy, 194
Sandy Flash, 93, 201, 251, 283
Sandy's Sable, 175, 179, 256, 344, 382
Sanford, John, 136
Sanrema Hanover, 175
Sansom, 302
Santa Claus, 51
Santee Hanover, 172
Santos, 41, 51, 57, 65, 111, 119, 171, 213, 267, 289, 321, 345, 359, 371, 377, 383
Sara Black, 47
Sara Loren Rd, 311, 314
Sara Van, 155
Sarah Napoleon, 155
Sarah Trick, 21, 23
Saraton, 24
Sassy Becky, 28
Sassy Margie, 292
Satan's Alley, 350
Satellite, 199, 300, 366
Satellite Hanover, 167
Saucy Wave, 356, 358
Saute, 110

Save Fuel, 110, 265
Savilla Song, 356
Say Hello, 34, 115
Scamp, 118, 286, 289, 297
Scandal, 350
Scarlet Skipper, 27, 140, 263, 280-281, 381
Scene Topper, 272, 274
Schnurr, Michael, 246
Schulsinger, Sam, 306
Scoot Herb, 55, 168, 170
Scoot Outa Reach, 168, 170, 273
Scoot To Power, 257-258
Scooter Hanover, 27, 29, 170, 175, 228, 235, 387, 395
Scooter Sampson, 30
Scorch, 100
Scotch Claire, 171, 259, 327
Scotch Jewel, 211
Scotland, 20, 55, 93, 135, 140, 143, 155, 163, 169, 171, 179, 185, 187, 192, 195, 199, 201, 221, 251, 256-257, 259, 264, 272, 293, 297, 300, 305, 315, 321, 327, 340, 342-345, 349-350, 353, 363, 366, 368-369, 371, 378, 397
Scott Frost, 305, 326
Scottish Pence, 210, 272, 357
Sea Biscuit, 12
Seabert Hanover, 279, 380-382
Seahawk Hanover, 16, 27, 32-33, 108-110, 183, 191, 250, 265, 279-280
Sealed N Delivered, 192-194, 295
Sean Douglas, 148
Searights, 56
Seascape, 159, 163
Seatrain, 266, 278
See You There, 69, 153, 205, 311
Seedling Herbert, 29
Seeley, Jonas, 12
Seelster Farms, 144-145, 148
Segal, George, 72, 75, 238, 242, 390, 393
Self Control, 26
Semalu D'Amour, 286-288
Semer, Dr. Jerry, 336
Senator Mare, 207
Senor Skipper, 146
Serious Fun, 152
Serpico Hanover, 382
Set The Style, 26
Seth Jay, 170
Seven O'Clock, 29, 250, 344, 384, 387
Sexy Dolly, 27
Shadow Almahurst, 358
Shadow Dan, 358

Shadow Dance, 21, 24, 98-100, 186, 357
Shadow Grattan, 101, 155, 163, 187, 206, 221, 305, 315, 327, 354, 359, 397
Shadow Lane Farms, 246
Shadow Star, 159, 357-358
Shadow Wave, 16, 20-21, 33, 47-48, 50, 54, 97, 99, 101, 154-155, 159-161, 163, 169-170, 183, 187, 206, 221, 264, 272, 302, 305, 311, 315, 327, **354-359**, 372, 397
Shadow's Finale, 49, 356
Shady Character, 192-194
Shady Counsel, 356, 358
Shady Daisy, 29, 192, 194, 196, 211
Shadyside Trixie, 319-320
Shana Hanover, 23
Shanghai Mary, 207
Shania, 30
Shannon Fancy, 357
Shannon Spirited, 281
Sharp Attack, 28, 170, 303
Sharpe Sam, 186
Sharper Image, 24, 159
Sharpshooter, 28
She's A Great Lady, 28, 153-154, 222
She's A Ten, 24, 39
She's So Misty, 192-193
Shehan, William, 243, 372
Sheppard, Lawrence, 45, 378
Sherman Almahurst, 25, 77-78
Sherry Almahurst, 159
Shiaway St. Pat, 88
Shifting Sands, 356, 372
Shifting Scene, 356, 372
Shipp's Fella, 55
Shipp's Purser, 392
Shipp's Saint, 218
Shipp's Scorch, 100
Shipps Schnoops, 311
Shock Treatment, 344
Shocking Secret, 349
Shogun Hanover, 369, 388
Sholty, George, 146, 180, 360
Shop Till Ya Drop, 363, 375
Shore Patrol, 63, 293-294, 296
Short, Harry, 202
Shotgun Scott, 30, 394-396
Showmethewayhome, 313
Shy Ann, 89, 93, 229, 250-251
Sickem Cindy, 28
Sidney Dillon, 41, 51, 57, 111, 119, 171, 359, 371, 377
Sienna, 111, 171

Sierra Kosmos, 354
Sign Of Rain, 244
Signed N Sealed, 220, 378
Signfeld, 244
Sigrid Volo, 41, 46, 51, 57, 65, 71, 79, 85, 93, 101, 111, 119, 129, 135, 143, 149, 163, 179, 187, 195, 229, 237, 245, 251, 259, 289, 297, 305, 315, 333, 339, 353, 359, 365, 371, 377, 389
Silent Brook, 57, 101, 187, 237, 359
Silent Byrd, 114, 354
Silent Grattan, 57, 101, 155, 163, 187, 206, 221, 237, 305, 315, 354, 359, 397
Silent Majority, 16, 24-25, 28, 32-33, 37-38, 41, 70-71, 79, 154, 186, 235, 237, 242, 245, 272, 327, 349, 351, 381-382
Silent Spring, 25, 109, 311-312, 314
Silent T., 57, 101, 163, 187, 237, 305, 315, 359
Silk Cord, 111
Silk Stockings, 19, 96, 270, 272, 274, 279, 340, 342, 381-382
Silky's Gal, 76
Silky Stallone, 63, 76, 138, 158, 238, 304
Silly Gamble, 29
Silver Almahurst, 16, 21, 24, 116-117, 156, 268, 293-294, 296
Silver Direct, 339
Silver Queen, 297
Silver Reign, 147
Silver Similie, 204
Silver Wraith, 147
Silverheel, 27, 40, 324, 393
Silverman, Jerry, 156
Silverman, Richie, 74, 156, 158
Silverman Stable, 158
Silvertail, 12
Simcoe Hanover, 214
Simon, William, 325
Simply Ravishing, 39
Simpson, Sr., John, 58
Simulcast, 387
Sir Carlton, 24
Siren Almahurst, 25, 357
Siskiyou, 155, 163, 221, 301, 305, 397
Sister Tami, 281, 293, 295
Six Day War, 293, 296
Sixty Six Spur, 387
Skilful, 65
Skip By Night, 25, 331
Skip By Night Jud, 25
Skip To Glory, 255
Skipa Napoleon, 205
Skipper Dexter, 96, 150

Skipper Pace, 225
Skipper Walt, 29
Skipper's Romance, 279
Skippy Rhythm, 154
Slapstick, 24-25, 31-32, 99, 196, 218, 264, 343, 381-382
Slick Pavement, 387
Slipstream, 344
Slotting Allowance, 69
Slug Of Jin, 332
Sly Attorney, 205-206
Sly Yankee, 380-381
Smart, Wayne
Smart Son N., 21, 24
Smartest Remark, 286-288
Smarty Britches, 69-70
Smarty Pants, 24
Smashing Vic, 56
Smicker, 370
Smile As You Go, 161-162
Smiling Rebecca, 293, 295
Smith, Jerry, 366
Smog, 147
Smoke Robertson, 176, 178, 288
Smooth Fella, 271, 312
Smooth Millie, 312
Sniffles Hanover, 279
Snug Feeling, 331-332
Snyder, Jeffrey, 130
So Cozy, 366, 384, 387-388
So Excited, 27, 236
So Fresh, 133, 152, 234-236
So Misty, 192-193
So Precious, 26
So Western, 394-396
Soaring Falcon, 186
Soft Light, 368, 370
Soky's Atom, 55, 62, 64, 123
Solicitor, 17, 135, 141, 143, 155, 163, 167, 195, 210, 221, 260, 300, 305, 319, 321, 378, 397
Some Kinda Dream, 25
Something Persistent, 337
Something Present, 338
Something Windy, 142
Sometime Lobell, 282
Son Of Afella, 24
Songcan, 354
Sonic Sam, 186
Sonsam, 16, 19, 23-24, 26, 28-30, 32-33, 61-62, 77, 110, 134, 140, 147, 152, 160, 177, 186, 228, 244, 293-294, 300, 312, 320, 331, 338, **360-365**, 375, 381, 394

Index

Sonsam's Dream, 26, 28
Sonsamette, 362
Sonuva Best, 142
Sophy, 383
Sorceress, 152
Sorpresa Rosa, 204
Souffle, 93, 196, 198-201, 229
Southampton V., 381
Southern Gentleman, 287
Southsider, 99
Southwest Art, 78
Spare Hand, 115, 118
Sparkling Hanover, 27
Spectacle, 64, 343
Spectacular Deal, 27
Speculation, 133, 224, 360
Speed Bowl, 196, 198
Speedster, 257
Speedy Count, 167
Speedy Crown, 42, 61, 169
Speedy Pick, 301
Speedy Romeo, 301
Speedy Scot, 83
Spencer, 65, 85, 93, 143, 171, 179, 187, 195, 201, 251, 259, 289, 293, 297, 342, 345, 353, 365, 371
Spencer Scott, 187
Spengay, 44
Spiked Boots, 320
Spiked Byrdie, 24, 116-117
Spinster, 22, 65, 71, 79, 85, 93, 143, 155, 163, 179, 195, 201, 245, 251, 257, 289, 297, 333, 342, 345, 353, 365, 371, 397
Spinster Hanover, 93, 196, 198-199, 201, 229
Splendid Splinter, 25, 90, 92
Spoiled Royal, 159
Sports Town, 24, 99, 159-162, 233, 387
Sportsmaster, 39, 220, 390
Spring Rumpus, 194
Springtime Romeo, 142
Spud Hanover, 93, 201, 229
Spurred On, 83
St. Patrick's Morn, 117
Stabilizer, 83-84
Staff Officer, 27
Stafford, Jody, 328
Stampede Hanover, 27, 394-396
Stand Alone, 224, 256-257, 387
Stand And Deliver, 72
Stand By, 211
Stand Forever, 20, 23, 175, 177-178, 288
Stand Together, 76

Standing Around, 29, 186, 224
Star Ring, 26
Star's Pride, 14, 93, 167, 171, 201, 229, 259, 327
Stardrift, 93, 171, 201, 229, 259
Starfire Almahurst, 29
Start The Fire, 63, 74, 158, 293-294, 296
Starter Hanover, 220
Startsman, Florence, 94
Staying Together, 19, 23, 139
Steady Beau, 15, 17, 27, 83, 380
Steady Freedom, 27
Steady Johnnie Sue, 27
Steady Star, 14-15, 17, 23, 33, 69, 91, 182, 380, 386
Stephan Smith, 204, 206
Stern, Howard, 188
Steven's Bald Chief, 207
Stewart, Steve, 346
Stewart, Tom, 263
Sticky Two Step, 230
Stienam, 184-186, 351
Stienam's Girl, 28, 184
Stienam's Place, 28, 76, 78, 184, 294-295
Stock Boy, 69-70
Stoddard, John, 325
Stone Dragon, 29, 176-178
Stonebridge First, 146-148, 192
Stonegate Farm, 66, 68, 70, 123, 349
Stoner Creek Stud, 86, 89, 196, 198, 263, 268
Stoneridge Scooter, 27, 170
Storm Cloud, 292-293, 297
Storm Compensation, 27, 265, 369-370
Storm Damage, 16, 23-28, 31-33, 55, 63, 69, 107-110, 133, 140, 166, 191, 193, 273, 281, 284, 320, 340, **366-371**, 375, 384
Storm Prince, 369-370
Storm Tossed, 368-370
Stormcliffe, 267
Stormin Jesse, 74, 370
Storming Jessie, 74
Stout, 24, 30, 115, 331-332
Strike Out, 16, 19, 24, 28, 33, 107-110, 147, 149, 154, 159, 191, 212, 219, 250, 343, 357, **372-377**
Strike Le Ru, 205, 376
Striking Force, 146, 372
Striking Image, 16, 23, 29, 91, 109, 126, 144, 146, 149, 159, 191, 298, 372, 374
Strong Clan, 25, 40, 168, 170
Strong Life, 242, 244
Stubbs, George, 246

Stud Muffin, 220
Styx And Scones, 83
Suave Hanover, 89, 93, 229
Such A Hoot, 161-162
Sugar Dust, 342, 344
Sugar Loaf, 12
Sultry Song, 244
Sumatra, 41, 85, 111, 171, 195, 259, 275, 371, 377
Sumkinda Wonderful, 183
Summa Cum, 319
Sun Damage, 55, 369
Sun Lamp, 89
Sun Prince, 89
Sunbelle Hanover, 89, 93, 229
Sunburn, 24, 89, 93, 229
Sundance Skipper, 38, 91
Sunnie Tar, 380-382
Super Bird, 63
Super Bowl, 42, 169, 320
Super Bradshaw, 69
Super Clint, 94, 116-117
Super Seeled, 194
Super Star, 349
Super Trooper, 147-148
Super Wave, 116, 146, 356, 358
Superstar Killean, 351-352, 374
Surburbanite, 100
Surf Party, 90, 92
Surmo Hanover, 24
Survival Kit, 28
Survivor Gold, 29, 39, 300, 392-393
Susan Wayne, 221
Sweet Dragon, 246, 322
Sweet Miss, 289, 297
Sweet N Legal, 134
Sweet Reflection, 98, 100, 273
Sweet Surrey, 84
Sweetgeorgiabrown, 170, 219-220, 313
Sweetness, 51
Swinebroad, George, 45
Swing Back, 293, 295-296
Swingin Glory, 30
Swingin Single, 26, 220
Sydney Hill, 194
T. K.'s Skipper, 20, 23, 115, 150
T M I, 29, 300
Tabloid, 25
Tackey, 51, 119, 213, 383
Taffeta Silk, 171
Taffolet, 171, 259
Take A Look, 19, 46, 115, 125, 168-169,
186, 219, 244, 263, 270, 272, 274, 276, 294, 343, 346
Take Down The Flag, 30, 394-396
Take Flight, 394-396
Take Home The Gold, 313, 352
Take The Points, 152
Tallulah Belle, 78, 295
Tallulah Hanover, 78-79
Talon Almahurst, 176
Tambourine, 311
Tandy, 83
Tango Almahurst, 24, 185
Tanzy Lobell, 280-282, 381
Tar Boy, 381
Tar Heel, 14-15, 17, 20-23, 26-27, 33, 37, 39, 41, 47-48, 55, 60, 62, 65, 70-71, 77, 79, 82, 85, 89-91, 93, 97-99, 102, 107-109, 111, 115-116, 129, 135, 143, 149, 155, 159, 163, 169, 175-177, 179, 192, 195, 205, 210, 221, 228-229, 237, 242, 244-245, 250-251, 259, 272, 279-281, 289, 294-295, 297, 300, 302-303, 305, 312, 315, 319, 326-327, 332-333, 338-339, 342-344, 349-351, 353, 357, 363-365, 369, 371-372, 377, **378-383**, 384, 386, 389, 394, 397
Tara Hills Stud, 326
Tarport Addy, 387
Tarport Cheer, 22, 177, 179, 251, 303, 344, 382, 384, 386-387, 389
Tarport Clarabell, 26
Tarport Count, 146
Tarport Crystal, 384
Tarport Duchess, 22, 387
Tarport Effrat, 381
Tarport Hap, 146, 160, 184, 270, 272, 274, 311, 350, 381-382, 384
Tarport Kathy, 22, 177, 303, 344
Tarport Lib, 250
Tarport Martha, 250-251
Task Force, 233, 237
Tate Lobell, 55, 281
Tawnee Herbert, 351-352
Taylor, Don, 112
Teen Talk, 219
Tempered Yankee, 380-381
Temptres Almahurst, 176
Temujin, 16, 30, 33, 122, 340, 342-344, 381
Tender Loving Care, 263-266
Terka Hanover, 155, 257, 302
Terri Terrific, 311

414

Terrie Letsgo, 168
Tesio, Federico, 70
Thais Direct, 101
Thankful, 93, 201, 229
That'll Be Me, 311, 314, 325
The Abbe, 14, 16, 21, 41, 46, 51, 57, 65, 69, 71, 79, 85, 93-94, 96, 98, 101, 111, 119, 129, 171, 179, 187, 195, 201-202, 204-205, 207, 213, 217, 221, 237, 245, 251, 259, 267, 275, 279, 283, 289, 297, 305, 310, 315, 321, 339, 345, 353, 359, 365, 371, 377, 389
The Big Dog, 24, 153-154
The Big Stable, 94
The Booger Lady, 23
The Broncho, 65, 85, 93, 129, 187, 201, 237, 259, 267, 275, 283, 289, 353, 365, 389
The Denman, 362, 364
The Gay Princess, 41, 71, 79, 237, 245, 327
The Great Miss Morris, 21, 235
The Hobo, 377
The Intruder, 316
The Iron Byrd, 118
The King Direct, 199, 363, 365
The Laurel Hall, 85, 107, 111, 129, 195, 297, 365, 371, 377
The Miss Stokes, 65, 143, 221, 345, 371
The Moor, 51, 101, 207, 213
The Old Maid, 20, 65, 71, 79, 85, 93, 135, 153, 155, 163, 196, 199, 201, 229, 245, 257, 264, 289, 294, 297, 327, 333, 342-344, 350, 353, 363, 365, 369, 397
The Senator, 41, 242, 353
The Starting Gate, 106, 133, 225, 240, 249, 330, 336
The Tang Man, 387
The Widow, 383
The Widower, 20, 38, 41, 71, 77, 79, 205-206, 217, 221, 237, 245, 327
The Wrath of Pan, 27, 40
The Zombro Belle, 171, 259, 283
Theda Patch, 217, 221
Thelma's Dream, 26
Thirty G's, 293, 357
Thithter Thavage, 25
Thistle Bird, 221
Thomas, Dick, 150
Thomas, Henry, 44
Thomas, Thomas, 44, 150, 187, 278
Thompson Sisters, 227
Thor Hanover, 47, 243
Thorpe Hanover, 15, 17, 33, 48, 62, 116, 196, 229, 257, 264, 272, 294, 342, 344, 354, 369, 380, 387
Three Diamonds, 27, 49, 61-62, 75-76, 192, 234, 238, 242, 245, 256
Three Mile Island, 24, 344
Three Wizzards, 61, 72, 156, 158-159
Threefold, 97, 100, 146, 192, 242
Thruway Hershey, 30, 311, 314
Tibet, 265, 311, 314
Ticket To Heaven, 302
Tidewater Nick, 282
Tidewater Trick, 140
Tiger's Milk, 242
Tika Belle, 9
Till We Meet Again, 86, 88, 362-364
Tillie Thompson, 345, 371
Tilly Tonka, 201
Tilly's Sam, 199
Timberton, 220
Timbo Timbo, 90
Time Goes Bye, 117
Time O Nic, 342, 344
Time Well Spent, 110
Timely Adora, 26
Timely Beauty, 211-212, 326
Timely Knight, 211-212
Timely Napoleon, 211-212
Times Square, 286
Timothy Haymaker, 186
Timothy Lobell, 55
Tinsel, 233, 237
Tiny Gold, 97, 101
Tiny Wave, 97, 101, 206, 356
Titan Hanover, 183
Tmolus, 41, 51, 57, 65, 111, 119, 187, 201, 213, 267, 275, 283, 321, 345, 359, 371, 377
Toddington, 41, 85, 111, 195, 275, 371, 377
Toddling Van, 155
Tom Hal Jnr, 51, 57, 111, 213, 267, 321, 345, 359, 383
Tom Kendle, 111, 119, 171, 267, 321, 377, 383, 389
Tom Walsh, 246, 249
Toneworthy, 353
Tony Bucks, 9
Too Good, 55, 168, 368
Too Much Trouble, 29
Toofunnyforwords, 220
Tooter Scooter, 74, 83-84, 138, 168-169, 222, 331
Tootie Roll, 381
Topnotcher, 27, 38-40, 127, 273
Torpid, 83, 146, 149
Torresdale, 149
Torris, 83
Total Freight, 382
Totally Ruthless, 170, 265, 393
Touch Of Spring, 177, 194-195, 340, 366
Tough Hombre, 140
Towel Me, 90, 92
Town Dreamer, 303
Town Jester, 292
Town Judge, 292
Town Leader, 280
Town Pro, 98, 100, 109
Town Sweetheart, 23, 99, 147
Town Tramp, 29
Townation, 100
Towner's Big Guy, 32, 97, 99, 170, 186, 303, 313, 381
Towner's Image, 98-100
Toy Poodle, 271-272
Traci Miss, 28
Tracy Blue Chip, 312
Tracy's Jackpot, 23
Trader Hanover, 52
Traveling Man, 273
Treasure, 152, 315
Treecoscious, 350-352
Trenton, 24, 27, 122, 263-266, 281, 300, 320, 340
Trenton Time, 250, 284, 342, 344
Tres Grand Vitesse, 185
Trickster, 133
Trim The Tree, 233, 320
Trimtex, 168, 170
Trini Hanover, 98
Trini's Best, 142
Trinity Lobell, 242
Triple B, 112
Trombone, 133
Tropic March, 110
Troublemaker, 16, 24-25, 27, 29, 31-32, 37, 133, 194, 238, 268, 270-272, 274, 308-309, 344, 350, 375
Truancy, 29
Truax, 41, 85, 111, 155, 163, 171, 195, 221, 259, 275, 305, 371, 377, 397
True Athlone, 149
True Charm, 289, 297
True Duane, 25, 106, 194
True Genius, 84
True Lady, 101, 207, 283
True Tone, 353
Truluck, 126, 146, 149
Trump Casino, 20, 23, 192-194
Trutone Lobell, 280-282
Tucker, Robert, 66, 123, 349
Tucson Hanover, 61-62, 64, 238, 242
Tuff Choice, 309
Tulane, 20, 23, 236
Tulsa Blue Chip, 273, 312
Tululu, 287-288
Tune Town, 20, 23, 28, 98-100
Turn The Tide, 61-62, 320
Turnpike Token, 141
Tucson Hanover, 61-62, 64, 238, 242
Tuxedo Hanover, 104
Twilight June, 339
Twin B Fabio, 147
Twin B Playboy, 190
Twin B Reno, 351-352
Twist In The Wind, 133
Two Gaits Farm, 44, 113, 209, 340-341, 378-379
Ty Cobb, 331
Tyler B, 16, 18-19, 22, 24-26, 29-33, 76, 108, 124, 134, 144, 154, 161, 169, 175, 177, 179, 186, 212, 227-228, 243, 246, 249-251, 256, 268, 270-272, 284, 300, 310, 313, 330, 338, 343-344, 366, 369-370, 375, 381-382, **384-389**, 394
Tyler Town, 24, 99, 161, 387-388
Tyler's Mark, 16, 23-24, 31-33, 144, 175, 250, 268, 271, 281, 310, 343, 375, 384, 386-388
Tyler's Point, 388
Tyrannical, 384
Tyrant, 374
Ultimate Falcon, 19, 23, 186, 192-194
Ultra Bright, 109-110
Ultra Jet, 40, 287-288
Umbrella Fella, 194
Under Orders, 28, 186
Union Depot, 152
Untamed Heart, 233
Upstream Farm, 300
Uptown Stable, 86, 89
Uptown Swell, 100
Uptown Weezie, 148
Vacation Bagel, 26
Vacationing, 273, 311-312, 314
Val D'or Farm, 156
Valedictory, 120-121
Valentina, 384, 387
Valhalla Lobell, 150
Valiant Bret, 108
Valley Victory, 60, 220, 292
Van Kirk, John, 325
Vance Hanover, 32, 62

Index

Veda Hanover, 20, 41, 62, 71, 77, 79, 116, 237, 245, 327
Vengeance, 152
Venus, 51, 57, 111, 359
Vernie Wilkes, 129, 275, 389
Vernon Dancer, 318
Very Fast Cass, 146
Very Rare, 388
Vibrant Hanover, 20, 60, 62, 65, 71, 77, 79, 85, 116, 135, 155, 163, 245, 289, 297, 327, 333, 365, 397
Vicanora, 41
Vicar Hanover, 382
Victoria Lind, 38
Victory Abbey, 235
Victory Song, 20, 166, 171, 198, 235, 259, 327, 356-357, 374
Vignette Childer, 152
Viking Commander, 29
Viking Fury, 152
Viking Princess, 152, 155
Viking Renegade, 152
Viking Temptress, 152
Viking Terror, 152, 257-258
Viking Treasure, 152
Viking Vengeance, 152
Viking's Princess, 152
Village Connection, 30, 40, 125, 128, 144, 224, 226
Village Jasper, 30, 40, 218-220
Village Jewel, 25, 30
Village Jiffy, 22, 24, 125, 128, 144, 170, 211, 238, 241, 281, 325, 336
Village Jig, 24, 168, 170
Village Jove, 24, 128, 170, 281
Vine Street, 26, 273, 336, 369-370
Virginia Alta, 101, 207, 221, 283, 315
Virginia Grattan, 57, 143, 354
Virginia O, 305
Visi D'Arte, 29
Vivian Hanover, 41, 60, 65, 71, 79, 85, 135, 155, 163, 237, 245, 262, 289, 297, 327, 333, 365, 397
Volga E., 21, 185, 195, 199, 212, 302, 305, 321, 326, 345, 371
Voodoo Hanover, 58, 60, 65, 71, 79, 85, 135, 155, 163, 245, 289, 297, 327, 333, 365, 397
W R H, 83

Wainscot, 101, 207, 283
Walkin On Air, 349
Wall Street Stable, 290
Wallace, John, 13
Wallace McKinney, 71, 85
Walnridge Farm, 89, 166, 284
Walnut Hall Farm, 34, 37, 139, 176
Walsh, Martin, 346
Walsh Jr., Tom, 246
Walsh III, Tom, 246
Walt Hanover, 123, 381, 393
Walter Dear, 208
Walter Direct, 17, 41, 65, 93, 101, 111, 119, 129, 171, 179, 187, 201, 251, 259, 267, 275, 283, 289, 305, 315, 321, 353, 371, 377, 383, 389
Walton Hanover, 14, 16, 23, 27, 31-32, 40, 63, 96, 98-100, 127, 160, 204, 220, 387, 393
Wannamaker, 37
Waples, Keith, 372
Waples, Ron, 230, 336
War Chief's Sister, 30
Warm Breeze, 16, 24-25, 27, 29, 32-33, 107-110, 169, 191, 193, 195, 212, 255, 312, 320, 340, 351, 366
Warner, Harry, 44-45
Warrior For Peace, 242
Warwell Worthy, 93, 143, 171, 179, 195, 201, 221, 237, 251, 327, 345, 353, 371
Watch Him Step, 282
Water Tower, 28
Watering Can, 28, 161, 265
Watering Hole, 37
Waverly Nero, 282
Waxman, Robert, 156
Way Wave, 149, 159, 163, 211-212
Wayblaze, 397
Waycross, 357
Wealthy Skipper, 252
Weather Related, 370
Webster, Ben, 34, 298
Wedgewood, 51, 213
Well Endowed, 24
Wellwood Hanover, 393
Wendy Hanover, 393, 397
Wendy M. Hanover, 393
Wendy Sue Hanover, 393, 397
Wendyann Hanover, 393
Wendymae Hanover, 28, 393, 397

Western Azure, 394-396
Western Canada, 90, 306, 308
Western Dreamer, 20, 23, 393-396
Western Hanover, 16, 23, 27-28, 30-32, 61, 63, 97, 124, 144, 159, 170, 211, 217, 238, 268, 270-271, 301-302, 304, **390-397**
Western Slide, 394
Western Spirit, 396
Weston Seelster, 147
Whamo, 196
What's Next, 271-272, 274
Whata Baron, 114, 134, 210, 278
Whatanut, 380
Whenuwishuponastar, 146-148, 364
Whimsical Lobell, 29
Whirlwind, 22, 25, 332
Whisper, 119, 213, 383
Whispering Sands, 356, 372
White Dawn, 337, 339
White Mountain Boy, 337, 339
Whiteland Fella, 350
Whiteland Trouble, 350
Wicomico Shamy, 339
Widow Grattan, 41, 71, 79, 206, 221, 237, 245, 327
Widow Maggie, 111, 187, 201, 383, 389
Widower Peter, 41
Wilco's Kosby, 238
Wilcutts, John, 58
Wild Fire, 101
Wilellen, 41, 71, 79, 237, 245, 327, 353
Wilkes Boy, 57, 119, 267, 321, 354, 359
Wilkesberry, 207
Will It Matter, 152
Willglow, 41, 71, 79, 237, 245, 353
William L, 213, 359
William Time, 316
Williams, Sam, 208
Willina H, 259
Willola, 41, 71, 79, 237, 245, 327, 353
Wilmington, 41, 71, 79, 179, 237, 245, 251, 327, 353, 389
Windshield Wiper, 39, 117, 228-229, 263-264
Windy Answer, 368-369
Winnie Davis, 119, 383
Winning Goalie, 26, 28, 152, 226
With Thanks, 78
Without Reproach, 22, 24, 272

Witsend's Wizard, 172
Witty Dragon, 249
Wolverine, 34, 209, 366
Wonderful Thing, 183
Woolworth, Norman, 86, 196, 260
World Trade Center, 92
Worthy Bowl, 192
Worthy Boy, 14, 17, 93, 109, 140-141, 143, 167, 171, 179, 185, 195, 201, 221, 229, 233, 237, 251, 259, 319, 326-327, 343, 345, 353, 357, 366, 368, 371
Worthy Petress, 221
Worthy Sis, 301
Worthy Spirit, 41, 57, 353
Worthy Wick, 185
Wrestling Matt, 152
Wyatt, W. H., 276
Yankee Aspen, 161
Yankee Cam, 303
Yankee Cashmere, 55
Yankee Coed, 55, 301
Yankee Finesse, 170, 395
Yankee Hanover, 104, 170
Yankee Kent, 281-282
Yankee Maid, 349, 353
Yankee Scott, 349, 353
Yankeeland Farm, 56
Yankeetone, 349, 353
Yarmila, 25
Yes Dear, 23
Yo Eleven Lo, 186
Young Chicago Maid, 38
Young Daisy, 213
Young Jim, 383
Young Miss, 119, 207, 383
Your The Top, 375
Youra Jinx, 84
Zanzara, 70
Zeinfeld, Morris, 52
Zelica, 101, 207
Zero Inflation, 325, 387
Zombrewer, 41, 65, 85, 143, 187, 201, 267, 275, 283, 321, 339, 345, 371
Zombro, 65, 119, 171, 187, 201, 213, 259, 267, 275, 283, 315, 321, 345, 371, 383
Zulu Belle, 101, 187, 359
Zupnick, Stanley, 164